W9-DFT-019

Contents

The Canadian population figures in this guide are based on the official 1991 Canadian census.

Addresses, telephone numbers, opening hours and prices published in this guide are accurate at the time of publication. We apologize for any inconveniences resulting from outdated information, and we welcome corrections and suggestions that may assist us in preparing the next edition.

MAP OF PRINCIPAL SIGHTS

GREENLAND

Worth the trip ★★★		Town described
Worth a detour ★★	▲	Other point of interest
Interesting ★	⑦	National park

The names in black type indicate the cities and sights described in this guide.
(See index p 246)

🍁 Trans-Canada Hwy
⑯ Yellowhead Hwy
㉟ U.S. Interstate
㊗ Other route

Highway
Provincial route
60 Road distance (km)

New England

MICHELIN
Green Guide
available

0 ————— 450 km

LABRADOR SEA

NEWFOUNDLAND

Labrador

Cartwright

Goose Bay

Churchill R.

Churchill Falls

Smallwood Reservoir

R. Romaine

Lewisporte

ST JOHN'S

725

910

Gros Morne

See map p 218

Burin Peninsula

Havre-St-Pierre

Mingan Archipelago

Côte Nord   R. Moisie

Sept-Îles   pp 156-157

Port-Cartier

Anticosti Island

Channel-Port aux Basques

GASPÉ PEN.

Percé

Magdalen Islands

P.E.I.

Louisbourg

733

NEW BRUNSWICK

651

FREDERICTON

NOVA SCOTIA

HALIFAX

See map pp 182-183

Saint John

MONTREAL

...anada Village

New England

Boston

Hudson R.

NEW YORK

New York City

PHILADELPHIA

ATLANTIC OCEAN

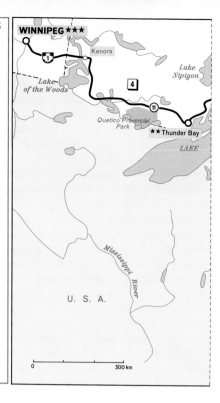

4 Northern Ontario. – *Trip of 2,271km/1,411mi from Ottawa to Winnipeg. Time: 10 days.* On this tour, visitors can experience the wild, untouched beauty of the Canadian Shield country with its rocks, trees and lovely lakes. The drive around Lake Superior is particularly attractive.

Days	Itinerary	Visits
1-2		Ottawa★★★ *(p 117)*
3	**Ottawa – North Bay** 363km/226mi	North Bay★ *(p 116)*
4	**North Bay – Sault Ste Marie** 427km/265mi	Sudbury★★ *(p 127)*
5		Sault Ste Marie★★ *(p 125)*
6	**Sault Ste Marie – Thunder Bay** 705km/438mi	Lake Superior Drive★★ *(p 126)* North Shore Lake Superior★★ *(p 129)* (described in other direction)
7		Thunder Bay★★ *(p 128)*
8	**Thunder Bay – Kenora** 569km/353mi	Kakabeka Falls★★ *(p 129)*
9-10	**Kenora – Winnipeg** 207km/129mi	Winnipeg★★★ *(p 94)*

5 Southern Ontario. – *Round-trip of 1,737km/1,079mi from Niagara Falls. Time: 18 days.* This tour combines the vibrant city of Toronto with the magnificent falls on the Niagara River, the highly cultivated southern Ontario, some Canadian Shield country and the nation's capital of Ottawa.

1-2	60km/37mi	Niagara Falls★★★ *(p 113)* Niagara Parkway (north)★★ *(p 114)*

Days	Itinerary	Visits
3	**Niagara Falls – Toronto** 147km/91mi	Hamilton★ *(p 108)*
4-7		Toronto★★★ *(p 130)*
8	**Toronto – Kingston** 269km/167mi	Oshawa★★ *(p 117)*
9		Kingston and the Thousand Islands★★ *(p 110)*
10	**Kingston – Ottawa** 201km/125mi	Upper Canada Village★★★ *(p 144)*
11-12		Ottawa★★★ *(p 117)*
13	**Ottawa – Gravenhurst** 406km/252mi	Gravenhurst★ *(p 108)*
14	**Gravenhurst – Midland** 56km/35mi	Orillia★ *(p 116)* Ste-Marie among the Hurons★★ *(p 106)* Midland★ *(p 106)*
15		Penetanguishene★ *(p 106)* Georgian Bay★★ *(p 105)*
16	**Midland – Goderich** 249km/155mi	Wasaga Beach★ *(p 106)* Blue Mountains *(p 107)* Goderich★ *(p 107)*
17	**Goderich – London** 140km/87mi	Stratford★ *(p 127)* London★ *(p 112)*

Optional 2-day excursion, 482km/300mi, can be made to Windsor★ (p 145) and Point Pelee National Park★★ (p 125); overnight stop at Leamington.

18	**London – Niagara Falls** 209km/130mi	Brantford★ *(p 105)*

6 Quebec. – *Round-trip of 2,359km/1,466ml (not including ferries) from Montreal. Time: 17 days.* This tour combines the charm of Quebec City, the ancient capital, with the impressive fjord on the Saguenay; the beautiful Gaspé peninsula culminating in the scenic wonder of Percé; and the modern vibrant city of Montreal.

1-3		Montreal★★★ *(p 160)*
4	**Montreal – Quebec City** 277km/172mi	Trois-Rivières★★ *(p 179)*
5-6		Quebec City★★★ *(p 170)*
7	**Quebec City – Île aux Coudres** 107km/67mi and ferry	Beaupré Coast★★ *(p 175)* Charlevoix Coast★★★ *(p 152)* Île aux Coudres★★ *(p 152)*
8	**Île aux Coudres – Tadoussac** 104km/65mi and ferry	Charlevoix Coast★★★ *(p 152)* Tadoussac★★ *(p 178)*
9		Whale-Watching Cruise★★ *(p 178)* or Cruise on the Saguenay Fjord★★★ *(p 178)*
10	**Tadoussac – Matane** 204km/127mi (ferry Les Escoumins – Trois-Pistoles)	Gaspé Peninsula★★★ *(p 155)* Métis Gardens★★ *(p 155)* Matane★ *(p 155)*
11	**Matane – Percé** 404km/251mi	Forillon National Park★★ *(p 156)* Gaspé★ *(p 156)*

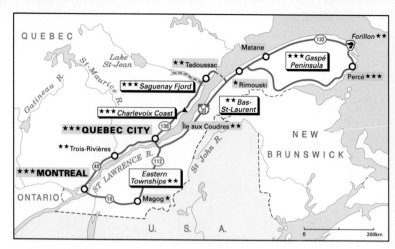

Days	Itinerary	Visits
12-13		Percé★★★ (p 156)
14	**Percé – Rimouski** 466km/290mi	Gaspé Peninsula★★★ (p 155) South Coast (p 156) Rimouski★ (p 152)
15	**Rimouski – Quebec City** 312km/194mi	Bas-St-Laurent★★ (p 151) (described in opposite direction)
16	**Quebec City – Magog** 275km/171mi	Eastern Townships★★ (p 154) Magog★ (p 154)
17	**Magog – Montreal** 210km/130mi	Richelieu Valley★★ (p 176)

7 Maritime Provinces. – *Round-trip of 4,235km/2,632mi (not including ferries) from Halifax. Time: 22 days.* This tour of the three Maritime provinces is an interesting blend of seascapes, rocky headlands, sandy beaches and the high tides of the Bay of Fundy with historical highlights such as the French fortress of Louisbourg, Halifax and its citadel, the Acadian country and the important port of Saint John.

1-2		Halifax★★ (p 207)
3	**Halifax – Antigonish** 261km/162mi	Sherbrooke★ (p 212)
4	**Antigonish – Sydney** 212km/132mi	Louisbourg Fortress★★★ (p 210)
5	**Sydney – Ingonish** 127km/79mi	Glace Bay (Miners' Museum★★) (p 207) Cabot Trail★★ (p 204) (described in opposite direction) Ingonish (p 206)
6	**Ingonish – Baddeck** 233km/145mi	Cabot Trail★★ (p 204) Cape Breton Highlands National Park★★ (p 205) Chéticamp (p 204) Baddeck★ (p 204)
7	**Baddeck – Charlottetown** 263km/163mi and ferry	Prince Edward Island (p 213) Charlottetown★★ (p 214)
8-9-10	800km/500mi (maximum)	Prince Edward Island Scenic Drives (pp 214-216)
11	**Charlottetown – Newcastle** 259km/161mi and ferry	

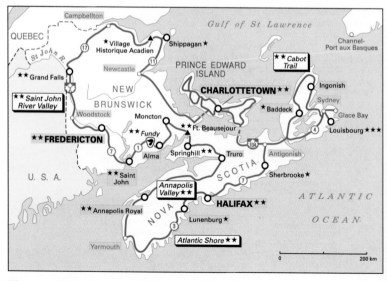

Days	Itinerary	Visits
12	**Newcastle – Campbellton** 301km/187mi	Shippagan★ *(p 196)* Village Historique Acadien★ *(p 196)*
13	**Campbellton – Woodstock** 311km/193mi	Saint John River Valley★★ *(p 195)* (described in opposite direction) Grand Falls★★ *(p 195)* Hartland★ *(p 195)*;
14	**Woodstock – Fredericton** 101km/63mi	Kings Landing★★ *(p 195)*
15	**Fredericton – Saint John** 109km/68mi	Fredericton★★ *(p 188)*
16		Saint John★★ *(p 193)*
17	**Saint John – Alma** 143km/89mi	Fundy National Park★★ *(p 190)*
18	**Alma – Truro** 254km/158mi	Hopewell Cape★★ *(p 190)* Moncton *(p 191)* Fort Beausejour★★ *(p 188)* Springhill★★ *(p 212)*
19	**Truro – Annapolis Royal** 243km/151mi	Truro *(p 212)* Annapolis Valley★★ *(p 200)* (described in other direction)
20	**Annapolis Royal – Yarmouth** 131km/81mi	Annapolis Royal★★ *(p 198)* Port Royal Habitation★★ *(p 199)*
21	**Yarmouth – Lunenburg** 311km/193mi	Atlantic Shore★★ (described in opposite direction) Liverpool *(p 203)* Ovens Natural Park★ *(p 203)* Lunenburg★ *(p 202)*
22	**Lunenburg – Halifax** 176km/109mi	Atlantic Shore★★ *(p 201)* Peggy's Cove★★ *(p 201)*

⑧ **Newfoundland.** – *Round-trip of 2,073km/1,288mi (not including ferries) from North Sydney, Nova Scotia. Time: 12 days.* This tour of Canada's most easterly province enables visitors to discover the scenic wonders of Gros Morne, the French island of St-Pierre and the old port city of St John's.

1	**North Sydney – Port aux Basques** by ferry *(it is advisable to spend the previous night in Sydney)*	
2	**Port aux Basques – Wiltondale** 305km/190mi	
3	191km/119mi	Gros Morne National Park★★ *(p 220)*
4	**Wiltondale – Gander** 356km/221mi	
5-6	**Gander – Trinity** 182km/113mi	Terra Nova National Park★ *(p 227)* Cape Bonavista★ *(p 228)* Trinity★★ *(p 227)*
7	**Trinity – Grand Bank** 333km/206mi	Burin Peninsula *(p 219)* Grand Bank *(p 219)*
8	**Grand Bank – St-Pierre** by ferry from Fortune	St-Pierre★ *(p 226)*
9-10	**Saint-Pierre – St John's** 362km/224mi	St John's★★ *(p 223)*
11	**St John's – Cape Shore** 175km/109mi	Placentia (Castle Hill★) *(p 219)* Cape St Mary's★ *(p 220)*
12	**Cape Shore – North Sydney** by ferry from Argentia	

Introduction

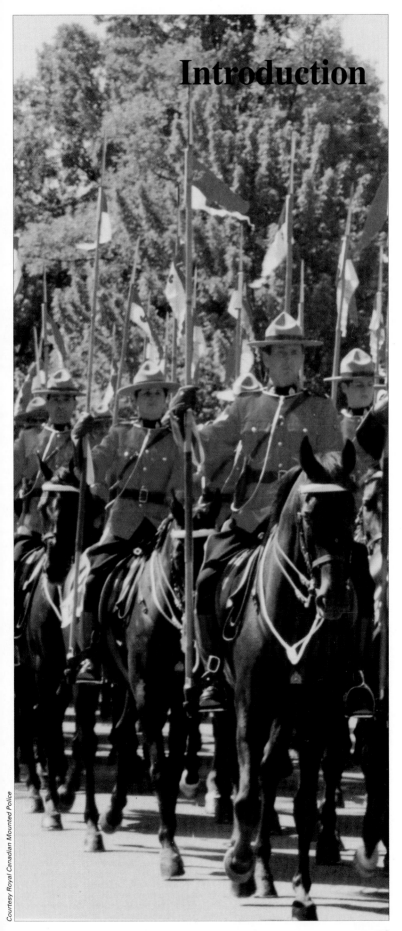

CANADA'S LANDSCAPE

Covering nearly 10 million sq km/3.9 million sq mi, Canada is the second largest country in the world in terms of physical size. It is exceeded only by Russia, whose landmass totals some 17 million sq km/6.6 million sq mi. Having shores on three oceans (Atlantic, Pacific and Arctic), Canada occupies most of the northern part of the North American continent. Yet its inhabitants, largely concentrated along the Canadian/US border, number only some 27 million—roughly 3 million less than the state of California.

The country stretches from latitude 41°47' N at **Pelee Island** in Lake Erie (the same latitude as Rome, Italy) to 83°07' N at **Cape Columbia** on Ellesmere Island, a mere 800km/500mi from the North Pole. This north-south extension of about 4,600 km/2,900mi is countered only by its width. Canada covers more than 5,500km/3,400mi from **Cape Spear** in Newfoundland (longitude 52°37' W) to the **Yukon/Alaska** border (141° W). One of the most remarkable features is the immense bite cut out of the coastline by **Hudson Bay**. This enormous gulf or inland sea could be considered part of either the Atlantic or the Arctic Ocean. In common with the US, Canada shares another noteworthy feature—the **Great Lakes**, which together form the largest body of fresh water in the world. Finally, the country is characterized by its extremely mountainous western rim.

The Great Ice Ages. – The physiographic regions described below have been extensively modified in more recent geological times by the advance and retreat of glacial ice. Four times during the past million years, the North American climate has become progressively colder. Snowfall became increasingly heavy in the north and was gradually compressed into ice. This ice began to flow south, reaching its maximum extent at the Ohio and Missouri river valleys in the US before retreating. At peak coverage, 97 percent of Canada was submerged under ice up to 3km/2mi deep at the centre and 1.6km/1mi deep at the edges. Only the Cypress Hills and the Klondike region of the Yukon escaped this cover. The last ice age receded more than 10,000 years ago.

A sheet of ice of such thickness exerts a great deal of pressure on the earth below. As the ice from each glacial advance retreated, hollows were scoured out of the land and filled with water, and mountain ranges were worn away and sculptured. Today, about 2 percent of Canada is covered by glacial ice, mainly in the Arctic islands, but glaciers are found in the western mountains (Columbia Icefield and St Elias Mountains).

The Great Natural Regions

Physiographically, Canada has at its centre a massive upland known as the Canadian Shield, which forms the geological platform for the whole country. This upland is partially surrounded by areas of lowland that in turn are rimmed by mountain ranges on three of Canada's four sides; to the south, the country lies open to the US. Only in parts of the north do these mountain rims flatten out to form a coastal plain.

Seven major physiographic regions can be distinguished:

The Canadian Shield. – This massive horseshoe-shaped region surrounding Hudson Bay encompasses nearly half of Canada's area. The terrain is formed of ancient, hard rocks of the **Precambrian** era (over 500 million years old) known for their great rigidity and strength. This strength and the region's shape are the origin of the name "Shield." The region is characterized by its innumerable lakes and rivers (Canada possesses as much as one-quarter of the world's total supply of fresh water, largely concentrated in the Shield), by its rugged nature (a combination of rock and bog that makes much of the area inaccessible) and by its lack of agricultural soil. However, the region is also the source of much of the country's extensive mineral, forest and hydro-electric wealth.

Great Lakes/St Lawrence Lowlands. – Despite their comparatively small size, these lowlands, which extend south into one of the great industrial and agricultural belts of the continent, are home to over 50 percent of the country's inhabitants. They were created in Paleozoic times (200-500 million years ago) when great stretches of the region were flooded by the sea for long periods. During this flooding, thousands of feet of sedimentary rock accumulated on top of the Shield, providing fertile soil that has made the region important for agriculture today. This factor, combined with a favourable climate and proximity to the US, have made these lowlands Canada's richest and most industrialized area as well as its most populous.

Prairies and Mackenzie Lowlands. – The geologic history of these lowlands is similar to those of the Great Lakes/St Lawrence region. Material eroded from the Shield and the marginal mountains (in particular, the Rockies) was first deposited in shallow seas. Subsequently swept by glaciers, the flat plains in the south consist of fertile soils ideal for wheat and general farming. The Mackenzie Lowlands begin north of a low divide between the Saskatchewan and Athabasca rivers, and support little agriculture because of their northerly latitude. In places where the Mackenzie Plain joins the Shield, there are large natural basins partially filled with water. Indeed, the dividing line between these two regions is marked by a series of great lakes—Winnipeg, Athabasca, Great Slave, Great Bear, and others.

Hudson Bay and Arctic Archipelago Lowlands. – The northern counterpart of the Great Lakes/St Lawrence region, these lowlands are widely scattered portions of a partially drowned plain of Paleozoic rock that once covered the northern part of the Shield. They slope gently away from the latter with little relief. Owing to its northerly latitude, severe climate and frozen soil, this area supports little except a vegetation of moss and lichens.

Appalachian Mountains. – About 200 million years ago, these mountains, which stretch from Alabama in the US to Newfoundland, were the first to be folded on the edges of the continent. Since then, extensive erosion by ice, rivers and sea has reduced them to mere stumps of their former heights. Today, the region is a series of generally flat to rounded uplands, with few sharp peaks rising to no more than 1,280m/4,200ft. Prince Edward Island, and the Annapolis, Restigouche and Saint John river valleys are notable areas of plain where ancient glacial lakes have left fertile soil.

Canadian Cordillera. – The Canadian Cordillera consists of five major parts (from east to west): the Rocky Mountains, the interior basins and plateaus, the Coast Mountains, the Inside Passage along the coast, and finally the outer system of islands *(map is below)*. Covering the western quarter of the country, this great sweep of mountains is part of North America's long mountain systems known as the Western Cordillera. The Canadian Cordillera is a relatively recent geological development. About 70 million years ago, enormous earth forces thrust these mountains up with a great deal of faulting, folding and volcanic activity. Since then, erosion and uplifting by glaciers, and partial drowning by sea have produced a deeply indented coast.

Arctic Ranges. – These mountains in the extreme north of the country probably rose after the Appalachians. They consist of two fairly distinct parts: the rounded hills of the Parry Islands and the folded peaks of Ellesmere Island.

Vegetation. – The tree line crosses Canada in a rough diagonal from the Mackenzie Delta to Hudson Bay and the Atlantic. North of this line lies the **tundra**, a land of lichens, miniature flowering plants and stunted shrubs. South of this line, the **boreal forest** of black and white spruce, tamarack and other conifers gradually begins, becoming increasingly dense as it extends south. More deciduous trees are found until it becomes a **mixed forest**. But only in southern Ontario are the conifers of the north completely left behind and a true **deciduous forest** exists. In the Prairies, the trees almost completely disappear, making way for the flat former **grasslands** that are now highly cultivated. The mountain region of the West also has its own vegetation pattern, the trees thinning out as they approach the alpine tree line in the same way as they do in the north.

Climate. – Canada's climate is as varied and extreme as its geography. In a large area of the country, winter lasts longer than summer, yet the latter, when it comes, can be very hot. In the north, long hours of daylight cause prolific plant growth. The central provinces receive the most snow, far more than the Arctic, which in fact, receives the least precipitation of any region.

One major factor influencing climate is proximity to large bodies of water: chiefly, the Pacific and Atlantic oceans, Hudson Bay, and the Great Lakes. Such expanses tend to make winters warmer and summers cooler. Regions distant to them, therefore, are inclined to have much colder winters and hotter summers. But terrain is also a factor. In the West, the high Coast Mountains shield the interior of British Columbia and the Yukon from the mild and moist Pacific air, making their climate more extreme than their location would indicate. The Rockies intensify this trend, leaving the Prairies vulnerable to both Arctic winds and hot southern breezes.

Each regional introduction has a summary of climatic conditions with average summer temperatures and precipitation.

"Few Englishmen are prepared to find it [Canada] what it is.
Advancing quietly; old differences settling down, and being fast forgotten;
public feeling and private enterprise alike in a sound and wholesome state;
nothing of flush or fever in its system, but health and vigour throbbing in
its steady pulse: it is full of hope and promise."

Charles Dickens, *American Notes*, 1842

TIME LINE

Pre-Colonial Period

BC	
c.13,000	Asiatic peoples migrate to North American continent.
AD	
c.1000	Norse reach Newfoundland *(p 222)*.
1492	Christopher Columbus lands on San Salvador.
1497	**John Cabot** explores east coast of Canada.

New France

1534	**Jacques Cartier** claims Canada for France *(p 148)*.
1565	St Augustine, Florida, the oldest city in the US, is founded by Spaniards.
1583	Sir Humphrey Gilbert claims Newfoundland for England.
1605	Samuel de **Champlain** establishes **Port Royal** *(p 199)*.
1610	**Henry Hudson** enters Hudson Bay.
1620	Pilgrims found Plymouth, Massassachusetts.
1670	**Hudson's Bay Company** is formed *(p 17)*.
1713	Treaty of Utrecht is signed. France cedes Acadia to Britain.
1722	The **Six Nations Iroquois Confederacy** is formed.
1730s-1740s	La Vérendrye family explores Canadian West *(p 75)*.
1755	Acadians deported *(p 184)* from Nova Scotia.
1756-1763	Seven Years' War.
1759	British defeat the French in Quebec City *(p 175)*.
1763	**Treaty of Paris** is signed. France cedes New France to Britain.

British Regime

1775	War of Independence begins in American colonies.
1778	James Cook explores coast of British Columbia.
1783	American colonies gain independence from Britain. Loyalists migrate to Canada.
1791	**Constitutional Act** creates Upper Canada (Ontarlo) and Lower Canada (Quebec).
1793	Alexander Mackenzie crosses British Columbia to the West Coast.
1812-1814	War of 1812.
1837	Rebellions in Upper and Lower Canada *(pp 130 and 160)*.
1841	**Act of Union** creates the United Province of Canada.
1847	**Responsible government** system is implemented in Canada *(p 18)*.
1848	California Gold Rush begins.
1858-1861	British Columbia's gold rushes *(p 25)*.
1861-1865	American Civil War.

Canadian Confederation

1867	British North America Act establishes Canadian Confederation.
1869-1870	The Riel Rebellion occurs in Red River Valley.
1870	Canadian Confederation buys Hudson's Bay Company land; Manitoba is created *(p 75)*.
1872	**Dominion Lands Act** is passed *(p 75)*.
1874	NWMP (Royal Canadian Mounted Police) is established.
1881-1885	The Canadian Pacific Railway is constructed *(p 18)*.
1885	The Northwest Rebellion occurs. Canada's **first national park** is created *(p 43)*.
1896	Gold is discovered in the Klondike *(p 26)*.
1914-1918	World War I.
1931	**Statute of Westminster** grants Canada control of external affairs.
1939-1945	World War II. Canada receives large numbers of European immigrants.
1942	Alaska Highway is completed *(p 28)*.

Contemporary Canada

1959	**St Lawrence Seaway** is opened *(p 148)*.
1962	The Trans-Canada Highway is completed *(p 37)*.
1968	The Québécois Party is founded.
1982	The **Constitution Act** is passed. Quebec refuses to sign the new constitution.
1986	Nunavik *(p 170)* is created.
1987	**Meech Lake Accord** calls for special status for Quebec *(p 149)*.
1990	Manitoba and Newfoundland refuse to sign the Meech Lake Accord before the deadline. Quebec refuses to sign the 1982 constitution.
1992	A national referendum to grant Quebec special status is defeated. Establishment of Nunavut *(p 231)*.
1993	Negotiation of **North American Free Trade Agreement** among Canada, Mexico and the US.

HISTORICAL NOTES

The First North Americans. – Man is not indigenous to North America. According to recent archaeological findings, prehistoric tribes from the mountains of Mongolia and the steppes of Siberia crossed to the continent some 15,000 years ago by a land bridge that once existed across the **Bering Strait**. They gradually moved south across the whole continent and into South America. Their descendants are the native Indian and Inuit peoples of Canada today, and they can be divided into six groups:

The **Northwest Coast tribes** constituted a highly developed civilization, well known for its totem poles and other carved objects. Principal tribal groups are the Bella Coola, Coast Salish, Haida, Kwakiult, Nootka (along the West Coast), Tlingit and Tsimshian (including the Gitksan). Also known as the Plateau culture (named after the Columbian Plateau region), the **Cordillera Indians** eked out an existence in the British Columbia interior as hunters and fishermen. The Athapaskan, Salishan and Kutenai language families represent this native culture. The **Plains Indians**—the Assiniboine, Blackfoot, Cree, Gros Ventre and Sarcee tribes—were nomadic buffalo hunters who lived in teepees and wore decorative clothing made of animal skins. The Beothuk, Cree, Dene, Montagnais, and other **Sub-Arctic Indians** lived a nomadic existence hunting caribou and other animals. The Algonquian and the Iroquoian peoples formed the **Eastern Woodlands** culture of bellicose farmers who lived in fortified villages, growing corn and squash. Nomadic inhabitants of the most northerly regions, the **Inuit** traditionally lived in ice houses in winter, and in tents and sodhouses during the summer. Using their highly developed navigational skills, they hunted seals and whales off the coast and caribou and waterfowl in the interior.

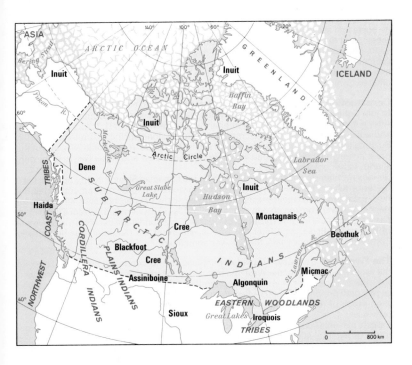

The Arrival of the Europeans. – Long after the migrations of Asiatic peoples from the west, Europeans arrived on the shores of present-day Canada and proceeded to conquer the land and impose their own civilization. The Norse explored the coast of Labrador in the 10C and are believed to have founded the earliest known European settlement in North America around AD 1000 *(p 222)*. Basque and English fishermen knew of the rich resources of the Grand Banks as early as the 15C.

However, the first permanent settlements began in the 17C. Within seven years of each other (1603-1610), Frenchman **Samuel de Champlain**, and Englishmen Henry Hudson and John Guy claimed the riches of the continent for their respective kings. Their claims led to nearly two centuries of war among the empires of France and England and the native peoples for hegemony. The rivalry in North America revolved mainly around the lucrative fur trade. In 1713, the **Treaty of Utrecht** secured a temporary peace that lasted until the **Seven Years' War** (1756-1763), in which France, Spain, Austria and Russia opposed Britain and Prussia. Before their final defeat by the British on the **Plains of Abraham** in 1759 *(p 175)*, the French not only established enduring settlements in the St Lawrence Valley, but also explored half the continent, founding an empire known as **New France**, which, at its greatest extent, stretched from Hudson Bay to New Orleans (Louisiana) and from Newfoundland nearly to the Rockies. This empire thrived on the fur trade. However, England's **Hudson's Bay Company (HBC)**, founded in 1670, gained control of all the lands draining into the great bay and exercised a monopoly over that area, challenged only by Scottish merchants who established themselves in Montreal after the British conquest of France and formed the **North West Company** in 1783.

The Movement towards Confederation. – In 1763, when the fall of New France was confirmed by the **Treaty of Paris**, the population of the future confederation of Canada was overwhelmingly French. A few settlements in Newfoundland and Halifax in Nova

Scotia were the only English-speaking exceptions. This imbalance was not to endure. The aftermath of the American Revolution brought thousands of **Loyalists** to the remaining British colonies (Nova Scotia, Prince Edward Island and Lower Canada, later named Quebec) and led to the creation of two more colonies—New Brunswick and Upper Canada (later Ontario).

Lower Canada and Upper Canada were reunited by the British Parliament's **Act of Union** in 1841. This law was prompted by a report by then-governor general, Lord Durham, based on his investigation of the 1837 rebellions in which Americans had participated. In addition to recommending union, the report proposed **responsible government**, a system of majority party rule in the assembly (the British government did not formally implement this system until 1847), partly in the hope of reducing American influence.

Threats and incursions by Americans during the War of 1812, the Rebellions of 1837, the American Civil War and the Fenian Raids of 1866-1870 convinced the British government that more settlers were needed if their colonies were to survive. The policy of offering free land to potential settlers played a significant role in the development of Canada during the 19C and early 20C.

Fear of American takeover encouraged the small groups of British colonists to unite for common defence. Their actions helped to propel the British Parliament into ratifying the **British North America Act** of 1867, which provided for **Canadian Confederation**. The resulting new political entity, initially composed of four founding provinces—**Ontario**, **Quebec**, **New Brunswick** and **Nova Scotia**—adopted a parliamentary system of government and separation of federal and provincial powers. Even as Confederation was negotiated, chief proponents John A. Macdonald and George-Étienne Cartier envisaged a dominion stretching from coast to coast. Between the eastern provinces and the small colony of British Columbia on the West Coast lay the immense, empty domain of the Hudson's Bay Company. Pressured by the British government, the company finally agreed in 1868 to relinquish its lands to the new Confederation for a cash settlement and rights to its posts and some land. As the new Dominion of Canada took possession, the Métis rebellion in the Red River Valley led to the creation of the fifth province, **Manitoba**, in 1870. Meanwhile, **British Columbia** began negotiations to become the sixth province, prompted by fear of an American takeover, and **Prince Edward Island** joined its sister maritime provinces in Confederation in 1873. The Yukon Territory was created in 1898 and entered Confederation in the same year.

Construction of the Canadian Pacific Railway. – To encourage British Columbia to join Confederation in 1871, the province was promised a transcontinental rail link. After a few false starts, construction finally got underway in 1881. It was an immense and difficult project, the western mountain ranges alone posing a formidable barrier. Building the line over the steep grades of **Kicking Horse Pass**, for example, was one of the great achievements of railroad engineering. **Rogers Pass** and **Fraser Canyon** were only slightly lesser obstacles.

Serious problems beset the laying of track in the Canadian Shield country north of Lake Superior where, at one moment, tonnes of granite had to be blasted out and at the next, track lines would collapse into the muskeg. In the Prairies, however, all records for track laying were broken: in one day, a total of 10km/6mi were laid, a record never surpassed by manual labour. This progress was achieved under the dynamic management of **William Van Horne**, who later became president of the Canadian Pacific Railway Company. In only four years, the line was completed.

The Twentieth Century. – Canada's purchase of land, controlled by the HBC opened the way for settlement of the West; the building of the transcontinental rail line provided the means. Thousands of immigrants poured into the region, necessitating the creation of two new provinces in 1905—**Saskatchewan** and **Alberta**. Soon afterwards, what was then much of the remaining Northwest Territories was redistributed to the other provinces.

Canada played a substantial role in both world wars, and finally achieved complete control of its external affairs in 1931 by the **Statute of Westminster**, a British law that clarified Canada's parliamentary powers. After World War II, Canada's tenth province was added when the citizens of **Newfoundland** voted to join the Confederation in 1949. In the postwar years, Canada found itself becoming a major industrial country, with an influx of immigrants who provided the skills and labour vital to economic growth.

The 1960s saw the beginnings of Quebec's **separatist movement**, resulting from cumulative grievances of French Canadians. The Federal Government accelerated efforts to accommodate Quebecers' demands, including broader educational funding and official bilingualism. In 1969, institutional bilingualism was established at the federal level by the Official Languages Act. Separatists were defeated at the provincial polls in 1973, but were victorious in 1976. In 1980, a move toward independence was rejected by the Quebec electorate, but the controversy continued.

In 1982, the British North American Act (1867) was renamed the Constitution Act, which repatriated the constitution from London. Quebec refused to sign the constitution, mainly since the agreement did not provide for transfer of legislative powers between federal and provincial governments. In 1987, the **Meech Lake Accord** *(p 149)* called for special status for Quebec. Federal and provincial ratification was not forthcoming by 1990, however. In 1992, a national referendum that would have granted special constitutional status to Quebec was defeated.

Canada's native population continues to press for autonomy and land settlements. The defeated 1992 referendum included a provision for self-governing powers for native peoples. Earlier that year, however, Canadians had voted in favour of dividing the Northwest Territories to form a self-administered Inuit homeland called **Nunavut** *(map pp 3-4)* after a seven-year transitional period. A goal of the **Assembly of First Nations** (AFN), representing some 500,000 Indians of the country's nearly one-million native population, is constitutionally guaranteed rights of self-government.

Multiculturalism is nothing new to Canada, a nation of wide ethnic and racial diversity. It remains to be seen, however, if the current socio-political upheaval and resulting introspection will fracture national unity or restore it.

CANADA TODAY

Population. – This immense country is inhabited by a relatively small number of people: some 27 million in 1991, compared to over 250 million in the US. The United Kingdom's total area of only 244,019sq km/94,216sq mi is home to some 57 million people. Canada's inhabitants are largely concentrated in a band about 160km/100mi wide immediately north of the Canadian/US border. The regional distribution is approximately British Columbia, Rockies, Yukon 12 percent; the Prairie provinces 18 percent; Ontario 37 percent; Quebec 25 percent; the Atlantic provinces 9 percent; Northwest Territories 0.2 percent. Although 62 percent of the population lives in Ontario and Quebec, mainly between Quebec City and Windsor, Canada is strongly characterized by regional distinctions.

Language and Culture. – Canada is a land of immigrants. A population of 5 million in 1900 grew to 12 million by the end of World War II and to almost 26 million in 1988, thanks largely to immigration. Considered to be the **"founding" nations**, the British and the French are the largest populations (37 and 32 percent respectively). To reflect this composition, Canada is officially bilingual. The largest concentration of French-speaking people is in Quebec, but Francophones are found in every province. The Federal Government tries to provide services in both languages nationwide. There are significant numbers of Germans, Italians, Ukrainians, Dutch and Poles, especially in the Prairie provinces and, of native Indian and Inuit, resulting in an interesting mosaic of cultures across the country.

Food and Drink. – Food in Canada varies little from that in the US, but there are many regional specialities of interest. British Columbia is famous for its **seafood**, especially king crab and salmon. The province produces a variety of fruit, such as peaches, cherries, grapes, and its own wine in the Okanagan Valley in British Columbia and in the Eastern Townships of Quebec. In the Prairies, the **beef** is excellent, along with fresh lake fish in the north, wild rice (a great delicacy collected by certain Indian tribes), berries of all types, and the heritage of many immigrant cultures—cabbage rolls, *pierogis* (dumplings), and borscht, for example. Southern Ontario is the great fruit and vegetable area of Canada and another wine-producing region.

Owing to its French heritage, Quebec has a fine culinary tradition. Many French restaurants, especially in Montreal and Quebec City, serve traditional French-Canadian cuisine—pork dishes, meat pie *(tourtière)*, soups, and a generous use of maple syrup. The Atlantic provinces are another great **seafood** region, especially oysters, lobster, scallops, and mussels. In Newfoundland, **screech**, a heady dark rum, or one of the country's fine **beers** is popular with meals—Canadians are great beer drinkers. New Brunswick is famous for **fiddleheads**, the new shoots of ferns available fresh in May and June, and for **dulse**, an edible seaweed. **Moose meat** and fresh lake fish are available in the Northwest Territories, as is **Arctic char**, a delicacy similar to trout and salmon in taste.

Government. – Canada is a **federal state** with ten provinces. Each province has its own elected legislature controlling regional affairs. The central government in **Ottawa**—the federal capital—assumes responsibility for such matters as defence, foreign affairs, transportation, trade, commerce, money and banking, and criminal law. The Federal Government is also directly responsible for administering Canada's two territories, the Yukon and the Northwest Territories (which is only one territory despite its name), and for the affairs of state of Canada's native Indian and Inuit peoples.

Though officially part of the Commonwealth, Canada functions in actuality as an independent nation. The Canadian Head of State is the **British monarch**. Her authority is exercised by the **governor general**, who was at one time appointed by the monarch, but today is chosen by the elected respresentatives of the Canadian people. However, the governor general is little more than a figurehead as actual power lies in the hands of the Canadian **prime minister**, the leader of the majority party in Canadian **Parliament**. This latter institution consists of an elected legislature called the **House of Commons**, and an appointed **Senate**, members of which are chosen by the governing party. The prime minister rules through a cabinet drawn from the elected representatives (sometimes from members of the Senate also), and must submit his or her government for re-election after a maximum of five years, or if he or she is defeated in the House of Commons.

International Relations. – After World War II, Canada was catapulted to global leadership as a founding country in the United Nations and as a member of the North Atlantic Treaty Organization (NATO). The country retains diplomatic missions in over 80 countries and has earned respect as an international peacekeeper. In addition, Canada is a regular participant in international conferences, including the yearly economic summit of the seven major industrialized democracies, known as the G7. In 1992, Canada, Mexico and the US gave preliminary approval to the North American Free Trade Agreement. Ratification by each country's legislature is needed for implementation of the far-reaching trade pact.

ECONOMY

The following is a very general account of economic activity in Canada. Additional information can be found in the regional introductions. The Canada Year Book *(published by Statistics Canada, Ottawa, Ontario K1A 0T6) is an excellent reference for readers seeking detailed information.*

Canada's great strength lies in the wealth of its natural resources such as forests, minerals, and energy fuels that form the base of its economy. The country has become an important trading nation, exporting about a quarter of its production, mostly in raw or partially processed form (minerals, wood products, grain) and importing nearly a third of all manufactured goods and services.

The US is Canada's largest trading partner, although trade links exist with almost every country in the world. The proposed North American Free Trade Agreement among Canada, Mexico and the US has received mixed reception, but, if adopted, will have a far-reaching impact on Canada's economy.

Land of Forests. – Forestry is of prime importance to Canada; trees in one form or another are among the country's most valuable assets. Over a third of the total land area is forested, and the forestry industry exists in every province. The industry is of great importance to British Columbia, which is best known for its sawn lumber, and to Quebec, a major producer of **newsprint**. Canada is the world's largest exporter of the latter commodity, supplying more than a third of total world consumption.

Riches Beneath the Soil. – Mining is an important activity in every region of Canada; it is the principal industry in the Northwest Territories and the Yukon. The country is a leading international producer of nickel and zinc (Ontario), potash (Saskatchewan), asbestos (Quebec), molybdenum (British Columbia), uranium (Saskatchewan and Ontario) and lead (British Columbia, Northwest Territories and New Brunswick). The country's premier base metals are gold (Ontario, Quebec and the Northwest Territories), copper (British Columbia, Ontario and Quebec) and iron ore found in the Labrador Trough (Quebec–Newfoundland) and Ontario.

Alberta is the leading province for **fossil fuels**. Its oil and gas production are greater in dollar value than all of Ontario's mines. Alberta possesses immense reserves awaiting exploitation in its Athabasca oil sands, and shares substantial coal reserves with British Columbia. Although fossil fuels are almost entirely restricted to Western Canada at present, recent offshore oil discoveries on the continental shelf off Newfoundland could change this restriction in the future.

Hydro-electric Giant. – The abundance and power of Canada's water sources offer exceptional opportunities for generation of hydro-electricity. Almost two-thirds of the country's electricity comes from this source. Generating stations operate in every province except Prince Edward Island, and Quebec's massive **James Bay Energy Project** *(p 148)*, with a capacity of more than 10,000 megawatts, is one of the largest hydro-electric engineering projects in the world. In Labrador, a huge generating station is located on the Churchill River. Other examples are in British Columbia on the Peace and Columbia rivers, in Quebec on the Manicouagan and Outardes rivers combined, in both Ontario and Quebec on the St Lawrence, in Saskatchewan on the South Saskatchewan, and in Manitoba on the Nelson.

The electricity produced powers industries involved in natural resource utilization such as smelting businesses and pulp mills. Plentiful and inexpensive hydro-electricity has attracted other industries such as the aluminum industry to Canada (British Columbia and Quebec). Canada's energy is transported via high-voltage power lines to southern Canada to heat Canadian homes. Canada's surplus electricity is exported to the US.

Traditional Occupations. – Despite the tough climate and terrain of much of Canada (a mere seven percent of its land surface is cultivated), **agriculture** occupies an important position in the economy of several regions. Wheat has long been the cornerstone in the Prairie provinces and grain is exported all over the world. Beef cattle are also raised in the Western provinces, whereas dairy products are more important in Ontario and Quebec, tobacco in Ontario, and potatoes in the Maritime provinces.

Fishing and **trapping** were for centuries Canada's primary industries and today, Canada is still a leading exporter of fish in the world. The Atlantic Coast supplies the vast majority of this resource, although a quarter of the value is provided by the rich Pacific salmon fishery. Canada is one of the largest suppliers of animal pelts in the world.

Manufacturing and Transportation. – Canada's manufacturing industry, while largely resource processing (forest products, mineral smelting, food and beverages, for example), is rapidly shifting into secondary manufacturing. A significant petrochemical industry exists in Alberta, Ontario and Quebec; automobile manufacture is centered in Ontario and Quebec; electrical and electronics industries are strong in the same two provinces and petroleum refining is a growth industry across the country.

Because of Canada's size, transportation has always been of prime importrance. Until about 1850, waterways commanded the country's economic growth. Fishing and timber industries and the fur trade all depended on water transport. Since then, wheat farming, mining and pulp and paper industries have grown largely dependent on rail transport. Even in these industries, movement of goods by water is not insignificant. The network of locks and canals known as the **St Lawrence Seaway** was opened in 1959, a massive joint engineering achievement between Canada and the US. This 3,790km/2,350mi waterway through the St Lawrence River and the Great Lakes significantly boosted Canada's economy: in particular, the country became an exporter of iron ore after the Seaway facilitated exploitation of Labrador and Quebec's huge deposits. The road network has expanded since World War II with the completion of the Trans-Canada Highway and the opening of the great northern roads—the Alaska and the Dempster highways. Aviation is playing an increasing role, especially in the North. Airplanes are sometimes the only means of supplying mineral exploration teams there and may, in the future, be used to remove exploited resources.

FURTHER READING

BC – Rockies – Yukon

The National Dream and the Last Spike by Pierre Berton *(McClelland & Stewart, 1970)*
Looking at Indian Art of the Northwest Coast by Hilary Stewart *(Douglas & McIntyre, 1992)*
The Streets Were Paved with Gold by Stan Cohen *(Pictorial Histories Publishing Co, 1991)*

Prairie Provinces

Saskatchewan by Edward McCourt *(Macmillan, 1977)*
Wilderness Man - the Strange Story of Grey Owl by Lovat Dickson *(General Publishing, 1991)*
Who Has Seen the Wind? by W. O. Mitchell *(Bantam Books, 1985)*
The Promised Land - Settling the West by Pierre Berton *(McClelland & Stewart, 1984)*

Ontario

Toronto - No Mean City by Eric Arthur *(University of Toronto Press, 1986)*
Rideau Waterway by Robert Legget *(University of Toronto Press, 1986)*
The Invasion of Canada 1812-13 by Pierre Berton *(McClelland & Stewart, 1980)*
Roughing it in the Bush by Susannah Moodie *(McClelland & Stewart, 1989)*
The Man from Glengarry by Ralph Connor *(McClelland & Stewart, 1987)*

Quebec

Montréal Guide - An Architectural and Historical Guide by Joshua Wolfe and Cécile Grenier *(Libre Expression, 1991)*
Two Solitudes by Hugh Maclennan *(General Publishers, 1991)*
Maria Chapdelaine by Louis Hémon *(General Publishers, 1992)*

Atlantic Provinces

The Fascinating World of New Brunswick by Stuart Trueman *(McClelland & Stewart, 1970)*
The Town that Died by Michael Bird *(McGraw Hill Ryerson, 1967)*
The Acadians of the Maritimes by Jean Daigle *(Université de Moncton, 1982)*
Anne of Green Gables by Lucy Maud Montgomery *(McGraw Hill Ryerson, 1968)*
Saint-Pierre and Miquelon by William Rannie *(W.F. Rannie, 1975)*
Outport People by Claire Mowat *(McClelland & Stewart, 1983)*
A History of Newfoundland and Labrador by Frederick W. Rowe *(McGraw Hill Ryerson, 1980)*

Northwest Territories

Company of Adventurers by Peter C. Newmann *(Penguin Books, 1985)*
People of the Deer by Farley Mowat *(Seal Books, 1984)*
The Snow Walker by Farley Mowat *(Seal Books, 1984)*
Sculpture of the Eskimo by George Swinton *(McClelland & Stewart, 1972)*
Northwest Territories Data Book produced by Government of Northwest Territories *(Outcrop, 1990/91)*

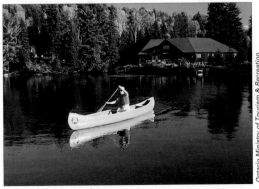

Ontario Ministry of Tourism & Recreation

British Columbia
Rockies ✤ Yukon

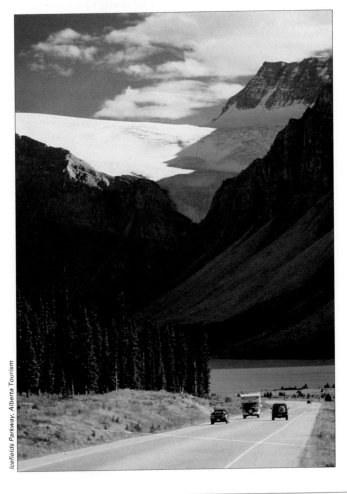

Icefields Parkway, Alberta Tourism

Known as the **Canadian Cordillera** *(map p 15)*, this region consists of the province of British Columbia, part of the province of Alberta, and the Yukon Territory. Covering the extreme west, it stretches from the Pacific Ocean to the Rockies and from the Canadian/US border to the Beaufort Sea. The high snow-capped peaks, massive glaciers, rugged ranges, mighty rivers, wild streams and tranquil lakes of this land of beauty attract millions of tourists every year.

GEOGRAPHICAL NOTES

Contrary to the belief that all mountains between the Prairies and the Pacific Ocean are the Rockies, this famous mountain range is only one of many in the region. Starting in the west, the **Coast Mountains** of British Columbia rise steeply out of the deeply indented and heavily forested Pacific Coast to over 3,000m/10,999ft. North of this chain in the Yukon are the high St Elias Mountains, which peak with Mount Logan at 5,959m/19,520ft, the highest point in Canada.

East of this coastal system lies an immense, elevated **plateau**. In the south, where it is nearly 300km/200mi wide, this plateau encompasses such diverse areas as the Cariboo ranch lands *(p 30)* and the irrigated Okanagan fruit-growing belt *(p 38)*. In the southeast, the plateau ends at the **Columbia Mountains** where the Cariboo, Purcell, Monashee and Selkirk ranges *(p 36)* are found. In the north, the plateau changes to an area of rugged hills—the Skeena and Cassier ranges—before spreading out into the vast Yukon Plateau, a basin-like area of rolling uplands, encircled by high mountains and drained by the Yukon River and its tributaries.

It is east of this interior plateau, across the Columbia Mountains and the Rocky Mountain Trench, that the **Rockies** are reached. About 150km/94mi wide at most, the Canadian Rockies stretch from the 49th parallel to the Yukon/British Columbia boundary. Rugged, with numerous peaks over 3,000m/10,000ft, they are spotted with glaciers, especially in the area of the Columbia Icefield *(p 48)*. In the east the rocky's front ranges rise abruptly above the foothills, giving the impression of a wall towering above the seemingly flat prairie lands of Alberta. At the Yukon/British Columbia boundary, the **Liard River**, a tributary of the Mackenzie River, carves a channel between the Rockies and the **Mackenzie Mountains**. North of the Mackenzies are the Richardson and British mountains, stretching almost to the Beaufort Sea.

Climate. – Tremendous variation marks the climate of this region, which extends from latitude 49° to north of the Arctic Circle, and has coasts on two oceans—the warm Pacific and the icy Arctic. Elevations range from sea level to nearly 6,100m/20,000ft.

The climate of coastal British Columbia is influenced by the warm waters of the Pacific, the prevailing westerly winds and the high Coast Mountains. Winters are mild (0°–5°C/30°–40°F) and summers warm, though not hot (15°–24°C/60°–75°F). Rainfall can be low in protected areas, but among the heaviest in the world in locations exposed to the full blast of winds off the Pacific *(p 61)*. Similarly, cloud cover can be light in protected places and heavy in exposed areas.

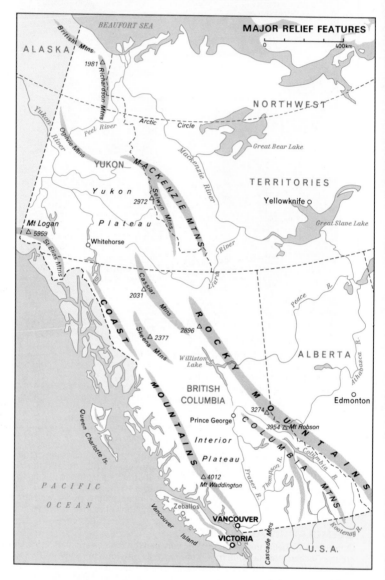

East of the Coast Mountains, one encounters a very different climatic regime with greater extremes of temperature and lower rainfall. Winters average –5°C/23°F and summers 22°C/72°F. Irrigation is needed in the Okanagan Valley to allow cultivation of its famous fruits, whereas the Selkirk Mountains have recorded the highest snowfall in Canada.

In the north, the towering St Elias Mountains cut the Yukon off from the moderating influences of the Pacific, but also from the high precipitation of the coast. Summers are pleasantly warm and dry (nearly 21°C/70°F and 23–43cm/9–17in of rain) with long hours of daylight (an average of 20 hours) during which the sun shines for a large percentage of the time. Winters, however, are dark and cold, though temperatures vary widely (Dawson City –27°C/–16°F, Whitehorse –15°C/–5°F).

HISTORICAL NOTES

The First Inhabitants. – Native peoples of this region fall into three basic groups: the wealthy, artistic tribes of the Pacific Coast; the tribes of hunters and fishermen who inhabited the British Columbia interior (known as the Cordillera Indians); and the Athapaskan-speaking tribes of the Yukon, whose lives were spent following the caribou in the same way as the Indians of the Northwest Territories *(p 230)*. The civilization created by the **Northwest Coast tribes** is unlike any other in North America.

Before the Europeans arrived, they enjoyed, in a country rich in resources, a high standard of living—far above the subsistence living of tribes in other regions. Wood from giant **cedar trees** that proliferated along the coast, and **salmon** from the ocean were the basis of their livelihood.

Having leisure time to devote to art, they developed a creative expression un-equalled on the continent north of Mexico. Tall tree trunks were carved with expressive forms and raised as **totem poles** before the houses of the chiefs. Carved with designs of birds, animals, humans and mythological creatures, these columns of cedar wood are not solely works of art. Each carving is a sign or crest of a family or clan, similar to coats-of-arms or heraldic emblems. Their purpose varied: some-times they were functional, serving as house corner posts; sometimes decorative, serving as the entrance to a house (a hole was made at the bottom of the pole); oth-er times they were memorials to dead relatives, or actually part of the grave. They represent an art form unique to the Northwest Coast Indians. The golden age of carving was 1850 to 1900, after the introduction of metal tools by Europeans. In recent years, there has been a revival of the art as Indians seek to re-create their traditions. The same designs were woven onto blankets, and carved into masks, chests, ornaments and jewellery. The more of the latter a man possessed, the wealthier he was, and the higher he ranked in the tribe's social structure.

The arrival of Europeans disrupted tribal life on the Northwest Coast, in the interior and in the Yukon. Indians were encouraged to hunt for furs to satisfy the demands of the European market. In exchange, they received firearms, alcohol and other imports, on which many tribes became dependent, and their lifestyle altered. In the Yukon, tribal life changed to a lesser degree because of the relative remoteness of the area. Along the Northwest Coast, perhaps because of the strength of the culture, many customs remain, however, and others are being revived *('Ksan p 54)*.

The Arrival of the Europeans. – European discovery of the region occurred from two directions. Small ships explored the coast, while fur traders, seeking new sup-plies and transportation routes, approached the interior. Although **Francis Drake** may have sighted the coast of British Columbia during his around-the-world voyage of 1579, the area was not explored until the 18C. Spaniards journeyed northward from California, and Russians travelled southward from Alaska. Capt **James Cook**, how-ever, made the first recorded landing during his voyage of 1778, sailing up the coast of British Columbia. Landing on Vancouver Island, he bought pelts from the Indians and sold them in China at great profit. News of this trade encouraged other Eng-lishmen and Spaniards to visit the North Pacific. A clash was inevitable. The British forced the Spaniards—who later retreated entirely—to declare the coasts open to all traders. To reinforce its claims, the British government sent an expedition under the command of Capt **George Vancouver**, who had been a midshipman on the Cook voyage, to map the coast. Between 1792 and 1794, Vancouver mapped practically the entire British Columbia coast.

Fur-Trading Empire. – The first European to glimpse the Canadian Rockies had come and gone with little fanfare. **Anthony Henday** of the Hudson's Bay Company (HBC) sighted the mountain wall in 1754, about 10 years after La Vérendrye's sons had viewed the range in Wyoming. Henday's report roused little interest at company headquarters. **Alexander Mackenzie** of the rival North West Company completed the first crossing of the continent north of Mexico in 1793, predating the **Lewis and Clark** expedition by 12 years. He climbed the Rockies by the Peace River, reaching the Pacific after a hazardous traverse of the British Columbia interior. Mackenzie had sought an easier route than the long canoe trek across the continent to the Pacific, where furs could be shipped to Europe.

Other "Nor'westers" sought alternative routes through the Rockies to the rich fur area west of the mountains. By following the Columbia and Kootenay rivers, **David Thompson** explored the Howse and Athabasca passes, the southeast corner of British Columbia, and northern Washington state between 1804 and 1811. Meanwhile **Simon Fraser** retraced Mackenzie's route in 1808 and descended the river that now bears his name.

While Fraser and Thompson were establishing posts and encouraging trade with Indians of the interior, an American fur-trading company created by **John Jacob Astor** founded a post at the mouth of the Columbia, beginning the American challenge to British ownership of the Oregon territory. In 1846, the rivalry was settled when the HBC (which merged in 1821 with its great competitor, the North West Company) was finally forced to accept the 49th parallel as the US frontier. The HBC moved its western headquarters from the Columbia River area to **Vancouver Island**, which was declared a crown colony in 1849 with Victoria as its capital. The rest of British Columbia (known as New Caledonia) remained the exclusive domain of the com-pany, as did the Yukon, where the firm established itself after 1842. Thus, in 1858, British Columbia, the Rockies and the Yukon were predominantly a fur trader's par-adise—a state of affairs that was to change very quickly.

Gold. – The discovery of gold in California in 1848 attracted countless people who hoped to make a fortune. Nine years later, the gold was gone, but prospectors did not stop looking. Many entered New Caledonia to search. In 1858, the news spread like wild fire—there was gold in the sandbars of the lower Fraser River. The small settlement of **Victoria** (pop 400) saw 20,000 people pass through en route to the gold fields. Afraid the influx of Americans would lead to an American takeover (as had occurred in California), the governor of the island colony, **James Douglas**, stepped in quickly to assert British sovereignty. The mainland was rapidly declared a British colony and named British Columbia, with Douglas as first governor. Poor trans-portation routes made control of the new territory difficult. When rich gold strikes in the Cariboo brought even more people, Douglas planned construction of a wagon road—the famous **Cariboo Road**, built between 1862 and 1865, which helped ensure British control of the area.

Confederation and a Railway. – The wealth from mining gold did not last long. The late 1860s saw economic disaster looming for the two western colonies (united in 1866; while in the east, the British colonies were discussing Confederation, which became a reality in 1867). US purchase of Alaska in 1867 again raised fears of an American takeover. Thus, negotiations concerning Hudson's Bay Company's domain were begun with the new Canada, located 3,200km/2,000mi away, and completed in 1871. British Columbia entered Confederation on the condition that, within 10 years, a railway would be built to connect the province with the east. The birth pains of such a massive project nearly led to British Columbia's withdrawal from the Confederation; but the project was completed in 1881 in the remarkably short time of four years *(p 18)*. When the last spike was hammered in at Craigellachie in November, 1885, and the transcontinental runs began the next year, the province was transformed. The railway brought tourists, settlers and capital to the impoverished region, and encouraged the search for mineral wealth and the utilization of natural resources that have made British Columbia what it is today.

"Ho for the Klondike". – When the Cariboo gold fields were exhausted, prospectors again moved north. Gold was found in the Omineca and Cassiar mountains. Then prospectors entered the Yukon, which was declared a district of the Northwest Territories in 1895 by the Canadian government, again because of fear of American encroachment. A detachment of the **Mounted Police** *(p 84)* was dispatched to maintain law and order—a timely move. The long-hoped-for big strike was made in 1896 on a small creek renamed "Bonanza," which drained into the Klondike River, a tributary of the Yukon. When news of the find became common knowledge, what has been described as "one of the world's greatest economic explosions" occurred. Thousands of men and women set off from all corners of the globe to reach the Klondike by a variety of means *(p 69)*. In eight years, $100,000,000 worth of gold was shipped out, providing an enormous stimulus for this western frontier.

THE REGION TODAY

British Columbia/Rockies. – In this century, especially since World War II, the growth of British Columbia has been spectacular. Discovery of gold in the Klondike spurred the search for minerals all over the Cordillera region, leading to the development of the Kootenays as the principal mining area *(p 35)* for the extraction of **lead, zinc** and **silver**. Copper and molybdenum are mined extensively in the province, especially in the Highland Valley near Kamloops. Sulphur, peat moss and gypsum are also found. The Crowsnest Pass area of the Kootenays is rich in **coal**, which is exported mainly to Japan. At Kitimat, there is a huge aluminum smelter (the bauxite, the principal source of aluminum, is imported), and asbestos is mined at Cassiar. Natural gas and oil are found in the Peace River area and farther north near Fort Nelson. They are transported south by pipeline where the oil is refined at Kamloops. Construction of the **Panama Canal**, opened in 1915, greatly stimulated exploitation and export of the province's minerals by providing a cheap means of transport to Europe. British Columbia's products were thereby competitive, worth exploiting. Roads and railways were built to carry the minerals to smelters and ports. This transportation network stimulated growth of the **forestry** industry. About a quarter of the marketable timber in North America is found in the province. In the moist climate of its coast, trees grow to great size. Annual timber cut is about 90.5 million cu m/3.2 billion cu ft, making forestry British Columbia's prime industry.
Hydro-electricity has also boomed since World War II. Two vast projects—the W.A.C. Bennett Dam with generating stations on the Peace River, and Mica Dam with a station on the Columbia—have capacities exceeding 2,000,000kW and 1,700,000kW respectively. Although British Columbia abounds with raw materials, it supports a large manufacturing industry. The province is also known for its rich coastal **fishing industry**: salmon, halibut, herring, clams, oysters and crab abound. Despite mountainous terrain and forest-covered slopes, **agriculture** thrives in some areas of the province. The lower Fraser Valley is a land of dairy cattle and crops; the Okanagan is famous for its tree fruits and wine industry; the Kootenays are also known for fruit; the great interior plateau called the Cariboo is cattle-raising country with large ranches, stampedes and rodeos; and the Peace River country east of the Rockies is British Columbia's chief grain-growing area.
Correspondingly, the **population** of British Columbia has increased from a little over 50,000 at the turn of the century to 3,282,000 today. The great majority of these inhabitants live in the southwest corner of the province, nearly half in the Vancouver metropolitan area.

The Yukon. – This territory's development has not been as spectacular as British Columbia's. The golden years of the Klondike Stampede were followed by years of economic stagnation, with the population falling from 27,219 in 1901 (even greater at the height of the Stampede) to 4,157 in 1921. World War II saw the construction of the Alaska Highway *(p 28)*, which has led to increased exploitation of the Territory's mineral wealth. Zinc, lead, silver, cadmium, copper, tungsten and gold are mined and transported south by road through the Coast Mountains to Skagway. Today, the population is once again at the turn-of-the-century level of some 27,000. Well over half the residents live in the territorial capital of Whitehorse.

"You cross the Rocky Mountains from the prairies to British Columbia, and you are in a different place: you are in another country....The Prairie Provinces are one place and British Columbia is another...a thing by itself: a vast Pacific Empire beside the sea."

Stephen Leacock, *My Discovery of the West,* 1937

Practical Information

Practical Information

** ALASKA HIGHWAY British Columbia, Yukon, Alaska

Map of Principal Sights p 2

This great road to the North, and adventure, passes through a land of mountains and lakes of rare beauty, largely untouched by mankind except for a scattering of small communities. Beginning at Dawson Creek in British Columbia, the highway parallels the Rocky Mountains, enters the Yukon along the valley of the Liard, touches the Cassiar and the Coast mountains of British Columbia, and follows the St Elias Mountains to enter Alaska, finally terminating in Fairbanks.

A Military Route. – To link Alaska and the Yukon with the road system farther south, the highway was constructed in 1942 by joint agreement between Canada and the US. When the Japanese bombed **Pearl Harbour** in 1941, landed in the Aleutian Islands, and threatened sea routes to Alaska, Americans feared an imminent invasion of mainland Alaska. A land route between the US and Alaska was considered essential. Thus, in only nine months, 2,451km/1,523mi of highway were built by the US Army Corps of Engineers. Traversing muskeg swamps, bridging wide rivers, climbing or avoiding mountain ranges, the road has become a legend in the annals of road construction. Upgraded after World War II and opened to civilian traffic, the highway is of major economic importance as a means of transporting the region's mineral wealth and the tourists who travel its length.

Practical Information. – The Alaska Highway is either a paved or treated bituminous surface over most of its length. Travel on it is possible all months of the year. The period of thaw in spring can make driving conditions difficult some years, but highway advisories are broadcast promptly. Service stations able to perform repairs are situated at regular intervals; however, vehicles should be in good mechanical condition before starting out. The speed limit varies from 70km/h (43mph) to 90km/h (55mph); watch posted signs. Headlights should be kept on at all times. For road conditions, contact the nearest tourist office.

Distances are marked by kilometre posts and measured from Dawson Creek, BC. For example, Watson Lake is at km 1,017/mi 632. **Historical miles** are measurements originally used in the 1940s by lodgings along the route. Although inaccurate now, these readings are traditionally employed by businesses as indicators of their location.

A most helpful annually updated publication is *The Milepost*, which describes natural and historical sights, eating establishments and overnight accommodation mile by mile. This book may be purchased from GTE Discovery Publications, Inc, PO Box 3007, Bothell, WA 98041-3007; ☎206/487-6100.

Many tourists stay in campgrounds provided by the governments of the Yukon and British Columbia. There are, however, motels and other accommodation.

FROM DAWSON CREEK TO FORT NELSON *483km/300mi*

The Alaska Highway begins at **Dawson Creek** (pop 10,981), BC, in the region of the Peace River. The rural nature of the area is immediately striking: green and gold patches of wheat, barley and other crops, neatly laid out in grid patterns. The descent into the river valley is lengthy and somewhat winding. At **Taylor**, which sits on a vast natural gas and oil field, the river is crossed. Gas processing plants can be seen along the highway and oil pipelines run beneath fields of crops all the way to **Fort St John** (pop 14,156).

** **Excursion to W.A.C. Bennett Dam.** – *234km/145mi round-trip. Allow 1 day. Take Hwy 29 W 11km/7mi north of Fort St John to Hudson's Hope, then Dam Access Rd. Caution: steep, winding roads. Speed limits indicated for dangerous curves.* Except for the steep inclines of valley ascent and descent, this is a pleasant drive through lovely farmland with several breathtaking **views**★★ of the Peace River.

The road follows the river valley, climbing above it to permit exquisite **views★** of the flat-topped hills and fertile fields. The little village of **Hudson's Hope** (pop 985) was the site of one of Simon Fraser's trading posts and the place where Alexander Mackenzie began his portage around the Peace River Canyon on his epic trek to the West Coast. From the village, the winding dam access road ascends into the mountains with views of snow-capped peaks ahead.

Built between 1963 and 1967, the enormous earth-filled dam wedges the upper end of the canyon, creating a reservoir, **Williston Lake**. Measuring 362km/225mi in length, the lake encompasses part of the valleys of the Parsnip and Finlay rivers, which meet in the Rocky Mountain Trench and flow out eastward as the Peace River. The dam itself (183m/600ft high and 2km/1.25mi across) was constructed of glacial moraine deposited during the last ice age, 7km/4mi away from the old valley of the Peace River. In the post-glacial period, the river cut a new channel, the aforementioned canyon. Material that blocked the river's course about 15,000 years ago was used to reblock it when the present dam was built.

At present, the project generates over 2,416,000kW of electricity—23 percent of the total electrical requirements for the province of British Columbia.

★ **G. M. Schrum Generating Station.** – *Visit by guided tour only Victoria Day–Thanksgiving. Off-season Mon–Fri. Reservations required. ✗ (summer) ৬ ☎604/783-5211.* The tour begins at the **visitor centre**, which houses several interactive exhibits on electricity, water wheels, magnets and motors. A film (*10min*) on the history of the site and building of the dam follows. Then visitors descend by bus to the powerhouse, 152m/500ft underground and hewn out of solid rock. At the manifold chamber, water is seen surging from the turbines into the tailrace discharge tunnel. Explanatory diagrams are installed at each tour stop.

West Side Lookout. – *3km/2mi across dam. Steep road.* Good views of Williston Lake and the spillway are obtained from this viewpoint. Part of the canyon of the Peace River is visible with the reservoir of the smaller Peace Canyon Dam downstream.

★ **Peace Canyon Dam.** – *8km/5mi south of Hudson's Hope, on Hwy 29. Visitor cen-tre open for self-guided tours same times as Schrum Generating Station, daily Victoria Day–Thankgiving. Off-season Mon–Fri.* ☏*604/783-9943.* Located 23km/14mi downstream, the Peace Canyon Dam reuses water from the larger W.A.C. Bennett Dam to generate additional electricity. The 200 tonne/220 ton turbine runners (or water wheels) were manufactured in Russia and the generators in Japan. The pow-erhouse can be visited and the control room viewed. The observation deck and walkway over the dam provide good **views**.

After the junction with Highway 29, the Alaska Highway passes through flat and heavily wooded country that gradually becomes more mountainous. There is a good **view★** of the Rockies at km 314/mi 195, across the Minaker River Valley.

These views continue through heavy forest until the road reaches **Fort Nelson** (pop 3,804), a lumber centre and base for oil and gas exploration. The Liard Highway to Fort Simpson (Northwest Territories) via Fort Liard commences at this point, offer-ing access to spectacular Nahanni National Park Reserve *(p 234).*

★★ FROM FORT NELSON TO WHITEHORSE 991km/616mi

After leaving Fort Nelson, the highway turns west and offers many sweeping views of the mountains as the road traverses the end of the Rocky Mountains. The coun-try is very open and during the initial part of the drive, the mountains are largely flat-topped, more akin to the "mesa" mountains of the Southern Rockies in the US than to the pointed peaks of the Banff-Jasper area *(p 43).*

★ **Stone Mountain Provincial Park.** – *Km 627/mi 389. Open daily May–Oct.* ☏*604/ 787-3407.* A rocky and barren area resembling a stone quarry, this park is named for a mountain to the north of the highway. The mountains at this point are more rugged than previously. The highlight of the park is **Summit Lake★**, a lovely green-coloured stretch of water lying beside the highway.

After leaving the lake, the road passes through the rocky gorge of Macdonald Creek.

★★ **Muncho Lake Provincial Park.** – *Km 688/mi 427. Open daily May–Oct.* ☏*604/ 787-3407.* This park is one of the most beautiful parts of the drive. At first the road follows the valley of the Toad River, a wide, rocky and rather desolate area softened only by the pale-green colour of the river. The vista widens ahead, and more moun-tains come into view, many snow-capped. Stone sheep can often be seen licking salt from the road bed. Reached after entering the park *(46km/29mi)*, **Muncho Lake★★** mirrors the surrounding folded mountains that rise over 2,000m/7,000ft. Its aqua-marine colour is attributed to copper oxide.

At km 788/mi 490, the first view of the **Liard River** is obtained. Rising in the Yukon, this wild and turbulent river flows south into British Columbia and finally north again into the Northwest Territories to join the Mackenzie River. Its valley marks the north-ern limit of the Rocky Mountains. The highway follows the river for approximately 240km/150mi, providing some good views.

★ **Liard River Hot Springs Park.** – *Km 765/mi 478. Take side road on right to park-ing area; follow boardwalk. Open year-round. Changing rooms provided. Visitor programs May-Labour Day.* ⚠ ☏*604/787-3407.* This small park consists of large, hot sulphur pools (temperature averages 42°C/107°F) in natural surroundings, deep enough for swimming.

At km 947/mi 588, the highway crosses the 60th parallel, entering the Yukon Ter-ritory. The exit from British Columbia is not yet final, however, as the highway crosses and recrosses the boundary several times. Fine views of the **Cassiar Mountains** are obtained along this road.

Watson Lake. – Pop 912. *Km 1,016/mi 632.* This transportation and communica-tions centre for southern Yukon is famous for its collection of **signposts** *(illustration p 237).* In 1942, a homesick soldier, employed in the highway's construction, erect-ed a sign with the name of his hometown and its direction. Tourists have kept up the tradition. Today, some 17,000 signs from all over the continent and abroad line the highway through town.

From the south, the **Stewart-Cassiar Highway** (Route 37) joins the Alaska Highway at km 1,044/mi 649. Winding 800km/500mi through western British Columbia, this road provides an alternative route to the Yukon. After this junction, the Alaska Highway begins to cross the Cassiar Mountains, with good views of snow-capped peaks on both sides of the road.

At km 1,162/mi 722, a rise of land is traversed that marks the divide between two great river systems, the Mackenzie and the Yukon, which empty into the Arctic and Pacific oceans respectively.

Teslin Lake. – *Km 1,290/mi 802.* The name of this stretch of water means "long lake" in local Indian dialect. The highway crosses Nisutlin Bay and hugs the shore of this long narrow lake for about 48km/30mi. Frequently, the mountains and lake are bordered by clusters of Yukon's adopted emblem, the pinkish-purple flower called **fireweed**, common throughout the Yukon and British Columbia. At the head of the lake, the road crosses the Teslin River by a high bridge, a remnant of the days when river steamers carried traffic in this area and needed clearance under bridges.

Teslin. – Pop 181. *Km 1,294/mi 804.* This tiny town is the home of the **George Johnston Museum** *(open daily Victoria Day–Labour Day; $2.50;* ♿ ☏*403/390-2550),* which con-tains native dress and artifacts. Featured are the black and white **photographs** by Johnston (1884-1972) of his fellow Tlingit (KLING-it) Indians during the early 1900s.

★ **Excursion to Atlin.** – *At Jake's Corner, km 1,392/mi 865, take road south for 98km/ 61mi. This is a fairly isolated drive on unpaved road. Travel Infocentre in the Atlin Museum, 1st and Trainor sts.* ☎604/651-7522. An old gold-mining town, the small community of Atlin in British Columbia has a pretty **site★** overlooking a beautiful lake of the same name, backed by majestic snow-covered peaks. From Warm Bay Road, **Llewellyn Glacier** can be seen beyond Atlin Lake on a clear day.

★★ **Marsh Lake.** – *Km 1,428/mi 887.* Surrounded by mountains, this beautiful blue-green lake is really an arm of the much larger **Tagish Lake** to the south, and therefore part of the Yukon River system. Because of its proximity to Whitehorse, the lake is not as deserted as others passed on the highway; many houses can be seen along its edge. The road follows the lake for about 16km/10mi, with several lovely view-points. At the end of the lake, the road crosses the Yukon River *(p 69)* at a dam.

At km 1,445/mi 898, there is a good **view★** from above of the steep, white cliffs and clear green water of the fabled **Yukon River**, which rises only 24km/15mi from the Pacific and meanders nearly 3,200km/2,000mi, crossing the Arctic Circle before it finally jettisons its waters into the ocean.

★ **Whitehorse.** – *Km 1,474/mi 916. Description p 67.*

★★ **From Whitehorse to Alaska Border** (Alaska Highway). – *491km/305mi. Description (in opposite direction) p 71.*

★ # The CARIBOO   British Columbia

Map of Principal Sights p 2

The Cariboo is the name given to the region in the valley of the Fraser River, north of the Thompson River. Part of the central plateau of British Columbia, this region is a vast rolling plain of low arid hills, lakes and sagebrush, bounded to the east by the Cariboo Mountains—from which the area gets its name—and to the west, by the Coast Mountains.

Opened by fur traders, the Cariboo first reached prominence with the Gold Rush of 1861, which led to the building of the Cariboo Road. Once the gold was gone, the miners left and farmers moved in. Today, the main economic activity is cattle rais-ing; some of the largest ranches in Canada are found in this region. The centre of the area is **Williams Lake** (pop 10,385), which holds an annual stampede—considered the premier rodeo of the province—in the first week of July. Cowboys come from all over North America to vie for trophies. The largest stockyards of British Columbia are located in Williams Lake. A popular tourist area, the region is known for its sports fishing, game hunting, dude ranches and other traditional features of "Western" living, and for the restored Gold Rush town of **Barkerville**.

The Cariboo Gold Rush. – Gold was first found in this area in 1859 by prospectors who had made their way from California to the lower Fraser and then north, fol-lowing the gold trail. By 1861, large quantities were being extracted from the upper part of Williams Creek when **Billy Barker**, a Cornish sailor who had jumped ship at Victoria to try his luck, hit pay dirt in its lower reaches. Within 48 hours, he had extracted $1,000 worth of gold. The area boomed and towns such as Barkerville (named for Billy), Camerontown and Richfield sprang up.

Ten years after the first discovery, no more gold could be found, and the towns of the Cariboo were almost deserted. In Williams Creek alone, more than $50,000,000 worth of gold had been extracted. Barkerville was inhabited until 1958, when the provincial government transformed the site into a museum-town, carefully restor-ing it to its former splendour.

The Cariboo Road. – To facilitate transportation to the boom towns of the gold discovery, the government of British Columbia (the province was created in 1858) decided to build a wagon road to Barkerville from the lower Fraser River near Yale, some 650km/403mi. Following the wild rocky canyon of the Fraser, the road, com-pleted in 1865, was the remarkable engineering achievement of Royal Engineers from Britain, army engineers and private contractors. Over much of the route, solid rock had to be blasted. The old road has since been replaced by the Trans-Canada Highway, the Cariboo Highway (97) and Highway 26.

The **drive★** *(Hwy 97 north, then Hwy 26)* from Quesnel to Barkerville penetrates the Cariboo Mountains, passing **Cottonwood House** *(open daily mid-May–mid-Sept)*, one of the few remaining roadhouses on the old wagon road, and **Wells**, a mining com-munity.

★★ ## BARKERVILLE HISTORIC TOWN
90km/56mi east of Quesnel by Hwy 26.

The old gold mining centre has a fine **site★** in the valley of Williams Creek, sur-rounded by mountains. The restored buildings of Barkerville include all the elements of a mining community such as stores, hotels, saloons and an assay office.

Visit. – *Open year-round daily 8am–8pm; winters dawn–dusk. $5.* ⚒ ⚙ ☎604/994-3332. In the **visitor centre**, the interesting video shows *(shown regularly in summer)* and displays on the town, the Gold Rush and methods of mining are a good in-troduction. Note the rather unusually shaped **St Saviour's Anglican Church**, a structure of whipsawn timber and square nails. At the far end of the street is the Chinese section with its **Chinese Freemasons' Hall** (the Chinese followed the other gold rushers north from California, but tended to stay within their own community). **Billy**

Barker's claim is marked, and the **Theatre Royal** stages typical Gold-Rush era shows *(Victoria Day–Jun Sun–Fri daily show; until Labour Day Sat–Thur two shows daily)*. A dramatized sketch of **Judge Baillie Begbie** is performed *(Jul–Aug Wed–Mon)* in the Richfield Courthouse *(1.6km/1mi walk up Williams Creek)*. Begbie was the famous Cariboo judge who enforced law and order in an unruly community. Visitors can also pan for gold in the Eldorado Mine *($3.50)*.

★★ DAWSON CITY   Yukon Territory   Pop 972

Map of Principal Sights p 2   Tourist Office ☎ 403/993-5575

Set on a dramatic **site★** on the east bank of the wide Yukon at its confluence with the Klondike, this historic frontier town—the heart of the Gold Rush—is truly a delight. Remarkably like a Western movie set, this former destination of thousands of fortune seekers retains its unpaved streets, pedestrian boardwalks and false facades, which enhance the feeling of being in a bygone era.

The Great Stampede. – News of the 1896 gold discovery on Bonanza Creek *(p 33)* spread like wildfire. Soon the whole area was staked by prospectors already in the Yukon. Instead of making a claim, a trader named **Joe Ladue** laid out a townsite on the level swampland at the mouth of the Klondike, amassing a fortune from his foresight. Lots were soon selling for as much as $5,000 a front foot on the main street. The heyday of Dawson was underway. Prices were skyhigh: eggs $1.00 each, nails $8.00 a pound; but everything was available: the latest Paris fashions, the best wines and foods. At more saloons than one could visit in a night, drinks were normally paid for in gold dust.

Dawson had a unique feature: despite being the biggest and richest of all the mining boom towns, it was the most law-abiding. The North West Mounted Police maintained tight control. Everything was closed down on Sundays. No one carried a gun except the police. Offenders were given a "blue ticket" (i.e., run out of town).

Decline and Revival. – The heyday was short-lived. By 1904, the rich **placer** fields were exhausted: $100 million in gold had been shipped out. Complicated machinery was needed to exploit any gold that remained. People left; the glamour departed. The age of the giant dredges began, and Dawson became a company town.

Dawson City c.1898

Yukon Archives/E.A Hegg

Once the largest Canadian city (pop 30,000) west of Winnipeg, Dawson City maintained its pre-eminence until World War II when Whitehorse—connected to the outside world by road (Alaska Highway), rail and air—took over, growing as Dawson shrank. In 1953, Whitehorse was made the capital of the Yukon. With this blow and the end of commercial gold mining in 1966, Dawson might have become a ghost town were it not for the tourist boom that is reviving the city. People still make a living mining the creeks, but little gold is found in comparison to the $22 million discovered in 1900.

The year-round population of nearly 1,000 swells in summertime with the arrival of tourists and seasonal residents. Situated less than 300km/200mi south of the Arctic Circle on fertile soil untouched by the last ice age, Dawson enjoys hot summers with nearly 24 hours of sunlight. Vegetables are cultivated in gardens, and flowers sprout through cracks along the streets. Many old buildings tell the story of a grandeur and wealth seen nowhere else so far north. Some sag sideways, however, because of permafrost. The Canadian government has embarked on a substantial restoration project that is returning the town to some of its former splendour.

Festivities. – Two important dates for tourists in Dawson are: June 21 when the midnight sun barely dips down behind the Ogilvie Mountains, and the third weekend in August when the anniversary of **Discovery Day** is celebrated with a parade, raft races on the Klondike River and other activities.

** DOWNTOWN *2 days*

Since Dawson's sights and tourist activities are numerous, it is best to first stop at the visitor centre (Front and King sts; open mid-May–mid-Sept ☎403/993-5566; year-round ☎403/993-5575) for a schedule of events and guided tours as well as a map. Informative audiovisuals and displays are also in the centre.

Historic buildings not open to the public usually have a window display [indicated (wd) below] depicting the structure's history.

Laid out in a grid pattern, this town lies in the shadow of the huge hill known as the Midnight Dome *(p 33)*, easily visible from downtown. On its face is **Moosehide Slide**, a natural landslide—thought to be the result of an underground spring—which has been less of a threat to the community than floods and fires.

On **Front Street** (also called First Avenue) stands the **SS Keno**, a sternwheeler once used to transport silver, lead and zinc on the Stewart River from the mines in the Mayo district *(p 70)*. Built in Whitehorse in 1922, the steamer also made trips to Dawson. After its last voyage there in 1960, it was permanently dry docked there. Because damage was extensive, the flood of 1979 led to the building of a sandgravel dike along the riverbank where the steamers once docked. Next to the *Keno* is the former **Canadian Imperial Bank of Commerce**, a stately building with a pressed-tin facade made to imitate stone. The plaque on the exterior refers to its famous teller, Robert Service.

The former **British North American Bank**, with its handsome polished wood teller enclosure, occupies the corner of Queen Street and 2nd Avenue. The **assay office** contains a wide sampling of the instruments used to weigh Klondike gold. South on 2nd Avenue is **Ruby's Place** *(wd)*, one of several restored town buildings.

At Princess Street and 3rd, the renovated **Harrington's Store** *(open daily mid-May–mid-Sept)*, built in 1900, contains the comprehensive photo exhibit, *Dawson As They Saw It*. Across the street is **Billy Bigg's** blacksmith shop *(wd)* and north on 3rd, note the **KTM Building** *(wd)*, which served as a warehouse for the Klondike Thawing Machine Company in 1912.

Formerly a Carnegie Library, the neoclassical **Masonic Temple** corners 4th and Queen, while diagonally across the street is **Diamond Tooth Gertie's** Gambling Hall. Named for a notorious female resident, this establishment boasts the only legalized casino of its kind in Canada *(floor shows Mon–Sat mid-May–mid-Sept; $4.76; contact Klondike Visitors Association for details)*. Behind Gertie's is the colourful **Fire Hall**, which also contains city offices.

Back on 3rd Avenue are the **Dawson Daily News** (1898-1953) *(wd)* and **Madame Tremblay's Store** *(wd)*, restored to its 1913 appearance. Opposite, a clapboard building with a squat tower houses a replica of the original 1900 **Post Office** *(open daily Jun–Labour Day)*, designed by Englishman **Thomas W. Fuller**, who served as Canada's chief architect for 15 years, influencing the country's federal architecture in particular. He also designed the Government House and the Old Territorial Administration Building *(see below)*. Across King Street stands a replica of the **Palace Grand Theatre★** *(open daily mid-May–mid-Sept)*, a distinctive pinewood structure with an elaborate false front. Built in 1899 by "Arizona Charlie" Meadows, the original theatre offered everything from opera to wild west shows. Draped with Old Glory and Union Jacks, the colourful two-tiered, U-shaped interior seats audiences in rows of padded "kitchen chairs." *Gaslight Follies,* turn-of-the-century vaudeville and melodrama, plays nightly *(performances Wed–Mon at 8pm; for reservations ☎403/ 993-6217).*

On Harper Street between 2nd and 3rd avenues is a photographer's favourite: the delapidated **Old Guns and Ammunition Shop**, victim to permafrost action. One street over is aptly named Church Street, site of the clapboard **St Paul's Anglican Church** built in 1902 with money collected from miners in the creeks.

Southward, double-porticoed **Government House**, where the Yukon's commissioner, or governor, lived in the early 1900s, overlooks Front Street. Designed by T. W. Fuller, the original residence had a more ornate exterior than the present structure, a replacement after a housefire in 1906. The house and grounds, once abundant with flowers, were the centre of Dawson's social life—host to afternoon teas, dinner receptions and summer garden parties. To the rear are the remains of **Fort Herchmer** *(not open to the public)*, a former North West Mounted Police barracks: married quarters, stables; jail; and commanding officer's residence. The renovated St Andrews **Presbyterian Manse** stands behind **St Andrews Church**, at 4th Avenue.

ADDITIONAL SIGHTS

★ Dawson City Museum. – *5th Ave. Open daily mid-May–mid-Sept. $3.25.* ✗ ও ☎403/993-5291. Dominating the upper section of 5th Avenue, the impressive Old Territorial Administration Building (1901, T. W. Fuller), in neoclassical style, houses the museum. The South Gallery has exhibits and re-creations of Dawson's Gold Rush; the North Gallery features early 20C city life in Dawson City. Locomotives of the short-lived Klondike Mines Railway are on display in an outdoor shelter.

Robert Service Cabin. – *8th Ave at Hanson St.* Overlooking the town from the southeast is a small log cabin with moose antlers over the door—the residence from 1909 to 1912 of the "poet of the Yukon" (1874-1958). Here he wrote his only novel, *The Trail of '98* and his last Yukon verses, *Rhymes of a Rolling Stone.* Though he arrived in Dawson shortly after the Gold Rush, his poetry—*Songs of a Sourdough* in particular—vividly re-creates the atmosphere of the times. Outdoor **recitals** of his poems are presented on the grounds *(daily mid-May–mid-Sept 10am & 3pm; 1hr; ☎403/993-5462).*

Jack London Interpretive Centre. – *8th Ave at Firth St.* The cabin of another writer who spent time in Dawson City during its heyday, American author **Jack London** (1876-1916), has been reconstructed on the property. His stories of the North,

Call of the Wild, White Fang and *Burning Daylight* are among his best-known works. The adjacent centre *(open daily Jun–mid-Sept; ☎403/993-5575)* houses a photo exhibit of London's life in the Klondike and of the mid-1960s search for his original cabin, found in the vicinity of Henderson Creek, some 73km/45mi south of Dawson City. There is also a **lecture** about his life and works *(daily at 1pm; 30min).*

EXCURSIONS

Midnight Dome. – *9km/5mi by Dome Road—a steep, winding road.* So named because of the midnight sun visible here on June 21, this mountain rises 884m/ 2,900ft behind the townsite. From the summit, the **view★★** is splendid, day or night. Below lies Dawson at the junction of the Yukon and Klondike rivers—the Yukon weaving its way south to north, wide and muddy; the Klondike making a clear streak that is absorbed as it enters the Yukon. Even Bonanza Creek can be seen entering the Klondike. The devastation of the whole area caused by the dredges is evident. There are mountains in all directions; to the north, the Ogilvie Mountains are particularly impressive.

★★ **Bonanza Creek.** – *4km/2.5mi by Klondike Hwy from town to Bonanza Creek Rd. Unpaved road, maintained for 16km/10mi.* The road along Bonanza Creek winds through huge piles of **tailings**, or washed gravel refuse, left by the mining dredges. Large-scale mining activity still takes place here and throughout the Klondike today. The largest remnant of earlier mining equiment is **No. 4 dredge** on Claim 17BD. (Claims of 152m/500ft were staked out and numbered in relation to the discovery claim: 17BD means 17 claims below, or downstream of, discovery; 7AD means 7 claims above discovery.) An enormous wooden-hulled, bucket-lined machine, the dredge consists of four basic parts *(shown in the exhibit panels)*: a barge for flotation; a series of steel buckets to excavate the gravel in front of the barge and to deliver it to the barge's housing; the housing itself where gravel was washed with water and the gold recovered; and a conveyor or stacker to disgorge barren gravel behind the barge, creating tailings.

Signs designate a claim provided by the Klondike Visitors Association for enterprising visitors who wish to **pan for gold** *(details available from the visitor centre).*

A simple plaque marks the place where the Klondike Stampede began: **Discovery Claim** itself *(14.5km/9mi from junction with Klondike Hwy).* Farther on *(19km/12mi from junction),* Eldorado Creek joins Bonanza. Some of the richest claims were located on Eldorado and the community at the junction, Grand Forks, was once a thriving place. Today, nothing remains.

Bear Creek. – *13km/8mi by Klondike Hwy from town to Bear Creek Rd. Visit by guided tour (1hr) only daily mid-May–mid-Sept. ☎403/993-5462.* Closed by the Yukon Consolidated Gold Company in 1966, this sizeable compound was once a busy community of over 2,000 workers engaged in the maintenance of a fleet of dredges. The visit includes the cavernous machine shop and the orderly **gold room**, where each step in the refining process is clearly described. An archival film *(5min)* closes the tour.

★ **FORT ST JAMES** British Columbia   Pop 2,058

Map of Principal Sights p 2

In a lovely setting beside Stuart Lake, this town, 154km/96mi northwest of Prince George, is one of the oldest settlements in British Columbia. Simon Fraser founded a trading post here in 1806 that became the chief Hudson's Bay Company post in New Caledonia *(p 25)* after 1821. It remained in operation until 1971.

★ **Fort St James National Historic Site.** – 🛈 *Beside lake in town. Open daily mid-May–Sept.* ♿ ☎604/996-7191. The park contains five restored Hudson's Bay Company buildings that date from 1884 to 1889. The **men's house**, trading store and officers' dwelling with their meticulously stored furnishings can be visited. Built off the ground, the **fish cache** with its displays of dried fish and pork and the dovetailed log **general warehouse** with its fur store can also be seen. The visitor centre has displays on the fort's history.

★★ **FRASER and THOMPSON CANYONS** British Columbia

Map of Principal Sights p 2

Between the city of Vancouver and Shuswap Lake, the Trans-Canada Highway follows deep valleys, cut by two of the wildest rivers in the province, through the rocky Coast Mountains and the dry, hilly scrubland of central British Columbia.

Taming an Impossible Route. – Alexander Mackenzie was the first European to see the Fraser River. On his epic journey to the Pacific in 1793, he followed its northern course. His partner in the North West Company, Simon Fraser, descended and reascended the river's entire length in 1808, traversing on foot along rock ledges and down ladders slung over rockfaces by the Indians. Fraser gave the river his name and that of David Thompson, geographer and another North Westerner, to its major tributary.

Too wild for a fur-trading route, the Fraser was little used until gold was discovered at **Hill's Bar** near Yale in 1858. Much of the metal was found in the ensuing rush, but the major strike occurred in the then-inaccessible Cariboo farther north. Above Yale, the river was too turbulent for steamboat passage (a few boats were winched through Hell's Gate, but a permanent water route was impossible). To solve the dilemma, the Cariboo Road was built *(p 30)*, the section through the Fraser Canyon taking two years to construct.

The Fraser and Thompson Canyons were again selected in the 19C for another substantial transportation venture: the Canadian Pacific Railway. The 20C has seen this once near-impassable passage become a major artery—now traversed by a second railway and the Trans-Canada Highway.

Billy Miner, who gained notoriety as the robber of Canadian Pacific Railway's Transcontinental Express, took up residence in Canada in 1904. Known for his courtesy during a hold-up, the American bandit is believed to have originated the command, "Hands up!"

★ FROM VANCOUVER TO HOPE   *141km/88mi*

The Trans-Canada Highway heads east from Vancouver along the wide valley of the Lower Fraser River, flanked by the Cascade Mountains—notably the pyramidal peak of Mount Baker to the south and the Coast Ranges to the north. Rich black soil, deposited over eons, supports dairy cattle, hay fields and market gardens.

★ Hope. – Pop 3,147. The mountains close in around this community as the valley narrows and swings northwards. The wildness and unpredictability of the region were well demonstrated by the **Hope Slide** of 1965. One January day, an immense amount of rock from Johnson Peak *(21km/13mi east by Rte 3)* slid into the valley, filling a lake and forcing its waters up the other side. Route 3 had to be rebuilt more than 45m/148ft above its original level.

Excursion to Manning Provincial Park. – *26km/16mi east of Hope by Rte 3.* After entering **Manning Provincial Park★** *(open year-round; hiking, horseback riding, bicycling, cross-country skiing; △ ⅄ ⴲ)*, Route 3 traverses an area called **Rhododendron Flats**, where these wild plants flower in profusion in mid-June and crosses **Allison Pass** (1,341m/4,400ft). In the **visitor centre** *(68km/42mi from Hope, just east of Manning Park Lodge; open daily May–Oct; off-season Mon–Fri; ☎604/840-8836)*, the three vegetation zones of the park are featured: the western slopes covered with the damp, dense growth of coastal British Columbia; the central area reflecting the transitional zone; and the eastern part with its dry and arid sagebrush country, so typical of the interior of the province. This park is one of only two places in Canada where visitors can drive to extensive subalpine meadows *(Mount Revelstoke p 37).*

★★ ① FRASER CANYON – From Hope to Lytton
Map p 38. 109km/68mi.

After Hope, mountains close in abruptly and farmland is left behind. The river changes into a rushing torrent, and the road is often situated on high rocky ledges or lower, at river level.

★ Yale. – Pop 18. Surrounded by high and impressive cliffs, this tiny hamlet was once a town of 20,000. During the Gold Rush, it was the terminus of river navigation and the beginning of the Cariboo Road.

Hill's Bar is located just to the south. To the north, the most spectacular part of the **canyon★★** begins. The cliffs are sheer, the valley narrow, tunnels are frequent, and the river below seethes along, around and over rocks.

Just after Spuzzum, the road crosses the river and continues on the east side.

★ Hell's Gate. – The canyon here is 180m/600ft deep, but the river, rushing past at 8m/25ft per second, is only 36m/120ft wide. The river was once wider, but during construction of the Canadian National Railway in 1914, a rockslide occurred, narrowing the gap. Thereafter, upstream passage was almost impossible for the salmon, their spawning grounds being the lakes and streams around Shuswap Lake. A sharp decline in the Pacific salmon fishing industry occurred until "fishways" were constructed between 1944 and 1946 to enable the salmon to bypass the turbulent water.

An **airtram** *(daily Apr–Thanksgiving; off-season Mon–Fri; $8; ⅄ ⴲ ☎604/867-9277)* descends 150m/500ft to river level, where the canyon and the incredible speed of the water can be appreciated. There are displays on the salmon and the fishways as well as a film *(20min)*. The fishways are visible in the river, but salmon are rarely seen because the water is murky.

The Pacific Salmon. – Every summer and autumn, British Columbia's five salmon species—sockeye, pink, coho, spring and chum—leave the ocean and swim far inland up the province's rivers and streams to spawn. In none are their numbers greater than in the Fraser River, where they travel as far as 48km/30mi a day. Soon after spawning, they die. Their offspring remain in fresh water for about two years before heading to the ocean, where they mature in two to five years. Then the epic return journey to their spawning grounds occurs.

After Hell's Gate, the canyon becomes less dark and formidable, and there are more trees on its rocky slopes. From **Jackass Mountain**, there is a fine **view★** of the canyon from high above the river, and at Cisco Creek two bridges can be seen as the railways switch sides.

Lytton. – Pop 335. This community regularly registers the highest temperatures in Canada. Rather than the green pine trees of the lower Fraser Canyon, the vegetation is more the sagebrush of central British Columbia. At this point, the clear blue waters of the Thompson River surge into the muddy brown Fraser, making a streak visible for a short distance downstream.

★★ ② THOMPSON CANYON – From Lytton to Shuswap Lake
Map p 38. 230km/143mi.

The Trans-Canada Highway and the two railways leave the valley of the Fraser and turn east along the Thompson, passing through a dry, treeless and steep-sided **canyon★★**. The road winds and weaves along, making sharp bends. Just before Spences Bridge, where the road crosses the river, the remains of a great landslide that occurred in 1905 can be seen.

Then the river **valley★** gradually widens into a semi-desert area where scrub vegetation and sagebrush predominate. Occasionally, there is some cultivation of the terraces above the river, but only for irrigation. The remains of one such attempt can be seen 17km/11mi after Cache Creek at a place once called **Walhachin** ("abundance of the earth"). Between 1907 and 1914, a group of young British aristocrats built irrigation flumes to carry water to their fields, and for a while, the area flourished. World War I ended the experiment, as most of the men left to fight and were killed. Odd bits of flume and withered apple trees are all that remain.

Just before Savona, the Thompson expands to form **Kamloops Lake**. From the Trans-Canada Highway, there are some pleasant **views★** of this blue lake set in rocky arid hills. Again, irrigation is bringing some of the land under cultivation. The highway bypasses the industrial city of **Kamloops** (pop 67,057), and follows the south branch of the Thompson to its headwaters in **Shuswap Lake**. Here the country changes from dry barrenness to verdant green with sparkling waters. Many salmon spawn in this region after their long swim up the turbulent Fraser and Thompson rivers.

★★ INSIDE PASSAGE British Columbia
Map of Principal Sights p 2

This protected inland waterway, the result of past glaciation, cuts between the wildly indented northwest coast and the myriad islands that stretch from Puget Sound in Washington state to Skagway, Alaska—a total distance of 1,060 statute mi/ 1,696km. The portion of the route served by Canadian ferries extends from Port Hardy on the northern tip of Vancouver Island to Prince Rupert (507km/314mi), on the northwest coast of British Columbia, ushering visitors into a world of lush, tranquil beauty.

Cruise. – *Departs Port Hardy May 22–Sept three times weekly 7:30am, arrives Prince Rupert 10:30pm. $85 plus vehicle charge. Off-season Sat only 4:30pm, arrival Sun 9am. Reduced rates during off-season. Check-in 60min before sailing. Reservations strongly suggested. For schedules, vehicle charges & reservations contact BC Ferries, 1112 Fort St, Victoria, BC, V8V 4V2* ☎604/386-3431. From Port Hardy, the ferry crosses the open sea at Queen Charlotte Strait, then enters the sheltered waters of Fitz Hugh Sound. The remainder of this voyage through the narrow, spectacular Inside Passage offers close-up **views★★**, weather permitting, of islands to the west and the fjord-slashed coast of western British Columbia to the east. The low, mountainous terrain, densely forested in spruce and hemlock, drops steeply into the sea. Virtually uninhabited, the area retains only one substantial community, the town of Bella Bella (pop 1,104), home to the native Heiltsuk. Several abandoned cannery communities are passed during the cruise.

Eagles and sea birds, as well as such marine mammals as seals, dolphins, orca and humpback whales may be sighted during spring and fall migration. The highlight of the voyage comes near its northern end as the ferry enters the 40km/25mi **Grenville Channel★★**. At its narrowest, the channel measures only 549m/1,800ft across, with a maximum depth of 377m/1,236ft.

★ The KOOTENAYS British Columbia
Map of Principal Sights p 2

A major tributary of the Columbia, the Kootenay River winds through the southeast corner of British Columbia—an area of mountains, beautiful lakes and lush valleys— giving the region its name. Rising in the Rockies, the Kootenay traverses its own national park *(p 51)*, misses the headwaters of the Columbia by just over a kilometre at Canal Flats, flows south into the US, loops and returns to Canada to form Kootenay Lake, and finally joins the Columbia at Castlegar.

At the south end of the lake, the valley around **Creston** (pop 4,205) is full of grainfields, orchards and other fruit-bearing plants. The **Crowsnest Pass** region has some of the largest soft-coal deposits in North America. Farther west, copper, lead, zinc and silver are mined and processed in the huge smelter at **Trail** (pop 7,919).

Gold in the Wild Horse Valley. – The first settlers came to the region in 1864 when gold nuggets were found in the valley of the Wild Horse River, a tributary of the Kootenay. At the junction of these rivers, a certain John Galbraith set up a ferry service, and the settlement that developed took the name Galbraith's Ferry. From New Westminister, the former capital of British Columbia, a road was pushed through the mountains to the site by a young English engineer, **Edgar Dewdney**. To this day, the road (Route 3) bears his name. After the gold dwindled, settlers increasingly turned to farming and ranching. Land disputes with the Kootenay Indians resulted. A detachment of the North West Mounted Police was sent under the command of the famed Mountie, **Sam Steele** (1849-1919). He restored peace and order to the settlement, which changed its name to Fort Steele to honour him and to mark the first posting of police west of the Rockies.

* **Fort Steele Heritage Town.** – *16km/10mi northeast of Cranbrook by Rte 95. Open daily year-round. $5.* ⚒ ⚙ ☎*604/489-3351.* This former centre of a mining boom that brought prosperity to the Kootenays has a fine **site★** at the foot of the Rockies. The townsite has been re-created to represent a typical Kootenay community at the turn of the century.

The town of Fort Steele flourished in the early 1890s. Its death knell sounded when the railway over Crowsnest Pass bypassed the town, going instead to Cranbrook. In 1961, the provincial government began restoration of the practically deserted townsite. Today, Fort Steele lives again.

Among the many restored buildings, the **museum**, set in an old hotel, is the most interesting, with excellent displays on the history of the region. The North West Mounted Police barracks can also be visited. Live entertainment is provided in the **Wildhorse Theatre** *(Jul–Labour Day Tue–Sun; $6.50;* ☎*604/426-5682).* An old steam locomotive offers rides *(20min; $4)* and there are stagecoach tours of the site. Overlooking the Kootenay River stands a large wooden water wheel, once used to haul water out of the mines.

★★ MONASHEES and SELKIRKS British Columbia

Map below

Part of the Columbia Mountain System, the Monashee and Selkirk ranges are located in southeastern British Columbia between the central plateau and the Rockies. Starting as rolling hills in the west, they soon develop sharp ridges, deep valleys and pyramid peaks—the results of heavy glaciation, especially in the Selkirks of Glacier National Park where several valley glaciers still exist. The Trans-Canada Highway crosses the two ranges by an often spectacular route through Eagle and Rogers' passes.

FROM SICAMOUS TO GOLDEN
219km/136mi by Trans-Canada Hwy. Allow 6hrs.

* **Eagle Pass.** – *71km/44mi from Sicamous to Revelstoke.* This pass through the Monashee Mountains (*Monashee* is a Gaelic word meaning "mountain of peace") was discovered by **Walter Moberly** in 1865. According to popular legend, Moberly fired his gun at an eagle's nest and watched the birds fly away up a valley. Following them, he discovered the pass, henceforth known as Eagle Pass, which eventually became the chosen route for the Canadian Pacific Railway as well as the Trans-Canada Highway.

From the small town of **Sicamous** (pop 2,501), set on the narrows between Shuswap and Mara lakes, the Trans-Canada begins to climb the valley of the Eagle River. After 26km/16mi, the highway reaches **Craigellachie**. On November 7, 1885, the last spike of the Canadian Pacific Railway, linking east and west, was driven here *(note the plaque erected beside the railway tracks off the road on the right)*. Craigellachie is Gaelic and refers to the rallying point of the Grant clan in Scotland, a symbol well known to the Banffshire-born directors of the railway.

The highway rises more steeply and the valley narrows before the road reaches **Three Valley Gap★** *(47km/29mi)*, occupying a lovely **site★** beside Three Valley Lake, edged with sheer cliffs. Soon afterwards, the road arrives at the top of the pass *(55km/34mi)*, and then begins a steep descent to the Columbia in the valley of Tonakwatla Creek.

★★ **Revelstoke.** – Pop 7,729. Set on the east bank of the Columbia River at its junction with the Illecillewaet, this small community has a picturesque **site**★ surrounded by mountains—the Selkirks to the east, the Monashees to the west. Named for **Lord Revelstoke**, head of the London banking firm of Barings, which financed completion of the Canadian Pacific Railway in 1885, the town has become a summer-winter sports centre because of its proximity to **Mount Revelstoke National Park** *(open year-round; hiking, fishing, skiing, cross-country skiing;* ☎*604/837-7500).*

Just to the north, the **Revelstoke Dam** can be seen rising 175m/574ft above the Columbia River. A visitor centre *(4km/2.5mi north by Rte 23; open daily mid-Mar–Oct; BC Hydro* ☎*604/837-6211)* features displays on its construction and a model of all Columbia River power projects.

★★ **Mount Revelstoke Summit Parkway.** – *27km/16mi of gravel road, unsuitable for trailers. Begins on Trans-Can Hwy 1.6mi/1mi east of Revelstoke turnoff. 45min to ascend.* This road ascends the southwest face of Mount Revelstoke in a series of switchbacks. After 5.6km/3.5mi, there is a **viewpoint**★ of the town of Revelstoke, spread out on the bank of the Columbia. The snow-capped twin peaks of Mount Begbie dominate the Monashees, which backdrop the river. Just east of the town, the valley of Tonakwatla Creek is visible, cutting its way through the mountains.

At the summit, the **view**★★ extends to the north. The Columbia's steep-walled valley and the glaciated mountains of the Clachnacudainn Range, with their jagged peaks and bare slopes, can be seen. A short distance from the parking area, a lookout tower has displays identifying the visible peaks. The vegetation has completely changed. Instead of the red cedars, hemlocks and spruce of the lower slopes, there are only stunted and wind-pruned firs. Paths at the summit descend into the **alpine meadows**, where multi-coloured wild flowers abound in summer: Indian paintbrush (red), lupines (blue), arnica (yellow) and valerian (white).

★★ **Rogers Pass.** – ☞ *148km/92mi from Revelstoke to Golden.* After crossing the Rockies by Kicking Horse Pass *(p 46)*, the Canadian Pacific Railway was supposed to follow the Columbia River loop *(map p 36)* because the Selkirks were considered an impenetrable barrier. In 1881, however, a determined surveyor, **Albert Rogers**, followed the Illecillewaet River into these same mountains and discovered the pass named for him. The railway was routed this way, saving 240km/150mi.

Avalanches. – From the beginning, incredibly high snowfall in the Selkirks (annual average 940cm/370in) and avalanches were obstacles to construction through the pass. Since the steep slopes of the mountains had been worn smooth by previous slides, nothing blocked the path of new avalanches. Kilometres of snowsheds were constructed over the railway, but the yearly winter battle with the elements proved too costly for Canadian Pacific. To avoid the most hazardous area, the Connaught Tunnel was built through Mount Macdonald in 1916.

For the next 40 years, the Rogers Pass section remained untouched. In 1959, however, after surveys were conducted, the decision was made to extend the Trans-Canada Highway through the pass, using the original railway roadbed. The highway was completed in 1962 when the section through the pass, the most expensive and challenging segment was finished. To double the track under Mount Macdonald, a second railway tunnel, the longest in North America (over 14km/9mi), was opened in 1988.

An elaborate defence system is in place. Concrete snowsheds deflect slides over the road, while rubble barriers divert and break up dangerous falls. Rangers stationed high in the mountains monitor snow pile-up; a howitzer is fired to trigger avalanches before they become too large.

★★ **From Rogers Pass to Golden.** – *May be temporarily closed when avalanche control is underway. Winter travellers must follow instructions by park wardens.* The Trans-Canada Highway follows the high-walled valley of the Illecillewaet River into the Selkirks, and soon passes through snowsheds that provide winter protection for the road. After 48km/30mi, the highway enters **Glacier National Park** *(open year-round; hiking, fishing, skiing, cross-country skiing;* △ ☎*604/837-6274).* Ahead, the four pointed peaks of the **Sir Donald Range** are visible: *(left to right)* Avalanche Mountain, Eagle Peak, Uto Peak, and the great slanting slab of Mount Sir Donald itself. To the north, the steep pyramidal form of **Mount Cheops** can be seen. To the south, there are views of glaciers across the rocky and bounding Illecillewaet River.

The road swings around the Napoleon Spur of Mount Cheops to reach the summit of the pass *(72km/45mi)*, where a double arch commemorates the completion of the highway in 1962. The **Rogers Pass Centre**★ *(open daily in summer; winter Wed–Sun)* has displays, models and films that explain the history of the pass and the annual battle against avalanches. The **view**★ includes the slide-scarred peaks of **Mount Tupper** and **The Hermit** to the north; the Asulkan Ridge and snowfields, including the Illecillewaet Glacier, to the south; and the peaks of the Sir Donald Range and Mount Cheops.

The road begins its steep descent between the bare slopes of Mount Tupper and The Hermit to the north and the looming form of **Mount Macdonald**. Passing through a series of reinforced concrete snowsheds, it swings into the valley of the Beaver River, a tributary of the Columbia, which separates the spiky Selkirks from the more-rounded Purcell Mountains. Then the road leaves the park, crosses the Columbia at Donald and follows the river south to **Golden** (pop 3,721) in the Rocky Mountain Trench.

If you love natural beauty, take care to pollute no stream, spoil no woodland, and leave only your footprint behind.

** OKANAGAN VALLEY British Columbia

Map of Principal Sights p 2

An important fruit-growing and wine-making region, this valley in south central British Columbia consists of a large lake (Okanagan), several smaller lakes, and the river of the same name (south of the US border, it is spelled Okanogan). Combined with lots of sunshine, intensive use of lake water for irrigation has made apple, peach, plum, grape, cherry, apricot and pear-growing possible in this area of low rainfall, arid hills and sagebrush. Beautiful lakes with sandy beaches have made the valley a popular resort.

FROM OSOYOOS TO VERNON
Map below. 177km/110mi by Rte 97. Allow 6hrs.

* **Osoyoos.** – Pop 3,403. This community lies on narrows in the middle of **Osoyoos Lake**. It is surrounded by arid hills and semi-desert country where sagebrush, grease-wood and cactus thrive, in sharp contrast to the green orchards on the lakeshore. **Anarchist Mountain** *(6km/4mi east on Rte 3)* provides a fine **view**★★ of the area.

** **Route 97 to Penticton.** – Through orchards and past fruit stands, Route 97 follows the Okanagan River to **Oliver** (pop 3,743). As the road approaches **Vaseux Lake**★, the scenery is impressive, with huge rocks and barren slopes. In contrast, the hills surrounding **Skaha Lake**★★ are sandy, covered with sagebrush and small trees. They offset the blue waters of this lovely lake.

** **Okanagan Game Farm.** – *8km/5mi south of Penticton. Open year-round daily 8am–dusk. $8.* ✗ ⅙ ☎*604/497-5405.* Overlooking Skaha Lake, this pleasant zoo is set among the low, rolling hills and scrub vegetation typical of the area. A circular drive *(5km/3mi)* enables visitors to view the animals from all parts of the world.

* **Penticton.** – Pop 27,258. A corruption of a Salish Indian word meaning "a place to live forever," Penticton has a pleasant **site**★ on narrows between Okanagan Lake and Skaha Lake, surrounded by rolling hills. It is a tourist resort with attractive beaches and parks on both lakes. Beside Okanagan Lake lies the *SS Sicamous*, a sternwheeler *(under renovation)* once used on the lake.

** **Route 97 to Kelowna.** – After leaving Penticton, Route 97 borders **Okanagan Lake**★★, offering lovely views. Near Summerland, steep white cliffs stand beside the lake. The road then passes through terraces of orchards and vineyards supported by irrigation. Note the lovely contrast between the blue of the lake, the green orchards, and the semi-desert sagebrush, rock and dry-soil hills.
The road follows the bend of the lake where, according to local Indian legend, the monster **Ogopogo** lives. Like his name, Ogopogo is supposed to look the same viewed from either end, but the descriptions of him are as varied as the people who claim to have spotted him. After Peachland, the road climbs up above the lake, leaving it temporarily to pass through the orchards before Kelowna.

★ **Kelowna.** – Pop 75,950. Route 97 crosses the narrows of Lake Okanagan to enter this town by a floating bridge, part of which can be raised to allow boats to pass. On this attractive **site★**, the town was founded by **Father Pandosy**, an Oblate priest who established a mission in 1859 and encouraged the settlers who followed him to cultivate the land. Today, Kelowna is the marketing centre for the Okanagan.

Route 97 to Vernon. – After Kelowna, the road skirts Wood Lake and winds along the eastern edge of **Kalamalka Lake★** where the rolling hills, still rocky but greener than farther south, descend directly into the water. This change of terrain continues as the fruit-growing area is left behind. North of the town of Vernon (pop 23,514), cattle raising predominates.

★★ **QUEEN CHARLOTTE ISLANDS** British Columbia Pop 5,316
Map of Principal Sights p 2

Separated from the northwest coast of British Columbia by the expansive Hecate Strait (50-130km/31-81mi), this remote archipelago comprises some 150 islands with a total landmass of approximately 10,126sq km/3,910sq mi. The two principal islands are Graham Island in the north, the largest and most populous; and, at the southern end, Moresby Island, which is predominantly a national park reserve. Essentially wilderness, the islands remain a habitat for a variety of marine mammals, sea birds and fish. The archipelago is renowned as the traditional homeland of the Haida, whose monumental totem poles are widely considered to represent the height of artistic expression among the **Northwest Coast cultures**.

Haida Gwaii. – The islands have long been known as Haida Gwaii, "Land of the Haida." Ethnically distinct from other Northwest Coast tribes, the Haida are believed to have inhabited this archipelago for over 7,000 years. Traditionally, they were superb craftsmen, seafarers, and fearless warriors given to plunder. Their villages were richly adorned with massive **totem poles** carved in the distinctive Haida style. Employing strong ovoid lines and animal motifs, the poles served different ceremonial and social purposes: house poles flanked doorways of clan longhouses; mortuary poles contained remains of important deceased villagers; memorial poles commemorated chiefs; heraldic poles recorded myths associated with a clan; and potlatch poles were raised during ceremonial feasts. The Haida were divided into two clans, Raven and Eagle, which were then subdivided into families. Kinship was traced matrilineally (through the mother's line).

European Contact. – In 1774, Spanish navigator Juan Perez Hernandez was the first European to sight these islands while on an expedition north from California. In the 1780s and 1790s, other Europeans sailed the Northwest Coast, bartering with natives for treasured sea otter pelts. George Dixon, a British trading captain, named the islands for **Queen Charlotte**, wife of King George III.
European contact introduced the Haida to iron tools that facilitated their wood carving. Larger, more elaborate totem poles were erected (some extant today) and more dugout canoes produced, allowing the Haida to trade and raid farther south. By the end of the 19C, however, Haida civilization was in decline: European diseases had decimated the population, and "pagan" potlatches and totem carving were halted as a result of missionary influence. By the early 20C, most of the traditional villages were abandoned as the Haida relocated to Graham Island.

The Islands Today. – Though located only 55km/34mi south of the Alaska Panhandle, the islands enjoy a temperate climate, thanks to the moderating effects of the warm Kuroshio Current. High annual rainfall and fertile soil support forests of Sikta spruce, hemlock and cedar. The southern third of the archipelago is a national park reserve that contains a World Heritage Site *(p 41)*. Year-round residents inhabit six communities on Graham Island and one on Moresby. Logging, fishing and tourism are major industries. A resurgence of Haida art and traditions, begun in the late 1950s, is evident today. Wood and argillite carvers, as well as silk-screen artists, are at work on Graham Island.

Practical Information

Access. – **Air** service to Sandspit from Vancouver is provided daily by Time Air (☎604/637-5660); to Masset from Prince Rupert by Waglisla Air Inc (☎604/626-5006) and Trans-Provincial Airlines (☎604/637-5355). Car rental available at airport (☎604/637-5688). Limo service offered by Twin Services Ltd ☎604/559-4461. BC Ferries offers year-round **ferry** service between Prince Rupert and Skidegate (departs Prince Rupert 11am; arrives Skidegate 5:30pm; one-way 7hrs; $17/person plus $65/vehicle; reservations strongly suggested; for schedules & fares contact BC Ferries, 1112 Fort St, Victoria, BC, V8V 4V2 ☎604/669-1211). Another ferry service connects Skidegate to Alliford Bay (departures year-round; hourly; fare: $0.75 vehicle, $2.25 passenger).
A **guide** ($3.95) giving information on history, attractions, parks, campsites and accommodation can be obtained by writing to Observer Publishing Co, PO Box 205, Queen Charlotte, BC, V0T 1S0 ☎604/559-4680. B&B's, full-service hotels, self-contained cottages and campgrounds offer a range of **accommodation**. For outfitters offering kayaking tours and cruises of varying lengths contact the Queen Charlotte Islands Chamber of Commerce, Box 420, Port Clements, BC, V0T 1R0 ☎604/557-4600 or the Canadian Parks Service *(p 244)*.

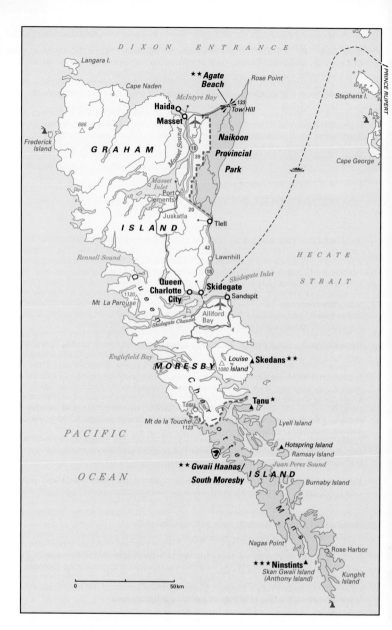

GRAHAM ISLAND   *Map above*

Largest of the Queen Charlottes, Graham Island is by far the most populous, home to roughly 4,600 inhabitants. The majority of residents live in the small logging, fishing and administrative towns and Haida villages on the east side of the island. A continuation of the mainland's Yellowhead Highway, Highway 16 runs in a north–south direction along the east side of the island, between Queen Charlotte City and Masset.

Queen Charlotte City. – Pop 1,200. This small town functions as the administrative heart of the islands. Catering to tourists from the mainland, many of whom arrive by ferry at nearby **Skidegate** (SKID-eh-get) **Landing**, the community centre consists of a line of hostelries, restaurants, gift shops and related services scattered along Skidegate Inlet *(information centre open daily year-round; Joy's Island Jewellers, 3922 Hwy 33 ☎604/559-4742).*

★ **Queen Charlotte Islands Museum.** – *1km/.6mi from ferry landing. Open daily Apr–Sept. Off-season Wed–Sun. $2.50.* ♿ ☎*604/559-4643.* Natural history exhibits and native artifacts, including argillite carvings and totem poles, are displayed in this museum. In the same complex, a reproduction longhouse serves as the Kinsàlang Haida Fine Arts Gallery and as the offices of the Haida Watchmen *(p 41).* An adjacent shed houses the stunning **Loo Taas**, an ornate 15m/50ft hand-crafted dugout canoe produced in traditional Haida style for Expo '86 in Vancouver.

Skidegate. – Pop 469. *1.5 km/.9mi from ferry.* Facing Rooney Bay, this long-time Haida community, locally called "the Village," serves as a political and cultural centre of the present-day Haida Nation. The offices of the Skidegate Band Council are housed in an impressive reproduction of a cedar **longhouse**, painted with Haida motifs. Internationally known Haida artist **Bill Reid** (b. 1920) created the elaborate frontal **totem pole★★**.

At the crossroads community of **Tlell**, the headquarters for Naikoon Provincial Park provides information on recreation and beach access *(open daily year-round; for additional information contact area supervisor ☎604/557-4390).*

Masset. – Pop 1,476. Located on Masset Sound, near its entrance to the open waters of McIntyre Bay, this community is the islands' largest municipality, owing in part to the presence of the Canadian Forces station. The town attracts sports anglers and beachcombers interested in exploring the island's spectacular northern beaches.

Haida. – Pop 632. Adjacent to Masset, this town, also known as Old Massett, overlooks Masset Harbour. An important hub of Haida culture, the community boasts several newly erected totem poles. Note especially the one located in front of St John's Anglican Church by acclaimed Haida artist **Robert Davidson**. The **Ed Jones Haida Museum** *(open Jul-Aug Mon-Fri; ☎604/626-3337)* displays old totem carvings, petroglyphs, silk-screen designs and natural history specimens from the islands. The works of Haida artists are sold in several village craftshops, including one whose exterior is painted with Haida designs and fronted by a finely carved totem pole by Davidson's brother, **Reg Davidson**.

Naikoon Provincial Park. – *9km/6mi east of Masset. Unpaved, but well-maintained beach access road. Open year-round. Park information centre in Tlell. Hiking, fishing, beachcombing.* △ This 72,640ha/179,421 acre park encompasses the lowlying northeast corner of Graham Island, with broad beaches and dunes fronting both Hecate Strait (east) and Dixon Entrance (north). At **Agate Beach★★** *(25km/15mi from Masset; public parking and beach access available at campground),* beachcombers congregate to search for the elusive stones that give the beach its name. To the north is a parking area for **Tow Hill** *(26km/16mi),* a forested basalt outcropping that rises 133m/436ft above the beach. An easy trail *(1hr round-trip)* leads to the summit, affording **views★** of the sweeping expanse of beach to the east and west. If weather permits, Alaska can be seen across the Dixon Entrance.

MORESBY ISLAND   *Map p 40*

Rimmed with inlets, fjords and smaller islands, the second largest island in the archipelago forms the bulk of the Gwaii Haanas/South Moresby National Park Reserve. The southern three-fifths of Moresby is encompassed by the park. The island's only town, **Sandspit**, traditionally a logging community, has become an access point for kayakers and cruise passengers beginning a tour of the reserve.
Moresby Island has been periodically logged since the mid-20C. Beginning in the mid-1970s, a 10-year conflict between logging interests, on the one hand, and Haida and environmentalists on the other, ultimately resulted in the creation of the park reserve. Scars of clear-cutting are still visible.
Forming the backbone of the island, the forested slopes of the Queen Charlotte Mountains (maximum elevation about 1,000m/3,300ft) often drop directly into the sea. Abundant rainfall has nourished impressive **rain forests★★** of towering spruce and cedar, luxuriant ferns and mosses. Bald eagles are frequently sighted in this wilderness, as well as deer, otters and bears. Seals, sea lions, porpoises and orca whales can sometimes be seen. A variety of fish, including red snapper, salmon, halibut and cod, abound in island waters.

★★ Gwaii Haanas/South Moresby National Park Reserve. – Deserving its Haida appellation, this wild and verdant 1,400sq km/541sq mi "Land of Wonder" nurtures a variety of wildlife and shelters the remains of a number of Haida villages. In 1988, the reserve was created to protect these natural and historical treasures.
Though many villages have reverted to forest, at several sites totem poles still stand and the remains of longhouses are clearly discernible. In an effort to protect their cultural heritage, the Haida implemented, in the mid-1980s, a program of caretakers, the **Haida Watchmen**, who are posted at the most popular sites during the summer.

Access. – *By sea or air only. Touring with an outfitter is strongly recommended since waters can be hazardous and weather is subject to sudden changes. For outfitters offering kayaking tours and cruises of varying lengths contact the Canadian Parks Service, Box 37, Queen Charlotte, BC, V0T 1S0 ☎604/559-8818; Sandspit ☎604/637-5362.*
Visitors are asked to register with the Canadian Parks Service or at the Haida Gwaii Watchmen office at Second Beach, Skidegate ☎604/559-4496.

Cruise. – *The following describes an outfitter cruise along the east and south coast of Moresby Island with disembarkation at sites described. Note: not all outfitters stop at these sites.* Situated on the east coast of Louise Island *(outside the national park reserve),* the remains of the village of **Skedans★★** contain a few erect totem poles, the overgrown and decaying remains of toppled ones and the depressions of several longhouses. Located on the east coast of Tanu Island, the ancient site of **Tanu★** also has the remains of fallen poles and longhouse depressions. Popular Hotspring Island offers three rock-lined natural **pools★★** *(open for public bathing)* in a fine coastal setting.
Added to the World Heritage list in 1981, Sgan Gwaii (also known as Anthony) Island occupies a spectacular site at the edge of the Pacific. Believed to have been occupied for 1,500 years, celebrated **Ninstints★★★** was one of the largest villages in the southern archipelago, with a population of 400 people. It faces a protected cove, and many of its totem poles have survived the effects of weathering. Today, a score of poles are still upright, giving the visitor a rare taste of what Haida civilization was like in the 19C.

★★★ **ROCKY MOUNTAIN PARKS** Alberta, British Columbia

Map of Principal Sights p 2

Internationally renowned for its spectacular mountain scenery, this chain of four contiguous national parks is one of Canada's most popular natural attractions, beckoning some six million sightseers a year. These terrestial wonders, with their diverse topography, vegetation and wildlife, are the jewels of western Canada.

Modern parkways dissect the region's wide river valleys, and hiking trails crisscross the back-country, allowing access to an awesomely rugged mountain world of soaring peaks, alpine lakes, waterfalls and glaciers.

Practical Information

When to visit. – The Rocky Mountain Parks are open year-round. The **summer season** is July to mid-September, peak season being July and August when daylight extends to 10pm. Visitors should be prepared for cold weather even in summer, since snowfall in August and September is not unusual. Throughout the **winter**, most park roads are open. Parkways are regularly cleared, but snow tires are recommended from November to February.

Access. – **Air** service to Calgary is provided daily by Canadian and US air carriers. Banff is 128km/79mi west of Calgary via Trans-Canada Highway and Jasper is 366km/227mi west of Edmonton via Highway 16. **VIA Rail** connects Jasper with Calgary, Edmonton and Vancouver. **Bus** service from Calgary to the Banff/Lake Louise area is offered by Pacific Western (☎403/762-4558), Brewster Transportation (☎403/762-6767) and Greyhound Bus Lines (☎403/265-9111). One-way fare $22. Car rentals (Avis, Hertz, Tilden/National) are available at Calgary Airport and in Banff.

Tourist Information. – Each national park has an information centre, operated by the Canadian Parks Service, where schedules, pamphlets, maps and permits are available. Information on Banff National Park can be obtained from **Banff Information Centre**, 224 Banff Ave ☎403/762-1550. At this location, the Banff/Lake Louise Chamber of Commerce Information Centre ☎403/762-8421 provides information on commercial facilities, services and activities in the area. The **Lake Louise Information Centre**, Samson Mall ☎403/522-3833 provides both information on Banff National Park and the Lake Louise area facilities and activities. A visitor guide to the area, *Where,* features activities, lodging, dining, shopping and maps.

Accommodation. – The Canadian Rockies are renowned for their **backcountry lodges**, generally accessible only by hiking, skiing or helicopter. These wilderness hostelries, most of them family-operated, range from rustic cabins to comfortable alpine chalets with fine food. Primitive cabins that rent for $11-16/night per person can be reserved through the Alpine Club of Canada, PO Box 2040, Canmore, AB, T0L 0M0 ☎403/678-3200. Many commercial campgrounds are located adjacent to the national parks. For information on campgrounds within the national parks, contact the park superintendent. A variety of accommodation such as hotels, resorts, motels, B&B's, chalets and condominiums is available in the area. For information on all types of lodging, contact the Banff/Lake Louise Chamber of Commerce Information Centre ☎403/762-8421.

Recreation. – All four national parks offer **hiking, backpacking, bicycling, horseback riding, canoeing, fishing, swimming** (except Yoho) and **winter sports**. Banff and Jasper have facilities for **tennis** and **golf**; boat tours and canoe rental are also available (for details contact Canadian Parks Service).

The Banff Springs Hotel boasts a 27-hole **golf** course. To reserve, contact the hotel ☎403/762-6801. Kananaskis Country Golf Course has two 18-hole courses; bookings should be made 60 days in advance ☎403/591-7070. Other area hotels offer golf. Outfitters specializing in **wilderness excursions** provide equipment, guides and transportation. Helicopter sightseeing excursions begin at $75. For more information contact the Banff/Lake Louise Chamber of Commerce Information Centre ☎403/762-8421.

The Banff/Lake Louise area offers **winter sports** from mid-November to mid-May including downhill skiing, heli-skiing, ice skating, dog sledding and cross-country skiing. There are three ski resorts: Lake Louise (☎403/522-3555); Sunshine Village (☎403/762-6500); Ski Mystic Ridge & Norquay (☎403/762-4421). Amenities include mountain lodges, daycare, ski rentals and professional ski schools. Access is offered with the purchase of a tri-area lift pass ($114/3 days). There is a free shuttle bus between hotels in Banff and Ski Mystic Ridge & Norquay.

The site of the 1988 Olympic nordic events features 56km/35mi of trails for the intermediate and advanced skier. Facilities include ski rentals, lessons and a day lodge; the use of trails is free (in summer mountain biking). Canmore Nordic Centre, Box 1979, Canmore, AB, T0L 0M0 ☎403/678-2400.

Useful Numbers (Area Code 403)
Canadian Parks Service Information:

Banff National Park	762-3324
Kootenay National Park	347-9615
Jasper National Park	852-6161
Yoho National Park	343-6324
Alberta Motor Association (CAA affiliate)	762-2711
Park Weather Forecasts	762-2088
RCMP	762-2226
Trail Conditions (summer) Avalanche Hazard (winter)	762-1460

The major parks in the Canadian Rockies are Banff, Jasper, Yoho and Kootenay National Parks and Mount Robson Provincial Park. Situated next to each other in the southern part of the mountain range, they form one of the largest mountain park-lands in the world, covering over 22,274sq km/8,600sq mi. The area contains other impressive provincial parks and reserves, notably **Mount Assiniboine** *(between Banff and Kootenay; not accessible by road);* and the **Kananaskis Country,** a preserve 90km/56mi southeast of Banff that includes three provincial parks. Waterton Lakes National Park *(p 66)* is situated apart from the other Rocky Mountain parks in the southwest corner of Alberta.

Canada's Rooftop. – Frequently rising over 3,000m/10,000ft, the Canadian Rockies constitute the easternmost range of North America's **Western Cordillera** *(p 15).* Beginning at the border with the US, the Canadian Rockies stretch roughly 1,550km/900mi through western Alberta and eastern British Columbia in a north-westerly direction. To the north, these mountains are bounded by the broad plain of the Liard River; to the east, by the Interior Plains; and to the west, by the **Rocky Mountain Trench** *(map p 48),* one of the longest continuous valleys in the world. The spine of the Rockies forms part of the **Continental Divide**.
Composed of sedimentary rock deposited by ancient seas some 1.5 billion years ago, the Rockies have a distinct layered appearance. They first began to uplift 120 to 70 million years ago because of the collision of tectonic plates. During the last ice age (75,000 to 11,000 years ago), glaciation carved the mountains into the terrain seen today: U-shaped valleys, glacially fed lakes, canyons, bowl-shaped cirques and hanging valleys with waterfalls and glaciers. Since the end of the Little Ice Age, or Cavell Advance, in 1870, the Rockies' glaciers have begun a significant retreat.

Fauna and Flora. – Still largely wilderness, the Rockies are inhabited by a variety of animal and plant life. Even along roadways, black bear, coyote, elk, moose, mule deer and mountain sheep, as well as squirrels and chipmunks, are often seen. More rarely, bighorn sheep and white-coated, short-horned mountain goats may be sight-ed, and in more remote areas, grizzly bears and wolverines make an infrequent appearance.
Plant life varies greatly, owing to drastic changes in elevation. Wildflowers are abun-dant throughout the vegetation zones. Their bloom follows the snowmelt up the mountainsides from late June through early August. Stands of Douglas fir, lodge-pole pine, white spruce and quaking aspen often cover the valleys, gradually giving way to alpine fir, Lyall's larch and Engelmann spruce on the higher slopes. Just below the tree line lies a band of krummholz vegetation—trees dwarfed by the severe conditions. Above the tree line (normally 2,200m/7,200ft on south-facing slopes, lower on north-facing), only the low, ground-hugging vegetation of the alpine tundra survives: hardy mosses, lichens, dwarf wildflowers and grasses.

From Wilderness to Watering Hole. – Archaeological evidence indicates early nomads traversed this region 10,000 years ago. The indigenous natives were over-whelmed, prior to European contact, by the **Stoney tribe,** who moved into the Rockies in the early 1700s. During the mid- to late-18C, the European **fur trade** burgeoned in the Rockies, and by the mid-19C, mountaineers and explorers had arrived.
By 1885, the **Canadian Pacific Railway** (CPR) line had crossed the Rockies and reached the West Coast. Recognizing the mountains' tourist potential, the CPR company con-vinced the government to establish "preserves"—the origin of the current parks. During the late 18C and early 19C, the railway company built a series of fine moun-tain chalets and hotels, a number of which are still in operation. By the 1920s, all four Rocky Mountain national parks had been established. In 1985, the combined four parks were designated a World Heritage Site.

★★★ ☐1 **BANFF NATIONAL PARK**　*Map p 49. Allow 2 days.*

Canada's first and most famous national park, Banff encompasses impressive peaks, scenic river valleys and the popular resort towns of Banff and Lake Louise. This pre-serve lies at the southeastern end of the chain of mountain parks.

The Growth of Siding 29. – In the 1880s, the construction of the transcontinental railroad and discovery of natural hot springs elevated Banff to national prominence. By 1883, the railway had reached Siding 29 (sidings are switch tracks from the main track). While prospecting for minerals, three rail workers found hot springs on Sulphur Mountain and attempted to stake a claim. But the interests of the railroad magnates, who had named Banff after Banffshire, Scotland, prevailed. The 26sq km/10sq mi Banff Hot Springs Reserve was established in 1885 by the government around Cave and Basin hot springs. In 1887, bathhouses were installed and a rail station built. The federal reserve was expanded to 673sq km/260sq mi and renamed Rocky Mountain Parks Reserve. In 1888, the CPR opened what was then the world's largest hotel, the **Banff Springs Hotel**. Built at the confluence of the Bow and Spray rivers, this renowned "chateau" remains the dominant landmark.
Banff gradually became a social gathering place for wealthy travellers, who arrived by train. Not until 1915, after a bitter fight, were automobiles admitted to the park, a factor that made the area more accessible to the general public. The reserve was renamed Banff National Park in 1930. One of Canada's major resort areas today, Banff draws an international crowd.

★★ **Banff Townsite and Area**　*Map p 44*

At the southeast end of the park system, this well-known resort town (pop 5,688) on the Bow River sits at an elevation of 1,380m/4,534ft amid breathtaking mountains. Though bustling with visitors much of the year, the community maintains the charm of a small alpine town.

Tourists and residents alike celebrate artistic creations during the annual, summer-long **Festival of the Arts**. An **information centre** *(224 Banff Ave, open daily year-round; closed Christmas; &. ☎403/762-1550)* operated by the Canadian Parks Service provides information on park activities. *Information on commercial facilities and services is available at the centre.*

★ **Whyte Museum of the Canadian Rockies [A].** – *111 Bear St. Open daily mid-May–mid-Oct. Off-season Tue–Sun. $3. &. ☎403/762-2291.* Opened in 1968, this contemporary building houses a heritage gallery that traces the history of mountaineering and tourism in the Canadian Rockies, and art galleries featuring changing exhibits by regional and international artists. The museum sponsors tours of the on-site heritage homes *(summer: Tue–Sun ; winter: weekends only)*.

★ **Banff Park Museum [B].** – ⊗ *93 Banff Ave. Open daily May–Oct. Off-season Thur–Mon. Closed Christmas & New Year's. &. ☎403/762-1558.* Constructed in the trestle-like "railway pagoda" style of the turn of the century, this historic museum maintains its 1905 appearance, both inside and out. Glass cases display a variety of minerals and taxidermied animals of the Rocky Mountains. Among the collections is a series of prints by renowned contemporary wildlife artist **Robert Bateman**.

★ **Cascade Gardens [D].** – *At the south end of Banff Ave, across Bow River Bridge. Open year-round.* These terraced gardens, with their rock-lined pools and cascades, provide an excellent **view★** of **Cascade Mountain**, the 2,998m/9,836ft peak that towers above the north end of Banff Avenue. The stone Gothic Revival building at the centre of the grounds houses the park administration offices.

★ **Luxton Museum.** – *1 Birch Ave, on the southeastern bank of the Bow River. Open daily year-round. $3.75. &. ☎403/762-2388.* A replica of a log fur-trading fort, this museum displays native artifacts and life-size dioramas depicting aspects of Plains Indian life. Formerly owned by the Glenbow Museum *(p 82)* of Calgary, the Luxton is now operated by the Buffalo Nations Cultural Society.

★ **Bow Falls.** – At the foot of the Banff Springs Hotel, the Bow River tumbles over a wide, low lip, just before flowing into the Spray River.

★★ **Cave and Basin Centennial Centre.** – ⊗ *Open Victoria Day–Labour Day daily 9am–7pm. Off-season daily 9am–5pm. Closed Christmas & New Year's. $3 (for pool). ☒ (summer) &. ☎403/762-1557.* The Canadian park system began at this site. The arched stone building, a re-creation of the 1914 bathhouse, surrounds an open-air swimming pool of hot springs water (average temperatures 30-35°C/86-95°F). The complex includes the natural cave pool fed by a hot spring *(not open for bathing)*, and a museum tracing the 100-year history of the Canadian parks system.

★★ **Sulphur Mountain.** – *3.5km/2.2mi from downtown. Access by gondola, 8-10min ascent. In operation daily Jan–mid-Nov. $8.50. ☒ &. ☎403/762-5438.* The 2,285m/7,500ft summit allows a 360° **view★★★** of the Bow Valley, Banff and the turreted Banff Springs Hotel (east and north); the Spray Valley (southeast); Mount Rundle and the more distant Fairholm Range and Lake Minnewanka (northeast); Mount Norquay (north), and the Sundance Range (southwest). Bighorn sheep frequently browse along the trails here.

★ **Upper Hot Springs.** – *3.5km/2.2mi from downtown. Open daily year-round. ☎403/762-1557.* Discovered a year after the Cave and Basin hot springs, the mineral waters (average temperature 38°C/ 100°F) now feed a large public pool.

★ **Hoodoos.** – These naturally sculpted pillars of cemented rock and gravel can be viewed from a scenic nature trail above Bow River *(1km/.6mi; trailhead off Tunnel Mountain Road)*.

★ **Lake Minnewanka Loop.** – *Begins 4km/2.4mi from downtown.* Along this 16km/10mi drive, three lakes serve as natural watersports playgrounds: Johnson; Two Jack; and Minnewanka, a dammed reservoir that is Banff Park's largest waterbody. Tour boats offer cruises down this lake to Devil's Gap *(departs daily mid-May–Sept; eight people minimum; $18; Minnewanka Tours ☎403/762-3473)*. Included on the drive is **Bankhead**, an abandoned early 20C coal-mining operation. An interpretive park trail explains the history of the site.

★ **Mount Norquay.** – *8km/5mi from downtown. Access by chair lift in winter only. In operation daily Dec–mid-Apr. Free transportation from major Banff hotels.* ✗. *For ski packages & schedules.* ☎403/762-4421. A well-graded switchback road climbs Stoney Squaw Mountain toward Mt Norquay's chair lift, providing increasingly better **views** south and east over Bow Valley and the townsite, backdropped by **Mount Rundle**, which is shaped like a tilted writing desk.

★ **Bow Valley Parkway to Lake Louise** (Highway 1A)
Map p 49. 48km/30mi. Begins 5.5km/3.5mi west of town.

An alternative to the faster-paced Trans-Canada Highway, this scenic parkway was the original 1920s road connecting Banff and Lake Louise. Sightings of elk, deer, moose and coyote are not uncommon along the road. Curving through evergreen forests along the north bank of the Bow River, the route offers **views**★ of the Sawback Range to the northeast—in particular, crenellated Castle Mountain—and of the Great Divide peaks to the southwest. Frequent lookouts feature interpretation of regional geology, flora and fauna. At **Johnston Canyon**★★ *(17km/11mi)*, a paved, often cantilevered, pathway over the narrow limestone canyon leads to **lower falls**★★ *(about 1km/.6mi)* and **upper falls**★★ *(about 1.6km/1mi)*. The Inkpots, a collection of cold springs, are located beyond the upper falls *(6km/4mi)*.

At Castle Junction, Hwy 93 leads west from Bow Valley Parkway to Kootenay National Park (see description p 5).

★★★ **Lake Louise and Area** *Map below*

Smaller and less congested than Banff, this townsite and its environs in the park's west-central section encompass massive, glaciated peaks and pristine lakes, most notably the legendary Lake Louise. Called "lake of little fishes" by the Stoney tribe, Lake Louise was first viewed by a non-native in 1882. Taken there by a Stoney guide, **Tom Wilson**, a packer for railway survey crews, named the waterbody Emerald Lake because of its brilliant blue-green colour. Two years later, the lake was renamed for Queen Victoria's daughter, Princess Louise Caroline Alberta. By 1890, a small guest chalet had been built on the shore. By the early 1900s, a road had been built to the lake, a larger chalet constructed, and guests were flocking there. In 1925, the CPR completed the present hotel, **Château Lake Louise**, which rises elegantly by the lake.

Lake Louise Village. – A small resort crossroads with several shops, hotels and visitor facilities, the village is located just off the Trans-Canada Highway. A park **information centre** *(open daily year-round; closed Christmas, Boxing Day & New Year's;* ♿ ☎403/522-3833) features excellent **displays** on the natural history of the area, including the Burgess Shale *(p 46)*, and provides information about drives, hikes and natural attractions.

*** Lake Louise. – *4km/2.5mi from village.* Set in a hanging valley backdropped by the majestic mountains of the Continental Divide, this beautiful glacier-fed lake, with the stately chateau near its shore, remains one of the most visited and photographed sites in the Canadian Rockies.

Visible at the far end, the **Victoria Glacier** once stretched to the site of the chateau. The 2km/1.2mi long, .5km/.3mi wide tarn (maximum depth 75m/246ft) was created when this glacier retreated, leaving enough morainal debris to serve as a dam. The chateau is actually built on the moraine. Fed by glacial meltwater draining off the surrounding peaks, the lake (maximum temperature 4°C/40°F) changes colour with light conditions and as the summer progresses. Known as glacial flour, fine powdery silt suspended in the water refracts the green rays of the spectrum and emits hues ranging from bluish-green to emerald.

The far end of the lake is dominated by **Mount Victoria** (3,464m/11,362ft). To the left of Victoria stands the rocky face of **Fairview Mountain** (2,744m/9,000ft), and to the right of Victoria rises the distinctive rounded shape of **The Beehive**. A 3km/1.8mi trail circles the lake. Additional trails ascend into the backcountry. Two popular day hikes lead to teahouses: one at Lake Agnes *(3.5km/2.2mi from the lake)* and another at the Plain of Six Glaciers *(5.5km/3.3mi from the lake)*. *Details on hikes available at the chateau and at park information centres.*

*** Moraine Lake. – *13km/8mi from village.* Smaller and less visited than Lake Louise, Moraine Lake nonetheless occupies a splendid **site**** below the sheer walls of the Wenkchemna peaks.

Moraine Lake Road climbs above Bow Valley, offering an impressive **view****, first of one of the park's highest peaks—ice-capped **Mount Temple** (3,543m/11,621ft)—and then of the glaciated **Wenkchemna** or **Ten Peaks**. A short walk leads up the rock pile damming the north end of the lake, providing the best **view*** of the surroundings. The pile is believed to be the result of a rock slide from the adjacent pinnacle of rock called the Tower of Babel. Other trails lead around the lake and to nearby backcountry lakes and valleys.

* Mount Whitehorn. – *Access by gondola. 12min ascent; in operation daily Jun–Sept, mid-Nov–mid-May.* ☒ ☎403/522-3555. From the top of the Friendly Giant gondola lift, a **panorama**** of Bow Valley is obtained, with the Wenkchemna peaks and Mount Temple filling the horizon. To the west, Lake Louise can be seen cupped below the Victoria Glacier.

** Great Divide Road (Highway 1A) *Map p 45*
14km/8mi from Lake Louise Village to western junction with Trans-Can Hwy; access 3km/1.8km west of the village.

Weaving through subalpine stands of fir, spruce and pine, this highway parallels the southwest side of the Trans-Canada Highway. An arch across the road *(10km/6mi from the village)* marks **Kicking Horse Pass** (1,625m/5,330ft), a point on the Great Divide, as well as the boundary between Alberta and British Columbia and between Banff and Yoho National Parks. The name of the pass derives from an incident here that befell geologist **James Hector** of the Palliser Expedition (1857-1860). Accidentally kicked by his horse, he became unconscious and, mistaken for dead, was almost buried by his men.

** 2 YOHO NATIONAL PARK
Map p 45. 1/2 day not including Burgess Shale.

Smallest and most compact of the parks, Yoho (a native word meaning awe) is a place of raging rivers and waterfalls. The preserve enjoys international renown as the site of the Burgess Shale, one of the most important fossil beds ever discovered. The Trans-Canada Highway cuts diagonally through the park. Situated in the centre of Yoho in the valley of the roaring Kicking Horse River, the small town of **Field** serves as a park hub. The **information centre** (open daily year-round ☎604/343-6324) features displays and videotapes on the Burgess Shale and other park attractions.

* Spiral Tunnels. – In the shape of an elongated figure eight, these tunnels allowed trains to make the treacherously steep, 4.5 percent descent down "The Big Hill" leading into the valley of the Kicking Horse River. A lookout about 9km/6mi beyond the northeast entrance to Yoho has interpretive signs tracing the history of the CPR's upper and lower tunnels. The opening of the lower tunnel in Mount Ogden can be seen from this vantage point.

** Yoho Valley. – *Access road of 13km/8mi with switchbacks; no trailers allowed.* Situated between Mount Field and Mount Ogden, lovely Yoho Valley is accessed by a climbing road that includes a lookout above the confluence of Yoho and Kicking Horse rivers. Near the road's end, Yoho Peak and Glacier can be seen straight ahead, with Takakkaw Falls to the right.

** Takakkaw Falls. – One of the highest waterfalls on the continent, this torrent of meltwalter from the Daly Glacier cascades in two stages for a combined total of 254m/833ft to join the Yoho River. A short paved walk leads to the base of the falls, which are visible from the road.

** Burgess Shale. – *Owing to the fragile nature of the sites, public visitation is by guided hike only. 4km/2.5mi round-trip to Mount Stephen's trilobite beds; 20km/12mi round-trip to Burgess Shale. Note: both are strenuous all-day hikes on steep trails. Jul-Sept three times weekly by reservation only. Space is very limited. Contact the park three weeks in advance ☎604/343-6524. For hikes led by licensed private guides contact Canadian Wilderness Tours ☎604/343-6470. Instead of hiking, visitors may choose to view Burgess Shale exhibits at, for example, Field and Lake Louise information centres.* Northwest of Field, a unique site on **Mount Burgess**

(2,583m/8,472ft) contains evidence of multicellular life found in the oceans 525 million years ago. Because of its abundant fossil deposits, the Burgess Shale enjoys world renown among professional paleontologists and amateur enthusiasts. In 1886, an employee of Canada's Geological Survey discovered rich trilobite beds on **Mount Stephen** (3,185m/10,447ft), which rises directly behind Field. In 1909, American paleontologist **Charles Walcott** found a rare fossil of a soft-bodied animal in a piece of shale, and later discovered a rich layer of fossil-bearing shale running through Mount Burgess. Since the Rockies were part of an ancient sea *(p 43)*, the fossils were well preserved in ocean sediment. Walcott spent three summers quarrying the site. Since his death, other scientists have intermittently worked the quarry. The Royal Ontario Museum is currently excavating the site.

The challenging trail to the Burgess Shale offers excellent **views★★** of Emerald Lake and the President Range, in particular. At the small, hillside quarry, visitors can observe researchers excavating shale by hand and see recent fossil finds.

★★★ **Emerald Lake.** – *Accessible via 8km/5mi road off Trans-Can Hwy. Refreshments; accommodation.* Aptly named by Tom Wilson in 1882, this beautiful lake lies at the foot of the President Range. Glacial runoff from these mountains gives the water its striking green colour.

Shortly after leaving the highway, the road to the lake offers views, from a parking area, of a **natural bridge** of limestone. Kicking Horse River has cut this passage for its narrowed, turbulent course. The **site★** is fine, with Mount Stephen rising above the river to the northeast and the mountains of the Van Horne Range visible downstream. The road ends at the lake. Situated at the southeastern end of the lake with Mount Burgess rising behind it, Emerald Lake Lodge traces its beginnings to a 1902 CPR chalet. Mount Wapta lies to the northeast and the peaks of the President Range to the west. A pleasant **trail★** *(5km/3mi)* circles the lake.

After the turnoff to Emerald Lake, the Trans-Canada Highway follows the scenic **lower gorge★★** of the Kicking Horse River to its junction with the Columbia River and the town of Golden.

★★★ ③ **ICEFIELDS PARKWAY** *Map p 49. Allow 1 day.*
    233km/145mi (Trans-Can Hwy junction to Jasper).

Designed expressly to dramatize the incredible landscape, this unequalled parkway (Highway 93) runs below the highest mountains in the Canadian Rockies. Following the valleys of five rivers, the road angles northwesterly along the eastern flank of the Continental Divide, connecting Banff and Jasper parks. Glaciers, lakes and waterfalls are abundant along the route, as are interpretive lookouts that explain the natural and human history of the area.

From its southern terminus, the parkway quickly climbs, with fine views of the Waputik Range.

★ **Hector Lake.** – *16km/10mi.* Named for James Hector *(p 46)*, the lake is set below the Waputik Range (south), Mount Hector (east) and Bow Peak (north).

★★ **Crowfoot Glacier.** – *33km/20mi.* After rounding Bow Peak, the parkway reaches a viewpoint for this glacier spread across the lower rock plateaus of Crowfoot Mountain. Now in retreat, the glacier has lost some of the ice that made it resemble a crow's foot.

★★ **Bow Lake.** – *37km/23mi.* Directly by the road, this lovely lake is best seen from the lookout leading to historic, red-roofed Num-ti-jah Lodge, visible on the north shore of the lake. The Bow Glacier hangs above the lake between Portal and St Nicholas peaks.

Passing through a green meadowland of birch and willow, the parkway reaches Bow Summit (2,069m/6,786ft), the highest pass on the route.

★★★ **Peyto Lake.** – *40km/25mi to spur road; park in upper lot where short trail leads to a viewpoint.* The striking turquoise waters of this lake are fed by Peyto Glacier. Both lake and glacier are named for turn-of-the-century guide, Bill Peyto. **Mistaya Mountain** rises sheerly from the opposite side of the lake, with Peyto Peak on its left. The Mistaya River Valley stretches north beyond the lake.

The road descends to the valley and passes a series of lakes. At **Upper Waterfowl Lake** lookout *(56km/35mi)*, there is a fine **view★** of the formidable stone expanse of the Great Divide peaks, especially towering Howse Peak (3,290m/10,791ft) and pyramidal Mount Chephren (3,307m/10,847ft).

★ **Mistaya Canyon.** – *72km/45mi to spur road for parking; follow trail into valley for 400m/1/4mi.* This narrow gorge, cut by the Mistaya River, is notable for its smooth, sculpted limestone walls.

Continuing northward, the parkway passes Mount Murchison (3,337m/10,945ft), which rises to the east, and the steep cliffs of Mount Wilson (3,261m/10,696ft), looming above the road. Both are part of the **Castle Mountain Syncline**, a downfold stratum that runs from Castle Mountain, outside Banff, to Mount Kerkeslin, near Jasper.

After the road descends into the valley of the North Saskatchewan River, a lookout *(76km/47mi; trail through trees)* affords a **view** of the Howse River Valley. David Thompson travelled this corridor in 1807 on his way to set up the first trading post west of the mountains, near present-day Invermere.

Very quickly, the parkway reaches its junction with Highway 11—the David Thompson Highway *(restaurant, services)*. The parkway then runs below the massive cliffs of Mount Wilson (to the east), with views first of Survey Peak and Mount Erasmus to the west and then the layer-cake facade of **Mount Amery**.

At 105km/65mi, the road hugs the base of Cirrus Mountain, the sheer cliffs of which are known as the **Weeping Wall** because streams cascade down them. Soon thereafter, the parkway rounds what is called the "big bend" and climbs quickly above the valley where a lookout allows a spectacular **view★★** of the North Saskatchewan Valley. A second, almost adjacent, lookout directly faces the filmy spray of **Bridal Veil Falls**.

★★ **Parker Ridge.** – *118km/73mi*. This ridgetop affords a magnificent **view★★★** of glaciated backcountry, particularly the **Saskatchewan Glacier**, one of the major glaciers of the Columbia Icefield *(see below)*. A switchback trail *(2.4km/1.5mi)* ascends through dwarf, subalpine forest and then through treeless tundra *(1.5hrs round-trip)*, carpeted in summer with dwarf alpine flowers.

At 122km/76mi, the parkway crosses Sunwapta Pass (2,035m/6,675ft) to enter Jasper National Park, with views ahead of Mount Athabasca and other peaks surrounding the Columbia Icefield.

★★★ **Athabasca Glacier.** – *127km/79mi*. This glacier is part of the vast **Columbia Icefield**, the largest subpolar icefield on the continent. The 325sq km/126sq mi Columbia lies along the Alberta/British Columbia border. The Athabasca and four other major outlet glaciers (Saskatchewan, Dome, Stutfield and Columbia), as well as smaller ones, flow off its eastern edge. Meltwater from these glaciers eventually feeds into three oceans: the Atlantic, Pacific and Arctic.

Situated along the high, remote tops of the Rockies at an altitude of over 3,000m/10,000ft, the icefield was apparently unknown until 1898, when a mountaineering expedition from Britain's Royal Geographical Society discovered and named it. From the parking lot of the Columbia Icefield Chalet, a **view★★★** encompasses the Athabasca, Kitchener and Dome glaciers. Nearby, the Columbia Icefield Information Bureau serves as the southern **information centre** *(open daily Victoria Day–Sept & ☎403/852-7030)* for Jasper National Park and functions as a small museum, with displays and an audio-visual presentation on glaciology.

Across the parkway is Sunwapta Lake, fed by the Athabasca Glacier. From the parking area, a short trail ascends to the toe of the glacier. In recent decades, the glacier has retreated dramatically. The progress of its recession is marked on signposts along the parking-lot access road and the trail.

★★ **SnoCoach Tours on the Glacier.** – *Access by commercial snow coach from ticket office beyond information centre, weather permitting. Note: expect long queues from 11am-2:30pm in July and August. Depart May–Oct daily 9am–5pm. $18.50.*

Columbia Icefield Snowmobile Tours ☎*403/762-6735.* These specially designed shuttle buses travel a short distance onto the upper end of the Athabasca Glacier and allow passengers to get off to briefly experience the glacial surface.

★ **Sunwapta Falls.** – *176km/109mi; 400m/1/4mi spur road to parking.* The Sunwapta River circles a small island, plunges over a cliff, makes a sharp turn around an ancient glacial moraine, and enters a deep limestone canyon.

Soon after the falls, the parkway enters the valley of the mighty **Athabasca River** and follows it to Jasper. This impressive valley is dominated on the west by the distinctive off-centre pyramid shape of **Mount Christie** (3,103m/10,180ft) and the three pinnacles of the Mount Fryatt massif (3,361m/ 11,024ft). To the northwest, the distant snow-capped summit of Mount Edith Cavell *(p 50)* slowly assumes prominence, while **Mount Kerkeslin** (2,956m/9,696ft), the final peak of the Castle Mountain Syncline, towers over the parkway to the east.

★★ **Athabasca Falls.** – *199km/123mi; turn left on Rte 93A for 500m/1/4 mi.* The silt-laden waters of the Athabasca River roar over a lip of quartzite and down a canyon smoothed by the force of the rushing waters. Backdropping the cataract, Mount Kerkeslin, slightly reddish from quartzite, has the same layering as the rock by the falls.

As the parkway approaches Jasper townsite, the Whistlers can be seen to the west. Straight ahead rises **Pyramid Mountain**, and to the east, the pinnacled peak of **Mount Tekarra**. At dusk, elk are frequently spotted grazing alongside the parkway near the Wapiti Campground.

★★★ 4 **JASPER NATIONAL PARK**
Map p 48. Allow 2 days.

The largest and northernmost of the four Rocky Mountain parks, Jasper National Park covers 10,878sq km/4,200sq mi, most of which is remote wilderness. In addition to spectacular terrain, Jasper also offers frequent opportunities to view wildlife.

BC, ROCKIES, YUKON

★ Jasper Townsite and Area *Map below*

This pleasant town sits in the valley of the Athabasca River near its confluence with the Miette River. Small and very beautiful lakes—**Pyramid**, **Patricia**, **Annette**, **Edith** and **Beauvert**, site of the well-known **Jasper Park Lodge**—surround the townsite. The peaks of nearby mountains are visible on the horizon, most notably Mount Edith Cavell to the south and rugged **Pyramid Mountain** (2,763m/9,063ft) to the north.

The Growth of Jasper. – In the early 19C, area natives saw increased European presence as fur traders used the Athabasca River and Pass as a route through the Rockies. In 1813, Jasper Hawes, a clerk for the North West Company, established a supply depot on Brule Lake, 35km/22mi north of the present townsite. The depot became known as "Jasper House," and ultimately gave the current townsite its name. In the 1860s, the **Overlanders**, a party of 125 gold seekers, passed through the region on their way to the goldfields of the Cariboo Mountains *(p 30)*. Except for mountaineers and trappers, the area had few inhabitants until the early 20C. In 1907, Jasper Forest Park, as it was then called, was created in anticipation of completion of the CPR across the Yellowhead Pass. The townsite grew from a railroad construction camp set up in 1911. Situated at the junction of the Yellowhead Highway and the Icefields Parkway, Jasper is the focal point of activity for the park and contains a park **information centre** *(Connaught Dr and Miette Ave. Open daily year-round;* & ☎403/852-6176).

★★ The Whistlers. – *Access by tramway; 5-7min ascent; in operation daily Apr–Oct. $9.65. ✗ & ☎403/852-3093.* The tramway ascends more than 900m/3,000ft to the terminal perched on the ridge of these 2,470m/8,102ft peaks named for the sound made by resident marmots. The **panorama★★★** from this elevation includes the townsite, the lake-dotted Athabasca Valley and the Colin Range to the northeast, and Mount Yellowhead and the Victoria Cross Ranges to the northwest. If visibility permits, the great white pyramid of Mount Robson *(p 51)* can be spotted beyond them. A trail climbs an additional 180m/600ft to the treeless ridgetop *(1.5hrs round-trip)*, offering a **view** to the south of Mounts Edith Cavell and Kerkeslin.

★★ Mount Edith Cavell. – *24km/15mi from townsite. Access via Icefields Pky to junction with 93A, then Mt Edith Cavell Rd.* Known as the queen of the range, this massif (3,368m/11,047ft) was named for an English nurse executed by the Germans in World War I for assisting Allied prisoners of war.
The narrow, twisting access road climbs steeply into the high country, paralleling the dramatic Astoria River Valley. By walking a short distance to **Cavell Lake** from the parking area for the Tonquin Valley trail *(26km/17mi)*, visitors can obtain a good **view** of the mountain. The lake's bright-green waters feed from the fast-receding, but lovely **Angel Glacier**, which is located on the mountain. At the end of the road *(2km/1.2mi drive)*, the trailhead is reached for the Path of the Glacier trail *(40min round-trip)*, which follows the toe of this ice river.

★★★ Maligne Valley *Map below and p 48*
96km/60mi round-trip by Hwy 16 and Maligne Lake Rd. 5hrs, including boat trip.

This valley cradles a magnificent lake and canyon, both also named Maligne (Ma-LEEN), which can mean malignant or injurious in French. Despite its name, the valley is among the most beautiful in the Rockies.

★★ Maligne Canyon. – *7km/ 4mi from Rte 93 junction.* The most spectacular of the Rocky Mountain gorges, this great slit carved in limestone reaches depths of 50m/164ft, while spanning less than 3m/10ft wide in places. A paved trail *(30min round-trip)* follows the top of the canyon, descending with the drop of the Maligne River. Bridges crossing the canyon serve as viewpoints.

★ Medicine Lake. – *22km/ 14mi.* The Colin Range to the north and the Maligne Range to the south hem in this lovely lake. From its highest levels during the snowmelt of early summer, the waterbody gradually shrinks as the season progresses, sometimes becoming only mud flats. Intriguingly, the lake has no surface outlet, draining instead through sink holes in the limestone bedrock and resurfacing in the waters of the Maligne River. The road follows the edge of the lake for 8km/ 5mi with several advantageous viewpoints.

★★★ **Maligne Lake.** – *For boat rentals, hiking trips, white-water rafting contact Maligne Tours Office* ☎*403/ 852-3370 or Maligne Lake Book Store in Jasper Park Lodge* ☎*403/852-4779.* At 23km/14mi long, Maligne is the largest natural lake in the Rockies and one of the most spectacular.

In 1875, surveyor Henry MacLeod was the first European to see the lake, naming it "Sore-foot." The lake and the peaks that rise from it were initially explored in detail in 1908 by an expedition led by Mary Schaffer, a middle-aged widow from Philadelphia who spent her summers in the Rockies.

The road ends at the northern shore of this glacial lake. As seen from the road, the twin peaks of **Mounts Unwin** (3,300m/10,824ft) and **Charlton** (3,260m/10,693ft) on the southwest side are most prominent. However, these peaks and the others at the southern end can be appreciated only by boating down the lake.

★★★ **Boat Trip.** – *Departs from Chalet at Maligne Lake May–Sept daily 9am–5pm. Round-trip 1hr 30min. $27.* ✗ ⅃ *Maligne Tours* ☎*403/852-3370.* As the boat proceeds down the lake, the water colour changes from green to deep turquoise because of the presence of suspended glacial silt. After passing Samson Narrows, the boat stops so passengers can disembark near tiny **Spirit Island** to enjoy the **view★★★** of the half-dozen glaciated peaks framing the south end of the lake.

★★ 5 THE YELLOWHEAD HIGHWAY *Map p 48*

Also designated Highway 16, this major thoroughfare runs east-west through Jasper and Mount Robson parks and continues westward to the Pacific at Prince Rupert *(p 52)*. The highway was named for a fair-haired Iroquois fur trader known as Tête Jaune ("yellow head") who, in the 1820s, set up a cache in the small town now named in his honour.

★★ From Jasper to Miette Hot Springs *49km/ 31mi. Allow 4hrs.*

Heading eastward from Jasper, the highway enters, and then follows, the broad valley of the Athabasca River. The craggy pinnacles of the Colin Range are soon silhouetted against the eastern horizon.

For the remaining 40km/25mi, the highway offers breathtaking **views★★★** of the braided course of the river and the peaks surrounding it. The road passes between **Talbot Lake** (east) and **Jasper Lake**, which is backdropped by the **De Smet Range**. At the Disaster Point **animal lick★** *(111km/69mi)*, small pools on the east side of the road attract mountain sheep and the less frequently sighted white-coated mountain goats. The close proximity of the highway has led to animals being hit by cars; hence the point's name. From approximately this location on, the drive holds fine views of **Roche Miette** (2,316m/7,599ft).

★ **Miette Hot Springs.** – *42km/26mi to junction with Miette Hot Springs Rd. Open daily Victoria Day–Labour Day. $2.50.* ⅃ ☎*604/852-6161.* A road winds 18km/11mi through a pleasant green gorge to the park's hot springs bathhouse. The springs are high in calcium and the hottest in the Canadian Rockies (maximum temperature 54°C/129°F). The natural **setting★★** for the springs, with mountains hovering close by, makes this the most spectacular location among all the mountain parks' bathhouses.

After this junction, the highway continues east another 7km/4mi to the east gate of Jasper National Park.

★ From Jasper to Rearguard Falls *100km/62mi. Allow 5hrs.*

West of Jasper, Highway 16 follows the narrowing valley of the Miette River. At **Yellowhead Pass**—the lowest pass on the Continental Divide, and also the boundary between British Columbia and Alberta—the road leaves Jasper National Park *(24km/ 15mi)* and enters Mount Robson Provincial Park.

★★ **Mount Robson Provincial Park.** – *East boundary at 24km/15mi. Open year-round. Hiking, boating, accommodation.* △ ✗. Encompassing magnificent mountain terrain, this 217,200ha/536,484 acre park is named for its greatest attraction: 3,954m/12,972ft **Mount Robson★★★**, the highest peak in the Canadian Rockies.

After entering the park, Route 16 picks up the course of the Fraser River, skirting Yellowhead Lake and larger Moose Lake. At **Overlander Falls★** *(88km/55mi; accessible by trail, 30min round-trip)*, the blue-green Fraser River drops off a wide ledge, and then narrows as it enters a canyon. Just beyond the falls, the park **information centre** *(open daily May–Sept; off-season Mon–Fri;* ⅃ ☎*604/566-4325)*, backdropped by Mount Robson, displays natural history exhibits on the area.

★ **Rearguard Falls.** – *3.2km/2mi walk, about 25min round-trip.* Part of a small provincial park by the same name, these wide, low falls on the Fraser River are particularly noted as a place where chinook salmon can be seen leaping upstream during the August spawning season. The salmon have made a 1,200km/744mi journey inland, from the Fraser outlet on the Pacific to this point.

The crossroads town of Tête Jaune Cache is 5km/3mi farther west.

★★ 6 KOOTENAY NATIONAL PARK *Map p 48*

This park was formed in 1920 as a result of the Federal Government's completion of the Banff-Windermere Highway (Route 93)—which would provide an important commercial link between southwestern Alberta and the Columbia Valley—in exchange for land bordering the road. Extending 8km/5mi from both sides of the highway, the strip of land became Canada's tenth national park.

From Castle Junction to Radium Hot Springs
105km/65mi by Rte 93. Allow 3hrs.

This picturesque **route**★★ through Kootenay National Park leaves the Trans-Canada Highway at Castle Junction and climbs steeply to the summit of **Vermilion Pass** (1,650m/5,412ft). The pass marks the Great Divide and coincides with the borders of Banff and Kootenay national parks and the provincial boundaries between Alberta and British Columbia.

★ **Marble Canyon.** – *17km/11mi from junction.* The rushing waters of Tokumm Creek charge through this narrow limestone gorge on their way to meet the Vermilion River. The **information centre** *(open daily mid-Jun–Labour Day; &.)* for the park's north entrance is located here. Interpretive signs explain the geology of white-dolomite outcroppings, a natural bridge and other features along a trail *(1.6km/1mi)* that leads through the canyon *(30min round-trip)*.

Paint Pots. – *20km/12mi from junction; trail of 1.2km/.7mi.* Of historic interest, this area contains pools of ochre clay first used as body paint and dyes by natives, and later mined by Europeans. The three cold **mineral springs**★ near the end of the trail were considered places of spiritual power by native tribes.

The highway follows the Vermilion River to its confluence with the Kootenay. At 89km/55mi, a lookout provides a sweeping **view**★ of the wide, wooded **Kootenay Valley** and the **Mitchell Range** flanking its west side. After topping Sinclair Pass (1,486m/4,874ft), the road follows Sinclair Creek's tumbling descent through **Sinclair Valley**★, passing between the precipitous red cliffs called the **Iron Gates**, because of the iron oxides that give them their colour.

★ **Radium Hot Springs.** – *103km/64mi.* The waters of Radium Hot Springs (average temperature 47°C/117°F) feed the swimming pool in a park complex known as the aquacourt. The mineral content of the springs is generally lower than that of other springs developed in the Rockies.

Immediately after the aquacourt, the highway passes through the rocky cleft of **Sinclair Canyon**★ before reaching the park's southern entrance gate. A park **information centre** *(open daily mid-Jun–Labour Day; until mid-Oct weekends only; ☎604/347-9505)* is located just inside the gate.

★★ # SKEENA VALLEY British Columbia

Map of Principal Sights p 2

Cleaving the rugged Coast Mountains of northwest British Columbia, this verdant river valley holds the second largest river in the province. Rising in the Skeena Mountains of the interior, the 565km/350mi "river of mists" flows south to the town of New Hazelton, then southwest toward its confluence with Hecate Strait, following a massive channel cut by Ice Age glaciers. The valley is noted for its spectacular scenery and for the rich Tsimshian culture of the **Gitksan** tribe, which still inhabits the riverbanks.

HISTORICAL NOTES

The Skeena and its tributaries have been the territory of the Gitksan Indians for close to 10,000 years. Part of the native **Northwest Coast cultures** *(p 24)*, the Gitksan traditionally based their subsistence on salmon, berries and western red cedar used to construct longhouses and to carve elaborate totem poles *(p 25)*. Pole-raisings, as well as weddings, funerals and other important occasions, were accompanied by great feasts called **potlatches**.

European Contact. – In the 19C, European fur-trading posts, dominated by the Hudson's Bay Company, were established along the Skeena. The area was further opened to European settlement in the 1880s with the coming of sternwheelers to the Skeena. During the same period, fishing and cannery operations, established near the mouth of the river, attracted Asians and more Europeans. In 1912, the Grand Trunk Pacific Railway was completed through the valley, an additional means of influx. Today, the Yellowhead Highway follows the Skeena from east of Prince Rupert to New Hazelton.

Native Decline and Renewal. – The native peoples were greatly affected by the arrival of Europeans. Several factors combined to decimate the aboriginal culture of the Northwest: old patterns of hunting and gathering were curtailed in favour of supplying furs to the new immigrants; missionary zeal and European misapprehensions about the potlatch led to its ban between 1884 and 1951; totem poles were de-stroyed; and the introduction of diseases such as smallpox significantly reduced the native population. The Gitksan, however, maintained their system of clans and of matrilineal descent. In the 1970s, a renaissance of native culture began. Today, their language, Tsimshian, is taught in reserve schools, and traditional crafts such as wood- and stone-carving have been revived. The technique of silk-screening, introduced in the past few decades, has allowed artists to develop innovative approaches to classic designs.

PRINCE RUPERT

Situated on Kaien Island near the mouth of the Skeena, this maritime city (pop 16,620) faces a scenic deep-water harbour dotted with islands. Canada's westernmost seaport, Prince Rupert was established in 1906 when its site was chosen as the terminus of the Grand Trunk Pacific. Located just south of the Alaska Panhandle, the town was expected to surpass Vancouver as Canada's major Pacific port. By

1922, however, Vancouver had secured that role. Today, with its ice-free harbour, the city is a fishing and fish-processing centre as well as a coal, grain, pulp and lumber port. It also serves as the major urban hub for northwest British Columbia. Known as the "City of Rainbows," Prince Rupert receives an annual rainfall of 254cm/100in. Fine reproductions of Tsimshian and Haida *(p 39)* **totem poles★** are scattered throughout the city.

★★ **Museum of Northern British Columbia.** – *Open Jun–Labour Day daily 9am–9pm. Off-season Mon–Sat 10am–5pm.* ♿ ☎*604/627-1129*. This museum has a fine collection of native Northwest basketry, argillite and wood carvings, as well as a carving shed where craftsmen demonstrate their talents. The small museum displays selections from its holdings of over 8,000 artifacts.

Additional Sights. – The **Mount Hays gondola** ride provides a good **view★** of the city's harbour and the surrounding islands of Chatham Sound. The **Cow Bay** area has a pleasant dockside atmosphere, with a few cafes and shops. The Grand Trunk Pacific Railway's small **Kwinitsa Station★** *(open daily mid-June– Labour Day)*, recently moved to the Prince Rupert waterfront, now serves as a railroad museum, which traces the history of railroading in this region through artifacts and old photographs.

from photo by Otto Nelson, Denver Art Museum

Chilkat blanket

★★ FROM PRINCE RUPERT TO NEW HAZELTON
300km/180mi by Rte 16. Allow 5hrs, including visits.

★★ **North Pacific Cannery Museum.** – *22km/14mi east of Prince Rupert, southeast of Port Edward, 1889 Skeena Dr. Open May–mid-Sept daily 10am–7pm. Off-season Wed–Sun 10am–4pm. Closed Christmas, Boxing Day & New Year's. $5.* 🍴 *(summer)* ♿ ☎*604/628-3538*. In the late 19C, this fish cannery was one of more than 220 on the British Columbia coast. Built in 1889 on an arm of the Skeena, the complex is the oldest surviving cannery village on the north coast. The picturesque village is still intact, as is the factory equipment, which has been out of operation since 1972. Fishing and canning methods are explained during the guided tours *(three times daily in summer, 30min)*. An historical drama about Prince Rupert is included on selected tours.

East of Port Edward, the road meets the Skeena River, paralleling it through its magnificent valley. The entire route provides excellent views of the broad, turbulent river and of the cloud-shrouded, snow-capped Coast Mountains rising to 2,000m/6,000ft above. In the town of **Terrace** (pop 11,433), the **Heritage Park**, a collection of eight old log buildings moved here from outlying areas, depicts pioneer life in the region. The river waters around the town and around nearby Kitimat to the south *(52km/31mi)* provide excellent sportfishing for trout and salmon. After Terrace, where the valley widens briefly, the road winds through the Hazelton Mountains. East of Terrace *(12km/7mi)* at the village of **Usk**, a small cable ferry breasts the treacherous waters of the Skeena.

★★ **Tour of the Totems.** – *Map p 54. Self-guided driving tour. Information on the native villages is available outside the band council office in Kispiox (see below) and at the New Hazelton visitor centre on Rte 16 (open mid-Jun–Sept ☎604/842-6071)*. Today, the Gitksan still inhabit five ancient villages along the Skeena and its tributaries. Four of these villages have impressive stands of **totem poles★★★** that date from the late 19C. The weathered poles, devoid of paint, range in height from 5-9m/15-30ft.

Kitwanga (Gwitwangan). – *Junction of Rte 16 and Rte 37 north, after crossing the Skeena River; then turn right on Bridge St.* Situated beside the Skeena River, a fine stand of about a dozen 19C totem poles graces a flat, grass-covered field against a backdrop of the impressive **Seven Sisters** Mountains (2,755m/9,039ft).

Kitwancool. – *Rte 37, 18km/11mi north of Kitwanga.* This village has the oldest existing stand of Gitksan totem poles, though several of its most venerable ones are now stored in a shed at the rear of the totem field for preservation. Active carving is still going on in this field.

Return to Rte 16 and continue east.

Kitseguecla. – *Rte 16, 19km/12mi east of junction with Rte 37.* The original totem poles in this village were destroyed by fire (1872) and by flood. New poles, however, now stand scattered throughout the village.

Kispiox. – *19km/12mi north of New Hazelton on Kispiox Valley Rd.* Situated near the confluence of the Skeena and Kispiox rivers, this large village boasts a dozen impressive totems in a field by the waters of the Kispiox.

'Ksan. – *Rte 62, 7km/4mi northwest of New Hazelton. Grounds open year-round.* ☎604/842-5544. A complex of totem poles and long-houses re-created in the traditional style, this historical village museum provides an insight into the Gitksan culture. 'Ksan, the Gitksan name for the Skeena, is situated on the site of an ancient village near the confluence of the Skeena and Bulkley rivers, with a magnificent view of Mount Rocher Déboulé.

The village consists of seven major buildings: an exhibit hall featuring travelling displays and fine examples of Gitksan basketry, carving and weaving; a carving house and silkscreen workshop, where native artists from throughout the Northwest Coast work; a gift shop; and three longhouses *(visit by guided tour only; $2.50)* where an extensive **native collection★★** of artifacts is used to explain the culture and lifestyle of these people. The acclaimed 'Ksan dancers perform in the summer *(Jul–Aug every Fri evening; call ahead for schedule).*

★★★ VANCOUVER British Columbia

Metro Pop 1,542,744

Map of Principal Sights p 2

Tourist Office ☎604/683-2000

Canada's third-largest metropolis, this West Coast city has a magnificent **site★★★** on a peninsula protruding into the Strait of Georgia. Situated between Burrard Inlet—the most southerly of a series of deep fjords cut into the coast of British Columbia—and the delta of the Fraser River, the city covers 113sq km/44sq mi of the peninsula's western end. A protected deep-sea port, accessibility to the Pacific Ocean, and a virtually snow-free climate have contributed to Vancouver's prosperity and rapid growth.

The city is almost surrounded by mountains. To the north, the Coast Mountains rise steeply, the most prominent peaks being **Hollyburn Mountain**, the twin summits of **The Lions**, **Grouse Mountain** with its ski slopes and **Mount Seymour** to the east. To the west across the Strait of Georgia stand the mountains of Vancouver Island and to the southeast rises the Cascade Range, topped by the snow-clad peak of **Mount Baker** in Washington state. Despite heavy snowfall that provides superb skiing conditions in these mountains, Vancouver itself rarely receives snow. Instead, the city has a high rainfall compared with the rest of the country (152cm/60in a year). Even in July and August, the sunniest months, a light rain and mist may shroud the mountains.

Early History. – The shores of the Strait of Georgia were the preserve of the Coast Salish Indians until 1791, when Spanish captain José Maria Narvaez was the first European to enter their waters. Surveying the coast for the British Navy, Capt **George Vancouver** explored Burrard Inlet a year later. In 1808, Simon Fraser saw the area from the land side, at the end of his descent of the river bearing his name. Bypassed by the Fraser River gold rushers, the site aroused little interest until three Englishmen opened a brickworks in 1862 on land stretching over much of the present downtown. Having poured their life savings into what is today reputed to be the most densely populated square mile in Canada, they received the epithet "the three greenhorns." The 1860s saw the opening of sawmills on both sides of the inlet to process the area's rich timber. In 1867, John Deighton *(p 57)* opened a saloon for the mill workers. The community that developed around it became known as Gastown and was eventually named Granville in 1869, when a townsite was laid out by government surveyors.

The Coming of the Railway. – The location of the terminus of the Canadian Pacific Railway was a long-standing controversy. When it was finally decided to route the railway down the Fraser Valley to Burrard Inlet, land prices skyrocketed at Port Moody, a tiny settlement at its head *(map p 61)*. The prices and lack of space there caused **William Van Horne** in 1884 to extend the line farther down the inlet to the site of Granville. Overnight, a town was born. At its official incorporation in 1886, the city was baptized Vancouver, Van Horne's choice. Almost immediately thereafter, fire destroyed the community, but by 1887, it had recovered sufficiently to welcome the first trans-Canada passenger train.

Vancouver Today. – Vancouver has become the largest city in the province, with a metropolitan population of over 1.5 million; in Canada, only Toronto and Montreal have greater populations. The financial, commercial and industrial centre of British Columbia, Vancouver is also the province's major port—indeed, Canada's largest port. Bulk loads of grain and potash from the Prairies, and of lumber, logs, coal, sulphur and other minerals from interior British Columbia arrive by train and are exported chiefly to Japan and other countries bordering the Pacific Ocean. Vancouver is a centre for forestry and fishing as well. The city and its environs continue to be a popular tourist destination.

In 1986, Vancouver hosted the world exposition, **Expo '86**, as part of its centennial celebrations. The exposition site on the north and east shores of False Creek *(map p 56)* has been cleared for commercial and residential development.

Practical Information

Public Transportation. – The Vancouver Regional Transit System operates an integrated network of rapid transit, ferries and buses. Hours of operation vary among the different services. **SkyTrain**, the city's rapid transit, services downtown and the New Westminster route; daily 5:30–1am; every 2-5 min. **SeaBus**, passenger harbour ferries, operates between Vancouver and the North Shore: Mon–Sat 6–1am, Sun 8am–11pm; every 15-30min. Adult fare during off-peak hours is $1.35; weekdays before 9:30am and from 3-6:30pm fares are based on zone boundaries. Fares are the same for all services; exact fare is required. FareSaver books of 10 tickets ($13.75) and a DayPass ($4) are available from ticket machines and outlets. Transfers are free for 90min of unlimited travel. **Bus** service connects SkyTrain and SeaBus at all stations. Buses operate 7 days/wk. A *Transit Guide* map ($1.25) is sold at TicketMaster outlets and convenience stores. For route information & schedules ☎604/261-5100.

Taxis. – Advance Cabs ☎604/876-5555; Black Top Cabs ☎604/731-1111; Yellow Cabs ☎604/681-1111.

Car Rentals. – Avis ☎604/682-1621; Hertz ☎604/688-2411; Tilden/National ☎604/685-6111.

Tourist Office. – Tourism Vancouver operates the Vancouver Travel InfoCentre at Plaza Level, Waterfront Centre, 200 Burrard Street (*open summer daily 8am–6pm; winter Mon–Fri 8:30am-5pm, Sat 9am–5pm*) or contact Tourism Vancouver, Waterfront Centre, Vancouver, BC, V6C 3L6 ☎604/683-2000, or 800/888-8835 (toll-free US).

Newspapers. – Daily: *The Vancouver Sun* and *The Province.* Monthly guide (free) to entertainment, shopping and restaurants: *Where.*

Entertainment. – Consult arts and entertainment supplements in local newspapers (Thur & Fri edition) for schedule of cultural events and addresses of principal theatres and concert halls. Ticketmaster ☎604/280-4444 (major credit cards accepted).

Sports. – BC Lions Football Club. Home games are played at BC Place Stadium. Season: Jul–Nov. For schedules ☎604/583-7747. Vancouver Canadians (baseball). Home games are played at National Bailey Stadium. Season: Apr–Sept. For schedules ☎604/872-5232. Vancouver Canucks (ice hockey). Home games are played at Pacific Coliseum. Season: Oct–Apr. For schedules ☎604/254-5141. Tickets for all events are sold through Ticketmaster ☎604/280-4400 (major credit cards accepted).

Useful Numbers (Area Code 604)

BC Rail (North Vancouver)	1311 W 1st St	984-5246
VIA Rail	1150 Station St	669-3050
BC Ferries		685-1021
Canadian Automobile Association	999 W Broadway	732-3977
CAA Emergency Road Service (24hr)		293-2222
Greyhound Lines of Canada (bus)	150 Dunsmuir St	662-3222
Shoppers Drug Mart (24hr) drugstore	1125 Davie St	685-5752
Main Post Office	349 W Georgia St	662-5725
Road Conditions		660-9770
Weather (24hr)		664-9010

★★★ STANLEY PARK   *Map p 56*

Vancouver's outstanding attraction, this 405ha/1000 acre park has a magnificent **site★★★** at the end of a peninsula that almost closes Burrard Inlet at **First Narrows**. Washed on three sides by the inlet waters, this densely forested expanse offers splendid views of the North Shore Mountains, the peaks of Vancouver Island, the city and the port.
In 1886, the month-old city of Vancouver asked the Canadian government for the peninsula, planning to convert the former military reserve into a public park. The idea of a woodland reserve was rather advanced at the time, primarily because Vancouver consisted of almost nothing except forest. Ottawa agreed, and Governor General **Lord Stanley** dedicated the park.

★★★ **Scenic Drive.** – *10km/6mi. About 1hr.* Circling the park in a counterclockwise direction, the drive begins and ends at Georgia Street. The route follows the edge of Coal Harbour, offering views of the yacht clubs, port and city as far as **Brockton Point**, with its fine panorama of the inlet and North Shore Mountains. Just before the point, note the display of brightly painted **totem poles**, the work of the Northwest Coast Indians. The road continues to **Prospect Point** where ships, passing through First Narrows in and out of port, can be observed. Then the road turns inland, but paths lead to the sea wall near **Siwash Rock**, cut off from the rest of the peninsula. From **Ferguson Point**, there are views of Third Beach; Point Grey Peninsula, where the University of British Columbia is situated; and the mountains on Vancouver Island. The road continues past Second Beach, various sports facilities and Lost Lagoon.

★★★ **Aquarium.** – *Open July–Aug daily 9:30am–8pm. Off-season daily 10am–5:30pm.* $8.50. ⬤ ▣ ☎604/682-1118. Home to more than 8,000 animals, this lauded aquarium is known for its extensive marine mammal centre featuring a variety of whales, seals and sea otters. Several galleries are devoted to ocean and freshwater fish native to British Columbia and exotic fish of the world.

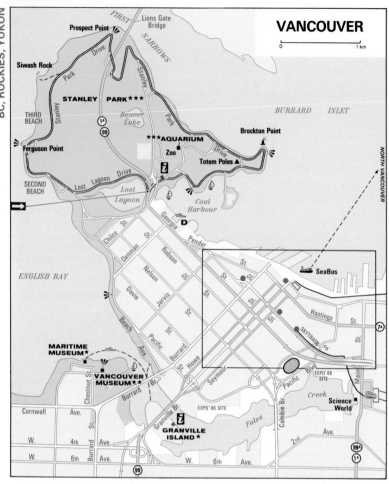

The aquarium was first to publicly exhibit **killer whales** (also known as orcas), distinguished by their black and white colouring and dorsal fin. Performing regularly for visitors in their 5 million litre/1.3 million gallon outdoor habitat, these large mammals demonstrate their amazing power, grace and intelligence.

A special feature of the Arctic Canada section is the **beluga whales**, seen through large viewing windows swimming underwater.

Indoors, a highlight is the walk-in **amazon rain forest** where crocodiles, anacondas, turtles, lizards and two-toed sloths live in a steamy environment, complete with suitable vegetation and a multitude of brightly coloured birds. Adjacent to the rain forest, tanks contain sharks, piranhas, electric and moray eels and other tropical creatures.

Surrounding the aquarium is the **zoo** *(open daily year-round; railway $2;* & ⌷ ☎*604/ 681-1141)* and at its entrance, there is a bronze sculpture of a killer whale by acclaimed Haida sculptor **Bill Reid**.

★★ DOWNTOWN   *Map p 57. 5hrs.*

Positioned along Granville Street, the commercial centre is closed to all traffic except buses for a six-block pedestrian thoroughfare known as **The Mall**. The major department stores and extensive underground shopping developments called the Pacific and Vancouver centres are located here. At the northern end is Granville Square, a plaza with views of port activities at the wharves below. Steps lead to the attractively renovated rail station from which a passenger ferry service known as SeaBus crosses Burrard Inlet, offering good views of the harbour and city.

★★ **Canada Place.** – Designed by architect Eberhard Zeidler, this gleaming-white structure resembles a flotilla of sailing ships at anchor in Burrard Inlet. Constructed as the Canada Pavilion for Expo '86, the complex consists of a hotel, office tower and convention centre. Exhibition halls are enclosed by the "sails" of fibreglass yarn coated with teflon, tensioned to appear as though they are catching the ocean winds. Along with cruise ships that moor at its sides, Canada Place has transformed the waterfront.

★★ **Harbour Centre.** – *Observation deck open daily 8:30am–10:30pm. Winter daily 10am–sunset. $5.50.* ✕ & ☎*604/689-0421.* Visitors ascend this distinctive office building via exterior elevators to arrive at the circular observation deck with its magnificent **panorama★★★** of the city, mountains, ocean and Fraser River delta. An interesting multimedia **film** *(12min)* provides a good introduction to the city.

★★ **Art Gallery.** – *Open May–Sept Mon–Sat 10am–5pm (Thur 9pm); Sun noon–5pm. Off-season closed Tue. Closed Christmas & New Year's. $4.25.* ⚒ & 🅿 ☎*604/682-5621.* Designed in 1907 by Francis Rattenbury, the neoclassical building served as the city courthouse for 70 years. It was tastefully converted by Arthur Erickson so that galleries open off the central rotunda with its glass-topped dome, through which natural light enters.

A highlight is the collection of paintings and drawings by Emily Carr, including such famous works as *Big Raven* (c.1931) and *Scorned as Timber, Beloved of the Sky* (c.1936). There are also changing exhibitions of regional, national and international interest from the permanent collection.

★★ **Robson Square.** – Stretching from Nelson Street almost to Georgia Street, this complex was also designed by Arthur Erickson. Opened in 1979, the square houses most of the offices of the provincial government in Vancouver and has transformed the downtown area.

A seven-storey **law court building [J]** with a spectacular slanted-glass roof complements a series of terraced gardens with waterfalls and plants on top of offices *(between Smithe and Robson)*. A plaza under Robson Street contains outdoor cafes, a skating rink and an exhibition area.

★★ **BC Place Stadium.** – Resembling an enormous quilted marshmallow, this stadium is the largest air-supported domed amphitheatre in the world. Designed by Phillips Barratt, it opened in 1983. Inflated by huge fans, the teflon and fibreglass roof is secured by steel cables. Containing heating elements to melt winter snow, the roof is self-cleaning with the aid of area rainfall and translucent enough so that artificial lighting is rarely required. The stadium seats up to 60,000 with no interior supports. A glass-enclosed concourse on the upper level offers a city **panorama**.

★ **Chinatown.** – *Pender St between Carrall St and Gore Ave.* This colourful quarter is the centre of Vancouver's large Chinese community. Many restaurants and shops sell oriental foods and other wares. The neighbourhood is particularly lively during the Chinese New Year.

★ **Dr Sun Yat-Sen Classical Chinese Garden.** – *578 Carrall St behind Chinese Cultural Centre on Pender St. Open daily year-round. Closed Christmas. $3.50.* & ☎*604/689-7133.* Modelled after classical gardens developed in the Chinese city of Suzhou during the Ming dynasty (14-17C), this garden is a small oasis of contemplative calm. Pine, bamboo and flowering plum trees grow amid sculpted rocks, water, arched bridges and covered walkways.

★ **Gastown.** – This attractive area between Carrall and Richards streets combines restored buildings of the late 19C with modern buildings constructed to blend with their surroundings. Gastown has not always been chic. In the 1860s, sawmill owners on Burrard Inlet had strict rules against consumption of alcohol on their premises. Thirsty mill employees had to walk 19km/12mi to New Westminster until an enterprising Englishman, John Deighton, arrived at the edge of mill property with a barrel of whisky. Nicknamed **Gassy Jack** because of his garrulousness, he enticed mill workers to build his saloon, rewarding them with whisky. Soon he had a lively trade and the resulting community took his name—Gassy's town or Gastown.

Over the years, the character of the area has changed several times. Today, its centre is **Maple Tree Square**, where a statue of Gassy Jack stands. **Water Street** is one of the attractive surrounding streets with its gaslights and shops. On the corner of Cambie stands a **steam clock [B]**, powered by a steam engine. The mechanism actually works by gravity and the clock "hoots" out the hour, half hour or quarter hour.

★ **Harbour Tour [D].** – *Map p 56. Departs from Coal Harbour Jun–mid-Sept Mon, Thur–Sun 11:30am & 1:30pm. Round-trip 1hr 30min. $13.50. Commentary on board.* 🅿 *($5)* ⚒ & *Harbour Ferries Ltd* ☎*604/688-7246.* This boat trip by paddle-wheeler makes a pleasant excursion, enabling visitors to see Vancouver's busy port and offering fine views of the city and mountains.

Vancouver

Stefan Schulhof

SIGHTS OUTSIDE DOWNTOWN

★★★ **UBC Museum of Anthropology.** – *Map p 59. Open Jul–Labour Day daily 11am–5pm (Tue 9pm). Off-season Tue–Sun. Closed Christmas. $5.* ㅎ ㅁ ☏*604/822-3825.* At the end of Point Grey Peninsula, the University of British Columbia has a large campus overlooking the Strait of Georgia and the mountains of Vancouver Island. Known for its site and for its research facilities in agriculture, forestry and oceanography, the university is also famous for its collection of Northwest Coast Indian art. Opened in 1976, the **museum building★★**—the work of Arthur Erickson —is an architectural masterpiece. A glass and concrete structure, it admirably complements the site. Flanked by exhibits, a ramp leads down to the **Great Hall★★**. Glass walls rise 14m/45ft around the magnificent collection of Haida and Kwakwaka'wakw **totem poles** and other large wood carvings. The trees, sea, sky and mountains are visible through the glass walls, giving visitors the impression of seeing the poles in their original surroundings, not in a museum. The poles and other carvings in the museum grounds are copies of older carvings now decayed.

In contrast to the immense sculptures in the Great Hall, the carvings in the **Masterpiece Gallery** are tiny and intricate. Works in silver, gold, argillite, horn, bone, ivory, stone and wood bear the same designs in miniature as the monumental sculpture elsewhere.

One corner of the museum is devoted to **Raven and the First Men**, a massive modern carving in yellow cedar by Bill Reid *(p 40)*, symbolic of birth. A huge raven stands on a clam shell that is being pushed open by a series of small figures.

The remainder of the building is predominantly "visible storage" galleries, where the museum's worldwide collections from ancient times to the present are on display, catalogued by region and civilization. There are also galleries for changing exhibitions.

★★ **The North Shore.** – *Map p 59.* The mountains descend quite precipitously towards Burrard Inlet on its north side, cut not only by deep fjords such as Indian Arm and Howe Sound, but by steep valleys or canyons of several small rivers and creeks—Capilano, Lynn and Seymour being the best known. Houses on the north shore are, for the most part, expensive and often cling to mountain slopes that permit good views of the inlet and city.

★★ **Mount Seymour Provincial Park.** – *31km/19mi from downtown by Second Narrows Bridge; take the third exit (Mt Seymour Parkway) and follow signs. Open year-round. Hiking, horseback riding, mountain biking, skiing. For trail maps contact park office ☏604/929-1291.* From the park entrance, a road climbs steeply to Deep Cove Lookout *(8km/5mi)* from which there is a **view★★** to the east. The village of Deep Cove, Indian Arm and Simon Fraser University in Burnaby are visible. From just below the ski centre *(13km/8mi)*, there is a fine **view★★** of the city and Vancouver Island on clear days. In the distance, the peak of Mount Baker in Washington state can usually be seen above the clouds.

A **chair ride** takes visitors to the summit of Mount Seymour *(operating daily Nov–Apr 9am–10pm; for ski passes & schedules ☏604/986-2261).*

★★ **Grouse Mountain.** – *Also map p 61.13km/8mi from downtown by Lions Gate Bridge, Capilano Rd and Nancy Greene Way. Tram operates year-round daily 9am–10pm; $14.93;* ╳ *☏604/ 984-0661.* The aerial tram rises to an elevation of 1,100m/3,700ft, offering, as it ascends, a splendid **view★★** of the city, and from the summit, a panorama embracing, on clear days, Vancouver Island, the Fraser delta and Burrard Inlet.

★ **Capilano Canyon.** – This deep canyon can be appreciated by visiting the narrow pedestrian **suspension bridge★ [B]** *(9km/6mi from downtown by Lions Gate Bridge and Capilano Rd; open daily year-round; closed Christmas; $5.98;* ╳ *☏604/985-7474)* 70m/230ft above the Capilano River. Built in 1889, it is 137m/450ft long and sways as visitors walk across it. On the far side is a pleasant glade of Douglas firs and Western red cedars.

Farther along Capilano Road, **Capilano Canyon Park** offers pleasant walks and views of the canyon from below. At the northern end of the park (*access from Nancy Greene Way*) are Cleveland Dam and Capilano Lake, a reservoir for the city of Vancouver. Across the lake, there is a **view★** of the double peak of The Lions.

★★ **Queen Elizabeth Park.** – *Map below. W 23rd Ave and Cambie St.* This beautiful park lies at the geographic centre and highest point (150m/500ft) of Vancouver. In clear weather, there are extraordinary **views★★★** of the city and mountains by day and night, including the fine snow-capped peak of Mount Baker of the Cascades more than 110km/70mi away. The road from the entrance climbs through an arboretum to the **Bloedel Floral Conservatory★**, a geodesic-domed structure of glass and aluminum. Inside *(open daily year-round; $3;* ⚒ ♿ 🅿 ☎*604/872-5513)* are examples of tropical and desert vegetation, enlivened by a number of colourful birds.
The other attraction of the park is the lovely **Sunken Gardens★★**. Paths weave among the flowers to a waterfall and a bridge, from which there are views of the gardens and city.

★★ **Simon Fraser University.** – *Map below. In Burnaby. Gaglardi Way. For guided tours* ☎*604/ 291-3210.* This architecturally famous, albeit controversial, university has a lovely site on Burnaby Mountain, with views of the North Shore Mountains. The unique ensemble of interconnected buildings constructed along a tree-lined, partially covered pedestrian mall and around a large quadrangle with a pond was designed by Vancouver natives **Arthur Erickson** and **Geoffrey Massey**. The harmony of these somewhat harsh concrete structures derives from their design and construction as a unit. Erickson went on to design other interesting structures, among them the UBC Museum of Anthropology, Robson Square and the renovated Art Gallery, the Bank of Canada in Ottawa and Roy Thomson Hall in Toronto.
Since its opening in 1965, the university has gained a reputation as a progressive educational institution. It operates year-round on a trimester system, each term being independent so that students can study continuously or take only one or two terms a year.

★★ **Vancouver Museum.** – *Map p 56. In Vanier Park. Open May–Sept daily 10am–9pm. Off-season Tue–Sun 10am–5pm. $5.* ⚒ ♿ 🅿 ☎*604/736-7736.* Through permanent and rotating exhibits, this museum specializes in the history and art of Vancouver, native peoples, Asia, Europe and the US.
Representing the creature that traditionally guards the harbour in Indian legend, a huge stainless steel **crab★**—the work of sculptor George Norris—dominates the front entrance in an ornamental pool. There is an excellent **view★★** of the city and North Shore Mountains from the parking area or from the terrace of the museum cafeteria. The **Northwest Coast galleries** cover aspects of the lives of the Northwest Coast tribes. Artifacts on display show an extraordinary artistic finesse: note the tiny woven baskets of cedar and bear grass, the argillite carvings and the masks. Some masks have two faces—the first, an animal, opening to reveal the second, a human, reflecting the union between these two lifeforms. There are interesting displays on whaling (note the large Nootka canoe) and the uses for the wood of the cedar tree.
In the **Exploration and Settlement galleries**, Vancouver's past is traced from the first arrival of Europeans. A Hudson's Bay Company trading store has been re-created, along with steerage quarters on an immigrant ship. The birth of Vancouver as a lumber village is shown with its growth after the arrival of the "iron horse." A series of room reconstructions of the 1910 era illustrates the city's rapid development.

The buildings of the museum surround the distinctive conical dome of the **MacMillan Planetarium** *(open daily late-Jun–Labour Day; off-season Tue–Sun; $5;* ⚒ ♿ 🅿 *for laser light show ($7) schedule* ☎*604/736-3656),* which has become a Vancouver landmark since its opening in 1968. In the **Southam Observatory**, visitors can look through the giant telescope at the sun, moon, planets and stars.

★ **Maritime Museum.** – *Map p 56. In Vanier Park. Ferry to Granville Island departs from the museum wharf. Open daily Victoria Day–Thanksgiving. Off-season Tue–Sun. $5.* ⚅ ▯ ☏*604/737-2211.* Ship models and artifacts illustrate the maritime history of Vancouver and British Columbia. The highlight of the collection is the **St Roch**★★, a Royal Canadian Mounted Police patrol ship, which navigated the Northwest Passage in both directions.

After Roald Amundsen's completion of the passage *(p 231)*, various countries sought control of the Arctic. To assert sovereignty over the northland, the Canadian government decided to send a ship through the passage. Under Capt Henry Larsen, the *St Roch* left Vancouver in June 1940 and, after being frozen in several times, reached Halifax in October 1942. In 1944, the return trip of 7,295 nautical mi/ 13,510km in ice-strewn waters took only 86 days. Not only was the *St Roch* the first ship to navigate the passage both ways, but the first to complete the east-west voyage in one season. The 32m/104ft wooden vessel has been completely restored, with authentic items in all the cabins *(visit by 45min guided tour only; every hour).*

★ **Granville Island.** – *Map p 56. Accessible by car from the Granville Bridge and W 4th Ave, by ferry from beside Vancouver Aquatic Centre on Beach Ave or from Maritime Museum.* This one-time industrial area under Granville Bridge has been renovated to house restaurants, art galleries, boutiques, theatres and a hotel, in addition to some surviving industry. Its highlight is the **public market** *(open daily)* where stalls of fresh produce vie with products of Vancouver's many ethnic groups.

★ **Vanterm [E].** – *Map p 59. At north end of Clark Dr; take overpass to visitor parking lot. For schedule of guided tour* ☏*604/666-6129.* The enormous container-handling complex can be viewed from an observation lounge that overlooks the loading and unloading docks for ships, trucks and trains, against a backdrop of the North Shore Mountains.

Van Dusen Botanical Garden [K]. – *Map p 59. On 37th Ave at Oak St. Open daily year-round. Closed Christmas. $4.80.* ⚅ ▯ ☏*604/266-7194.* This garden offers fine displays of plants in geographic as well as botanical arrangements. In addition to a rosaceae, a magnolia garden and a rhododendron walk, there are sections devoted to vegetation of the Southern Hemispheric, Mediterranean and Sino-Himalayan areas. MacMillan-Bloedel Place features displays on the province's forests.

Science World. – *Map p 56. Quebec St and Terminal Ave. Open daily year-round. $7.* ✗ ⚅ ☏*604/687-7832.* Situated on the Expo '86 site overlooking False Creek, this stimulating centre, opened in 1989, features interactive exhibits such as a plasma ball that demonstrates the properties of an electric current, and a tornado chamber that re-creates nature's forces.

The centre includes an Omnimax theatre, where films are shown on a wrap-around, domed screen; the Music Machines Gallery, where visitors can operate a huge synthesizer; and a children's problem-solving gallery.

EXCURSIONS   *Map p 61*

★★★ **Howe Sound.** – Extending some 48km/30mi into the mountains, this deep fjord provides some of the province's most dramatic coastal scenery.

Howe Sound can be admired by train, boat or car. A large steam engine that once pulled trains across Canada, the **Royal Hudson 2860**, makes regular trips to Squamish from the rail station in North Vancouver *(departs Jun–mid-Sept daily at 10am; return by boat arriving Vancouver at 4:30pm; off-season Wed–Sun; round-trip 6hrs 30min; $45; for reservations* ☏*604/688-7246).* The return trip is a spectacular voyage aboard the **MV Britannia**. The views of both sides of the fjord are excellent, as are those of Vancouver harbour, the point of disembarkation.

By car *(66km/41mi, allow 3hrs),* travellers follow Route 99, a road built through virtually sheer cliffs, providing incredible **views**★★★ of the mountains and the blue-green waters of the Sound between Horseshoe Bay and Squamish.

★★ **BC Museum of Mining.** – *In Britannia Beach, 53km/33mi from Vancouver. Open Jul– Aug daily 10am–5pm. May, Jun & Oct Wed–Sun 10am–5pm. $7.* ✗ ☏*604/896-2233.* Set in the Britannia mine, which was once the largest copper producer in the British Empire, this museum provides a fascinating introduction to mining. An audio-visual presentation traces the mine's history from discovery in 1888 to closure in 1974. Then follows a **guided tour** *(1hr 30min)* into one of the tunnels: equipment is demonstrated, and the old gravity-fed mill is viewed. The mining house *(three levels)* has displays on mining in British Columbia, with particular emphasis on the Britannia mine.

★★ **Shannon Falls.** – *60km/37mi.* These impressive falls cascade 198m/650ft over a cliff in pleasant surroundings.

Squamish. – *Pop 10,157. 66km/41mi.* This lumber centre occupies a fine site at the foot of snow-capped peaks, including Mount Garibaldi (2,678m/8,786ft).

★ **Fort Langley National Historic Site.** – ⊗ *56km/35mi southeast of Vancouver by Trans-Can Hwy and Glover St or Rte 7 and ferry. Open daily Victoria Day–Labour Day. Off-season Thur–Sun. $4.* ⚅ ☏*604/888-4424.* The fort was one of a network of trading posts established by the Hudson's Bay Company in British Columbia in the early 19C. Fur trading was the predominant occupation, though a large farm was operated, and salmon were caught and packaged for trade.

Today, the restored buildings of the wooden-palisaded fort can be visited. The warehouse has a fine collection of **furs**★ and of the trading goods once exchanged for them. In the Big House, quarters of the resident Hudson's Bay Company officials can be seen. There is also a reconstructed blacksmith's shop and cooperage.

★★★ **VANCOUVER ISLAND** British Columbia

Map of Principal Sights p 2

Covering an area of more than 32,000sq km/12,000sq mi, Vancouver Island is the largest of the islands off the Pacific Coast of North America. Mountains rise over 2,100m/7,000ft to form the central core. The west coast is deeply indented by inlets or fjords that almost dissect the island. The east coast slopes gradually, with wide beaches in the south and mountains farther north.

The climate is temperate throughout the island, but rainfall varies greatly: Victoria in the southeast receives 680mm/27in annually, whereas Zeballos *(map p 62)* on the west coast receives 6480mm/255in. This high rainfall supports dense forest growth. Not surprisingly, the island's major industry is logging: saw mills and pulp mills are located in many places.

The population is concentrated mainly in the southeast corner around Victoria and along the shores of the Strait of Georgia.

Access. – *Vancouver Island is served by ten ferry services (map p 62).*

★★★ **Victoria.** – *Description p 63.*

★★ **FROM PARKSVILLE TO PACIFIC RIM** Map p 62
154km/96mi by Rte 4. Allow 2hrs, 4.5hrs including visits.

This winding route traverses the mountain backbone of the island through lovely scenery. Some parts are wild and untouched by mankind; other parts are the scene of great activity, particularly that of the logging industry.

★ **Englishman River Falls.** – *5km/3mi from Parksville; turn left for 8km/5mi.* This river tumbles over two sets of falls. The upper ones are narrow and deep, dropping into a gorge. A path bridges the river, following it to the lower falls *(3/4hr round-trip)* through a dense forest of tall trees, ferns and moss-covered rocks. The lower falls are twin jets dropping around a rock into a deep pool.

Route 4 leaves the plain behind and begins to enter the mountains.

★ **Little Qualicum Falls.** – *26km/16mi from Parksville; turn right to parking area.* The Little Qualicum River descends over two sets of falls connected by a gorge. The lower falls are small, but the walk to the upper falls *(1/2hr round-trip)* through forest is pleasant, providing views of the canyon. The **upper falls★** are on two levels, with a pool between them.

Route 4 follows the south side of **Cameron Lake** with occasional views of it through the trees.

★★ **Cathedral Grove.** – *35km/22mi from Parksville, part of MacMillan Provincial Park. Parking beside highway.* As the name suggests, Cathedral Grove contains some of the original tall trees. Elsewhere, Douglas firs have been cut for their wood, but fortunately this grove was preserved by the MacMillan Bloedel Paper Company and donated to the province.

61

A walk *(3/4hr)* under these giants is impressive, especially for those who have not seen the redwoods of California. Many of these firs rise to 60m/200ft or more. One is 3m/9.5ft in diameter and nearly 76m/250ft tall. The largest trees are 800 years old. Between them grow red cedar and hemlock trees.

Route 4 descends to the coast and bypasses **Port Alberni** (pop 18,403), an important lumber centre that is situated at the head of Alberni Inlet. This arm of Barkley Sound reaches within 19km/12mi of the east coast of the island. The road then follows **Sproat Lake** with good views. Signs of logging activity are evident along the road, from cut areas to huge logging trucks. After leaving the lake, Route 4 begins to climb Klitsa Mountain along the valley of the Taylor River.

After reaching the height of land, the road begins its winding descent to the Pacific along the Kennedy River, offering **views★** of snow-capped peaks. The river widens into **Kennedy Lake,** the largest stretch of fresh water on the island. The road follows the lake, alternately rising above it and dipping to water level. Pacific Rim National Park Reserve is reached near the junction with the Tofino-to-Ucluelet road.

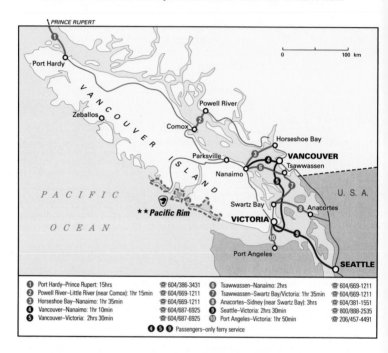

❶ Port Hardy–Prince Rupert: 15hrs	☎ 604/386-3431	❻ Tsawwassen–Nanaimo: 2hrs	☎ 604/669-1211
❷ Powell River–Little River (near Comox): 1hr 15min	☎ 604/669-1211	❼ Tsawwassen–Swartz Bay/Victoria: 1hr 35min	☎ 604/669-1211
❸ Horseshoe Bay–Nanaimo: 1hr 35min	☎ 604/669-1211	❽ Anacortes–Sidney (near Swartz Bay): 3hrs	☎ 604/381-1551
❹ Vancouver–Nanaimo: 1hr 10min	☎ 604/687-6925	❾ Seattle–Victoria: 2hrs 30min	☎ 800/888-2535
❺ Vancouver–Victoria: 2hrs 30min	☎ 604/687-6925	❿ Port Angeles–Victoria: 1hr 50min	☎ 206/457-4491

❹ ❺ ❾ Passengers–only ferry service

★★ PACIFIC RIM NATIONAL PARK RESERVE

Open year-round. Hiking, fishing, canoeing, sailing, swimming. Park information centre open daily mid-Mar–mid-Oct. △ ✗ ᗒ ☎604/726-4212 (summer) or 604/726-7721 (year-round).

Situated on the rugged west coast of Vancouver Island, this reserve is a long narrow strip of rocky islands and headlands, stretching intermittently for about 130km/80mi between Port Renfrew and Tofino. The park consists of the 72km/45mi **West Coast trail** for backpackers between Port Renfrew and Bamfield *(each end is accessible by road)*, about 100 islands and rocky islets in Barkley Sound known as the **Broken Group Islands** *(departs from Argyle St dock in Alberni Jun–mid-Sept Mon, Wed, Fri & Sun at 8am; round-trip 9hrs; $32; commentary on board; reservations suggested; Alberini Marine Transportation ☎604/723-8313)* and famous Long Beach.

★★ **Long Beach.** – *Visitors can enjoy exceptional surfing and swimming. However, the water is cold (10°C/50°F) and can be extremely dangerous. Attention must be paid to tides and currents. For details, contact the park information centre.* Pounded by the surf, this 11km/7mi curve of sand and rock is backed by a dense rain forest and mountains rising to 1,200m/4,000ft. Offshore, sea lions bask on the rocks, and Pacific gray whales are often spotted. Numerous birds make the beach and forest their home, while many more visit seasonally.

The heavy rainfall and moderate temperatures of this coast have produced thick rain forests where Sitka spruce flourishes, and red cedar and hemlock grow. Breakers of the Pacific Ocean crash in, depositing huge drift logs over the beach one day and carrying them away the next. The power of these waves is immense; variation in sand level can be as great as 1.8m/6ft between winter and summer in one year. At low tide, the beach is nearly 1km/.5mi wide, and a variety of creatures can be seen in tidal pools among the rocks.

There are several points of access to Long Beach. Paths weave through the high trees and mossy, fern-covered rain forest, offering views of the beach and ocean. From Combers Beach, the **sea lion rocks** can be seen offshore *(binoculars advisable)*.

★★ **Radar Hill.** – *22km/14mi from Ucluelet junction. Take road to left, ascending 1.6km/1mi to viewpoint.* From this point above the forest, a splendid **panorama★★** of the area is obtained *(telescope available)*. The mountains behind the park can be seen, as well as the wild and rocky coastline.

Facing the **Juan de Fuca Strait** and the **Olympic** and **Cascade mountains** in Washington state, the capital of British Columbia occupies the southeast tip of Vancouver Island. Famous for its beautiful gardens, its elegance and gentility and its British traditions, the city contrasts with the rest of Vancouver Island, which is largely untamed forest and rugged mountains pounded by raging seas. Canada's "gentlest" city, with its annual rainfall of 680mm/27in and large amount of sunshine, is a popular tourist destination. Author Stephen Leacock *(p 116)* wrote of it, "If I had known of this place before, I would have been born here."

From Trading Post to Gracious Capital. – When it became clear that the location of their Pacific headquarters would be declared US territory, the Hudson's Bay Company built a trading post in 1846 on the site of present-day Victoria, naming the new post after the Queen of England. An important provisioning centre, the post grew in the 1850s and 1860s during British Columbia's gold rushes *(pp 30 and 34)*. In 1849, the settlement was made the capital of the crown colony of Vancouver Island. When the island was united with the mainland, Victoria became the capital of British Columbia (except between 1866 and 1868, when New Westminster was the capital). A centre of gracious living, the city avoided industrial development when the Canadian Pacific Railway was terminated at Vancouver (trains cross to the island by ferry), which grew into a major commercial centre. Other than the Canadian Forces' Pacific Naval base in nearby **Esquimalt** (pop 16,192), major employers for the Victoria area are the government and the tourism industry. The city's pleasant climate also has attracted a large retirement population.

★★ **DOWNTOWN** *Map below. 1 day.*

The city centre is situated along Government Street, which is the main shopping area, and around the James Bay section of the harbour where ferries from Port Angeles and Seattle dock. Intriguing little squares and alleys such as Nootka Court, Trounce Alley and Bastion Square house elegant shops, restaurants and sidewalk cafes. Just north, Market Square, a collection of older renovated buildings, has shops around courtyard gardens.

To the south, located off Belleville Street, is Heritage Court. The narrow columns and arches on the ground floor of this group of striking modern buildings add a distinct Islamic flavour. The complex houses the provincial archives and the Royal British Columbia Museum. At the front stands the **Netherlands Carillon Tower [A]**, an

open-sided 27m/ 88ft tower containing 62 bells given to the province by Canadians of Dutch origin. At the north end of the museum, an arcade called the **Glass House** contains a collection of totem poles from all over the province.

In the main entrance hall, a Cowichan Indian **welcome figure** greets visitors. Carved for the Indians of the Expo '67 Canada Pavilion, the figure is that of a chief wearing a cedar bark hat and chief's blanket.

★★★ **Royal British Columbia Museum.** – *Open May–Sept daily 9:30am–7pm. Off-season daily 10am–5:30pm. $5. ⅃ 🅿 ($1.50) ☎604/387-2164.* One of the top museums in the world, this eminent institution has focused on the natural and human history of the province for over 100 years. Since 1972, the museum has welcomed some one million visitors annually.

British Columbia's **natural history** is featured on the second floor. A series of spectacular dioramas of the coastal forest and seashore regions in-

includes animal, bird and fish life. An unusual **Open Ocean** exhibit is based on William Beebe's deep-sea dive in 1930. Visitors follow his adventure through a succession of theatres, dioramas, observation platforms and models that portray life in the open seas. In the future, there will be dioramas of other natural regions, such as mountains, valleys and interior drylands.

The third floor is devoted to British Columbia's **human history**. Starting with the province today, visitors walk backwards through time. Highlights are the reconstruction of a turn-of-the-century street, complete with shops, hotel, movie house and station; vivid re-creations of a sawmill, fish-packing plant, farmyard and mine, illustrating the development of industry; and, in the section on European discovery of the province, a reconstruction of part of George Vancouver's ship, *The Discovery*. The **Indian History Gallery** contains an extensive collection of Indian art, arranged in striking dioramas. These exhibits depict the way of life prior to the arrival of Europeans and the changes after contact, such as smallpox epidemics, land settlement disputes and the banning of potlatch ceremonies. Note especially the totem poles, and the reconstructed house and furnishings that once belonged to a Kwakiutl chief.

* **Parliament Buildings.** – On the south side of James Bay stands a long squat stone building with a central dome, topped by a gilt statue of Capt George Vancouver. Designed by **Francis Rattenbury** (1867-1935) and completed in 1898, "the buildings," as they are known, house the British Columbia legislature and government offices. Stationed in front of them is a bronze statue of Queen Victoria. A highly decorated arch beneath the dome marks the entrance *(open daily Jun–Labour Day; off-season Mon–Fri; closed legal holidays; ☎604/387-3046)*. On summer evenings, thousands of tiny lights illuminate the buildings, adding a romantic flair.

* **Empress Hotel.** – Also designed by Francis Rattenbury, and built by the Canadian Pacific Railway in 1908, this enormous turreted, ivy-covered hotel is a city landmark. For many years "tea at the Empress" was considered an essential part of gracious living. Still served at the hotel *(daily; reservations suggested; ☎604/384-8111)*, tea is more a tourist attraction now than a facet of gracious living.

* **Thunderbird Park [B].** – This small park has a fine collection of replicas of totem poles and other Indian carvings. Many of the original works, on which these copies are based, were executed by Chief Mungo Martin, a famous carver. As each carving decays, it is copied and replaced *(carvers can sometimes be seen at work)*.

Next to Thunderbird Park stands a white clapboard building, **Helmcken House [D]** *(visit by 45min guided tour only May–Sept Thur–Mon; $3.25; & ▯ ☎604/387-4697)*, which was built in 1858.

* **Maritime Museum.** – *Open daily year-round. Closed Christmas & New Year's. $5.* & ▯ ☎604/385-4222. A lighthouse beacon stands in front of the law court building that houses this museum. Inside, there are model ships, marine paraphernalia and displays on Northwest Coast explorers. Of special interest are the *Tilikum*, a converted Indian dugout canoe that sailed from Victoria to England in the early 1900s, and the *Trekka*, a 6m/20ft sailing boat built in Victoria that sailed around the world from 1955 to 1959, the smallest boat ever to undertake such a voyage.

* **Emily Carr Gallery [F].** – *Open daily Jul–Nov. Off-season Tue–Sat. $2.* & ☎604/384-3130. This gallery is devoted to one of Canada's best-known and original painters, British Columbian **Emily Carr** (1871-1945). Her portrayals of West Coast landscapes and Indian villages are striking, and examples of her work can be found in most major collections across the country. On a rotating basis, the gallery exhibits original works by Carr and other related material including letters, manuscripts, newspaper articles and photographs.

Crystal Garden. – *Open daily year-round. Closed Christmas. $5.* ✗ & ☎604/381-1213. The immense glass house was once the location of orchestral concerts, art exhibits and a large underglass seawater swimming pool. Today, it houses a tropical garden filled with exotic birds, monkeys and plants. It is also a pleasant place to have tea.

Undersea Gardens. – *Open daily year-round. $6.* ☎604/382-5717. Situated in the inner harbour, this structure enables visitors to descend below the water's surface to see fish in aquariums. During the shows, divers bring various species such as small sharks and octopuses close to the glass walls for spectators to view.

Classic Car Museum [M¹]. – *Open daily year-round.* ☎604/382-5717. Over 40 cars, many of historic interest, are on display.

** **SCENIC DRIVE** *Map p 65. 13km/8mi. Allow 1hr.*

Leave from Thunderbird Park and take Douglas St south.

This beautiful drive enables visitors to appreciate Victoria's grand site on the Strait of Juan de Fuca and the lovely gardens maintained by the city's residents. Skirting the large, flower-filled **Beacon Hill Park★**, the road passes a plaque [L] marking the initial kilometer of the nearly 8,000km/5,000mi **Trans-Canada Highway**, which stretches to St John's, Newfoundland. From Finlayson and Clover points, there are fine **views★★** of the Olympic Mountains. The drive enters the community of **Oak Bay** (pop 17,815), a wealthy suburb with large houses, beautiful gardens, pretty views and a very English population. Harling Point provides a good view of the rocky coastline and the houses perched along the coast. Directly below on the right, Gonzales Bay is visible and the Trial Islands can be seen offshore to the left. The drive continues around McNeill Bay with several more viewpoints. Bisected by the road, the Oak Bay golf course on Gonzales Point is one of the continent's most attractive courses with **views★★** of the sea *(weather permitting)*, the San Juan Islands and the snow-clad peaks of the Cascades, dominated by Mount Baker.

The drive then passes through **Uplands Park★**, a pleasant section of Oak Bay with lovely homes and gardens. From **Cattle Point**, there are views of the coast.

ADDITIONAL SIGHTS

★ **Craigdarroch Castle.** – *Map above. Open daily year-round. $5.* 🅿 ☎604/592-5323. Built by Robert Dunsmuir, a Scot who made a fortune from coal, the huge stone mansion has towers, turrets and a carved carriage entrance. This former centre of Victoria's society (one Dunsmuir son became the premier of the province and later the lieutenant-governor) once stood amid 11ha/27 acres of gardens. Today, the house is gradually being restored to its 1880s grandeur. Note the wood-panelled hall and massive oak staircase. An enormous dance hall is found on the fourth floor, and from the top of the tower, there is a good view of Victoria.

★ **Fort Rodd Hill.** – 🐾 *Map below. 14km/9mi west by Rtes 1, 1A and Ocean Blvd. Open daily year-round. Closed Christmas, Boxing Day & New Year's.* ♿ 🅿 ☎604/363-4662. Set in 18ha/44 acres of land at the southwest corner of Esquimalt harbour, the fort contains the remains of three coastal artillery-gun batteries and displays on the shore defences of this area. Built to protect the approaches to the naval base at Esquimalt, the batteries were in operation until 1956. From beside Fisgard Lighthouse, there are fine **views**★ of Juan de Fuca Strait, the Olympic Mountains and the naval base.

★ **Anne Hathaway's Cottage.** – *Map opposite. In Esquimalt, 429 Lampson St, part of Olde England Inn. Visit by guided tour (30min) only daily year-round. $5.75.* ✖ 🅿 ☎604/388-4353. Covered with a thatched roof, this black and white half-timbered building is a replica of the Stratford (England) home of William Shakespeare's wife. Inside, there are ten rooms with period furniture. Note especially the wooden panelling on the ground floor. An attractive "old world" English garden surrounds the house.

Art Gallery of Greater Victoria. – *Map above. 1040 Moss St. Open daily year-round. Closed Christmas & Good Friday. $4.* ♿ 🅿 ☎604/384-4101. The nucleus of the gallery is a Victorian mansion built in 1890. Several modern additions have been made, but the house remains the focal point with its Japanese garden and a fascinating dollhouse on the second floor. The gallery is known for its collection of Asian art, shown in regularly changing exhibitions.

Craigflower Heritage Site. – *110 Island Hwy at Gorge Rd. Visit by guided tour (45min) May–mid-Oct Sun only. Grounds open year-round. $3.25.* 🅿 ☎604/387-4697. This Georgian clapboard house was constructed in 1856 by Kenneth McKenzie, bailiff for Puget Sound Agricultural Company, the first organization to develop the island for farming. One of the earliest buildings in Victoria, the house was partially fortified in case of Indian attack (note the studded oak door and heavy wooden shutters). Most of the manor is original and contains period furnishings.

EXCURSIONS *Map p 65*

*** The Butchart Gardens. – *21km/13mi north by Rte 17 and Keating Rd or by 17A. Open year-round daily at 9am. Closing times vary with season. $11; reduced rates in off-season.* ✗ ♿ ☏*604/652-5256.* Expanded to approximately 20ha/50 acres, these internationally famous gardens were started in 1904 by Jennie Butchart to beautify the quarry pit resulting from her husband's cement business. Still operated by the family, the grounds are maintained by a small army of gardeners in summer.

The floral showpiece is the beautiful **Sunken Garden***** with its green lawns, trees and exquisite flower arrangements that create a whirl of colour. The flowers change from season to season, but the effect is always striking. Set in a huge hole with ivy-covered sides, the garden is best viewed from above or from the rock island at its centre. Paths weave down into it through a rockery.

The other gardens include the **Ross Fountain** with changing water displays in a rocky pool; the **Concert Lawn** *(concerts: Mon–Sat Jun–Sept; fireworks: Sat Jul–Aug)*, the **Rose Garden***, full of blooms overhead and on both sides *(Jun–Sept)*; the dark, secluded **Japanese Garden*** with its lacquered bridges and wooden teahouses; and the formal **Italian Garden*** with its star-shaped lily pond and statues. On summer evenings, the lighting of the gardens provides an entirely different perspective *(mid-Jun–mid-Sept)*.

* Malahat Drive. – *Begins 16km/ 10mi along Trans-Can Hwy.* This attractive stretch of road crosses Malahat Ridge with good **views**** of Finlayson Arm, Saanich Inlet, the Gulf Islands and the mainland. If the day is clear, the peak of Mount Baker *(p 54)* is visible through the trees.

* British Columbia Forest Museum. – *65km/40mi north by Hwy 1, just after Duncan. Open daily May–Sept. $5.* ✗ ♿ ☏*604/746-1251.* Covering 40ha/100 acres, this museum provides some background to the province's most important industry. Visitors can walk through a forest of Douglas fir trees, visit a log museum displaying the evolution of logging techniques, see a reconstructed logging camp and ride the narrow-gauge steam railway.

** WATERTON LAKES NATIONAL PARK Alberta

Map of Principal Sights p 2

Situated in the southwest corner of the province, this lovely preserve in the Canadian Rockies forms an International Peace Park with the larger Glacier National Park in Montana. Because its gently rolling hills (rarely over 1,200m/4,000ft) meet a vertical rock wall towering another 1,200m/4,000ft or more above the plains, the park has been described as the place "where the prairies meet the mountains."

The underlying sediment of these mountains, which once were part of an inland sea, was thrust up and sculptured by erosion and glaciation into sharp peaks, narrow ridges and interlocked U-shaped valleys. Among them, the three Waterton Lakes lie in a deep glacial trough. Formerly a Blackfoot Indian stronghold, the mountains of Waterton were first visited by Thomas Blakiston of the Palliser Expedition, who explored the area in 1858 and named the lakes for an 18C English naturalist, **Charles Waterton**. Oil was discovered a few decades later, but never proved profitable. The area was designated a national park in 1895.

VISIT

Open year-round. Hiking, horseback riding, swimming, fishing, boating, golf, winter sports. $5/day per car; $10/4 days per car. △ ✗ ♿ ☏*403/859-2445.*

Waterton Townsite. – Built on delta materials deposited by Cameron Creek, the town has a lovely **site**** near the point where Upper Lake narrows into the Bosporus Strait, which separates it from Middle Lake. Just south behind the townsite, the flat face of **Mount Richards** can be distinguished. Beside it stands **Mount Bertha**, marked by pale green streaks down the otherwise dark-green surface. The streaks were caused by snowslides that swept trees down the mountainside. Across the lake rise **Vimy Peak** and **Vimy Ridge**. Upper Lake stretches south into Montana, separating the mountains of the Lewis and Clark ranges, which tower steeply above it. In summer, **tour boats** make trips down the lake to the US ranger station at the southern end *(depart daily mid-May–Sept; Jul–Aug five cruises daily; round-trip 2hrs; $14; commentary on board; ♿ Waterton Shoreline Cruises* ☏*403/859-2362).* Behind the townsite, **Cameron Falls** can be seen dropping over a layered cliff.

** Cameron Lake. – *17km/11mi from townsite by Akamina Hwy.* Before reaching the lake, the highway passes the site of the first oil well in western Canada. The **lake**** itself is set immediately below the Continental Divide and, like Upper Waterton, it spans the international boundary. Dominating the view across the lake are, to the left, **Mount Custer** with the **Herbst Glacier**, and to the right, **Forum Peak**.

* Red Rock Canyon. – *19km/12mi from townsite; turn left at Blakiston Creek.* The drive to this small canyon offers good **views*** of the surrounding mountains. A **nature trail** follows the narrow canyon *(2km/1.2mi)*, where characteristic colour is due to iron compounds in the rock that oxidized to form hematite.

* Buffalo Paddock. – *400m/.2mi from park entrance. Auto circuit 3km/2mi.* A small herd of buffalo occupies a large enclosure on a fine **site*** with Bellevue Mountain and Mount Galway as a backdrop.

Situated on flat land on the west side of a big bend in the Yukon River, Whitehorse is the capital of the Yukon Territory and a regional service centre. Above it, sharp cliffs rise to a plateau where the airport is located and across which the Alaska Highway passes. On the river's east side, barren hills become mountains known as the Big Salmon Range.

Transport Town. – The city owes its existence to the difficulty encountered by the Klondike Stampeders in negotiating Miles Canyon and the Whitehorse Rapids (now tamed by a hydro-electric plant) on the Yukon River. A tramway was built to carry goods around these obstacles so that the boats could be piloted through with greater ease. The completion of the White Pass and Yukon Route Railway in 1900, from Skagway *(p 68)* through the Coast Mountains, changed methods of transport in the area. The town soon bustled in summer with the transfer of passengers and goods from railway to riverboat, and from railway to overland stage in winter. The railway company's decision to end its line at Whitehorse (and not to continue to Dawson City) resulted in the birth of the city.

The presence of the railway and of a small airport were major factors when the decision to build the Alaska Highway *(p 28)* was made in 1942. Whitehorse became a major base for the road's construction, changing overnight at a time when Dawson City was declining in importance. Reflecting this change, the territorial capital was moved here in 1953. Today, the city is a centre for tourism as well as communications in the Yukon. Proud of its part in the Klondike Stampede, the community stages a celebration every February called the **Sourdough Rendezvous** when people dress in the costumes of 1898 and race dog teams on the frozen Yukon River.

SIGHTS *1 day*

No longer a frontier town in appearance, Whitehorse retains, nevertheless, some historic structures, notably: the **old log church** on Elliott at Third, built in 1900; the "**sky-scrapers**" on Lambert between Second and Third avenues, built after World War II when there was a housing shortage, and still in use today; and the log **railway station** on First Avenue at Main. In contrast is the modern steel and aluminum Yukon government **Administration Building** on Second Avenue, opened in 1976. Its light and airy interior, finished in wood, features an acrylic resin mural that looks like stained glass. The Yukon Permanent Art Collection installed here features contemporary art as well as traditional native costumes and artifacts.

★ **MacBride Museum.** – *First Ave at Wood St. Open daily mid-May–mid-Sept. Off-season by reservation. $3.25. �&. ☎403/667-2709.* Situated in a log building (1967) built with a sod roof, this museum features Gold Rush memorabilia, native Indian cultural objects, trapping equipment and a splendid collection of old **photographs** of the men and women of the Yukon. A large number of preserved animals are displayed side by side, enabling the visitor to appreciate the relative size and characteristic markings of each, such as the differing antlers of moose, elk and caribou. Of particular interest are the navigational **maps** of the Yukon River, hand-drawn by riverboat captains ("masters") and their pilots, mounted on hand-cranked spools so their length can be appreciated. Outside are relics of Yukon transport, examples of early machinery, Sam McGee's cabin and a government telegraph office c.1900.

★★ **SS Klondike.** – ⑨ *Second Ave near Robert Campbell Bridge. Open mid-May–mid-Sept daily 9am–7pm. ☎403/667-4511.* One of over 200 sternwheelers that once plied the waters of the Yukon between Whitehorse and Dawson City, this well-restored 1937 craft is the only remaining steamboat open to the public in the Territory. Carrying passengers, ore and supplies, the vessel required 32 cords of wood to fuel the 40-hour, 700km/436mi downstream trip to Dawson. The return trip against the current took 96 hours and burned 112 cords of wood. Visitors can see the huge boiler, engine room and cargo space; from the wheelhouse, envision the captain's vantage point; and view the galley and first-class passenger accommodation, including the observation room and dining area with its elegant tablesettings.

Cross the river via Robert Campbell Bridge and stop to see the **fish ladder** at **Whitehorse Dam**, built to enable the chinook salmon to circumnavigate the dam and reach their spawning grounds upriver *(usually occurs in August)*. Interpretive panels and windows for viewing the fish as they "climb" the ladder are provided. These salmon are near the end of the longest-known chinook migration in the world—3,200km/2,000mi. The dam is best viewed from the fishway's observation deck.

★★ **Miles Canyon.** – *9km/6mi south of Whitehorse via Canyon Rd.* Following the edge of Schwatka Lake, **Canyon Road** passes the *MV Schwatka* dock *(see below)* and climbs above the canyon *(sharp curves and steep grades)* where there is a good **view★** from the lookout. Near the parking lot above Miles Canyon, another fine **view★** is possible. The river can be crossed by a footbridge for other clifftop views.

For more than 1km/.75mi, the Yukon River passes through a narrow gorge of sheer columnar basalt walls, grayish-red in colour. Created by the shrinkage of volcanic lava upon cooling, these walls rise straight up, 9-12m/30-40ft above the river. Here the Yukon still flows through rapidly, swirling around Devil's Whirlpool. But construction of the power dam downstream has very much lessened the speed and navigational hazards the stampeders experienced.

Canyon **cruises** *(MV Schwatka departs daily in summer; round-trip 2hrs; $15; ☎403/668-3161; take South Access Rd towards centre of Whitehorse, turn right onto unpaved road immediately past railroad tracks)* afford good **views★** of the deep green waters of the Yukon and the steep canyon walls. The tremendous force of the river is better appreciated from the water level than from the viewpoints above. Interesting historical commentary is given.

Yukon Transportation Museum. – *Alaska Hwy near airport. Open daily mid-May–mid-Sept. $2.* ⅃ ☏*403/668-4792.* Exhibits include archival photos of Yukon aviation and a replica of the 1920s mail carrier float plane, *Queen of the Yukon.*

★★ EXCURSION TO SKAGWAY 1 day

Note: Skagway is in Alaska. Canadian citizens need identification to enter the US. Other visitors need US visas, which are available from any US consulate, but not in Whitehorse.

An impressive trip in the Yukon is the traverse of the Coast Mountains to the Pacific tidewater at Skagway—terminus of the Klondike Highway—on the Alaska Panhandle. Tiny frontier towns, dramatic lake systems, barren flatlands, abandoned mines and coastal vistas season this outing with diversity, while summoning images of earlier sojourners struggling to reach the fields of gold.

★★ Klondike Highway to Skagway. – *180km/112mi by Alaska Hwy and Klondike Hwy (Rte 2). About 3hrs; Canadian/US border open 24hrs year-round.* ☏*907/983-2725 or 907/983-2325.* Adjoining the Alaska Highway south of Whitehorse, the Klondike Highway passes through forest and gradually enters the mountains, with views of snow-capped peaks ahead. At small, historic **Carcross** (pop 183)—where the final rail was laid for the White Pass and Yukon Route—the scenery changes dramatically as the road follows the shores of **Tagish Lake, Windy Arm** and **Tutshi** (TOO-shy*) **Lake***. The sight is striking: imposing mountains rise straight out of the blue waters of the lakes. After leaving Tutshi Lake, the road begins the traverse of the White Pass with another change in scenery. The pass is desolate, almost lunar—treeless flatlands with lichen-covered rocks. The steep descent to Skagway on the coast permits views of the **Taiya Inlet** in the Lynn Canal far below.

★ Skagway. – Pop 692. The wide Pacific lying at its door, the historic little community, known as the "Gateway to the Klondike," occupies a lovely **site**★ with snow-capped peaks as a backdrop. A port of call on the Inside Passage route *(p 35),* this tourism centre, with its pervasive frontier flavour, attracts scores of visitors annually via road, rail and seaway.

Skagway was born with the Klondike Stampede. Until the first boatload of gold seekers docked in July of 1897, Capt William Moore and his son were the only European settlers in the area, having arrived in 1888. Amid supplies, horses and equipment, tents and huts sprouted up everywhere. In three months, the population swelled to roughly 20,000 and a grid pattern of streets sported saloons, casinos, dance halls and stores. Lawlessness was rife as the town became home to notorious characters such as **Soapy Smith**, a con artist *par excellence* who succeeded in divesting many greenhorn gold rushers of their money. In 1898, construction of the White Pass and Yukon Route Railway *(see below)* and a crackdown on crime helped to stabilize the community.

Northern terminus of the southeast ferry system, the small but busy port has received regular calls since 1963. The Klondike Highway from Skagway to Carcross was laid in 1978, and the railway restored in 1988. Several times a day, the train's whistle can be heard in town.

Visit. *2.5hrs.* – Designated an historic district by the US National Park Service, the area along **Broadway** from First to Seventh avenues contains several turn-of-the-century wooden structures housing hotels, saloons and shops restored to evoke the days of the Gold Rush.

The former railroad depot, a handsome 1898 building, serves as the Park Service **visitor centre** *(open May–Sept;* ☏*907/983-2921)* and departure point for walking tours conducted by park rangers. Particularly noteworthy are the **Arctic Brotherhood Hall** *(Broadway between 2nd & 3rd aves; Skagway visitor centre; open daily mid-May–mid-Sept.* ☏*907/983-2855)* with its fanciful driftwood facade, and the small **museum** *(city hall building on 7th Ave and Spring St, open late-May–Sept;* ☏*907/983-2420)* featuring artifacts and documents from Skagway's colourful past.

The adventurous can relive the stampeder experience by hiking the legendary **Chilkoot Trail** *(p 70),* which starts at the abandoned site of Skagway's former rival, **Dyea** *(15km/9mi north of Skagway by dirt road)* and ends at Lake Bennett. The arduous 54km/33mi trek can take up to five days and requires proper equipment *(for trail information and maps, apply to National Park Service in Skagway).*

★★ White Pass and Yukon Route Railroad. – *Train departs May–Sept daily 8:45am & 1:15pm. Round-trip 3hrs. $72. Commentary on board. Through-service to Whitehorse leaves Skagway 12:45pm, transfer in Fraser, BC to motorcoach, arrival Whitehorse 6:30pm. $92/one way. Reservations suggested.* ⅃ *White Pass & Yukon Route* ☏*907/983-2217.* Conceived in 1898 as an alternative to the treacherous ascent of the White Pass and Chilkoot trails, this narrow-gauge railroad stands as a testimony to the inventiveness and determination of the stampeder spirit. The route, which originally linked Skagway to Whitehorse, functioned commercially from 1900 to 1982. Operating solely as a tourist attraction since 1988, the refurbished railroad cars climb, in a mere 32km/20mi, to an elevation of 873m/2,865ft, providing **views**★ of Skagway and the rugged peaks dominating the town. On-board commentary points out noteworthy features, such as waterfalls, bridges and remnants of the White Pass trail. After reaching the summit at White Pass, the train concludes its thrilling 45km/28mi run at the Canadian station in Fraser, BC.

"I don't even know what street Canada is on."

Al Capone, 1931

Map below

Covering a 483,450sq km/186,660sq mi triangle in Canada's northwest corner, the legendary Yukon conjures up images of raging rivers, snow-capped mountains, deserted valleys, long winters, the midnight sun and gold. An adventure to one of the truly faraway places of the globe, this scenic journey rewards travellers willing to traverse a relatively isolated frontier to witness nature's grandeur and mankind's diversions. The majestic Yukon River, a silent, but ever-present companion, dominates half the circuit.

The Mighty Yukon. – One of the longest rivers in North America, this giant of the remote North—its Loucheux Indian name *Yu-kun-ah* means "great river"—traverses 3,185km/1,975mi of rugged territory. Originating in Tagish Lake on the Yukon/British Columbia boundary, the river flows northward through the Yukon Territory and Alaska to empty into the Bering Sea. The Teslin, Pelly, Stewart and White are its primary Canadian tributaries. Over the centuries, this river's natural resources have sustained a native population, its wealth has lured fur traders and gold miners, its currents have transported scows and sternwheelers, and today, its awesome beauty beckons adventurers from many countries.

Home of the Klondike. – On August 16, 1896, **George Carmack** and his Indian brothers-in-law, Skookum Jim and Tagish Charlie, found gold on **Bonanza Creek**, a tiny stream emptying into the bigger **Klondike River**, itself a tributary of the mighty Yukon. When news of their find reached the outside world, an estimated 100,000 people left their homes as far away as Australia to begin the long, arduous trek to Dawson City, the town that sprang up at the mouth of the Klondike. Stories of their travels are legion. Many never made it; of those who did, few made a fortune.

The Routes of '98. – There were several routes to Dawson City during the Gold Rush. The longest, yet easiest, was by sea to the mouth of the Yukon and then by riverboat the 2,092km/1,300mi upstream to the city of gold. But this passage was only for the rich. A few people tried an overland course from Edmonton, Alberta, through almost impassable muskeg and bush, following more or less the present-day route of the Alaska Highway. The majority, however, sailed up the Pacific Coast via the Inside Passage (p 35) to Skagway or Dyea, tiny way stations on the Alaska Panhandle, and trudged into the Yukon across the Coast Mountains.

Treacherous Trails. – From Skagway, Alaska, the trail followed the **White Pass**, a narrow and slippery climb of 879m/2,885ft. More than 3,000 horses were forced along this route in 1897. Most died before reaching the summit. Their remains were quickly trampled underfoot by the mass of humanity behind them. Dead Horse Trail, as it became known, was closed that same winter.

Stampeders who insisted on continuing turned to the more difficult **Chilkoot Pass**. Starting in Dyea, this route was 183m/600ft higher than the White Pass and much steeper—it climbed at an angle of 35° in places. Raw rock in summer, the pass became slick ice and snow in winter, and with temperatures of -50°C/-58°F, it was a nightmare to climb. Yet over the winter of 1897-1898, 22,000 people scaled it, not just once but 30 to 40 times! The North West Mounted Police at the Canadian border insisted that anyone entering Canada have a year's supply of food and equipment because of shortages in the Territory. To carry this "ton" of goods over the pass, stampeders had to make numerous trips! Thus the Chilkoot was a stream of climbing humanity for the entire winter.

The trek by foot ended at **Lake Bennett**, where boats were constructed to complete the journey to Dawson. Hazards on the voyage, such as Miles Canyon *(p 67)* and Five Finger Rapids *(see below)*, seemed minor after the traverse of Chilkoot.

Today, thousands of people follow in their footsteps, not to hunt for gold but to discover, as the Klondike Stampeders did, the beauty of that wild northland, and to experience what the poet Robert Service called *The Spell of the Yukon:*

> It's the great, big, broad land 'way up yonder,
>
> It's the forests where silence has lease,
>
> It's the beauty that thrills me with wonder,
>
> It's the stillness that fills me with peace.

VISIT *1 week, not including excursion to Skagway, Alaska.*
About 1,450km/900mi from Whitehorse via Klondike, Top of the World, Taylor and Alaska hwys. Lengthy drive over stretches of dirt or gravel road. 4-wheel drive recommended. For road conditions, see p 27. Service facilities are few and infrequent. Prepare for emergencies with food, warm clothing and vehicle supplies. Be familiar with protection against weather and wild animals. The Milepost (p 28) is a useful reference for this trip.

★ From Whitehorse to Dawson City
540km/335mi by Klondike Hwy (Rte 2). Allow 1 day.

★ Whitehorse. – *Visit: 1 day. Description p 67.*

The Klondike Highway skirts **Lake Laberge** *(barely visible from the road)*, through which the Yukon River runs. At the end of the unpaved access road to the campground, there is a lovely **view** of this lake and the mountains beyond.

Passing through hilly and largely deserted country, the highway rejoins the river at **Carmacks** *(178km/110mi)*, named for the discoverer of Klondike gold.

After 196km/ 122mi, just beyond a bend in the Yukon, a series of small rock islands, varying in size, can be seen. These formations have divided the river into five fast-flowing channels, known as **Five Finger Rapids★**. A hazard to navigation even today, these rapids caused problems during the stampede; riverboats often had to be winched through the narrowest channel by cable. From the lookout *(panel exhibit)*, a good view of the rapids is afforded.

In the vicinity of Minto, about 2km/1mi past Minto Resorts, an unpaved road leads to the riverside *(1.6km/1mi)*. Here, amid the ruins of earlier log structures, a sign marks the Overland Trail, a wagon road built in 1902 and the winter mail route from Whitehorse to Dawson City. The **view★** of the Yukon from the bank is grand.

Leaving the Yukon Valley, the highway crosses the central plateau and bridges the Pelly and Stewart rivers. At Pelly Crossing, descriptive **panels** tell the history of the native **Selkirk** people whose tradition it was to fish the area in spring, years prior to the coming of Europeans to the Yukon.

Note at Stewart Crossing, Route 11 *(unpaved between Mayo and Keno)*, designated the **Silver Trail**, begins its 111km/69mi northeast traverse through Mayo (pop 243) to Keno (pop 36), a boom town in the 1920s when mining of the area's vast silver deposits was in its heyday *(p 32)*.

After Stewart Crossing, the vast **Tintina Trench** runs parallel to the highway. From the designated lookout about 61km/38mi south of Dawson City, a good **view** of this valley can be obtained. Stretching through the Yukon and Alaska, the trench is another example of plate tectonics *(p 221)*.

There is a **viewpoint**, after 483km/300mi, of the valley of the Klondike River from above, with the Ogilvie Mountains to the northeast. The road then follows the Klondike, but the river is not always visible because of the great mounds of tailings *(p 33)* left by mining dredges.

At 494km/307mi, note that the **Dempster Highway** heads northward to Inuvik in the Mackenzie Delta *(p 234)* across the Ogilvie and Richardson mountains. Named for Corporal Dempster of the North West Mounted Police who pioneered the route by dogsled at the turn of the century, it is the only road in North America that crosses the Arctic Circle *(open all year except spring break-up and fall freeze-up when Peel and Mackenzie river ferries do not operate)*.

The Klondike Highway crosses the famous Klondike River after 538km/334mi and enters Dawson City. The word *Klondike* is a Han Indian adaptation for "hammer water," suggestive of the posts hammered into the riverbed to make salmon traps.

★★ Dawson City. – *Visit 2 days. Description p 31.*

From Dawson City to Whitehorse

905km/562mi by Top of the World, Taylor (both closed in winter), and Alaska hwys. Allow 2-3 days. Caution: Reduced speeds necessary, usually 40–64km/h/25–40mph on winding and often unpaved road. Drive with headlights on. Canadian/US customs. Border open daily 24hr year-round. ☎907/983-2725 or 907/983-2325.

★★ **Top of the World Highway.** – *108km/67mi to Alaska border; road closed in winter. Entry only when US Customs open, 9am - 9pm daily.* Route 9 is called Top of the World Highway because most of its length is above the tree line, allowing magnificent **views**★★★ in all directions. It leaves Dawson by the ferry *(continuous 24hr service May–Oct)* across the vast Yukon. At this point, the river's waters are no longer the sparkling green colour of Miles Canyon *(p 67)*, but a light gray-blue, resulting from the earth brought in by major tributaries—the Pelly, the White and the Stewart. For about 5km/3mi, the road climbs to a **viewpoint** at a bend in the road providing a different perspective of the city and rivers from that seen from Midnight Dome. After 14km/9mi, there is another **viewpoint** of the Ogilvie Mountains, the Yukon Valley and, visible to the north, the Tintina Trench *(p 70)*. From then on, the road follows the ridgetops 90km/50mi, winding up and down for some distance. Ever-changing vistas of mountains and valleys greet travellers on this route.

The Route in Alaska. – *306km/190mi. At Alaskan border, set watches back 1hr.* Route 9 joins the Taylor Highway (US Route 5) after 23km/14mi *(services available at Boundary, Alaska)* and heads south along the valley of the Fortymile River. Shortly before the great Klondike discovery, gold was found here. In the creeks along the highway, evidence of mining remains today. **Chicken**, Alaska, *(food and fuel)* offers ocal colour and frontier history. Wanting to name their camp "ptarmigan" for a local bird, miners settled on "chicken" instead, it is said, because they could spell it! The community was home to Ann Hobbs, who chronicled her life as Chicken's teacher in the book, *Tisha*. *(Daily guided tour of the old mining camp, including author's home. Contact Chicken Creek Cafe, Airport Rd.)* At **Tetlin Junction**, take the Alaska Highway south to the Canadian border *(set watches forward 1hr)*.

★★ **Alaska Highway.** – *491km/305mi from Alaska border to Whitehorse. Along the highway, posts indicate the distance from Dawson Creek, BC, where the highway begins (p 28). Thus the kilometres/miles in this section are shown in descending order to conform with these post readings.* North of the Canadian/US border, in the vicinity of Northway (Alaska), is the Tetlin National **Wildlife Refuge** *(open daily Memorial Day–Labour Day;* ☎907/883-5312*)*, a 384,620ha/950,000 acre preserve of boreal forest, wetlands, lakes and glacial rivers. At km 1982/mi 1229, the US Fish and Wildlife Service **visitor center** features exhibits of wildlife and flora indigenous to the Upper Tanana River Valley.

After crossing the Canadian border *(km 1969/mi 1221)*, the highway *(caution: intermittent bumps)* passes through flat muskeg country and later bridges the White and then the Donjek rivers, full of glacial silt. From the course of the latter *(km 1810/ mi 1125)*, there is a **view** of the Icefield Ranges of the **St Elias Mountains** *(see below)*.

★★ **Kluane Lake.** – Just before Burwash Landing *(km 1759/mi 1093)*, the road approaches this vast lake, paralleling it for 64km/40mi and offering excellent **views**★★. The highest and largest lake in the Yukon, Kluane (kloo-ON-ee) is ringed by mountains and fed by glaciers, the factor in its incredibly beautiful colour. To the south and west lie the **Kluane Ranges**, to the north and east the **Ruby Range**. All of them are reflected in the icy blue waters of this lake, the surface of which can change from a rippling mirror to a heaving mass of waves in a very short period.

In Burwash Landing (pop 77), the **Kluane Museum of Natural History** *(open daily mid-May–mid-Sept; $3;* &. ☎403/841-5561*)* is housed in a six-sided log building. **Dioramas**★ of native wildlife line the building's interior while a reconstructed mountain occupies the center, covered with preserved birds and animals of varying sizes. There is also a large relief map of the mountain ranges of Kluane National Park.

★★ **Kluane National Park Reserve.** – 🐾 *Park office in Haines Junction (see below) Limited 4-wheel-drive vehicle access to park's interior (streams must be forded). Arrangements to visit interior must be made in advance with park authorities. Park open year-round. Hiking, rafting, fishing, cross-country skiing.* ⚠
Plane excursions: Daily flights (weather permitting) from Victoria Day–Labour Day; $60/person (40min) or $160/person (2hrs); 24hr advance reservation; for schedules & reservation contact Glacier Air Tours ☎403/841-5171*. Trans-North Air offers charters by helicopter year-round; $600/hr plus fuel; for schedules & reservations* ☎403/634-2242*. Excursion by float plane daily May–mid-Oct. $270/hr, maximum 3 passengers. Reservations suggested. Sifton Air* ☎403/668-4916*.* The scenic variety and beauty of this World Heritage Site (inscribed in 1980) are stunning. The park occupies the entire 22,000sq km/8,494sq mi southwest corner of the Yukon, including most of the St Elias Mountains in Canada. From the Alaska Highway, the rugged, snow-capped Kluane Ranges (as high as 2,500m/8,000ft) of these mountains can be seen. Behind them and largely invisible from the highway are the **Icefield Ranges**. Separated from the Kluanes by a narrow trough called the Duke Depression, these ranges contain the highest mountains in Canada, with many peaks exceeding 4,500m/15,000ft. Best known are **Mount Logan** (5,959m/19,546ft) and **Mount St Elias** (5,488m/18,008ft). Mount Logan is second in height only to **Mount McKinley** (6,193m/20,320ft) in Alaska, the highest point on the continent. Forming the base of these peaks is an ice-covered plateau 2,500-3,000m/8,000-10,000ft high, from which many glaciers radiate.

At km 1707/mi 1061, the Alaska Highway passes **Sheep Mountain** *(satellite visitor centre)*, a rocky and barren peak so named for the white Dall sheep sometimes seen on its slopes. The Alaska Highway crosses the large delta *(km 1707-2/mi 1061-58)* of the **Slims River**, its sandy streak of glacial silt from the Kaskawulsh Glacier penetrating the blue of Kluane Lake for some distance, until absorbed.

Haines Junction. – Pop 559. *Km1635/mi1016. Kluane National Park Reserve visitor centre open mid-May–mid-Sept daily 8:30am–9pm. Off-season Mon–Fri 8:30am–4:30pm.* ☎*403/634-2251.* At the junction of the Alaska and Haines (Route 3) highways, this community has a fine **site**★ at the foot of the Auriol Range and is the location for Kluane National Park Reserve headquarters. The **visitor centre** provides information and registration services, and offers interpretive panels and a poetic audio-visual presentation of the park's diversity and grandeur *(25min).*

Affording views of Kathleen Lake as it parallels the park to the south, Haines Highway then crosses the Chilkat Pass before entering Alaska and reaching the town of Haines (pop 1,151) on the Lynn Canal.

About 20km/12mi south of Haines Junction via Route 3, there is a lookout for a **view**★★ of lovely **Kathleen Lake**★★. However, at the park's only campground, visitors can drive to the edge of the lake with its shimmering blue waters. When untroubled by frequent winds, the lake's surface mirrors the imposing forms of King's Throne Mountain and Mt Worthington, rising above.

Returning to Haines Junction, travellers can continue to Whitehorse (km 1474/mi 916) on the Alaska Highway, with views of the Coast Mountains to the south most of the way. About 13km/8mi after the junction, there is a **view**★ from the Alaska Highway *(weather permitting)* of two white pinnacles protruding above the Auriol and Kluane ranges up the valley of the Dezadeash River: Mts Hubbard and Kennedy of the Icefield Ranges.

Prairie Provinces

Barb & Ron Kroll

Alberta, Saskatchewan and Manitoba, known collectively as the Prairie provinces, are often declared flat and monotonous by visitors who drive the long 1,500km/930mi journey from Ontario to Banff. But few who spend time exploring this vast region of nearly 1,963,000sq km/758,000sq mi come away with this impression. There is something awe-inspiring about the wide open spaces, extensively cultivated, yet sparsely populated (just over 4.6 million people). Despite the seemingly endless plain, there are variations. Rivers have cut deep valleys into the soft soil, and in some of these, **badlands**—the eery lunar landscape of another age—can be seen.

The countryside is an ever-changing rainbow of colours. Green in the spring, the wheat turns gold before harvest. Flax has a small blue or white flower, rapeseed a yellow one. Tall colourfully painted **grain elevators**—the "cathedrals of the plains"—rise beside the railway tracks. Above extends an infinite blue sky, dotted with puffy white clouds, sometimes black as a storm approaches. Prairie sunsets are a sight not to be missed, and night-time skies are so full of stars, it is rarely dark.

Yet among ample evidence of man's handiwork, wildlife survives. Wild ducks, geese and other birds are frequently seen on prairie **sloughs** (small ponds), and ground squirrels (gophers) are a common sight along the roadside.

The people of this land represent an amazing mélange of ethnic groups and cultures, each maintaining its identity, perhaps because of the distances between communities. From afar, villages with their onion-domed churches rise like mirages from the wheat fields.

GEOGRAPHICAL NOTES

The idea that the word prairie is synonymous with endless fields stretching to the horizon is a recent phenomenon. The word is, in fact, of French origin and means "meadow." It was given to the large area of natural grassland that existed in the interior of the North American continent before the arrival of the Europeans. Characterized by its flatness and lack of trees, this grassland was an area where the buffalo, roaming in huge herds, were hunted by the various Plains Indians. Today, little natural grassland survives, and in Canada the term "Prairies" now applies to the whole of the three provinces, despite the fact that this immense region is geographically quite diverse.

Semiarid Southwest. – The southernmost part of Alberta and Saskatchewan is a relatively dry land of short grass. In 1857, a scientific expedition led by **John Palliser**, commissioned by the British government to study the possibilities for settlement in the Prairies, decided that the southwestern corner would never be productive agriculturally. Palliser did not foresee the widespread use of irrigation, which has brought much of the region into cultivation today, nor did he fully realize the nutritional value of the native grasses, which today provide adequate pasture for cattle. This region, especially the vicinity of Cypress Hills, rates second in importance to British Columbia's Cariboo for cattle raising in Canada.

Wheat-Growing Crescent. – To the north of the arid lands lies a crescent-shaped region of fertile soil, graced with more abundant rainfall. Once, the grass grew shoulder high, and few trees blocked the view of distant horizons over the flat plain. Today, this is the wheat belt, the prairie of many people's imagination. Prim farm buildings dot the enormous fields of thriving crops, contributing to a general air of prosperity.

Aspen Parkland. – North of the wheat belt is another roughly crescent-shaped region where trees grow in good soil and mixed farming flourishes. This is a region of rolling parkland, a transitional zone between the prairie and the forest of the north. It is in this region that the majority of the inhabitants of the three provinces live.

Boreal Forest and Tundra. – Nearly half of the total area of the three provinces lies directly on the Precambrian rock of the Canadian Shield. This is a pristine, largely uninhabited land of lakes, trees and rocks. The few people who do call it home are involved either in the forestry industry or in mining. Along the shores of Hudson Bay in northern Manitoba, a small region of tundra thrives. Its treeless and forbidding winter landscape turns startlingly beautiful in summer.

Prairie "Steps". – Despite their reputation, the Prairies are not actually flat. Apart from deep valleys cut by rivers, the Prairies rise gradually in three main levels or steps, from sea level at Hudson Bay to nearly 1,200m/4,000ft west of the Rockies. The first Prairie step ends with the **Manitoba Escarpment**, which rises to a maximum 831m/2,727ft. Encompassing the flattest lands, the second step ends with the **Missouri Coteau**, rising to a maximum 879m/2,885ft and visible from Moose Jaw. The third step borders the Rockies. The Prairies are broken by numerous ranges of small hills in the north, in addition to these steps, and by the Cypress Hills in the south.

Climate. – The Prairies experience a climate of extremes that varies from year to year, making average conditions difficult to gauge. Winter is generally long and cold; summer is short and hot. Precipitation is low (380-500mm/15-20in a year), frequently arriving in the form of blizzards in winter and violent thunderstorms in summer, often after periods of drought. Sunshine is plentiful, especially in July, the driest and hottest month of the year (mean maximum for Calgary is 24°C/76°F, Regina 27°C/81°F, Winnipeg 27°C/80°F). In the southwest, winter is alleviated by the chinook winds, which blow warm air from the Pacific through the Rockies. In a few hours, temperatures can rise by as much as 28°C/50°F.

PEOPLE OF THE PRAIRIES

Indians of the Plains. – Once the only inhabitants of this region, the Assiniboine, Blackfoot, Cree, Gros Ventre and Sarcee Indians lived almost exclusively on buffalo. The animals were driven over cliffs or stampeded into pounds. Their meat was often dried and made into **pemmican**—a nutritious mixture of pounded meat, animal fat and sometimes saskatoon berries—which could be preserved for up to a year. Buffalo hides were used to make moccasins, leggings and tunics; the wool was left on to fashion robes for winter. Clothing was decorated with fringes and later, beads. Home was a **teepee**, a conical structure of poles (some almost 12m/40ft tall) covered with buffalo hides.

These nomadic tribes followed buffalo herds all summer, then dispersed in winter. Possessions were put on a **travois**, a structure of crossed poles pulled by a dog and later a horse (horses were in general use in the Canadian Plains by the mid-18C). In spring, they reassembled to await the return of the buffalo and to celebrate the **sun dance** or medicine lodge dance.

Existing rivalry and warfare among the tribes grew more lethal when fur traders began supplying guns. Since buffalo hunting was easier with guns, their use resulted in the gradual extinction of the great herds which, in turn, destroyed the traditional life of the hunters. By the 1880s, the herds were gone, and European settlers had arrived to cultivate and fence the once-open prairie. The Indians signed treaties and moved to reservations, but a sedentary life of farming did not come easily to the former nomadic hunters.

Fur Traders. – The lucrative fur trade inspired the French to establish the first permanent settlements in mainland Canada in the 17C, and sent them farther into the continent in search of the elusive beaver. Eager to reduce the long journey by canoe between Ville-Marie (present-day Montreal) and Lake Superior, two traders, **Pierre Radisson** and **Sieur des Groseilliers**, proposed a quicker, cheaper way to transport furs to Europe via Hudson Bay, the huge waterway discovered by Henry Hudson in 1610. This scheme met with little interest in France, but "Radish and Gooseberry," as they became known, found a warmer reception at the English court of Charles II. The ketch *Nonsuch* was equipped and sailed to Hudson Bay in 1668, returning with a rich load of furs. In 1670, Charles II granted a royal charter to the "Governor and Company of Adventurers of England trading into Hudson's Bay." The **Hudson's Bay Company** (HBC), as it became known, held sole right to trade in the vast watershed that drains into the bay. Forts or factories were quickly established on its shores and trade thrived.

The first European to explore the interior of this large region was **Henry Kelsey** who travelled across northern Manitoba and Saskatchewan in the early 1690s. Threatened by Kelsey's contacts with the Indians, the **Sieur de la Vérendrye** established the first French trading posts on the plains in 1730. While travelling through Alberta in 1754, **Anthony Henday** of the HBC found the French so entrenched on the plains that he recommended the company abandon its policy of letting Indians bring their furs to the bay, and establish posts in the interior of the land. However, the fall of New France in 1759 seemed to diminish the threat, and Henday's suggestion was not heeded.

Bitter rivalry developed among fur traders in the Prairies during the late 18C and the early 19C. The Scots quickly established themselves in Montreal and founded the North West Company, soon a ferocious competitor of the HBC. Rival posts sprang up along the Prairie rivers; every load of furs was grounds for contention. Competition finally ended in 1821 when the two companies merged; Hudson's Bay kept the upper hand.

The Métis and the Creation of Manitoba. – A consequence of the fur trade was the creation of a new ethnic group, the Métis—offspring of Indian women and French *coureurs des bois* (and later of Scots and English traders). Though mainly French-speaking Roman Catholics, the Métis preserved the traditional lifestyle of their Indian forebears, hunting buffalo and making pemmican to sell to fur traders. The first threat to their lifestyle came with the arrival of settlers along the Red River in 1812 *(p 94)*. Conflict ensued since farms and fences could not share the prairie with wandering herds of buffalo and their hunters. In 1870, the situation escalated when the new Dominion of Canada decided to take over the vast lands of the Hudson's Bay Company. The Métis not only saw their traditional life disappearing with the arrival of more and more settlers, but also feared the loss of their language. When Dominion surveyors began marking out long narrow strips of Métis land into neat squares, these people turned to 25-year-old **Louis Riel**. Soon after his return from Montreal, where he had completed his religious training, Riel declared the surveys illegal, since sovereignty had not yet been established, and set up his own provisional government to ensure the recognition of Métis rights in the new government. Although supported by his own people, Riel gained no sympathy from English Métis and other settlers, particularly many Ontarians of Irish origin who had recently moved to the area in anticipation of the Canadian sovereignty. After foiling a plot to assassinate him, Riel executed a boisterous adventurer from Ontario, **Thomas Scott**, an act which he was long to regret. Nevertheless, his plea on behalf of his people was heard. In July 1870, the new province of Manitoba was created (the name, chosen by Riel, means "the spirit that speaks"). Land was set aside for the Métis, and both French and English settlers were given equal status. Riel was elected to Parliament several times, but was unable to take his seat in Ottawa because of anger in Ontario over Scott's death. Eventually, Riel went into exile in the US, but resurfaced again 15 years later *(p 93)*.

A Human Mosaic. – Once the Hudson's Bay Company had ceded its immense territory to the government, several matters had to be settled. First, treaties had to be negotiated with the native peoples of the region. Though established by 1877, the treaties proved unsuccessful as the Northwest Rebellion of 1885 showed *(p 93)*. Second, some means of enforcing law and order was required. In 1873, the **North West Mounted Police** force was created *(pp 84 and 91)*. Third, land had to be distributed. The **Dominion Lands Act** of 1872 allowed prospective homesteaders to register for a quarter section (65ha/160 acres). Title was given after three years if a homestead had been built and a certain amount of the land cultivated. Settlers also had an option on an additional quarter section. Finally, a means of reaching the region and transporting produce to market was required. To solve this problem, construction of the **Canadian Pacific Railway** was begun in 1881. By the year of its completion (1885), the population of the Prairies was about 150,000; by 1914, it had reached 1.5 million.

The prospect of free land attracted inhabitants of an overcrowded Europe, especially those who lived in industrial cities, where factory hours were long and hard. The area also appealed to religious refugees who hoped to have the freedom to worship and live as they pleased. The Canadian government under **Sir Wilfrid Laurier** advertised all over the world: "Canada West—the last best west. Free homes for millions." Millions indeed came—from Ontario, the Maritimes (New Brunswick, Nova Scotia, Prince Edward Island), the US, Iceland, England, Scotland, Ireland, Germany, Austria, France, Scandinavia and Russia, especially the Ukraine. Mennonites, Hutterites and Doukhobors arrived from Russia, and Orthodox Christians from Eastern Europe. These immigrants were joined by Roman Catholics, Mormons, Jews and Protestants belonging to a variety of denominations. The provinces of **Alberta** and **Saskatchewan** were created in 1905. Since 1915, these peoples have been joined by those seeking refuge from political unrest in their homelands. They have made the Prairies a veritable mosaic of cultures. The population today stands at more than 4.6 million (Alberta 2,545,553; Saskatchewan 988,928; Manitoba 1,091,942).

ECONOMY

King Wheat. – Between 1876 and 1915, the land where the fur trade once reigned supreme suddenly developed a wheat economy. The region where giant bluestem and needle grass thrived and prairie flowers bloomed in millions vanished under the plough. Several factors contributed to the striking changes. In 1842, David Fife, a Scottish farmer living in Ontario, developed a strain of wheat that later proved ideal for cultivation on the prairies. Called **Red Fife** for its rich colour, it was resistant to rust and thrived in the drought-ridden short summer season. It is the ancestor of all the strains used today.

Another factor was the building of the Canadian Pacific Railway, which brought settlers to cultivate the land and provided transport for their produce to market. Loading platforms and elevators sprang up along the tracks, while trains moved grain to Thunder Bay, Vancouver, Prince Rupert and Churchill. By 1915, the wheat-growing regions were unrecognizable to those who had seen them 40 years earlier. However, wheat did not always flourish in this region of changeable and unpredictable climate. Drought and hardships in the 1930s caused many farmers to abandon the land. Today, farmers depend less on wheat than in the past. Barley, oats, rye, flax, rapeseed, mustard, buckwheat, peas, sunflowers and potatoes are all widely cultivated; nevertheless, 50 percent of the land annually seeded to field crops is devoted to wheat. More than 32 million tonnes/35 million tons of wheat are produced in the western provinces every year, about three-quarters of which is exported.

Cattle Country. – Although grain is by far the major economic staple of the Prairies, ranching is firmly established as a secondary industry. Canadian ranching began in British Columbia and spread into southern Alberta and Saskatchewan after the Indian treaties of the 1870s. The dry, short-grass country turned out to be fine pasture for cattle, and the chinook winds made winter grazing possible as they melted the snow, exposing the grass.

Slowly, as ranchers discovered that cattle would not run off with buffalo or be killed by winter or Indians, the number of ranches increased. By the turn of the century, cattle raising attained its present position as the second most important economic activity. To this day, southern Alberta and Saskatchewan remain "cowboy country." Horseback riders among the herds are a common sight, and rodeos abound. The most popular cowboy event is the Calgary Stampede (p 81).

Riches Below the Earth. – The first mineral exploited in the Prairies was **coal**, found in Lethbridge, Alberta, in 1869. Later, coal was also mined near Estevan in Saskatchewan. The giant **zinc**, **cadmium** and **copper** field at Flin Flon, Manitoba, was established in 1915. Today, mining activity has spread across the border into Saskatchewan. Copper was discovered near Lynn Lake, Manitoba, and gold in the Lake Athabasca area of Saskatchewan.

In the 1880s, Kootenay Brown found **oil** in the Waterton Lakes area of Alberta and sold it as machine grease. In 1914, oil was discovered in Turner Valley (p 81), marking the beginning of Alberta's petroleum industry. The year 1947 saw the discovery of the Leduc oilfield (p 86); subsequently, numerous other small fields underlying Alberta were exploited. Alberta accounts for the vast majority of Canada's oil and **natural gas** production. Alberta's reserves are supplemented by the **Athabasca oil sands** in the northern part of the province.

Uranium was found in the late 1940s in the Beaverlodge area of Saskatchewan, north of Lake Athabasca, and in the 1960s, the giant **nickel** field of Thompson, Manitoba, came into production. The first **potash** was mined in 1951 near Esterhazy in Saskatchewan. This province's potash reserves are estimated at more than 25 percent of the world's total supply and, at current rates of consumption, enough to supply world needs for 2,000 years. Just as oil and natural gas underlie Alberta, potash underlies Saskatchewan in a wide arc roughly corresponding to the aspen parkland zone (p 74). Saskatchewan also has **sodium sulphate** and oil in the Lloydminster, Swift Current and Estevan areas.

Other Resources. – In the northern regions of all three provinces, the traditional industry of fur trapping still flourishes, along with thriving forestry concerns. All three provinces also generate hydro-electric power, the biggest projects being the **Gardiner Dam** on the South Saskatchewan River in central Saskatchewan, and in northern Manitoba the Limestone generating station on the Nelson River.

Principal Festivals

Feb	Trappers' Festival Festival du Voyageur (p 96) Winter Festival	The Pas, MB St-Boniface, MB Prince Albert, SK
Jun	Provincial Exhibition of Manitoba Western Canada Farm Progress Show Red River Exhibition	Brandon, MB Regina, SK Winnipeg, MB
Jul	Yorkton Exhibition Folk Festival Saskatoon Exhibition Manitoba Highland Gathering Manitoba Threshermen's Reunion (p 80) Calgary Exhibition and Stampede (p 81) Klondike Days (p 86) Big Valley Jamboree	Yorkton, SK Winnipeg, MB Saskatoon, SK Selkirk, MB Austin, MB Calgary, AB Edmonton, AB Craven, SK
Jul–Aug	National Ukrainian Festival Pioneer Days Buffalo Days	Dauphin, MB Steinbach, MB Regina, SK
Aug	Whoop-up Days and Rodeo Icelandic Festival York Boat Days (boat race) Folklorama (p 94) Folkfest	Lethbridge, AB Gimli, MB Norway House, MB Winnipeg, MB Saskatoon, SK
Nov-Dec	Canadian Western Agribition	Regina, SK

Practical Information

How to get there. – Major domestic and international airlines provide service to the following gateway cities: Calgary, Edmonton, Regina, Saskatoon and Winnipeg. Several regional carriers offer connections to cities within all three provinces: Calm Air (☎204/778-6471); Prairie Flying Service (☎306/525-5055); Time Air (☎306/569-2307).
VIA Rail Canada has regularly scheduled transcontinental service to all three provinces. In Canada, consult the telephone directory for nearest office; from the US ☎800/561-3949 (toll-free).

Accommodation and Tourist Information. – The government tourist offices produce annually updated guides listing approved hotels, motels, Bed & Breakfast lodgings and cabins. Camping guides and discovery guides give detailed information on golf courses, outfitters, guest ranches and fishing camps. Winter vacation guides list ski areas, winter sports activities, hotels and ski lodges. These publications and maps are available free of charge from:
Alberta Tourism, 10155 102 St, Edmonton, AB, T5J 4L6 ☎403/427-4321 or 800/661-8888 (toll-free Canada/US).
Travel Manitoba, Tourism Division, 155 Carlton St, Winnipeg, MB, R3C 3H8 ☎204/945-3777 or 800/665-0040 (toll-free Canada/US).
Tourism Saskatchewan, 1919 Saskatchewan Dr, Regina, SK, S4P 3V7 ☎306/787-2300 or 800/667-7191 (toll-free Canada/US).
Most major hotel chains have facilities in these provinces *(p 242)*. Average overnight rates range from $90 to $180 in resort areas during high season ($55-$120 off-season). Many independent hotels and Bed & Breakfast lodgings can be found along major routes. **Farm vacations** are offered in all three provinces, but Saskatchewan is especially popular. Alberta in particular boasts many **guest ranches** offering trail riding with overnight camping for the experienced or the novice rider, as well as families.

Road Regulations. – All three provinces have good paved roads. Unless otherwise posted, speed limits are: Alberta: 100km/h (60mph) in daylight, 90km/h (55mph) at night. Manitoba: 90km/h (55mph). Saskatchewan: 100km/h (60mph). Use of **seat belts** is compulsory. The wearing of motorcycle helmets is compulsory in Manitoba and Saskatchewan.

Time Zones. – Alberta: Mountain Standard Time. Manitoba: Central Standard Time. Both observe Daylight Saving Time from the first Sunday in April to the last Sunday in October. Most of Saskatchewan is on Central Standard Time all year; thus it is the same as Alberta in summer, the same as Manitoba in winter. However, some border communities prefer to keep the same time as the neighbouring province all year.

Taxes. – In addition to the national 7% GST *(see p 242 for rebate information)*, Manitoba levies 7% and Saskatchewan 8% sales tax on all items and an additional 7% on restaurant bills. In Alberta, there is a 5% hotel tax but no sales or restaurant tax. Manitoba offers a rebate of its provincial sales tax to non-residents; contact Retail Sales Tax Office, 115-401 York Ave Winnipeg, MB, R3C 0P8 ☎204/945-6444.

Liquor Laws. – The legal drinking age is 18 in Manitoba and Alberta, 19 in Saskatchewan. In all three provinces, liquor and wine can be purchased only in government stores. In isolated parts of the North where no government stores exist, grocery stores are licensed.

Provincial Holidays *(see National Holidays p 240)*
Family Day *AB* .... 3rd Monday in February
Civic Holiday *MB and SK* .... 1st Monday in August

Outdoor Activities. – The Prairies are especially prized by outdoor enthusiasts. **Water sports**—boating, sailing, canoeing, water skiing and swimming—are particularly popular, owing to the large number of lakes and river systems. Saskatchewan is famous for its **white-water rafting**, especially along the Churchill River.
The region is well endowed with national parks *(p 244)* and provincial parks, offering hiking trails and campsites in summer and cross-country skiing, snowshoeing and snowmobiling in winter.
All three provinces offer good **fishing**, but northern Manitoba and Saskatchewan are particularly famous for their numerous fly-in lodges. Lac la Ronge in Saskatchewan is perhaps the best-known region for sport fishing. Fishermen and hunters must have a valid license, obtainable in most sporting goods stores. The *Anglers' Guide* and *Hunting and Trapping Guide* (available free of charge from provincial tourist offices) give valuable information such as hunting and fishing regulations, species and limits.

Special Excursions. – The **Prairie Dog Central**, a turn-of-the-century steam train, makes weekly excursions from Winnipeg northwest to Grosse Isle (from CN St James Station, 1661 Portage Ave; Jun–Sept Sun 11am & 3pm; round-trip 2hrs; $13; ☎204/284-2690).
To relive the days of the Wild West, join a **covered wagon trek** and travel through the wide expanses of Saskatchewan. Experienced scouts take visitors from May to September on three- or six-day excursions that include campfire dinners (contact Tourism Saskatchewan for details).

★★★ The ALBERTA BADLANDS Alberta

Map of Principal Sights p 2

The meltwaters of the last continental glacier eroded a deep and sometimes wide valley across southern Alberta, which today is occupied by the Red Deer River. In so doing, they exposed rocks formed during the Cretaceous period (between 64 and 140 million years ago) and created the Alberta Badlands, a striking panorama of steep bluffs and fluted gullies. During this period, the area was a subtropical lowland inhabited by huge reptilian creatures known as dinosaurs. A number of these were fossilized and preserved to this day.

Haunt of the Dinosaurs. – The word *dinosaur* is derived from Greek, meaning "terrible lizard," a reference to the predatory habits and great size of some of these creatures. In fact, there were many types: some were small and most were plant eaters, but the biggest weighed as much as 27 tonnes/30 tons and grew to 24m/80ft in length. The **duckbilled dinosaur** walked on its hind feet, which were webbed for swimming, and sported a snout resembling a duck's bill, thus its name. The **horned dinosaur** walked on four feet and had horns—usually one over each eye and one on the nose. The **armoured dinosaur** was equipped with a row of bony plates on its back and spikes on its tail as a form of protection. All of these were herbivorous, slow moving and prey to the ferocious **carnivorous dinosaur** with its sharp claws and teeth, and muscular hind legs for running.

Dinosaur bones have been found on all continents, but no region is as rich as this valley in Alberta. The first fossils discovered in 1884, along with the bones and several hundred complete skeletons unearthed since then, are on display in many world museums, including the Royal Ontario Museum *(p 139)* and the Canadian Museum of Nature *(p 122)*.

DINOSAUR TRAIL *Map below. 51km/32mi circular drive. 2hrs.*

Connecting the sights of the Drumheller area, this loop on the plain above Red Deer River offers good views of the Badlands.

★ **Drumheller.** – Pop 6,277. *Tourist Office ☎403/823-5885.* This former coal-mining town, 138km/86mi northeast of Calgary, lies amid the badlands of the Red Deer River as does Dinosaur Provincial Park *(p 79).* Drumheller is surrounded by a fertile wheat-growing plain, unbroken except by occasional oil pumps known as "donkey heads" because they bob up and down continuously. Upon the approach to the town, the extensively eroded valley, nearly 120m/400ft deep and about 1.6km/1mi wide, comes as something of a surprise.

★ **Dinosaur and Fossil Museum [M].** – *335 1st St E in Tourist Office building. Open daily May–mid-Oct. $2. & ☎403/823-2593.* Devoted to the region's geology, this museum features examples of dinosaur fossils. The most impressive is **Edmontosaurus**, a 9m/30ft long, 3.5m/11ft high duckbilled dinosaur with webbed feet and a strong tail for use when swimming.

★★★ **Tyrrell Museum of Palaeontology.** – *6km/4mi northwest of Drumheller by Hwy 838 (North Dinosaur Trail). Open year-round Victoria Day–Labour Day daily 9am–9pm. Off-season Tue-Sun 10am–5pm. $5 (free on Tue). & ✗ ☎403/823-7707.* This splendid museum, which opened in 1985, is one of the largest in the world devoted to the study of lifeforms from past geological periods. It has a fine setting in the badlands and blends well with its surroundings in a series of innovative structures designed by Douglas Craig of Calgary.

The highlight is the enormous **Dinosaur Hall**, where the major types of dinosaurs formerly inhabiting this area are re-created, some with original fossils, others with modern casting materials. The huge Tyrannosaurus rex, Albertosaurus, the armoured Stegosaurus and some smaller bird-like dinosaurs can be seen. One part of the hall represents the bottom of the ancient Bearpaw Sea, which covered the western Canadian interior 70 million years ago. Here, mosasaurs—large marine reptiles up to 15m/50ft long—can be viewed.

In the **palaeoconservatory**, visitors can admire a large collection of plants descended from those the dinosaurs would have known. Some have changed little in 140 million years.

The museum's main theme is a "celebration of life," featuring displays, films and slide shows on such topics as the creation of the universe, evolutionary theories, diverse environments, the age of the dinosaurs and the mystery of their disappearance, mammals (including species now extinct), the ice ages and the evolution of *Homo sapiens.*

After passing the museum, Dinosaur Trail provides a good view of the badlands from **Horsethief Canyon★**, with its rounded, almost barren hills stretching to the river. The trail crosses the river by the **Bleriot cable ferry** and climbs to a fine **view★** of the valley. The green pastures beside the river provide an interesting contrast to the cactus-strewn bluffs and gullies immediately below. Continue south for 26km/16mi to Drumheller to reach **Prehistoric Parks** *(open daily Apr–mid-Oct; $3;* ☎*403/823-6144),* where life-size models of some of the largest dinosaurs stand among low hills covered with sagebrush and cactus.

ADDITIONAL SIGHTS

★ **Horseshoe Canyon.** – *18km/11mi southwest of Drumheller by Rte 9.* Paths leading through the hillocks to the river provide some of the best **views** of the badlands in the area.

★ **Hoodoos.** – *16km/10mi southeast of Drumheller by Rte 10.* These strange rock formations, which look like giant mushrooms, illustrate the work of erosion in the valley. Soft rock has been worn away, leaving harder pieces behind.

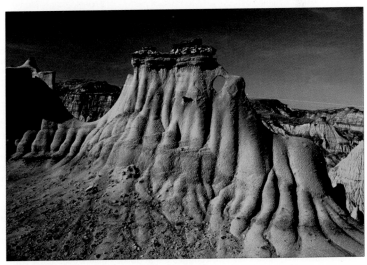

Hoodoos

Alberta Tourism

★★ **Dinosaur Provincial Park.** – *174km/108mi southeast of Drumheller by Rte 56 and Trans-Can Hwy east to Brooks. Take Hwy 873 for 10km/6mi, then right on Hwy 544, and left on Hwy 551. Open year-round sunrise to sunset.* △ ☎*403/378-4587.* The park is set in the most spectacular part of the Red Deer River Valley and the richest fossil area. In 1979, UNESCO recognized its importance by placing it on the World Heritage List.

Immediately upon entrance to the park, an excellent **viewpoint★★** overlooks nearly 3,000ha/7,000 acres of badlands cut by the Red Deer River. The road then descends to the valley.

A **circular drive★** *(5km/3mi)* takes the visitor through this wild and desolate, almost lunar, landscape where little except sagebrush flourishes. At several points, short walks can be taken to see dinosaur bones preserved where they were found. Explanatory panels offer details on the type of dinosaur and its size. Longer nature trails enable visitors to better appreciate this pristine terrain. Most of the park, however, is accessible only by special bus tours *(1hr 30min, daily)* or by conducted hikes *(contact park office for details).*

Tyrrell Museum Field Station. – *1.6km/1mi from park entrance. Open year-round daily Victoria Day–Labour Day. Off-season Tue-Sun.* ☎*403/378-4342.* Opened in 1987, this research satellite of the provincial museum *(p 78)* is located within Dinosaur Provincial Park. The interpretation centre features habitat and fossil displays and an observation post for watching staff prepare fossils.

★ AUSTIN Manitoba

Map of Principal Sights p 3

Set in the centre of a rich agricultural region, the little community, 123km/76mi west of Winnipeg, is renowned for its collection of operating vintage farm machinery.

★ Manitoba Agricultural Museum. – *On Hwy 34, 3km/2mi south of Trans-Can Hwy. Open daily May–Sept. $2.50.* ⓖ ☎*204/637-2354.* This museum has a splendid collection of "prairie giants"—steam tractors, threshing machines, and the cumbersome gasoline machines that replaced them in the early part of this century. Every year at the end of July, these machines are paraded and demonstrated in the Manitoba **Threshermen's Reunion and Stampede.** Drawing thousands of visitors from all over the continent, this festival features threshing, sheaftying and stooking contests, a stampede and steam engine races. A **homesteaders' village** illustrates rural life at the end of the last century

Steam tractor

when the first giant steam engines were breaking the prairie sod and bringing it under cultivation. The village includes several log homes, a church and a school. The centennial building houses a large collection of pioneer artifacts.

★ The BATTLEFORDS Saskatchewan   Pop 18,457

Map of Principal Sights p 3   Tourist Office ☎306/445-6226

Surrounded by rolling country, the twin communities of **Battleford** and **North Battleford**, 138km/86mi northwest of Saskatoon, face each other across the valley of the North Saskatchewan River. North Battleford has a fine **site★** overlooking the river.

Fur traders established posts on the Battleford (south) side of the river in the 18C, but it was not until 1874 that the first settlers arrived. A North West Mounted Police post was established in 1876, and the settlement was chosen as the home of the government of the Northwest Territories. A bright future seemed assured. Then the Canadian Pacific Railway Company decided to route its line through the southern plains, and in 1883, Battleford lost its status as capital when the government offices were moved to Pile O'Bones Creek (later Regina). To add insult to injury, the settlement of Battleford was looted and burned by Poundmaker Crees during the Northwest Rebellion of 1885 *(p 93)* while the fearful inhabitants took refuge in the police fort. The death knell sounded in 1903 when the Canadian Northern Railway was built along the opposite side of the river, creating a new community, North Battleford, which grew as Battleford shrank. Today, North Battleford, served by the Yellowhead Highway as well as the railway, is a distribution centre of no small importance.

★ Battleford National Historic Site. – ☞ *Central Ave, Battleford. Open daily May–Oct.* ⓖ ☎*306/937-2621.* This North West Mounted Police post was the fifth established by the police in the Northwest Territories. Enlarged after the Northwest Rebellion, it was abandoned in 1924. Today restored, it provides insight into police life in the late 19C.

The **commanding officers' residence** suggests that police officers lived fairly comfortably. The **officers' quarters** house an office for the police. Just outside the palisade, a former barracks has been converted into an **interpretation centre**, which provides a particularly good account of the 1885 rebellion.

★ Western Development Museum. – *On Hwy 16 at junction with Rte 40 in North Battleford. Open daily May–mid-Sept. $3.50.* ⓖ ☎*306/445-8033.* Devoted to agriculture, this branch of the Western Development Museum—one of four (Moose Jaw, Saskatoon, Yorkton) in the province—displays a large collection of agricultural machinery and domestic artifacts used on farms in the 1920s.

Outside, an interesting **heritage farm and village** of 1925 *(closed in winter)* is set out with homes and churches reflecting the diverse origins of the peoples who settled this province. Note the Ukrainian Orthodox Church with its onion dome, and the thatched *dacha* displaying the handicrafts and household fittings of a pioneer Ukrainian home. Also featured are a general store, a police post and a railway station complete with train.

We welcome your assistance in the never-ending task of updating the texts and maps in this guide. Send us your comments and suggestions:

Michelin Tires (Canada) Ltd.
175 Bouchard Boulevard
Dorval, Quebec H9S 5T1 CANADA

Set in the foothills of the snow-capped peaks of the Canadian Rockies, this thriving city lies at the confluence of the Bow and Elbow rivers, two mountain torrents of clear blue water. Covering the largest land area of any city in Canada (420sq km/ 162sq mi), Calgary was Canada's fastest-growing, most prosperous metropolis in the early 1980s, mainly because of Alberta's vast oil wealth and the city's own importance as a transportation centre. Blessed with a pleasant climate (moderate rainfall, low humidity, lots of sunshine and a moderately cold winter, tempered by warm chinook winds), this tourist mecca is known for its internationally famous Stampede and remembered fondly by millions around the world as host of the 1988 Winter Olympic Games.

Origins. – In 1875, a North West Mounted Police post was built on this site and named Fort Calgary by Col James MacLeod *(p 88)*, commander of the police in the Northwest, for his home in Scotland. The name is derived from a Gaelic word probably meaning "clear, running water."

A small community grew up around the post, which quickly developed in the 1880s when the Canadian Pacific Railway Company decided to route its railway south through Calgary and the Kicking Horse Pass, rather than through Edmonton and the Yellowhead Pass. This momentous decision resulted in a huge influx of settlers to the lush grazing lands of the region. The Dominion Lands Act *(p 75)* also encouraged owners of great cattle herds to move north from the US.

Calgary rapidly became a marketing and meat-packing centre, gaining the epithet of Canada's Cowtown—a title it still has not relinquished, although cattle constitute a relatively minor part of its life today.

"Black Gold". – The discovery of oil in 1914 at Turner Valley, just southwest of Calgary, marked the birth of western Canada's petroleum industry. For about thirty years, this valley was the country's major oil producer. Then in 1947, a great discovery was made at Leduc *(p 86)*, and Calgary began a period of phenomenal growth. Although recent oil and gas discoveries have been closer to Edmonton, Calgary has predominated as the headquarters of the industry.

Calgary Convention & Visitors Bureau

Saddledome, Calgary

"The Greatest Outdoor Show on Earth". – The **Calgary Stampede**, a grand ten-day event held in early July, attracts hundreds of thousands of spectators and competitors every year *(reservations are recommended)*. The entire population dons western garb (boots, jeans and hats) and joins the festivities. There are flapjack breakfasts, street dances, and a huge parade in the city. Livestock shows and the famous **rodeo** and **chuckwagon races** are held in Stampede Park. Invented in Calgary, the races recall the wagon races held by cowboys after a roundup. They are, without doubt, an exciting part of the stampede. *Details of all events can be obtained from the tourist office.*

DOWNTOWN *Map pp 82-83. 1/2 day.*

Calgary's downtown has undergone a phenomenal transformation since World War II and continues to develop. In recent years, the Calgary Tower, surrounded by a host of attractive glass-fronted highrises, has been overshadowed by the sloping-top brown marble headquarters of **Petro-Canada**. A pedestrian **mall** stretches four blocks along 8th Avenue. At the western end lie the big bank blocks: the reflecting glass Royal Bank Centre, the Scotia Centre and the black towers of the Toronto Dominion (TD) Square, all connected to one another and to The Bay and Eaton's department stores by second-floor pedestrian bridges.

Toronto Dominion Square boasts a fine indoor greenhouse featuring tropical plants called the **Devonian Gardens★** *(4th floor, access from Eaton's or, outside store hours, via elevator from TD Square entrance on mall; open year-round daily 9am–9pm).* East of the mall, the tiered, blue-reflecting glass structure of Calgary's **Municipal Building** rises around a 12-storey atrium. Across 2nd Street Southeast stands the **Centre for the Performing Arts**, an attractive series of brick buildings.

★★ **Glenbow Museum.** – 130 9th Ave SE, in Convention Centre complex. Open year-round Tue–Sun 10am–6pm. Closed Christmas, Boxing Day & New Year's. $3. ↺ ☎403/ 237-8988. Administered by the Glenbow-Alberta Institute, this museum contains displays from an outstanding **Plains Indians collection★★**. Note particularly the fine beadwork.

European settlement in the province is traced through exhibits focusing on the fur trade, the North West Mounted Police, missionaries, the Canadian Pacific Railway, the arrival of the first farmers, ranching, the discovery of oil and Alberta life in the 1920s and 1930s.

Displays on weapons and arms, tracing their development from medieval times to recent years, are featured. In addition, the museum mounts temporary exhibits of art and sculpture. A large acrylic and aluminum sculpture by James Houston, entitled **Aurora Borealis**, is the museum's focal point.

★★ **Calgary Tower.** – In Palliser Square, 101 9th Ave SW. Observation deck open year-round. Jun–Sept 7:30am–midnight. Off-season 8:30am–midnight. $3.75. 🅿 ↺ ╳ ☎403/266-7171. This 191m/626ft tower provides an excellent **view★★** of the city and its site. To the west, the snow-capped peaks of the Rockies rise above the rolling, arid foothills on which the city is built. Immediately below the tower, the maze of railway lines attests to the city's importance as a transportation centre.

ADDITIONAL SIGHTS

★★ **Crescent Road Viewpoint.** – Map p 83. Standing above the Bow River and Prince's Island Park, this crescent offers a fine view of the downtown buildings and, on clear days, the snow-capped Rockies to the west.

Fort Calgary. – Map p 83. 750 9th Ave SE. Open daily year-round. Closed Christmas, Boxing Day & New Year's. ↺ ╳ ☎403/290-1875. An interpretation centre on the site of the original North West Mounted Police post recounts the history of the city. The location of the post itself is indicated on the ground, and the house of the NWMP superintendent can be visited. Paths afford **views★** of the Bow River, and a pedestrian bridge allows access to St George's Island and the zoo.

★★ **Zoo and Prehistoric Park.** – 1300 Zoo Rd SE, on St George's Island. Parking on Memorial Drive and on the island. Open Victoria Day–Labour Day daily 9am–6pm. Off-season daily 9am–4pm. $7.50. 🅿 ↺ ╳ ☎403/232-9300. Located on an island in the Bow River, this attractive zoo houses a wide variety of animals from all over the world and a tropical greenhouse filled with exotic plants, flowers, butterflies and birds. The **prehistoric park★★** (same hours as zoo but closed Nov–Apr) re-creates western Canada as it might have looked in the age of the dinosaurs between 225 and 65 million years ago. Life-size reproductions of these giant creatures stand among mountains, volcanoes, hoodoos, swampland and Canadian Shield country, along with the vegetation that might have existed in their day.

★ **Grain Academy.** – South of downtown by Macleod Trail, in Roundup Centre, Stampede Park, 17th Ave and Second St SE. Open Apr–Sept Mon–Sat. Off-season Mon–Fri. 🅿 ↺ ☎403/263-4594. This museum, Alberta's only grain interpretation centre, focuses on one of mankind's basic food sources. It presents a working model of a Prairie grain elevator, a model railway showing the movement of Prairie grain through the Rocky Mountains, and a film (12min) on the history of grain growing in western Canada.

The museum is located in Stampede Park near the distinctive 20,140-seat Olympic **Saddledome★** (illustration p 81) constructed in 1983. The flowing saddle design of the stadium's roof echoes Calgary's cowboy past (public tours year-round Mon–Fri; ☎403/261-0400).

★ **Heritage Park.** – 16km/10mi southwest of downtown. Take Macleod Trail SW to 1900 Heritage Dr SW. Open daily Victoria Day–Labour Day; until mid-Oct weekends only. $6. 🅿 ↺ ╳ ☎403/259-1910. Occupying a pleasant **site★** in a recreation area overlooking Glenmore Reservoir, this park re-creates prairie life of a bygone era with a pioneer community and a reconstructed Hudson's Bay Company post. The turn-of-the-century town features a church, drugstore, bakery, general store, post office, newspaper office, pool hall, police post, houses and a station for a functioning steam train that gives tours of the site *(daily; $1.25)*. Beside the tracks stands a working grain elevator, and on the outskirts of the town are farm buildings and a windmill. A replica of the *SS Moyie*, a sternwheeler once used on Kootenay Lake, offers boat trips on the reservoir *(every 35min; $1.75)* and memorable rides can be taken on the antique **midway** *($0.75)*.

CARDSTON Alberta   Pop 3,480

Map of Principal Sights p 2

This small town, 25km/16mi north of the Montana (US) border, is an important Mormon centre. Founded in 1887 by **Charles Ora Card**, a son-in-law of Brigham Young, it boasts one of the few Mormon temples in Canada—an imposing white granite structure completed in 1923 *(visitor centre open daily mid-May–mid-Sept; ☎403/653-3787)*. Also known as the Church of Jesus Christ of the Latter Day Saints, the sect was founded in 1830 by **Joseph Smith** at Fayette, New York. After his death, most of his followers moved to Utah under the leadership of **Brigham Young**, establishing Salt Lake City in 1847. The Mormon doctrine is based on the Bible and Smith's writings, notably, *The Book of Mormon*. In Canada, the sect numbers about 126,000 and is largely concentrated in southern Alberta.

★★ CHURCHILL Manitoba   Pop 1,143

Map of Principal Sights p 3

On the shores of Hudson Bay, on the east side of the estuary of the wild and beautiful Churchill River, lies the little town of Churchill, Canada's most northerly deep-sea port. Situated north of the tree line, Churchill is bleak in winter, but during the summer months, a carpet of flowers covers the tundra, beluga whales abound in the blue waters of the bay, and myriad birds and scavenging **polar bears** visit the townsite. Because it experiences some of the world's most amazing spectacles of the Northern Lights *(p 230)*, the town has attracted much scientific interest.
Churchill also boasts an interesting history. A fur-trading post was founded at the mouth of the river in 1685 by the Hudson's Bay Company. Named for the governor of the company, **John Churchill**, later Duke of Marlborough, it remained an important fur-gathering and export centre until this century when wheat took over. A railway was built in 1931, and a grain elevator and port facilities shortly thereafter. The Hudson Bay and Strait are navigable only three months a year *(Aug–Oct)*. During this period, trains arrive constantly and ships of many nations visit the townsite to take on grain.

Access. – *Regularly scheduled flights from Winnipeg. Also accessible from Winnipeg by VIA Rail (summer daily Mon–Fri; winter Mon, Wed, Fri).*

Town Centre Complex. – Opened in 1976, the centre combines recreational and health facilities, library, high school, and business offices under one roof. This low-lying complex with its **views** of the bay displays interesting art work.

** **Eskimo Museum.** – *Beside Roman Catholic Church. Open Victoria Day–Labour Day Mon–Sat 9:30am–4:30pm. Off-season Tue–Sat.* ☎204/675-2030. This museum houses a fine collection of Inuit carvings in stone, ivory and bone. Collected over 40 years by the Oblate fathers, these carvings depict various aspects of life. Many refer to Inuit legends and others to the arrival of the first airplanes or snowmobiles in the North. A recorded commentary describes some of the works.

* **Fort Prince of Wales.** – ☞ *Across Churchill River estuary from town. Access by boat depending on tides and weather conditions. Visit by guided tour (1hr) only Jul 2–Aug 31 daily. Contact visitor centre* ☎204/675-8863. Built by the Hudson's Bay Company to protect its fur trade, this large stone fortress took 40 years (1731-1771) to complete. The long-standing threat from the French was eliminated after the defeat of New France on the Plains of Abraham in 1759. Subsequently, a group of Montreal traders, who later founded the North West Company, challenged the Hudson's Bay Company's monopoly. In 1782, a French fleet attacked the fort, then under the command of the explorer Samuel Hearne. Not knowing that England and France were again at war, Hearne surrendered without a shot being fired. Most of his garrison was inland preventing the Montreal traders from taking all the furs. The French commander, Comte de La Pérouse, blew up parts of the walls and set fire to the fort. Returned to the British soon afterwards, the fort was never again used by the HBC, which preferred to establish outposts farther upstream.

Visit. – The boat trip to the fort is an excellent means of viewing the beluga whales that inhabit the estuary of the Churchill River in July and August.

The **visitor centre** *(open daily Victoria Day–mid-Nov; off-season Mon–Fri;.* ☎204/675-8863*)* offers films, and a slide show on the HBC's warehouse and **York Factory National Historic Site**, the remains of a major HBC trading post located 240km/149mi southeast of Churchill on Hudson Bay near the mouth of the Hayes River *(accessible only by canoe or charter plane. For information, contact the visitor centre)*.

In the fort itself, note the massive stone walls nearly 12m/40ft thick at their base and 5m/17ft high, and 40 huge cannon.

** CYPRESS HILLS   Alberta-Saskatchewan

Map of Principal Sights p 3

Straddling the Alberta/Saskatchewan boundary, 70km/43mi north of the state of Montana, the plains give way to rolling, forested hills cut by numerous coulees, valleys, lakes and streams. These verdant hills rise prominently in the midst of otherwise unbroken, sunbaked, short-grass prairie. On their heights grow the tall, straight lodgepole pines favoured by Plains Indians for their teepees or lodges—thus the name. The trees were probably mistaken by early French voyageurs for the jack pines *(cyprès)* of eastern Canada. Although no such trees are in the vicinity, a bad translation further compounded the error, and the name Cypress Hills was born.

Oasis in the Desert. – In 1859, John Palliser camped in these hills during his tour of the western domains for the British government *(p 74)*. "A perfect oasis in the desert we have travelled," was his brief description. Later, settlers found the hills ideally suited for **ranching** and today, much land is devoted to cattle raising.

Not only is the scenic beauty of the hills a surprise, but they also present unique geographical features. The highest elevations in Canada between Labrador and the Rockies, they rise to nearly 1,500m/5,000ft. A 200sq km/80sq mi area of their heights was untouched by the last ice age, which covered the rest of this vast area with ice more than 1km/.6mi deep. The hills form a divide between two great watersheds: Hudson Bay and the Gulf of Mexico. Streams flow south to the Missouri-Mississippi system and north to the South Saskatchewan River, Lake Winnipeg and Hudson Bay. The flora and fauna of the hills offer a remarkable diversity. Wild flowers and songbirds normally associated only with the Rockies flourish here, cactus grows on the dry south-facing slopes and orchids thrive beside quiet ponds.

The Cypress Hills Massacre. – An event that occurred in these hills influenced the creation of that revered Canadian institution: the **Royal Canadian Mounted Police**. In the early 1870s, several trading posts were established in the Cypress Hills by Americans from Montana. In exchange for furs, they illegally traded "fire water," an extremely potent and lethal brew. During the winter of 1872-1873, Assiniboine Indians were camped close to two of these posts—Farwell's and Solomon's. They were joined by a party of American wolf-hunters from Montana, whose entire stock of horses had been stolen by Cree raiders. Thinking the Assiniboines were the thieves, the "wolfers," fired up by a night's drinking, attacked and destroyed the Indian camp, killing about 20 people.

When news of this massacre reached Ottawa, Prime Minister Sir John A. Macdonald acted quickly. He created the **North West Mounted Police** (renamed the Royal Canadian Mounted Police in 1920) and dispatched them to the Northwest to stop such border incursions and end the illegal whisky trade. The perpetrators of the massacre were arrested but later acquitted for lack of evidence. However, the fact that European men had been arrested impressed the Indians with the impartiality of the new police force and helped establish its reputation.

Sitting Bull in Canada. – In 1876, a force of Sioux warriors under their great chief, Sitting Bull, exterminated an American army detachment under Gen **George Custer** on the Little Big Horn River in southern Montana. Fearing reprisals from the enraged Americans, Sitting Bull crossed into Canada with nearly 5,000 men. Inspector **James Walsh** of the North West Mounted Police was given the difficult task of trying to persuade the Sioux to return, in order to avoid war between the Sioux and their traditional enemies, the Cree and the Blackfoot, who inhabited the region. Riding into the sizeable Sioux encampment near Wood Mountain *(350km/217mi east of Fort Walsh)* with only four constables and two scouts, he informed Sitting Bull that he must obey Canadian law. Although this act of bravery won the respect of the chief, it was four years before Sitting Bull consented to returning to the US to live on a reservation.

★★ **Cypress Hills Provincial Park.** – *In Alberta, 65km/40mi southeast of Medicine Hat by Trans-Can Hwy and Hwy 41 south. Park office in Elkwater. Year-round recreation, accommodation, service station. Campsites ($10.75–$17.25) for reservations* ☎403/893-3782 *after May 1. For road conditions check at park office in Elkwater* ☎403/893-3777. *Visitor centre offers interpretive programs mid-May–Labour Day.* ᕕ ᕤ. This park encompasses the highest part of the Cypress Hills. From Elkwater Lake, an interesting drive *(40km/25mi)* leads past **Horseshoe Canyon** to **Head of the Mountain**, which affords pleasant views of coulees and hills as far as the Sweet Grass Hills and Bear Paw Mountains of Montana. The drive proceeds to Reesor Lake and the park boundary.

This road crosses the provincial boundary and continues to Fort Walsh, approximately 18km/11mi south.

★ **Fort Walsh.** – ☯ *In Saskatchewan, 52km/32mi southwest of Maple Creek by Hwy 271. Open daily mid-May–mid-Oct.* ᕕ ᕤ ☎306/662-3590. Reached from Cypress Hills Provincial Park or by a pleasant drive from Maple Creek, this North West Mounted Police post, named for its builder, Inspector James Walsh, was constructed close to the site of the Cypress Hills Massacre. From 1878 to 1882, it served as the force's headquarters.

At the **visitor centre**, displays and films provide a good introduction. The fort *(guided tours, 2-3hrs)* can be reached by foot or by park bus service. The white-washed log buildings include barracks, stables, a workshop and the commissioner's residence. At **Farwell's Trading Post★** *(2.5km/1.5mi south of fort, access by park bus; 30min guided tour),* visitors are shown around by "Farwell," who re-creates the lawless atmosphere of the times before the arrival of the police when "a man's life was worth a horse, and a horse was worth a pint of whisky."

★★ EDMONTON Alberta

Pop 616,741

Map of Principal Sights p 2

Tourist Office ☎403/988-5455

The capital of Alberta spans the deep valley of the North Saskatchewan River in the geographic midpoint of the province. This thriving metropolis is the heart of Canada's oil industry. Located in a rich agricultural area, Edmonton is also a meat-processing and grain-handling centre as well as the major distribution hub for northern Canada.

From Fur Trade Post to Provincial Capital. – By the end of the 18C, both the North West and Hudson's Bay companies had erected fur-trading forts in the vicinity of present-day Edmonton. When the two merged in 1821, **Edmonton House** became the most important post in the West, serving not only Alberta but the territory west of the Rockies.

Settlement developed around the post, with goods arriving by York boat from York Factory or overland from Winnipeg by Red River cart. The growing community suffered a relapse when the Canadian Pacific Railway Company decided to build its line through Calgary, but recovered when other rail lines were built at the end of the century. People poured in, especially during the Klondike Stampede of 1896-1899 en route to Dawson City, the beginning of Edmonton's development as a "gateway to the North." In 1905, the city became Alberta's capital; its strategic location

Oil pump near Leduc

Alberta Tourism, Edmonton

between rich central farmland and northland resources was a major determinant. Edmonton might have remained a quiet administrative centre had it not been for **Leduc**, a small community located to the south. In February 1947, oil was found 1,771m/5,810ft below the ground, the first strike of what proved to be a 300-million-barrel bonanza. In 1948, the Redwater field was opend, followed by other discoveries. The city is the major service and distribution centre for the vast Athabasca oil sands to the north. More than 80 percent of Canada's oil reserves lie in Alberta, and over 80 percent of the producing oil wells are concentrated in the Edmonton area. Refineries and petrochemical plants line **Refinery Row**.

Klondike Days. – Every year in July, Edmonton celebrates its role in the great **Klondike Stampede**. Bedecked in costumes of the Gay Nineties, inhabitants and visitors parade, eat flapjacks, dance in the streets, gamble at the casino, pan for gold at the Chilkoot Mine, compete in raft races on the river, and in general "whoop it up" for about ten days.

DOWNTOWN   *Map below. 1/2 day.*

Edmonton's downtown is generally considered to be the vicinity of Sir Winston Churchill Square and Jasper Avenue. The square is surrounded by a collection of modern buildings including City Hall **[H]**, the Court House **[J]**, the Art Gallery, the elegant glass and brick Citadel Theatre **[T]** with its three stages, the attractive Centennial Library **[L]**, and Edmonton Centre with its shops, restaurants and offices.
Two blocks south, the steel and glass structure of the Edmonton **Convention Centre** rises opposite Canada Place, which houses offices of the Federal Government.

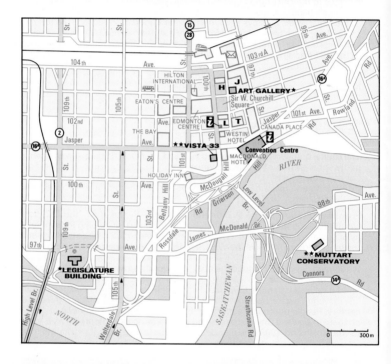

* **Art Gallery.** – *2 Sir Winston Churchill Sq. Open daily year-round. Closed Christmas & New Year's $3.* 🕭 ☎*403/422-6223*. Constructed in 1969, this modern building with its open central stairway, presents regularly changing and permanent exhibits. The development of Canadian art is traced by a selection of works from the gallery's collections.

** **Vista 33.** – *10020 100th St. Open year-round daily 10am–8pm. $1.* 🅿 🕭 ☎*403/493-3333*. This observatory on the 33rd floor of the Alberta Government Telephone Tower offers a **panorama**★★ of Edmonton. Immediately to the south, the river is visible in its winding steep-sided valley. The other three sides afford good views of the downtown highrises.

** **Muttart Conservatory.** – *9626 96A St. Open year-round daily 11am–9pm. Closed Christmas. $4.* 🅿 🕭 ✗ ☎*403/428-5226*. The four glass pyramids of this striking architectural ensemble provide a fine setting for displays of plants from three different climatic zones—tropical, temperate and arid. One pyramid is reserved as a showplace for changing displays of ornamental plants.

* **Legislature Building.** – *Legislature Centre. Open daily year-round. Closed Christmas, New Year's & Good Friday.* 🅿 🕭 ✗ ☎*403/427-7362*. Set in pleasant gardens overlooking the North Saskatchewan River, the yellow sandstone Alberta Legislature building (1912) occupies the original site of Fort Edmonton. The main entrance *(north side)* leads into an impressive hall from which a stairway ascends to the **legislative assembly**. The fifth floor of the dome presents an interesting display on Alberta history.

ADDITIONAL SIGHTS *Map below*

★★ **Fort Edmonton Park.** – *Open May–Aug daily 10am–6pm; Sept weekends only. $6.* ☐ ♿ ✗ ☎*403/428-2992.* Set in the ravine of the North Saskatchewan River, this park re-creates the history of European settlement in Edmonton. Inside a high palisade, the buildings of **Fort Edmonton**—the 1846 fur-trading post—have been reconstructed. Dominant is the Big House, a four-storey residence with a third-floor balcony from which the chief factor, or governor of the fort, could survey his domain. Quarters of the other 130 inhabitants, such as clerks, artisans, labourers and servants, have been meticulously re-created. Also on view are trade and storage rooms, the forge, stable and boatshed where York boats *(p 97)* are under construction (a completed one can be seen on the river), and the chapel built for the Rev **Robert Rundle**, the first missionary in Alberta, who spent the years 1840 to 1848 at Fort Edmonton.

The **pre-railway village** contains a reconstruction of Jasper Avenue in 1885, notable for its width and boardwalks. Along the avenue stand stores selling furs, jewellery, drugs, and hardware, as well as the North West Mounted Police post, the Dominion Land Office, and the offices of the local newspaper. One original building, the McDougall Church, erected downtown in 1873, was moved to this site. Built by the Rev **George McDougall**, it was the first Protestant church in Alberta. The village gradually becomes **1905 Street**, which shows Edmonton at a time of great growth. A street car *(continuous service)* runs down the middle of the road lined with a penny arcade, Masonic Hall, two churches, a firehall, civic centre and other structures.

Eventually, 1905 Street becomes **1920 Street**, which is currently under development. Commercial concerns such as a brickyard and greenhouse complex can be visited along with a Ukrainian bookstore and the train station *(continuous service)*.

Fort Edmonton Park

Alberta Tourism, Edmonton

West Edmonton Mall. – *170th to 178th sts, 87th to 90th aves. Open daily year-round.* ☎*403/444-5200.* Covering over 483,000sq m/5.2 million sq ft, this huge shopping centre is reputedly the largest in the world. It encloses an amusement park, full-size ice rink, aquapark, hotel and some 800 stores and restaurants.

★★ **Provincial Museum.** – *12845 102nd Ave. Open Victoria Day–Labour Day daily 9am–8pm. Off-season Tue–Sun 9am–5pm. $3 (free on Tue).* ☐ ♿ ✗ ☎*403/427-1786.* A showcase of Alberta's culture and human and natural history, this complex occupies an attractive **site**★ in a park overlooking the river beside the former residence of Alberta's lieutenant-governor.

On the ground floor are **dioramas**★ of the wildlife of the four great natural regions of the province—prairie, parkland, forest and mountain. The **Indian Gallery**★★ details the life of the Plains Indians in Canada. Note their exquisite beadwork and the displays on food, clothes, shelter, transportation, recreation and religion.

The second floor features displays on Alberta's geology and mineral wealth. Giant mammals and dinosaurs are exhibited in the Fossil Gallery, opened in 1988. Educational displays on bird, mammal and insect life complete the exhibit. The

historical exhibits★ trace European settlement, with displays evoking life in the province in previous times. Of particular interest is the section on the religious backgrounds of the province's population.

★ **Edmonton Space and Science Centre.** – *11211 142nd St. Open daily end-Jun–mid-Sept. Off-season Tue–Sun. $5.* ▣ ⅙ ✕ ☎*403/451-7722.* Resembling a large space ship with its white steel cladding over a steel frame, the centre houses an IMAX theatre as well as a planetarium. Featured are exhibits on the planets and meteorites, the telescope, space exploration and a full-size model of the **Canadarm**, a remote manipulator system developed in Canada and used on US space shuttles. Housed separately, an **observatory** offers a close-up view of the stars and planets *(weather permitting; Fri & Sat 8–11pm; Sun 1-4pm).*

EXCURSIONS

St Albert. – *Pop 42,146. 19km/12mi north by Rte 2.* In 1861, a Roman Catholic mission was founded here on the banks of the Sturgeon River by Father **Albert Lacombe** (1827-1916). The simple log structure that served as his **chapel** still stands today and is the oldest building in Alberta *(St Vital Ave).*
The crypt of the modern-day church contains Father Lacombe's tomb and that of Bishop **Vital Grandin** (1829-1902), whose adjoining residence can also be visited.

★ **Ukrainian Cultural Heritage Village.** – *On Hwy 16, about 50km/30mi east. Open daily mid-May–Nov. $3 (free on Tue).* ▣ ⅙ ✕ ☎*403/662-3640.* This reconstructed village traces Ukrainian settlement in Alberta since the 1890s. Displays in the visitor centre provide insight into the mass migration of Ukrainian people to the Canadian Prairies. Homestead development—from early sod-covered dugout to white-washed dwelling—is explained in great detail by costumed interpreters. The village also includes a rural community and an early town, complete with a grain elevator, train station, provincial police post, domed church and shops.

★ **FORT MACLEOD** Alberta   Pop 3,112

Map of Principal Sights p 2

South of Calgary (165km/102mi), this small town on the Oldman River was the site chosen for the first North West Mounted Police post in the West. In October 1874, a band of weary men arrived after a long and arduous trek from Manitoba. They had been quickly trained and dispatched to stop the illegal whisky trade and border incursions, such as the one leading to the Cypress Hills Massacre *(p 84).* Under the command of **Col James Macleod**, they built permanent barracks on an island in the river.
Today, Fort Macleod is a thriving agricultural community. Grain is grown with the aid of irrigation, and cattle are raised on the ranchland of nearby Porcupine Hills.

★ **Fort Museum.** – *On Hwy 3, one block from centre of town. Open daily May–mid-Oct. Off-season Mon–Fri, except holidays. $3.50.* ⅙ ☎*403/553-4703.* This museum re-creates life in and around police posts during the early settlement of Alberta. Inside the wooden palisaded walls stand a number of log structures. The **Kanouse House** with its sod roof is devoted to the early settlers of the region. The **Mounted Police Building** houses a model of the original fort and exhibits on the police. In the canteen, there are video presentations *(24min)* on the police and on Head-Smashed-In Buffalo Jump *(see below).*
In summer, students dressed in the police uniforms of 1878 (red jackets, black breeches, white pith helmets) perform a musical ride *(daily Jul–Aug).*

★ **Head-Smashed-In Buffalo Jump.** – *18km/11mi northwest by Hwy 785 (Spring Point Rd). Open daily mid-Mar–Nov. Off-season Tue-Sun. $5.* ⅙✕ ☎*403/553-2731.* This buffalo jump has the most extensive deposits (9m/30ft deep) of any in North America. Its importance was recognized by UNESCO in 1981, when the site was inscribed on the World Heritage List.
For over 5,000 years, buffalo were driven to their deaths over this cliff. The buffalo provided most of the necessities of life for the native Indians—meat, hides for clothing and shelter, and bone for scrapers and needles. A visitor centre contains displays and films on buffalo-hunting cultures.

★ **LETHBRIDGE** Alberta   Pop 60,974

Map of Principal Sights p 2   Tourist Office ☎403/320-1222

Located in southern Alberta, 216km/134mi southeast of Calgary, this city overlooks a deep coulee cut by the Oldman River. Constructed into the side of this coulee are the striking buildings of the University of Lethbridge, and crossing it is the High Level Railway Bridge (about 1.5km/1mi long and 96m/314ft high).
Lethbridge was founded in 1870, after coal deposits were discovered in the valley. Today, the city is the centre of a productive agricultural region. Widespread irrigation and the relatively mild winters moderated by the warm chinook winds *(p 74)* have made the cultivation of grain and vegetables, especially sugar beet, very profitable. Livestock are also raised here.

★ **Nikka Yuko Japanese Garden.** – *In Henderson Lake Park on Mayor Magrath Dr. Open daily mid-May–Sept. $2.75.* ⅙ ☎*403/328-3511.* The city built this garden in 1967 as a symbol of Japanese-Canadian amity *(Nikka Yuko* means Japan-Canada). It is a wonderfully serene place where visitors can gain an appreciation for traditional

Japanese landscape architecture. When Canada declared war on Japan in 1941, about 22,000 Japanese-Canadians living on the West Coast were placed in internment camps in central British Columbia and Alberta, although in many cases they were Canadian citizens. About 6,000 of these Japanese-Canadians were resettled in Lethbridge, where they chose to stay after the war. Five types of formal landscapes are linked by meandering paths. At the centre lies a pavilion of Japanese cypress wood, laid out for a tea ceremony.

★ **Fort Whoop-up.** – *In Indian Battle Park by river, access from Hwy 3. Open daily mid-May–Labour Day. $2.* & ☎403/329-0444. In the deep coulee of the Oldman River stands a replica of this once-notorious whisky trading post. Founded by Americans from Fort Benton, Montana, the post attracted Indians from far and wide to trade buffalo skins, furs, and indeed almost anything, for a particularly lethal brew bearing little resemblance to whisky (ingredients included chewing tobacco, red peppers, Jamaican ginger and black molasses, as well as alcohol).

Such illegal liquor forts, of which Whoop-up was the most important, sprang up all over southern Alberta and Saskatchewan in the early 1870s. The Canadian government formed the North West Mounted Police to counter this American encroachment of Canadian territory and to stop a trade that was demoralizing the Indians. In 1874, the force that arrived at the gates of Whoop-up found the premises vacated. The founding by the force of Fort Macleod *(p 88)*, and later Fort Calgary *(p 82)*, effectively ended the illegal trade and brought law and order to the West.

The reconstructed fort flies not "the Stars and Stripes" (the American flag) but the trading flag of the original Fort Benton company. Below it, wooden buildings form a fortified enclosure. In the **interpretation centre**, a video presentation *(20min)* presents the history of the post in the context of the development of the Canadian West.

★ MOOSE JAW Saskatchewan   Pop 33,593

Map of Principal Sights p 3

Rising out of the flat wheat lands of southern Saskatchewan, 71km/44mi due west of Regina, is the province's third-largest city. Named for a sharp turn in the river that resembles a protruding moose jaw, this industrial centre, with flour mills, grain elevator and stock yards, is an important railway junction for agricultural produce of the area. The city is also involved in the refining of Saskatchewan's oil.

★ **Western Development Museum.** – *At junction Trans-Can Hwy and Hwy 2. Open daily Apr–Dec. Closed Christmas. $3.50.* & ✗ ☎306/693-6556. One of four museums on Western development in the province, this one is devoted to transportation in Saskatchewan. The water section has displays about the *Northcote*, a steam ship used to take supplies up the South Saskatchewan River during the Northwest Rebellion, and on cable ferries, particularly that of St-Laurent *(p 94)*. The land section features a Canadian Pacific locomotive, a reconstructed station and a 1934 Buick converted to run on rails and used as an inspection vehicle for 20 years. In addition, there is an interesting collection of other automobiles. The air section presents several Canadian planes, including a 1927 Red Pheasant, and a gallery devoted to the British Commonwealth Air Training Plan.

★ PRINCE ALBERT NATIONAL PARK Saskatchewan

Map of Principal Sights p 3

Located in the geographic centre of Saskatchewan, this large park consisting of wooded hills dotted with lakes and streams constitutes a fine example of Canada's southern boreal plains, an area where the aspen forest of the south mixes with the true boreal wilderness. Isolated pockets of grassland near the southern boundary support prairie animals—coyotes, badgers and ground squirrels. The northern forests are home to wolves, moose, elk, bears, beaver, otter, mink and a small herd of woodland caribou. In the extreme north, white pelicans nest on Lavallée Lake.

Grey Owl. – Famous for his writings and lectures on the fate of the beaver and the vanishing wilderness, this man posed as an Indian, dressing in buckskins and wearing his long hair in braids. He travelled throughout North America and Europe with a conservation message, even lecturing to the British monarch, George VI, in 1937. Trying to re-establish beaver colonies, he worked for Canada's national park service, first in Riding Mountain National Park *(p 92)* and then in Prince Albert. At his death in 1938, he was exposed as an Englishman, **Archie Belaney**, who had taken the Indian name *Wa-sha-Quon-Asin* (the Grey Owl) about 1920. Though discovered to be an impostor, Grey Owl remains one of Canada's finest nature writers and among the first to preach the importance of the wilderness. His most famous books are *Tales of an Empty Cabin, Pilgrims of the Wild* and *Sajo and Her Beaver People.*

Access. – *80km/50mi north of Prince Albert by Hwys 2 and 264.*

Visit. – ☞ *Open year-round; hiking, canoeing, swimming, golf, tennis, winter sports; accommodation in Waskesiu Lake. Admission $5/day per car or $10/4 days per car. Map available at information office (open daily year-round).* ⚠ ☎306/663-5322. The **nature centre** *(open daily Victoria Day–Labour Day)* in Waskesiu (meaning "place of the elk") Lake provides an introduction to the park. The roads following both shores of Lake Waskesiu and **boat trips** on the lake in a paddlewheeler afford pleasant views *(daily Jul & Aug; 1hr; $6)*. On the southernmost edge of the park, visitors can drive around a **buffalo enclosure** in which a small herd roams a prairie landscape. Hiking trails and canoe routes crisscross the park. One interesting hike takes the visitor to the cabin and grave of Grey Owl *(15km/9mi)*.

PRAIRIE PROVINCES

Map of Principal Sights p 3 · Tourist Office ☎ 306/789-5099

Set in an extensive, fertile, wheat-growing plain and located on the main line of the Canadian Pacific Railway and the Trans-Canada Highway, this provincial capital has long been an important agricultural centre. Regina is the headquarters for the province's rich potash industry.

Pile O' Bones. – Few cities have been established in less congenial surroundings—treeless plains stretching to the horizon; a scanty water supply from a sluggish creek; soil of gumbo clay, muddy in wet weather, dusty in dry. Nevertheless, in the early 1880s, the Canadian Pacific Railway Company decided to build its line across the southern plains, leaving the existing capital of the vast Northwest Territories at Battleford *(p 80)* high and dry. Determined to move the capital, the Dominion government, in collaboration with the railway company, chose a location where the future rail line would cross a creek long favoured by Indians and Métis for running buffalo into pounds to slaughter them. Testifying to their once great number, the remains of these animals had given this spot (as recorded by John Palliser, *p 74*) the Cree name, *Oskana,* translated as "pile o'bones." The choice was controversial, especially since the lieutenant-governor of the then Northwest Territories, Edgar Dewdney *(p 35),* owned land at that place. In August 1882, when the first train arrived, Princess Louise, wife of Canada's governor general, rechristened it Regina ("Queen" in Latin) after her mother, Queen Victoria.

Historic Court Case. – After the defeat of the Northwest Rebellion in 1885 *(p 93),* the Métis leader, Louis Riel *(p 75),* was taken to Regina for trial. The court immediately became a centre of controversy. To Quebecers, Riel—a Catholic Métis who had studied for the priesthood in Montreal—was a patriot who had fought for the rights of his people. To Ontarians, he was a common rebel who had gone unpunished after murdering Thomas Scott during the Red River Rebellion *(p 75).* Defence counsel pleaded that Riel was insane: he had spent several years in asylums and had wished to set up a new Catholic state on the Saskatchewan River, with Bishop Bourget of Montreal as Pope. Riel himself rejected the plea and convinced the jury he was sane. But if sane, he was guilty: the verdict was death by hanging. Prime Minister Sir John A. Macdonald was inundated with petitions from both sides. The sentence was delayed while doctors studied Riel's mental health. The prime minister weighed the political consequences of hanging Riel and decided the sentence had to be carried out. Riel lost his life on November 16, 1885.

Queen City of the Plains. – Regina became the capital of Saskatchewan when that province was created in 1905. As immigrants poured in from all parts of the world, the city burgeoned. Their enterprising spirit helped overcome the physical shortcomings of the city's site. To solve the water problems, Wascana Creek was dammed, creating an artificial lake. Trees were planted and carefully nourished, defying the notion of a treeless wilderness.

Though the city's development in the 20C has been precarious, Regina has experienced steady growth since World War II. The downtown core has been revitalized, and imposing buildings constructed. Today, from 80km/50mi distant, Regina rises above the flat, treeless prairie like a mirage, its quiet grace testifying to its epithet, Queen City of the Plains.

Every summer, the MacKenzie Art Gallery is the setting for a dramatic re-enactment of the **Trial of Louis Riel★★** based on actual court transcripts *(3475 Albert St; Wed, Thur, Fri in Aug 8pm; tickets available at door or ☎306/525-1185).*

DOWNTOWN
Map opposite. 1/2 day.

★★ **Museum of Natural History.** – *College Ave and Albert St. Open May–Labour Day daily 9am–8:30pm. Off-season daily 9am–4:30pm. Closed Christmas.* 🅿 ♿ ☎306/ 787-2815. This long, low building of Tyndall stone housed one of the finest museums of natural history in Canada until the remarkable life sciences dioramas, highlight of the museum, were destroyed by fire in 1990. Plans to re-create them are

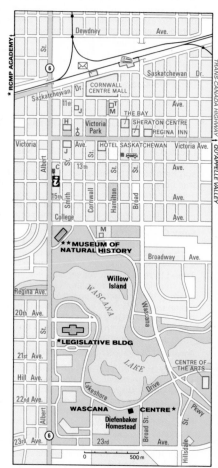

under way. Exhibits in the Earth Sciences Gallery include dinosaurs and woolly mammoths, volcanoes and glaciers from the province's geological beginnings to the appearance of mankind in Saskatchewan. A new First Nations Gallery is scheduled to open in the future.

★ **Legislative Building.** – *2405 Legislative Dr. Visit by guided tour (30min) only daily year-round. Closed legal holidays.* 🅿️ ♿ ✕ ☎*306/787-5358*. Completed in 1912, this graceful building of Tyndall stone was built in the shape of a cross topped by a dome. It occupies a fine **site★** overlooking gardens and Wascana Lake.
The guided tour visits the legislative chamber, legislative library, the rotunda, and art galleries named after the rivers of the province.

★ **Wascana Centre.** – *Picnicking, swimming, boating. Open year-round* ☎*306/522-3661.* This 930ha/2,300 acre park is Regina's pride and joy. Formal gardens of beautiful flowers and trees surround the western part of the artificial Wascana Lake. **Willow Island** is a picnic site accessible by ferry *(ferry reservations required; daily Victoria Day–Labour Day; $2).*
Also in the park, which can be toured by car, are the provincial legislative building and the **Diefenbaker Homestead**, a three-room pioneer dwelling *(open daily Victoria Day–Labour Day;* ☎*306/522-3661),* home to John George Diefenbaker, Prime Minister of Canada from 1957 to 1963 *(p 93).* This house was moved from its original site in Borden, Saskatchewan, where the Diefenbaker family homesteaded between 1905 and 1910.
East of Wascana Parkway, the park is a bird sanctuary. Many species of waterfowl can be spotted, but by far the most common is the **Canada goose**. Some of these birds are year-round residents of the centre, benefiting from crops grown nearby. Visitors can also tour a waterfall display pond *(open daily Victoria Day–Labour Day).*

ADDITIONAL SIGHTS

★ **Royal Canadian Mounted Police Training Academy.** – *West of downtown by Dewdney Ave. Visit by guided tour (30min) only daily year-round. Closed Christmas & New Year's.* 🅿️ ♿ ☎*306/780-5838*. People who know nothing else about Canada have heard of the **Mounties**, the country's federal police force. Stories about them are legion, and many films have portrayed their ability to "always get their man." Created in 1873 as the **North West Mounted Police**, the force had to formulate as well as to preserve law and order in the Canadian West. Faced with problems such as the illegal sale of "fire water" to Canadian Indians by American traders, the police quickly established themselves as an effective force. They helped the various Indian tribes accept treaties and life on reservations, gave valuable aid to new settlers in the West, and enforced law and order during the Klondike Stampede *(p 31).*
In 1920, they were united with the Dominion Police as the **Royal Canadian Mounted Police.** Today, they enforce federal laws across Canada and act as the provincial police in all provinces and territories except Ontario and Quebec. They are famous for their **musical ride**, a collection of early cavalry drills performed on horseback and culminating in a rousing "charge." All new recruits undergo a six-month basic course at the academy. Guided tours vary, depending on the number of recruits and their activities.

★ **Museum.** – *(same hours)* This museum illustrates the history of the Mounties and recalls such famous incidents as Sitting Bull's years in Canada *(p 84),* the Northwest Rebellion *(p 93),* the Klondike Stampede and the voyage of the *St Roch (p 60).* Displays also explain the work of the force today.

EXCURSION

★ **Qu'Appelle Valley.** – *Map p 6.* From Lake Diefenbaker to the Manitoba border, the Qu'Appelle (kap-PELL) Valley cuts a deep swath across the otherwise flat prairie. It was carved out 12,000 years ago by meltwaters from a retreating glacier that left a wide valley with only a small stream at its midst, surrounded by low, round-topped hills. As visitors approach the Qu'Appelle from any direction, the prairie seems endless, and then suddenly the road drops and a 2km/1.2mi wide stretch of verdant green comes into view. As much as 120m/400ft deep in places, with several sparkling lakes, the valley presents a complete contrast to the surrounding plains. The name derives from Indian lore. According to legend, a brave in his canoe heard his name called. *Qu'appelle?* ("who calls?" in French) he shouted, but only an echo answered him. On returning home, he found his sweetheart lifeless—she had called his name moments before dying.

★ **The Fishing Lakes.** – *73km/45mi east of Regina by Trans-Can Hwy, northeast by Rte 10; 1/2 day.* The best way to appreciate the Qu'Appelle Valley is to drive alongside the river where it forms the Fishing Lakes—Pasqua, Echo, Mission and Katepwa. North of Lake Echo, there is a particularly attractive stretch of road on Route 56 leading to **Echo Valley Provincial Park★** *(open year-round; visitor centre open daily Victoria Day–Labour Day; limited facilities during off-season;* ♿ ⛺ ☎*306/332-3215).*

Canada's 7% Goods and Services Tax (GST), effective since January 1991, replaced the federal sales tax. The GST is a personal consumption tax levied, for example, on groceries, vehicles, accommodation, and health, dental, financial and educational services. Non-residents are entitled to a rebate. For information, see p 242.

** RIDING MOUNTAIN NATIONAL PARK Manitoba

Map of Principal Sights p 3

Established in 1933 on the Manitoba plain, this lovely park is a rolling plateau of wooded slopes and lakes. Approached from the east and north, it rises 457m/1,500ft above the surrounding countryside (756m/2,480ft above sea level) and does indeed look like a mountain—or at least a hill.

Early fur traders named it "Riding" Mountain, as it marked the place where they exchanged canoes for horses to continue west. It is, in fact, part of the **Manitoba Escarpment**, a jagged 1,600km/1,000mi ridge winding across North Dakota, Manitoba and Saskatchewan—a series of hills cut by many rivers, rather than a continuous ridge.

The park is also a crossroads where northern, western and eastern environments and habitats meet. High areas are covered with an evergreen forest of spruce, pine, fir and tamarack. Lower sections support a deciduous forest of hardwoods, shrubs, vines and ferns. In the west, wild flowers thrive on meadows and grassland (July and Aug), forming some of the only true prairie left on the continent.

Access. – 197km/122mi west of Winnipeg by Trans-Can Hwy, then 91km/56mi north of Brandon by Rte 10.

Visit. – ⌖ Open year-round; hiking, boating, tennis, golf, winter sports; accommodation in Wasagaming; $5/day per car and $10/4 days per car; map available at visitor centre. ⌂⌖✕ ☎204/848-2811. The **interpretation centre**★★ (open mid-May–mid-Oct daily 8am–8pm) in Wasagaming features excellent displays on the park's geological history, the different habitats therein and the native wildlife. Visitors can view films on related subjects.

Near Lake Audy (47km/29mi from Wasagaming), a herd of about 30 buffalo roams a large enclosure. From a viewpoint above the Audy plain, these animals can be seen in their true prairie environment. An exhibit explains how they nearly became extinct. Visitors can drive around the enclosure (4km/2.5mi).

A fine **view**★ of the Manitoba Escarpment is obtained from Route 19 (31km/19mi east of Wasagaming or 5km/3mi from park's east gate).

* SASKATOON Saskatchewan   Pop 186,058

Map of Principal Sights p 3   Tourist Office ☎306/242-1206

Built on both sides of the South Saskatchewan River, this city, 259km/161mi northwest of Regina, occupies a pleasant **site**★ enhanced by wide, tree-lined streets as well as parkland beside the water (in particular, **Kiwanis Park** with its views of bridges and the University of Saskatchewan). The largest city in Saskatchewan, this manufacturing and distribution centre is set in a fertile wheat-growing area, amid the province's vast potash reserves. Surrounding prairie landscape is a little more rolling than around Regina, but is nonetheless dominated by the "heights" of **Mount Blackstrap** (91m/300ft), an artificial ski hill rising south of the city (40km/25mi).

Temperance Town. – Founded in 1883 by Methodists from Ontario, the city was to be the capital of a temperance colony. A leader of this venture, **John Lake**, selected the name Saskatoon, a small purplish berry native to the region. However, the teetotallers' paradise did not attract many settlers and two decades later, numbered only 113 souls. In 1908, the whole area quickly experienced a boom when colonists arrived by the new rail lines. German, Scandinavian, Ukrainian and British settlers transformed the city, and the early temperance ideals were laid to rest. Today, they are honoured once a year in July during **Pioneer Days**.

SIGHTS *Map p 92. 1/2 day.*

★ **Mendel Art Gallery.** – *950 Spadina Crescent E. Open daily year-round. Closed Christmas & Good Friday.* & ☎306/975-7610. This attractive modern gallery overlooking the river is named for **Fred Mendel**, a wealthy Saskatoon meat-packer of German origin who launched the idea of an art gallery and spent much of his time and money developing it.

The permanent collection includes works by the Group of Seven *(p 143)*, Emily Carr and David Milne in the Canadian section, and Feininger, Chagall, Utrillo and Pissarro in the **European section**. The gallery also displays visiting exhibits. At one end there is an attractive conservatory of exotic flowers and plants.

Ukrainian Museum. – *910 Spadina Crescent E. Open daily Jun–Aug. Off-season closed mornings & Sat. $2.* & ☎306/244-3800. This museum presents displays of traditional costumes, tapestries, pioneer tools, wood-inlaid objects, and other handicrafts illustrating the heritage of the people who have played such a large role in the settlement of the Prairies.

Boat Trip. – *Departure points, see map p 92. Jun–Labour Day daily 1-8pm; 1hr; commentary; $6.50.* 🅿 & *Northcote River Cruises* ☎306/665-1818. This cruise on the South Saskatchewan River is a pleasant way to discover the scenic beauty of the area.

★ **John Diefenbaker Centre.** – *On University of Saskatchewan campus, off Rte 5. Open daily year-round.* & ☎306/966-8384. Upon his death in 1979, the former Canadian prime minister left his papers to the university. They have been assembled to form a veritable shrine to this man, a legend in his own time. A lawyer by training, well known for his defence of the "little man," Diefenbaker entered politics and became a strong proponent of Western Canadian ideas in the Conservative Party. Elected party leader in 1956, he served as prime minister from 1957 to 1963, remaining influential in federal politics until his death.

In addition to displays on his life and works, the centre features a replica of the office of the prime minister and the Cabinet Chamber as they existed in the Diefenbaker era.

★★ **Western Development Museum.** – *In Prairieland Exhibition Grounds, 8km/5mi south of downtown by Rte 11/16. Open year-round daily 9am–5pm. Closed Christmas. $3.50.* & ✗ ☎306/931-1910. The grand attraction of the Saskatoon branch of this museum *(p 80)* is **Boomtown**, a faithful reconstruction of an entire street of 1910 vintage, complete with its Western Pioneer Bank, garage, stores, Chinese laundry, school, church, pool hall, theatre, hotel and railway station. Several period automobiles and horse-drawn vehicles line the street.

Separate halls house a large collection of automobiles and agricultural equipment, including steam tractors. The museum also features the Eaton collection of mechanized Christmas window displays, crafted from surplus World War II aircraft motors.

Wanuskewin Heritage Park. – *3km/2mi north of downtown by Hwy 11. Open daily year-round. $6.* & ✗ ☎306/931-6767. A series of archaeological sites on the banks of the South Saskatchewan River forms the basis of this testament to the survival of the Northern Plains Indians. Translated from Cree as "seeking peace of mind," *Wanuskewin* was a meeting place and hunting ground for native nomadic peoples for more than 6,000 years until their removal to reservations in the 1870s. Several trails in the 120ha/290 acre park link the prehistoric sites. Opened in 1992, a striking **visitor centre** features displays and demonstrations of native culture and allows observation of excavations and laboratory work.

EXCURSION

★★ **Batoche National Historic Site.** – ☞ *88km/55mi northeast of Saskatoon by Rte 11 to Rosthern, Rte 312 east and Rte 225 north; 1/2 day. Open year-round.* This quiet and beautiful spot on the banks of the South Saskatchewan River was the site of the final stand of the Métis in 1885.

The Northwest Rebellion. – The seeds of the last armed conflict on Canadian soil were sown in Manitoba's Red River Valley early in the 19C when the Métis learned that land did not necessarily belong to those born and living on it. The uprising led to Louis Riel's provisional government of 1869, the formal creation of the province of Manitoba (1870) and the allocation of 567,000ha/1.4 million acres of land for Métis settlement *(p 75)*.

Unfortunately, the Métis, left leaderless when Riel was banished for five years, were prey to speculators who bought their land for a fraction of its worth. Many moved northwest to the valley of the South Saskatchewan River, hoping to lead traditional lives of buffalo hunting and to avoid survey groups and European settlers. The buffalo were nearly extinct, however, and the march of "progress" continued. Again the Métis found they had no right to land they farmed. The Dominion government consistently ignored their petitions. In 1884, they sent for Louis Riel.

Riel hoped to repeat his earlier victory at Red River. He allied the Métis with Cree Indians who were also discontent with changes in their lifestyle. An unfortunate incident resulting in the deaths of some members of the North West Mounted Police at **Duck Lake** destroyed all hope of a peaceful solution. In eastern Canada, there was outrage at the thought of police being killed by "lawless rebels," and a military force was quickly dispatched to the West under Maj-Gen **Frederick Middleton**.

Restrained by Riel, the Métis—under their military leader, **Gabriel Dumont**, an experienced buffalo hunter—were unable to deter the advancing army by guerrilla tactics. Instead, they made a stand at Batoche, which never could have succeeded against

Middleton's overwhelming numbers. It was a heroic defence that lasted four days because of the strength of the Métis position. Afterwards, Riel surrendered and was taken to Regina to stand trial for murder. He was found guilty and hanged (p 90). Dumont fled to the US, though he was later pardoned for his part in the revolt and returned to Batoche. The struggle was not in vain, however, for in the wake of the rebellion, the Métis were offered the land title they had sought unsuccessfully for such a long time.

Visit. – Today, the park is a poignant tribute to the Métis. Little remains of the village except the tiny **church** dedicated to St Anthony of Padua, the **rectory** with its bullet holes and a cemetery of Métis graves, including Dumont's burial place. The buildings have been restored to the period and house historic artifacts.
The **visitor centre** (open daily Victoria Day–Thanksgiving; & ✗ ☎306/423-6227) offers a moving audio-visual presentation on the rebellion and displays on Métis history and culture.

The return trip to Saskatoon can be made by the St-Laurent cable ferry (10km/6mi north of Batoche), past the small community of Duck Lake on Route 11, where the rebellion had its beginnings.

★★★ WINNIPEG Manitoba   Pop 616,790

Map of Principal Sights p 3   Tourist Office ☎ 204/943-1970 or 204/945-3777

Set on the banks of the Red and Assiniboine rivers, the capital of Manitoba occupies the geographic heart of Canada and is often described as the place where "the West begins." Indeed, for over a century, it has been the traditional first stop for immigrants to the West. Not far to the east and north, the hilly and rocky tree-covered terrain of the Canadian Shield with its multitude of lakes gives way to the open fertile prairie with its endless horizons. This dramatic change clearly marks the division between east and west.
Named for the large and shallow lake to the north called win-nipi (murky water) by the Cree, Winnipeg developed as the distribution and financial centre of the West. Although challenged by Vancouver and Alberta's cities in recent years, it retains a huge **commodity exchange** (the most important in Canada), vast stock and railway yards, a manufacturing industry and headquarters of the Hudson's Bay Company, so influential in the growth of the fur trade in the Prairies.

The Red River Settlement. – In the early 19C, Thomas Douglas, Earl of Selkirk, obtained title from the Hudson's Bay Company to a large piece of land covering much of present-day southern Manitoba called **Assiniboia**. In 1811, he began resettling some of his poverty-stricken compatriots from the Scottish Highlands there in the Red River Valley.
The success of this colony was slow in coming, mainly because of the Red River's tendency to flood, plagues of crop-eating grasshoppers and rivalry between the great fur-trading companies—the Hudson's Bay and the North West. The latter allied with the Métis, who had seen their traditional lifestyle gradually disrupted by settlers.
During the **Seven Oaks Massacre** of 1816, the Métis nearly succeeded in wiping out the colony: some 20 settlers were killed and the rest temporarily abandoned the settlement. Selkirk re-established his colony, however, and it gradually grew in size as a commercial centre with brigades of Red River carts going to and from St Paul, Minnesota and steamboats chugging along the Red River. The city's connections below the border made annexation by the US seem likely, but the Northwest Rebellion and the creation of Manitoba in 1870 prevented it.

Winnipeg Today. – The community's future was assured when the Canadian Pacific Railway Company chose the site as a major maintenance and repair centre and built a rail line through town. Floods of immigrants poured in by train. Winnipeg (the name was adopted at the time of the rebellion) not only assumed an outfitting role, but became a distribution centre for the entire Northwest. In the 19C, the population consisted of Scots, Irish, English, French, Métis and Indians. During the 20C, Germans, Eastern Europeans and especially Ukrainians joined their ranks. Winnipeg's skyline, dotted with spires, towers and domes of Catholic, Protestant and Orthodox churches, reflects this diversity.
Winnipeg is rich in cultural institutions—the Manitoba Theatre Centre, the Symphony Orchestra, the Manitoba Opera Company and, most famous of all, the Royal Winnipeg Ballet. Every August, the city's diverse cultural background is celebrated in **Folklorama**, a festival held in pavilions throughout Winnipeg. The Folk Festival held in July is also a popular event.
The **Forks**, 26ha/65 acres of riverfront property refurbished by the city, includes a **public market** housed within former stables, a National Historic Site and a waterside walkway.

DOWNTOWN Map p 95. 2 days.

The intersection of **Portage Avenue** and **Main Street** has traditionally been considered the centre of Winnipeg. In a bygone era, it was said these principal thoroughfares were wide enough for ten Red River carts to rush along side by side. Today this corner, long known as the windiest in Canada, is dominated by tall buildings, all connected underground by an attractive shopping area, **Winnipeg Square**. Extending for three blocks to the west, between Vaughan and Carlton streets, is **Portage Place★**, a shopping and office complex with restaurants, three movie theatres and a giant-screen IMAX theatre.

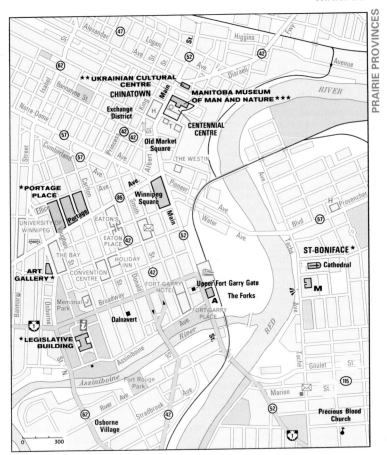

Just south of the intersection at Portage and Main, in a small park below the Fort Garry Hotel, stands a stone gateway. It is all that remains of **Upper Fort Garry**, once the local headquarters of the Hudson's Bay Company. The present-day headquarters **[A]** rises a block away.

North of the intersection lies the **Exchange District**, which has some remarkable examples of early 20C architecture *(walking tours daily Jul & Aug leaving from museum see below)*, and attractive boutiques and restaurants around the **Old Market Square** *(King, Albert and Bannatyne sts; weekend market in summer)*. Close by is **Centennial Centre**, a complex enclosing a concert hall, theatre, museum and planetarium connected by terraced gardens. Just north is Winnipeg's **Chinatown**.

Another interesting quarter for shopping and dining is **Osborne Village**, south of the Assiniboine River between River and Stradbrook avenues.

★★★ **Manitoba Museum of Man and Nature.** – *190 Rupert Ave, across from City Hall. Open Victoria Day–Labour Day daily 10am–6pm. Off-season Tue–Fri 10am–4pm, weekends 10am–5pm. Closed Christmas. $3.50.* 📧 ⅙ ✕ ☎*204/943-3139.* This excellent museum presents the history of human occupation in Manitoba by means of fascinating dioramas, displays and audio-visual presentations. It also portrays the great natural regions of the province.

On entering, the visitor is first struck by the magnificent diorama of a Métis rider, his spear poised, chasing several buffalo. The **Earth History Gallery** explains the geological creation of Manitoba. The mural by Daphne Odjig portrays the creation of the world according to Odawa Indian tradition.

The **Arctic/Sub-Arctic Gallery** is devoted to the northernmost part of the province. At its entrance stands an **inukshuk** *(illustration p 233)*, a stone sculpture used as a navigational aid, campsite or hunting marker, or reminder of special occasions. Artifacts and photographs illustrate the interdependency of the Inuit and Chipewyan Indians with their environment; displays on Hudson Bay marine life and the phenomenon of the Northern Lights complete the exhibit.

In the **Boreal Forest Gallery**, dioramas present the area's indigenous animals. One impressive "walk-through" diorama with a waterfall and cliffs depicts Cree Indians, one of whom is painting on a rock symbols that illustrate religious aspects of the hunt. Other displays feature life on the trapline and modern developments. A mural by Jackson Beardy depicts a world view of the native peoples.

The **Grasslands Gallery** is devoted to the southern part of Manitoba. Insightful displays describe the Assiniboine Indians and first European settlers. There is an example of a **Red River cart**, the major means of pioneer transportation on the prairies: the axles never required greasing and the wheels were easily removed for river crossing. The gallery also has interesting displays on the diverse ethnic and religious groups of Manitoba's population.

The **Urban Gallery** captures a fall evening in Winnipeg in the 1920s. The wooden side-walks, the railway station, shops, restaurant, rooming house, mission hall and theatre showing period movies have been frozen in time.

The highlight of the museum is the **Nonsuch★★★**, a replica of the ship that sailed from England to Hudson Bay in 1668 in search of furs. The successful enterprise led to the creation of Hudson's Bay Company two years later *(p 74)*. Built for the company's tricentenary in 1970, the 15m/49ft ketch is anchored in a reconstructed 17C Thames River wharf. The wooden houses and the inn set around the harbour vividly re-create the scene.

A **planetarium** *(daily shows; $4)* and an innovative science gallery, **Touch the Universe**, exploring sensory perception, *(open Victoria Day–Labour Day until 7pm; off-season same hours as museum; $3)* are located on the lower level.

★★ **Ukrainian Cultural Centre.** – *184 Alexander Ave E. Open year-round Tue–Sat 10am–5pm, Sun 2-5pm. Closed holidays.* ☎204/942-0218. A visit to this centre, one of the largest of its kind outside the Ukraine, forms an interesting introduction to the history and culture of Manitoba's second largest ethnic group, whose influence on the province is very marked.

The **museum★★** *(5th floor)* features exquisite examples of Ukrainian traditional embroidery, wood carving, ceramics and beautifully painted *pysanky* (Easter eggs). The centre also houses an art gallery, library and archives.

★ **Art Gallery.** – *300 Memorial Blvd. Open year-round Tue–Sun. Closed legal holidays. $3.* ⚒ ☎204/775-7297. Designed by Winnipeger Gustavo Da Roza, this unusual wedge-shaped structure contains a beautiful art gallery. Shown in a constantly changing series of exhibits, the permanent collection is large and varied. The gallery is best known for its **Inuit art**, a selection of which is always exhibited, and for the Lord and Lady Gort Collection of Gothic and Renaissance panel paintings.

★ **Legislative Building.** – *Broadway and Osborne St N. Open daily Jul–Labour Day.* ⚒. *For further information call Travel Manitoba* ☎204/945-3777. This harmonious neoclassical building stands in an attractive park, close to the residence of Manitoba's lieutenant-governor. Completed in 1919, the Tyndall stone building forms an "H" with a dome at its centre. Above the dome stands the **Golden Boy**, cast by Charles Gardet, a bronze gold-plated statue clutching a sheaf of wheat in one hand and holding a torch aloft in the other to symbolize Manitoba's glowing future. Above the main entrance *(north side)*, a pediment depicts Canada's motto "From Sea to Sea"; at the centre is Manitoba, the keystone province, another cast by Gardet, joining east and west.

The main entrance hall opens onto a stairway flanked by two **bronze buffalo**, the provincial emblem. The tour enables visitors to view the horseshoe-shaped legislative **assembly chamber** and two reception rooms.

The statues around the building and in the park represent important figures in Manitoba history. Across Assiniboine Avenue stands a striking modern **monument** to Louis Riel *(p 75)* by Étienne Gaboury.

Dalnavert. – *61 Carlton St. Visit by guided tour (1hr) only year-round Tue–Sun. $3.* ☎204/943-2835. This large, brick Victorian house was built in 1895 by Sir Hugh John Macdonald, the only son of Sir John A. Macdonald, Canada's first prime minister. At the time of its construction, Dalnavert was equipped with numerous luxuries and state-of-the-art amenities, such as walk-in closets, electric lighting, indoor plumbing and central hot-water heating. Beautifully restored today, it reflects the life of this philanthropic politician (member of Parliament from 1893 to 1899, and premier of Manitoba from 1899 to 1900), who reserved part of his basement as a lodging for the homeless.

★ **St-Boniface.** – In 1818, Fathers Provencher and Dumoulin arrived from Quebec to establish a Roman Catholic mission on the banks of the Red River. They were followed by other French-Canadians who created, with the largely French-speaking Métis, a lively community. St-Boniface was incorporated into the City of Winnipeg in 1972, but it retains its distinctive French character. Every February, a **Festival du Voyageur** is held, celebrating the early fur traders with ethnic food, dancing and outdoor activities.

★ **Museum [M].** – *494 Ave Taché. Open daily year-round. Closed legal holidays.* ⚒ ☎204/237-4500. This attractive frame structure of white oak was built for the Grey Nuns in 1846, making it the oldest building in Winnipeg. Inside are scenes portraying the work of this religious order and mementos of St-Boniface residents, in particular of Louis Riel.

Cathedral. – Six churches have stood on this site since 1818. The fifth building was largely destroyed by fire in 1968, except for its large white stone facade, which stands immediately in front of the new cathedral. Designed by Étienne Gaboury, the church features an attractive wooden interior. The **cemetery** contains the grave of Louis Riel.

Precious Blood Church. – Also the work of Gaboury, the little brick and shingle church is built in the shape of an Indian teepee.

ADDITIONAL SIGHTS *Map p 97.*

★ **The Mint.** – *Trans-Can Hwy at Hwy 59. Open May–Aug Mon–Fri. $2.* ☎204/257-3359. This branch of the Royal Canadian Mint is housed in a spectacular half-pyramid structure of rose-coloured reflecting glass. Inside, fountains and exotic plants surround a coin collection and displays on the history of coinage in Canada. The process of minting coins can be viewed.

Riel House. – 🕭 *330 River Rd, St Vital. Open daily Victoria Day–Labour Day; until Sept 30 weekends only.* &. ☎*204/257-1783.* The tiny wooden house was built in 1881 by the Riel family who occupied it until 1968. Although Louis Riel *(p 75)* never actually lived in the house, his body lay in state there after his execution in November, 1885. The residence has been meticulously restored to reflect the period immediately after his death. An interpretive display on the Riel family is presented outside.

Seven Oaks House. – *127 Rupertsland Ave E. Open daily Victoria Day– Labour Day. $1.* ☎*204/ 339-7429.* This nine-room log structure was completed in 1853 by John Inkster, a wealthy merchant. It is believed to be the oldest remaining habitable house in Manitoba. It lies in the parish of West Kildonan, part of the original Selkirk settlement, and near the site of the Seven Oaks Massacre of 1816 *(p 94).* Inkster's store and post office, both furnished with period pieces, stand beside the house.

Zoo. – *In Assiniboine Park. Open daily year-round.* &. ✗ ☎*204/883-3634.* This large and pleasant zoo offers a **tropical house**, home to a variety of monkeys and birds, who thrive among the exotic plants.

Western Canada Aviation Museum. – *Ellice and Ferry roads at airport. Open daily year-round. Closed Christmas & New Year's. $2.50.* &. ☎*204/786-5503.* Over 20 aircraft are on display, ranging from early bush planes to jets. Others can be seen in the process of restoration.

EXCURSIONS

★★ **Lower Fort Garry.** – 🕭 *32km/20mi north of Winnipeg by Hwys 52 and 9.* This stone fort was built between 1830 and 1847 by the Hudson's Bay Company to replace district headquarters at Upper Fort Garry *(p 95),* which was regularly subjected to flooding. An important company post until 1911, the fort received goods from the firm's warehouse at York Factory on Hudson Bay by means of **York boats.** These wooden-hulled boats were much larger and more unwieldy than canoes, but they could be sailed across lakes.

Visit. – *Open daily mid-May–Labour Day. $3.25.* ✗ ☎*204/785-6050.* One-day excursions by boat/bus on the Red River from Winnipeg: *River Rouge Tours* ☎*204/ 947-6843* and *Paddle Wheel Greyline Tours* ☎*204/942-4500.* A visit begins at the **visitor centre,** where an audio-visual presentation *(20min)* forms a good introduction. Restored to reflect life in its mid-19C heyday, the fort itself is surrounded by stone walls. At its centre stands a large and gracious stone dwelling with high chimneys, built to house the offices and residence of the governor. Nearby, the trading store and warehouse display a wide range of goods; note in particular the **furloft** with its splendid collection of furs. On the grounds, a York boat and a Red River cart are on display.

★ **Mennonite Heritage Village.** – *In Steinbach, 61km/38mi southeast of Winnipeg by Trans-Can Hwy and Hwy 12.* This village presents the life of the first Mennonites who settled in Manitoba about 1874. Two groups of Mennonites exist in Canada: the Dutch-Germanic of Ontario and the Russian Mennonites of the West. Extreme pacifists who refuse to fight in any war, both are descended from the Protestant sect led by **Menno Simons.**

Persecuted in 17C Europe, some fled to the US, some to Russia. Meeting persecution again, some of the Americans moved to Ontario and the Russians to Manitoba. The sect numbers approximately 100,000 in Canada—the majority live in Manitoba and Ontario *(p 112).*

Visit. – *Open daily May–Sept.* ✗ ☎*204/326-9661.* Of particular interest is the farmhouse built in characteristic style with the kitchen and stove in the centre (to heat all rooms) and a barn on one end. Other buildings include a church, school and windmill. A museum displays pioneer artifacts and a map of the various Mennonite migrations. The cafeteria serves Mennonite specialities.

Prairie Dog Central. – *Steam train to Grosse Isle. Description p 77.*

"If some countries have too much history,
we have too much geography."
William Lyon Mackenzie King, 1936

Map of Principal Sights p 3

This city, 187km/116mi northeast of Regina on the Yellowhead Highway, was first settled by farmers from York County, Ontario. They were soon followed by a variety of other nationalities, especially Ukrainians. Today, Yorkton is known as a manufacturing centre for agricultural equipment and for stockyards and poultry marketing plants.

Western Development Museum. – *Hwy 16 on west side of city. Open daily Apr–Sept. $3.50.* & *204/783-8361.* The Yorkton branch of this museum is devoted to the various ethnic groups found in Saskatchewan, in particular in the Yorkton area. There are interesting displays on the local Indians and the Métis, and dioramas of Ukrainian, German, Swedish, English and American pioneer homes. In addition, there is a collection of antique steam and gas traction engines and a display on Saskatchewan inventions.

Ontario

CN Tower, Toronto/CN Tower Limited

Canada's richest and most populous province (10,084,885 inhabitants), Ontario is the country's industrial, economic, political and cultural heartland. Stretching from the Great Lakes in the south to Hudson Bay in the north, the province encompasses a wide variety of scenery, the majority of its natural beauty spots being in or near water. Possessing nearly 200,000sq km/70,000sq mi of lakes, Ontario takes its name from the Iroquoian word meaning "shining waters."

GEOGRAPHICAL NOTES

A Land Shaped by Glaciers. – When North America's last ice age receded about 10,000 years ago, it left the region that is now Ontario scarred and completely reshaped. Great holes gouged out of the earth had gradually filled with water and over much of the land, the geological core of the continent was revealed. The Precambrian rocks of this forested, lake-filled terrain known as the **Canadian Shield** *(p 14)* are still exposed over a large part of the province today. Only in the north and in the extreme south are they covered with sedimentary deposits that allow a landscape other than one of rock, water and rock-clinging trees, so typical of the Shield.

The Great Lakes. – These vast expanses of fresh water are one of the most extraordinary legacies of the glaciers. **Lake Superior,** the largest, deepest and coldest of the lakes, was created before the ice ages by a fault in the Shield. The other four (Lakes **Huron, Michigan, Erie** and **Ontario**) were formed by erosion of the original sediment over millions of years. With each advance and retreat of the glaciers, their basins were reshaped. At one time, they drained south to the Gulf of Mexico. Today, their waters flow northeast down the St Lawrence to the Atlantic. All but Lake Michigan border Ontario, giving the province a freshwater shoreline of 3,800km/2,360mi, which greatly affects its climate.

The North. – The large region north of an imaginary line from the Ottawa River to Georgian Bay via Lake Nipissing *(map p 100)* is referred to as "Northern Ontario." Sparsely populated except in areas of rich mineral deposits *(p 102),* the land rarely rises above 460m/1500ft, other than a few higher rocky ridges near Lake Superior. Although a small number of farms exist in the clay belt between Lake Timiskaming and Cochrane, it is an unproductive region agriculturally. However, Northern Ontario does provide a large harvest of wood for the pulp and paper mills, and its many lakes have created a sportsman's paradise.

The South. – The smaller region south of the Ottawa River–Georgian Bay dividing line is the most densely populated and industrialized part of Canada, especially the area at the western end of Lake Ontario, known as the **Golden Horseshoe**. Approximately a third of the region lies directly on the Canadian Shield. This section of the Shield cuts the rest of southern Ontario in two. To the east lies a small agricultural triangle in the forks of the Ottawa and St Lawrence rivers. To the west are the fertile farmlands of the **Niagara Peninsula** and the region called southwestern Ontario. Once, hardwood forests of maple, beech, walnut, elm and ash trees grew here. Today, agriculture dominates Canada's most southerly and climatically favourable region.

Climate. – The climate varies widely in this province. Northern Ontario experiences long, bright but cold winters, and sunny summers with hot days and cool nights. In the south, the winters are less severe owing to the moderating influence of the Great Lakes. The summers are also longer than in the north but much more humid, again due to the Great Lakes.

Average daily temperatures:

	January low	January high	July low	July high
Ottawa	-15°C/5°F	-6°C/21°F	15°C/59°F	26°C/79°F
Toronto	-7°C/18°F	-1°C/30°F	17°C/63°F	27°C/81°F
Thunder Bay	-21°C/-6°F	-8°C/16°F	11°C/52°F	23°C/75°F
Windsor	-9°C/16°F	-1°C/30°F	17°C/63°F	28°C/82°F

Evenly distributed throughout the year in most regions, the amount of precipitation varies over the province (660–1016mm/26–40in) and includes 200–250cm/80–100in of snow in the north. July rainfall is about 100mm/4ins in Ottawa and 76mm/3in in Toronto and Thunder Bay. The number of frost-free days varies from 179 on the Point Pelee peninsula in the south to 60 on the shores of Hudson Bay.

The roads outlined in green are
particularly attractive to follow.

HISTORICAL NOTES

Before the Europeans. – Northern Ontario was inhabited by Indians of the sub-Arctic culture whose subsistence lifestyle in a meagre environment was similar to that of the tribes in the Northwest Territories. The south, on the other hand, was the realm of Indians of the Algonquian and Iroquoian language groups commonly known as the **Eastern Woodlands culture** *(map p 17)*. These tribes generally lived a fairly sedentary life in organized villages around which fields of beans, corn and squash were cultivated. No crop rotation was practised; every ten or so years when the land was exhausted, the village was moved to a new site. Travelling by birchbark canoe in summer, and snowshoe and toboggan in winter, the men hunted and fished extensively, never staying away long from their palisaded villages. Tribes lived in large rectangular huts made of a framework of poles covered with hides. These **long-houses** accommodated several families, each having their own fireplace and sleeping platform (some of the Algonquian tribes built circular dome-shaped huts instead of longhouses). Minimal in summer, clothing consisted in winter of deerskin leggings, fur robes and moccasins.

Iroquoian society was matrilineal (descent was from the mother) and the women of these tribes wielded considerable power, selecting the male chiefs, for example. In contrast, Algonquian society was patrilineal. Rich traditions of distinct religious and mythological beliefs and practices permeated both groups. To frighten away disease or other evils, the Iroquoian **False Face Society** performed dances in elaborate masks of wood and human hair. Many of these tribes grew militant, owing, in particular, to their increasing dependency on European trade. Composed of five tribes (Mohawk, Onondaga, Seneca, Cayuga, Oneida), the **League of the Iroquois** warred repeatedly with the early French settlers, and defeated and dispersed the **Huron**, another Iroquoian group. Today, little remains of the Eastern Woodlands Indians' former way of life.

Part of New France. – The region that is now Ontario was crisscrossed by most of the 17C and 18C French explorers. First to visit was **Étienne Brulé**, soon followed by **Champlain** himself, **Radisson** and **Groseilliers** in their search for a route to Hudson Bay, Marquette and Jolliet in their search for a river flowing west from Lake Superior, and **La Salle** on his famous trip down the Mississippi. Fur trade was the main reason for exploration, and trading posts were set up all over the province. There were also two attempts at permanent settlement. In 1639, the **Jesuits** established a mission on the shores of Georgian Bay to convert the Huron to Christianity. Settlement lasted only until 1650 because of fierce attacks by the Iroquois who captured and martyred five of the Jesuit fathers. Then in the early 18C, farms were laid out on the shores of the Detroit River in southwest Ontario. At the time of the fall of New France, about 400 people were living there.

At the same time, the **Hudson's Bay Company** was establishing itself in the province's northern section. In 1673, a post was founded at **Moosonee** on James Bay, which claims to be Ontario's oldest settlement. Despite these attempts at settlement, Ontario, or Upper Canada as it was known, was still very much the realm of Indians at the time of the American Revolution.

The Arrival of the Loyalists. – When the American colonies revolted against British rule in 1775, many people refused to join the rebels. Called Loyalists (or "Tories," to use the American term) primarily because of their loyalty to King George III, they may have numbered as many as 1.25 million—a third of the population. When the American Revolution ended, Loyalists found themselves very unpopular; most were forced to leave their homes and flee for their lives.

An estimated 80,000 Loyalists settled in Canada—in Nova Scotia, New Brunswick, Prince Edward Island, the Eastern Townships of Quebec, the St Lawrence Valley and the Niagara Peninsula. They also fled to England and the West Indies, but Canada was popular because they were promised free land. Among the Loyalists in Ontario were Indians of the **Six Nations Iroquois Confederacy** (the Tuscarora joined the five-nation Iroquois league in 1722) who, under their great chief **Joseph Brant** (p 105), had fought for the British. The arrival of such a great number of people—one of the largest mass movements of the time—created, almost overnight, the province of Upper Canada (Lower Canada being present-day Quebec). In 1791, a separate administration was established in Niagara-on-the-Lake and later in Toronto. Although many more immigrants have settled in Ontario since that date, the influence of the descendants of these Loyalists is still strong in Ontario today.

Meanwhile, the waters and lakes of the province were alive with the brigades of fur traders of both Hudson's Bay and North West companies. Indeed, the latter set up its great rendezvous point at Fort William on Lake Superior.

American Invasion. – In 1812, the Americans, infuriated by British high-handedness on the open seas, declared war and invaded Canada, hoping to seize it quickly while the British were preoccupied fighting Napoleon in Europe. They were confident that the inhabitants would rush to join their standard. Instead, they found the population of Upper Canada united in its dislike of the US, if not in its loyalty to Britain. The ensuing war was fought mainly in Upper Canada. Naval encounters occurred on the Great Lakes, during which Toronto was looted and burned. There was much fighting in the Niagara Peninsula where **Isaac Brock** and **Laura Secord** engraved their names in Canadian history; along the St Lawrence, particularly at Crysler's Farm (p 145); and in the province of Quebec at Chateauguay. Battles were often indecisive, but the Americans were kept out of Canada, and in Ontario at least, a sense of nationhood was born.

Toward Confederation. – As a result of the war, the British government decided to encourage immigration to Upper Canada to bolster the population against further possible American attack. Free land was offered and, since economic distress in Britain was great, approximately 1.5 million people crossed the Atlantic from 1820 to 1840 to seek a better life in Ontario. Farms, villages and towns sprang up where previously there had been only bush. The face of the province was changed immeasurably.

These new settlers brought not only their industry but also their political ideas. Fresh from a struggle to promote electoral reform in England, they found Canada backward. Real political power lay not with the elected assembly but with the governor and a council dominated by several well-connected groups known as the **Family Compact**. Opposition to this system was led by a fiery Scot, **William Lyon Mackenzie**, who eventually resorted to armed revolt in 1837. While the uprising was quickly suppressed by colonial authorities, it did persuade Britain to grant "responsible government" (p 18). In 1841, Upper and Lower Canada were reunited as the Province of Canada in a kind of confederation with equal representation for each. This union led to a movement to unite all British colonies in North America, led by an Ontario politician, **John A. Macdonald** and his Quebec colleague, **George-Étienne Cartier**. When union (see Confederation p 18) was achieved in 1867, Upper Canada officially took the name of Ontario.

Since Confederation, Ontario has grown enormously in population, attracting immigrants from all over the world. This large influx, added to the province's abundant natural resources and strategic location in relation to the rest of Canada and the US, led to Ontario's rapid industrial development and its pre-eminence in modern Canada.

RESOURCES AND INDUSTRIES

Agriculture. – Farming of various types has been practised in Ontario since earliest times, and it is still an important activity today. The southern part of the province boasts some of the richest soil in Canada as well as the country's longest frost-free season. Dairy farming is the predominant activity in the southeast corner, along the shores of Lake Ontario and in the Upper Thames Valley. Other livestock are raised in the Georgian Bay–Upper Grand River region. Soybean and Field corn are the staple crops of the southwest, but crops such as sweet corn, tomatoes and other vegetables are also grown. The section of the Niagara Peninsula on the shores of Lake Ontario sheltered by the Niagara Escarpment is Canada's most important **fruit-growing** region. Not only are peaches, cherries, strawberries and grapes grown, but a **winemaking** industry thrives.

Mining. – No other province is as rich in minerals as Ontario, one of the world's largest suppliers of nickel, and a major producer of gold, silver, platinum, uranium, zinc, copper and a range of structural materials. The province is an important source of salt, gypsum and nepheline syenite. Ontario produces more non-fuel minerals for commercial use than any other Canadian province.

The vast majority of these minerals come from the Canadian Shield, which covers much of Ontario. The **Sudbury Basin** (p 127) is the largest single source of nickel in the world. Nickel from Sudbury accounts for 66 percent of Canada's total production, over 70 percent of which is exported to the US. Platinum, copper, cobalt, silver, gold, selenium, sulphur compounds and tellurium are also extracted from the ore. In 1903, the great **silver** deposits of Cobalt were found during the building of a railway, followed by the discovery of **gold** in the Timmins-Kirkland Lake region. Gold was found at Red Lake to the west as well, and iron ore at Wawa, taken to Sault Ste Marie for smelting. During World War II, the iron ore deposits of Atikokan were developed, and a huge mining boom ensued in the wake of the war. In the 1950s, the vast **Manitouwadge** field of copper, zinc and silver deposits was exploited, and the uranium of Elliot Lake was tapped for the first time. In the 1960s, the Timmins-Kirkland Lake region was revived by zinc, copper, lead and iron finds to replace the exploited gold. Most notable was the Kidd Creek copper-zinc-silver discovery. Recent gold discoveries at Detour Lake and Hemlo continue to demonstrate the wealth of the Shield.

Not all of Ontario's minerals are found in the Shield, however. Southwestern Ontario has produced a small amount of oil and gas since 1859. **Salt** is mined extensively at Goderich *(p 107)*, and gypsum and a range of structural materials are found in sizable quantities. Mining is an essential base of Ontario's economy, reflected by the number of mining interests listed on the Toronto Stock Exchange.

Forestry, Fishing, Furs and Hydro-Electricity. – These four resources significantly affect Ontario's economy. The province is still largely covered with forest, despite serious depletion in the last century. Today, pulp, paper and sawn lumber are the main products, and Ontario ranks third after British Columbia and Quebec in the value of production. The province leads the rest of Canada in the value of fish taken from inland waters, thanks to the Great Lakes. Fur production, the province's oldest industry, is still carried on both by trapping and fur farms. The development of hydro power has accompanied the province's overall economic growth in this century, especially since Ontario has little oil or gas and no coal. The harnessing of the Niagara River, the St Lawrence and other waters was essential for industrial development. Today, Ontario ranks third after Quebec and British Columbia in hydro-electric output.

Manufacturing. – About half of Canada's total output of finished goods comes from Ontario. The province's largest industry, manufacturing has made Ontario Canada's industrial heart. Motor vehicles and parts rank first in production value, but also important are the production of heavy electrical machinery, agricultural implements and rubber, iron, steel and chemical goods as well as printing, publishing and food processing. Most of these industries are concentrated in the Golden Horseshoe around Toronto and Hamilton—Canada's largest marketing area. The region's high industrial ranking in North America is partly due to Hamilton's vast primary iron and steel industry. Other important industrial regions are: Windsor (motor vehicles), Sarnia (petro-chemicals) and Sault Ste Marie (iron and steel).

St Lawrence Seaway. – Cheap water transportation on this system of lakes, rivers and canals has been of unparalleled importance to the development of Ontario. Raw materials are transported to smelters and factories; finished products are moved to markets. Heaviest traffic is among the Upper Lakes; the locks at Sault Ste Marie, for example, are busier than the Panama Canal.

Principal Festivals

Feb	**Winterlude**	*Ottawa*
Mar	**Maple Syrup Festival**	*Elmira*
Apr–Nov	**Shaw Festival** *(p 115)*	*Niagara-on-the-Lake*
May	**Blossom Festival**	*Niagara Falls*
May	**Canadian Tulip Festival**	*Ottawa*
May–Nov	**Stratford Festival** *(p 127)*	*Stratford*
Jun	**Metro International Caravan** *(p 132)*	*Toronto*
Jun–Jul	**International Freedom Festival**	*Windsor*
Jul	**Great Rendezvous** *(p 128)*	*Thunder Bay*
	Molson Indy	*Toronto*
Jul–Aug	**Rockhound Gemboree**	*Bancroft*
	Glengarry Highland Games	*Maxville*
	Caribana *(p 132)*	*Toronto*
Aug	**Six Nations Native Pageant** *(p 105)*	*Brantford*
	Summerfolk	*Owen Sound*
Aug–Sept	**Canadian National Exhibition** *(p 132)*	*Toronto*
Sept	**Festival of Festivals**	*Toronto*
	Niagara Grape and Wine Festival	*St Catharines*
Oct	**Oktoberfest** *(p 112)*	*Kitchener-Waterloo*
Nov	**Royal Agricultural Winter Fair**	*Toronto*
Nov–Jan	**Winter Festival of Lights**	*Niagara Falls*

Practical Information

How to get there. – **Air** service to Toronto's Pearson International Airport is offered by major domestic and international carriers. Inter-Canadian (☎800/776-3000) and its affiliates provide connections to regions throughout the province. **VIA Rail** Canada links many cities within the province and is the starting point for the Transcontinental route to Vancouver. In Canada consult the telephone directory for the nearest office; from the US ☎800/561-3949 (toll-free). Major **bus** lines are Voyageur Colonial, Gray Coach Lines and Greyhound (for local numbers consult the telephone directory).

Accommodation and Tourist Information. – The government tourist office produces annually updated guides: *Accommodation, Camping, Country Inns, Cruises, Adventures* and *Fishing Packages. Travel Ontario* suggests driving tours, events, and gives general travel tips. All publications and a map are available free of charge from: **Ontario Travel**, Queen's Park, Toronto, ON, M7A 2E5 ☎800/668-2746 (toll-free Canada/US). For information on campground vacancies, spring blossoms and fall colours, or skiing conditions ☎416/314-0998.

Road Regulations. – Speed limits, unless otherwise posted, are 100km/h (60mph) on freeways, 90km/h (55mph) on the Trans-Canada routes, and 80km/h (50mph) on most highways. The speed limit in cities and towns is 50km/h (30mph). **Seat belt** use is mandatory. For listings of the **Canadian Automobile Association (CAA)** consult the local telephone directory.

Time Zone. – Most of Ontario is on Eastern Standard Time. Daylight Saving Time is observed from the first Sunday in April to the last Sunday in October. In the western third of the province (west of longitude 90) Central Standard Time applies.

Taxes.– In addition to the national 7% GST *(rebate information p 242),* Ontario levies an 8% provincial sales tax, a 10% alcoholic beverages tax and a 5% accommodation tax. Non-residents can request rebates of the provincial tax from Retail Sales Tax, 2300 Yonge St, Toronto, ON, M4P 1H6 ☎416/487-1361.

Liquor Laws. – The legal drinking age is 19. Liquor is sold in government stores.

Provincial Holiday *(see National Holidays p 240)*
Civic Holiday............................... 1st Monday in August

Outdoor Activities. – An abundance of lakes and waterways offers the outdoor enthusiast a wide variety of **water sports**. Scenic routes to explore by boat are the Rideau Canal and lakes from Ottawa to Kingston, and the Trent-Severn system from Trenton to Georgian Bay via the Kawartha Lakes and Lake Simcoe. **Canoeing** is one of the most popular outdoor activities ranging from lake and river to white-water canoeing.
Many outfitters offer an array of excursions that include transportation, lodging, equipment and the service of experienced guides. The best-known regions are: **Algonquin Provincial Park** (☎705/633-5572), which has 1,600km/1,000mi of canoe routes and **Quetico Provincial Park** (☎807/597-2735), through which the Boundary Waters Fur Trade Canoe Route passes with 43 portages along 523km/325mi. For additional information contact the Canadian Recreational Canoeing Assocation, 1029 Hyde Park Rd, Hyde Park, ON, N0M 1Z0 ☎519/473-2109.
Hiking is a favoured activity during the summer. The famous Bruce Trail follows the Niagara Escarpment for 692km/430mi across the southern part of the province *(map p 100)*. Hikers are lead through wilderness on the Coastal Trail along the shores of Lake Superior in **Pukaskwa National Park** (☎807/229-0801).
Ontario is a fisherman's paradise particularly in the north, where many fly-in lodges arrange **fishing** expeditions. Non-residents must obtain a license available from local sporting good stores. For information on seasons, catch and possession limits contact the Ministry of Natural Resources, Information Centre, 900 Bay St, Toronto, ON, M7A 2C1 ☎416/314-1177.
In winter, cross-country skiing and snowmobiling are prevalent recreational activities. Thunder Bay, Blue Mountain, Burrie and Searchmont are among the province's popular alpine ski centres.
For more information on outdoor activities contact Ontario Travel *(see above)*.

Special Excursions. – Several **white-water rafting** excursions, led by experienced guides, are available on the Ottawa River. Packages include equipment and meals. Season: May–Sept. Raft trip 4-6hrs. Rates start at $76. Accommodation & camping extra. Wilderness Tours, Box 89, Beachburg, ON, K0J 1C0 ☎613/646-2291.
A fascinating all-day train trip, the **Polar Bear Express**, takes the traveller from Cochrane across terrain of giant forests, bushland and muskeg through the Arctic watershed to Moosonee on Hudson Bay. Arriving around midday, visitors have ample time to tour Ontario's oldest English settlement, founded by the Hudson's Bay Company in 1673 on Moose Factory Island. Departs mid-Jun–Labour Day Sat–Thur 8:30am, returns to Cochrane at 9:20pm. Connecting bus service to Timmins. Round-trip $44. Reservations required. ✕ &. Ontario Northland ☎416/314-3750 or 705/472-4500.
Luxury steamboat cruising, retracing routes of early explorers through inland waters, can be enjoyed aboard **MV Canadian Empress**. Cruises include shore-visits to historic sites and to Ottawa, Montreal, Quebec City and other cities. Departs Kingston mid-May–mid-Oct. 2-5 day trips available. &. For schedules & reservations contact St Lawrence Cruise Lines, Inc, 253 Ontario St, Kingston, ON, K7L 2Z4 ☎613/549-8091.

Named for Six Nations chief Joseph Brant, this manufacturing city is also famous as the family home of Alexander Graham Bell.

Brantford stands on what was once part of a grant of land in the valley of the Grand River given to the Six Nations Indians *(p 102)* in 1784 by the British government. Led by Chief Brant, these Indians fought on the British side in the American Revolution and, like other Loyalists at the end of the war, were forced to flee the US. To show his personal gratitude to his Indian subjects, George III provided money for the construction of a chapel known as **Her Majesty's Chapel of the Mohawks** (it is of course "His" if the monarch is male), the oldest Protestant church in Ontario *(on Mohawk St 3km/2mi southeast by Greenwich St; open daily Jul–Sept)*. European settlers purchased land from the Indians in 1830, and the present city was founded, retaining the old name of the location—Brant's Ford, because the chief had crossed the river there. The Indian reserve still exists to the south, though much reduced in size. It is the scene every year of the **Six Nations Native Pageant** during which the Iroquois tribes commemorate their history and culture *(Aug)*.

Telephone City. – **Alexander Graham Bell** (1847-1922) moved to Ontario from Scotland with his parents in 1870. Soon afterwards, he took a job as a teacher of the deaf in Boston, a profession he shared with his father. While trying to find a means of reproducing sounds visibly for his deaf pupils, he solved the problem by transmitting and receiving speech along an electrified wire. From this solution, he developed the telephone, an idea he conceived in Brantford in 1874 while visiting his parents. He tested his invention in Boston the next year. The first "long distance" call was made from Brantford when Bell, in Paris, Ontario *(about 11km/7mi away)*, was able to hear his father's voice. The telephone's invention made Bell a fortune, enabling him to undertake research, in addition to his work for the deaf. Much of this research was carried out at his summer home in Baddeck, Nova Scotia *(p 204)*.

SIGHTS *3hrs*

★ **Bell Homestead.** – *94 Tutela Heights Rd. From downtown, take Colborne St W across Grand River, turn left on Mount Pleasant St and left again on Tutela Heights Rd. Open daily mid-Jun–Labour Day. Off-season Tue–Sun. Closed Nov–Mar. $1.* ☎519/756-6220. This pleasant house with its covered veranda is furnished much as it would have been in Bell's day, with many original pieces. There is an interesting display on his life, inventions and research.

Next door stands a smaller clapboard structure moved to this spot from the centre of Brantford. Among other things, it housed the first telephone business office in Canada. Inside, there is an early telephone exchange and displays on the development of the telephone since Bell's day.

Museum of the Woodland Indian. – *In Woodland Indian Cultural and Educational Centre, 184 Mohawk St near chapel (see above). Open daily year-round. Closed Christmas–New Year's. $3.* ☎519/759-2650. This museum houses an interesting collection of artifacts depicting the way of life of the Eastern Woodland Indians of which the Six Nations Indians are a part.

The country around this small manufacturing centre was first settled by black slaves who had escaped their masters in the US and fled to freedom in British North America. Among them was **Josiah Henson**, who arrived in Ontario with his family in 1830. With the aid of donations from Britain, Henson purchased land in the Dresden area, established a refuge for fugitives from slavery and founded a school to teach children skills their parents had never learned. Unable to write, Henson dictated the story of his life *(The Life of Josiah Henson–Formerly a Slave)*, which was subsequently published. This manuscript so impressed **Harriet Beecher Stowe** that she met him and used him as the model for her influential novel, *Uncle Tom's Cabin*.

★ **Uncle Tom's Cabin Historic Site.** – *1.6km/1mile west off Hwy 21. Open daily mid-May–Sept. $3.* ☎519/683-2978. This collection of wooden buildings includes Henson's house (Uncle Tom's Cabin), a simple church where he preached, a fugitive slave's house and some agricultural buildings. In the museum, there are such items as posters advertising slave sales, a ball and chain similar to those slaves were forced to wear to prevent escape, slave whips, handcuffs and clubs. A recorded commentary explains the exhibits and tells Henson's story. His grave is outside.

Named for George IV of England, this immense bay is almost a lake in itself, cut off from the rest of Lake Huron by the Bruce Peninsula and Manitoulin Island. The variety of its landscapes makes Georgian Bay a popular area to visit.

Immortalized by the Group of Seven painters, the eastern and northern shorelines are wild and rocky with numerous indentations and thousands of islands. Some of these islands are mere slabs of rock with perhaps a few wind-swept pines or other hardy plants maintaining a precarious hold. The western, and part of the southern, shores form a section of the **Niagara Escarpment** with one gently rolling slope and one steep escarpment. This ridge of limestone crosses Ontario from Niagara Falls, mounts the Bruce Peninsula, submerges and then resurfaces to form Manitoulin and other islands, and ends in Wisconsin. A complete contrast to these rocky shores, the coast along the western side of the Midland peninsula has long sandy stretches, especially in the region of Wasaga Beach. Summer cottages line its shores and islands. Most attractive sailing and boating country, it is more than a resort area, however, as Owen Sound, Collingwood, Midland, Port McNicoll and Parry Sound are fair-sized ports with grain elevators and considerable light industry. Located in the southeast corner of the bay are 59 islands that form Georgian Bay Islands National Park, established in 1929.

Huronia. – Étienne Brulé, one of Champlain's men, visited Georgian Bay in 1610. Fur traders and Jesuits soon followed, arriving via the 1,300km/800mi canoe route from Quebec. Eager to convert Huron Indians to Christianity, the Jesuits built a mission post called Sainte-Marie near the present site of Midland in 1639. At this time, the Huron were suffering frequent attacks from the Iroquois tribes to the south and, weakened as they were from the "white man's diseases," they were unable to resist the onslaught. Caught in the middle, several Jesuit fathers were killed after suffering incredible torture. The atrocities led to the abandonment of Sainte-Marie in 1649. After the Jesuits' return to Quebec, and the Huron's defeat, peace was restored until the early 19C when warfare erupted between the British and Americans over control of the Great Lakes. With peace, the present borders were established, and the region has seen no fighting since.

HISTORICAL SIGHTS

★ **Midland.** – Pop 13,865. *Map p 100.* This busy city on the bay is well known for its numerous historical and natural attractions.

★★ **Sainte-Marie among the Hurons.** – *5km/3mi east on Hwy 12. Open mid-May–mid-Oct daily 10am–5pm; Moon of Wintertime (Dec 6) & Christmas. $5.75.* ✗ ⅙ ☎705/526-7838. Consisting of 22 structures enclosed within a wooden palisade, the mission established by the Jesuits in 1639 and destroyed by them before their retreat in 1649, has been reconstructed.

An audio-visual presentation (*17min*) explains the mission's history and should be viewed before the rest of the visit. The chapel, forge, sawpit, carpentry shop, residences and native area are "peopled" by historical interpreters in 17C costume. The mission is divided into separate sections for the Jesuits, the lay workers (called *donnes*) and the Huron. A rectangular, bark-covered longhouse and a hospital where the Jesuits tended the sick have been constructed in the native section. In the **museum★★**, slide shows illustrate Sainte-Marie in the context of its times. Topics such as 17C Europe, New France, the Jesuits and the Huron are explained in excellent displays.

Beside Sainte-Marie is the **Wye Marsh Wildlife Centre** (*open daily year-round; $4.50;* ☎705/526-7809) where nature trails, a boardwalk and an observation tower allow visitors to appreciate the life of a marsh. There are also slide and film shows, and a display hall.

★ **Martyrs' Shrine.** – *5km/3mi east of Midland on Hwy 12 near Wildlife Centre.* This twin-spired stone church was built in 1926 as a memorial to the eight Jesuit martyrs of New France, who were declared saints in 1930. They were killed by the Iroquois between 1642 and 1649, the first five while they were missionaries at Sainte-Marie. On the front portico stand **statues** of Jean de Brébeuf and Gabriel Lalemant, the two Jesuits who were severely torture before death. The church has a striking **interior** with wood panelling and a roof of sandalwood from British Columbia.

★ **Huron Indian Village.** – *In Little Lake Park on King St. Open daily mid-May–mid-Nov. Off-season Mon–Fri. $4.75.* ✗ ⅙ ☎705/526-2844. This village is a replica of a 16C Huron community. After viewing an introductory **film** (*15min*), visitors pass through the wooden palisade to examine examples of the long rectangular bark-covered frame houses in which the Huron lived communally. Animal skins, plants and herbs are hanging to dry. The medicine man's house, a sweat bath, storage pits and a canoe-making site can also be visited.

Beside the village in the park is the **Huronia Museum** (*same as village*), which has an art gallery, a collection of Indian artifacts and pioneer displays.

★ **Penetanguishene.** – *Pop 6,643. 12km/8mi west of Midland by Rtes 12 and 93.* The southern entrance to this town, which has a large French-speaking community, is guarded by two angels symbolizing the harmony between the Huron and French cultures.

★ **Naval and Military Establishments.** – *At end of Church St. Open daily mid-May–Labour Day; Christmas Events. $5.75.* ✗ ⅙ ☎705/526-7838. On a pleasant site above Penetang harbour stands this reconstruction of a British Naval dockyard and military garrison established here after the War of 1812.

An audio-visual presentation (*15min*) in the visitor centre presents the site's history. In the Naval Establishment, which existed from 1817 to 1834, costumed interpreters evoke the life of the commanding officer and his staff who worked in the naval storehouse and dockyard. At the wharf, there is a replica of the schooner, *Bee.* The military garrison was located here from 1828 to 1856. The original officers' quarters and the restored home of the fort adjutant can be visited.

★ **Wasaga Beach.** – Pop 6,224. *Map p 100.* This popular resort is well known for its 14km/9mi stretch of white sand.

★ **Nancy Island Historic Site.** – *In Wasaga Beach Provincial Park, Mosley St off Hwy 92. Open daily mid-May–Labour Day.* ⅙ ☎705/429-2728. The museum stands on a small island near the mouth of the Nottawasaga River. The island was created by silt collecting around the hull of a sunken schooner, the **Nancy**. During the War of

1812, the vessel was requisitioned by British forces to act as a supply ship for their military bases. After the American victory at the naval battle of Lake Erie, this British ship—the only one left on the Upper Lakes—was tracked down and sunk by the Americans while hiding in this spot on the Nottawasaga.

In 1927, her hull was recovered from the silt and is now displayed in the museum building with explanations of its history, and that of the War of 1812.

NATURAL SIGHTS   *Map p 100*

★ **Thirty Thousand Islands.** – An excellent means of appreciating the natural beauty of Georgian Bay and its many islands is one of three boat cruises: from **Midland** town dock *(departs daily May 9–Oct 12; summer 4 cruises daily; round-trip 2hrs 30min; $13; commentary on board; reservations suggested; ✗ ᐊ PMCL Boat Cruises ☎705/526-0161);* from Penetanguishene town dock *(departs daily late-Jun–Labour Day; round-trip 3hrs; commentary on board; reservations suggested; ✗ ᐊ Argee Boat Cruises ☎705/549-7795);* and from **Parry Sound** town dock *(departs daily Jun–mid-Oct; summer 4 cruises daily; round-trip 3hrs; reservations suggested; ✗ ᐊ 30,000 Island Cruise Lines ☎705/746-2311).*

★ **Tobermory.** – This tiny village is located at the tip of the Bruce Peninsula where the Niagara Escarpment becomes submerged and the waters of Georgian Bay meet those of Lake Huron. Tobermory provides hundreds of protected moorings around its double harbour known as Big Tub and Little Tub. The clear waters, underwater rock formations and number of old shipwrecks also attract divers. The **SS Chi-Cheemaun** provides regular ferry service to Manitoulin Island *(departs daily May–mid-Oct; summer 5 crossings daily; 2hrs; $23/car plus $10.50/adult; commentary on board; ✗ ᐊ Ontario Northland Marine Services ☎705/596-2510).*

★ **Bruce Peninsula National Park.** – ☞ *Open year-round; visitor centre on Little Tub harbour; open daily Jun–Labour Day;* ᐊ ☎519/596-2233. Established in 1987, this national park is known for its trails along the spectacular Niagara Escarpment. There is a 242-site campground at Cyprus Lake, 15km/9mi south of Tobermory.

★ **Fathom Five National Marine Park.** – This "underwater" preserve, Canada's first national marine park, encompasses 19 islands and the treacherous waters off Tobermory. The remains of 19 known wrecks of sail and steam vessels from mid-19C to 20C can be viewed close up with scuba-diving or snorkeling equipment, or from above by **glass-bottomed boat** *(departs daily May–Sept; round-trip 1hr 30min; drop-off at Flowerpot Island possible; $11; commentary on board;* ᐊ *Blue Heron ☎519/596-2250).*

Tiny **Flowerpot Island★**, the best known of the park islands, was at one time completely covered by the waters of Lake Huron. Caves high up in the rocks and two coastal islets, or rock pillars, known as the **flowerpots,** are evidence of water erosion. These pink and grey pillars have a limestone base that has been eroded and a harder dolomite top. They stand 15m/50ft and 11m/35ft high and can be closely approached by boat or on foot from the island. The tour boats circle the island, affording good views of the flowerpots.

Beausoleil Island. – *Part of the Georgian Bay Islands National Park. Access by private boat or water taxi only from Honey Harbour (about 40km/25mi northeast of Midland via Rte 12, Hwy 69 and Rte 5). Information & maps available at park office in Honey Harbour* ☎705/756-2415. There are walking trails and an interpretation centre *(open summer only)* on this island.

The Blue Mountains. – *56km/35mi from Wasaga Beach to Meaford by Rte 26.* This drive is pretty, with the waters of Georgian Bay on one side of the road and the Blue Mountains, the highest part of the Niagara Escarpment, on the other.

> *"The Americans are our best friends whether we like it or not."*
> Robert Thompson, in the House of Commons, 1960s

★ GODERICH   Pop 7,452

Map p 100

Built on a bluff above the point where the Maitland River joins **Lake Huron**, this town was founded in 1828 as the terminus of the Huron Road, a right-of-way built in the early 19C to encourage settlement. The town has wide, tree-lined streets that radiate like the spokes of a wheel from central, octagonal **Court House Square.** Goderich has a sizeable harbour and several industries, including rock-salt mining.

Huron County Museum. – *110 North St. Open daily year-round. Sept–Apr closed legal holidays. $2.50.* ᐊ ☎519/524-2686. All aspects of the region's history are depicted in this museum. Outside stands a stump puller used by pioneer farmers in clearing their land.

Huron Historic Gaol. – *181 Victoria St N. Open daily May–Labour Day. Off-season Sun–Fri. Closed Dec–Mar. $2.* ☎519/524-6971. This unusual 150-year-old octagonal stone structure housed the county jail *(gaol is British spelling)* until 1972. The governor's house constructed in 1901 can also be visited.

★ GRAVENHURST   Pop 9,988

Map p 100

This attractive town with its tree-lined streets, elegant houses and opera house on the main street (now a summer theatre) lies at the southern end of the **Muskoka Lakes**, Ontario's most popular vacation region. Lake Joseph, Lake Rosseau and Lake Muskoka itself, on which Gravenhurst stands, are picturesque bodies of water with indented shorelines and numerous islands.

Birthplace of Dr Bethune. – Gravenhurst is the birthplace of Norman Bethune, surgeon, inventor, advocate of socialized medicine and national hero of the Chinese people. Born in Gravenhurst in 1890, the son of a Presbyterian minister, Bethune studied in Toronto. He then practised in Detroit, where he contracted tuberculosis. Confined to a sanitorium in Saranac Lake, he learned of a little-known method of treating tuberculosis by collapsing a lung and insisted that this operation be performed on him. The operation was successful. Between 1928 and 1936, he worked as a chest surgeon in Montreal but, disillusioned with the lack of interest in socialized medicine in Canada, he departed for Spain to fight on the Republican side in the civil war. There, Bethune set up the first mobile blood-transfusion unit to treat soldiers where they fell. In 1938, he went to China and worked alongside the Chinese Communists fighting the Japanese. The surgeon organized a medical service for the Chinese army, but died of blood poisoning late in 1939. Fame in his own country stemmed from Bethune's status as a hero to the Chinese.

★ **Bethune Memorial House.** – *235 John St. Open daily year-round. Closed legal holidays in winter.* ⚅ ☎705/687-4261. The doctor's birthplace contains several rooms restored to their 1890s appearance, and an excellent **interpretive display** in three languages (English, French and Chinese) on his life and importance. A visitor centre offers an orientation video *(15min)*.

Steamship cruises from Gravenhurst's wharf aboard the **RMS Segwun** enable visitors to appreciate the beauty of the lakes and see some of the summer homes along their shores *(daily cruises Jun 13–Oct 12; round-trip 1hr 30min to 7hrs. $12-$45.95; dinner cruise 3hrs 30min; $42.50; reservations suggested; Muskoka Lakes Navigation ☎705/687-6667).*

★ HALIBURTON HIGHLANDS

Map p 101

Wooded hills and lovely lakes have made the Haliburton Highlands of central Ontario a popular resort area. The small towns of Minden and Haliburton are the chief centres. One popular activity is canoeing, because many of the lakes are interconnected and the rivers flow south to the Kawartha Lakes. To the north is **Algonquin Park**, an impressive wilderness famous for having inspired the painter Tom Thomson and for its web of canoe routes.

★**Kanawa International Museum.** – *29km/18mi north of Minden by Hwy 35. Open daily by appointment May–Oct. $2.* ☎705/489-2644. A series of log buildings houses this fascinating collection of some 600 canoes, kayaks and rowing craft of all types and construction. Examples of craft used by various native peoples include West Coast dugouts, Inuit kayaks, a Kutenal canoe from central British Columbia and a Mandan Bull boat used by the Prairie Indians to cross rivers. Several finely crafted canoes made by immigrant artisans are displayed. In addition, there are paddles, models, related artifacts and an art collection depicting watercraft.

★ HAMILTON   Pop 318,499

Maps pp 100 and 109   Tourist Office ☎416/546-2666

The city of Hamilton, "Canada's Pittsburgh," lies at the extreme western end of Lake Ontario. This city has a fine land-locked harbour bounded on the lake side by a sand bar. A canal has been cut through the bar to enable ships of the seaway to reach port with their loads of iron ore for Hamilton's huge steel mills. The sand bar is crossed by Burlington Skyway, part of the **Queen Elizabeth Way (QEW)**, which connects Toronto with Niagara Falls. Hamilton is set on the Niagara Escarpment, which swings around the end of Lake Ontario at this point, rising steeply to 76m/250ft in the city. Known locally as the "mountain," it provides pleasant parks and views.

★ **City Centre.** – Hamilton has a modern downtown area *(along Main Street between Bay and James streets)* with many attractive buildings, in particular City Hall **[H]**; the Education Centre; the Art Gallery; and Hamilton Place, a cultural centre with two theatres. A few blocks west is **Hess Village★** *(junction Hess and George streets)*, a collection of attractive older homes now containing fashionable boutiques, restaurants and cafes.
Also in the vicinity is the **farmers' market** *(York Blvd; open year-round Tue, Thur, Fri, Sat)*, one of Ontario's largest indoor markets selling the produce of the Niagara peninsula, Canada's chief fruit-growing region.

★ **Art Gallery.** – *Open year-round Tue–Sun. Closed legal holidays. $2.* ⚅ ☎416/527-6610. This distinctive concrete structure stands across a plaza from City Hall. Its attractive interior is open and airy with wooden ceilings. Changing exhibits from its extensive permanent collection are displayed, as well as visiting shows.

Whitehern [A]. – *Visit by guided tour (1hr) only daily Jun–Labour Day. Off-season Tue–Sun. $2.* ☎416/522-5664. In small but pleasant gardens surrounded by Hamilton's city centre, this Georgian house was the residence of three generations of the

McQuestern family until 1968. It reflects the life of a prosperous Ontario family between the years 1840 and 1960. The McQuesterns, who settled in Hamilton in the early 19C, were pioneers in the heavy industry that is now Hamilton's lifeblood. Involved in public life, they inspired such projects as the Royal Botanical Gardens and the Niagara Parkway. The house contains the original furnishings.

★ **Dundurn Castle.** – *Open daily year-round. Closed Christmas & New Year's. $3.75.* ♿ ☎*416/522-5313.* This grand stone house with its neoclassical portico entry stands on a hill overlooking Hamilton Bay. A showplace of 19C privilege, it illustrates the wealth and power of the Family Compact.

The residence was completed in 1835 by Sir Allan Napier MacNab—soldier, lawyer, politician and member of the Family Compact. In 1838, he was knighted by Queen Victoria for fighting against Mackenzie. From 1854 to 1856, MacNab served as prime minister of the Province of Canada.

The interior is elaborately furnished, though the contents are not original. Of particular interest is the basement, the domain of the army of servants needed to run a house of this magnitude in the mid-19C. (MacNab actually died in debt, however.) The house is situated in Dundurn Park which commands a good **view** of the bay and the city. A small military museum and a summer theatre for children are situated in the grounds.

★ **Royal Botanical Gardens.** – *Open daily year-round. Closed Christmas & New Year's. $4.25* ⚒♿ ☎*416/527-1158.* These gardens occupy 1,000ha/2,700 acres of land at the western tip of Lake Ontario. Much of this area is natural parkland with walking trails. Several featured gardens are worth visiting *(car required).*

At the Royal Botanical Gardens Centre, the **Mediterranean garden** can be visited *(open daily; $2.50).* This conservatory houses vegetation from the five regions of the world that have this climate (the Mediterranean Rim, Southern Africa, Australia, California and Chile). Across the road, the **rose garden**★ has magnificent displays *(Jun–Oct).* Nearby, the **Laking garden** has irises and peonies *(May–Jun),* and herbaceous perennials *(May–Oct).* Farther afield, the **rock garden**★ is a whirl of colour in summer, with its flowering plants and shrubs set amid water and rocks. In the arboretum *(return along Rte 2/6 and turn right),* the **lilac garden** is lovely *(late May–early Jun).*

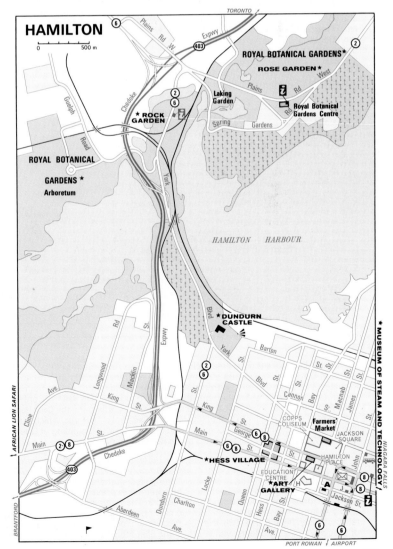

ONTARIO

* **Museum of Steam and Technology.** – *900 Woodward Ave, just south of Queen Elizabeth Way (QEW). Open daily Jun–Aug. Off-season Tue–Sun. Closed Christmas & New Year's. $2. ☎416/549-5225.* Hamilton's former waterpumping station completed in 1859, now provides a rare example of 19C steam technology. Architecturally interesting with its arches and cast-iron Doric columns, the engine house contains two Gartshore steam-powered beam engines of 1859 in full working order. They once pumped as much as 5 million gallons of water a day, until they were replaced in 1910. The old boiler house has displays on the use of steam power and a working model of the beam engines.

EXCURSION

* **African Lion Safari.** – *32km/20mi northwest by Hwy 8, right on Rte 52N after Rockton and left on Safari Rd. Open daily year-round. $13.* ✗ & ☎519/623-2620. Visitors drive their own cars *(safari tram available at additional cost)* through various enclosures of African and North American free-roaming animals. One enclosure called the monkey jungle contains about 70 African baboons that will climb over your car and steal any removable part they can.

★★ KINGSTON and the THOUSAND ISLANDS

Map p 101

The city of Kingston lies on the north shore of Lake Ontario, at the point where the St Lawrence River leaves the lake in a channel full of islands.

★★ KINGSTON
Map below   Tourist Office ☎613/548-4415

This one-time capital (pop 56,597) of the Province of Canada owes its political and economic development to its location at the junction of Lake Ontario and the St Lawrence River. One of the main shipbuilding centres on the Great Lakes in the 19C, the former colonial stronghold is home to several military colleges.
On the site of the present city in 1673, a French fur-trading post, called Cataraqui and Fort Frontenac at various times in its history, was established. Abandoned when New France fell, the area was later resettled by Loyalists, who called their community Kingston. The settlement soon became an important British naval base and dockyard, and a fort was built to protect it during the War of 1812. After the war, Kingston's importance increased with the building of the Rideau Canal and of a stone fortress, Fort Henry. Having served as capital of the Province of Canada from 1841 to 1843, Kingston lost that honour, but remained a vital military centre. Today,

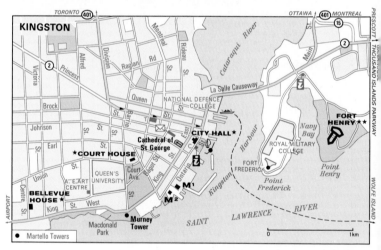

the **Royal Military College** (Fort Frederick), the Canadian Army Staff College and the National Defence College are evidence of the military's continuing presence. Kingston is a pleasant city, with tree-lined streets, parks and public buildings constructed of local limestone. Among these is the handsome **City Hall★** in Confederation Park on the harbour, built as a potential home for parliament; the **Court House★** with a small dome similar to that of City Hall; the **Cathedral of St George**, which is reminiscent of Christopher Wren's London churches; the **Grant Hall** building of Queen's University; and some of the buildings of the Royal Military College.

* ★★ **Fort Henry.** – *Open Jun 21–Labour Day daily 10am–6pm. Off-season daily 10am–5pm. Mid-Oct–mid-May by reservation only. $8.75.* ✗ & ☎613/542-7388. Completed in 1837, this large, exceedingly strong stone fortress is set on a peninsula above Lake Ontario. Its main defences face inland, expressly to guard the land approach to the naval dockyard at Point Frederick. The water approaches were covered by Martello towers built later. Having never been attacked, the fort eventually fell into decay. Restored in 1936, it is now best known for the **Fort Henry Guard**, a troop of specially trained students who re-create the life of the 19C British soldier, guide

visitors around the restored quarters and storerooms, and perform military manoeuvres. In particular, the **sunset ceremony** should not be missed *(Jul–Aug Wed & Sat 7pm)*. The Guard travels extensively to perform these professional military drills.

★ **Bellevue House.** – 🎞 *Open daily year-round. Closed legal holidays.* & ☏613/545-8666. Variously named the "Pekoe Pagoda" and "Tea Caddy Castle," this somewhat exotic Italian-styled villa contrasts sharply with Kingston's more traditional stone buildings. When completed in 1840, it caused quite a sensation and, for a short time (1848 to 1849), served as the residence of Canada's first prime minister.
A Scot by birth, **Sir John A. Macdonald** (1815-1891) spent much of his youth in Kingston, and opened his first law office in the city in 1835. He went on to enter provincial politics, becoming one of the chief architects of Canadian Confederation in 1867. During his terms in office (1867-1873, 1878-1891), the building of the Canadian Pacific Railway was the realization of one of his dreams. The house is furnished to reflect Macdonald's time of residence. In the visitor centre, there are exhibits and an introductory film *(8min)*.

★ **Marine Museum of the Great Lakes [M¹].** – *Open daily Apr–Dec. Off-season Mon–Fri. Closed Christmas & New Year's. $3.25* 🍴 *(summer)* & ☏613/542-2261. Set in old shipbuilding works beside Lake Ontario, this museum has displays on sail and steam vessels that have plied the Great Lakes. An interesting shipbuilders' gallery explains various construction methods, and a special section is devoted to Kingston's shipbuilding days. There are audio-visual presentations and changing exhibits on various aspects of marine life.

Murney Tower. – *Open daily Victoria Day–Labour Day. $3.* ☏613/544-9925. This squat stone tower in a pleasant park beside the lake is one of Kingston's Martello towers, a National Historic Site. It is in good repair with fine stonework and vaulting. Inside, living quarters of the garrison have been re-created, and the gun platform with its 15kg/32lb cannon on a circular traverse can be seen.

Pump House Steam Museum [M²]. – *Open daily Victoria Day–Labour Day. $3.25.* & ☏613/546-4696. Kingston's 1849 pumping station has been restored to pay tribute to Canada's steam age. Among the many operating machines and scale models are two enormous steam pumps once used in the pump house, restored as they were in 1897.

★★ THE THOUSAND ISLANDS
Tourist Office ☏315/482-2520

As it leaves Lake Ontario, the St Lawrence River is littered, for an 80km/50mi stretch, with about 1,000 islands (the exact number varies from 995 to 1,010, depending upon how many boulders are counted as islands!). Among the oldest and most popular vacation areas in northeastern North America, the islands with their sparkling waters and pink granite rocks attract Americans and Canadians.
All of the islands are of Precambrian rock, the remnants of the **Frontenac Axis**, which links the Canadian Shield with the Adirondacks of New York state. The islands are large and lushly forested, small with a few ragged pine trees, or barren—mere boulders of rock worn smooth by retreating glaciers. The international border passes among them, leaving the greater number on the Canadian side.

★★ **Boat Trip.** – *Departures from Gananoque, 28km/17mi north of Kingston by Rte 2; departs from customs dock daily mid-May–mid-Oct; Jun 26–Labour Day 9am–5pm hourly. Round-trip 3hrs ($15); 1hr ($10). Commentary on board.* 🍴&. *Gananoque Boat Lines* ☏613/382-2144. *Also cruises from Ivy Lea (10km/6mi north of Gananoque by Hwy 648) daily May–Oct. Round-trip 1hr 30min. $10.* 🍴 *Ivy Lea Boat Tours* ☏613/659-2295. *From Rockport (7km/4mi north of Ivy Lea by Hwy 648) daily mid-May–mid-Oct. Round-trip 1hr. $9.* 🍴& *Rockport Boat Ltd* ☏613/659-3402. This relaxing cruise through the maze of islands affords views of trees, rock and water interspersed, at times, with summer homes. These dwellings range from small shacks on rocky islets to the palaces of Millionaire's Row on Wellesley Island. The huge ships of the St Lawrence Seaway, which follows the American coast, can be seen alongside private cruisers, yachts and canoes. A stop can be made at Heart Island to visit **Boldt Castle**, built by a German immigrant at great cost, but never finished *(in US, non-Americans must have identification to land)*.

★ **Thousand Islands Parkway.** – *Begins 3km/1.8mi east of Gananoque at Interchange 648; 37km/23mi to Interchange 685, south of Brockville.* This scenic drive follows the shore of the St Lawrence, offering many good views. The **Skydeck** *(open daily May–Oct; $4.95;* 🍴& ☏613/659-2335) on Hill Island provides a fine **view★** of the islands and surrounding area *(take bridge to island, toll $2. Do not enter US).*
At Mallorytown Landing, the headquarters of the **St Lawrence Islands National Park** can be visited *(open daily Victoria Day–Labour Day; for camping fees, docking fees, water taxi and boat rental information contact the park office ☏613/923-5261)*. Beside the interpretion centre, a hut encloses the remains of the wreck of an early 19C gun boat.

Before planning your trip to Canada be sure to consult:
- *the Map of Principal Sights (pp 2-5);*
- *the suggested driving tours (pp 6-11).*

KITCHENER–WATERLOO
Pop 239,463

Attractive, orderly and clean, these twin industrial cities in southern Ontario reflect their German heritage. The skills and industriousness of their immigrant founders created a diverse economy still evident today.

At the beginning of the 19C, the first settlers here were Pennsylvania Dutch or **Mennonites**, a Protestant sect persecuted in Europe for its religious ideas and pacifism (members refused to serve in any army). Many emigrated to Pennsylvania in the 17C, but during the American Revolution, their pacifism again got them into trouble. Many moved with the Loyalists to Ontario, where they were granted land in the Kitchener area. Strict Mennonites live a simple, frugal life as farmers. They use no modern machinery, cars or telephones. They can sometimes be seen in the country to the north and west of Kitchener–Waterloo, driving along in horse-drawn buggies that display a fluorescent triangle on the back as a modern-day safety precaution. The men wear black suits and wide hats, the women ankle-length black dresses and small bonnets *(see also p 97)*.

Other German-speaking people came to this area in the 19C, and the German influence remains strong. Every fall, there is a nine-day **Oktoberfest** featuring German food and drink, oompah-pah bands and dancing. At the **farmers' market** *(entrance Market Square at Frederick & Duke sts; St Jacobs Market: year-round Thur & Sat 7am–3pm, also Tue in summer; Kitchener Market: year-round Sat 5am–2pm, also Wed in summer)*, German specialities are for sale. On Queen Street stands the **Centre in the Square**, which comprises a concert hall, studio theatre and art gallery.

★★ **Seagram Museum.** – *57 Erb St W, Waterloo. Open May–Dec daily 10am–6pm. Off-season Tue–Sun 10am–6pm. Closed Christmas & New Year's.* ✗ & ☎519/885-1857. This museum is devoted to the activities of the world's largest producer and marketer of distilled wines and spirits. Located on the site of the original Seagram distillery, the museum is housed in an old barrel warehouse with a modern extension. A series of fascinating displays covers the entire distilling process, augmented by short videos on key aspects.

Woodside National Historic Site. – ⌖ *528 Wellington St N, Kitchener. Open daily year-round. Closed legal holidays in winter.* ☎519/742-5273. This low-lying brick Victorian house stands in an attractive park. Built in 1853, it was for some years the boyhood home of **William Lyon Mackenzie King**, prime minister of Canada 1921-1926, 1926-1930, 1935-1948. It has been restored to reflect the period of King's residence in the 1890s. In the basement, an audio-visual presentation *(10min)* provides an introduction, and there is an excellent **display** on King's life and association with Woodside. The influence of his grandfather, the rebel leader William Lyon Mackenzie, is of particular note.

Joseph Schneider Haus. – *466 Queen St S, Kitchener. Open daily Victoria Day–Labour Day. Off-season Tue–Sun. Closed Christmas, Boxing Day & New Year's. $1.35.* & ☎519/742-7752. This Georgian frame house was built about 1820 by Kitchener's founder, Joseph Schneider. It is restored and furnished to the period of the mid-1850s. Special events and seasonal activities reflect the family's Mennonite roots.

Doon Heritage Crossroads. – *About 3km/2mi from Hwy 401; Exit 275; turn north. Open daily May–Dec. $3.75.* ✗ ☎519/748-1914. Many authentic buildings have been removed to this site to reflect life in a small rural Waterloo village in the early 20C through 1914. Note the **Gingerbread House** of 1890 Victorian vintage, which has a display of dolls, and the **museum**, with its interesting exhibits on the first European settlers of Waterloo County, as well as on the native Indians.

★ LONDON
Pop 303,165

This major industrial centre serves Ontario's rich agricultural south. London is also the location of the University of Western Ontario. In 1792, **John Graves Simcoe**, Lieutenant-Governor of Ontario, chose the present site of London as his capital. He considered the existing administrative centre, Niagara-on-the-Lake, too close to the American border. He named the site for the British capital and called the river on which it stood, the Thames. However, approval of the choice of capital from higher authorities was never forthcoming, and York (Toronto) received the honour instead. Today, London is a pleasant city of tree-lined streets and attractive houses.

★★ **Regional Art and Historical Museum.** – *421 Ridout St N. Open year-round Tue–Sun noon–5pm. Closed Christmas.* ✗ & ☎519/672-4580. Set in a park overlooking the River Thames, this spectacular museum is remarkable chiefly for its architecture. Designed by Toronto architect Raymond Moriyama, and opened in 1980, the unusual structure is covered by concrete barrel vaults of aluminum and baked enamel. Each vault contains skylights—Moriyama's answer to the problem of providing indirect natural lighting without damaging the art. The result is a series of airy and spacious galleries where changing exhibits are displayed. Selections from the permanent Canadian collection of 18C and 19C works are usually on view. The historical museum features exhibits on the city's past.

★ **Eldon House.** – *481 Ridout St N. Open year-round Tue–Sun. $3. Closed Christmas.* ✗ ☎519/661-5165. Just north of a series of restored Georgian houses stands this large and elegant frame residence, completely surrounded by a veranda. Constructed in 1834 by John Harris, a retired Royal Navy captain, London's oldest house was for many years a centre of social and cultural activities in 19C southern Ontario. Its furnishings reflect a refined way of life at a time when most pioneer settlers were living in log cabins. Owned by four generations of the Harris family, the house was donated to the City of London. The library and drawing room are particularly noteworthy.

EXCURSIONS

Fanshawe Pioneer Village. – *In Fanshawe Park, 15km/9mi northeast. Open daily May–Labour Day. Off-season Wed–Sun. Closed Dec 25–Apr. $5.* ✗ ♿ ☎*519/457-1296.* This reconstructed 19C community is part of a large park beside Fanshawe Lake, a reservoir constructed to control flooding by the River Thames. The village contains several houses and shops, the Lochaber Presbyterian Church with a Gaelic bible, a fire hall, and an Orange Hall— the social centre of the community. A Protestant fraternity founded in Ireland in 1795 and named for William III (of Orange), the **Orange Order** had considerable influence in the foundation of Ontario. In summer, costumed guides lend life to the village.

Ska-Nah-Doht Indian Village. – *In Longwoods Road Conservation Area, 32km/20mi southwest by Hwy 2. Open daily mid-May–Labour Day. Off-season Mon–Fri. Closed legal holidays. $5/car.* ♿ ☎*519/264-2420.* This village is a re-creation of the type inhabited by prehistoric Iroquois in Ontario 800 to 1,000 years ago. These Indians cultivated the land, trapped animals and fished.
The village is surrounded by a stake palisade with a complicated entrance to make it easy to defend. Inside, daily life is depicted through displays and artifacts such as three longhouses where the families lived, a primitive sauna called a sweat lodge, drying racks for smoking meat, stretching racks for hides, storage pits and a fish trap. In the fields outside the palisade, corn, squash and tobacco crops are grown. The park resource centre nearby has audio-visual programs and displays.

★★★ NIAGARA FALLS

Map p 100   Tourist Office ☎416/356-6061

Roughly halfway along its course from Lake Erie to Lake Ontario, the Niagara River suddenly changes its level by plunging over an immense cliff, creating one of earth's great natural wonders. These famous falls are the most visited in the world, attracting more than 12 million people a year.

There are, in fact, two sets of falls separated by tiny Goat Island, which stands at their brink. The so-called **American Falls** (because they are on the US side of the river) are 300m/1,000ft wide and more than 50m/160ft high. The Canadian or **Horseshoe Falls** (named for their shape) are nearly 800m/2,600ft wide, about the same height, and contain 90 percent of the water allowed to flow down the river. It is the latter falls that people think of as Niagara.
The river's water volume varies by hour and season. By means of canals, major power developments divert up to 75 percent of the water above the falls to generating stations downstream. Flow of water over the falls is reduced at night when additional electricity is needed to illuminate them. In winter, so much water is diverted that the falls partially freeze—a spectacular sight. Standing on the brink of the falls, watching the mighty rush of water, visitors should consider today's water diversion, and try to imagine the cataract's appearance in 1678 when **Louis Hennepin** was the first European to view it. Hennepin heard such a mighty noise on Lake Ontario that he followed the river upstream to discover its source.

The Erosion of the Falls. – In geological terms, the falls are not old. At the end of the last ice age, the waters of Lake Erie created an exit channel for themselves to old Lake Iroquois. The edge of the ancient lake was the present-day Niagara Escarpment, over which this new river plunged to the lake. The water's force immediately began to erode the underlying soft shale, causing the harder limestone to break off. A gorge was eventually created.
Today, the waters of Lake Iroquois have receded to the present level of Lake Ontario, and the Niagara River has cut a gorge some 11km/7mi back from the edge of the escarpment at Queenston to the present position of the falls *(map p 115)*. In another 25,000 years or so, unless mankind intervenes, the gorge will extend back to Lake Erie, and the falls as we know them will practically cease to exist.

The Site. – In the 19C, Niagara was a hucksters' paradise where every conceivable ruse was employed to separate tourists from their money. The Province of Ontario and the State of New York stepped in, buying all the land on both sides of the river adjacent to the falls. Today, beautiful parks full of flowers line the riverbank. Hucksterism still exists in the city of Niagara Falls (pop 75,399), but visitors can enjoy the natural dignity of the falls without being bothered. The following text describes attractions that concern only the natural beauty and history of the site.

★★★ THE FALLS   Map p 114

The falls can be viewed from the riverbank level, from the water level at the bottom of the cataract and from the summit of various towers constructed especially for viewing purposes.

★★★ **The Walk from Rainbow Bridge to Table Rock.** *About 1.6km/1mi.* From Rainbow Bridge, visitors can wander along the bank beside the river, passing **Queen Victoria Park** and its beautiful flowers *(especially fine in April when the daffodils are in bloom)*. The American Falls are seen, and it is possible to stand on the brink of Horseshoe Falls at Table Rock. Watching the water cascade over the edge is an impressive experience. In Table Rock House, elevators descend and visitors can walk along **tunnels★** to see this immense curtain of falling water *(open daily year-round. $5. ☎416/354-1551).*

★★★ **The Maid of the Mist [E].** – *Access from River Rd. Descend by funicular ($1.07). Elevator & boat ride daily mid–May–mid-Oct (weather permitting), $8.30. ☎416/358-5781.* This boat trip is exciting, memorable and wet *(visitors are equipped with raincoats and hoods).* After passing the American Falls, the boat goes to the foot of the horseshoe cataract, the best spot to appreciate the mighty force of the water.

★★★ **The View from Above.** – Three towers in Niagara Falls provide a spectacular elevated **view★★★** of the cataract. The best view is from the **Skylon [B]** *(Robinson St; open daily year-round; $5.95 ☎416/356-2651),* which looks like a miniature CN Tower *(p 132)* and is ascended by exterior elevators known as yellow bugs.

EXCURSIONS *Map below and p 115*

From the Falls to Niagara-on-the-Lake
26km/16mi. 5hrs with visits.

Niagara Parkway (north)★★ follows the river to its junction with Lake Ontario. Maintained by the Niagara Parks Commission, the parkway has good viewpoints and attractive gardens. From the falls, the parkway passes under Rainbow Bridge, through a pleasant residential area and past the Whirlpool Bridge.

★★ **Great Gorge Adventure.** – *4km/2.5mi. Open late-Apr–late-Oct daily 9am–5pm. $4. ☎416/374-1221.* An elevator descends to the bottom of the gorge. It is here that some of the world's most hazardous water can be seen thundering, broiling and rising into huge **rapids★★**.

★★ **The Whirlpool.** – *5km/3mi.* A colourful Spanish aero car *(daily Apr–Oct; weather permitting; $4.25; ☎416/354-5711)* crosses the gorge high above the river, with excellent **views★★** of the water as it swirls around the whirlpool and the rocky gorge. By driving another 1.5km/1mi, visitors reach the far side of the whirlpool. There is a **view★** from Thompson's Point scenic look.

★ **Niagara Glen.** – *7.5km/4.7mi.* There is a view of the river from above. Trails lead to the water's edge *(15min to descend, 30min to ascend).*

★ **Niagara Parks Commission School of Horticulture [F].** – *9km/5.5mi. Open daily year-round. ☎416/356-8554.* A beautiful display of flowers, shrubs and trees is maintained by the students at this school, which offers a three-year course in horticulture. The **rose garden★** is particularly fine in early June. The industrial side of Niagara is reached about 1.6km/1mi from the school. Across the river on the Canadian side, the immense **Robert Moses Generating Station** can be seen, and farther on, the **Sir Adam Beck Generating Station** is passed. These two stations use the water diverted from the river above the falls to generate electricity.

Just after the power stations, note the large **floral clock**.

★ **Queenston Heights.** – *12km/8mi. Open daily year-round.* These heights are part of the Niagara Escarpment and were once the location of Niagara Falls. Today, they have been made into a pleasant park that provides good views of the river. At the centre of the park stands a monument to **General Sir Isaac Brock**, the Canadian military hero of the War of 1812. The heights were captured by the Americans during the war. Brock was killed while leading the charge to recapture them. The heights were recaptured, and now Brock's statue overlooks them from the top of his monument *(open daily mid-May–Labour Day; ☎416/468-4257).*

★ **Queenston.** – *14km/ 9mi.* This village at the foot of the escarpment has attractive houses and gardens.

Laura Secord Homestead. – *Partition St. Open daily Victoria Day–Labour Day. ☎416/262-4851.* In 1813, Laura Secord set out from her home in enemy-held Queenston and walked 30km/ 19mi through the bush to warn the British of a surprise attack planned by the Americans. Forewarned, the British won a great victory at the subsequent Battle of Beaver Dams. Her rather plain house has been beautifully restored by the candy company named after this Canadian heroine. An interpretive display about Secord's life stands outside.

As visitors continue along the parkway, they can look back to see the statue of Brock at the summit of the escarpment. For the remainder of the drive to Niagara-on-the-Lake, there are several parks with picnic tables, and occasional fine views of the river. In summer, stalls selling the produce of the Niagara peninsula line the route.

★★ **Niagara-on-the-Lake.** – Pop 12,945. Situated at the north end of the Niagara River where it joins Lake Ontario, this town resembles a picturesque English village. Settled by Loyalists, it was the first capital of Upper Canada. Burned to the ground by the Americans in 1813, it was rebuilt soon afterwards, and seems to have remained unchanged. The town is filled with tree-lined streets and gracious 19C houses with beautiful gardens. Pleasant shops, restaurants, teahouses, hotels and the **Niagara Apothecary**, an 1866 pharmacy *(open daily May–Labour Day; �& ☎416/ 962-4861)* line a wide, main thoroughfare, **Queen Street★**, with a clock tower at its centre. Niagara-on-the-Lake is also a cultural centre, home to the **Shaw Festival**, a season of theatre devoted to the works of the Irish playwright, **George Bernard Shaw** (1856-1950). The main theatre, a brick structure with a beautiful wood interior, stands at the junction of Queen's Parade and Wellington Street. There are two other theatres in the town. *For details regarding performances (Tue–Sun) contact Box Office, PO Box 774, Niagara-on-the-Lake, ON, L0S 1J0 ☎416/468-2172.*

★ **Fort George.** – 🎫 *On River Rd near theatre. Open daily mid-May–Labour Day; until Thanksgiving, weekends only. $2.25. �& ☎416/468-4257.* Built by the British in the 1790s, this fort played a key role in the War of 1812, being alternately captured by the Americans and recaptured by the British. Restored in the 1930s, it has grassy earthworks and a wooden palisade enclosing officers' quarters, a forge, powder magazine, guard house and three blockhouse barracks of 25cm/10in thick timbers housing military displays.

★★ Welland Canal

From Niagara Falls, take Queen Elizabeth Way (QEW) to St Catharines; exit at Glendale Ave interchange, follow Glendale Ave and cross canal by the lift bridge; turn right or left on canal service road (Government Rd).
From Niagara-on-the-Lake, take the Niagara Stone Rd (Rte 55) to its end, turn left on the south service road, right on Coon Rd to Glendale Ave turn right and cross canal as above. The early explorers and fur traders portaged their canoes around the falls and rapids on the Niagara River, but navigation of anything larger between Lakes Ontario and Erie was impossible until canals and locks were built in the 19C. The present canal, part of the St Lawrence Seaway, is 45km/28mi long, crossing the Niagara peninsula between St Catharines and Port Colborne. Its eight locks raise ships 99m/326ft—the difference in level between the two great lakes.

★★ **Drive alongside Canal.** – *About 14km/9mi from Lake Ontario to Thorold on Government Rd.* There are fine views of the huge ships on the seaway negotiating seven of the eight locks of this section. Lock 3 *(just north of the lift bridge)* has a **viewing platform★** *(open daily year-round; closed Christmas, Boxing Day & New Year's; $3;* ✗ ☙ ☎*416/685-3711)* and information centre *(same hours)* at the seaway. The times ships pass through the lock are posted and are fairly continuous *(it takes nearly an hour for a ship to negotiate a lock).* Locks 4, 5 and 6 in Thorold raise ships up the Niagara Escarpment. They are twin-flight locks having two parallel sets of locks, so that one ship can be elevated as another comes down.

From the Falls to Fort Erie *32km/20mi. 1hr.*

Rushing along at 48km/h (30mph), Niagara River is impressive, revealing its **rapids★★** as it prepares to plunge over the cliff. **Niagara Parkway (south)★** crosses to **Dufferin Island,** where a pleasant park *(open daily year-round)* has hiking trails, streams and a swimming area. The parkway passes the large international control dam and gates that divert water along canals to the generating stations downstream. In complete contrast to its lower stretch, the river slowly becomes a broad, quietly flowing stream. There are some pleasant views of the US shore and Grand Island.

At the city of **Fort Erie** (pop 26,006), the Peace Bridge crosses the river to the large American city of **Buffalo.** There are good **views★** of the Buffalo skyline.

Fort Erie. – *Open daily mid-May–Labour Day. $3.50.* ✗ ☎*416/871-0540.* A reconstruction of the third fort built on this site, the star-shaped stone stronghold is set at the mouth of Lake Erie. The first two forts were destroyed by storm and flood, the third by the Americans in 1814. Visitors enter by a drawbridge and can tour reconstructed officers' quarters, barracks, a guard house and powder magazine. Students in early 19C uniforms perform manoeuvres and serve as guides.

★ NORTH BAY   Pop 55,405

Map p 100   Tourist Office ☎705/472-8450

This resort centre on the shores of **Lake Nipissing** was located on the old canoe route to the West. The La Vase portage connected the waters of Trout Lake and the Ottawa and Mattawa rivers with Lake Nipissing, the French River and Georgian Bay.

Today, these waters are used solely for recreational purposes. From the government dock on Main Street, there are **cruises** across Lake Nipissing and down the attractive French River, with several stops *(depart from Government Dock on Memorial Drive Jul–Labour Day Wed–Fri & Sun 10am; moonlight cruise Wed & Fri 7pm; round-trip 3hrs & 6hrs; commentary on board;* ✗ ☙*; for schedules & fares contact Ontario Northland* ☎*705/472-4500).*

North Bay is also the centre of a rich fur-trapping industry. Every summer *(Jul–Aug 7pm)* beaver, marten, muskrat and other furs are auctioned at the Fur Harvesters' Auctions, which rank among the largest in the world.

Quints' Museum. – *Beside tourist office on Hwy 11/17. Open daily mid-May–mid-Oct. $2.50.* ☙ ☎*705/472-8480.* On May 28, 1934, the **Dionne quintuplets** were born in this house. These five little girls quickly became the world's sweethearts. The museum displays "quint" memorabilia.

EXCURSION *Map p 100*

Sturgeon Falls. – *37km/23mi west by Hwy 17.* Just southwest of this community is the **Sturgeon River House Museum** *(open daily Victoria Day–Labour Day; off-season Mon–Fri;* ☙ ☎*705/753-4716),* which tells the story of the fur-trapping industry. Exhibits include a trapper's cabin complete with equipment, pelts that can be touched and a wide range of traps.

★ ORILLIA   Pop 25,925

Map p 100

Set on the narrows between Lakes Simcoe and Couchiching, this small industrial centre and resort town has a reputation out of all proportion to its size. Orilla served as the model for "Mariposa" in *Sunshine Sketches of a Little Town* by famed humourist and author **Stephen Leacock** (1869-1944). Possibly the best known of Canada's literati, this political-science professor at McGill University spent his summers here, finding inspiration for some of his finest works.

★ **Stephen Leacock Museum.** – *In Old Brewery Bay off Hwy 12B. Open daily mid-Apr–mid-Oct. Off-season Mon–Fri. $4.* ☎*705/326-9357.* Set amid pleasant grounds overlooking Brewery Bay, this attractive house was designed and built by Leacock in 1928. The nonsensical, uproarious humour of this man, who stated he would rather have written *Alice in Wonderland* than the whole of the *Encyclopaedia Britannica,* pervades the house and the tour guides.

Sights described in this guide are rated:

   ★★★ **Worth the trip**

    ★★ **Worth a detour**

     ★ *Interesting*

★★ OSHAWA

Tourist Office ☎416/728-168

ONTARIO

This industrial city on the north shore of Lake Ontario is one of the main centres of Canada's automobile industry. Its name has long been synonymous with industrialist and philanthropist, **Robert S. McLaughlin** (1871-1972).

★★ **Parkwood Estate.** – *270 Simcoe St N, 2.5km/1.5mi north of Hwy 401. Visit by guided tour (1hr) only Jun–Aug Tue–Sun 10:30am–4:30pm. Off-season Tue–Fri 1:30–4pm, Sun 1:30–4pm. $5.* ☎*416/579-1311.* This gracious, imposing residence was built by McLaughlin in 1917. Bequeathed by him to Oshawa General Hospital, the house is open to the public, maintained by the hospital as it was at his death.

Apprenticed in his father's carriage works, McLaughlin converted the manufacturing business into a motor company, and used an American engine in his famous **McLaughlin-Buick**. In 1918, he sold the company to the General Motors Corporation of the US, but remained chairman of the Canadian division, whose main plant is in Oshawa.

A visit to Parkwood provides insight into the lifestyle of the immensely wealthy McLaughlin family. Beautifully and tastefully appointed, the house contains priceless antiques from all over the world. Every room has furnishings of the finest woods and fabrics representing the work of skilled craftsmen.

This gem of a house is set in some of the finest **gardens** in the eastern half of Canada. Containing mature trees, manicured lawns and shrubbery, formal gardens, statuary and fountains, they are a delight to wander in. A visit is further enhanced by a stop at the pleasant **teahouse** *(light lunches, English teas, Jun–Aug)* set beside a long pool with fountains.

★ **Canadian Automotive Museum.** – *99 Simcoe St S, about 1.5km/1mi north of Hwy 401. Open daily year-round. $5.* & ☎*416/576-1222.* The history of the automobile industry in Canada is explained by means of photographs, illustrations, models, and of course, by actual vehicles. Primarily from the 1898-1930 period, about 70 automobiles, in mint condition, are on display. Noteworthy among them are the 1903 Redpath Messenger built in Toronto—the only remaining example of its type, the 1912 McLaughlin Buick, and the 1917 Rauch and Lang electric car.

Cullen Gardens. – *In Whitby, 5km/3mi north of Hwy 401 by Hwy 12 and Taunton Rd. Open daily mid-Apr–Dec 23. $8.50.* ⚑& ☎*416/668-6606.* These attractive gardens combine flower beds, a rose garden, topiary, ponds and a stream with miniature reproductions of historic houses from all over Ontario.

Robert McLaughlin Gallery. – *Civic Centre near city hall. Open year-round Tue–Sun.* ⚑& ☎*416/576-3000.* Originally built in 1969, the expanded gallery designed by Arthur Erickson collects the works of the **Painters Eleven**, a group of artists who united in the 1950s to exhibit abstract art in Toronto. Changing exhibits feature contempory Canadian art.

★★★ OTTAWA

Tourist Office ☎ 613/237-5158 or 613/239-5000

Defying the stereotypical image of a capital city, this seat of national government lacks the imposing architecture, sweeping vistas and vast monuments of other world capitals. The city's attraction is its charm, captured in such scenes as joggers following the Rideau Canal, briefcase-clutching civil servants skating to work, Sunday bicycle brigades rounding a corner, or colourful tulips crowding the parks.

The city sits on the south bank of the **Ottawa River** at the point where it meets the **Rideau River** from the south and the **Gatineau River** from the north. The capital is due west of Montreal, about 160km/100mi upstream from the confluence of the Ottawa and St Lawrence rivers. The Ottawa River marks the boundary between the provinces of Ontario and Quebec, but the National Capital Region spans the river, encompassing a large area in both provinces that includes the cities of Ottawa and Hull.

HISTORICAL NOTES

Although the region was known to the Outaouais Indians and visited by French explorers, there was no settlement in the Ottawa area until 1800. The first settler was **Philemon Wright**, an American who harnessed the **Chaudière Falls** to power gristmills and sawmills on the Hull side of the river. He cut wood and floated the first raft of squared timber to Quebec in 1806, beginning what was to be a vast industry.

The Rideau Canal. – The War of 1812 exposed the dangers of the St Lawrence as a communications and supply route from Montreal for the military in Upper Canada. Ships were vulnerable to perilous rapids and gunfire from the US. After the War, the **Duke of Wellington** sent men to Canada to look for a safer passage. The route selected followed the Ottawa, Rideau and Cataraqui rivers and a series of lakes to reach the Royal Navy base at Kingston on Lake Ontario. Construction of the canals and locks necessary to make the route navigable was entrusted to **Lt-Col John By** of the Royal Engineers in 1826. The lieutenant-colonel established his base at the present site of Ottawa. Soon a thriving settlement developed known as Bytown. By 1832, the canal system was completed, but its cost was so great that By returned to England unemployed and penniless.

Lumbertown. – The completion of canal construction did not signal the end of Bytown's boom. By the mid-1830s, the community had become the centre of Ottawa Valley's squared-timber industry. Using the power of Chaudière Falls, as Philemon Wright had, residents built sawmills on the Bytown side of the Ottawa River. Splendid stands of red and white pine fell victim to the new industry. Over the century, the industry concentrated more on exporting lumber to the US and less on floating timber to Quebec for export to England. Having never been used militarily, the Rideau Canal blossomed briefly as a means of transporting the lumber south. Bytown became a rowdy centre for lumberjacks and rivermen skilled at negotiating the rapids (so skilled that the British government recruited them to negotiate the hazardous cataracts of the Nile in order to relieve General Gordon at Khartoum in 1884).

Westminster in the Wilderness. – The 1850s saw great rivalry among Montreal, Toronto, Kingston and Quebec, over which should be selected as the capital of the new united Canada. Contention was so intense that the government asked **Queen Victoria** to decide the issue. She chose Bytown, which had hastily changed its name to Ottawa as a more suitable appellation for a capital. The choice did not please everyone: "the nearest lumber village to the north pole" wrote Torontonian **Goldwin Smith**. But the American press discovered Ottawa's advantage—it eluded capture by the most courageous of invaders, because they would become lost in the woods trying to find it! Despite such quips, the parliament buildings were begun in 1859 and completed enough by 1867 to be used by representatives of the new Confederation, of which Ottawa was accepted as the capital—this time without demur.

Ottawa Today. – A city of parks, pleasant driveways and bicycle paths, Ottawa is also a city of flowers, especially in May when thousands of tulips bloom—a gift from the Dutch whose queen spent the war years in Ottawa. It is a city that has capitalized on the the cause of its founding—the **Rideau Canal**. Flanked by tree-lined drives, this waterway is a recreational haven: canoeing, boating, jogging, strolling, biking in summer, skating and cross-country skiing in winter. The canal can be followed its entire 200km/125mi length to Lake Ontario through picturesque countryside and lovely lakes. Ottawa boasts other driveways that follow the Ottawa and Rideau rivers (p 123), and more are planned.

Although still a centre for forestry and for the rich agriculture to the south, Ottawa is chiefly a city of government. Not here do "temples of finance" rule the skyline as in Toronto and Montreal. Instead, highrises contain government departments and ministries, the most dominant being government-owned **Place du Portage** across the river in Hull.

Finally, Ottawa is a cultural centre, with a fine selection of museums and music, and dance and drama at the **National Arts Centre**. The city is particularly lively in February during the winter festival titled **Winterlude**, in May for the **Canadian Tulip Festival**, and in late June/early July when **Oh Canada Days** are celebrated in style on Parliament Hill.

** PARLIAMENT HILL AND AREA *Map p 119*

Approached from Wellington Street, Parliament "Hill" seems to belie its name. Canada's Parliament actually stands on a bluff overlooking the Ottawa River and must be viewed from that angle to appreciate its designation.

The "Hill," as it is familiarly known, was purchased in 1859 from the British military, which used it for barracks during the building of the canal. Construction began immediately on the parliament buildings, which were occupied in 1866 but completed in 1876. The present three Gothic-style sandstone structures do not all date from the mid-19C. In 1916, a disastrous fire destroyed the middle building; it was rebuilt in 1920. The **Peace Tower** at its centre was added in 1927 as a monument to Canadians killed during World War I. Today, the **Centre Block** contains the Houses of Parliament—Commons and the Senate. The **East Block**, with its whimsical windowed tower designed to look like a face, and the **West Block** contain the offices of members of Parliament and senators. Once, these three buildings were sufficient to house not only Parliament, but the entire civil service.

Visit *1 day*

Parliament Hill is "guarded" by the Mounties—members of the Royal Canadian Mounted Police, attired in their famous ceremonial uniforms of stetsons, red tunics, riding breeches, boots and spurs *(summer only)*. Regiments of Foot Guards wearing bearskin caps, scarlet tunics and blue trousers are also stationed on the Hill in summer. A **Changing of the Guard**** is performed in summer *(mid-Jun–mid-Sept)*, resembling the ceremony held outside Buckingham Palace and a seasonal **sound and light** show presents Canada's history *(nightly May 6–Labour Day; different hours for English & French productions; in case of rain show will be cancelled; & ☎613/ 239-5609)*.

* **Centre Block.** – *Visit by guided tour (30min) only daily Victoria Day–Labour Day. Off-season Mon–Sat.* & ☎613/992-4793. Tours enable visitors to enter the House of Commons, the Senate, the Library, Confederation Hall and the Hall of Honour. Separately, the peace tower can be ascended for a fine **view*** of the sprawling capital. Parliamentary proceedings are open to the public if the House is in session *(T&C)*. Each session begins with the **Speaker's Parade** through the Hall of Honour to the Commons.

* **East Block.** – *Visit by guided tour (30min) only daily Jun–Aug. Off-season weekends only. Closed Christmas, New Year's & Canada Day.* & ◻ ☎613/992-8483. The interior of this mid-19C building has been restored to its 1872 appearance. Some of

the offices have been authentically furnished to represent their occupants at the time: Prime Minister Sir John A. Macdonald; his Quebec colleague and fellow Father of Confederation, Sir George-Étienne Cartier; the governor general, Lord Dufferin; and the Privy Council.

The Grounds. – In front of the parliament buildings is a low-lying fountain called the **Centennial Flame [A]** because of the natural gas always burning at its centre. Symbolizing the first 100 years of Confederation, it was lit at midnight on New Year's Eve, 1966. Around the flame, the 12 shields of Canada's provinces and territories are displayed, with the date they entered Confederation.

The walk around Centre Block is pleasant, affording **views★** of the river and of Hull (p 158), which has rapidly changed from an industrial city to a Federal Government annex containing large office complexes. A notable collection of statues graces this walk, many of which are the work of well-known Quebec sculptor **Louis-Philippe Hébert**. Most commemorate Canadian prime ministers, with the exception of the Queen Victoria statue.

At the back of Centre Block stands an attractive polygonal building housing the **Parliamentary Library★**, the only part of the original structure to escape the 1916 fire. The library is modelled on the reading room of the British Museum, but its exterior looks like the chapter house of a Gothic Cathedral.

★★ **Ottawa River Boat Trip.** – Departs from Ottawa locks May–mid-Oct daily from 11am–7:30pm; cruise departs from Hull dock 30min earlier; round-trip 1hr 30min. $8.50. ⚓ & Paul's Boat Lines ☎613/235-8409. This is an excellent trip, especially at dusk, affording close-up views of Parliament Hill, the Rideau Falls and the houses along Sussex Drive overlooking the river, in particular the prime minister's residence. The sheer size and force of the Ottawa River are impressive. The boat descends as far as Pointe Gatineau, a pretty village on the Quebec shore where log booms can be seen in the mouth of the Gatineau River.

★ **Rideau Canal.** – ⌖ Heritage Canal. From Wellington Street, visitors can descend into the small gorge where the Rideau Canal begins. Eight **locks★** raise boats from the Ottawa River to the top of the cliff. There is also a **boat trip** on the canal (departs from Conference Centre May–mid-Oct daily from 10am–8:30pm; round-trip 1hr 15min; $8.50; ⚓ & Paul's Boat Lines ☎613/235-8409).

Beside the locks stands the **Old Commissariat Building**, completed by Colonel By in 1827 as a military supply depot and treasury. The historic edifice now houses the **Bytown Museum** (open mid-May–mid-Oct Wed–Mon; off- season Mon–Fri; closed Dec– Mar; $2.25; & ☎613/234-4570) and a display on the canal builders. Across the canal stands the **Château Laurier**, Ottawa's most distinguished hotel, easily recognizable by its turrets and steeply pitched copper roofs in true "chateau" tradition. Facing the canal, the **National Arts Centre★** consists of interrelated concrete structures. Opened in 1969, the complex contains theatres and a charming cafe with an outdoor terrace (summer only) located beside the waterway. Across the canal stands the **Rideau**

Centre, a hotel, convention and shopping complex. Across Confederation Square is **Sparks Street Mall**, a pleasant pedestrian mall with trees, seating and cafe tables between the shops. Note the **Royal Bank Centre**, and the attractive **Bank of Canada**★ designed by Arthur Erickson and opened in 1980. Set within a 12-storey court, this neoclassical building is now flanked by two 12-storey towers of solar-tinted glass and oxidized copper. In the court are trees, shrubs, a pool and the Currency Museum

★★ **Nepean Point.** – Situated high above the river beside Alexandra Bridge, this point offers a splendid **view**★★ of Parliament Hill, Hull and the Gatineau Hills across the river. The statue is of **Samuel de Champlain**, who sailed up the Ottawa River in 1613 and 1615.

In nearby Major's Hill Park stands the **noon-day gun [B]**, a muzzle-loaded ship's cannon that is fired every day *(10am on Sun; loud report, do not stand too close)*. On clear days, the gun can be heard over a 22km/14mi area.

Rideau Canal, Ottawa

Ontario Ministry of Tourism & Recreation

★ **Basilica of Notre Dame.** – This church with its twin spires is a Roman Catholic cathedral built between 1841 and the 1880s. Note the gold-leaf statue of the Madonna and Child between the steeples. To the right of the basilica, there is a statue of Joseph-Eugene Guigues, the first bishop of Ottawa, who was responsible for the cathedral's completion.

The very fine **woodwork**★ of the interior was carved in mahogany by Philippe Parizeau. Around the sanctuary, there are niches that contain statues of the prophets, patriarchs and apostles carved in wood by Louis-Philippe Hébert, though they have been painted to look like stone.

★ **Tin House Court.** – In this pleasant square with its stone houses and fountain, a strange object can be seen hanging from the wall. It is the facade of a house built by Honore Foisy, a tinsmith. Foisy spent his time decorating the front of his home with sheet metal, making it look like wood or stone. When his house was destroyed, the facade was moved here to preserve this example of tinsmithing.

★ **Byward Market.** – Stretching over several blocks, this colourful market *(indoors in winter)* has existed since 1846. From spring to fall, there are stalls of flowers, fruit and vegetables. Year-round, people are also attracted to the neighboring shops, cafes and restaurants.

Supreme Court. – *Visit by guided tour (30min) only daily May–Aug. Off-season Mon–Fri.* & ☎613/995-4330. Created in 1875, but not "supreme" until 1949 (when appeals to England's Judicial Committee of the Privy Council were abolished), Canada's Supreme Court occupies a building with green roofs overlooking the Ottawa River. The court itself consists of nine judges, five of whom constitute a quorum. Visitors can listen to the legal arguments if the court is in session, and visit two other court rooms.

★★★ THE MUSEUMS

As befitting a capital city, Ottawa has a fine collection of museums. Several of them moved into new quarters in the late 1980s. Some are expanding or altering their present location. Thus, the following descriptions are subject to change.

★★★ **National Aviation Museum.** – *Map p 123. Rockcliffe Airport. Open May–Labour Day daily 9am–5pm (Thur 9pm). Off-season Tue–Sun 9am–5pm (Thur 9pm). $4.28.* ✗ & ₽ ☎613/993-2010. This enormous triangular-shaped, high-tech building recalls the three-sided pattern of the numerous airfields built across the country during World War II, when Canada was known as the "Aerodrome for Democracy." Opened in 1988, the museum is devoted to the history of aviation from pioneer days to the present, with special emphasis on Canadian contributions.

A selection of old aviation films and videos accompanies the exhibits, presenting an interesting glimpse of the past. There is a replica of the *Silver Dart,* the first aircraft to fly in Canada *(p 204).* There are fighters and bombers used in both world wars: a Nieuport 17, a Sopwith Snipe, a Hawker Hurricane, a Supermaine Spitfire and a Lancaster Bomber. The beginnings of modern passenger service can be traced to the Boeing 247, the Lockheed 10A and the DC-3, examples of which are on view. Early "bush" float planes illustrate the importance of aviation in opening up Canada's vast northland.

The **RCAF Hall of Tribute,** a memorial room adjacent to the entrance lobby, honours men and women of the Royal Canadian Air Force.

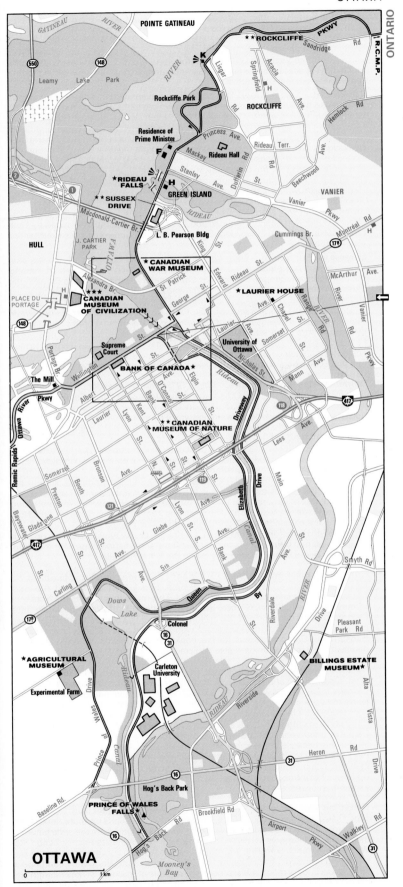

★★★ National Gallery. – *Map p 119. 380 Sussex Dr. Open May–mid-Oct daily 10am–6pm (Wed–Fri 8pm). Off-season Wed–Sun 10am–5pm (Thur 8pm). $5.* ✗ ⴕ 🄟 ☎613/990-1985. This magnificent glass, granite and concrete building (1988, Moshe Safdie), capped by prismatic glass "turrets" rises on the banks of the Ottawa River across from the Victorian Gothic parliament buildings. Its bold beauty, light and airy exhibit spaces and tranquil interior courtyards provide a unique setting for the remarkable national collections.

Canadian Art. – *Second floor.* This collection is displayed in a series of galleries arranged to trace the development of Canadian art. In the centre is the reconstructed **chapel** of the Convent of Our Lady of the Sacred Heart (1887) with its decorative fan-vaulted ceiling, cast-iron columns and carved woodwork. Other highlights include the Croscup Room murals, painted in Nova Scotia in the mid-19C; early Quebec religious art, including Louis Jourdain's gold gilt tabernacle and Plamondon's *Portrait of Sister Alphonse*; the works of Paul Kane and Cornelius Krieghoff; Lucius O'Brien's *Sunrise on the Saguenay*; a series of paintings by Tom Thomson and the Group of Seven (notably Thomson's *The Jack Pine,* Jackson's *The Red Maple,* Harris' *North Shore, Lake Superior* and the Group of Seven murals from the MacCullum-Jackman cottage on Georgian Bay). Emily Carr and David Milne are represented along with Marc-Aurele Fortin, Jean-Paul Lemieux, Alfred Pellan *(On the Beach),* Goodridge Roberts, Molinari and Tousignant. Contemporary works by Paul-Émile Borduas, Harold Town, Jack Shadbolt, Michael Snow and Yves Gaucher are also featured.

European and American Art. – *Third floor.* In addition to its Canadian art, the National Gallery owns an impressive and comprehensive collection of European art. Among the highlights are Simone Martini's *St Catherine of Alexandria,* Lucas Cranach the Elder's *Venus,* Bernard Van Orley's *Virgin and Child,* Hieronymous Bosch's tiny yet superbly detailed *Temptation of St Anthony,* Rembrandt's *The Toilet of Esther,* El Greco's *St Francis in Meditation with Brother Leo,* Bernini's fine bust of *Pope Urban VIII* and Benjamin West's *Death of General Wolfe,* the original of this much-reproduced painting. Impressionists are well represented, as are such 20C masters as Fernand Leger *(The Mechanic),* Picasso and Gustav Klimt. Galleries devoted to Inuit and Asian art should not be overlooked.

The large collection of contemporary art is exhibited on both floors.

★★ Canadian Museum of Nature. – *Map p 121. Open May–Labour Day daily 9:30am–5pm (Mon, Thur, Sun 8pm). Off-season daily 10am–5pm (Thur, Sun 8pm). Closed Christmas. $4.* ✗ ⴕ 🄟 ☎613/996-3102. In 1989, the museum took over the entire building at McLeod and Metcalfe streets, which it formerly shared with the Canadian Museum of Civilization. The earth's geological history and the origin of life are the predominant topics of this comprehensive museum.

Interesting exhibits on the creation of oceans and continents, particularly North America, and an outstanding display on **dinosaurs★★** with several complete reconstructions of skeletons, await visitors.

Also noteworthy are films and fine **dioramas★★** of Canadian mammals, such as the muskox of the Northwest Territories, the pronghorn antelope of Saskatchewan, British Columbia's grizzly bear and the moose of New Brunswick. An interesting **Birds in Canada** gallery features life-like dioramas from all regions of the country. Note in particular the Canada geese, complete with sound effects.

Other galleries explore animal life in a more general way with displays on such topics as animal geography, animal behaviour and relationships with mankind. Finally, there is a large conservatory called the **Hall of Plant Life**.

★★ Currency Museum. – *Map p 119. In Bank of Canada complex, 245 Sparks St. Open May– Labour Day Mon–Sat 10:30–5pm, Sun 1–5pm. Off-season Tue–Sun. Closed legal holidays. $2.* ⴕ ☎613/782-8914. This museum presents the history of money from early China, Greece, Rome, Byzantium, Medieval and Renaissance Europe, to its introduction and use in North America. The development of Canadian money is highlighted, with examples of wampum, the card money of New France, Hudson's Bay Company tokens, the first banknotes and decimal currency. The emergence of the Bank of Canada is also depicted.

★★ National Museum of Science and Technology. – *Map p 123. 1867 St Laurent Blvd. Open May–Labour Day daily 9am–5pm (Thur 9pm). Off-season Tue–Sun. Closed Christ-mas. $4.28.* ⴕ 🄟 ☎613/991-3044. The flashing beacon of the old Cape North (Nova Scotia) lighthouse marks the museum's location. Visitors can tour the lighthouse *(visit by 30min guided tour only Victoria Day–Labour Day daily 10am & 2pm)* and see outdoor exhibits such as an Atlas rocket and a steam locomotive.

Displays inside concentrate on transportation. The hall of **steam locomotives** is impressive because of the sheer size of the vehicles. An exhibit on early automobiles (1900-1914) in Canada, ship models and agricultural machinery are also featured. Other sections of the museum are devoted to such themes as the development of printing, communications, computers, physics, astronomy and the exploration of space.

★ Canadian War Museum. – *Map p 119. 330 Sussex Dr. Open daily May–Labour Day. Off-season Tue–Sun. $2.50.* ⴕ ☎613/992-2774. Exhibits on three floors trace the history of war in Canada and wars involving Canadians, from the strife between the French and Iroquois in the 17C to the Korean War. A lifesize reconstruction of a World War I trench complete with sound effects, a room commemorating the soldiers who stormed Vimy Ridge in 1917, a diorama of the Normandy Landings in 1944, and a large armoured Mercedes Benz capable of reaching 217km/135mph and used by Adolf Hitler in the 1930s are featured. In addition, there are changing exhibitions on various military themes.

★ **Laurier House.** – ⑨ *Map p 121. 335 Laurier Ave E. Visit by guided tour (1hr) only Apr–Sept Tue–Sun. Closed legal holidays.* ♿ ☎*613/992-8142.* This yellow brick house with a veranda pays tribute to three Canadian prime ministers. In 1897, Canada's first French-speaking prime minister, **Sir Wilfrid Laurier** (1896-1911), moved into the house. After his death, Lady Laurier willed the house to Canadian prime minister, **William Lyon Mackenzie King,** grandson of the rebel William Lyon Mackenzie. King resided here until his death in 1950, bequeathing the house to the nation, along with his estate in the Gatineau Hills *(p 158).*

The visit includes King's study, bedroom, dining room, two rooms containing Laurier memorabilia and a reconstruction of the library of **Lester Bowles Pearson,** 1957 Nobel Peace Prize winner and prime minister from 1963 to 1968. Pearson did not live in the house, but the photographs and cartoons in his library are fascinating.

★ **Billings Estate Museum.** – *Map p 121. 2100 Cabot St. Open May–Oct Sun–Thur.* ♿ ☎*613/564-1363.* This attractive clapboard house with its dormer windows is one of Ottawa's oldest houses. Built in 1828 by Braddish Billings, the dwelling was inhabited by four generations of his family before becoming the property of the City of Ottawa in 1975. The rooms are full of documents, artifacts, photographs and furniture relating to all four generations.

★ **Agricultural Museum.** – *Map p 121. Building 88, on grounds of Experimental Farm. Open daily Mar–Nov. Off-season weekends only. Closed Christmas & New Year's.* ♿ 🅿 ☎*613/993-4802.* This museum is housed in a barn dating from the 1920s. The machinery displayed, the techniques, even the smells, are evocative of farming in times past. The **Experimental Farm** is the headquarters of the Department of Agriculture. Its fine collection of dairy cattle *(in the basement)* and draught horses can be seen. There are also ornamental gardens and an arboretum *(for information & tours ☎613/995-5222).*

★★ DRIVES AROUND THE CAPITAL

Ottawa is well known for its lovely drives beside the river, along the canal and in the Gatineau Hills to the north.

★★ **Sussex Drive and Rockcliffe** – *Map p 121. 5.5km/3.5mi from Confederation Square. Allow 1.5hrs.* This drive along the river and through the prestigious residential area of Rockcliffe is a pleasant one. After passing the Basilica of Notre Dame and the Canadian War Museum, motorists will see on the right, immediately after the Macdonald-Cartier Bridge to Hull, a modern structure of darkened glass and concrete—the **Lester B. Pearson Building,** which houses the Department of External Affairs. The road then crosses the Rideau River to Green Island past **Ottawa City Hall** [**H**], which offers a pleasant view★ of the river from the top floor *(under renovation).*

★ **Rideau Falls.** – *Park beside French Embassy* [**F**]. On both sides of Green Island, the Rideau River drops over a sheer cliff into the Ottawa River. The falls are said to resemble a curtain, hence their name meaning "curtain" in French. The intensity of the flow depends on the time of year. The falls are best viewed in the spring, or in winter when they are frozen. To see the second set of falls, visitors can cross the first set by a bridge. There are good views of the Ottawa River and Hull.

Along Sussex Drive, the entrance to the official residence of Canadian prime ministers, **24 Sussex Drive,** is seen on the left. Hidden among the trees, the stone house overlooks the river and is best viewed from the water. Around the corner is the gate to Rideau Hall, official residence of the governor general, guarded by military personnel *(open late-Jun–Aug)*. There are **walking tours** of the grounds *(daily Jun 22–Aug 30; for off-season schedule ☎613/998-7113/4)*.

The road then passes through **Rockcliffe Park** via a one-way route. On the return, there are good views of the river. Farther on, however, there are excellent **views★★** from a covered pavilion **[K]** of Pointe Gatineau on the Quebec shore, of log booms in the river and of the Gatineau Hills in the distance. The steepled church in Pointe Gatineau is St François de Sales, built in 1886.

Rockcliffe is an area of large stone houses, tree-lined streets and lovely gardens, occupied by senior civil servants and members of the diplomatic corps. The drive ends at **RCMP Rockcliffe**, where members of the famous **musical ride** and their horses are trained. When the troupe is not on tour, the horses can be seen in training *(stables under renovation; sometimes performances are given; follow signs to visitors' parking outside administration building)*.

★ **Rideau Canal Driveways.** – *Map p 121. About 9km/6mi from Confederation Square. 1hr.* This drive is especially picturesque in tulip time *(May)*. In all seasons, the canal is a centre for sports.

The **Queen Elizabeth Driveway** follows the canal's west bank; the **Colonel By Drive** parallels the east bank. The University of Ottawa is soon passed on the left. Later on, Carleton University will also be seen. At **Dow's Lake** where the canal widens out, there are fine tulip displays in May and paddle boats can be rented. At this point, the two driveways diverge, the Colonel By continuing along the canal, the Queen Elizabeth entering the Experimental Farm. From Colonel By Drive, there are views of Prince of Wales Falls and the Rideau Canal locks before the drive ends at Hog's Back Road.

★ **Prince of Wales Falls.** – *Free parking in Hog's Back Park.* After leaving Mooney's Bay, the Rideau River drops over these falls and rushes through a small gorge. The result of a geological fault that exposed underlying formations and strata, the falls are particularly impressive in the spring thaw. The dam was built by Colonel By in 1829. **Mooney's Bay** marks the end of the canal section of the Rideau Canal, after which the river is navigable. The Bay, with its beach and picnic grounds *(access from Riverside Drive)*, is one of Ottawa's main recreational areas.

★ **Ottawa River Parkway.** – *Map p 123. 11km/7mi starting from Confederation Square. 1hr.* Wellington Street passes the parliament buildings, the Bank of Canada and the Supreme Court, and becomes the parkway just south of Portage Bridge to Hull. Almost immediately, there are signs on the right to **The Mill.** Built in 1842, this old stone structure was once a sawmill and gristmill, standing near a log flume—a means by which timber could be floated downstream without being battered by the Chaudière Falls. The drive beside the Ottawa River is lovely, offering several lookout points for the Remic Rapids. The best view of these rapids is from **Bate Island★** *(take Champlain Bridge to Hull and exit for island)*. The parkway continues, affording other good viewpoints.

★★ **Gatineau Park (Quebec).** – *Map p 123. Circular drive of 55km/34mi from Confederation Square. Allow 3hrs.* Cross Portage Bridge to Hull, turn left on Rte 148 for just over 2km/1.2mi, then turn right on the Gatineau Parkway. *Description p 158.*

PETERBOROUGH   Pop 68,371

Map p 101   Tourist Office ☎705/742-2201

This pleasant city is set on the Otonabee River where it widens into Little Lake, and on the Trent Canal, part of the Trent-Severn Waterway, which links Lake Ontario with Georgian Bay. At this point, there are three locks on the canal, including the famous lift lock.

The Peterborough area is also known for its Indian relics. The largest concentration of petroglyphs anywhere in Canada is protected in **Petroglyphs Provincial Park** on Stony Lake to the north *(open daily May–Sept; $6/car; ☎613/332-3940)*. About 900 carvings of between 500-1,000 years of age can be seen.

★ **Lift Lock.** – ⌚ *In operation daily year-round.* This hydraulic lift lock built in 1904 is one of only eight in the world. In two chambers mounted on large rams, the lift raises and lowers boats 20m/65ft. Water is displaced from one cylinder to the other, causing one chamber to descend as the other rises. Visitors can watch the lock in action from the park beside it.

There are displays and a film on the building and the operation of the lock in the **visitor centre** *(open daily year-round; closed legal holidays; ☎705/745-8389)* administered by the Canadian Parks Service. A slide show *(13min)* explains the Trent-Severn Waterway, which, in addition to 40 regular locks, includes a second lift lock at Kirkfield and a marine railway on the Severn River. Visitors who lack their own marine transportation can experience the lift lock by taking the **boat cruise** *(from Holiday Inn downtown; two cruises daily mid-May–mid-Sept; 2hrs; $14; commentary on board; reservations suggested; Liftlock Cruises ☎705/742-9912)*.

Times given in this guide are approximate. When given with the distance, times allow the visitor to enjoy the scenery; when given for sightseeing, times are intended to provide an idea of the possible length of a visit.

★★ POINT PELEE NATIONAL PARK

Map p 100

Situated on a pointed peninsula extending into **Lake Erie**, this park is one of the few places where the true deciduous forest of eastern North America still exists. Well known to ornithologists across on the continent, the southernmost tip of the Canadian mainland possesses a unique plant and animal life, owing largely to its latitude of 42°N, the same as that of Rome.

The peninsula took its shape 10,000 years ago when wind and lake currents deposited sand on a ridge of glacial till under the waters of Lake Erie. Today the ridge is covered with as much as 60m/200ft of sand. The sand bar continues under the waters of the lake for some distance, creating a hazard for shipping. The sandspit is itself mantled with a lush forest of deciduous trees (there are few evergreens). Covered with vines, white sassafras flourishes alongside hop trees, sumac, black walnut, sycamore, shagbark hickory, hackberry and red cedar. Beneath them, many species of plants thrive, including the prickly pear cactus with its yellow flower.

An Ornithologists' Paradise. – For most people, **birds** are Point Pelee's major attraction. Its location at the convergence of two major flyways, its extension into Lake Erie, and its lack of cultivation have combined to foster large bird populations. Spring and fall migrations can be spectacular—as many as 100 species have been sighted in one day. Over 300 species have been recorded in the park, approximately 100 of them remaining to nest. September is the month of the southern migration for the **monarch butterfly**. Visitors can see trees covered with these beautiful insects.

Access. – 10km/6mi from Leamington.

VISIT

❂ Open year-round. Hiking, fishing, bicycling (canoe & bicycle rental), swimming, ski trails, skating. $5/day per car; $10/4days per car. ⚠. For additiional information & reservation contact park superintendent ☎519/322-2365. Excellent flora and fauna displays await discovery in the **visitor centre★★** (7km/4mi south of park entrance; open daily year-round; closed legal holidays in winter; ✗ & ☎519/322-2371), together with an interesting account of the peninsula's creation. Slide presentations and films about the park can also be viewed. A nature trail (2km/1.2mi) begins from the centre.

Marshland between the sand bars can be toured by a **boardwalk★** (1km/.6mi) and two lookout towers provide good **views★** of the marsh, where muskrats, turtles and fish as well as birds can be seen.

From the end of the transit ride, visitors can walk to the tip of the peninsula, which is an ideal place, in the fall, to observe birds across the lake beginning their southern migration. The modern lighthouse offshore stands on the sand bar. From the peninsula's tip, paths lead in both directions along the park's 22km/14mi fine sandy beaches (accessible from other places also).

★ PRESCOTT — Pop 4,512

Map p 101

This small industrial town on the St Lawrence is the only deep-water port between Montreal and Kingston. Originally settled by Loyalists, the community was the chosen location for a fort to protect ships from American attack during the War of 1812. It was also the site of the **Battle of the Windmill** in 1838 when rebel supporters of Mackenzie (p 130) and their American sympathizers were dislodged, only with difficulty, from a windmill on the riverbank. Today, relations with the US are more cordial; an international bridge spans the river near the town.

★ **Fort Wellington.** – ❂ On Hwy 2, just east of town. Open daily mid-May–Labour Day. Off-season Mon–Fri. Mid-Oct–mid-May by reservation only. & ☎613/925-2896. Built by the British, this small earthen fort includes officers' quarters and a three-storey stone **blockhouse**, restored to reflect its 1840s appearance. The third weekend in July, the fort becomes the annual setting of an historic **military pageant**. Performers are attired in British and American regimental uniforms of the period.

East of the fort (1.5km/1mi), between Highway 2 and the river, stands the **windmill** of battle fame. Today, it serves as a lighthouse, but there are displays on the battle and a pleasant **view** of the river (picnic tables).

★★ SAULT STE MARIE — Pop 81,476

Map of Principal Sights p 4   Tourist Office ☎705/949-7152

Connected to Michigan's city of the same name by road and railway bridges, this Ontario city is an industrial centre with huge steelworks and a pulp mill. The "Soo," as it is commonly called, lies on the north side of **St Mary's River**, the international boundary and waterway that connects Lakes Superior and Huron, forming an important link in the St Lawrence Seaway.

The rapids in the river between the two cities were a gathering place from earliest times when Ojibwa Indians came to catch whitefish here. Étienne Brulé visited the rapids in 1622, as did many of the great explorers of New France: Nicolet, Radisson, Groseilliers, Marquette, Jolliet, LaSalle, the La Vérendrye family and others. In 1668, Pére Marquette established a mission beside them, calling it Sainte Marie du Sault (sault means "falls" in French). Gateway to the wild and uninhabited **Algoma** wilderness, Sault Ste Marie today is also the headquarters of the Firebirds, the province's aerial firefighters who control the spread of forest fires by such methods as water-bombing.

★ **The Soo Locks.** – These locks are the busiest section of the entire seaway, handling up to eighty lockages per day and an average of more than 90 million tonnes/100 million tons of cargo annually. To bypass the rapids, the **North West Company** completed the first lock and canal in 1798 (destroyed during the War of 1812). Since then, locks of increasing size have been constructed and today, the enormous ships of the Great Lakes are able to bypass the rapids by four parallel locks on the American side of the river.

The vast lock system in the river can be appreciated either by driving to the base of Huron Street, where, nearby, there is a reconstruction of the **first lock [A]**, or by taking a **boat trip** *(departs from dock off Foster Dr daily Jun–mid-Oct; round-trip 2-3hrs; $14; dinner-cruise Thur–Sat $40; & Lock Tours ☎705/253-9850)* that passes through one of the large American locks.

★ **City Hall.** – At the base of Brock Street, Sault Ste Marie has a pleasant riverfront area dominated by its attractive City Hall, built of copper-coloured reflecting glass. Nearby stands the permanently berthed *MS Norgoma* **[B]**, the last overnight passenger ship used on the Great Lakes *(docked next to Holiday Inn, open daily Jun–Aug)*. On board the ship is a museum of Great Lakes history.

★ **Ermatinger House.** – *Open daily Jun–Sept. Off-season Mon–Fri. Closed Dec–Mar. & ☎705/759-5443*. This attractive Georgian stone house was built in 1814 by Charles Oakes Ermatinger, a partner in the North West Company, for his wife Charlotte, an Ojibwa princess. It has been restored to reflect this period when it stood almost alone in the region and received many eminent visitors.

Among the guests was **Paul Kane** (1810-1871), who made several long canoe trips across Canada, sketching and making notes about the Indians of the Great Lakes, Plains and Pacific Coast regions. On his return to Toronto, he wrote *Wanderings of an Artist among the Indians of North America,* which was published in 1859. On the second floor, there are interesting displays on the history of Sault Ste Marie and of the Ermatinger family.

Bellevue Park. – From this park on the river, there are fine **views★** of the ships using the locks and of the bridge to the US.

EXCURSIONS

★ **Gros Cap.** – *26km/16mi west by Hwy 550*. From this headland, there is a good **view★** of Lake Superior and the beginning of the St Mary's River.

Train Trip to Agawa Canyon. – *183km/114mi by Algoma Central Railway; departs from Bay St daily at 8am Jun–mid-Oct, returns at 5pm. Snow train Jan–Mar weekends only. $42.75. Commentary on board. Reservations suggested. ✗ & Algoma Central ☎705/254-4331*. The train traverses some of the Algoma wilderness north of Sault Ste Marie. At a stopover in Agawa Canyon *(2hrs, except in winter)*, travellers can climb to a lookout for a fine **view★** of the canyon and the Agawa River. The trip is especially popular in late September for viewing the autumn colours.

★★ **Lake Superior Drive.** – *Map p 4. 230km/143mi by Trans-Can Hwy (Rte 17) to Wawa*. This drive is ruggedly beautiful. The road cuts through some of the oldest rock formations in the world, the Canadian Shield. After Batchawana Bay, the wild shore of Lake Superior is followed for a lengthy stretch, with views of headlands, coves, islands, rocks and high granite bluffs pounded by the waters of this, the deepest of the Great Lakes. The drive is especially fine around **Alona Bay★** *(viewpoint after 108km/67mi)* and **Agawa Bay★** *(viewpoint after 151km/94mi)*. Lookouts have been built beside the road.

For 84km/52mi, the road passes through **Lake Superior Provincial Park** *(open daily mid-May–Sept; swimming, hiking; boat rental; ⚠ & ☎705/856-2284)*, a wilderness area of forested hills and cliffs rising straight out of the lake. The park is known for its Indian **pictographs**—primitive rock paintings often commemorating great events or relating to nature. After 153km/95mi, a side road leads to a parking lot from which a rugged trail *(10min)* descends to the lake. A series of pictographs possibly several hundred years old can be found on **Agawa Rock★**, a sheer rock face rising out of the water. The **view★** of the lake is excellent.

★ STRATFORD
Pop 27,666

Map p 100   Tourist Office ☎519/271-5140

This community is home to the annual **Shakespeare Festival**, a major theatrical event of the English-speaking world that attracts people from all over North America. Though the focus is still Shakespearean, the festival offers a wide variety of drama and music.

The festival is said to have had its beginnings in 1830 when one William Sargint called his establishment on the Huron Road to Goderich the Shakespeare Inn. The community that grew up around the hostelry adopted the name of the birthplace of the famous English dramatist, and named the river the Avon. In 1952, local journalist **Tom Patterson** dreamed of creating a festival to celebrate the works of the town's namesake. From modest beginnings in a tent a year later, the festival has grown to its present seven-month season *(May–Nov)* in three theatres, drawing a yearly audience of nearly 500,000. *For performance schedule & reservations contact the Box Office, Stratford Festival, PO Box 520, Stratford, ON, N5A 6V2.* ☎519/273-1600.

Festival Theatre. – Reflecting the tent of its origin, this building resembling a circus "big top" contains an *apron* or thrust stage, surrounded by audience seating on three sides. This modern development of the Elizabethan stage used in Shakespeare's day was revolutionary in the 1950s (but much copied since) because no elaborate scenery could be used and no member of the audience was more than 20m/65ft from the stage.

The theatre is set at the edge of a pleasant park that stretches down to the river, dammed at this point to form **Victoria Lake**, the home of many swans. Before evening performances in the summer, the beautifully manicured lawns and the small island in the lake are covered with picnicking theatre-goers. At intermission, the elegantly attired crowd wanders among the formal flower beds and over the lawns surrounding the theatre.

★★ SUDBURY
Pop 92,884

Map p 100   Tourist Office ☎705/673-2171

Located on the largest single source of nickel in the world, Sudbury is one of the biggest and most important mining centres in Canada. The nickel-bearing rock strata are part of the **Sudbury Basin**, an approximately 60km/37mi long and 27km/17mi wide geological formation created by meteoric impact or volcanic eruption millions of years ago. Geological opinion is divided on the issue.

Whatever its origins, the basin's wealth (platinum, copper, cobalt, silver and gold, in addition to nickel) was discovered in 1883 during the construction of the Canadian Pacific Railway. A blacksmith named **Thomas Flanagan** noticed a rust-coloured patch of rock while working with a crew in a recently blasted area just west of the present city.

Today, the discovery is commemorated by a plaque *(on Hwy 144 near the Murray Mine)*, and Sudbury claims the world's largest integrated nickel mining, smelting and refining complex. The **Super Stack**, an enormous smoke stack rising 380m/1,250ft above the surrounding countryside, tops the complex. Despite its industrial importance and reputation for pollution, the Sudbury region is typical Canadian Shield country of beautiful lakes, rocks and trees. A number of lakes are encompassed within city limits, including **Lake Ramsey**, which has enough pickerel to supply local fishermen, and beaches just a short walk from the civic centre.

Sudbury is also one of the principal centres of francophone culture in Ontario. The **Franco-Ontarians** make up about a quarter of the population of this region, which they prefer to call *Le Nouvel Ontario* rather than Northern Ontario. **Laurentian University**, which serves the northeastern part of the province, is bilingual, and there are a variety of other French cultural organizations and festivals.

SIGHTS *1/2 day*

★★★ **Science North.** – *About 1.5km/1mi south of Trans-Can Hwy by Paris St on Ramsey Lake Rd. Open Jul–Labour Day daily 9am–6pm. Off-season 10am–4pm. Closed Christmas & Boxing Day. $7.50* 🍴 ♿ *☎705/522-3701.* Perched on a rock outcropping on the shores of Lake Ramsey, this dramatic science centre was designed by Raymond Moriyama in association with local architects. A hexagonal exhibit building resembling a snowflake (to represent the glacial action that shaped Northern Ontario) is set over a cavern blasted out of the rock (to represent the probable creation of Sudbury Basin by a meteor). Exhibits emphasize first-hand experience with science and northern technology in a vivid way.

Visitors enter a small reception building (also hexagonal in shape), and proceed to the centre proper via a **rock tunnel**. Raw rock is exposed as it is in the impressive **rock cavern** (9m/30ft high by 30m/100ft in diameter), where a 3D-film on the Northern Ontario wilderness is shown. Visitors then ascend to the exhibit floors via a spiral ramp that zigzags over the **Creighton Fault**, a geological fracture within the Canadian Shield, active over 2 billion years ago, that left a groove 4m/13ft deep at this point. Hanging over the fault is a 23m/72ft fin whale skeleton, weighing 1800kg/4,000lb, recovered from Anticosti Island. The glass walls of the ramp offer views of Lake Ramsey. Museum staff are on hand in the fitness centre, for example, where visitors can be tested for correct body weight, or in the Alex Baumann Human Performance Lab, where visitors can discover their fitness level. There is a section devoted to endangered species. Seen in the small creatures area are such insects as a "walking-stick" or the museum's pet porcupine, who grows his furry coat in summer when the building is air-conditioned and loses it in winter when his home is heated.

There is a weather station, an atmosphere laboratory that records the pollution of the Sudbury Basin, a seismic station, and a dynamics laboratory. Displays on computers and communications can be seen as well. Science shows are presented regularly in the Discovery Theatre, and there are films and demonstrations from time to time.

From the dock, **boat tours** of the lake can be taken *(depart daily mid-May–Sept; 1hr; $7.50; commentary on board; reservations suggested; ✗ & Cortina Cruise Boat* ☎*705/673-7844)*, and there are also bus tours of the area *(see below)*.

★★ **Big Nickel Mine.** – *On Trans-Can Hwy just west of city. Visit by guided tour (1hr) only mid-May–Thanksgiving daily 9am–5pm. $6* ☎*705/522-3701.* Operated by Science North, this mine is the only authentic hard-rock mine open to the public in Ontario. Visitors descend 21m/70ft by a miners' cage to the underground "drifts" or tunnels where the mining process (drilling, blasting and other procedures) is explained and demonstrated. There is even a simulated blasting sequence. Near the mine stands the **Big Nickel**, a replica of the 1951 Canadian commemorative five-cent piece. Long a Sudbury landmark, the replica is 9m/30ft high and 0.6m/2ft thick.

Path of Discovery. – *Visit by organized tour only twice daily Jul–Aug. 2hrs 30min. $11.* ☎*705/522-3701.* Organized by Science North, this bus tour enables visitors to appreciate the giant mining, smelting and refining operations of the Sudbury Basin. Highlights are the visit to the Inco refinery and to Super Stack. A stop is made at the Big Nickel Mine.

★★ THUNDER BAY
Pop 113,946

Map of Principal Sights p 4   Tourist Office ☎807/625-2149

Situated almost in the centre of Canada on the shores of Lake Superior, the city of Thunder Bay is an important port and the Canadian "lakehead," or western extremity, of the St Lawrence Seaway. Its clutter of rail lines transport a wide range of commodities—wheat from the Prairies being the most important—to docks for transfer to the huge ships of the seaway.

Linchpin of the Fur Trade. – This exchange of goods and transportation is not the result of the St Lawrence Seaway's construction. For many years, the area was the linchpin of the fur trade. Every summer, brigades of canoes left the widespread posts of the North West Company in the northwest to transport a year's collection of furs to a fort called Fort William. There these "wintering" partners (so named because they spent the winter in the wilds) met the Montreal partners who had made the long canoe trek through the Great Lakes with the trading goods their counterparts would need for the next year. Lasting about six weeks, the "**rendezvous**" was a time of wild celebration, as well as serious discussion of trading policy and strategy against the rival Hudson's Bay Company, who took their furs to market by way of the great bay. When the two fur-trading companies merged in 1821, Fort William lost its position as the place of the great rendezvous, but remained a fur-trading post until late in the century. In 1970, the communities of **Fort William** and **Port Arthur** were amalgamated to create the city of Thunder Bay. The city has 15 enormous grain elevators dominating the skyline, with a capacity of more than 2 million tonnes/2.2 million tons; one of them, the **Saskatchewan Pool Terminal No. 7**, alone holds 362,650 tonnes/398,915 tons, making it one of the largest in the world.

Today, the fort has been re-created as it was at its peak, and every year the rendezvous is re-enacted *(July)*.

VISIT 1 day

★★ **Harbour Cruise.** – *Departs Port Arthur Marina at foot of Red River Rd (Hwy 102) mid-May–Thanksgiving daily 2pm. 2hrs. $12.50. Reservations suggested. & Welcome Ship* ☎*807/344-2512.* This fascinating cruise is the only way to appreciate the impressive port, and the sheer size of the grain **elevators** and **lakers** that load from them. The largest of these ships may be 222m/728ft by 23m/75ft, capable of carrying a million bushels of grain—the yield of 20,650ha/51,000 acres of land, which requires 5 trains to carry it to Thunder Bay! Also seen are the ore docks, shipyards and drydock; the Coast Guard centre with its hovercraft used to break ice in the winter; and the breakwater protecting the harbour from the storms of Lake Superior. Waves can be 12m/40ft high in autumn. In summer, the lake is calmer, and sailboat races are held weekly within and outside of the breakwater.

★★ **Old Fort William.** – *Map p 129. 16km/10mi south by Broadway Ave. Also accessible by boat; departs Port Arthur marina mid-Jun–early-Sept daily 10am. $15. & Welcome Ship* ☎*807/344-2512. Fort open mid-May–mid-Oct daily 10am–5pm. $7.25 ✗ &* ☎*807/577-8461.* Located on the Kaministikwia River, part of the trade route to the northwest, the fort of the great rendezvous has been superbly reconstructed. From the visitor centre, visitors can walk through the woods to the palisaded fort, which is almost a town. Inside the palisade, there is a large square of dovetailed log buildings, several raised above the ground on stilts (the river still floods). Some 50 structures represent all aspects of early 19C fur-trade society. Costumed guides help re-create fort life. The North West Company partners can be seen discussing business in the council house; the warehouses are full of furs and trading goods; and birchbark canoes, ships and barrels are under construction or repair. Other highlights include a farm, apothecary, Indian encampments, living quarters and a jail.

★ **Viewpoints.** – Thunder Bay is surrounded by the hills of the Canadian Shield. The city is hemmed in across the bay by a long peninsula that rears its head at the end to form a cape called **Sleeping Giant** because its resembles the prone figure of a man.

* **Mount McKay**. – *At end of Mountain Rd on Indian reservation.* This prominent flat-topped peak is the highest (488m/1,600ft) of the Norwester Chain. From a ledge 180m/600ft high, there is a fine **view** on clear days of the city, port and Sleeping Giant guarding the entrance to the harbour.

* **Hillcrest Park**. – *High St between John St Rd and Red River Rd.* Located on a cliff above Port Arthur, this park provides a good **view** of the port, elevators, ore dock and, in the distance, Sleeping Giant and the islands that close the harbour mouth.

EXCURSIONS *Map below*

** **Kakabeka Falls**. – *29km/18mi west by Trans-Can Hwy (Rte 17). Provincial park open year-round. $6/vehicle. ☐ △ For information & reservations ☎807/473-9231.* The Kaministikwia River plunges 39m/128ft over a cliff around a pinnacle of rock into a narrow gorge. A bridge crosses the river to enable visitors to view the falls from both sides. These falls were the first obstacle negotiated by the fur traders of the North West Company when leaving Fort William on their return trip to the north-west.

** **North Shore Lake Superior**. – *211km/131mi to Schreiber by Trans-Can Hwy.* This route passes several interesting features northeast of Thunder Bay.

Terry Fox Monument and Scenic Lookout. – *1km/.6mi east of Hodder Ave.* The fine bronze monument commemorates the heroic efforts of Terry Fox to raise money to fight cancer. Deprived of his right leg by the disease at age 18, he undertook a cross-Canada run in 1980, starting in Newfoundland. Two months later, he was forced to abandon his run close to this spot because of recurring cancer from which he died in 1981. The monument overlooks Lake Superior.

* **Sleeping Giant Provincial Park**. – *After 51km/32mi, take Rte 587. Open mid-May–mid-Oct. $6/vehicle. ☐ △ For information & reservations ☎807/933-4332.* Occupying most of the peninsula that has the Sleeping Giant at its end, this pleasant park features trails, high cliffs, fine **views**★ of Lake Superior, and the remains of the village of Silver Islet. This community was formed in 1868 when a rich silver vein was discovered on the tiny islet offshore. The vertical vein yielded $300 million worth of ore before the shaft flooded at a depth of 400m/1,300ft.

Amethyst Mine. – *After 56km/35mi, take East Loon Rd for 8km/5mi. Open daily mid-May–mid-Oct. ☐ ☎807/622-6908.* Amethyst is found in many places along the north shore of Lake Superior. This open-pit mine is a rockhound's delight as pieces of the purple quartz can be collected *(charge of $1/lb)*, or polished stones purchased.

** **Ouimet Canyon**. – *After 76km/47mi, take road for 12km/8mi. Open daily mid-May–mid-Oct. ☎807/933-4332.* This incredible canyon is quite a startling find in the country north of Lake Superior. Gashed out of the surface of the Canadian Shield during the last ice age, possibly along an existing fault line, the canyon is 100m/330ft deep, 150m/500ft across and more than 1.5km/1mi long. It is rocky and barren except for a few Arctic flowers that grow on its floor; the cold, sunless environment will support little else.

Just after the Red Rock turnoff on the Trans-Canada Highway, a cliff of layered limestone coloured red by hematite can be seen. Called the **Red Rock Cuesta**, this unusual geological formation is nearly 210m/690ft high and about 3km/2mi long.

** **Nipigon Bay**. – *88km/55mi from Nipigon to Schreiber.* After crossing the Nipigon River, the Trans-Canada Highway runs along the shore of this bay, offering **views**★★ of rocky islands covered with conifers and rocks worn smooth by the action of Lake Superior.

The **view**★★ of Kama Bay through the Kama Rock Cut *(27km/17mi from Nipigon)* is particularly fine. The rock itself indicates the type of problems involved in the construction of this highway in 1960, the same encountered in the building of the Canadian Pacific Railway.

★★★ TORONTO

Map of Principal Sights p 4

Dynamic, cosmopolitan, stimulating, Toronto is the heartbeat of Canada. Having surpassed Montreal in size in 1977, the country's largest city ranks ninth in North America.

A forward-looking metropolis protective of its past, Toronto has restored its architectural treasures and preserved its history. Waves of immigrants have repeatedly integrated with the population, enhancing the city's cultural legacy. Toronto's size, heritage and diversity have much to offer: world-class exhibits, colourful neighborhoods, lively markets, stately hotels, historic mansions, a vibrant harbourfront, wide-ranging cuisine and cultural events, and multiple recreational activities.

Sprawling over 600sq km/372sq mi in the southeast leg of the province, the metropolis is set on the broad north shore of **Lake Ontario**. An active port thanks to the St Lawrence Seaway, Toronto is the hub of the **Golden Horseshoe**, the 60km/100mi wide arc stretching from Oshawa to Hamilton where 24 percent of Canada's manufacturing is based. Its fine harbour is almost landlocked by a chain of offshore islands *(p 133)* that provide the city with its major parkland.

Flat beside the lake, the land rises noticeably about 5km/3mi inland at the old shoreline of prehistoric Lake Iroquois. The plain is intersected by a number of small rivers that have created a network of ravines. On the west, Toronto is bordered by the **Humber River** *(map p 142)* and to the east, the **Don**. In the recent past, the ravines and river valleys have largely been used for parks.

HISTORICAL NOTES

In their search for food and trade, native inhabitants of the area had long used the rivers as a transportation system. Prior to 1600, the **Huron** and **Petun** peoples abandoned their north shorelands to the warring **Iroquois Confederacy**. The Iroquois occupied the vacated territory to strengthen their fur trade, only to be evicted themselves by French traders, to whom this "Toronto Passage" of trails and canoe routes between Lakes Huron and Ontario was well known.

The French Regime. – The site of Toronto was important to the burgeoning fur trade. As early as 1615, it was visited by **Étienne Brulé**, one of Champlain's men who travelled widely in Ontario. Years later, French traders under royal command met native and English traders at a bartering post on the banks of the Humber River in the vicinity of what is now Toronto, a Huron word for "meeting place." Attempting to curb competition, the French began construction in 1720 of several forts around mammoth Lake Ontario. The remains of **Fort Rouillé** have been found in Toronto's Exhibition Grounds. To prevent British use, the French destroyed the fort in 1759 during the Seven Years' War, the war that signalled the end of French presence in the area.

Muddy York. – The site was first ignored by the new British rulers, but in 1787, **Lord Dorchester**, the governor-in-chief of Canada, made arrangements to buy land equivalent in size to present-day metropolitan Toronto from the **Mississaugas**, who had occupied it after the Iroquois. Loyalists fleeing the US had also settled along the lake; their demands for English law eventually led to the formation of Upper Canada (now Ontario) in 1791. Col **John Graves Simcoe**, lieutenant-governor of the new territory, decided upon Toronto, despite its swamps, as the site for a new capital, because of its fine harbour and distance from the American border. (The existing capital, Niagara-on-the-Lake, was considered too close to the enemy.) Baptized **York** after the victorious soldier-son of George III, the new outpost grew slowly, despite such grandiose projects as the building of **Yonge Street**. By the outbreak of the War of 1812, the unpaved streets of this swamp town gave the village the unfortunate sobriquet, "Muddy York."

In April 1813, the town was jolted by an American fleet that captured and set fire to the Legislature and other imposing buildings. In retaliation for this assault and the burning of Niagara-on-the-Lake, the British attacked and set fire to part of Washington, DC, the capital of the US, in 1814.

The Family Compact. – After 1814, York grew as waves of immigrants from Britain came to Ontario in the wake of the Napoleonic Wars. A small group of wealthy, privileged men with strong British ties dominated the government of York—and the whole of Upper Canada. By appointing officials only from their ranks, they guarded their exclusive elite. New arrivals began to challenge the power of what was called "the Family Compact." A fiery Scot named **William Lyon Mackenzie** (1795-1861) attacked the group in his newspaper, *The Colonial Advocate*. In 1828, he was elected to the legislative assembly, becoming leader of the radical wing of the Reform Party. Expelled by the compact, he was re-elected and re-expelled five times. However, in 1835, he was elected the first mayor of the City of Toronto, newly incorporated in 1834 (the city's original name had fallen from favour as its namesake, the Duke of York, continued to lose in battle). Mackenzie then reassumed his seat in the Legislature. The assembly was dissolved in 1836 by Gov **Sir Francis Bond Head**, and subsequent elections brought the defeat of the Reform Party.

Gaining no satisfaction from the British Parliament, Mackenzie turned to armed rebellion in December 1837. When Toronto's garrison was away in Lower Canada, he gathered supporters at **Montgomery's Tavern** (which stood near the present intersection of Yonge Street and Eglinton Avenue) and marched towards the city. Loyal citizens hurriedly formed a defence, but quickly dispersed after a skirmish with Mackenzie's men. Unknown to them, Mackenzie's forces had also retreated. Reinforcements arrived under Col Allan MacNab the following day, the revolt collapsed, and Mackenzie fled to the US.

ONTARIO

Toronto the Good. – Although two of Mackenzie's men were publicly hanged, the revolt was effective in that British Parliament ultimately granted "responsible government" to the Canadian colonies. The united Province of Canada was created *(p 18)*, and Mackenzie was permitted to return in 1849. The revolt bred among Torontonians an enduring hatred of violence and a resulting support for government. By the end of the 19C, Toronto's reputation was one of Anglo-Saxon rectitude. As a major manufacturing centre, the city had become immensely wealthy. Prosperous financiers, industrials and merchants were united in their desire to preserve Sunday as a day of rest and church-going, and in their belief that intemperance was a fundamental social problem. Toronto was nicknamed "The Good," but considered dull.

Toronto Today: The Urban Miracle. – As late as 1941, Toronto was 80 percent Anglo-Saxon, but since World War II, this once-homogeneous city has opened its doors to immigrants from around the world. Today, Italians, Germans, Ukrainians, Dutch, Poles, Scandinavians, Portuguese, East Indians, Chinese, West Indians and other nationalities have made their home here, giving Toronto a stimulating mix of indigenous and imported cultures. **Kensington Market**, several adjacent streets containing outdoor and indoor vendors, is the realm of the Portuguese and East Indian communities *(best time to visit is Mon-Sat mornings)*. One of the largest Chinese districts in North America, **Chinatown** *(Dundas St from Elizabeth to Spadina sts)* is also vibrant with street vendors, notably exotic-produce merchants. The Italian districts *(College St west of Bathurst St)* evoke the mother country. Particularly active between Spadina and John streets, **Queen Street West** has become a colourful area of trendy bistros, unusual bookstores and young designer boutiques.

The last 25 years have seen the Toronto skyline transformed. Shining glass-fronted skyscrapers and "spacescraper" CN Tower overshadow the once-dominant **Royal York Hotel** and old **Bank of Commerce**. Rapid development has been highly controversial, however. Citizen-action groups formed to halt destruction of residential areas for proposed freeways and highrises. The city was the first in North America to adopt a tiered system of metropolitan government to solve problems caused by 19C municipal boundaries.

Toronto's port has suffered since the opening of the St Lawrence Seaway when the era of containerization began. Cargo unloaded at ports such as Halifax and St John's on the East Coast is containerized, and shipped inland via rail, bypassing Toronto's waterways.

Practical Information

Public Transportation. – The Toronto Transit Commission (TTC) operates an extensive public transport system comprising buses, streetcars and subway. Hours of operation: Mon–Sat 6–1am, Sun 9–1am. Adult fare is $2 one-way ($3 two-way) for unlimited travel with no stopovers. Day Pass $5. Tokens 10 for $13. Exact fare is required. Free transfers to buses & streetcars. System maps & timetables available free of charge. For route information & schedules ☎416/393-INFO.

Taxis. – Co-op ☎416/364-8161; Diamond ☎416/366-6868; Metro Cab ☎416/363-5757.

Car Rentals. – Avis ☎416/777-AVIS; Hertz ☎416/620-9620; Tilden/National ☎416/925-2072.

Parking. – Toronto has a strictly enforced tow-away policy. Motorists should park in designated parking areas; public, off-street parking facilities are located throughout the city. For parking fee information & free map ☎416/393-7275.

Tourist Office. – Visitor Information Centre, Yonge St outside Eaton Centre (open late-May–Labour Day Mon–Sat 9am–7pm, Sun 9:30am–6pm; off-season Tue–Sat 9:30am–5:30pm; ☎416/368-9821) or write to Metropolitan Toronto Convention & Visitors Association, 207 Queen's Quay West, Toronto, ON, M5J 1A7 ☎800/ONTARIO, or 800/363-1990 (toll-free US).

Newspapers. – Daily: *The Toronto Star, The Toronto Sun,* and *The Globe and Mail.* Monthly guides (free) to entertainment, shopping, and restaurants: *Where, Now.*

Entertainment. – Consult arts and entertainment supplements in local newspapers (Thur & Fri edition) for schedule of cultural events and addresses of principal theatres and concert halls. Ticketmaster ☎416/870-8000 for concerts or 416/872-1111 for theatre & arts (major credit cards accepted).

Sports. – Toronto Blue Jays (baseball). Home games are played at SkyDome. Season: Apr–Oct. For tickets ☎416/341-1111. Toronto Maple Leafs (ice hockey). Home games are played at Maple Leaf Gardens. Season: Oct–Apr. For schedules ☎416/977-1641; tickets ☎416/872-5000 (Ticketmaster). Toronto Argonauts (football). Home games are played at Skydome. Season: mid-Jun–Nov. For schedules ☎416/595-1131; tickets ☎416/872-5000 (Ticketmaster).

Useful Numbers (Area Code 416)

Toronto (Pearson) International Airport		676-3506
Union Station (VIA Rail)	*Front & Bay sts*	366-8411
Bus terminal	*610 Bay St*	393-7911
Canadian Automobile Assoc. Travel Store	*2 Carlton St*	593-7479
CAA Toronto Emergency Road Serivce (24hr)		222-5222
Road Conditions		235-1110
Weather (24hr)		676-3066

Cultural and Sports Centre. – The centre of English-language culture in Canada, Toronto boasts the Toronto Symphony and the Mendelssohn Choir at Roy Thomson Hall, concerts at Massey Hall, the National Ballet of Canada, the Toronto Dance Theatre, Harbourfront Centre's Premiere Dance Theatre, and the Canadian Opera Company at the O'Keefe Centre. The St Lawrence Centre for the Arts, the Royal Alexandra, and the Elgin and Winter Garden Theatres stage traditional and popular drama. Every fall, the city hosts a world film festival, and summer brings a variety of outdoor entertainments. Several annual events draw visitors: the **Canadian National Exhibition** *(at the Exhibition Grounds three weeks before Labour Day)*, reputedly the world's largest exhibition, now primarily of consumer goods; the **Metro International Caravan**, a festival of ethnic cultures *(late Jun, pavilions throughout the city, special buses)*; the **Dragon Boat Race Festival**, a Chinese celebration *(Jun)*, and **Caribana**, a West Indies festival of steel bands and floating nightclubs on the lake *(Aug)*. Spectators sports are plentiful: *Toronto Blue Jays* baseball, *Maple Leaf* ice hockey games, an annual canoeing and rowing regatta *(July 1)*, horse shows *(particularly the Royal Winter Fair)*, soccer and auto racing. *For details contact the Metropolitan Toronto Convention & Visitor Association ☎416/368-9821.*

Maple Leaf ice hockey game

Graig Abel, Toronto

** **THE WATERFRONT** Map p 138. 2 days.

Built largely on land reclaimed in the mid-19 to mid-20C for the city's growing port installations, the area south of Front Street contains Toronto's foremost landmarks and its largest lakefront revitalization.

Crucial to the city's founding, the waterfront experienced growth and eventual decline of its maritime functions, now transferred to the commercial port east of Yonge Street. Lake shipping waned in the 1960s, and recession subsequently idled the harbourfront. Although scarred by remains of defunct industries, the area underwent gradual revitalization beginning in the early 1970s. Over the following 20 years, land north of the expressway was selected as the site of two major building projects—the CN Tower and SkyDome.

While further development of the railroad corridor and lakefront is anticipated, several quays have already been overhauled to house colourful shops, galleries, performance arenas, restaurants and sailing schools. Recent construction of an outdoor stage known as Molson Place confirms the area's growing popularity.

*** **CN Tower.** – The city's most prominent landmark, this concrete, rocket-like structure reaches 180 storeys (over 553m/1,815ft in height). Constructed at a cost of $52 million, the tower is the tallest free-standing structure in the world and a popular Toronto tourist attraction (1.4 million visitors a year).

Beginning in 1972, the tower was built over a four-year period by federally owned Canadian National (formerly Canadian National Railways) to provide telecommunications services. Topped by a powerful antenna, the tower serves FM radio and television stations *(telecommunications facilities not open to the public)* whose transmitters line the mast.

Visit. – *Access from Front St.* ●*Union, then via Skywalk. Open mid-May–mid-Oct Mon–Sat 9am–midnight, Sun 10am–10pm. Off-season daily 10am–10pm (Fri & Sat 11pm). $11.95.* ✗ ♿ ☎*416/360-8500.* In only 58 seconds, visitors are "beamed up" 346m/1,136ft (nearly the height of the Empire State Building) in an exterior glass-front elevator to **Skypod**, a circular steel "turban" seven storeys high. From its observation decks, **views**★★ of the city and suburbs, the lake and shoreline are suberb *(illuminated panels identify buildings and parks)*, providing a vivid aerial orientation to Toronto. Digital read-outs of current time, temperature, visibility, barometric pressure, humidity, atmospheric pollution and wind velocity can be checked.

Not for the faint-hearted is an ascent 33 storeys higher to the smaller observation gallery named **Space Deck**, a flying-saucer shaped, windowed ring 447m/1,465ft above the ground, reached via an elevator inside the tower. The sweeping **views**★★★ of the cityscape and Lake Ontario are spectacular. The feeling of height is reinforced by planes from nearby Toronto Island Airport flying below. If visibility is good, Niagara Falls and Buffalo, 120km/75mi away, can be seen.

** **SkyDome.** – Dominating railway land next to CN Tower—one of the few central locations big enough to hold it—this huge domed sports/entertainment complex is home to American League Baseball's *Toronto Blue Jays*. The multi-purpose stadium hosts rock concerts, opera, conventions and trade shows as well as sports. Designed by architect Roderick Robbie and engineer Michael Allen, SkyDome was built (1986-1989) by a private consortium in partnership with local and provincial governments for $585 million.

Visit. – ● *Union. Guided tours offered; times depend on event schedule.* ✗ ⅁ ⚡ *⚡416/341-2770. For general information ⚡416/341-3663.* Projecting from the Front Street facade 5m/16ft above street level, Michael Snow's collection of 15 painted-fiberglass sculptures *(The Audience)* towers over arriving visitors.

The stadium boasts an 3ha/8 acre **retractable roof**, a 346-room hotel overlooking the ballfield, a 150-seat cinema, shops, several restaurants and underground parking for 575 vehicles. In the open-air mode, the four roof panels are stacked over the north end of the field. In 20 minutes, the panels can be closed by pushing a button to activate a computer-controlled operation. Tall enough to accommodate a 31-storey building, the roof is 206m/675ft at its widest and rises to a height of 96m/310ft at its centre. The arena's flexible field (basketball, football, tennis, track or hockey configurations) and seating can be arranged for a crowd of 53,000 or an audience of 10,000.

★ **Fort York.** – *Access by Bathurst streetcar or by car: from Lakeshore Blvd take Strachan just before Princes' Gate entrance to Exhibition Grounds, then right on Fleet St and left on Garrison Rd (under Gardiner Expressway). Open daily year-round. Closed Christmas, Boxing Day, New Year's, Good Friday. $4.75.* ✗ ⚡ *⚡416/392-6907.* In stark contrast to the backdrop of Toronto's towering skyline stand the dwarfed remains of this historic garrison. Once strategically positioned on the lake's edge, Fort York was the primary guardian of Toronto's harbour.

Constructed in 1793, the post was fortified 18 years later when Anglo-American relations soured. Devastated in 1813 during American capture, the fort was rebuilt by the British. As US threats subsided, its military importance diminished. A new fort was constructed to the west after 1841. Renovated for the city's centennial in 1934, this popular tourist attraction celebrated its 200th birthday in 1993.

The wooden blockhouses, powder magazines and barracks, completed in 1815, have been faithfully restored. The **officers' barracks** is furnished to show the lifestyle of senior officers of the period. Canada's military history is revisited in the junior officers' barracks, the only 20C building. Other exhibits include York in 1816 and an illuminated map of Toronto's changing lakeshore. Costumed staff conduct tours and perform demonstrations and, in summer, military manoeuvres *(Jul–Aug).*

Marine Museum of Upper Canada. – *In Exhibition Grounds. Open year-round Tue–Sun. Closed Christmas, Boxing Day, New Year's, Good Friday. $3.25.* 🅿 ☎*416/ 392-6827.* Housed in barracks of the fort built in 1841, the museum is a tribute to Toronto's waterways and the Great Lakes. There are well-presented displays on navigational aids, shipwrights' tools, warships, whistles, underwater archaeology and other maritime themes.

The 25m/80ft steam tug *Ned Hanlan* stands restored outside the museum *(May– Oct)*, one of the last to ply the Great Lakes.

★★ **Ontario Place.** – *955 Lakeshore Blvd W, access from Exhibition Grounds. Open Victoria Day–Labour Day daily 10:30–1am. Some attractions close at dusk.* ✗ ⅙ 🅿 ☎*416/314-9900.* Like a space-age lunar base, this innovative, modular-piece leisure complex emerges from an extraordinary setting of lagoons, marinas and man-made islands on lakefront bordering the Exhibition Grounds. The park's emphasis is on entertainment and leisure activities.

Metallic and fabric structures glorify the geometric shapes of modern technology, a trademark of architect **Eberhard Zeidler** (b.1926). The metal "pods" suspended above the lake enclose children's play areas and a theatre in which 3D films are shown. Resembling a giant golf ball, **Cinesphere** features IMAX films on a screen six storeys high. The **Forum**, a large, outdoor performance space with a suspended tent roof, sits in a hollow so that audiences can enjoy, from grassy slopes or provided seating, a variety of local and international performers. In the **waterplay area**, a series of wading pools full of water jets and games is a popular attraction.

At the large marina, Canadian **HMCS Haida★**, veteran of World War II and the Korean War, can be boarded and toured *(open daily Victoria Day–Labour Day; $1.25).*

★★ **Harbourfront** . – *Access from York, Spadina and Bathurst sts;* ● *Union or Spadina, transfer to bus 77B; information centre at York Quay Centre* ☎*416/973-3000. For event schedule contact Box Office* ☎*416/973-4000.* Initiated in 1976, this colourful 40ha/100 acre waterfront development has transformed Toronto's previously neglected lakeshore into an attractive mix of marinas, outdoor cafes, antiques and crafts markets, modern hotels, sleek condominiums and pleasant mini-parks. A focal point of the city's cultural life, especially in summer, Harbourfront is also the scene of year-round recreational, educational and commercial activities, commonplace in the renovated quays and warehouses as well as out-of-doors.

The granddaddy of the waterfront warehouses, **Queen's Quay Terminal** (1927), with its imposing clock tower and rectangular solidity, was completely overhauled, perforated from top to bottom with wide bottle-green windows, and opened in 1983. Designed by Eberhard Zeidler, the refurbished terminal accommodates airy offices, plush living spaces, fashionable boutiques and eateries, the 450-seat Premiere Dance Theatre and, on the 5th floor, the Metro Toronto Convention and Visitors Association. Nearby, renovated **York Quay Centre** houses an art gallery, craft studios and summer theatre. Fronting the **Power Plant**, now a contemporary art gallery *(open year-round Tue–Sun; closed holidays;* ☎*416/973-4949)*, the multi-purpose **du Maurier Theatre Centre**, with its glass-faceted foyer, evolved from a former 1920s ice house. **Molson Place** (1992), an open-air 1,750-seat concert facility, occupies the southwest corner of the quay. Sailing schools, nautical stores and restaurants are located at **Pier 4**, and the Marine Division of the Metro Police is based at John Quay.

★★ **Toronto Islands.** – *Ferries (10-15min) depart from Queen's Quay foot of Bay St to three points: Centre Island, Ward's Island and Hanlan's Point. Depart daily year-round every 15min from 6:35am–11:45pm. $2.75.* ⅙ ☎*416/392-8193. Visit: 1/2 day minimum.* A popular retreat from the bustle of nearby downtown, these islands function as Toronto's principal public parkland. Formed from the erosion of Scarborough Bluffs *(p 143)*, this narrow landmass was a peninsula until 1853, when a violent storm severed it from the mainland, creating the present string of islands. Extending 6km/3.7mi from end to end, the islands are graced with expansive lawns, age-old shade trees, sandy beaches, marinas and spectacular **views★★** of downtown Toronto. Attractions on **Centre Island** include restaurants, cafes, a beach *(on the Lake Ontario side)* and a delightful theme/amusement park for youngsters *(open daily mid-May–mid-Sept; $14;* ☎*416/363-1112).* On foot or by bike *(motor vehicles prohibited on the islands)*, visitors can explore the adjacent islands, particularly **Algonquin** and **Ward's islands**, whose quaint roads lined with small, privately owned cottages lend a decidedly rural charm. Near the small airport located on the islands' western end is Hanlan's Point, renowned for its **views** of the city *(a trackless train operates continuously between Centre Island and Hanlan's Point).*

For visitors pressed for time, the hour-long **harbour cruise★** *(departs from Yonge St or York St hourly May–Thanksgiving; 1hr; $9.95; commentary on board; Grey Line* ☎*416/364-2412)* offers a waterside perspective of the harbourfront and the islands from glass-roofed boats. The return trip provides fine **views** of downtown.

★ **OLD TOWN OF YORK** *Map p 138. 1/2 day.*

In 1793, Governor Simcoe approved a surveyor's gridiron plan for York—ten city blocks bordered by present-day Front, George, Adelaide and Berkeley streets. By 1813, Jarvis Street marked the west boundary. The block between Front and King streets served as a public market.

Although not original to Simcoe's town, some remaining historic structures date from the first half of the 19C, including an active marketplace, the **South St Lawrence Market** *(95 Front St E at Jarvis St,* ● *King; open daily year-round)*, a cavernous brick building sheltering a two-storey food hall. Especially lively on Saturday mornings when early-bird shoppers converge on countless fruit stands, bakeries, meat counters and delicatessens, the market encases the surviving portion of the **Second City Hall** (1845-1899), built in 1844. The former second-floor council chamber houses the

Market Gallery of the City of Toronto Archives, which presents rotating exhibits of historical documents and paraphernalia *(open daily year-round)*. To the west, along Front Street, stands a handsome row of brick and stone 19C commercial buildings.

Directly across the street is **North St Lawrence Market**, a bustling farmers' market *(open daily year-round)* housed in a smaller building, where farm-fresh, or prepared, food is available. From the entrance, there is a good view, to the west, of Toronto's **flatiron building**, the Gooderham (1892) on Wellington Street, against a backdrop of the towers of BCE Place *(see below)*.

Adjoining the market via a charming pedestrian mall is the neoclassical **St Lawrence Hall** *(King and Jarvis sts)*, distinguished by its domed cupola. Former site of the city's market and social gatherings, this renovated mid-19C building houses various commercial enterprises.

Farther east is Toronto's **First Post Office★** *(260 Adelaide St E; open year-round Mon–Fri)*, formerly York's fourth post office, opened in 1833. Re-created to the period, it operates again, with replicas of the original boxes and a reading room, complete with fireplace, where residents once read their mail. Costumed staff demonstrate quill-and-ink letter-writing.

★★ DOWNTOWN   *Map p 138. 2 days.*

Containing the city's formidable financial core, Toronto's downtown exudes a sense of momentum and prosperity, exemplified in its soaring skyscrapers and early-20C halls of commerce. Site of the country's leading banks, legal, insurance and brokerage firms, and the Toronto Stock Exchange, the area of King and Bay streets constitutes Canada's "Wall Street."

By the 1840s, growing commerce fostered creation of several banks. Warehouses and offices followed within the next 10 to 20 years. At the time of Confederation *(p 18)*, 11 financial institutions had head offices in Toronto, and another 9 had branches. The desire to appear forward-looking led to successive replacement of these mid-19C stalwarts with newer-styled buildings.

Except for Sun Life Centre, the skyscrapers are connected by an **underground city** of shops, eateries, banks, concourses and passageways—a welcome haven in inclement weather. Reputed to be the largest in the world, this subterranean "city" extends six blocks from Union Station to Sheraton Centre.

One of the best-known and longest roads (1,896km/1,178mi) in Canada is **Yonge Street**, the city's east-west dividing line. Built by Simcoe in 1795 as a military route, this thoroughfare sports fancy boutiques, colourful flower stands, trendy restaurants, inviting bookstores, and classy antique shops.

★★ Financial District   ●*King or St Andrew*

A stunning ebony-coloured ensemble covering an entire city block, the **Toronto-Dominion Centre★★** was the first component of the current financial district. A fine example of International Style, the spartan black-glass towers, known locally as the T-D Centre, reflect the design of eminent 20C architect Mies van der Rohe, consultant for the project. Begun in 1964, the headquarters of the Toronto Dominion Bank consisted originally of three structures; today the towers number five. Fronting Bay Street, the Ernst & Young tower (1992) incorporates the former Art Deco Stock Exchange Building (1937) within its base. On view thoughout the centre are works by contemporary artists, predominantly Canadian.

The downtown abounds in other skyscrapers by noted architects, among them, the adjacent **Royal Bank Plaza★ [A]** designed by Boris Zerafa. Completed in 1976, the 41-storey and 26-storey gold, reflecting-glass towers are linked by a 40m/130ft high glass-walled banking hall, entry point to the underground city. A suspended sculpture of 8,000 aluminum tubes, the work of renowned Venezuelan artist Jesus Rafael Soto, dominates the interior of the hall.

The tiered, aqua-glass towers of **BCE Place**, designed by Spanish architect Santiago Calatrava, abut a lower central building bisected into matching office wings by an elaborate arched, aluminum **atrium★**. The southernmost tower is topped by a square telecommunications "cross." A 1990s newcomer to the financial district, the complex is the headquarters of Bell Canada Enterprises, and the new home of Exhibition Park transplant, the **Hockey Hall of Fame**, where the Stanley Cup is generally on display *(open daily year-round)*.

Four buildings (1931 to 1972) form **Commerce Court**, an office complex surrounding an outdoor courtyard of trees, benches and a central fountain. The dominant 57-storey stainless steel tower, head office of the Canadian Imperial Bank of Commerce, was designed by famed architect I. M. Pei.

Opposite Commerce Court, the ruby-coloured **Scotia Plaza** (1988) by Boris Zerafa is a striking addition to Toronto's skyline. At street-level, an "erector-set" canopy marks the entrance to the slender 68-storey building, distinguished by a V-shaped wedge in its summit.

First Canadian Place consists of a 72-storey white tower (1975) housing the Bank of Montreal and the 36-storey tower (1983) containing the **Toronto Stock Exchange [B]** *(open year-round Mon–Fri; 45min presentation by reservation only; ☎416/947-4676)*. Richly coloured wall hangings adorn the white-marbled lobby at the King Street entrance. Connecting the towers is a three-level plaza with elegant shops and an attractive water wall. Under Adelaide Street, a passageway called the "tunnel" *(located toward northwest corner of the complex)* leads to the Lanes, a shopping development, which extends as far as Sheraton Centre.

Designed by Boris Zerafa, the multi-faceted glass towers of **Sun Life Centre★** (1984) frame the east and west sides of University Avenue at King Street. Near the entrance to the 28-storey east tower, an outdoor sculpture by Sorel Etrog suggests a massive wheel-based tool.

** **Roy Thomson Hall.** – *60 Simcoe St.* ● *St Andrew. Visit by guided tour (45min) only Labour Day–April Mon–Sat at 12:30pm. Reduced schedule in summer. $3. Reservations suggested.* ☎416/593-4822. Resembling a large inverted bowl, this glass-sheathed concert hall, named for Canadian newspaper magnate Roy Thomson and designed by Arthur Erickson, dominates King and Simcoe streets. Transparent at night when illuminated, the diamond-shaped exterior panels shimmer in daylight, their blue cast a reflection of the sky.

Opened in 1982, the home of the Toronto Symphony retains its architectural uniqueness and acoustical superiority. To insulate the performance area, a thick circular passageway with entry doors at intervals creates a "sound lock." Fabrics for the seats, carpet and ceiling decorations are designed to enhance acoustics. An illuminated double-ringed *oculus* forms the ceiling's centerpiece, while a shower of suspended metal "raindrops" lights the stage below. Woven, tubular hanging banners can be raised or lowered to achieve desired resonance.

On Front Street, south of Roy Thomson Hall, the concrete box-shaped **Canadian Broadcasting Centre** sports a red and white grid-patterned exterior, interrupted at intervals by glass geometric-shaped components. Illustrative of the so-called Deconstructivist style, the ten-storey building was constructed in 1992 and designed by noted architect Philip Johnson.

★ **City Hall Area** ● *Osgoode or Queen*

These crescent-shaped towers and mushroom-like council chamber have been the symbol of Toronto since completion in 1965. Today, its former glamour somewhat diminished, the internationally acclaimed masterpiece by Finland's **Viljo Revell** remains a landmark nevertheless.

Unequal in height, the towers are clad in concrete on one side, windows on the other. They rise from a two-storey podium, as does the "stem" of the mushroom, the only support for the council chamber at the summit. Spacious **Nathan Phillips Square** (named for a former mayor) with its wide, arch-covered reflecting pool attracts crowds of ice-skaters in winter. Henry Moore's outdoor bronze sculpture, *The Archer,* was the precursor for the sizeable collection of his pieces in Toronto's Art Gallery of Ontario.

Occupying the east side of the square, **Old City Hall★ [D]**, designed by Toronto-born **Edward J. Lennox** (1855-1933), houses the provincial courts. Dominated by its clock tower, the massive Richardsonian Romanesque exterior of this previous home (1899-1965) of the city fathers conceals an ornate interior of patterned tile floors and copper-painted capitals atop marble columns. Backing the grand iron staircase is a large stained-glass window with scenes symbolizing the city's growth.

Extending several blocks on Yonge Street between Queen and Dundas streets is **Eaton Centre★** *(● Queen; open daily year-round;* ☎*416/598-8700),* a 5-level office/shopping complex with over 300 stores. Designed by Eberhard Zeidler, the megastructure, with its trees, plants, fountains and natural lighting, was a novel approach to shopping mall construction when it opened in 1977.

Long-time retailer, the Hudson's Bay Company ("The Bay"), can be reached by a covered walkway across Queen Street.

The Thomson Gallery. – *9th floor of The Bay department store at 176 Yonge St.* ● *Queen. Open year-round Mon–Sat. Closed legal holidays. $2.* ✗ ♿ ▯ ☎*416/861-4571.* Ken Thomson, owner of The Bay, has transformed a portion of the ninth floor into a showplace for his fine collection of Canadian art. The larger **20C gallery★** features important paintings by the **Group of Seven**, while works by 19C artists such as Cornelius Krieghoff are displayed in the adjacent gallery.

★ **Elgin and Winter Garden Theatres [E].** – *189 Yonge St, opposite Eaton Centre north of Queen St.* ● *Queen. Other than performances, visit by guided tour (1hr) only year-round Thur 5pm & Sat 11am. $4.* ☎*416/314-3580.* Reopened in 1989 after extensive restoration, this splendid edifice houses one of the few remaining double-decker theatres in the world. Designed by Thomas Lamb, the 1,500-seat Elgin and 1,000-seat Winter Garden opened in 1913 and 1914 respectively as vaudeville, and later, silent film houses. The Winter Garden closed in 1928; the Elgin became a movie palace.

The plush amphitheatre of the Elgin, with its ornate box seats and gold-patterned ceiling, is reached through a gilded lobby of Corinthian pilasters and arched mirrors. A seven-storey marble staircase leads to the fanciful Winter Garden, with its unique ceiling of hanging beech boughs. Original *olios* (hand-painted scenic drops) are on display.

★ **Mackenzie House [F].** – *82 Bond St.* ● *Dundas. Visit by guided tour (30min) daily year-round. Closed Christmas, New Year's, Boxing Day, Good Friday. $3.25.* ☎*416/392-6915.* This 19C brick row house, with its four chimneys and single dormer, was the last home of William Lyon Mackenzie. Friends purchased the house in 1859 for the publisher-turned-politician, who resided there until his death.

Rooms on the three floors have been restored to the 1850 period. In the kitchen, visitors can sample baked goods based on 19C recipes and baked in the cast-iron oven. In the modern annex at the rear, a small display chronicles Mackenzie's life and times, and a replica of his **print shop** includes a hand-operated flatbed press on which his newspapers were printed *(demonstrations).*

★ **Osgoode Hall.** – *130 Queen St W.* ● *Osgoode. Quiet is necessary, since courts may be in session. Visit by guided tour (45min) only Jul–Aug Mon–Fri.* ☎*416/947-3300.* Home of the Supreme Court of Ontario and the Law Society of Upper Canada, this stately neoclassical edifice graces expansive lawns west of Nathan Phillips Square. Erected in 1867 allegedly to keep cows out, an ornate cast-iron fence isolates the judicial bastion from the city's bustle.

Begun in 1829, the hall consisted of only the east wing. Damaged by troops quartered there after Mackenzie's rebellion, the building was upgraded in 1844. The central pavilion and west wing were added, and the facade and interior were altered. Until as late as 1991, sporadic changes continued.

Enclosed by a rectangular stained-glass roof, the two-tiered arched interior courtyard induces admiration, as does the magnificent **Great Library**—said to be "perhaps the noblest room in Canada." Supported by rows of Corinthian columns, a 12m/40ft vaulted ceiling, richly adorned with intricate plaster work, crowns its interior. A small **museum** features the history of Ontario's legal profession.

North of Osgoode Hall stands the Metro Toronto **Court House [J]**, with its circular rotunda and walkway to Nathan Phillips Square.

★ **Campbell House.** – *University Ave at Queen St.* ● *Osgoode. Visit by guided tour (30min) only daily Jun–Sept. Off-season Mon–Fri. Closed Christmas, Boxing Day & New Year's. $2.50.* ☎*416/597-0227.* Once belonging to **Sir William Campbell** (1758-1834), Chief Justice of Upper Canada from 1825 to 1829, the Georgian brick mansion was moved to this site in 1972 from its location in historic York. As it had been in the old town, the house is only a short walk from the city's courthouse.

The restored rooms contain some fine period pieces and surviving portraits of the Campbell family. On the second floor, a model of York of 1825 can be seen. The property once belonged to the Canada Life Assurance Company, whose headquarters rises just behind Campbell House. A prominent landmark, the building is distinguished at night by its tower, the lights of which indicate the barometer reading.

★★ **Art Gallery of Ontario.** – *317 Dundas St W.* ● *St Patrick. Open Wed–Sun 10am-5:30pm (Wed & Fri 10pm). $7.50.* ✗ & ☎*416/977-0414.* Occupying nearly a city block, this low-rise, brick and concrete building with its distinctive metal tower retains the world's largest public collection of works by renowned British sculptor **Henry Moore** (1898-1986). The permanent collection ranges from 15C European paintings to international contemporary art, and includes Canadian art from 18C to the present. Tastefully incorporated into the complex is an historic 19C mansion, the Grange—original home of the AGO.

Established in 1900 as the Art Museum of Toronto, the gallery was permanently housed in the Grange by 1911. Adjacent quarters were constructed in 1918 and enlarged twice in less than 50 years. As its scope expanded, the publicly supported institution underwent name changes. Modified in 1919, the Art Gallery of Toronto adopted its provincial status in 1966. After visiting Toronto to see his work in situ at the new City Hall, Moore announced, in 1968, his momentous gift to the gallery of over 150 of his works. He returned in 1974 to officially open the new sculpture centre named in his honour. Extensively renovated with additions in 1977, and again 10 years later, the AGO now possesses a permanent collection of over 16,000 pieces.

★★ **Henry Moore Sculpture Centre.** – The centre owns over 1,000 of Moore's works, including 689 prints, 139 original plasters and bronzes and 74 drawings. Many were donated by the artist when he learned that the AGO intended to devote a gallery to him. Occupying a spacious room on the upper level, the centre was designed by the artist to use natural light from the glass-panelled roof. More than 20 massive forms—all plaster casts or original plasters for some of Moore's famous bronzes—electrify this spartan space. At night, the effect of artificial lighting, with its interplay of shadows on these sculpted shapes, is stunning. Selected smaller bronzes and miniature maquettes are on display in the entryway.

★★ **The Permanent Collection.** – *Selections change regularly; not all of these works may be seen at one time. The galleries are sometimes used for visiting exhibitions.* Housed in galleries around Walker Court, the **European Collection** covers the Old Masters, Impressionism and early 20C movements. Highlights include works by Peter Brueghel the Younger, Tintoretto, Rembrandt, Franz Hals, Gainsborough, Reynolds, Renoir, Degas, Monet, Van Gogh, Gauguin, Picasso and Dufy.

Displayed in several galleries, the **Canadian Collection** features 18C to contemporary works. Early Quebec artists are represented along with Cornelius Krieghoff, Tom Thomson (*The West Wind*) and the Group of Seven, Emily Carr, David Milne and Paul Peel, to name a few.

Contemporary **Inuit art** on exhibit dates from 1948 to the present. Carved in ivory, whalebone, gray stone or mottled greenstone, the sculpture (mostly miniatures) depicts native animals or Inuit people. Large fabric hangings of embroidery and felt, as well as prints (stonecuts and stencil on paper) complete the collection.

★ **The Grange.** – *Entrance through Art Gallery. Call for specific opening hours* ☎*416/977-0414.* This Georgian brick mansion (c.1817) once stood on a 41ha/100 acre site reaching from Queen to Bloor streets. Socio-political life in Upper Canada during Family Compact days revolved around the residence of the Boulton family, Loyalists from New England who became leaders in the oligarchy.

Lawyer and politician **Henry John Boulton** (1790-1870) was largely responsible for four of the five expulsions of William Lyon Mackenzie from the Legislature. In 1875, The Grange became the home of a well-known scholar, **Goldwin Smith**, Regius Professor of History at Oxford, who made it a centre of intellectual pursuits and progressive ideas. After Smith's death in 1911, his widow bequeathed the house to the Art Gallery of Toronto.

Restored to its mid-19C appearance in 1973, the mansion is meticulously furnished to give the aura of Family Compact days. Although few pieces are original to the home, much of the furniture is from the Georgian and Regency periods. All three floors are open to visitors. Of special interest is the beautiful, curved staircase in the entry hall. The basement contains kitchens typical of a 19C gentleman's house. The residence faces lovely Grange Park, from which visitors can appreciate the mansion's gracious facade. The present entrance portico is a stone version of the original wooden one.

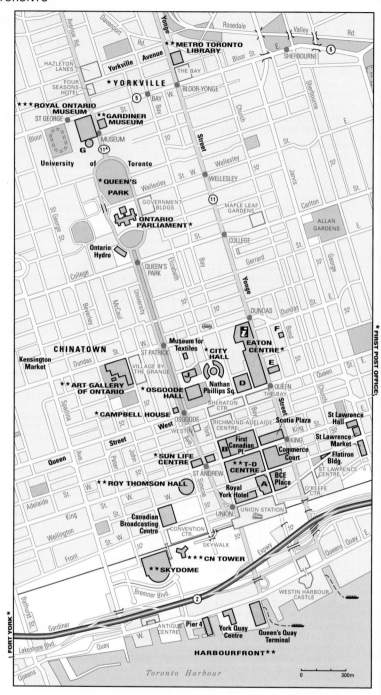

Museum for Textiles. – *55 Centre Ave.* ● *St Patrick. Open year-round Tue–Sun. Closed legal holidays. $3.50.* ♿ 🅿 ☏ *416/599-5321.* Occupying two floors of a high-rise hotel/condominium complex, the only Canadian museum devoted exclusively to the study, collection and display of textiles features traditional and contemporary works from around the world. The permanent collection of 18,000 pieces is presented alongside loaned works, on a rotating basis, in a series of temporary exhibits.

★ **QUEEN'S PARK** *Map above. 1 day.*

This oval-shaped park in the heart of Toronto is the setting for Ontario's Parliament. Based on E. J. Lennox's landscape scheme of 1876, its trees, statues and flowerbeds border nearby government buildings. To the west and east sprawls the **University of Toronto**, Canada's largest institute of higher education, perhaps best known for its medical school where, in 1921, **Frederick Banting** and **Charles Best** succeeded in isolating insulin. To the south, the curved, mirrored, multi-storied headquarters of **Ontario Hydro** (1975, Kenneth R. Cooper) rises above the surroundings. Inside, energy radiated by artificial lighting, equipment and people is stored in basement thermal reservoirs to be recirculated throughout the building, which has no furnace or heating plant.

★ **Ontario Parliament.** – ●*Queen's Park. Open daily Victoria Day–Labour. Off-season Mon–Fri.* & ☎*416/325-7500.* Dominating the south end of the park, the imposing, sandstone **Legislative Building** typifies the solidity and mass of Richardsonian Romanesque architecture. Also called the Parliament Buildings, this seat of provincial government opened in 1893 after a controversial six-year, million dollar construction. The focus of the dispute, American-based architect **Richard Waite** (1846-1911), had awarded himself the project after serving as a judge in a fizzled design competition.

The ponderous exterior belies the interior's elegant beauty, particularly the white-marbled **west wing**, rebuilt after a fire in 1909, and the stately **legislative chamber** with its rich mahogany and sycamore. On view is the 200-year-old mace *(ground floor)*, a ceremonial gold "club" mandatory at House proceedings. Taken by the Americans during their 1813 assault on York, it was returned years later by President F. D. Roosevelt.

★★★ **ROYAL ONTARIO MUSEUM** *Map p 138.* ● *Museum. Allow 1/2 day.*

Renowned for extensive research, this enormous museum consists of the H-shaped, five-floor main building at Avenue Road and Bloor Street —commonly referred to as the ROM—and the separately housed McLaughlin Planetarium and Gardiner Museum of Ceramic Art. Maintaining over 20 departments in art, archaeology and the natural sciences, the museum, known especially for its East Asian holdings, possesses a remarkable collection of six-million-plus artifacts and artworks from around the world.

Archaeological Base. – In the early 1900s, Toronto banker Sir Byron E. Walker campaigned to start a public museum. United in effort was archaeologist **Charles Trick Currelly**, whose world travels provided the first treasures for a collection. In 1912, the Ontario Legislature passed an ROM Act, and in 1914, the museum first opened as part of the University of Toronto. Independent by 1968, the ROM became a separate body under the provincial government. Officially reopened in 1982 after an ambitious 4-year, $55 million expansion, the ROM remains one of the country's leading museums, attracting visitors and scholars worldwide.

Main Building. – *Open Victoria Day–Labour Day daily 10am–6pm (Tue & Thur 8pm). Off-season Tue–Sun 10am–6pm. Closed Christmas & New Year's. $6.* ✗ & ☎*416/586-5551. The ROM continues to undergo renovation and rearranging of galleries. Some sections may be temporarily closed, or collections may be exhibited in locations other than those indicated. Formerly off-site, the Canadian Decorative Arts Collection has been moved to the main building for selected display in the future. The museum's floor plan, available at the information desk in the entrance rotunda or near the Mankind Discovering exhibit, is especially useful.*

Ground Floor. – The grand entrance **rotunda** is vaulted, with an exquisite domed **ceiling** of golden mosaic *tessarae*—tiny squares of imported Venetian glass. The marble in the floor, with its radiant sun pattern, was extracted from an Ontario quarry.

Before entering the galleries, note the two **totem poles** in the stairwells. Crafted of red cedar by the Nisgaas and Haida peoples of British Columbia in the second half of the 19C, the poles are so tall that their upper sections can be viewed from the second and third floors. The taller pole, 25m/81ft in height, depicts the family history of the chief who owned it.

The small centrepiece exhibit, **Mankind Discovering**, offers an excellent overview of the museum's research activities, illustrating through photos, documents, artifacts and equipment, the scientific process of artifact collecting.

The remainder of this floor is devoted to the outstanding **Chinese collection★★★**, one of the largest and most important of its kind outside China. Spanning nearly 4,000 years, the exhibits range from the Shang dynasty 1523 BC (the Chinese Bronze Age) to the overthrow of the Qing or Manchu dynasty (1644-1911) and the setting up of the Republic in 1912.

Artifacts were gathered mainly by **George Crofts**, a fur merchant who lived in Tientsin and, after his death in 1925, **William C. White**, Anglican Bishop of Honan. Assisted by Dr Currelly, these men procured Chinese works of art when such pieces were little known to the Western world. Later in 1960, the museum acquired the coveted treasures of **Dr James Menzies**, a missionary-scholar who lived in China for many years. The collection is noted for its clay **tomb figures**, small replicas of people and animals buried with the dead as their "servants," and dating from the 3C AD. The star attraction, however, is the **Ming Tomb**, the only complete example in the Western world. Within the archways, larger-than-life statues of animals and humans guard the "spirit way" to the tumulus, or mound, that marked the position of the subterranean chamber containing the coffin. This tomb is reportedly the burial place of Zu Dashou (1644-1911), a general who served the last Ming emperors and lived into the Qing period.

A series of interconnected galleries is devoted to **Later Imperial China** (10-19C). Traditional room settings, a life-size Chinese courtyard and a moon gate re-create the life of the gentry during the Ming (1368-1644) and Qing dynasties. Ceramics pieces, including the ROM's famous Ming porcelain, are also on display.

Remarkable for its ink and colour clay wall paintings, the **Bishop White Gallery** simulates the interior of a Northern Chinese temple. Flanked by two Daoist frescoes from Shanxi province with a probable date of 1325, the largest painting —"The Paradise of Maitreya"—is Buddhist, c.1298. Life-sized polychromed and gilded statues of *bodhisattvas* (those enlightened, compassionate individuals destined for Buddha status) of 12-14C stand in the centre.

Second Floor. – Natural history exhibits occupy this floor, the highlight of which are the magnificent reassembled **dinosaurs** in authentic settings. These skeletons come from upper cretaceous rocks exposed in the badlands of the Red Deer River Valley in central Alberta, one of the richest collecting sites in the world. The glass atrium of the **Bird Gallery** is filled with Canadian geese, turkeys, owls, ducks, and an assortment of smaller birds, preserved in flight. A somewhat eery, but sensory sound-and-light experience is a walk through the **Bat Cave**, a lifelike reconstruction of the St Clair Cave in Jamaica, complete with hundreds of hand-made bats. Favourites from the ROM's possessions such as ceremonial headdresses, West African masks, Japanese ceramics, manuscripts and furniture are featured in **From the Collections**.

Third Floor. – Interlinked galleries present a fascinating look at civilization around the Mediterranean basin in Egypt, the Classical World and the Near East. Opened in 1992, the **Ancient Egypt★** exhibit depicts **daily life** via tools, utensils, jewellery and miniature figures. The section on **religion** includes coffins, animal mummies and canopic jars, the remarkably preserved **Antjau mummy** and the colourful upright **mummy case** of a female musician. A chronological survey from pre-dynastic times to the Ptolemaic period is featured on the **history** wall. The **Punt wall reliefs★**, sculptural casts from the temple of Queen Hatshepsut (1503-1482 BC), illustrate her trade mission along the Nile. The exhibit on **Nubia**—a region south of the Sahara in present-day Lower Egypt and Northern Sudan whose early cultures date to 4500 BC—features pottery, glassware, arms and jewellery from 2000 BC to the 19C.

Ming Tomb

Royal Ontario Museum

Classic forms of marble sculpture, gold coins, decorated amphora and a model of the Acropolis are displayed in the **Greek World Gallery** (1100-100 BC) while the **Islamic** section reproduces a life-size Middle East house and bazaar.

The **Samuel European Galleries★** are devoted to decorative arts from Medieval times to the present. Note the elaborately carved coconut cups with their decorative silver mounts from the **Lee Collection**, exquisite medieval and Renaissance wares of gold and silver. In the **Arms and Armour** gallery, armaments from medieval chain mail to modern-day weaponry can be examined. Judaica, metalwork (1300 to the present), glass, and ceramics are given separate sections. Exemplifying straight cut, draping, shaping and tailoring methods throughout history, **Costume and Textiles** is a well-organized exhibit with an evolutionary perspective. **Culture and Context** presents partial-room reconstructions, such as a Victorian parlour (1860-1885).

Caravans and Clipper Ships unfolds an engaging 2,000-year "journey" over East-West trade routes, concentrating on mapmaking, the commerce in luxurious spices, transmission of religion and other evolutions of trade. Especially noteworthy are the finds from a remote Persian castle on the silk route through present-day Iran.

Lower Level. – In the **Ontario Prehistory** gallery, human-scale dioramas capture the life of the early Algonquian and Iroquoian peoples. Reproductions of limestone petroglyphs and a large mural of red-ochre rock paintings can also be seen.

The **Discovery Gallery** *(2nd level below; open Jul–Aug Mon–Fri 11am–4pm, weekends 1–5pm; off-season Mon–Fri noon–1pm, weekends 1–5pm)* is a "hands-on" room where visitors can examine a dinosaur bone, inspect a Ming vase or don a medieval helmet, among other activities. Exposure to this gallery can change the museum visitor from a passive spectator to an active observer.

★ **McLaughlin Planetarium** [G]. – *Adjacent to ROM main building, accessible from ground floor. Open daily Victoria Day–Labour Day. Off-season Tue–Sun. Closed Christmas & New Year's. Entrance included in museum admission.* ✗ & ☎416/586-5736. This distinctive white-domed observatory was constructed with donations from automobile magnate R. S. McLaughlin. The **Astrocentre** features floor-to-ceiling panels (some interactive) on the star system, examples of early charting instruments, a solar telescope for viewing the sun "live" and the **Stellarium**, a unique model of the Milky Way Gallaxy *(continuous 5min shows)*. Under the dome in the Star Theatre, computer-designed **star and laser shows** use 200 projectors to create a convincing "sky" that envelops the viewer.

ONTARIO

** **Gardiner Museum of Ceramic Art.** – *111 Queen's Park across from ROM main building. Open year-round Tue–Sun daily 10am–5pm. Closed Christmas & New Year's. Entrance included in museum admission.* ✗ ⚐ ☎*416/586-8080.* Located in a modern granite building, this museum, the project of collectors George and Helen Gardiner, features pottery and porcelain from a variety of countries and cultures. The Pottery Gallery *(ground floor)* showcases **pre-Columbian** works from Mexico, and Central and South America dating from 2000 BC to about AD 1500—primarily figurines, vessels and bowls of Olmec, Toltec, Aztec and other cultures. The orange Mayan pottery and *plumbate* (fired with silica glaze) vases are especially noteworthy. Made in Italy in the 15C and 16C, **Italian maiolica** is colourful tin-glazed earthenware. Blues, greens and bright yellows dominate the exhibited pieces, mostly large plates with intricate designs and religious scenes. Tin-glazed earthenware made in England in the 17C became known as **delftware**, probably because of its similiarity to wares from the Dutch town of Delft. Note the "chargers" or large plates with an English monarch painted on each. A gallery for temporary exhibits is also housed on the ground floor.

The Porcelain Gallery *(2nd floor)* features **18C porcelains** of Du Paquier, Sèvres (characterized by bright yellows), the great English companies—Worcester, Derby, Chelsea—and others. Highlights are the Meissenware pieces, in particular, the large tea service (c.1740-1745) in a fitted leather travel case, and the *commedia dell' arte* figures *(in the centre of the gallery)* crafted throughout Europe after this 16C form of improvised theatre spread from Italy. There is also an assemblage of tiny, exquisite scent bottles (1750-1755) made in England.

ADDITIONAL SIGHTS   *Maps pp 133 and 142*

* **Yorkville.** – ●*Bay.* Once the hangout of drug addicts and dropouts, Yorkville today represents all that is chic in Toronto—and a remarkable transformation. Between Yonge Street and Avenue Road, **Yorkville Avenue** presents charming Victorian houses converted to expensive boutiques or trendy cafes sporting the latest architectural facades.

In York Square at the corner of Avenue Road and Yorkville Avenue, shops surround an interior brick courtyard where summer dining is *al fresco.* Behind the square, on University Avenue, lies posh Hazelton Lanes *(open during business hours),* a labyrinthian shopping/office/condominium complex designed by Boris Zerafa (1978). On the other side of Yorkville Avenue, Cumberland Court is a rambling enclosure of old and new shops, eateries and offices, with a passageway to Cumberland Street.

** **Metro Toronto Library.** – *789 Yonge St.* ●*Bloor-Yonge. Open May–Thanksgiving Mon–Thur 9am–9pm (Jul–Aug 8pm), Fri 9am–6pm, Sat 9am–5pm. Off-season also open Sun 1:30–5pm.* ⚐ ☎*416/393-7141.* An architectural gem from renowned architect **Raymond Moriyama**, this massive brick and glass building contains Canada's most extensive public library. The 5-storey structure, completed for $30 million in 1977, contains nearly 1.5 million volumes.

Rising from a wide, light-filled centre, the tiered balconies are bordered by solid undulating balustrades. Special baffles in the ceiling reduce sound to a minimum. The Gallery on the main floor regularly showcases materials, often rare, from the library's collections.

In a cozy corner on the fifth floor is a tiny room brimming with the **Arthur Conan Doyle Collection**—famed Sherlock Holmes stories, Sherlockian criticism, Doyle's autobiography, historical novels, poetry and other writings. Worn Victorian furnishings complement mementos of the great detective's presence, felt chiefly in his pipes, a slipper and the inevitable deerstalker on the hat rack.

** **Casa Loma.** – *1 Austin Terrace;* ●*Dupont, then climb steps. Open daily 10am–4pm. Closed Christmas & New Year's. $8.* ✗ ⚐ ☎*416/923-1171. Visit 2 hrs (including gardens).* This enormous sandstone castle (1911 to 1914) was the lavish 98-room residence of prominent industrialist **Sir Henry Pellatt.** Maintained since 1937 by the Kiwanis Club, the medieval mansion is a popular tourist attraction.

Casa Loma's creator amassed a fortune largely from hydro-electric exploitation of Niagara Falls. E.J. Lennox combined sketches of castles Pellatt drew as a youth during world travels to design a home to the owner's liking. Three years and $3.5 million later, the interior was still not finished; nevertheless, in 1914 the Pellatts moved in, staying less than 10 years. High upkeep plus a reversal in Sir Henry's enterprises led to his losing Casa Loma to the City of Toronto for back taxes.

The "house on the hill," as its Spanish name translates, stands on the crest of Davenport Ridge—the edge of glacial Lake Iroquois, which existed after the last ice age. Seven storeys in height, the castle boasts two towers—one open-aired, the other enclosed—which offer good views of the city; secret passageways; and a lengthy underground tunnel to the magnificent **carriage house** and stables. The palatial residence includes 21 fireplaces, a **great hall** (22m/70ft ceiling), a marble-floor **conservatory**, an oak-panelled drawing room, and a **library** for 10,000 books. Especially well-appointed are the **Round Room★** with its exquisite Louis XV tapestry furnishings, the **Windsor Room** and **Lady Pellatt's suite.** Awash in conveniences uncommon to pre-World War I homes, the estate features an unfinished indoor swimming pool, 52 telephones, an elevator, a pipe organ and concealed steampipes.

* **Spadina.** – *285 Spadina Rd.* ●*Dupont, then climb steps. Visit by guided tour (30min) only daily year-round. Closed legal holidays. $4.75.* ⚐ *($2.25)* ☎*416/392-6910.* Built on a former 32ha/80 acre hillside estate outside mid-19C Toronto, Spadina overlooks its remaining 2.5ha/6 acre grounds amid a fashionable residential district. The 50-room brick mansion was home to businessman **James Austin** and his heirs, who adapted the structure to prevailing architectural styles and family size. In 1866, Austin acquired the estate, replacing the existing 1836 dwelling with a new

Georgian-styled house. His successful grocery store business had enabled him to become a major shareholder in, and eventually head of (1874-1897), the Consumers' Gas Company. He later founded Dominion Bank, incorporated 1869, serving as its first president. Austin's son added the spacious billiard room in 1898, and in 1907, the terraces and porte-cochère. The third floor, with its hipped roof and pedimented dormers, was added in 1912.

Reflecting the grandeur of Victorian and Edwardian styles, the spacious **drawing room** with its matching striped seating, and the airy wicker-furnished **palm room** show the comforts the Austin family expected.

METRO SIGHTS *Map below*

★★★ **Ontario Science Centre.** – *770 Don Mills Rd, 11km/7mi from downtown (22km/ 14mi by car via Don Valley Pkwy to Eglinton Ave); ● Don Mills or Eglinton bus E. Open year-round daily 10am–6pm (Fri 9pm). Closed Christmas. $6.25.* ✗ ♿ 🅿 *($2)* ☎416/696-3127. *Visit 1/2 day. Demonstrations and shows daily. For times and locations, check notice board at the bottom of escalator, level C.* Cascading down Don River ravine, this sizeable centre takes full advantage of its natural site. Raymond Moriyama designed a series of concrete and glass buildings on different levels connected by enclosed escalators. Opened in 1969, this popular attraction consists largely of interactive exhibits on science and technology.

Visitors learn, for example, by pushing buttons, rotating cranks, pedalling bicycles and turning wheels. Chemistry, printing, electricity and laser demonstrations, to name a few, provide another means of education.

HAMILTON / NIAGARA FALLS

The five levels are designated by letters, levels C, D and E being the exhibit/activity floors. Level C's **Earth/Food** section has a 5m/15ft high stack of grocery-filled shopping carts to illustrate "Food for a Year," while **Space** includes a rocket chair, hydroponics, super-gravity and other exhibits. Highlights of level D are the **Hall of Transportation** with its ascending model hot-air balloon, CA-3 powerboat and old-fashioned bicycles; the **Science Arcade** with humourous electricity demonstrations; and **Communications**, where visitors can participate in papermaking and television production. The **Hall of Technology** features, among other displays, life-size and model cantilever bridges for observing the effects of strain.

★★★ **Metro Toronto Zoo.** – *35km/22mi from downtown. ● Kennedy, transfer to bus 86A. Open mid-Mar–mid-Oct daily 9am–7:30pm. Off-season daily 9:30am–4:30pm. Closed Christmas. $9.* ✗ ♿ 🅿 ☎416/392-5900. *Visit 1/2 day. A useful site map is available at the entrance gate. In season, it is recommended that visitors begin by boarding the narrated shuttle, the zoomobile (daily May–Labour* ✗ *Day; $2), which provides an excellent overview of principal attractions. Disembark at the Serengeti station and begin the visit on foot.* Opened in 1974, this world-class zoological park features a remarkable variety of wildlife on 287ha/710 acres of tableland and forest. The 4,000 animals are divided into 6 "zoogeographic" regions: Africa, Australasia, Eurasia, the Americas, Indo-Malaya and Canada. Among the 440 species represented are numerous endangered or rare animals such as the Siberian tiger, the snow leopard, the Malayan tapir, the pygmy hippopotamus and the Liberian mongoose. Designed by Raymond Moriyama, harmoniously integrated glass and wood pavilions provide shelter for animals unadapted to Canada's climate.

The popular **Africa Pavilion**, abundant with tropical vegetation and exotic birds, is home to lowland gorillas, mandrills and other primates. Nearby resides Canada's largest herd of African elephants. The smaller Indo-Malayan and the Americas pavilions should not be overlooked. The **Edge of Night** exhibit *(adjacent to Australasia Pavilion)* provides a journey into a nocturnal world inhabited by seldom-seen species like the Tasmanian devil.

The main exhibit area is surrounded by rugged woodland, visible only by monorail *(operates year-round, weather permitting; $2; board at the main entrance area)*. On the 25min ride, visitors can view indigenous North American species such as caribou, Arctic wolves and grizzly bears, roaming freely.

★★ **Black Creek Pioneer Village.** – *In North York, 29km/18mi northwest of downtown. 1000 Murray Ross Parkway.* ● *Yonge and Finch, transfer to Steeles bus 60. Open May–Sept daily 10am–5pm (weekends 5:30pm). Off-season daily 10am–4:30pm. Closed Jan–mid-Mar. $7.* ⚒ ♿ 🅿 ☎ *416/736-1733. Visit 2hrs 30min. Site plan is distributed at the entrance.* This 12ha/30 acre re-created farming community evokes the traditions and architecture of Ontario's rural past. Opened in 1960, the village comprises 40 buildings, including 5 from the original farm established between 1816 and 1832 by Pennsylvania-German settlers, and a collection of 19C structures moved to the site.

Upon exiting the modern structure housing the **orientation centre**, visitors enter 19C Ontario. Set among abundant greenery and dirt roads flanked by wooden sidewalks and split-rail fences, the ensemble exudes a bygone-era charm, marred only by the din of the nearby freeway and the sight of neighbouring highrises above the trees. The restored buildings are appointed with furnishings characteristic of the 1860s. Highlights include: the tinsmith shop; the **Stong farm**; the Half Way House, a spacious white inn with a two-tiered veranda; **Roblin's Mill**, a handsome 4-storey stone, water-powered grist mill; and the printing office, complete with a working flatbed press. Costumed guides conduct continuous demonstrations of traditional 19C crafts and trades.

Scarborough. – *Map p 142.* Canada's seventh largest city, this sprawling urban centre with its sizeable Asian population has seen rapid growth in the last 10 years. Named by Governor Simcoe's wife, who kept a diary of their life in early York, it is known for picturesque cliffs along Lake Ontario, which reminded her of the town in Yorkshire, England.

★ **Scarborough Civic Centre.** – *150 Borough Dr, south of Hwy 401 at McCowan Rd, 35km/22mi from downtown Toronto. Open daily year-round.* ⚒ ♿ 🅿 ☎ *416/396-7216.* One of the area's first civic showplaces, the gleeming white concrete and glass complex, designed by Raymond Moriyama, was opened in 1973 by Queen Elizabeth II.

The interior is airy, filled with natural light from a central open shaft rising five storeys. Plant-bedecked balconies curve around in tiers that contain the office space. The council chamber is underground—the architect's solution to the necessity of constructing a large room without sacrificing structural lines.

Separating the centre from an adjacent shopping plaza is Albert Campbell Square. Located outdoors, the square accommodates concerts and other activities in summer, and ice skating in winter.

★ **Scarborough Bluffs.** – Easily Toronto's most dramatic geographical feature, these buff-coloured cliffs, sprouting finger-like hoodoos *(p 79)*, protrude into Lake Ontario for about 16km/10mi along its shoreline. The focus of much interest from scientists around the world, the bluffs contain layers of fossil-rich sand and clay—a unique geological record in North America of the final stages of the Great Ice Age.

The **Scarborough Bluffs Park** *(from Kingston Rd south, turn left on Midland Ave, then immediate left onto Kelsonia and right onto Scarborough Crescent; at end, park on Drake Crescent)* offers good **views**★ of the high sand structures branching out from the cliffs, the vast lake and Bluffers Park below.

Bluffers Park. – *Return to Kingston Rd and travel east to Brimley Rd; turn right and follow to the end.* The road descends the cliffs, emerging onto an artificial peninsula that has been constructed to protect the bluffs. This is a pleasant park on the lake with a marina.

★ **Spencer Clark Collection of Historic Architecture.** – *On grounds of Guild Inn, 201 Guildwood Parkway off Kingston Rd. Open daily year-round.* ⚒ ♿ ☎ *416/261-3331.* This unusual sculpture park contains architectural features from about 60 demolished Toronto buildings. The collection was the idea of Rosa and Spencer Clark, who founded a haven for artists called "The Guild of All Arts" on this site in 1932. Among the most striking artifacts on view are the Corinthian columns and capitals of the Bank of Toronto (demolished 1966), which have been assembled to form a Greek theatre, and the white marble facade of the Imperial Bank of Canada (demolished 1972). Modern sculpture works, many by Guild members, adorn the grounds.

EXCURSIONS

★★ **McMichael Canadian Art Collection.** – *Map p 142. In Kleinburg, approx 40km/25mi north. Hwy 400 to Major Mackenzie Dr, then west about 6km/4mi to Islington, then north 1km/.6mi. Open Apr–Oct daily 10am–5pm (Wed 9pm). Off-season Tue–Sun 11am–4:30pm. Closed Christmas. $5.* ⚒ ☎ *416/893-1121.* Housed in square-hewn log buildings among the wooded hills of the Humber Valley, this gallery has the largest display in existence of paintings by the first truly Canadian school—the **Group of Seven.**

The centre also owns a sizeable collection of contemporary Indian and Inuit art. Eight Canadian painters are credited with forging a uniquely Canadian art by painting, in a revolutionary way, the colours and landscapes of the country's wilds. Though pioneer **Tom Thomson** (1877-1917) died before the group was formed, his influence was substantial. The original members were **Lawren Harris, A. Y. Jackson, J. E. H. MacDonald, Franklin Carmichael, Arthur Lismer, Frederick Varley** and **Frank Johnston.** Johnston left after the first exhibition; **A. J. Casson** joined the group in 1926. The group officially disbanded in 1932, but some members formed the Canadian Group of Painters, which had much the same aims. In 1952, **Robert and Signe McMichael** bought land in rural Kleinburg, decorating their home with Group of Seven paintings. In 1965, they

McMichael Canadian Art Collection 1966.16.76

Afternoon, Algonquin Park 1914, by Tom Thomson

donated their famed collection and property to the province of Ontario. Subsequent gifts by such individuals as R. S. McLaughlin have enlarged the collection. The ground level is largely devoted to the group's precursor, Tom Thomson; to A.Y. Jackson, "grand old man of Canadian art"; and to Lawren Harris, the "soul" of the group and a prime leader in Canadian art for decades. Examples by artists influenced by the seven, notably **Clarence Gagnon, Emily Carr,** and **David Milne,** are also displayed. On exhibit upstairs are fine works of contemporary Indian artists such as **Clifford Maracle, Norval Morrisseau, Daphne Odjig,** and **Arthur Shilling.** There are excellent samples of **Inuit Art** as well, principally stone carvings and lithographs.

★ **Ontario Agricultural Museum.** – *5km/3mi west of Milton on Tremaine Rd (Hwy 401, Exit 312 or 320B). Open daily mid-May–mid-Sept. $4.* ✗ ᵫ ▯ ☎ *416/878-8151.* This collection of period homes, barns and museum buildings portrays the evolution of Ontario agriculture from early settlement to the 20C. Featured are vehicles of transport, agricultural equipment, farmsteads of different eras and displays on the province's agri-food industry. A crossroads community with a forge, harness shop, carriage works, shingle mill and a rare octagonal barn of the 1890s has been re-created.

Canada's Wonderland. – *In Vaughan. 30km/19mi north by Hwy 400 and Rutherford Rd; special buses from* ● *Yorkdale or York Mills; $2.50 one-way; buy tickets first. Open daily mid-May–Labour Day. Off-season weekends only. Closed mid-Oct–mid-May. $25.95.* ✗ ᵫ ☎ *416/832-7000.* The North's answer to Disneyland, this theme park opened in 1981 and features areas such as International Street, Medieval Faire, Grande World Exposition of 1890 and Hanna Barbera Land. Visitors can climb a man-made mountain, browse in the shops and experience a variety of rides and shows.

★★★ **Niagara Falls.** – *130km/81mi, 1 day trip. Description p 113.*

★★ **Parkwood Estate.** – *Oshawa. 61km/38mi, 1/2 day trip. Description p 117.*

★ **Royal Botanical Gardens.** – *Hamilton. 70km/44mi, 1/2 day trip. Description p 109.*

★★★ UPPER CANADA VILLAGE

Map p 101

Reflecting 1860s community life in Ontario, this 27ha/66 acre living museum is without equal in Canada, and is one of the finest restoration projects in North America. Lying in an area settled by Loyalists after the American Revolution, the village was created when plans were made to flood a large part of the St Lawrence River Valley during the construction of the St Lawrence Seaway and the control dam at Cornwall. Some of the older homes and buildings were moved to this site to preserve them.

Access. – *11km/7mi east of Morrisburg by Hwy 2 (Exit 758 from Hwy 401 at Upper Canada Rd) in Crysler Farm Battlefield Park.*

Visit. – *Open mid-May–mid-Oct 9:30am–5pm. Off-season 10am–3:30pm. Horse-drawn transportation (free) on grounds. $9 (off-season $3.25).* ✗ ᵫ ☎ *613/543-3704.* The first impression upon entering the village is one of bustling activity. Visitors are transported at once to the 19C. Suitably attired "inhabitants" walk the streets or travel about by stagecoach or other 19C conveyance. They perform a variety of activities: cheese and bread making, quilting, cabinetmaking, printing and tinsmithing, in addition to farm chores. The progress in the life of the first settlers from pioneer shanties to substantial dwellings of brick and stone is excellently illustrated. Note in particular the elegant refinement of the **Robertson House**, the solid prosperity of the **farm**, and the evident wealth and luxury of **Crysler Hall** with its Greek Revival architecture. There are churches and schools, a village store, doctor's surgery and a tavern. An 1860s-style meal can be eaten at **Willard's Hotel**.

The **sawmill**, **woollen mill** (where woollen cloth was and is once again being produced) and flour mill operate on water power, and show the gradual trend toward industrialization evident in Ontario by 1867. Regular demonstrations are given for visitors. The flour mill has an 1865 steam engine. A boat trip can be taken in a **bateau**, a wooden boat of the early 19C, which was pulled along canals or rivers by a horse on the bank.

Battlefield Monument. – *Beside Upper Canada Village in the park.* This monument commemorates the Battle of Crysler Farm in 1813 when a small force of British and Canadian troops routed a much larger American force. It stands beside the St Lawrence River with a fine **view** over the site of the farm now flooded by the Seaway.

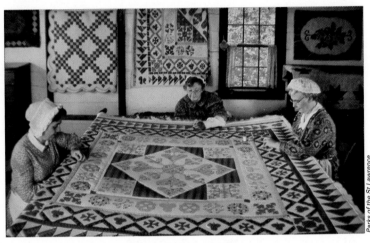

Parks of the St Lawrence

Quilting at Upper Canada Village

★ WINDSOR

Pop 191,435

Map p 100

Tourist Office ☎ 519/255-6530

The city of Windsor lies on the south side of the **Detroit River** opposite the American city of that name. A suspension bridge and tunnel connect both cities. Like Detroit, this industrial centre is a major automobile manufacturer and a port on the St Lawrence Seaway.

The Windsor/Detroit area was first settled by the French in the early 18C. In 1701, **Antoine de la Mothe Cadillac** built a post on the north side of the Detroit River that became the headquarters of the French fur trade in the Great Lakes/Mississippi River area. It was captured by the British in 1760. After the American Revolution, the fort and town were handed over to the Americans, and the Detroit River became the international border, except for a brief period during the War of 1812. The town of Sandwich developed on the Canadian side, but it was later engulfed by Windsor, founded in the early 1830s. In 1838, there were several invasions across the river by the American supporters of William Lyon Mackenzie, but since that time, relations between the two cities have been very cordial.

Every year, an **International Freedom Festival** is celebrated *(Jun–Jul)* to include the national holidays of both countries: July 1st and 4th. Today, Windsor is one of Canada's busiest points of entry.

★★ **Dieppe Gardens.** – The outstanding attraction of this park, which stretches several blocks along the river west of the main thoroughfare *(Ouellette Street)*, is its **view★★** of the Detroit skyline across the water. It is also a good vantage point from which to watch the huge ships of the Seaway.

★ **Art Gallery.** – *445 Riverside Dr W. Open year-round Tue–Sun. Closed legal holidays.* ☒ ⏱ ☎519/258-7111. Housed in a restored waterfront warehouse, the gallery displays changing exhibits from its permanent collection, which encompasses the Group of Seven, Inuit sculpture and East Asian art. From the third-floor cafeteria, there are fine **views** of the river.

EXCURSIONS

★ **Fort Malden.** – ☞ *In Amherstburg, 29km/18mi south. Open daily year-round. Closed legal holidays.* ⏱ ☎519/736-5416. This fort, built by the British at the end of the 18C when they had abandoned Detroit to the Americans, occupies a fine **site★** overlooking the Seaway. Some ramparts remain, now grass-covered, and a barracks has been restored to its 1819 state. In the **visitor centre**, a slide show *(6min)* explains the fort's role in the War of 1812 and the Rebellions of 1837. In the **interpretation centre**, military displays include an example of Mackenzie's rebel flag.

Route 50. – *31km/19mi from Malden Centre to Kingsville.* This quiet road runs along the coast of Lake Erie, offering vistas of the lake. It affords opportunities to view the many marshland birds and the market gardens that grow a variety of fruit and vegetables.

Jack Miner's Bird Sanctuary. – *On Rte 18 in Kingsville. Open Mar–Dec Mon–Sat.* ♿ ☏*519/733-4034.* Founded by conservationist **Jack Miner** (1865-1944), this sanctuary, one of the earliest in Canada, is a well-known stopping place for wildfowl on their seasonal migration. The best time to visit is late October and November when an estimated 40,000 geese and ducks land to feed.

★★ **Point Pelee National Park.** – *65km/40mi by Rtes 3 and 33. Description p 125.*

Quebec

Lower Town and Château Frontenac, Quebec City, *Tourisme Québec*

Encompassing an area of 1,540,680sq km/594,860sq mi, or one-sixth of Canada's total landmass, this vast province is first and foremost the bastion of French-Canadian culture. More than 80 percent of its population of 6.9 million are francophone, the survivors of an empire founded in the early 17C, which once covered half the continent. Very proud of this long tradition, the **Québécois** have maintained their own culture and lifestyle, creating a unique society in a North American milieu. About nine percent of the province's population claim British origin and are concentrated largely on Montreal island. The remainder of Quebec's population hails from a wide variety of ethnic origins, and includes Indians as well as Inuit who live in small settlements in the Great North.

GEOGRAPHICAL NOTES

Regional Landscapes. – Stretching almost 2,000km/1,240mi from the US border to Hudson Strait, Quebec is Canada's largest province. The extreme north is a forbidding land of treeless tundra underlain with permanently frozen ground that gradually turns to forest farther south. This forest covers most of the province, leaving only a sliver of arable land near the St Lawrence River. The majority of Quebec's population is concentrated in the St Lawrence Valley.

Three main physiographic regions can be distinguished in Quebec. The northern tundra and vast forested area lie on the **Canadian Shield** *(map p 15)*, a rocky expanse consisting of extensive plateaus interrupted by a few mountain massifs. In Quebec, the Shield rises to heights of 1,166m/3,824ft at Mount Raoul Blanchard in the Charlevoix region *(p 152)*, but otherwise presents a flat and monotonous surface, strewn with lakes. The extreme south of the province and the Gaspé Peninsula, on the other hand, are part of the **Appalachian Mountains**. These chains reach heights of 972m/3,188ft in the Eastern Townships *(p 154)* and 1,268m/4,159ft in the Gaspé Peninsula *(p 155)*, and provide large sections of arable land, especially in the south. Lodged between these two regions, the **St Lawrence Lowlands**, a triangular wedge graced with fertile soils and a moderate climate, support most of the province's agricultural production.

Climate. – Quebec experiences a wide range of temperatures because of its location. Although bright and sunny, the winters can be bitterly cold, especially in the north. Snowfall can accumulate up to 150cm/5ft in much of the central interior.

Following a short spring season, the southern regions of the province are suddenly plunged into summer, when hot weather and extremely humid conditions predominate. Summer departs slowly, and fall arrives with its beautiful colours. Sometimes, after all the leaves have dropped in late October or early November, summer returns briefly for a last fling. This "Indian summer" is another characteristic of Quebec's climate.

January temperatures in Montreal average -5°C/23°F, with an average of 254cm/100in of snowfall for the entire winter season. Located farther north, Sept-Îles registers -10°C/14°F with 422cm/165in of snow—the heaviest recorded snowfall in eastern Canada.

In July, Montreal registers maximum means of 26°C/79°F, Quebec City 25°C/77°F and Sept-Îles 20°C/68°F. Temperatures in excess of 32°C/90°F are not uncommon, however, in the southern regions, and humidity frequently exceeds 80 percent. Total annual precipitation in the south varies from 750–1000mm/30–40in and is fairly evenly distributed throughout the year.

ECONOMY

Although over 70 percent of the gross domestic product stems from manufacturing and services, Quebec's economy relies on the province's abundant natural resources and on traditional activities such as fishing, trapping and agriculture.

Since the opening of the **St Lawrence Seaway** in 1959, linking the Atlantic Ocean to the Great Lakes, the economy of Quebec has been closely tied to that of the US. Over 75 percent of the province's exported goods are bound to the US, which in turn exports 50 percent to Quebec.

Forest, Mines and Water Resources. – Covering more than 1,550,000sq km/600,000sq mi, the province's extensive forest has been exploited for centuries. Quebec is the Canadian leader in production of **pulp and paper**, manufacturing about one-third of the country's total output, and about 20 percent of the world's supply of **newsprint**. The province supports some 60 processing mills located along the St Lawrence, Ottawa, St Maurice and Saguenay rivers and in the Eastern Townships. Mining is concentrated in several regions lying on the Canadian Shield whose age-old rocks are a great source of mineral wealth. The Abitibi and Témiscamingue regions (Noranda, Matagami, Chibougamau) contain large deposits of **copper** as well as gold, silver, zinc, lead and nickel in smaller quantities. Copper is also found at Murdochville in the Gaspé Peninsula. Quebec is the world's largest exporter of asbestos, a fibrous silicate mineral found mainly in the Eastern Townships region *(p 154)*. An additional source of income stems from the recent exploitation of **iron ore** in the Labrador Trough *(p 185)*.

The province's industrialization has been closely linked to its abundant **hydro-electric resources**. The St Lawrence, St Maurice and Saguenay rivers generate large amounts of electricity mainly for industrial use. The Manic-Outardes *(p 154)* project, located on the north shore of the St Lawrence, produces in excess of 6.5 million kilowatts. The enormous project on the La Grande River, which runs into James Bay, has a capacity of more than 10 million kilowatts.

The low-cost energy generated from hydro-electric plants has spurred the province's electro-metallurgic industries. With smelters located at Beauharnois and Bécancour on the St Lawrence, Shawinigan on the St Maurice and Arvida on the Saguenay River, Quebec has become a major producer of **aluminum**.

Agriculture, Fishing and Trapping. – These regionally based activities still form the traditional supports of the province's economy. Agriculture predominates in the southern regions of Quebec, in particular the island of Montreal, St Lawrence Valley and Lake St-Jean area, which produce fruit, vegetables, beef and dairy products in sufficient quantities to supply the province's population. The major fishing centres are located on the Gaspé Peninsula, Magdalen Islands and Côte-Nord. Although trapping is no longer as important as it was during the settlement of the province, it is still practised in the northern areas.

HISTORICAL NOTES

Birth of New France. – Before the arrival of Europeans, Quebec's territory was inhabited by Indians of the Eastern Woodlands culture, including Algonquins and Montagnais. During the 15C, Basque fishermen came to fish off the coast. A century later, during the era of European explorers, French navigator **Jacques Cartier** (1491-1557) set out across the Atlantic Ocean in search of riches and a route to the Orient. He landed on the Gaspé Peninsula in 1534 and claimed this new land for the King of France, François I. Although Cartier returned to the New World in 1535 and 1542, France did not establish a firm presence on the continent until 1608, when **Samuel de Champlain** (c.1570-1636) left Port Royal in Acadia *(p 199)*, ascended the St Lawrence, and founded Quebec City.

Soon after establishing his *habitation (p 170)*, Champlain and his young colony suffered repeated attacks by Indians of the Iroquois nations. The **Iroquois Wars** continued until 1701, when the Montreal Peace Treaty established a temporary truce. The wars, combined with France's lack of interest in the colony, kept settlement to a minimum. The administration of New France consisted of an appointed governor responsible for conducting the colony's military and external affairs, and an intendant in charge of administrative and economic functions. The young colony was organized according to the feudal system that existed in France until the Revolution in 1789. A *seigneurie* or piece of land was granted to a **seigneur** or landowner who swore loyalty to the king. He in turn granted parts of his land to tenant farmers who paid him various dues. To provide as many people as possible with access to the river, the major means of transport, the land was divided into *rangs*—long thin strips that started at the river bank.

A Vast Empire. – During the mid-17C, the *coureurs des bois* (fur traders) and missionaries from New France explored wide areas of the continent. Champlain himself discovered the lake named after him, as well as the Ottawa River, Georgian Bay, Lake Simcoe and Lake Ontario. His followers, Étienne Brulé, Jean Nicolet and Nicolas Perrot, reached Lake Superior. In the 1650s, Pierre Radisson and the Sieur des Groseilliers travelled through the Great Lakes and north perhaps as far as Hudson Bay. They planned a quicker trade route to Europe via the bay that would avoid the long canoe/portage route back to Montreal. When France showed no interest in this scheme, Radisson and Groseillers turned to the British who eventually founded the Hudson's Bay Company.

The greatest explorers of them all were the **La Vérendrye family**. Pierre Gaultier de Varennes, Sieur de La Vérendrye, explored much of Manitoba and Saskatchewan between 1731 and 1738, setting up a series of trading posts. His sons François and Louis-Joseph explored even farther west, reaching the foot of the Rockies in present-day Montana in 1742, the first Europeans to behold this mountain range.

Anglo-French Wars. – Part of a broader struggle in Europe and elsewhere, the conflict between France and England in North America centred on the profitable fur trade. Repeated assaults by the British led to the capture of Quebec City in 1629. The French regained control of the city three years later. The Treaty of Utrecht ushered in a period of peace that lasted until the Seven Years' War *(p 17)*. On September 13, 1759, British Gen **James Wolfe** (1728-1759) defeated French Gen **Louis-Joseph de Montcalm** (1712-1759) on the **Plains of Abraham** *(p 175)* in Quebec City, signaling the end of the French colony. After Montreal's surrender in September 1760, France capitulated. The colony was ceded to England in 1763 by the Treaty of Paris.

A British Colony. – Faced with a Roman Catholic, French-speaking population, the new governor, **Sir Guy Carleton**, decided to recognize the rights of the Roman Catholic church, the seigneurial system and French civil law as a basis for government. These rights were enshrined in the **Quebec Act** of 1774.

During the American Revolution, the inhabitants of the 13 colonies tried unsuccessfully to persuade the French Canadians to join them. After the Revolution, many Loyalists moved to the Eastern Townships *(p 154)*. In order to satisfy their demands for representation, the British government divided the colony into Upper and Lower Canada in 1791. Both colonies were granted elected assemblies, but their powers were strictly limited. Frustration over these limitations led to the **Rebellions of 1837** *(p 130)* in both colonies. The issue was further inflamed in Quebec because the governor and his council were British and the assembly French. Led by **Louis-Joseph Papineau** (1786-1871), the **Patriots** petitioned for the right of self-government. Rejection of their demands by the British government ultimately resulted in fighting that left 325 soldiers and rebels dead. The Patriots were defeated, but full representative government was eventually granted.

Both colonies were joined by the Act of Union as a result of the Durham Report *(p 18)*. Although the union was to usher in a period of political liberalism, frequent crises finally led the British Parliament to ratify the British North America Act in 1867, establishing **Canadian Confederation** *(p 18)*. Facing a progressive loss of rights, Quebec entered an era of nationalism that advocated greater autonomy for the province.

A Sovereign State? – During the 1960s, a climate of social, economic and political change, labelled the "Quiet Revolution," emerged in Quebec. Provincial powers grew and an increased nationalist ideology continued to dominate the political landscape. Spearheaded by the leader of the Parti Québécois (1968), **René Lévesque** (1922-1987), the issue of Quebec sovereignty became a hotly debated topic. In May 1980, however, Lévesque's party lost a referendum on Quebec sovereignty when 60 percent of Quebecers voted against separation. Two years later, still under Lévesque's leadership, Quebec refused to sign the Canadian Constitution *(p 18)*. When the Liberal government of Robert Bourassa took power in 1985, negotiations with the other Canadian provinces resumed. The **Meech Lake Accord** (April 30, 1987), which provided a special status for Quebec as a "distinct society," had to be ratified by the Federal Government and all ten provinces before June 23, 1990. The provinces failed to reach a consensus, and Quebec was left debating sovereignty, or adherence to the Canadian Constitution. In October 1992, a national referendum on, among other issues, Quebec's status as a distinct society was voted down by a majority of Canadians. Canada will continue, however, to face the thorny issue of integrating the French-speaking province's demands into a constitution that is acceptable to the rest of the country.

Principal Festivals

mid-Feb	**Quebec Winter Carnival** *(p 171)* **Carnival** **Winterlude**	*Quebec City* *Chicoutimi* *Hull*
mid-Mar May	**Beauce County Maple Festival** **Grand Prix Molson**	*Saint-Georges* *Montreal*
Jul	**International Jazz Festival** **Drummondville World Folklore Festival** **International Summer Festival**	*Montreal* *Drummondville* *Quebec City*
late Jul	**International Swim Marathon** *(p 179)*	*Roberval*
Jul–Aug	**Orford Festival**	*Magog*
Aug	**Blueberry Festival** **Hot-Air Balloon Festival** **Montreal World Film Festival**	*Mistassini* *Saint-Jean-sur-Richelieu* *Montreal*
Sept	**International Canoe Classic** **Americas Cycling Grand Prix (World Cup)**	*Trois-Rivières* *Montreal*

Practical Information

How to get there. – **Air** service to Montreal's Mirabel and Dorval airports is provided by international and domestic airlines. Inter-Canadian (☎800/776-3000) and other affiliated carriers offer connections to many cities within Quebec.

Amtrak links Montreal and the US with two daily connections: one from Washington DC and one from New York City. **VIA Rail** train service is extensive within the province. In Canada consult the local telephone directory for nearest office; from the US ☎800/ 561-3949 (toll-free). Intercity **bus** service and connections to the regions of Bas-Saint-Laurent and Gaspé Peninsula are offered by **Orléans Express** (☎514/842-2281). The province has an extensive **ferry** boat system; for schedules contact Tourisme Québec *(see below)*.

Accommodation and Tourist Information. – The official government tourist office publishes annual summer and winter vacation brochures as well as regional guides that include points of interest, driving tours, hotels, activities, camping, etc. These publications and road maps can be obtained free of charge from: **Tourisme Québec**, CP 20 000, Quebec City, PQ, G1K 7X2 ☎514/873-2015 or 800/363-7777 (toll-free Canada/US).

Major hotel chains can be found in urban areas ($80–$175/night). Small hotels and Bed & Breakfast lodgings offer quality accommodation at moderate prices ($45–$90) throughout the province. **Farm holidays** ($30/day) may be especially appealing to families. For the guide, *Gîtes du Passant* ($7.95), listing facilities throughout the province, contact Ministère du Loisir, de la Chasse et de la Pêche, 4545 Ave Pierre-de-Coubertin, Montreal, PQ, H1V 3R2 ☎514/252-3000.

Language. – The official language of Quebec is French, spoken by 83% of the population. However, in urban areas, English is spoken. Tourist information is generally available in both languages. Telephone operators are bilingual.

Road Regulations. – Quebec has a network of highways *(autoroutes)* and well-maintained secondary roads. Road signs are in French only. The speed limit on highways, unless otherwise posted, is 100km/h (60mph), on secondary roads 80km/h (50mph) to 90km/h (55mph), and 50km/h (30mph) within city limits. Turning right on red is prohibited. **Seat belt** use is mandatory. **Canadian Automobile Association (CAA)**, Montreal ☎514/861-7111.

Time Zone. – Quebec is on Eastern Standard Time. Daylight Saving Time is observed from the first Sunday in April to the last Sunday in October.

Taxes. – In addition to the national 7% GST *(rebate information p 242)*, Quebec levies a provincial sales tax of 4% for all services and 8% for goods. Non-residents can request rebates of the provincial tax from Revenue Québec, 3800 rue de Marly, Sainte-Foy, PQ, G1X 4A5 ☎418/659-4692.

Liquor Laws. – The legal drinking age is 18. The sale of wine and liquor is regulated by the provincial government and sold in "Société des Alcools" stores. Beer and wine are also sold in grocery stores.

Provincial Holiday *(see National Holidays p 240)*
Saint-Jean-Baptiste Day............ June 24

Outdoor Activities. – The Canadian Parks Service operates three **national parks** offering year-round activities such as hiking, backpacking, nature programs, biking, sailing, canoeing, fishing, camping and winter sports. For trail maps, brochures and camping reservations ☎418/648-4177.

The guide, *Quebec Parks and Wildlife Reserves, Activities and Services,* obtainable free of charge (☎418/890-6527), gives in-park accommodation, boat or ski equipment rentals, and hunting and fishing information for the numerous **provincial parks** and **wildlife reserves**.

Canoeing is practised on most of the rivers except those used for logging. **Kayaking** is popular in the northern regions of Saguenay and Nunavik, where camps have been set up. Ranch vacations that include **horseback riding** are prevalent in the Eastern Townships, Gaspé Peninsula and Bas-Saint-Laurent regions. For further information on all outdoor activities contact Regroupement Loisir Québec ☎514/252-3000.

Major ski areas offering alpine and cross-country **skiing** are the Laurentians (Mont Tremblant ☎819/425-8711), the Eastern Townships (Mont Orford ☎819/843-6548) and the Quebec City region (Mont Ste-Anne ☎418/827-4561). Abundant snowfall extends the ski season to mid-April. **Snowmobiling** is a popular outdoor activity. A network of well-marked trails crisscrosses the countryside interspersed with heated cabins and other accommodation. For a free copy of the *Trans-Quebec Snowmobile Trail Network Map* contact Tourisme Québec *(see above)*.

Many regions in Quebec are known for excellent **hunting** and **fishing**. Outfitters' lodges *(pourvoiries)*, easily reached by land or air, offer packages that include accommodation, transport to remote locations, equipment rental, permits and game registration. Above the 52nd parallel, non-residents are required to hire the services of an outfitter. Write to Ministère du Loisir, de la Chasse et de la Pêche, CP 22 000, Quebec City, PQ, G1K 7X2 for the *Directory of Outfitters' Establishments*. The rivers of the Gaspé Peninsula are well known for salmon fishing.

Special Excursions. – Organized nature tours for canoeing, rafting, horseback riding, biking or hiking are offered through New World River Expeditions ☎819/242-7238. Activities such as rock climbing, dogsledding, canoeing and kayaking can be arrranged through CÉPAL ☎418/547-5728 or Nortour ☎514/987-9941. For information on additional adventure travel contact Tourisme Québec *(see above)*.

★★ ANTICOSTI ISLAND

Map of Principal Sights p 5

Stretching more than 222km/138mi in length and 56km/35mi at its widest point, Anticosti Island is mantled with coniferous forests and crisscrossed by over 100 rivers teeming with Atlantic salmon and trout. Well known by deer hunters for the abundance of game, the island is also a pleasant vacation spot for nature lovers.

French industrialist **Henri Menier**, who purchased Anticosti for the sum of $125,000 in 1895, transformed the island into his private paradise, constructing a sumptuous hunting lodge (destroyed by fire in 1953) and importing animals, in particular, white-tailed deer. In 1926, the island was sold for $6.5 million to the Anticosti Corporation. The Quebec government acquired Anticosti in 1974, and the majority of the island is now part of a reserve (4,575sq km/1,766sq mi).

Access. – *Air service available through Inter-Canadian ☎418/962-8321 or Aviation Québec Labrador ☎418/962-7901. Boat service available through Relais Nordik Inc., from Rimouski ☎418/723-8787 and Sept-Îles ☎418/968-4707. A four-wheel drive vehicle is indispensable on the island.*

A tour of the island from **Port-Menier**, the island's only remaining permanent settlement, leads past such scenic wonders as Kalimazoo Falls and La Patate Cavern, **Vauréal Falls and Canyon★★**, with a 70m/230ft waterfall, and **Tour Bay★★**, renowned for its spectacular limestone cliffs that plummet dramatically into the sea. Located to the west of Port-Menier, Baie-Sainte-Claire provides an ideal setting for observing **white-tailed deer**, sometimes seen in herds of up to 100.

★★ BAS-SAINT-LAURENT

Map p 153

Situated on the south shore of the St Lawrence River, between Quebec City and the Gaspé Peninsula, this region is characterized by fertile plains, plateaus and, to the north, the foothills of the Appalachians. The peaceful, rural landscapes along the shore are divided into long, narrow strips of farmland, perpendicular to the river. To the north, the Laurentian Mountains plunge into the St Lawrence, creating picturesque scenery.

Route 132 passes through the principal communities of this region, affording superb views of the St Lawrence and of various islands dotting the river.

★ **Lévis.** – Pop 39,452. *250km/155mi east of Montreal by Hwy 20 or Rte 132. A ferry connects Lévis to Quebec City.* Located on the south shore of the St Lawrence, opposite Quebec City, this important business centre is noted for its port and its wood-related industries. The city is also the birthplace and headquarters of the Desjardins cooperative savings and loan company *(Caisse populaire Desjardins).* Founded in 1900 by journalist Alphonse Desjardins (1854-1920), this people's bank sought to bring economic independence to French Canadians.

At the corner of Avenue Mont-Marie and Rue Guenette, the white clapboard **Maison Alphonse-Desjardins★** *(open daily year-round; ☎418/835-2090)* presents a video and photographic displays.

★ **Fort No. 1 National Historic Site.** – ☞ *Open May 12–Jun 21 Sun–Fri; daily Jun 22–Labour Day; until end-Oct Sun only. ☎418/835-5182.* Forming an irregular pentagon, the fort (1865-1872) stands atop Pointe-Lévis, the highest point on the south shore of the St Lawrence. It is the sole vestige of three such forts built to protect Quebec City from possible American attack after the threat of the American Civil War, and from the Fenian Raids. The fort is composed of a series of massive earthen ramparts with a tall embankment protecting the casemates, ditches and vaulted tunnels leading to the *caponiers*—stone and brick structures armed with small cannon.

★ **Grosse Île National Historic Site.** – ☞ *Visit by guided tour only Jun 1–Labour Day. Two daily cruises 9am & 1:30pm. Round-trip $29. Departures from Berthier-sur-Mer and Montmagny (39km/24mi and 55km/34mi east of Lévis respectively by Hwy 20 or Rte 132). Reservations required ☎418/248-4832.* The ever-increasing number of European immigrants to Canada prompted the government to establish, in 1832, a quarantine station on Grosse Île, one of 21 islands making up the Île aux Grues archipelago.

In the station's first year of operation, some 50,000 immigrants were examined in an effort to limit the spread of cholera into Canada. The western part of the island was known as the Hotel Sector. The Village Sector in the island's centre housed employees of the station and their families. To the east, the Hospital Sector included 21 hospitals of which one is still standing. In 1990, the Canadian Parks Service opened the site to the public.

Route 132 continues through **L'Islet-sur-Mer**, a small maritime community known as the birthplace of famed Arctic explorer, Capt Joseph-Elzéar Bernier (1852-1934), and through **Saint-Jean-Port-Joli★**, the craft and wood-carving capital of Quebec.

★ **La Pocatière.** – Pop 4,648. *60km/37mi from Montmagny.* Situated on a terrace above the coastal plain, this community is a leading centre for agricultural research. The **François Pilote Museum★** *(open daily May–Oct; off-season closed Sat; $3; ☎418/856-3145)* illustrates rural life in the province at the turn of the century. Collections focus on agriculture, the natural sciences and education.

Route 132 passes across a wide flood plain, affording expansive views of the Laurentian Mountains across the St Lawrence. Perpendicular to the shoreline, eel-traps extend into the river. From the pleasant community of **Kamouraska★**, lines of stakes can be seen in the tidal flats. These traps divert fish and eels into enclosures where they can be netted.

★ **Rivière-du-Loup.** – Pop 14,017. *72km/45mi from La Pocatière.* Situated halfway between Quebec City and Gapsé Peninsula, this town has developed into a commercial and resort centre. A walk through the downtown leads past several buildings of interest, including the imposing Gothic Revival **St Patrick's Presbytery**, surrounded by verandas, and the **Viatorian Clerics Residence**.

North of downtown, the Loup River drops over the cliff terrace in 38m/125ft high falls. Steps lead to a lookout providing an expansive view of the town and river.

★ **Bic Park** (Parc du Bic). – *81km/ 50mi from Rivière-du-Loup.* This 33sq km/13sq mi provincial conservation park, created in 1984, boasts a variety of flora, including both deciduous and boreal forests. The small town of **Bic** is known for its spectacular **setting**★★ on the shores of the St Lawrence.

★ **Rimouski.** – Pop 30,873. *25km/ 16mi from Bic Park.* Built along the banks of the St Lawrence, this industrial city has developed in a semicircular pattern around the mouth of the Rimouski River and is now considered a major metropolis of eastern Quebec. Among sights of interest, note the **Maison Lamontagne**, one of the few remaining examples of masonry half-timbering in North America *(open daily Jun 24–Labour Day; off-season by request only. $2;* ♿ ☎*418/722-4038).* Located 10km/6mi from town, the **Maritime Museum**★ *(open daily Jun 1–Labour Day; $3.50;* 🍴 ☎*418/724-6214)* at Pointe-au-Père displays hundreds of artifacts recovered from the wreck of the *Empress of Ireland*, nicknamed the "Titanic of the St Lawrence."

★★★ **CHARLEVOIX COAST**

Map p 153

One of Quebec's loveliest, most varied regions, this rugged coast is best appreciated by following Routes 138 and 362, which weave up and down, affording magnificent clifftop or water-level views of forested hills, the pristine shore and mountains that sweep down into the mighty St Lawrence. Named for Jesuit historian Pierre-François-Xavier de Charlevoix (1682-1781), this resort spot has long attracted and inspired painters, poets and writers.

★★ **Ste-Anne Falls.** – *52km/32mi east of Quebec City. Open May 10–Oct 1 8am–sundown. $5.* ♿🍴 ☎*418/827-4057.* Pleasant paths lead to this steep and narrow waterfall, which drops a total of 74m/243ft over the edge of the Canadian Shield, creating a mass of shattered rocks and whirlpools at its base.

★★ **Baie-Saint-Paul.** – *58km/36mi.* Route 138 offers spectacular **views**★★ on the descent to this celebrated artist haunt. Surrounded by rolling green hills, the charming community boasts more than a dozen art galleries and an **arts centre** *(open daily year-round;* ☎*418/435-3681)* that displays the work of local artists.

Departing by Route 362, visitors will find an overlook that provides another splendid **view**★★ of the town, the St Lawrence and the south shore.

★★ **Île aux Coudres.** – *Access by ferry year-round from Saint-Joseph-de-la-Rive (22km/14mi from Baie-Saint-Paul,* ☎*418/438-2743.* Named by Jacques Cartier in 1535 for its abundant hazel trees *(coudriers)*, this enchanting island, home to farmers, boat builders and fishermen, occupies a spectacular offshore **site** linked by ferry to the mainland. Each year, the island's inhabitants demonstrate their canoeing skills on the icy river at the Quebec Winter Carnival *(p 171).*

A tour of the island *(21km/13mi)* by car or bicycle reveals splendid views of both the north and south shores of the St Lawrence. Remnants of a past age—beached "voitures d'eau" or schooners—dot the coast. The **Musée des Voitures d'Eau**★ *(open daily Jun–Oct; $4.50;* ♿🍴 ☎*418/438-2208)* presents the region's maritime history.

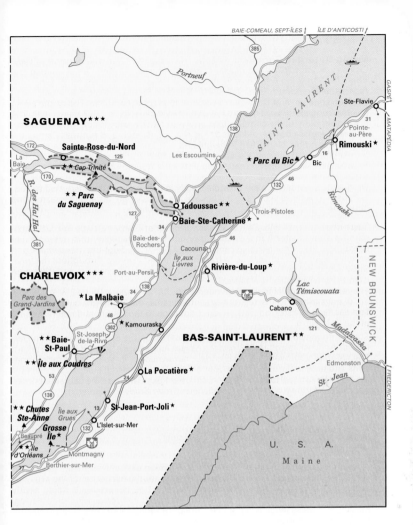

The **Île aux Coudres Mills★** *(open daily mid-May–mid-Oct; $2.75; & ☎418/438-2184)*, both dating from the 19C, provide a rare opportunity to compare the mechanisms of a windmill and a water mill. At La Baleine, the **Maison Leclerc**, a simple stone dwelling, is among the oldest homes on the island.

★ **La Malbaie.** – Pop 3,968. *26km/16mi northeast of Île aux Coudres.* Occupying a beautiful **site★**, this resort community was named "Malle Baye" (bad bay) by Samuel de Champlain in 1608, when he discovered his anchored ships had run aground. After the British defeated the French *(p 175)*, Scottish soldiers renamed it Murray Bay in honour of the colony's chief administrator. The picturesque **Manoir Richelieu** *(in Pointe-au-Pic)* is a grand reminder of the resort hotels that sprung up during the 19C.

★ **Baie-Sainte-Catherine.** – Pop 312. *74km/46mi northeast of La Malbaie.* Located at the mouth of the Saguenay River, this small community was settled in the 1820s. **Whale-watching cruises★★** have become a popular attraction, just as in Tadoussac *(p 178)* across the fjord. Overlooking the mouth of the Saguenay in the **Pointe-Noire Saguenay Marine Park** *(open daily Jun 15–Oct 1; $3; ☎418/237-4348)*, a lookout tower provides occasional glimpses of the large mammals frolicking in the water below.

★ CÔTE-NORD

Map of Principal Sights p 5

Extending from the mouth of the Saguenay River north to the Labrador border, Côte-Nord is divided into three regions: the southernmost stretching from Tadoussac to Sept–Îles; the central North Shore from Sept–Îles to Havre-Saint-Pierre; and the northernmost region *(accessible only by boat or plane)*, encompassing the vast expanse of taiga and the villages between Havre-Saint-Pierre and Blanc-Sablon. Long known as an untamed wilderness of forests with occasional fishing villages, Côte-Nord underwent gradual industrialization with the development of **pulp mills** in the 1920s and 1930s and later, the discovery of rich **iron-ore** deposits. In the 1960s, the region's enormous hydro-electric potential was harnessed, prompting another surge of economic growth. A drive along Route 138 leads through desolate stretches of pristine, rocky landscape, occasionally interrupted by developing towns and hydro-electric plants.

Manic-Outardes Complex. – *Manic 5 is located 210km/130mi north of Baie-Comeau (422km/262mi northeast of Quebec City) on Rte 389. Visit by guided tour only (1hr 30min) in French daily mid-Jun–Labour Day; English for groups only, reservations required. Free.* △ ✗ ☎418/294-3919. Begun in 1959, the harnessing of the Manicouagan and Outardes rivers took 20 years to complete. Today, the seven plants strung along both rivers have a combined capacity of 6,597 megawatts. The first power plant of the complex to produce electricity was **Manic 2★**. The spectacular **Daniel Johnson Dam★★** of **Manic 5★★** is the largest arch-and-buttress dam in the world, measuring 214m/702ft in height and 1,313m/4,307ft in length. Named for a former premier of Quebec, it was completed in 1968. During construction, two semi-circular lakes were united, creating the distinctive doughnut-shaped reservoir, with a diameter of 65km/40mi.

On the tour, guides explain how electricity is produced and transmitted to consumers. A bus takes visitors to the base of the massive arches and then across the dam where good views of the reservoir and surrounding landscape are permitted.

★ **Sept-Îles.** – Pop 24,848. *640km/397mi northeast of Quebec City by Rte 138.* Occupying a superb **site★★** in a circular bay on the St Lawrence, this dynamic city constitutes the administrative centre of the Côte-Nord. Sept-Îles' deep-water port enables ocean-bound vessels to tranship coal and iron ore throughout the year. Stroll along the old wharf to enjoy views of the magnificent bays and the seven islands for which the city is named.

The reconstructed **Old Trading Post** *(open daily Jun 24–Labour Day; $2;* ⅀ ☎418/968-2070)* pays tribute to the region's first inhabitants, the Montagnais. Offshore, the **Sept-Îles Regional Park★** offers a good introduction to the history and natural beauty of the Côte-Nord.

The community of **Havre-Saint-Pierre** (pop 3,344) marks the end of Route 138. The ferries for Anticosti Island *(p 151)* and the **Mingan Archipelago★★** depart from the wharf. The string of approximately 40 islands is renowned for its spectacular rock formations and unique flora and fauna. Havre-Saint-Pierre is also the departure point for the boat trip *(3 days)* to Blanc-Sablon, situated 1.5km/1mi from the Labrador border. *For more information, consult the Michelin Green Guide to Quebec.*

★★ EASTERN TOWNSHIPS (Estrie)

Map p 177

A region of lush rolling hills named for its location east of Montreal, "the Townships" as they are generally called, occupy the southwest corner of the province along the US border. This area of deep valleys, tree-covered hills rising nearly 1,000m/3,280ft, and beautiful, sparkling lakes such as Brome, Memphrémagog, Magog and Massawipi, is a popular retreat for Montrealers, offering a variety of recreational activities.

After the American Revolution, land parcels along the border were granted to Loyalists fleeing the US. The towns and villages these first settlers established reflect their New England heritage. After 1850, increasing numbers of French-speaking people moved into the region, and today its population is predominantly francophone. The northeastern section, in particular the towns of **Asbestos** and **Thetford Mines**, is known for its asbestos production. Directly north of Asbestos lies the Bois-Francs (hard woods) area, named for the predominant maple tree. To the east, drained by the Chaudière River, the flat fertile farmland referred to as the **Beauce** contains the greatest concentration of maple groves in Quebec. In spring, sugaring-off parties are a popular pastime.

★ **Sherbrooke.** – Pop 76,429. *150km/93mi east of Montreal by Hwy 10 and Rte 112.* Straddling the confluence of the Saint-François and Magog rivers, this industrial centre is the principal city of the townships. The **Museum of Fine Arts** *(open year-round Tue–Sun, closed holidays;* ☎819/821-2115)* exhibits a fine collection of Quebec art, focusing on the Eastern Townships. Standing atop the Marquette Plateau, the imposing Gothic Revival **cathedral★** was designed in 1958 by Napoléon Audet, who also designed the basilica at Sainte-Anne-de-Beaupré *(p 175)*. From this vantage point, the **view★** encompasses the entire city.

★ **Magog.** – Pop 14,034. *124km/74mi east of Montreal by Hwy 10.* This popular resort community enjoys a splendid **setting★** on the shores of Lake Memphrémagog, which stretches over 50km/31mi, crossing the border into Vermont. **Scenic cruises★** *(depart daily Jun 24–Labour Day; off-season Sun only; 1hr 45min with commentary; $9;* ✗ ☎819/843-8068)* on this long and narrow lake afford splendid views of the snow-capped peaks of Mount Orford, Sugar Loaf and Owl's Head.

★ **Saint-Benoît-du-Lac Abbey.** – *20km/12mi south of Magog by Rte 112 W; follow signs. Open daily year-round.* ⅀ ☎819/843-4080. The pleasant drive to this Benedictine monastery offers lovely glimpses of the sparkling lake waters. Distinguished by its impressive bell tower, the complex was designed by Dom Paul Bellot (1876-1944), who is buried in the cemetery. The monks are famous for their Gregorian chant and for the cheese (L'Ermite and Mont-Saint-Benoît) they produce on the premises.

★ **Mount Orford Park.** – *116km/72mi east of Montreal by Hwy 10 (Exit 115) and Rte 141. Open daily year-round. Sailing, hiking, golf,* △ *summers only.* ⅀ ☎819/843-6233. Created in 1938, this provincial park is dominated by Mount Orford (881m/2,890ft), a well-known ski centre. Follow a short path around the television tower at the summit for a sweeping **panorama★★** north to the St Lawrence Valley, west to the Monteregian Hills, south to Lake Memphrémagog and east to the Appalachians.

Orford Arts Centre. – *Open Jul–Aug Tue–Sun.* ሙ ※. *For information on concerts, workshops & exhibitions* ☎819/843-3981. Founded in 1951, the centre is renowned for its annual summer music festival *(Festival Orford)*. The great concert hall was formerly the Man and Music pavilion of Montreal's Expo '67.

Compton. – Pop 899. *172km/107mi east of Montreal by Hwy 10 and Rtes 143 and 147.* This quiet village is the birthplace of **Louis-Stephen Saint-Laurent** (1882-1973), Canada's 12th prime minister. An ardent Canadian nationalist, Saint-Laurent fought to establish a distinct Canadian identity during his years in office (1948-1957).

★ **Louis-Stephen Saint-Laurent National Historic Site.** – ⬤ *Rue Principale. Open May 14–Oct 14 Tue–Sun. Off-season weekends only.* ሙ ☎819/835-5448. The simple clapboard house, full of mementos of the Saint-Laurent family, has been restored to represent various periods of the prime minister's life. The adjoining general store, originally run by Saint-Laurent's father, is stocked with replicas of goods sold here at the turn of the century. A **multimedia biography** *(20min)* presents the highlights of Saint-Laurent's life and career.

Granby. – Pop 42,804. *80km/50mi southeast of Montreal by Hwy 10 (Exit 68) and Rtes 139 and 112.* Set on the banks of the Yamaska River, this small industrial centre was settled by Loyalists in the early 19C. Today, it is especially known for its **zoo**★ *(Blvd Bouchard; open daily May–Oct; $12;* ሙ ※ ☎514/372-9113) one of the largest in Canada, featuring over 1,000 animals, including 220 species of mammals and birds. Of particular interest is the reptile house, with over 350 reptiles displayed in a near-natural environment.

Valcourt. – Pop 2,284. *130km/81mi east of Montreal by Hwy 10 (Exit 90) and Rtes 243 and 222.* Long a small agricultural community, Valcourt is today the centre of a thriving **snowmobile** industry, begun by one of its residents. Joseph-Armand Bombardier (1907-1964) first developed a drive-wheel and track mechanism to power vehicles over snow in 1937. In 1959, he introduced the **ski-doo**, which went on to transform life in the north. Today, Bombardier Industries develops and sells snowmobiles all over the world.

★ **J.-Armand Bombardier Museum.** – *1001 Ave J-A Bombardier. Open daily Jun 24–Labour Day. Off-season Tue–Sun. $4.* ሙ ☎514/532-2258. Divided into three sections, this fascinating museum highlights the life and work of Valcourt's native son. One section illustrates the ski-doo's assembly and usage; another section re-creates the garage where Bombardier worked as a mechanic and inventor.

Drummondville. – Pop 35,462. *110km/68mi east of Montreal by Hwy 20 (Exit 177).* Founded as a military outpost after the War of 1812, this community is today an important industrial centre for the garment industry.

★ **Québécois Village of Olden Times (Village québécois d'antan).** – *Rue Montplaisir, Exit 121 off Hwy 20. Open daily Jun 1–Labour Day (weekends only until first week in Oct). Off-season by reservation only. $9.* ※ ☎819/478-1441. Over 50 authentic buildings (church, school, tavern, forge, farm and homes) were relocated to this pleasant site to re-create life in the region during the 19C. Costumed interpreters explain the daily life of the former occupants.

★★★ GASPÉ PENINSULA

Maps pp 156-157

This peninsula extends along the southern shore of the St Lawrence, advancing into the gulf of the same name. The interior is largely an impenetrable wilderness of mountains and forest, dominated by a continuation of the Appalachians—the **Chic-Choc Mountains**, which rise to their highest peak at **Mount Jacques Cartier** (1,268m/4,160ft). Tiny fishing villages dot the wild and rocky northern coast of the peninsula, culminating in the breathtaking beauty of Forillon and Percé. Agriculture and forestry are the primary industries along the southern coast. In addition to spectacular scenery that attracts visitors year-round, the region offers excellent cuisine and some of the best salmon fishing in Quebec.

THE NORTH COAST

★★ **Métis Gardens** (Jardins de Métis). – *350km/217mi southeast of Quebec City. Open Jun 1–Sept 8 daily 8:30am–8pm; until Oct 15 Mon–Fri 8:30am–4:30pm. $3.20.* ሙ ※ ☎418/ 775-2221. In 1918, Elsie Meighen Reford inherited this tract of land from her uncle, Sir George Stephen, president of the Canadian Pacific Railway Company. She transformed the estate into magnificent gardens. Since 1961, the property has been owned and maintained by the government of Quebec.
Over 600 varieties of flowers and ornamental plants, including many rare species, flourish in six distinct gardens that rank among the most beautiful in the world. Pleasant paths wind along a stream, revealing beautifully coloured plants, such as lilies, rhododendrons, azaleas, Asiatic gentians and Tibetan blue poppies. In the centre of the gardens stands the **Villa Reford**, an elegant mansion erected by Stephen. Inside, displays re-create aspects of regional life.

Matane. – Pop 12,756. *55km/34mi east of Métis Gardens.* This small industrial centre is known for its salmon fishing and shrimp production. In the town centre, a **salmon ladder**★ enables the fish to travel upstream from mid-June to October. The 44m/144ft channel passes through the lower level of an observation tower, in which several port holes provide a close-up look at the salmon.

GASPÉ PENINSULA

QUEBEC

★ **Gaspésie Park.** – *103km/ 64mi east of Matane. Open year-round. Hiking, mountain climbing, fishing, cross-country skiing. For camping & chalet reservation contact SEPAQ ☎418/763-2288.* Created in 1937, this park encompasses 800sq km/309sq mi devoted to the conservation of plant and animal life indigenous to the province. It is the only place in Quebec where caribou, moose and white-tailed deer are known to coexist.

The **Mount Albert Sector** reflects vegetation characteristic of the northern tundra. In the **Lake Cascapédia Sector**, the ridges of the Chic-Choc Mountains offer spectacular **views**★★ of the Appalachians. From the summit of Mount Jacques Cartier, home to caribou and arctic-alpine flora, an expansive **view**★★ extends to the McGerrigle Mountains. The **nature centre** *(open daily Jun–mid-Oct; & ☎418/763-7811)* presents exhibits, films, lectures and slide shows.

★★ **Scenic Route.** – Past Gaspésie Park, Route 132 follows the contours of the coastline, up and over rocky cliffs, affording splendid views of hills, valleys, picturesque fishing villages and the ocean. Of particular interest are the impressive shale cliffs around **Mont-Saint-Pierre** and the expansive views of the gulf from the bustling fishing village of **Rivière-au-Renard**.

★★ **Forillon National Park.** – ☞ *217km/134.5mi east of Gaspésie Park. Open year-round. $4.25/day per car, $9.50/4 days per car. ⚠&✗ ☎418/368-5505.* Located on the eastern tip of the peninsula, this 245sq km/95sq mi park includes limestone cliffs towering over the sea; mountains of spruce, fir, poplar and cedar; wildflower meadows; and sandy beaches tucked away in hidden coves. The interpretation centre *(open daily mid-Jun–Labour Day; & ☎418/892-5040)* features displays and films on the park, as well as saltwater aquariums. A road leads to **Cape Bon Ami**, providing magnificent **views**★★ of the sea and the limestone cliffs. At **Cape Gaspé**★, a pleasant walk affords **views**★ of the Bay of Gaspé and Île Bonaventure. Nearby, in the former fishing village of **Grande-Grave**★, several historic buildings have been restored.

★ **Gaspé.** – Pop 16,402. *42km/26mi south of Forillon National Park.* Occupying a pleasant site at the point where the York River empties into the Bay of Gaspé, this city is now the administrative and commercial centre of the peninsula. The **Musée de la Gaspésie**★ *(open daily year-round; closed holidays; $2.50; & ☎418/368-5710)*, dedicated to the preservation of Gaspesian culture and heritage, highlights historical events such as Jacques Cartier's discovery of the peninsula in 1534, the native Micmac population and regional geography. Completed in 1969, the **Cathedral of Christ the King**★ is distinguished by its unusual lines and a cedar exterior that blends harmoniously with the environment.

THE SOUTH COAST

★★★ **Percé.** – Pop 4,028. *76km/47mi south of Gaspé.* This bustling town was named for the massive offshore rock pierced *(percé)* by the sea. The landscape, a culmination of all the scenic beauty of the peninsula, is marked by reddish-gold limestone and shale rock, pushed and folded into a wonderful variety of cliffs, bays and hills. A tiny fishing village until the advent of tourism at the turn of the century, Percé now boasts some of the finest restaurants and tourist facilities on the peninsula.

★★ **Percé Rock.** – Once attached to the mainland, this mammoth rock wall is 438m/1,437ft long and 88m/289ft high. At one time, the limestone block may have had up to four archways. One of them crumbled in 1845, leaving a detached slab called the Obelisk. Today, only a 30m/94ft arch remains. The sculptured limestone rock is connected to **Mont-Joli**★★ by a sand bar, accessible at low tide.

★★★ **The Coast.** – The shoreline along Route 132 offers spectacular **views**★★ of the area. Just before entering Percé, a path leads up to **Cape Barré**, which affords a commanding view to the west of the the cliffs known as Trois-Sœurs. South of Percé, a promontory at **Côte Surprise** offers another superb view of the rock and the village.

Rising 320m/1,050ft above Percé, **Mount Sainte-Anne** features extraordinary red-rock formations. Lookouts stationed along the way to the summit *(2hr trail)* provide increasingly expansive **views**★★★ of Percé Rock, the village and the surrounding

156

area. Following the top of the sheer cliff on the west side of Mount Sainte-Anne, another trail provides views of the **Great Crevasse★**, a deep fissure in the red conglomerate rock.

★ **Île Bonaventure and Percé Rock Park**. – *Open daily Jun 24–mid-Oct.* 🚻 ✗ ☎*418/782-2240.* In summer, this flat-topped island is home to North America's largest **gannet** colony, with some 50,000 birds. These large white sea birds nest in the crevices, cracks and ledges of the cliffs lining the island. A pleasant **boat trip** *(departs daily mid-May–mid-Oct from Percé harbour; round-trip 1hr; $11; commentary on board; ✗ Les Bateliers de Percé, Inc ☎418/782-2974)* leads past Percé Rock and then around the island, affording superb views. Passengers can disembark on the island for a closer look at the birds and walk along the nature trails.

Bonaventure. – Pop 2,844. *131km/81mi southwest of Percé.* Founded in 1760 by Acadian settlers, this village is known for its salmon river and for its **Acadian Museum** *(open daily year-round; $3.25;* 🚻 *☎418/534-4000),* which illustrates the influence of these people on Quebec's culture.

Carleton. – Pop 2,749. *63km/39mi west of Bonaventure.* Nestled between the mountains and the sea, this community was founded by Acadians in the late 18C and has since become a choice resort, hosting a sailing festival every July. Carleton

View of Percé Rock from Mount Sainte-Anne

Sylvain Majeau/Tourisme Québec

is dominated by **Mount Saint-Joseph**, rising to 558m/1,830ft. From the summit, near a small stone shrine, the **panorama★★** encompasses Chaleur Bay from Bonaventure to the Miguasha Peninsula, and extends south to New Brunswick.

★ **Miguasha Park** – *24km/15mi west of Carleton. Open daily Jun 1–Oct 1.* ⚐ ✗ ☏*418/794-2475*. This national conservation park lies on an escarpment jutting out into Chaleur Bay, which contains fossils embedded in sedimentary rock since the Devonian Period (400 million years ago). Visitors are introduced to the world of fossils through exhibits at the interpretation centre, demonstrations in the laboratory, and on-site observation of the cliff.

Battle of the Restigouche National Historic Site. – ☏ *44km/27mi from Miguasha Park*. France's last attempt to save its North American colony from British domination during the Seven Years' War was thwarted in the estuary of the Restigouche River in 1760. An **interpretation centre** *(open daily mid-Jun–Labour Day; off-season Tue–Fri; mid-Oct–mid-May by reservation only;* ⚐ ☏*418/788-5676)* features exhibits on the battle and displays the hull and anchor of the French warship *Le Machault*, which sank nearby.

★ HULL   Pop 60,707

Map of Principal Sights p 4

Facing Ottawa across the wide waters of the Ottawa River, this bustling community was founded in 1800. Though Hull remains an important lumber, pulp and paper centre, today it functions primarily as an annex to the federal capital. In recent years, the downtown area has witnessed a great deal of change, including construction of two large federal government complexes and creation of a new campus for the University of Quebec.

★★★ **Canadian Museum of Civilization** (Musée canadien des civilisations). – *Map p 121. 100 Rue Laurier. Open May–Labour Day daily 9am–5pm (Thur 8pm). Off-season Tue–Sun 9am–5pm. Closed Christmas & New Year's. $4.50.* ⚐ ✗ ☏*819/776-7000*. Inaugurated in 1989, this sizeable museum is dedicated to the history of Canada since the arrival of the Vikings, and to the art and traditions of indigenous peoples and ethnic groups. The sweeping curves of the two large buildings designed by Douglas Cardinal evoke the emergence of the North American continent and its subsequent molding by wind, water and glaciers. The **Canadian Shield Wing** houses administrative offices and conservation laboratories, while the **Glacier Wing** provides 16,500sq m/33,792sq ft of exhibit halls.

In the **grand hall**, six cultural regions of the Canadian Pacific Coast are illustrated through the wooden homes of village chieftains and eleven totem poles, rising to the ceiling. In the **history hall**, reconstructed houses re-create 1,000 years of Canadian heritage. Guides in period costumes involve the visitor in the lifestyle of bygone eras. The delightful **children's museum** encourages young people to explore the world, from a Mexican village to a Pakistani street. A costume room, puppet theatre, games section and art studio complete the exhibit. In the **Cinéplus-Theatre** *($6.50)*, a seven-storey IMAX screen and an OMNIMAX dome provide unparalleled viewing opportunities for 295 spectators.

★★ **Gatineau Park.** – *Map p 123. Open year-round. Parkways closed from first snowfall until early May. Beach access $5.50/day per car. Skiing $6/day.* ⚐ ✗ ☏*819/827-2020*. Cover-ing 356sq km/137sq mi, this enchanting place lies nestled between the valleys of the Ottawa and Gatineau rivers. Formerly Algonquin and Iroquois territory, the land was designated a park in the 1930s with the assistance of **William Lyon Mackenzie King** *(p 123)*, tenth prime minister of Canada. Today, the park encloses several Federal Government buildings. A scenic parkway winding its way through dense hardwood forests leads to **Champlain Lookout**, which offers a magnificent **panorama★★** of the Ottawa Valley.

★ **Mackenzie King Estate.** – *Open daily May 16–Labour Day; until Oct 12 Wed–Sun. Parking $5.50.* ⚐ ✗ ☏*613/239-5000*. King willed his former estate to the Canadian people in 1950. His primary residence, **Moorside**, features exhibits and an audio-visual presentation, and houses a delightful tea room. On the grounds is a collection of ruins that he salvaged from buildings slated for demolition.

★★ LAURENTIANS

Map p 176

Stretching along the north shore of the St Lawrence, this range of low, rounded mountains rises to a maximum altitude of 960m/3,149ft at **Mount Tremblant**. Part of the Canadian Shield, the Laurentians, formed more than a billion years ago in the Precambrian era, are among the oldest mountains in the world.

The area north of Montreal between Saint-Jérôme and Mount Tremblant is especially noted for its string of resort towns that offer an attractive blend of recreational activities and fine cuisine. In winter, alpine skiers have a choice of over 100 ski lifts and tows, while cross-country enthusiasts can explore a variety of lengthy trails. In summer, water sports prevail on the innumerable lakes, and the surrounding hills cater to hikers, horseback riders and golfers. In the towns, several renowned summer theatres open their doors to visitors.

Weaving through forest-clad hills, the drive along Route 117 from Saint-Jérôme to Saint-Jovite is particularly splendid in fall, when the mountains display a dazzling array of colours.

* **Sainte-Adèle.** – Pop 4,916. *68km/42mi north of Montreal by Hwy 15 and Rte 117.* This resort community nestled around a small lake is popular with artists and writers. The reconstructed **Séraphin Village★** *(4km/2.5mi north of town; open daily Jun 21–Sept 7; off-season Wed–Sat; closed Oct 5–May 15; $8.25; ☎514/229-4777)* comprises some 20 buildings re-creating the life of the first settlers in the area. Inspired by Claude Grignon's 1933 work, *The Woman and the Miser,* several structures illustrate episodes in the life of Séraphin Poudrier, the novel's protagonist.

* **Sainte-Agathe-des-Monts.** – Pop 5,452. *18km/11mi north of Sainte-Adèle by Rte 117.* Set on the shores of the H-shaped **Sables Lake★★**, this lively town is the capital of the Laurentians region. A **scenic cruise** *(departs from dock Rue Principale daily mid-May–mid-Oct; round-trip 50min; $10; Les Bateaux Alouette Inc ☎819/326-3656)* is recommended to discover the magnificent lake and the sumptuous homes lining its shores.

* **Mount Tremblant Park.** – *About 140km/87mi north of Montreal. Open year-round. Summer activities May–Oct; winter activities mid-Dec–Apr.* △ ఉ *For information ☎819/688-2336.* Dominating the long, narrow Lake Tremblant, Quebec's oldest provincial park abounds in lakes, waterfalls and hiking trails. This recreational wonderland is also home to rich and diverse fauna and a multitude of birds.

Laurentides. – Pop 2,336. *62km/38mi north of Montreal by Hwy 15, then east on Hwy 158.* This small industrial town is known as the birthplace of **Sir Wilfrid Laurier** (1841-1919), the first French-Canadian prime minister of Canada (1896-1911). The **National Historic Site** *(open daily mid-May–Labour Day; off-season by reservation only; ☎514/439-3702),* a simple brick structure, stands on the place of Laurier's presumed birthplace. Next to it, an interpretation centre exhibits displays on the influential role Laurier played in Canadian politics.

★★ MAGDALEN ISLANDS Pop 13,991

Map of Principal Sights p 5 Tourist Office ☎418/986-2245

Located in the middle of the Gulf of St Lawrence, this isolated, windswept outpost consists of eight islands and numerous islets connected by sandspits that form a hook-shaped mass about 72km/45mi long. The archipelago's most striking features are the spectacular rock formations, cut into the stone by the pounding sea. Contrasting with the red sandstone, expansive white beaches stretch to the blue sea. Though discovered in 1534 by Jacques Cartier, the islands were not permanently inhabited until 1755, when they became a refuge for **Acadians** deported from Nova Scotia—the ancestors of many of the present population known as *Madelinots.* Supplemented by agriculture, logging and a growing tourism industry, fishing remains the primary economic activity of the archipelago. Today, the islands offer a wealth of outdoor recreation, from sightseeing to swimming and hiking.

Access. – *Car ferries run from Souris, Prince Edward Island, daily in summer, limited off-season service; no service Feb-Mar; $55/car $27.50/person; 5hrs; reservations recommended Coopérative de Transport Maritime ☎902/687-2181. Daily flights from Halifax, Nova Scotia, and from Gaspé. For information on guided tours, scenic cruises, restaurants and accommodation contact the tourist information office in Cap-aux-Meules ☎418/986-2245.*

* **Cap-aux-Meules Island.** – The largest of the islands is also the archipelago's administrative and commercial centre. Cap-aux-Meules' highest point, **Butte du Vent,** affords extensive **views★★** of the entire chain of islands. The western coast features some of the most dramatic **rock formations★★** on the Magdalen Islands. The sea has carved the red sandstone into deep crevasses and defiant promontories, creating a spectacular landscape of crumbled arches and solitary columns of stone.

* **Havre-Aubert Island.** – Marked by gentle, rolling hills, this southernmost island is the centre of the archipelago's cultural life. At the **Maritime Museum★** *(open daily year-round; $2.50; ఉ ☎418/937-5711),* displays of boats and navigational instruments acquaint visitors with the maritime history and culture of the Magdalen Islands. The historic site of **La Grave★** encompasses some 15 buildings, including stores, ironworks, *chaufauds* (sheds where cod was dried) and warehouses.

* **Havre-aux-Maisons Island.** – This elongated island has retained its rural charm and features some of the best examples of local domestic architecture, including the **baraque,** a small building designed to shelter hay. At **Dune du Sud★,** a fine beach and elaborate rock formations attract visitors.

On **Grande Entrée Island★,** coastal hiking trails afford spectacular **views★★★** of jagged cliffs and jutting promontories, tidal pools and vast beaches, twisted trees and colourful wildflowers. The **Grande Échouerie Beach★★** on **Île de l'Est** is considered the archipelago's loveliest.

*For in-depth information on the sights found in the province of Quebec, consult the **Michelin Green Guide to Quebec,** which highlights over 1,150 points of interest throughout the French-speaking province. In addition, insightful essays trace Quebec's history, geography and artistic heritage, while detailed city and regional maps accompany various walking and driving tours.*

★★★ MONTREAL

Metro 1,775,871

Canada's second-largest metropolis after Toronto *(p 130)* is located on a large island wedged into the mighty St Lawrence River, some 1,000 miles from the Atlantic. Owing in part to its key geographical position, this cosmopolitan city has emerged as a leading industrial, commercial and financial centre.

Home to the world's largest francophone population outside Paris, Montreal presents a unique combination of Old World cultures and North American modernity. A sizeable English-speaking community is particularly prominent in the business sector. The city offers visitors a wealth of cultural attractions and a diversity of urban settings, each with its distinctive ambience—from the charming cobblestone streets of Old Montreal to the landmark skyscrapers dominating the downtown cityscape.

HISTORICAL NOTES

While searching for riches and a route to the Orient in 1535, Jacques Cartier landed on the island of Montreal and visited the Mohawk village of **Hochelaga**. After founding Quebec City *(p 148)*, Samuel de Champlain sailed upriver and set foot on the nearby island of St Helen *(p 169)* in 1611. However, European settlement of the area did not occur until the arrival, in 1642, of Paul de Chomedey, **Sieur de Maisonneuve** (1612-1676), who is considered the founder of Montreal.

Under the French Regime. – Early in the 17C, two superiors of the Sulpician order in France decided to found a mission on the island of Montreal, as part of an effort to revive Roman Catholicism in the aftermath of the Protestant Reformation. They chose Maisonneuve to sail across the Atlantic with some 40 companions and establish the mission of **Ville-Marie** (City of Mary).

Amid continued fighting between native Iroquois inhabitants and the French settlers, Ville-Marie slowly developed into a commercial centre and was renamed Montreal in the early 18C. Seeking profit, the French set off across the Great Lakes to trap fur-bearing animals. The furs were highly prized in Europe, where they were transformed into luxurious apparel, and the trade boomed. By the time of the surrender of Montreal in 1760 *(p 149)*, the city had become a well-established, thriving community. After the British victory, most of the French nobility returned to France. A large number of Scots, attracted to the fur trade, and an influx of Loyalists from the US swelled the anglophone population.

From Rebellion to Confederation. – The fur trade reached its heyday in the late 18C and early 19C, bringing great prosperity to Montreal. Two partnerships, the **North West Company** (based in Montreal) and the **Hudson's Bay Company**, established trading posts all over northern Canada and monopolized the market. By the time the companies merged in 1821, however, Montreal's dominance in the trade was in decline.

Montreal was the centre of one of the **Rebellions of 1837** *(p 149)*, a political uprising against British rule, which, in Lower Canada, contested the power held by the Crown-appointed governor and his council. Led by Louis-Joseph Papineau, George-Étienne Cartier and other French Canadians, the **Patriots** engaged in several armed revolts against British troops. Although the insurgents were defeated, the British government subsequently decided to grant Quebec a representative government. By the time of Confederation in 1867, Montreal stood at the forefront of railway development and claimed the largest grain port in the world. The financial institutions sprouting along Rue Saint-Jacques promoted development of the city and the country and contributed to Montreal's dominance in Canada's financial sector until the 1970s.

Montreal Today. – Following a period of slow growth after the Great Depression, Montreal experienced a revival in the 1950s and 1960s, manifested in restoration projects throughout the city. Montreal has emerged as an international centre of commerce and culture. In addition to hosting such events as the 1967 World Fair

Place Jacques-Cartier

(Expo '67), the 1976 Olympic Games and the 1980 International Floralies, the city features annual international festivals in jazz, film and comedy, attracting thousands of visitors. Internationally acclaimed artists regularly perform at Montreal's premier cultural complex, **Place des Arts★★**, home to the Montreal Symphony Orchestra, the Grands Ballets Canadiens and the Montreal Opera.

The city remains a major centre of francophone culture. Its numerous cafes and restaurants, especially along Saint-Denis and Crescent streets, reflect Montrealers' *joie de vivre*. Visitors to this vibrant city will also enjoy the variety of shops and boutiques. In 1992, Montreal celebrated the 350th anniversary of its foundation.

In Montreal, the Sun Rises in the South. – The St Lawrence River generally flows in a west-to-east direction, and its banks are referred to as the north and south shores. At Montreal, however, the river takes a sudden turn northward. The streets parallel to the river are called east-west streets, although they actually run north-south, and the perpendicular streets are designated north-south, although they extend east-west.

Practical Information

Public Transportation.– Société de Transport de la Communauté de Montréal STCUM operates the **Metro** and the city buses. Hours of operation: 5:30am–12:30am. Tickets are available individually ($1.50), or in books of six ($6); monthly passes also available. Metro lines are colour-coded and directions indicated refer to the station at the end of the line. Transfers to the bus system are free. For route information & schedules ☎514/2886287. The **bus** system covers the island of Montreal. Exact change is required, tickets are transferable from the Metro. For route information ☎514/AUTOBUS.

Taxis. – La Salle ☎514/277-2552; Diamond ☎514/273-6331; Champlain ☎514/273-2435.

Car Rentals. – Avis ☎514/866-7906; Hertz ☎514/842-8537; Tilden/National ☎514/878-2771.

Tourist Office. – Tourisme Québec ☎514/873-2015; Infotourist, *1001 Rue Square-Dorchester (● Peel).*

Newspapers. – Daily: *La Presse, Le Journal de Montréal, Le Devoir, The Gazette.* Monthly guides (free) to entertainment, shopping and restaurants: *En Ville, Montréal Scope.*

Entertainment. – Consult arts and entertainment supplements in local newspapers (Sat & Sun editions) for schedule of cultural events and addresses of principal theatres and concert halls. Ticketron tickets may be purchased at Sears and La Baie department stores or from Admissions ☎514/522-1245 or 800/678-5440 (major credit cards are accepted).

Sports. – Hockey: Montréal Canadiens (National Hockey League). Season Oct–Apr ☎514/932-2582. Major League Baseball: Montréal Expos (National League). Season Apr–Oct. For tickets ☎514/522-1245 or 800/678-5440.

Useful Numbers (Area Code 514)

Dorval International Airport		633-3105
Mirabel International Airport		476-3010
Central Station (VIA Rail)	*935 Rue de la Gauchetière Ouest*	871-1331
Terminus Voyageur (Bus terminal)	*505 Blvd de Maisonneuve Est*	842-2281
Canadian Automobile Association	*180 Rue Drummond*	861-7111
Post Office	*1025 Rue Saint-Jacques Ouest*	283-1281
Road Conditions		873-4121
Weather (24hr)		636-3026

★★★ **OLD MONTREAL** *Map p 163. 1 day. ●Place d'Armes.*

Bounded by the Old Port, Saint-Jacques, Berri and McGill streets, Montreal's historic core was originally enclosed within imposing stone walls erected in the early 1700s. During the 19C, the settlement expanded and Montrealers moved outside the fortifications. Warehouses and commercial buildings gradually replaced stone dwellings and gardens, and the area fell into decline. Interest in Old Montreal was revived in the 1960s: the surviving 18C homes were renovated, warehouses were transformed into apartment buildings, and restaurants and shops opened. Today, Old Montreal is a pleasant area that caters mainly to tourists.

★ **Place d'Armes.** – Designed in the 17C by the Sulpician Dollier de Casson, this square long served as military drill grounds. A **monument★ [1]** (Louis-Philippe Hébert) in the centre honours the founder of Montreal, Sieur de Maisonneuve, who, according to legend, killed the local Indian chief on this site during a 1644 battle. The west side of this charming green space is dominated by the **Bank of Montreal★** (1847), one of the city's finest examples of the neoclassical style.

Extending south, **Rue Saint-Jacques★**, the financial heart of Canada until the 1970s, is lined with elegant 19C and 20C edifices. Note in particular the Canadian Imperial Bank of Commerce *(no. 265),* with its facade of fluted Corinthian columns, and the **Royal Bank of Canada★** *(no. 360),* whose tower is a distinct feature of the city's skyline.

★★★ **Notre-Dame Basilica.** – *Open Jun 25–Labour Day daily 7am–8pm; rest of the year until 6pm.* ♿. This twin-towered church rises on the south side of the Place d'Armes. Completed in 1829 under the supervision of James O'Donnell, the Gothic Revival basilica is especially renowned for its magnificent **interior**. The opulent decor, designed by Victor Bourgeau, features sculptures, wainscoting and giltwork typical of provincial religious architecture. The main nave, lined on both sides by deep-set double galleries, measures 68m/223ft long, 21m/69ft wide and 25m/82ft high. As visitors enter, eyes are drawn to the ensemble of white oak statues, part of the imposing **reredos** that stands out against the background's soft blue hues. Behind the choir, the Sacred Heart Chapel is dominated by an impressive bronze reredos representing mankind's difficult journey to heaven.

The **Old Sulpician Seminary★**, the oldest structure in the city, stands beside the basilica. Note the facade clock, installed in 1701, believed to be the oldest public timepiece in North America.

★★ **Place Jacques-Cartier.** – *Illustration p 160.* Lined with outdoor cafes and flower parterres, this charming cobblestone square is lively all summer, especially in the evenings, when street musicians and acrobats entertain the crowds. Created in 1847, the square was named for the famous explorer who, according to tradition, docked his ship here in 1535. Marking the north end of the plaza, a **statue [2]** of Horatio Nelson (1809) commemorates the British general's victory at Trafalgar. Montreal's **City Hall★** *(open year-round Mon–Fri; closed holidays;* ♿ 🅿 ☎*514/872-3355),* an imposing Second Empire building, stands across Rue Notre-Dame. Charles de Gaulle delivered his famous "Vive le Québec libre" speech in 1967 from the balcony overlooking the main entrance. The southern end of the square leads to **Rue Saint-Paul★★**, a charming street lined with lovely 19C buildings. Along with Rue Notre-Dame, this narrow street is one of the oldest in Montreal.

★ **Old Port (Vieux-Port).** – Stretching along the St Lawrence River, at the foot of Place Jacques Cartier, the former port has been transformed into a pleasant waterfront park with bike and walking paths, a skating rink, exhibition spaces, an IMAX cinema and a flea market. Stroll along the wide boardwalk or take a harbour cruise *(departing from Victoria Pier)* to enjoy scenic **views★** of the city and the majestic river.

★★ **Jet Boat Trips on the Lachine Rapids.** – *Departure from Victoria Pier. Protective clothing provided. Warning: not for the faint-hearted. Depart last week in Apr–mid-Oct. Round-trip 1hr 30min. $45.* 🅿 *($5). Reservations required. Lachine Rapids Tours Ltd* ☎*514/284-9607.* On this wet and exciting voyage, passengers are whisked upriver in specially designed vessels that mount and descend the ferocious Lachine Rapids. The **views★★** of Montreal and the surrounding areas are spectacular.

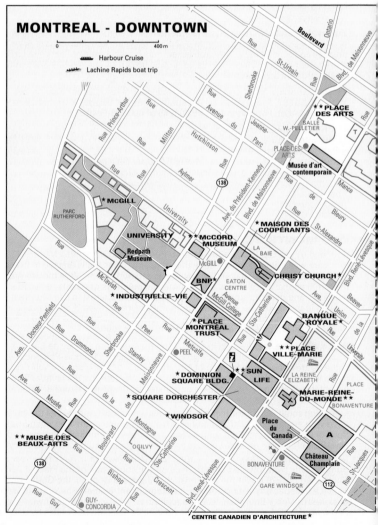

★★ **Château Ramezay.** – *280 Rue Notre Dame. Open Jun 15–Labour Day daily 10am–4:30pm. Off-season Tue–Sun. $2.50.* . . *☎514/861-3708.* Situated across from City Hall, this squat, fieldstone residence (1705) is a lovely example of early-18C domestic architecture. Constructed for Claude de Ramezay, 11th governor of Montreal during the French Regime, the building has undergone several renovations, yet remains relatively unchanged in appearance. It was acquired by the British government to serve as the official gubernatorial residence until 1849.

Restored and transformed into an **Ethnographic Museum** in 1895, the interior presents Montreal's history, with a focus on the French Regime. The highlight is the exquisite, hand-carved mahogany **panelling★** produced in 1725 in Nantes, France.

★ **Sir George-Étienne Cartier National Historic Site.** – ⚲ *458 Rue Notre-Dame. Open daily May–Sept. Off-season Wed–Sun.* . *☎514/283-2282.* This limestone, mansard-roofed structure, composed of two adjoining houses, was the home of George-Étienne Cartier (1814-1873), one of the Fathers of Confederation. Displays trace his life and career as a lawyer, businessman and politician. Refurbished in the Victorian style, period rooms illustrate the lifestyle of 19C middle-class society.

★ **Rue Bonsecours.** – This attractive street leading from Rue Notre-Dame to Rue Saint-Paul offers a charming perspective of the little Notre-Dame-de-Bonsecours Chapel *(see below)*. At no. 440 stands the **Maison Papineau**, a large grey edifice topped by a steeply pitched roof that is pierced by two rows of dormer windows. During an 1831 reconstruction, the original stone walls were covered in wood, sculpted and painted to resemble limestone. The building was home to six generations of the Papineau family, including Louis-Joseph, leader of the Patriots during the 1837 Rebellions *(p 149)*. The fieldstone walls, firebreaks, corner consoles, tall chimneys and pitched gables of the **Maison du Calvet★** (1798), located at the corner of Rue Saint-Paul, are characteristic of a traditional 18C urban residence.

★ **Notre-Dame-de-Bonsecours Chapel.** – *400 Rue Saint-Paul E.* This small church, topped by a copper steeple, stands on the site of a wooden edifice commissioned by Marguerite Bourgeoys in 1657 and destroyed by fire in 1754. Facing the St Lawrence, a 9m/30ft statue of the Virgin Mary crowns the rear of the church. Climb the observatory, accessible from the tower, to enjoy a **view★** of the river, Old Montreal and the Old Port.

Located in the basement, the **Marguerite Bourgeoys Museum** *(open year-round Tue–Sun; $2; ☎514/845-9991)* features a collection of dolls that re-creates the life of Bourgeoys (1620-1700), who came to Montreal with Maisonneuve in 1653 to found the Congregation of Our Lady. Bourgeoys was canonized in 1982.

Near the church, on Rue Saint-Paul, stands the **Bonsecours Market★**, a large neoclassical stone structure crowned by a lofty dome. It served as the city hall from 1852 to 1878, housing municipal offices thereafter. Plans are underway to convert the interior into a commercial space.

★ **Place d'Youville.** – Located south of Place d'Armes, this pleasant square is surrounded by grand edifices. Housed in a brick structure reflecting the Dutch baroque architectural style, the **Montreal History Centre★** *(open year-round Tue–Sun; closed holidays; $4.25; ᪣ ☎514/872-3207)* presents the city's rich past through interactive displays, artifacts, animated mannequins and a slide show. To the east of the square stand the **Youville Stables**, an ensemble of grey stone structures (1828) enclosing a lovely garden courtyard. Located in a former warehouse, the **Marc-Aurèle Fortin Museum★** *(118 Rue Saint-Pierre; open year-round Tue–Sun; closed Dec 22–Jan 8 & Good Friday; $3; ᪣ ☎514/845-6108)* exhibits the works of this 20C Québécois artist. His subjects include regional flora and fauna and St Lawrence River landscapes. Spanning the block between Saint-Pierre and Normand streets, the **Grey Nuns Convent** was erected in 1692 and extended in 1753 by Marie d'Youville, founder of the Grey Nuns order.

Pointe-à-Callière. – Maisonneuve established the settlement of Ville-Marie on this small triangle of land. A 10m/33ft **obelisk [3]** commemorates the occasion of his landing in May 1642. The recently opened **Montreal Museum on Archaeology and History** *(open year-round Tue–Sun; $6; ᪣ ☎514/872-9150)*, composed of a modern building, a crypt and an 1838 neoclassical edifice, presents Montreal's fascinating history through permanent and temporary exhibits and a multimedia presentation. Located under Place Royale, the crypt displays vestiges recovered during archaeological excavations.

★★ **DOWNTOWN** *Map p 162. 1 day. ● Rue Peel.*

Bordered by Rue Saint-Jacques to the east, Rue Sherbrooke to the west, and Saint-Denis and Atwater streets to the north and south, the city's commercial and cultural heart lies to the west of Old Montreal. The downtown developed into a prosperous and bustling quarter during the late 18C and 19C, and today features some of Montreal's most famous buildings and institutions. A walk along Sherbrooke, one of the most prestigious arteries in the city, reveals a lively retail sector alongside choice residences. Rue Sainte-Catherine is home to major department stores (Ogilvy, La Baie, Eaton) and commercial centres, while Avenue McGill College is lined with the city's landmark 20C skyscrapers.

★ **Dorchester Square.** – Formerly known as Dominion Square, this pleasant green space was renamed in 1988 in honour of Lord Dorchester, Governor of British North America during the late 18C. Long considered the centre of the city, the square is surrounded by a group of remarkable buildings, including the imposing Renaissance Revival **Dominion Square Building★** (1929) and the elegant **Windsor Hotel★**, with its mansard roof pierced by dormer and œil-de-bœuf windows. The **Sun Life Building★★**, an imposing Beaux-Arts edifice erected in 1913, dominates the north side of the square. Note the colossal colonnades adorning all four facades.

Facing Dorchester Square is **Place du Canada**, a small green plaza bordered by more recent constructions. Of particular interest are the **Château Champlain Hotel** (1967), marked by convex, half-moon windows and **1000 de la Gauchetière [A]** (1992), Montreal's tallest skyscraper.

★★ **Marie-Reine-du-Monde Basilica-Cathedral**. – *Main entrance on Blvd René-Lévesque.* Commissioned by Msgr Ignace Bourget to reinforce the Catholic presence in a predominantly Protestant district, this monumental church is distinguished by large Greek columns, ornate decoration and a row of statues crowning the cornice. Designed by Victor Bourgeau and modelled after St Peter's in Rome, the Baroque Revival edifice was consecrated in 1894. Inside the magnificent gold-leaf **baldachin** (1900), a replica of the 16C ornamental canopy created by Bernini for St Peter's Basilica. On the left side of the nave, a mortuary chapel (1933) decorated with beautiful mosaics contains the tombs of several archbishops and bishops as well as Msgr Bourget's mausoleum.

★★ **Place Ville-Marie.** – This four-building complex ushered in the renaissance of the downtown area. Completed in the 1960s, it became the centrepiece of Montreal's **underground city,** an extensive network of spacious corridors connecting various hotels, office buildings, department stores, railway stations, cultural and conventions centres, as well as boutiques, cinemas and restaurants.

Dominating the complex is I. M. Pei's 42-storey **Banque Royale Tower★** (1962), a cruciform structure sheathed in aluminum. Along with the other three buildings, the Banque Royale encloses a concrete esplanade that affords an unparalleled **vista★** west to McGill University and Mount Royal.

Extending from Place Ville-Marie to McGill University, Avenue McGill College is a veritable showplace for the city's post-Modern architecture. Completed in 1989, the enormous **Place Montréal Trust★** *(no. 1500)* features a pastel-blue, glass cylinder encased in a square base of rose marble and glass. Across the street *(no. 1981)* rise the sprawling, metallic-blue twin towers of the **National Bank of Paris/Laurentian Bank★ (BNP)**. Designed in intricate geometric shapes, the towers were completed in 1981. The granite-clad **Industrial Life Tower★** *(no. 2000)* presents an elegant exterior enlivened by post-Modern ornamentation, such as the huge fanlight window.

QUEBEC

★ **Christ Church Cathedral.** – *Entrance from Rue Sainte-Catherine between Rue University and Ave Union.* Topped by a single, slender spire and distinguished by its triple portico, ornate gables and gargoyles, this handsome edifice (1859) exemplifies the Gothic Revival style. The ivy-covered church preserves a graceful interior, embellished by magnificent stained-glass windows and a beautifully carved stone **reredos**. The capitals of the arcaded nave are decorated with leaves representing trees indigenous to Canada.

Rising behind the church is a prominent landmark, the **Coopérants Building★**. Designed to be viewed in tandem with the church, the copper-coloured edifice features colonnades, pointed entrances, arched windows and a pitched roof.

★★ **McCord Museum.** – *690 Rue Sherbrooke W. Open year-round Tue–Fri 10am–6pm (Thur 9pm); weekends 10am–5pm. $5. ♿ ✕ ☎514/398-7100.* One of Canada's foremost historical museums, the McCord was founded in 1922 and underwent extensive renovation in 1991. Holdings provide a fascinating insight into Canadian history, from the era of Indian settlement to the present day. In addition to more than 80,000 ethnological artifacts, the museum houses an outstanding compilation of over 700,000 photos that chronicle Canadian life in the 19C and 20C.

★ **McGill University.** – *End of Ave McGill College.* Set on the slopes of Mount Royal, Canada's oldest university (1821) is a bastion of Montreal's anglophone population, claiming an enrollment of over 30,000 students. The 60 buildings gracing the campus reflect a variety of architectural styles.

Housed in a large building designed in the style of an antique temple, the **Redpath Museum of Natural History** *(open year-round Mon–Fri; closed Jun 24–Labour Day on Fri and legal holidays; ☎514/398-4086)* displays vertebrate and invertebrate fossils, minerals, zoological artifacts, African art objects and Egyptian antiquities.

★★ **Montreal Museum of Fine Arts (Musée des Beaux-Arts).** – *1380 Rue Sherbrooke W. Open year-round Tue–Sun 11am–6pm (Sat 9pm). Closed Christmas, New Year's & Good Friday. $5. ♿ ✕ ☎514/285-1600.* Ranked among Canada's finest museums, this 130-year-old institution boasts a permanent collection of over 25,000 objects ranging from Old Masters to contemporary Canadian art. The Beaux-Arts main edifice (1912) presents Canadian art on its three floors, while the recent annex (1991), created by renowned architect **Moshe Safdie**, displays masterpieces from all over the world. The buildings are linked by a series of underground galleries that exhibit Ancient, Asiatic, African and Islamic art.

Displayed in several galleries, the collection of **Canadian Art** ranging from the 18C to the 1960s includes paintings, sculpture, furniture and decorative arts. Of note are works by Paul Kane, Cornelius Krieghoff, J. W. Morrice, Suzor-Côté, the Group of Seven and modern artists Paul-Émile Borduas and Jean-Paul Riopelle.

Galleries devoted to **European Art** span the Middle Ages to the late 19C, with works by Mantegna, Memling, El Greco, Rembrandt, Daumier and Rodin. The 20C is represented by works of Picasso, Alexander Calder, Sam Francis and Betty Goodwin. The museum also contains a fine collection of English porcelains, Japanese incense boxes, prints and drawings, and Indian and Inuit carvings. Located in the annex, a set of five vaulted galleries showcases various temporary exhibits.

★ **Canadian Centre for Architecture.** – *Map p 166. 1920 Rue Baile. Open year-round Wed–Sun. $5. ♿ ▯ ☎514/939-7026.* Designed by Peter Rose and Phyllis Lambert, the CCA (1989) is both an acclaimed museum-research facility and an original example of post-Modern architecture. Forming the core of the horseshoe-shaped building is **Shaughnessy House**, a Second Empire mansion built in 1874.

The main building's interior is embellished with limestone, black granite, maple panelling and aluminum fittings. Seven galleries display temporary exhibits on architectural themes. Also open to the public are the Shaughnessy House reception rooms and the delightful conservatory and tea room, which have been restored to their 19C splendour.

Across Boulevard René-Lévesque is an **architectural garden** by Melvin Charney, featuring an array of sculptures illustrating architectural elements such as pediments and columns.

Museum of Contemporary Art. – *Place des Arts Complex. Visit by guided tour (1hr 15min) only. $5. ♿ ▯ ✕. For schedule of tours ☎514/844-1211.* Housed in the most recent addition to the Place des Arts complex, this museum presents modern Quebec art, with an emphasis on post-1940 artists such as Paul-Émile Borduas, Alfred Pellan and Jean-Paul Riopelle. The rotating exhibits are supplemented by selections of contemporary art from all over the world.

★★ **MOUNT ROYAL AND SURROUNDINGS** *Map p 166. 1/2 day.*

Known to Montrealers as "the Mountain," Mount Royal has become one of the city's most popular leisure spots. Rising abruptly from the otherwise flat plain, the 233m/764ft mountain forms part of the Monteregian Hills, a series of eight peaks located between the St Lawrence and the Appalachians. The peaks are actually igneous plugs of magma that solidified before reaching the surface. To the west of Mount Royal lies the former anglophone enclave of **Westmount**, one of the city's choicest residential areas. Gracing the hill's eastern flank is the town of **Outremont**, home to Montreal's francophone bourgeoisie.

★★ **Mount Royal Park.** – *Drive up Voie Camillien-Houde or Chemin Remembrance to the parking areas or climb on foot (20min) from Rue Peel at Ave des Pins. ●Mont-Royal. Open year-round sunrise–sunset. Park Info ☎514/872-1415. Sports & Recreation ☎514/872-2644.* Opened to the public in 1876, the city's premier urban park was designed by American landscape architect **Frederick Law Olmsted**, creator of New York City's Central Park. Along with various plants and animals, the park has a lake, two lookout points, a chalet and welcome centre, an illuminated cross and numerous winding paths. In summer, the park is lively with joggers; in winter, horse-drawn sleds plow the snowy paths.

Viewpoints. – The terrace fronting the **Chalet lookout [A]** *(7min walk from parking area)* affords a splendid **view★★★** of the bustling downtown. Looming on the horizon, the Monteregian Hills dot the southern St Lawrence shore. The walk around the summit leads to the **cross [B]**, a 37m/120ft metal structure, illuminated at night, that commemorates a wooden cross placed here by Maisonneuve *(p 160)*. From the popular **Camillien Houde lookout** *(accessible by car on the Voie Camillien-Houde)*, the superb **view★★** of eastern Montreal is dominated by the Olympic Stadium *(p 168)*.

★★ **St Joseph's Oratory.** – *Entrance on Chemin Queen Mary.* ● *Côte-des-Neiges. Open Jun 24–Labour Day daily 6am–10pm; rest of the year until 6pm.* & 🄿. Dominating the northern section of Montreal, this famed Roman Catholic shrine, set on the slope of Mount Royal, is distinguished by its colossal dimensions and an octagonal, copper-clad dome.

A small chapel dedicated to the healing powers of St Joseph was erected on this site in 1904 by Alfred Bessette, known as Brother André. Crowds of afflicted people came to pray with the friar. Leaving the chapel cured, they spread the lay brother's reputation as a healer. By the early 20C, a basilica was planned to receive the increasing number of visitors. Constructed under the supervision of the Benedictine monk and architect, **Dom Paul Bellot**, the monument was completed in 1966. Today, over a million pilgrims visit the shrine annually.

In the immense, austere interior, note the carved bronze doors executed by Roger Prévost, and the oak statues of the apostles and stone altar chiselled by Henri Charlier. From the wide terrace, an excellent **view★** of northern Montreal and the Laurentian Mountains can be obtained. Also contained within the edifice are a votive chapel, a 56-bell carillon and the **Brother André Museum** *(open daily year-round; ☎514/ 733-8211)*, which displays a collection of photographs and mementos tracing the friar's life. The **original chapel** and Brother André's room are open to the public. Fashioned in 1960, the **Stations of the Cross★** are located in a pleasant hillside garden.

Boulevard Saint-Laurent. – This bustling thoroughfare has traditionally divided the city into its predominantly francophone eastern section and the anglophone west. Today, the boulevard attracts a diverse crowd to its "in" boutiques, cafes, ethnic restaurants and specialty shops. Established in 1672, the artery long formed Montreal's principal passageway, hence its nickname "the Main." For centuries, the Main has welcomed immigrants. During the 19C, Chinese settled in the southern section, giving rise to a lively **Chinatown★** *(at Rue de la Gauchetière).* Jewish merchants arrived in the 1880s and moved into the northern section. The most recent arrivals include Greeks, Slavs, Portuguese and Latin Americans.

★★★ OLYMPIC PARK AREA *Map p 168. 1 day.*

This vast recreational area is situated in the eastern part of Montreal, which was known in the past as the city of **Maisonneuve**. Created by wealthy francophone businessmen, the prosperous community launched a program of development during

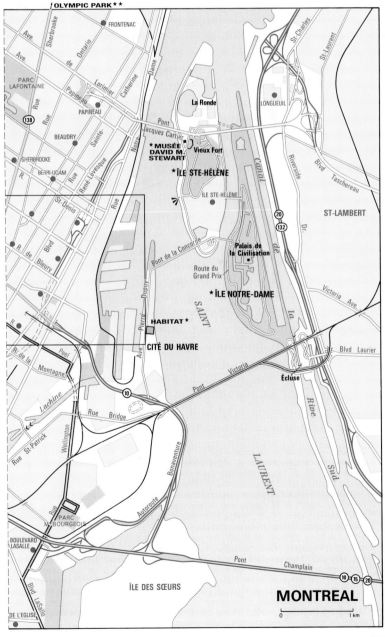

the late 19C, erecting grandiose mansions such as the Château Dufresne along its wide boulevards. The exorbitant cost drove Maisonneuve into bankruptcy, and the city was annexed to Montreal in 1918. Today, dominated by the striking silhouette of the Olympic Park, the area is home to Montreal's Botanical Garden and the 204ha/504 acre Maisonneuve Park.

★★ **Olympic Park.** – *4141 Pierre-de-Coubertin Ave.* ● *Rue Viau. Guided tours of buildings depart year-round from information desk at the base of the tower and include a multimedia presentation; tour of park (30min) by mini-train in summer.* & ✗ ☎514/ *252-8687.* Constructed to accommodate the 1976 Olympic Games, this gigantic sports complex has become the symbol of Montreal's East End. A stunning architectural achievement conceived by French architect Roger Taillibert, the park includes a stadium, an aquatic centre, and a velodrome, which now houses the **Biodome**—an innovative museum of environmental and natural sciences *(open daily year-round; $8.50;* & ✗ ☎514/872-3034)*. The Olympic Village, two striking 19-storey towers designed to lodge over 11,000 athletes during the Games, now contains a residential and commercial complex.

Begun in 1973, the project soon encountered a series of technical difficulties, delaying construction of the stadium's roof and tower until 1987. Tremendously expensive ($1.2 billion), the complex became the city's most controversial public project. However, it has made a valiant effort to remain lucrative and today receives over 4.5 million visitors yearly.

Stadium. – *The interior is accessible only by guided tour (1hr) or to spectators of sporting or cultural events. $7.* This immense concrete edifice, Taillibert's masterpiece, consists of 34 cantilevered ribs crowned by a structural ring and dominated by the world's tallest inclined tower. The building was originally designed to be covered by a retractable roof that could be hoisted into a niche at the summit of the tower by means of 26 cables and 46 winches anchored at the tower's base. Made of Kevlar—an ultra-thin synthetic fiber with the strength of steel—the roof has nevertheless been subject to deterioration.

With a seating capacity of 56,385, the stadium hosts sporting events, rock concerts, operatic productions and conventions. Hovering at a 45° angle above the stadium, the 169m/554ft **tower** *(open May 1–Labour Day daily 10am-11pm; off-season Mon noon–6pm, Tue–Sun 10am–6pm; closed mid-Jan–mid-Feb; $7;* & *)* can be ascended by a funicular elevator. From the observation deck, the **panorama**★★★ extends as far as 80km/50mi, weather permitting. Large skylights and windows afford breathtaking views of the stadium, downtown Montreal, the Laurentian Mountains and the Monteregian Hills. Located below the deck, an interactive **interpretation centre** presents exhibits on the stadium's construction.

** **Montreal Botanical Garden [A].** – *4101 Rue Sherbrooke.* ● *Pie IX. Open mid-May–mid-Oct daily 8am–9pm. Off-season daily 9am–6pm. Admission includes the Montreal Insectarium $7.* ⑤ ✗ ⒫ *($4)* ☎*514/872-1400.* Founded in 1931, this 73ha/180 acre botanical garden ranks among the world's finest horticultural facilities. Over 26,000 international plant species are exhibited in well-defined, specialized sections. The **conservatories★** present a wide range of tropical and semi-tropical plants alongside ferns, begonia, cacti and succulent plants. The Chinese greenhouse, called the jardin céleste, displays a magnificent collection of **bonsais**, trees that have been dwarfed through specialized cultivation. Opened in 1991, the **Chinese Garden★** is a replica of a typical Ming Dynasty (13C-17C) garden from southern China, with pavilions, a rock mountain and waterfall. The combination of mountains and water is thought to provoke contemplation. The 2.5ha/6.2 acre **Japanese Garden**, designed in the traditional Oriental style, creates a peaceful atmosphere. The main pavilion houses exhibit spaces, a tea room, library, Zen garden and a collection of bonsais. Other sections not to be missed include the Rose Garden, with over 10,000 specimens, the Marsh and Bog Garden, a re-created monastic garden, an Alpine garden, and an enclosure of poisonous plants. Covering two-thirds of the total area, the arboretum features over 9,000 tree specimens.

Near the Rose Garden, the **Montreal Insectarium**, built in the shape of a giant bug, offers a wide selection of preserved and living insects from all over the world.

** **Château Dufresne – Museum of Decorative Arts [B].** – *Entrance on Blvd Pie IX.* ● *Pie IX. Open year-round Wed–Sun 11am–5pm. Closed Christmas & New Year's. $3.* ⑤ ✗ ☎ *514/259-2575.* Erected in 1918, this sumptuous Beaux-Arts mansion, commissioned by Marius and Oscar Dufresne, evokes the lifestyle of Montreal's moneyed class in the 1920s and 1930s.

The five period rooms open to the public present a variety of styles. Note the beautiful mahogany panelling in the sitting room, the Moorish-style smoking room and the Adamesque dining room. Housed in the chateau since 1979, the **museum** displays an outstanding collection of furniture, glasswork, silver, textiles and ceramics from 1935 to the present *(ground and second floors).*

OTHER AREAS OF INTEREST *1/2 day*

* **St Helen's Island.** – *Map p 167. Access by car on Jacques-Cartier or Concorde Bridge;* ● *Île Sainte-Hélène.* Located east of Montreal, this small island, discovered by Samuel de Champlain in 1611, was named for his wife, Hélène Boulé. Transformed into a pleasant park, it has become a popular weekend spot.

After purchasing the island in 1818, the British government erected a citadel, now known as the **Old Fort**, on this strategic point *(open daily year-round; $4;* ⑤ ✗ ⒫. *Military drills Jun 24–Aug 31 daily 11am, 2:30 & 5pm).*

The island became Federal Government property after Confederation, and in the early 20C, it was annexed by the city. In 1967, along with Notre Dame Island, St Helen's hosted the world fair, Expo '67.

The shaded woods and clearings are interspersed with fortress remnants. Located in the Old Fort is the **David M. Stewart Museum★** *(open year-round Mon, Wed–Sun; closed Christmas & New Year's; $4;* ☎*514/861-6701),* which presents the history of European settlement in Quebec through displays of weapons, documents, maps and globes. Note the model of the city of Montreal as it appeared in 1760.

La Ronde, Montreal's major amusement park, occupies a pleasant site on the north end of the island *(open daily mid-May–Sept 7; $17.25;* ⑤ ✗ ⒫ *($6)* ☎*514/872-6222).*

The road skirting the island's western edge provides excellent **views★** of Old Montreal, the port installations, and **Habitat★** (Moshe Safdie), a futuristic, modular apartment complex built for Expo '67.

* **Notre Dame Island.** – *Map p 167. Access by car on Concordia Bridge or by free bus service from St Helen's Island metro station.* This artificial island, created in 1959 and enlarged in 1967, contains a Formula 1 race track, a pleasant lake and beach, and a superb floral garden designed for the International Floralies of 1980. The **Palais de la Civilisation**, the former French pavilion of Expo '67 *(open daily mid-May–Sept* ⑤ ✗ ☎*514/872-7663),* features cultural events.

Sault-au-Récollet. – *Map p 168. Located 12km/7mi north of Montreal by Sherbrooke E, Cartier and Rachel streets and Ave Papineau.* Set on rapids beside the Prairies River, Sault-au-Récollet is best known for its **Church of the Visitation of the Blessed Virgin Mary★**, the oldest religious structure on the island. The large nave and absence of lateral chapels illustrate the style of Récollet churches, which were popular in New France during the French Regime. The edifice boasts an elaborate **interior★★** fashioned by Louis-Amable Quévillon and his followers. Of particular interest are the turquoise and gold vault, adorned with diamond-shaped barrels; the sculpted decor in the chancel; and the magnificent **pulpit★**, one of the most beautiful pieces of liturgical furniture in Quebec.

For a listing of selected French terms used in this guide, see p 180.

★★ NUNAVIK

Map of Principal Sights p 4

Officially recognized in 1988 as the homeland of Quebec's **Inuit** population, the province's northernmost region offers the adventurous visitor a unique travel experience. Nunavik's spectacular expanses of rugged and pristine land, encompassing some 500,000sq km/193,050sq mi, appeal to travellers eager to explore one of the world's few remaining frontiers.

Located on the Ungava Peninsula, this vast territory also encompasses numerous off-shore islands and part of the James Bay region to the west. A multitude of lakes and waterways drain east into Ungava Bay, or west into Hudson Bay, named for the famed British explorer, Henry Hudson. The lack of vegetation is characteristic of regions with harsh climates. In fact, most of the peninsula is under permafrost, reaching 275m/902ft in depth in Nunavik's northernmost areas.

The region's first inhabitants were hunters from Asia who crossed the Bering Strait some 15,000 years ago. Travelling in small family groups, the Inuit ancestors caught marine mammals along the coast and ventured inland to hunt musk ox, caribou and waterfowl. The arrival of Europeans in the 17C dramatically transformed the traditional nomadic lifestyle and led to the creation of permanent settlements.

Today, the majority of the Inuit population inhabits 14 coastal villages and has access to schooling and professional training. Living in modern, prefabricated housing equipped with modern amenities, the Inuit have nevertheless maintained their traditional values and heritage.

Practical Information. – The 14 villages lining Nunavik's eastern and western shores are accessible by airplane only. Contact Canadian Airlines International (☏514/847-2211), First Air (☏613/839-1247), Air Inuit (☏514/634-7053) or Air Creebec (☏819/825-8355) for schedules and flight information. It is best to visit the region through organized tours, offered by the official travel agency for Nunavik, the Fédération des Coopératives du Nouveau Québec (FCNQ ☏514/457-9371). FCNQ also provides information on the various accommodation possibilities. Several outfitters organize fishing, hunting, hiking, canoeing and nature observation trips (contact FCNQ for information).

The largest among the 14 villages, **Kuujjuaq★** (pop 1,405) is the seat of regional government offices. Located to the west, **Inukjuak** (pop 1,044), serves as headquarters for the Avataq Cultural Institute, a non-profit organization devoted to the preservation and development of the Inuit heritage in Nunavik. The northeasternmost villages of **Kangiqsujuaq** (pop 404) and **Salluit** (pop 823) are especially remarkable for their spectacular **sites★★**, surrounded by rugged mountains and jagged cliffs. Located on the western shore, **Povungnituk** (pop 1,091) has gained recognition as a centre for Inuit sculpture. The village's **museum★** features a collection of Inuit tools, objects and crafts. Situated just north of James Bay, **Kuujjuarapik** (pop 605) is home to most of Nunavik's non-native population and to a sizeable number of Cree Indians.

★★★ QUEBEC CITY

Pop 167,517

Map of Principal Sights p 5   Tourist Office ☏418/692-2471

Built atop the Cape Diamant promontory jutting into the St Lawrence River, Quebec's capital has delighted visitors for centuries. Throughout the years, the city has retained its Old World charm, evident in the multitude of historic and religious monuments, fortifications and narrow cobblestone alleys. The distinctive French flavour is enhanced by fine restaurants, outdoor cafes and a lively nightlife. In 1985, the city became the first urban centre in North America to be inscribed on UNESCO's World Heritage List.

Birthplace of New France. – Long before Jacques Cartier's arrival in 1535, Indian hunters and fishermen inhabited the area of the village of Stadacona. Following a fruitless search for precious stones, Cartier soon abandoned the site, and interest in the area declined. Attempting to establish a fur-trading post, Samuel de Champlain set foot here in 1608 and constructed a rudimentary wooden fortress, known as the *habitation (p 148)*.

The first settlers arrived in Quebec during the 17C. Primarily craftsmen and merchants attracted to the profitable fur trade, they erected houses in the Lower Town *(p 172)*, which became the centre of commercial activity. Seeking protection offered by the fortifications, numerous religious institutions and colonial administration settled in the Upper Town.

The 18C and 19C. – Quebec City's location atop the 98m/321ft high Cape Diamant promontory provided the colony with a naturally fortified area. Despite this strategic military location, the French city was repeatedly attacked—first by the Iroquois, then by the British. The escalating hostility between the small French colony and Britain culminated in the Battle of the Plains of Abraham *(p 149)*, which precipitated the British Conquest of 1759.

Following the Treaty of Paris in 1763, Quebec City became capital of the new British dominion, and quickly assumed a dominant position. Owing mainly to its busy port activities, the city maintained a competitive position with Montreal until the mid-19C. As the population shifted westward, Quebec City gradually lost its position as centre of production and trade in New France.

Quebec City Today. – Since the turn of this century, most jobs have been related to public administration, defence and the service sector. Recent growth of the provincial government has provided the capital city with renewed vitality. Throughout its turbulent history, the city has remained a bastion of French culture in North

America. Although the anglophone community accounted for more than half the population in 1861, Quebec City today claims less than 5 percent British residents, a factor that contributes to the city's distinctly francophone character.

The main metropolitan event is the famous winter **Carnival** in February, which attracts thousands of visitors.

★★★ THE OLD CITY *Map p 173*

The oldest part of the city is divided into Upper Town, set atop the massive Cape Diamant, and Lower Town, nestled between the rocky cliff and the St Lawrence. It is best to visit the Old City on foot, in order to absorb the distinct character of the narrow, winding streets.

★★★ Upper Town *1/2 day*

The site of Samuel de Champlain's Fort Saint-Louis (1620), Upper Town was not developed until a group of wealthy merchants decided to increase settlement in the colony. Although a few houses appeared toward the end of the 17C, the area retained its administrative and religious vocation for over two centuries.

The handful of seigneurs and religious institutions who had established themselves on Cape Diamant, seeking protection from the military, refused to divide their land plots. It was only during the 19C that elegant residential neighbourhoods evolved along the Rues Saint-Louis, Sainte-Ursule and d'Auteuil, and Avenues Sainte-Geneviève and Saint-Denis. Today, Upper Town still functions as the city's administrative centre.

★★★ **Place d'Armes and Vicinity.** – Bordered by prestigious buildings and restaurants, this pleasant square, once used for military drills and parades, forms the heart of Old Quebec, attracting throngs of visitors. It is dominated by the city's most prominent landmark, the **Château Frontenac★★** *(illustration p 147)*. A massive structure erected in 1893 in the Chateau style, this renowned hotel stands on the site of the former governor's residence. Next to the chateau, the Governors' Garden, features the **Wolfe-Montcalm monument [1]** (1827), a joint memorial to the two enemies who died in combat and whose meeting resulted in the creation of the Canadian nation.

Located behind the chateau, **Dufferin Terrace★★★**, a wide wooden boardwalk, is perched 671m/2,200ft above the majestic St Lawrence, offering breathtaking **views★★** of Lower Town and the river. A **monument [2]** to Samuel de Champlain, founder of New France, marks the northern end of the terrace. At the southern end, a flight of steps ascends to the **Governors' Walk★★** *(closed in winter)*, a spectacular boardwalk, precariously suspended along the steep cliff that leads from the terrace to National Battlefields Park *(p 175)*.

In the narrow **Rue du Trésor**, a quaint pedestrian street off Place d'Armes, artists exhibit sketches and engravings of typical city scenes.

Fort Museum [M¹]. – *10 Rue Sainte-Anne. Open daily Jan–Nov. $4.50.* ☎*418/692-2175.* Housed in a castle-like structure, this museum features an audio-visual presentation that traces the city's military and civil history.

★ **Old Post Office [A].** – *3 Rue Buade. Open Mon–Fri.* Erected in 1873, this large edifice presents an imposing facade adorned with Beaux-Arts embellishments. Inside, the Canadian Parks Service presents exhibits on the development of historical and natural sites in Canada.

★ **Notre-Dame-de-Québec Basilica-Cathedral [B].** – Originally consecrated in 1674, the basilica was destroyed during the fighting between French and British forces in 1759. The church was reconstructed between 1768 and 1771 by Quebec's most prominent architects, the Baillairgé family. Jean Baillairgé rebuilt the south belfry with its two openwork drums surmounted by domes. François Baillairgé was responsible for the interior and designed the plans for the magnificent **baldachin**. His son, Thomas, designed the monumental neoclassical facade in 1843. Although the structure was destroyed by fire in 1922, it was rebuilt to reflect its original appearance. Of note in the interior are the stained-glass windows, the baldachin and the Casavant organ.

The majestic **City Hall** dominates the Place de l'hôtel de ville across from the basilica. In the square stands a **monument [3]** to Elzéar Alexandre Taschereau, the first Canadian cardinal.

Located north of the basilica, Quebec City's **Latin Quarter★** is the oldest residential district in Upper Town. Narrow, crisscrossing streets add to the charm of the quarter, today inhabited mainly by students.

★★ **Quebec Seminary.** – *2 Côte de la Fabrique. Visit by guided tour (1hr 30min) only Jun 24–Labour Day daily 10am–5pm.* ✦ ☎*418/692-2843.* Founded in 1663 by Msgr François de Laval to train priests for the colony, this institute of higher learning is the oldest in Canada. In 1852, the seminary was granted a university, Université Laval, which grew within the seminary walls until the Sainte-Foy campus opened in 1950.

The seminary comprises three buildings arranged around an inner court. Note the sundial on the facade of the Procure Wing, erected in 1678. The highlights of the guided tour include the **Msgr Olivier Briand Chapel★**, noteworthy for the fine wood paneling adorning its walls, and the **Congregational Chapel**, featuring a statue of the Virgin Mary crafted by Thomas Baillairgé.

The **outer chapel★** contains one of the most important collections of relics outside St Peter's in Rome. A funeral chapel added in 1950 houses Laval's tomb.

Reputedly the oldest museum in the province, the **Seminary Museum★ [M²]** *(9 Rue de l'Université; open daily year-round; closed Christmas & New Year's;* ✦ ☎*418/692-*

2843) presents items that reflect the life and work of the seminary since its inception. The vast collections include European religious paintings, oriental art, liturgical objects, documents and scientific instruments used for didactic purposes.

★ **Augustine Monastery.** – *32 Rue Charlevoix.* Founded by Augustinian Nuns in the 1640s, this monastery is best known for its hospital, the Hôtel-Dieu, which still operates today. The **church★**, designed by Pierre Émond in 1800, features a neoclassical facade adorned with a sculpted Ionic portal. Highlights of the interior, crafted by Thomas Baillairgé, include the high-altar tabernacle, the retable and the basket-handle wooden vault.
Opened in 1958, the **Augustine Museum★ [M³]** *(open year-round Tue–Sun; closed holidays; ☎418/692-2492)* presents a collection of objects and artworks tracing the Augustinian Nuns' history and heritage. The museum includes one of the foremost collections of **paintings★** dating back to the time of New France.

★ **Rue Saint-Louis.** – This charming, bustling street is home to a variety of restaurants and boutiques. It also features some of the city's oldest architectural gems. The **Maison Maillou★ [C]** (1736), located next the Château Frontenac, now houses the Quebec City Chamber of Commerce. The offices of the Consulate General of France occupy the adjacent house, the **Maison Kent [D]**, dating from the 1830s. Standing at the corner of Rue Desjardins, the **Maison Jacquet★ [E]** was built in 1699. Reputedly the oldest house in Quebec City, it is one of the only remaining examples of late-17C domestic architecture in the province. Today, a renowned restaurant occupies it.

★ **Ursuline Monastery.** – *Rue Donnacona.* Founded in 1639 by Madame de la Peltrie and Marie Guyart (Mère Marie-de-l'Incarnation), the monastery is the oldest educational institution for young women in North America and is still in operation today. The chapel (1902) is particularly remarkable for its **interior decoration★★**. Most of the ornaments were crafted between 1726 and 1736 under the supervision of Pierre-Noël Levasseur. Of particular interest are the wood sculptures of St Augustin, St Ursule and St Joseph, the nuns' choir surmounted by a wooden vault, and the collection of paintings.
The **Ursuline Museum★ [M⁴]** *(12 Rue Donnacona; open Jan–Nov Tue–Sun; $2.50; slide presentation by request; ☎418/694-0694)* occupies the former site of the house belonging to Madame de la Peltrie, the order's benefactress, in the 17C. Reflecting the occupations of the Ursuline Nuns, the collection features documents, furnishings, paintings, sculptures and numerous **embroideries★** of rare beauty. The museum also contains altar frontals and ecclesiastic vestments of the 17C.

★ **Price Building.** – *65 Rue Sainte-Anne.* This 17-storey Art Deco-style edifice, the Old Town's only high-rise, was built in 1930 to accommodate the head office of Price Brothers, famed for introducing the pulp and paper industry to the Saguenay region *(p 178)*. Its copper roof blends well with the surrounding buildings.

★ **Holy Trinity Anglican Cathedral [F].** – *31 Rue des Jardins.* Modelled after London's Church of St Martin-in-the-Fields, this edifice (1804) was the first Anglican cathedral built outside Great Britain. King George III provided the funding and sent English oak from the royal forests of Windsor for the pews.
In summer, the cathedral courtyard is a gathering place for artists.

★★★ **Lower Town** *1/2 day*
Access from Dufferin Terrace by funicular (in service May 1–Oct 31 8am–midnight; off-season 7:30am–11pm; fare $.85) or by Frontenac steps.

This narrow stretch of land dominated by Upper Town was the site of Champlain's **habitation**, a small wooden fortress erected in 1608. The first settlers arrived here in the late 17C and established shops and residences around the fort and the market square, now known as Place Royale *(see below)*. As commerce, shipbuilding and port activities grew, residents filled in parts of the shores, constructed numerous wharves and created new streets. By the 19C, the area of Lower Town, the city's commercial centre, had doubled in size.
As port activities declined in the 1860s, the neighbourhood lost its appeal and fell into decay. In 1970, the Quebec government began restoring the area. Today, restaurants, cafes and boutiques abound in the historic quarter of Place Royale. Lined with boutiques and art galleries, the pedestrian **Rue du Petit-Champlain★** reflects the quarter's 18C appearance.
Facing the Place de Paris, a **visitor centre** *(215 Rue du Marché-Finlay; open daily Jun 15–Sept 30; ☎418/643-6631)* offers guided tours of the area.

★ **Maison Chevalier.** – *Corner of Rue du Marché-Champlain and Blvd Champlain. Open daily Jun 15–Sept 30. & ▣ ☎418/643-9689.* This imposing stone structure, topped by a red roof and high chimneys, is composed of three separate buildings. The west wing was built in 1752 for a wealthy merchant, Jean-Baptiste Chevalier. Restored in 1956, the house now serves as part of the Museum of Civilization and features exhibits on traditional Quebec architecture and furniture.

Royal Battery. – *At the end of Rue Sous-le-Fort. Open year-round. Cannon animation Jun 24–Labour Day daily 10am–5pm. ☎418/643-6631.* Constructed in 1691, this thick, four-sided earthen rampart formed part of the fortifications of the city. It was destroyed during French-British fighting in 1759 and gradually buried. Archaeologists excavating the area unearthed it in 1972. It has been reconstructed and replicas of 18C cannon are positioned in the 11 embrasures.

★★ **Place Royale.** – Today the heart of Lower Town, this charming, cobblestone square was the hub of the city's economic activity until the mid-19C, when the port, and subsequently the area, fell into decline. Bordered by typical 18C stone houses, topped by steep roofs and chimneys, the square features a bronze bust of King Louis XIV as its centrepiece.

OLD QUEBEC

The 1656 **Maison Fornel [G]** *(entrance on 25 Rue Saint-Pierre; open daily Jun 15–Sept 30; ☎418/643-6631)* houses an interpretation centre featuring a permanent exhibit on Place Royale. Highlights include a replica of a map of New France drawn in 1688, a scale model of a 17C house and numerous artifacts uncovered during excavations in the square.

On the north side of the square, three stone structures, **Maisons Bruneau, Drapeau and Rageot [K]** *(open daily Jun 15–Sept 30),* have been transformed into an interpretation centre focusing on the importance of commerce in the development of Place Royale. The interior has been refurbished as a shop of the early 18C.

★ **Notre-Dame-des-Victoires Church.** – *On Place Royale.* Completed in 1723, this stone edifice topped by a single spire stands on the site of Champlain's *habitation.* It was named in thanksgiving for two successful occasions when Quebec City resisted the sieges of the British. Inside, the magnificent **retable** represents the fortified city.

★★ **Museum of Civilization.** – *85 Rue Dalhousie. Open Jun 24–Labour Day daily 10am–7pm. Off-season Tue–Sun 10am–5pm (Wed 9pm). Closed Christmas. $5.* ⤢ ✕ 🅿 ☎418/643-2158. Designed by Moshe Safdie, this acclaimed museum is housed in two stark, angular buildings crowned by copper roofs and a glass campanile. A monumental staircase links the buildings and leads to a terrace overlooking an inner court and the Maison Estèbe, a 1752 stone structure, which was integrated into the museum. Inside the spacious entrance hall, note *La Débâcle* (A. Reusch), a massive sculpture representing ice breaking up in spring.

The museum presents permanent and temporary thematic exhibits focusing on five broad areas: thought, language, natural resources, the human body and society. Among the permanent exhibits, **Objects of civilization** highlights Quebec furnishings, tools and costumes. Covering over four centuries of Quebec history and culture, the **Memories** exhibit takes visitors on a thought-provoking stroll down memory lane. The displayed artifacts illustrate a people's struggle to create a new life in a new land. The **barque** is one of several 18C flat-bottomed boats uncovered during archaeological excavations on Place Royale. It has been extensively restored to its original appearance.

★ **Rue Saint-Pierre.** – During the 19C, this busy thoroughfare emerged as the city's principal financial district. Among the noteworthy commercial buildings still lining the street are the **National Bank [L]** *(no. 71);* the former **Molson Bank [N]** *(no. 105),* now occupied by the Post Office; and the **Imperial Bank of Canada [P]** *(nos. 113-115).* Dominating the corner of Rues Saint-Paul and Saint-Pierre, the **Canadian Bank of Commerce [Q]** exemplifies the Beaux-Arts style.

The charming **Rue Saint-Paul★** is renowned for its antique shops and art galleries.

★ **Old Port** (Vieux-Port). – Located on the Louise Basin, the port played a major role in the development of Canada until the late 19C, when it fell into disrepair. Created by the Federal Government in the 1980s, the **Agora★** complex includes an amphitheatre, a modern shopping centre, a wide boardwalk on the river and a marina. The Old Port of Quebec **interpretation centre★** *(100 Rue Saint-André; open Apr–Nov Tue–Sun; $2.25;* & ⊓ ☎*418/648-3300)* is devoted to the port city's prominence during the 19C. Exhibits and audio-visual displays describe the logging and ship-building industries so vital to Quebec's economy. The glassed-in terrace on the top floor affords a fine **view** of Lower Town and the modern port.

★★ **Fortifications** *Map p 173. 1/2 day.*

Much of the charm of Quebec City stems from the fact that it is the only walled-in city in Canada. Although fortification projects were undertaken during the French Regime, most of the existing walls, batteries and the citadel were erected by the British after the Conquest, and never used. **Lord Dufferin**, Governor General of Canada between 1872 and 1878, initiated a beautification project that included refurbishing the fortified enceinte, rebuilding the gates to the city and clearing the ramparts.

★★ **Citadel.** – *Entrance at end of Côte de la Citadelle. Open May–Sept daily 9am–5pm (mid-Jun–Labour Day 7pm). Off-season Mon–Fri 9am–4pm (during Nov 2pm); Dec–Feb by reservation only. During Carnival open daily 10am–2pm. $4. Changing of the guard mid-Jun–Labour Day daily 10am.* & ⊓ ☎*418/648-3563. Some areas of the Citadel are off-limits as it is still a military base for the Royal 22e Régiment.* Erected between 1820 and 1832, this massive fortress, enclosing 16ha/40 acres, is typical of star-shaped fortifications. Advanced works, or outworks, were devised to protect entrances and ramparts from enemy fire, while sloping earthworks forced the enemy to expose itself to cannon fire from the garrison. The enceinte was composed of bastions, linked together by curtains (straight walls) that protected the ditches. The guided tour leads past the new powder house, the governor general's residence, the officers' mess, the old prison and the hospital. Occupying the old powder magazine, the **Museum of the Royal 22e Régiment** contains a collection of military objects from the 17C to the present.

Powder Magazine. – Located to the right of the Saint-Louis gate, this structure was built in 1810 on the Esplanade, a vast field used for military exercises between 1779 and 1783. The building now houses an **interpretation centre** *(open daily May 14 –Sept 30; off-season by reservation only; closed Oct 1–Mar 30)* displaying exhibits on the historical evolution of the city's fortifications.

Visitors can stroll south along the ramparts over the Saint-Louis, Kent and Saint-Jean gates to Artillery Park. The fortifications afford panoramas of the city and surrounding areas.

★ **Artillery Park National Historic Site.** – ⑨ *Entrance at corner of Rues Saint-Jean and d'Auteuil. Open daily Apr 1–Oct 31. Off-season Mon–Fri, weekends by reservation only.* ⑤ ⊡ ☎*418/648-4205.* This huge site that includes barracks, a redoubt and an old foundry, commemorates three centuries of military, social and industrial life in Quebec City. Designed by Chaussegros de Léry in 1750, the barracks, housed in a structure 160m/525ft in length, contained armouries, stock rooms, a guard room and six prison cells. The redoubt (1748) is remarkable for its massive stone buttresses added to the original building after 1763. Inside, an **interpretation centre** features costumes, paintings and artifacts that offer insight into a soldier's life in the 18C and 19C. The old foundry contains a **scale model**★★ of Quebec City, produced between 1806 and 1808 by British engineers, that presents a stunning picture of the city as it appeared at the beginning of the 19C.

★ **Rue des Remparts.** – Until approximately 1875, this street was a mere path that ran alongside the ramparts, connecting the various bastions and batteries. Today, a pleasant stroll down the street allows the visitor to recapture the atmosphere of the old fortified city.

OUTSIDE THE WALLS *1/2 day*

★ **Grande Allée.** – *Map p 173.* Departing from the Saint-Louis gate and extending southward of Old Quebec, this wide avenue is to the city what the Champs-Élysées is to Paris. Lined with innumerable restaurants, bars, outdoor cafes, boutiques and offices, the bustling thoroughfare provides an elegant setting for the city's nightlife.

★★ **Parliament Building.** – *Map p 173. Open Jun 24–Labour Day daily 9am–4:30pm. Off-season Mon–Fri 9am–4:30pm.* ☎*418/643-7239.* Overlooking the old city, this majestic edifice is the finest example of Second Empire architecture in Quebec City. Note the imposing facade, which presents a historic tableau wherein bronze figures commemorate the great names of Quebec history.
Inside, a grand staircase leads to the parliamentary chambers, which are accessed through finely chiselled doors. The Chamber of the National Assembly is used by Quebec's National Assembly, while the Chamber of the Legislative Assembly accommodates meetings of parliamentary committees and official receptions.

★ **National Battlefields Park.** – *Map p 173. Open year-round.* Stretching 107ha/250 acres along a cliff overlooking the St Lawrence, this park memorializes battles fought between the British and the French. A large section of the park occupies the former **Plains of Abraham**, where the French and British armies fought a major battle (1759) that eventually sealed the fate of the French colony. Both commanding generals, Wolfe and Montcalm, were mortally wounded during the short but decisive event.

Marie-Guyart Building. – *Map p 173. 1037 Rue de la Chevrotière. Open daily year-round.* ⊡ ⑤ ☎*418/644-9841.* The Anima G observatory occupying the 31st floor of this administrative building provides a splendid **view**★★ of Old Quebec, the citadel and forti- fications as well as the surrounding areas.

★ **Quebec Museum.** – *Map p 174. In National Battlefields Park. Open daily May 18– Sept 8. Off-season Tue–Sun. Closed Christmas & New Year's. $5.* ⑤ ✗ ⊡ ☎*418/ 643-2150.* Overlooking the parade ground, this imposing building features a monumental Beaux-Arts facade and a central staircase leading to an Ionic portico. The museum's holdings in Quebec art, spanning four centuries, represent the largest public collection in Canada. Displayed in six galleries are some 6,000 works of art, including watercolours, engravings, decorative arts and sculpture. The former "plains prison" was recently annexed and now houses several new galleries.

★ **Cartier-Brébeuf National Historic Site.** – ⑨ *Map p 174. 75 Rue de l'Espinay, 3km/2mi from Saint-Jean gate by Côte d'Abraham, Rue de la Couronne, Drouin Bridge and 1ʳᵉ Ave. Open daily May–Sept; Oct–Nov Mon–Fri. Rest of the year by reservation only.* ⑤ ☎*418/648-4038.* This park commemorates Jacques Cartier, who wintered on this spot in 1535, and Jean de Brébeuf, a Jesuit missionary. The **interpretation centre** features insightful displays that recall Cartier's second voyage to New France and his meetings with the Iroquois, as well as the Jesuit's first mission, established in 1627.
The highlight of the visit is a replica of **La Grande Hermine**★, the largest of Cartier's three vessels. Measuring less than 24m/80ft in length, the two-masted ship carried up to 60 men across the Atlantic.

EXCURSIONS

★★ **Beaupré Coast.** – Bordering the St Lawrence, this narrow stretch of land extends from Quebec City to Cape Tourmente. Its name is attributed to an exclamation made by Cartier, who, noting the lush green meadowland, said *"Quel beau pré!"* (what a fine meadow). A pleasant drive along Highway 360 leads through a string of charming communities dating from the French Regime.

★★ **Montmorency Falls.** – *Map p 174. 10km/6mi east of Quebec City. Open May 11–Oct 27 daily 8am–9pm.* ✗ ☎*418/622-4444.* Before emptying into the St Lawrence, the Montmorency River cascades over a cliff marking the edge of the Canadian Shield. The 76m/249ft high falls are spectacular year-round, and in winter, the spray creates a great cone of ice that sometimes exceeds 30m/98ft in height. From the **upper lookout**, visitors can fully appreciate the height and force of the falls. The **lower lookout** affords the opportunity to approach the base of the falls *(rain gear is advised).*

★★ **Sainte-Anne-de-Beaupré Shrine.** – *In Sainte-Anne-de-Beaupré, 35km/22mi east of Quebec City. Open May–Oct daily 6am– 9:30pm; rest of the year 7am–7pm.* ⑤. Named for the patron saint of Quebec, this Roman Catholic shrine is visited by over a million people yearly. An imposing, medieval-style basilica, consecrated in 1934, dominates the site. Divided into five naves separated by huge columns, the interior is lit by 200 stained-glass windows. Note also the glimmering mosaics adorning the barrel vault above the main nave. On the shrine's grounds are the memorial chapel and the chapel of the Scala Sancta. Life-size representations of the Stations of the Cross dot the hillside.

★★ **Saint-Joachim Church.** – *In Saint-Joachim, 40km/25mi east of Quebec City.* The small church (1779) is best known for its magnificent **interior★★**, fashioned between 1815 and 1825 by François and Thomas Baillairgé. Of particular interest are the panelling, enhanced by gilded bas-reliefs, and the main altar, surrounded by majestic columns and free-standing sculptures of the Evangelists.

★★ **Île d'Orléans.** – Pop 6,938. *10km/6mi east of Quebec City.* This almond-shaped island wedged in the St Lawrence was named Isle of Bacchus by Jacques Cartier in 1535, and renamed in 1536 to honour the son of King François I, the Duke of Orléans. Route 368 runs along the 67km/41mi circumference, passing through six communities, each with its distinct flavour. Driving along the road, the visitor will discover splendid scenery and magnificent **views★★** of the St Lawrence shoreline. The village of **Saint-Laurent★**, traditionally the island's maritime centre, still claims the island's only marina. In **Saint-Jean★**, the **Manoir Mauvide-Genest★** *(open daily Jun 1–Sept 3; off-season Tue–Sun; closed Thanksgiving Day–May 31; $2.50;* ✗ ☎*418/829-2630),* built in 1734, is considered the finest example of rural architecture under the French Regime. The manor now houses a restaurant and a museum featuring traditional Quebec furniture. The community of Sainte-Famille is best known for its tri-steepled **church★★** (1748), dating from the French Regime. In the neoclassical interior, note the sculpted vault by Louis-David Bazile, student of Quévillon, and the tabernacle crafted by the Levasseur family. This elaborate edifice contrasts with the **old church★** in Saint-Pierre, remodelled in the 1830s by Thomas Baillairgé.

★★ RICHELIEU VALLEY

Map p 177

Some 130km/81mi long, the majestic Richelieu River flows north from its source in Lake Champlain (New York) to join the St Lawrence at Sorel. Champlain discovered the waterway in 1609, named later for **Cardinal Richelieu**, chief minister of Louis XIII. The river served as an invasion route and was heavily fortified during the French Regime. The forts at Chambly, Saint-Jean-sur-Richelieu, Lennox and Lacolle were built initially to protect Montreal against attacks by Iroquois, and later by British and American troups. The valley also played an important role in the Rebellions of 1837 *(p 149)*, which resulted in several uprisings in Saint-Denis, Saint-Charles and Saint-Eustache. To facilitate transportation between the US and Quebec, an extensive canal system was built along the Richelieu in the mid-19C. Today, this region remains one of the richest agricultural areas in the province. A popular weekend retreat for Montrealers, the valley attracts thousands of travellers and tourists every summer.

★ **Chambly.** – Pop 15,893. *30km/19mi from Montreal by Hwy 10.* A residential suburb of Montreal, this community enjoys a beautiful site on the Richelieu. A pleasant walk along the river leads past the canal and Fort Chambly to **Rue Richelieu★**, lined with sumptuous 19C residences.

★★ **Fort Chambly National Historic Site.** – ☺ *Open May–Sept Tue–Sun 10am–6pm (Mon 1–6pm). Off-season Wed–Sun 9am–5pm.* ♿ ☎*514/658-1585.* Located in a magnificent park on the Chambly Basin, this fort is the only remaining fortified complex in Quebec dating back to the French Regime. Erected in 1711, the stone structure replaced an earlier wooden edifice constructed in 1695 by Jacques de Chambly.

The fort is laid out in a square with bastions at each corner. An **interpretation centre** features displays and dioramas on the history of the fort and a description of the restoration project. Located near the fort, the **Guard House** (1814) exemplifies the Palladian style adopted by the military throughout the British colonies. Inside, displays illustrate the period of British occupation of the city (1760-1851). Built in 1820, the small fieldstone **Anglican Church** served as the garrison's place of worship.

★★ **Mount Saint-Hilaire Nature Centre.** – *23km/149mi north of Chambly. Open Apr 1–Oct 31 daily 8am–6:30pm (Jun 1–Aug 31 until 8:30pm). Off-season daily 8am–4:30pm. $3.* ♿ ☎*514/467-1755.* Rising abruptly above the valley, Mount Saint-Hilaire (411m/1,348ft) is the most imposing of the Monteregian Hills. Several trails crisscross the lush forests covering the mountain, and lead to the summit, which affords sweeping **views**★★ of the Richelieu Valley.

★ **Saint-Denis-sur-Richelieu.**– Pop 1,038. *33km/20.5mi north of Nature Centre.* This agricultural community was the site of a Patriot victory in 1837. At the **Patriots' National House**★ *(open Jun–Nov Tue–Sun; off-season by reservation only; $2.50;* ☎*514/787-3623),* displays explain the background of the uprising and highlight the events leading to the Patriots' fight for freedom and democracy.

Saint-Jean-sur-Richelieu. – Pop 37,607. *40km/25mi southeast of Montreal by Hwys 10 and 35.* Today renowned as a manufacturing centre for pottery and ceramics, this industrial city once formed part of the chain of fortifications erected by the French along the Richelieu. The site of the former Fort Saint-Jean has been occupied since 1952 by the Collège Militaire Royal, where French-speaking officers are trained for the Canadian Armed Forces. The **Fort Saint-Jean Museum** *(open mid-May–mid-Aug Tue–Sun;* ☎*514/358-6810)* contains a collection of weapons, uniforms and other military artifacts.

Île aux Noix. – *48km/30mi south of Montreal by Hwys 10 and 35 S, and Rte 223.* This 85ha/210 acre island was fortified by the French in 1759 and captured by the British the following year. Having at various times served as a shipbuilding centre, a holiday resort and an internment centre, the island is now preserved as a national historic site.

★ **Fort Lennox.** – 🕐 *Visit by guided tour (1hr) only mid-May–Labour Day.* ♿ 🍴 ☎*514/291-5700.* Erected in the 1820s, this bastion-type fortress occupies a pleasant **site**★ overlooking the Richelieu River. A wide moat surrounds the fort, which forms a five-pointed star with corners protected by bastions. The neoclassical stone buildings have been restored to re-create life on a British army base in the mid-19C.

★★ **Safari Park.** – *63km/39mi south of Montreal by Hwy 15 and Rte 202. Open mid-May–mid-Sept daily 10am–5pm. $17; $65 per car.* ♿ 🍴 ☎*514/247-2727.* Situated in an apple-growing region west of the Richelieu, this zoological park is renowned for its hundreds of animals from all over the world that roam freely in large enclosures. Required to remain in their vehicles, visitors can follow the Safari Trail along which they can take photographs, touch and feed the animals. Highlights include an "Enchanted Forest," a jungle walk, a theatre and a circus.

★★★ SAGUENAY FJORD REGION

Maps pp 152-153

Located at the southern tip of the Saguenay region, the immense, saucer-shaped Lake Saint-Jean empties into the Saguenay River. Measuring 155km/96mi in length, this river flows into the southernmost fjord in the world, the majestic Saguenay Fjord, which discharges its waters into the St Lawrence.

Fed by a number of rivers, including the Péribonca, Mistassini and Ashuapmushuan, Lake Saint-Jean is a small remnant of an original lake created over 10,000 years ago by the meltwaters of retreating glaciers. First called Piékouagami ("flat lake") by the Montagnais, Lake Saint-Jean was renamed for **Jean Dequen**, the first Frenchman to visit its shores in 1647. The area remained unsettled until the mid-19C when the first sawmills were built, and the rivers harnessed for electricity.

Hydro-electric power plants, pulp mills and aluminum smelters still line the shores of the lake and the Upper Saguenay. Beyond Saint-Fulgence, the deep river channel was gouged in Precambrian rock by glaciers during the last ice age. Lined by rocky cliffs plunging into the water, the channel is 1,500m/4,920ft wide in places, having an average depth of 240m/787ft. The stark and untamed beauty of the river's southern section has attracted visitors for years. Most choose to take a scenic river cruise *(see below)*, but the fjord can also be enjoyed by exploring the villages nestled along its shores.

The spectacular, natural **Saguenay Park**★★ *(open daily May 15–Oct 20; car $6.50;* ⚠ ⚐ ☎*418/272-2267)* has been created to preserve part of the shoreline. The region is famous for the landlocked salmon known as **ouananiche**, a favourite catch for sports fishermen; the wild **blueberries**, or *bleuets*, found on the north shore of the lake; and the famous nine-day **International Swim Marathon** held in July.

★★★ SAGUENAY FJORD

★★ **Tadoussac.** – Pop 832. *220km/136mi northeast of Quebec City by Hwy 40 and Rte 138.* This tiny community occupies a magnificent **site**★★ at the mouth of the Saguenay on the cliffs and dunes lining the St Lawrence. The resort town is popular as a place to see migrating whales.

In 1600, Pierre Chauvin built Canada's first trading post here, and Tadoussac became an important centre for the fur trade. Settlers moved into the area in the mid-19C, and the community developed into a lovely vacation spot. Today, Tadoussac's principal attractions are whales that swim up the St Lawrence to the mouth of the Saguenay for a few months each year.

The village is dominated by the red roofs of the **Hotel Tadoussac**, dating from 1941. Facing the hotel, a boardwalk extends along the river, connecting a reconstruction of Chauvin's trading post and a tiny Indian chapel (1747). A short walk to the wharf affords fine views of the area. The 30m/98ft high sand dunes lining the St Lawrence are quite steep in places, and sand-skiing has become a local sport.

★★ **Whale-watching Cruises.** – *Departures from the wharf at Tadoussac May 31–mid-Oct daily 9:45am, 12:45 & 4:15pm; additional 2:45pm cruise mid-Jul–Labour Day. Round-trip 3hrs. $30. In high season advance reservations are recommended. Free parking at harbour.* ✗ *Croisières Navimex Inc* ☎*418/237-4274 (in season)* ☎*418/692-4643 (year-round).* At Tadoussac, the St Lawrence is more than 10km/6mi wide. Boats head for the centre of the river where whales surface to breathe, and to dive in search of food. Spray erupting from their blowholes makes them easy to see. The most common species sighted on cruises are the **fin**, **minke** and **beluga** whales. Occasionally, a fortunate visitor may glimpse a **humpback** or even the huge **blue whale**.

★★ **Scenic Cruises.** – *Departures from Tadoussac or Chicoutimi (see below) Jun 1–Oct 15 daily 8:30am, 12:30 & 4:30pm. Round-trip 3hrs. $30.* ✗ *Croisières du Grand Fleuve* ☎*418/235-4585 or* ☎*800/463-6761 (in season).* A boat trip is the most spectacular way to discover the Saguenay Fjord. The longer cruises lead to Éternité Bay, a lovely cove dominated by twin cliffs, Cap Éternité and Cap Trinité. Rising some 518m/1,700ft over the fjord, **Cap Trinité**★★ is renowned for the impressive statue of the Virgin Mary standing on a ledge 180m/590ft above the water. On the return trip, the **views** of Ha! Ha! Bay and of Chicoutimi itself are equally magnificent.

Sainte-Rose-du-Nord. – Pop 408. *94km/58mi from Tadoussac.* Founded in 1838, this charming village occupies an exceptional **site**★★ in a cove nestled between two rocky escarpments. The small nature **museum** *(open daily year-round; $2.50;* ⚐ ☎*418/675-2348)* contains a fascinating collection of nature's oddities.

★ **Chicoutimi.** – Pop 62,670. *200km/124mi north of Quebec City by Rte 175.* Meaning "where the deep waters end" in the local Montagnais language, Chicoutimi sits on the banks of the Saguenay, at the point where it becomes a spectacular fjord. Site of an important fur-trading post in the mid-17C, the town is today the cultural and administrative centre of the Saguenay region.

★ **Chicoutimi Pulp Mill.** – *300 Rue Dubuc. Open daily year-round.* This former pulp and paper mill (1887) was one of the most important industrial complexes in Quebec in the early 20C. The former workshop has been converted into an **interpretation centre** *(open daily May–Labour Day; off-season by reservation only;* ⚐ ✗ ☎*418/543-2729)* that features a fascinating audio-visual presentation on the mill and the lumber industry in general.

★ **Saguenay–Lac-Saint-Jean Museum.** – *534 Rue Jacques-Cartier Est. Open daily year-round. $3.* ⚐ ☎*418/545-9400.* This museum provides an insightful introduction to the Saguenay area. Exhibits focus on the Montagnais lifestyle, the first European settlers and the region's industrial development.

★★ **Scenic Cruises.** – *See description above.*

★★ LAKE SAINT-JEAN

Péribonka. – Pop 635. *270km/167mi north of Quebec City by Rtes 175 and 169.* After spending a few months in this charming community in 1912, the French author Louis Hémon (1880-1913) wrote his well-known novel, *Maria Chapdelaine, récit du Canada français.* Informative exhibits at the **Louis Hémon Museum★** *(open daily year-round; $3.50; & ☎418/374-2177)* trace the life and work of the author.

Saint-Félicien. – Pop 9,340. *67km/41.5mi west of Péribonka by Rte 169.* Located on the western shore of the lake, this agricultural community is best known for its **zoological garden★★** *(6km/4mi on Blvd du Jardin; open May 1–Sept 30 daily 9am–5pm; $13; & ✗ ☎418/679-0543).* A specially designed train takes visitors through the park, allowing them to admire a variety of animals roaming in natural surroundings. Of particular interest is the 324ha/800 acre park known as the **Nature Trails★★**, inhabited by native Canadian species.

Roberval. – Pop 11,628. *25km/15mi south by Rte 169.* Located on the southwestern shore of Lake Saint-Jean, this community is today an important service centre for the area. It is also the finish point of the annual International Swim Marathon.

Pointe-Bleue Amerindian Museum. – *9km/6mi north of Roberval by Blvd Saint-Joseph. Open daily Jun 15–Sept 15. Off-season Mon–Fri. $2.50. & ☎418/275-4842.* Located in Mashteuiatsh, an Indian reserve created in 1856, this museum traces the history of the Montagnais and displays traditional tools and clothing. Note the poignant mural, *Hommage to the Montagnais or Twilight of a People* by André Michel.

★ Val-Jalbert. – *9km/6mi south of Roberval by Rte 169. Open daily May 24–Sept 29. $3.50. ⚠ & ✗ ☎418/275-3132.* Today a ghost town, Val-Jalbert was once the site of a thriving pulp mill. Built in 1902, the mill produced up to 50 tonnes/45 tons of pulp a day at the height of production in 1910. By the late 1920s, stiff competition led to the mill's closing, and the village gradually fell into ruins. Visitors can wander through the old residential sector that once contained over 80 residences and shops. Today, most of these houses are in decay, creating an eerie atmosphere. The **Old Mill**, standing on the Ouiatchouan River, now contains an exhibit on pulp production. A steep stairway leads to the top of an impressive waterfall on the Ouiatchouan River. From this vantage point, the **view★★** encompasses Lake Saint-Jean and the surrounding area.

★★ TROIS-RIVIÈRES

Pop 49,426

Map p 177   Tourist Office ☎819/375-1222

Capital of the Mauricie Region, this industrial centre is located on the north shore of the St Lawrence River at the mouth of the Saint-Maurice. Just before joining the St Lawrence, the Saint-Maurice branches around two islands, creating the three "rivers" for which the city is named.

Sent by Champlain, **Sieur de Laviolette** established a fur-trading post here in 1634. Home to many great explorers, including Pierre Radisson, Sieur des Groseilliers and Sieur de la Vérendrye, the city flourished. In the 1850s, major logging companies began exploiting the surrounding forests, and a thriving pulp and paper industry took root in the area. By the 1930s, Trois-Rivières was the world capital for the production of newsprint, a distinction it still holds to this day. This bustling city is also the location of a University of Quebec campus.

★ Rue des Ursulines. – This charming street is lined with some of the surviving structures of a fire that destroyed most of the downtown in 1908. Distinguished by a gracious dome and large wall sundial, the **Ursuline Monastery★** is the jewel of Trois-Rivière's old quarter. Inside, the **museum** *(open May–Labour Day Tue–Sun; Oct–Apr Wed–Sun; closed Sept; $2; & ☎819/375-7922)* features fine collections of ceramics, silver, books and furniture.

Other buildings of interest on this street include St James Church, erected in 1742 by the Récollet Brothers, and the Gannes and Hertel de la Fresnière houses.

★ Waterfront Park. – This attractive terrace affords superb **views** of the river and Laviolette Bridge, erected in 1967. At its eastern end, a monument commemorates the Sieur de la Vérendrye, first European to reach the Rockies. At the **Pulp and Paper Industry Exhibition Centre** *(open daily Jun 24–Labour Day; May, Labour Day–Nov weekends only; $1; & ✗ ☎819/372-4633),* displays provide a fascinating introduction to the dominant industry of Trois-Rivières.

★ Scenic Cruise. – *Two daily cruises mid-May–mid-Sept. Round-trip 2hrs. $9 ✗ Croisières M/S ☎819/375-3000.* This cruise offers an unequalled **view** of the port at Trois-Rivières and the pulp and paper installations. The shrine at Cap-de-la-Madeleine *(see below)* is also visible.

EXCURSIONS *Map p 177*

★★ Cap-de-la-Madeleine Shrine. – *5km/3mi east of Trois-Rivières by Rtes 40 and 755 (Exit 10). Open May–Oct daily 8am–7pm; rest of the year 8am–4pm. &.* This shrine attracts thousands of people annually. Two events are credited with its renown as a pilgrimage site.

In the mid-19C, Father Luc Désilets decided his growing congregation needed a new church to replace the one built on this site in 1717. When unusually mild weather prevented the St Lawrence from freezing, Désilets could not transport stones across the river for the church's construction. The Father vowed to preserve the existing church in exchange for a miracle. In March 1879, ice appeared on the river, remaining just long enough for parishioners to take the stones across. On the night of the new church's consecration in 1888, another miracle is said to have occurred when the eyes of a statue of the Virgin reportedly opened before three witnesses. Begun in 1955 to accommodate an even larger congregation, the present basilica replaced Désilets' church and was completed in 1964.

The imposing octagonal basilica is adorned with magnificent **stained-glass windows**★ designed in the medieval style by Dutch Oblate father Jan Tillemans. Set in attractive grounds beside the basilica, the original 1717 church now serves as a votive chapel. The miraculous statue stands above the altar. Winding their way through the park, the Stations of the Cross end before the replicas of the Crucifixion and the tomb of Jesus in Jerusalem.

★ **Mauricie Region.** – Surrounding the valley of the Saint-Maurice River, this region ranks among the most industrialized in both the province and the nation. Forestry operations began in the 1850s, and hydro-electric plants were erected in the late 19C. Hugging the river, which is still used to transport logs from the forests to the pulp mills, the drive along Route 155 affords splendid **views**★ of the Saint-Maurice and the rocky cliffs lining its sides. Located northwest of Grand-Mère, the **Mauricie National Park**★★ offers a glorious landscape of dense forests interspersed with numerous lakes and rivers. *Open May 1–Nov 1 daily 7am–10pm. Off-season until sundown. Visitor centres open mid-May–Thanksgiving Day; Saint-Jean-des-Piles entrance open year-round. $4.25/day per car, $9.50/4 days per car. Hiking, bicycling, canoeing;* ⚠ & ✗ ☏*819/538-3232 (in season),* ☏*819/536-2638 (year-round).*

★★ **Saint-Maurice Ironworks National Historic Site.** – ☞ *13km/8mi from Trois-Rivières by Blvd des Forges. Open mid-May–Labour Day daily 9:30am–5pm; Sept & Oct Wed–Sun 9am–5pm. Nov by reservation only. Closed Dec–mid-May.* & ☏*819/378-5116.* Established in 1729, these ironworks produced a variety of implements, including stoves, guns, ploughshares and dumbbells until 1883, when the iron ore and wood of the region were depleted. Only ruins remain, but the shapes of the original buildings are suggested by metal structures resembling scaffolding. At the **blast furnace**, displays explain the smelting process. Beside the river, a spring known as **Devil's Fountain** emits natural gas.

French terms used in the text and on the maps in this guide:

anse	cove, bay
autoroute	highway
baie	bay
belvédère	viewpoint
cap	cape
centrale hydro-électrique	hydro-electric power station
centre d'accueil	welcome centre
centre d'interprétation	interpretation centre
chute	waterfall
côte	shore, coast
croisière	cruise, boat trip
Est	east
écluse	lock
église	church
gare	train station
hôtel de ville	city hall
île	island
jardin	garden
lac	lake
maison	house
manoir	manor
métro	subway
monastère	monastery
mont	mount
montagne	mountain
moulin	mill
musée	museum
Nord	north
Ouest	west
palais de justice	courthouse
parc	park
phare	lighthouse
place	square
plage	beach
pont	bridge
rapides	rapids
réserve faunique	wildlife conservation area
rivière	river
rocher	rock
rue	street
stationnement	parking
Sud	south
téléphérique	gondola
traversier	ferry boat
vallée	valley
ville	city, town

Atlantic Provinces

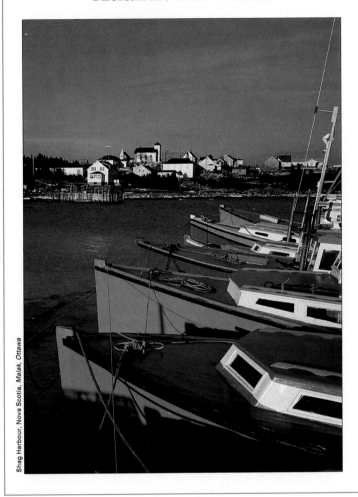

Shag Harbour, Nova Scotia, *Malak, Ottawa*

Battered by the Atlantic Ocean on one side and washed by the calmer Gulf of St Lawrence on the other, Canada's four Atlantic seacoast provinces—New Brunswick, Nova Scotia, Prince Edward Island and Newfoundland (including Labrador)—lie on the eastern side of the continent. The so-called Maritime provinces (New Brunswick, Nova Scotia and Prince Edward Island) together with Newfoundland, share the pervasive influence of the sea, which has molded, in great measure, their economic, political and cultural development.

GEOGRAPHICAL NOTES

Parts of the region, notably northern New Brunswick and Cape Breton Island, are hilly, lying near the end of the **Appalachian Mountain** chain. In the western part of Newfoundland, the **Long Range Mountains** (average height 610m/2,000ft) are a continuation of this chain. A harsh, mountainous land, Labrador contrasts to Prince Edward Island with its stretches of flat lowland.

Barren and rocky by the sea while densely forested inland, the landmasses possess some fertile areas, however—the Saint John River Valley, the Annapolis Valley, and the whole of Prince Edward Island. Their long, deeply indented coastlines are ruggedly beautiful, studded with bays, inlets, cliffs and coves (Newfoundland alone has 9,660km/6,000mi of shoreline). Remarkable for its rapid tides, the **Bay of Fundy** produces the phenomenal tidal bore *(p 191)*. The highest recorded tide in the world occurred at **Burncoat Head** *(map p 183)* on the Nova Scotia shore: a difference of 16.6m/ 54ft was measured between high and low tides.

Climate. – The sea determines the climate of this region. Moving south down the Atlantic coast, the cold **Labrador Current** enters the Gulf of St Lawrence by the Strait of Belle Isle. Because the region lies on the eastern side of an immense landmass, however, it receives air currents from the interior, since air masses generally move from west to east at these latitudes. Meeting warmer air currents off the continent, the cold waters of the Current can cause fogs throughout the year—less so in summer—along Newfoundland's and Nova Scotia's coasts especially.

Winters are stormy along the Atlantic but milder than inland. Coastal cities such as Halifax and St John's record a mean daily maximum in January of 0°C/32°F and 1°C/30°F respectively, whereas in northwestern New Brunswick extreme minimum temperatures of -34°C/-30°F are experienced.

Summers are cooler and less humid than in Ontario and Quebec at the same latitude. The coast is cooler than inland (Halifax 23°C/74°F, July mean daily maximum; Saint John 21°C/70°F) whereas extreme maximum temperatures in excess of 38°C/100°F have been recorded in northwestern New Brunswick.

In general, precipitation is evenly distributed throughout the year. Precipitation is greatest annually along the coasts of Newfoundland (St John's 1,345mm/53in) and Nova Scotia (Halifax 1,372mm/54in) and least in Newfoundland's interior (Gander 1,016mm/40in) and northwestern New Brunswick (1,016mm/40in). The Great Northern Peninsula of Newfoundland is the driest region. Snow falls in all the provinces, but is heaviest in northwestern New Brunswick (254-305cm/100-120in) and lightest along the coast (Halifax 163cm/64in). Labrador experiences a severer climate than other parts of the region with more extreme temperatures but less precipitation. Goose Bay registers a mean maximum of 14°C/7°F in January, and 21°C/70°F in July, with 737mm/29in of precipitation annually. With its sub-Arctic climate, Northern Labrador is colder: winter mean temperatures, recorded at sea level, average -20°C/-4°F.

Population. – More than two million people live in the Atlantic provinces, with Nova Scotia the most populous (899,942), followed by New Brunswick (723,900). Prince Edward Island has the lowest population (129,765). The majority of inhabitants claim origins in the British Isles (England, Scotland and Ireland). The most homogeneous of any province, Newfoundland sustains a population of 568,474 with 98 percent declaring English as their mother tongue. Yet there is a noticeable French-speaking minority in the region (largely Acadians), concentrated as follows: 1 percent in Newfoundland in the St George's/Port au Port region; 4 percent in Nova Scotia; 17 percent in Prince Edward Island; and 34 percent in New Brunswick (mainly in the north and east). Nearly 30 percent of Nova Scotia's population is of Scottish

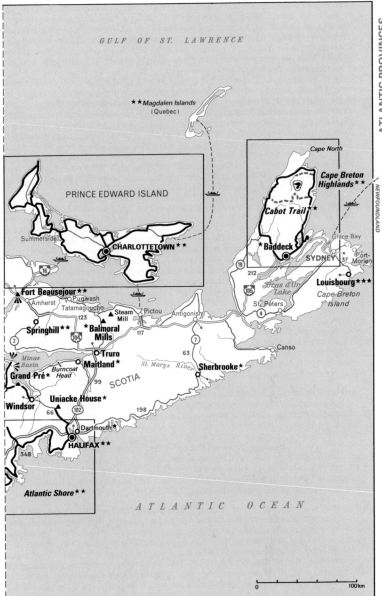

origin, living mainly in Cape Breton Island and on the shores of Northumberland Strait; another 4 percent living on the south coast, west of Halifax, have German origins. Micmacs are the most populous of native Indians in Newfoundland, New Brunswick and Nova Scotia. Inuit and Montagnais-Naskapi Indians are found primarily in northern Labrador. The black population, which accounts for less than 1 percent of the region's inhabitants, is concentrated primarily in the towns of Nova Scotia and New Brunswick.

HISTORICAL NOTES

Native Peoples. – Before the arrival of Europeans, the Atlantic provinces were inhabited by Indians of the **Eastern Woodlands** culture *(map p 17)*: **Micmacs** in New Brunswick, Nova Scotia and Prince Edward Island lived by hunting and fishing; **Maliseets** cultivated the land in southern New Brunswick like their Iroquoian brothers in Ontario *(p 101)*; and **Beothuk** in Newfoundland also fished and hunted. As their ancestors had done, the latter painted themselves with red-powdered ochre, perhaps the origin of the term "redskins." The Beothuk's belief that all goods were held in common increased hostilities with the early European fishermen who frequently found their supplies missing. Mass murder and European diseases diminished these natives greatly. The last known surviving Beothuk died in St John's in 1829.

The First Europeans. – Although he is credited as the first European arrival, **John Cabot** (1450-1498)—an Italian navigator on a 1497 voyage of discovery for England's Henry VII—was not the first European to set foot in the region. One school of thought claims the Norse settled in Nova Scotia about AD 1000, but irrefutable evidence is lacking. Archaeological remains prove that the Norse settled on the Newfoundland coast at that time *(p 222)*. There is reason to believe the **Irish** reached the province's shore in the 6C, and it is possible that **Basques** fished the North Atlantic as early as the 14C. At Red Bay in Labrador, archaeologists have discovered the presence of a large 16C Basque whaling port. Cabot's importance lies in his publicizing the region's rich fisheries. The Basques, English, French, Portuguese and Spanish came for the cod, especially abundant off Newfoundland's Grand Banks *(p 218)*. Dried on racks on shore, the fish was light, almost indestructible, and easily transportable to a ready market in Europe.

Settlement was discouraged by the English West Country merchant owners of the fishing fleets, who feared competition from a resident population. Before the close of the 16C, English fishermen established small communities on Newfoundland's coasts, despite stiff anti-settlement laws. In 1583, Newfoundland—the subject of great rivalry in Europe—was proclaimed the territory of Elizabeth I *(p 223)* at St John's. Only the French attempted to wrest control of the region from the English. **Jacques Cartier** *(p 213)* had claimed Prince Edward Island for France in 1534, renaming it Île-St-Jean, but serious attempts to colonize it were not forthcoming until the 18C. French efforts at settlement met with success in Nova Scotia, largely with the aid of the Micmacs who taught them survival skills, when Sieur de Monts and Samuel de Champlain established **Port Royal** in 1605 *(p 198)*.

"New Scotland". – Port Royal fell to a force from Virginia in 1613 and, although the French reestablished it later, in the interim it was British. In 1621, James I granted present-day Nova Scotia, Prince Edward Island and New Brunswick to **Sir William Alexander** to establish a "New Scotland" there (both men were Scots)—hence the Latin name *Nova Scotia* used on the original charter. The settlements Alexander founded were short-lived, and in 1632 Charles I, who apparently did not share his father's desire for a New Scotland, returned the region to the French by the Treaty of St-Germain-en-Laye. The future Nova Scotia had nonetheless been born—the coat of arms granted in 1621 is still the provincial emblem today.

"Acadie". – Acadie (Acadia) was what the French called a vague area covering much of Nova Scotia, New Brunswick, Prince Edward Island and Maine. The Acadians are descendants mainly of French colonists who came from western France to La Have and Port Royal between 1632 and 1651. As their numbers grew, settlements spread along the Annapolis Valley to the Minas Basin and Chignecto Isthmus *(p 188)*. Repeatedly attacked by expeditions from New England during the Anglo-French wars of the 17C, these settlements changed hands several times.

British Regime. – The English Crown granted a few charters in the 17C for colonies on Newfoundland, but authority for local law and order, granted in 1634 by Charles I, belonged largely to the **fishing admiral**—master of the first British ship to enter a harbour, regardless if there were residents. Fear of French expansion prompted the British to create permanent settlements in Newfoundland. Only with a strong, stable base could Britain properly defend her Atlantic harbours from the French who attacked from their colony at **Placentia**, established in 1662. French claims to the region ended in 1713 when, by the Treaty of Utrecht, France retained only the small islands of **Saint-Pierre and Miquelon** *(p 226)* and ceded all of mainland Nova Scotia to the British. Port Royal, renamed Annapolis Royal, became its capital *(p 198)*.

Nova Scotia Again. – The Treaty of Utrecht gave Acadians the choice of leaving British territory, or becoming British subjects. Taking an oath of allegiance to Britain would mean possibly having to bear arms against fellow Frenchmen. Leaving the area would deprive them of their rich farmlands. The Acadians maintained they were neutral, stating they would take the oath with exemption from military service. Initially the British governor agreed—his soldiers needed provisions that the Acadians supplied. In peaceful times the agreement may have lasted, but Anglo-French fighting in Europe was renewed and British rule in Nova Scotia was threatened by the building of Louisbourg *(p 210)*. Acadian sympathy for the French cause was undeniable, though it seems likely most Acadians were truly neutral. Then, in 1747, nearly 100 New England soldiers billeted in the village of Grand Pré were killed, as they slept, in a surprise attack by a French force from Quebec. Treachery among the Acadian inhabitants was suspected.

Acadian Deportation. – Fear of future attacks hardened the British toward the Acadians, especially after 1749 when Halifax was founded with 2,500 English settlers *(p 00)* who could provision the army. In 1755, **Governor Charles Lawrence** delivered his ultimatum—take an unqualified oath of allegiance or be removed from Nova Scotia. When the Acadians refused, Lawrence quickly issued the Deportation Order, with no reference to Britain. Over the next 8 years, 14,600 Acadians were forcibly deported. Others escaped to Quebec. Families were separated, some never to be reunited. Unwelcomed in the colonies, the Acadians were able to establish a new community only in Louisiana and, as **Cajuns**, survive to this day. Some escaped to Saint-Pierre and Miquelon. Others fled to Île-St-Jean until 1758 when the island was captured by a British expedition under **Lord Rolo**, and later annexed by Nova Scotia. Left untouched was a small settlement in the Malpeque area, the origins of Prince Edward Island's French-speaking population today. When peace was restored between England and France in 1763, most exiles returned to Nova Scotia only to find their rich farmlands occupied by new English colonists. The Acadians settled mainly in New Brunswick, where their descendants live to this day.

Scots, Loyalists and Other Settlers. – After Deportation, the British offered free land to anyone willing to settle in Nova Scotia. New Englanders from the south, groups from the British Isles and from the German states along the Rhine, and the first wave of Scottish Highlanders accepted the offer. Dispossessed by big landowners who sought profit in sheep raising over tenant farming, the first 200 Scots who arrived in 1773 settled mainly in Cape Breton *(p 204)*, Pictou, Antigonish and on Prince Edward Island.

In 1775 when revolution erupted in the American colonies, it appeared Nova Scotia would join the other 13. Instead it became a receiving point for 30,000 Loyalists who fled the new US after the war *(p 193)*. Their arrival transformed Nova Scotia. A separate administration was set up in 1784 and called New Brunswick for the German duchy of Braunschweig-Lüneburg, governed at that time by England's George III. Other Loyalists settled in Prince Edward Island, which was separated from Nova Scotia in 1769 and named in 1799 in honour of the father of Queen Victoria *(p 213)*.

Confederation. – In September 1864, representatives of Nova Scotia, New Brunswick and Prince Edward Island met with a delegation from Canada (then only Ontario and Quebec) to discuss British union in North America. This historic conference *(p 213)* paved the way for Confederation in 1867. The Island refused at first to join, but entered in 1873, pressured by Britain and threatened with impending bankruptcy from railway construction. Although its representatives attended the final conference in Quebec in October 1864, Newfoundland chose not to join, holding out until 1949 when it became Canada's tenth province.

RESOURCES

The Atlantic provinces benefit from their vast forests as well as from other land resources. Magnificent scenery has made tourism a major factor in the provincial economies, and the sea constitutes a rich resource on which the Atlantic provinces have long depended.

Fishing Industry. – Overtaken in value by manufacturing and mining, coastal fishing is still important to Newfoundland's economy. Cod remains the great catch as it has been since the 15C. (In Newfoundland cod is synonymous with "fish"; all other varieties such as herring, caplin or salmon are referred to by name.) Extending 500km/300mi from the coast, the submerged continental shelf known as the **Grand Banks** *(p 218)* is one of the most extensive fish breeding grounds in the world. In 1992, the Canadian government placed a two-year moratorium on cod fishing off the northeast coast of the island *(p 218)*.

Maritime Fishing. – Nova Scotia's commercial fishery ranks second in Canada behind British Columbia, while New Brunswick's share of the east coast fishing industry is 18 percent. Nova Scotia has an off-shore fleet that fishes the Banks, but 70 percent of its fishermen are based inshore. The most valuable catch for the three Maritime provinces is **lobster**. Since the season is tightly controlled, saltwater pounds keep the catch year round to be sold fresh on the world market. Most of these pounds are located in New Brunswick, notably on Deer Island *(p 192)*. The province is also known for its sardines and Atlantic salmon, Prince Edward Island is famous for Malpeque **oysters**, and Nova Scotia for Digby **scallops**. Giant **bluefin tuna** are caught off the shores of all three provinces. In New Brunswick and in Nova Scotia, north of Dartmouth, **aquaculture** is a provincial-supported industry, concentrating on the cultivation of mussels, clams and oysters.

Sealing. – The catching of seals for their skins and meat is as old as settlement in Newfoundland. In the spring, adult seals and their white-coated whelps leave their breeding grounds in the Arctic, floating south on ice floes carried by the Labrador Current. Scores of small boats set sail full of sealers for whom the mammals are an important part of their livelihood.
In recent years these hunts have become controversial, especially the means by which the seals are killed. A government ban now prohibits the use of long poles, which enable sealers to vault from ice floe to ice floe and double as clubs to kill the baby seals.

Agriculture. – Agriculture is important to the economies of the Maritimes, but it is the backbone of Prince Edward Island. While the Island supports a wide range of farming, it is most famous for its **potatoes**. Together with New Brunswick, Prince Edward Island produces more than 70 percent of Canada's domestic seed potatoes and 44 percent of the country's potato exports. The Saint John River Valley *(p 195)* and the Annapolis Valley *(p 200)* are the region's other great agricultural areas. Farms do exist in glacier-ravaged Newfoundland on **Avalon Peninsula** and in **Codroy Valley**, but they supply local markets only.

Forestry. – Land not under cultivation in New Brunswick (89 percent) and Nova Scotia (77 percent) supports a sizeable forest industry. Recently, New Brunswick's **pulp, paper** and **lumber** industries have expanded to overtake agriculture in domestic production. Previously dependent upon the fishing industry, Newfoundland's economy has diversified to include mining, and manufacture based on forest resources.

Mining and Energy. – **Iron ore** has been mined in Newfoundland since the turn of the century. The Bell Island works in Conception Bay, now closed, were important enough to be attacked twice by German submarines. Today the mines of the **Labrador Trough** in western Labrador produce most of the province's iron ore. Labrador City is the site of one of the world's largest open-pit mining, concentrate and pelletizing operations. Lead, zinc, copper, gold, silver, asbestos and gypsum are also mined in the province.
New Brunswick is the only Maritime province in which mining contributes to the economy. Zinc, lead and copper deposits are located near Bathurst, antimony near Fredericton and potash near Sussex. In Nova Scotia, **coal**, gypsum, salt, gold and tin are mined. Once a mainstay of the economy, Nova Scotia's coal industry slumped badly after World War II. Today, with renewed interest in coal as a fuel, several mines are operating again, producing metallurgical coal for refining steel, and thermal coal for generating electricity.
New Brunswick is also the only Maritime Province with significant electric power resources. The Saint John River has been harnessed in several locations, notably Mactaquac *(p 195)*. Labrador's **hydro-electric** potential is enormous. Virtually all the power produced by the huge generating station at **Churchill Falls** goes to the province

of Quebec. Technology is being developed for exploitation of the considerable **nat-ural gas** and **oil** reserves off Newfoundland and Labrador, hindered at present by drifting icebergs. Both New Brunswick and Nova Scotia plan to harness the mighty Bay of Fundy tides, a pilot project having opened at Annapolis Royal in 1983 *(p 199)*.

Manufacturing. – There is relatively little manufacturing industry in the Maritimes due to their distance from markets in central Canada, although Nova Scotia and New Brunswick have good road and rail links, and their ice-free ports are open all year. Except for scientific, medical and high tech industries in Halifax, what industry there is relies largely on local products—fish packing, food processing, etc. However, Nova Scotia supports an auto assembly and parts manufacturing industry, steel is refined at Sydney *(p 207)*, and oil at Saint John. Newfoundland's large-scale man-ufacturing includes a phosphorus plant at Long Harbour, shipbuilding at Marystown *(p 219)*, and paint manufacture at St John's.

RECREATION

Parks. – All four provinces have excellent national and provincial parks with camp-ing facilities and activities. Washed by the surprisingly warm waters of the Gulf of St Lawrence *(p 215)*, Prince Edward Island National Park has lovely beaches. Miles of sand dunes are part of New Brunswick's **Kouchibouguac National Park**. Hiking trails abound in the province's Fundy National Park *(p 190)*, Mactaquac Provincial Park and Mt Carleton Provincial Park, as they do in Nova Scotia's National Park in Cape Breton's Highlands *(p 205)* and Newfoundland's national parks *(pp 220 and 227)*.

Water Sports. – With so much coastline, the provinces offer unparalleled oppor-tunities for swimming, boating and sailing. Water temperatures are surprisingly warm off Prince Edward Island's northern shores and New Brunswick's North-umberland Strait, in the vicinity of Shediac's Parlee Beach Provincial Park. Those who find Atlantic waters rough for boating may prefer huge Bras d'Or Lake in Cape Breton, or the beautiful Saint John River *(p 195)* where **houseboats** can be rented by the week. Canoeing is gaining popularity in this region: **Kejimkujik National Park** *(p 199)* has several routes, and there are sailing and canoeing opportunities in Newfound-land's lakes and rivers. **Sea kayaking** is offered along Nova Scotia's eastern shore, off Cape Breton in particular, and **river rafting** is available on the province's Medway River, or even the Fundy Tidal Bore. **Windsurfing** is practiced on the bays and off the northshore beaches of Prince Edward Island, particularly Stanhope Beach, in the Eel River Bar of New Brunswick's Restigouche region and off the Acadian Peninsula.

Fishing. – Trout and salmon fishing in Newfoundland and Labrador are probably unequalled elsewhere in eastern North America. A famous place to watch the salmon leap *(August)* is **Squires Memorial Park** near Deer Lake *(map p 218)*. Especially noted for its Atlantic **salmon** are the Margaree Valley in Nova Scotia and the Miramichi and Restigouche valleys of northern New Brunswick. **Fly fishing** is the only legal method for anglers to catch salmon in Nova Scotia. **Deep-sea fishing** is popular in the Maritimes, where boats can be chartered.

Whale Watching. – Whales usually can be seen throughout the summer (August and September, especially) off the coasts of Newfoundland, New Brunswick and Nova Scotia. Cruises are available in Newfoundland in the vicinity of St John's *(p 226)*, Terra Nova National Park, Trinity and Twillingate. Deer Island, Grand Manan Island and St Andrews are departure points for whale-watching voyages in New Brunswick. In Nova Scotia, cruises depart from northern Cape Breton Island and from Digby Neck. Humpback, finback and minke are just some of the varieties that can be seen. Tour boats attempt to get close to the mammals for a memorable sound and sight experience.

Bird Watching. – There are many popular birding areas in the region, especially along the coasts. The bird population of **Grand Manan Island** *(p 193)* drew James Audubon to its shores to sketch its many species. In Nova Scotia, south of Liverpool, the **Seaside Adjunct** of Kejimkujik National Park protects a breeding grounds for pip-ing plovers. Yarmouth harbours cormorants and black-backed gulls. The **Bird Islands** attract a variety of sea birds to its protected sanctuaries and McNab's Island in Halifax harbour provides a nesting site for osprey. Bald eagles can be seen in the Bras d'Or Lake area as well as in Cape Breton Highlands National Park.
Of the 520 species found in Canada, 300 have been recorded in Newfoundland (and on Prince Edward Island as well). At its three famous sea bird colonies—**Cape St Mary's**, **Witless Bay** and **Funk Island** *(map p 218)*—gannets, murres, kittiwake gulls, razorbilled auks, puffins, guillemots and dovekies can be observed. Bald eagles, and even occasionally a golden eagle, are sighted along the south coast.

Other Activities. – **Adventure tours** on foot, by river boat or even **snowmobiles** (in Labrador) are offered by outfitters in the wilds of Newfoundland. Operating mainly out of Halifax, wilderness expeditions in Nova Scotia can include back-packing, pho-tography and even cross-country skiing.
Helicopter tours depart Prince Edward Island in March for the ice fields of the Gulf of St Lawrence where thousands of baby harp seals can be seen. Year-round flight-seeing tours of Newfoundland and Labrador, some by **seaplane** or helicopter, originate in St John's. Both Prince Edward Island and New Brunswick contain some excellent golf courses.

Winter Sports. – Downhill slopes and cross-country skiing trails are located in the northern part of Nova Scotia, notably Cape Breton Island. A number of snowmobile clubs have trails, accessible to the public, in the province's open fields and woods. Charlo bills itself as New Brunswick's cross-country ski capital. The province boasts some alpine ski centres as well. Skating on frozen ponds and lakes, and winter camping are popular in the region.

New Brunswick

Map p 182

Bounded by the US on the west and Quebec to the north, New Brunswick is the Atlantic provinces' connection to the continental mainland. Separated from Prince Edward Island by the Northumberland Strait, the province is linked to Nova Scotia by the narrow Chignecto Isthmus. An extensive coastline faces Chaleur Bay in the north, the Gulf of St Lawrence to the east and the Bay of Fundy in the south. Extending into the bay are the three **Fundy islands** of Deer, Campobello and Grand Manan *(p 191)*.

The 73,436sq km/28,354sq mi interior consists of mountainous uplands reaching 820m/2,690ft in the northwest, central highlands of hills 610m/2,000ft above sea level, the nearly L-shaped Saint John River Valley draining at the southern tidal shore, and a sloping plain extending east to Chaleur Bay.

Practical Information

How to get there. – Air Canada and its affiliates provide direct **air** service to Saint John and Fredericton. Northwest Airlink offers flights from the US. **VIA Rail** connects Saint John from Montreal (12hrs one-way). Government-operated ferries (free) provide service in the lower Saint John River area and to islands in the Bay of Fundy. A **ferry** connects Saint John with Digby, NS.

Accommodation and Tourist Information. – The official tourist office publishes an annual travel guide giving information on history, attractions and scheduled events. Government-inspected hotels and motels ($45-60/night), Bed & Breakfast and country inns, farm vacations and campgrounds are also listed. For a free copy of the guide and a map contact:

Tourism New Brunswick, PO Box 12345, Fredericton, NB, E3B 5C3 ☎800/561-0123 (toll-free Canada/US).

Language. – New Brunswick is officially bilingual; approximately 35% of the population speaks French. All road signs are in English and French.

Road Regulations. – Speed limits, unless otherwise posted, are 80km/h (50mph) on provincial highways and 50km/h (30mph) in cities. **Seat belt** use is mandatory. **Canadian Automobile Association (CAA)** Saint John ☎506/634-1400.

Time Zone. – New Brunswick is on Atlantic Standard Time. Daylight Saving Time is observed from the first Sunday in April to the last Sunday in October.

Taxes. – The national GST of 7% *(rebate information p 242)*, and a provincial sales tax of 11% (some items are exempt) are levied.

Liquor Laws. – The legal drinking age is 19. Liquor is sold in government stores.

Provincial Holidays *(see National Holidays p 240)*
New Brunswick Day .... 1st Monday in August

Principal Festivals

Jun-Jul	Salmon Festival	Campbellton
Jul	Loyalist Days Festival	Saint John
	Lobster Festival	Shediac
Jul-Aug	Foire Brayonne	Edmundston
Aug	Acadian Festival	Caraquet
Sept	Harvest Jazz and Blues Festival	Fredericton

The Saint John River. – Named by Champlain and de Monts *(p 199)* in honour of Saint John, this largely tranquil, 673km/418mi river flows northeast from northern Maine along the US/New Brunswick border to empty into the Bay of Fundy.

Between Edmundston and Grand Falls, rural villages intersperse the farmed river valley. Turbulent at Grand Falls gorge, the river cascades over 25m/76ft cataracts and 18m/59ft at Beechwood—both sites of hydro-electric dams. After the provincial capital of **Fredericton**, the river gradually broadens, traversing a picturesque valley of patchwork farmland. Fertile soil in its upper and lower regions sustains extensive cultivation, particularly the north's thriving **potato** industry. At the city of its namesake, the river is thrown back by the mighty Fundy tides in a slim gorge called **Reversing Falls** *(p 194)*. Fredericton and the major port city of **Saint John** are situated on the banks of this important waterway. Today, the river carries little except pleasure boaters and sailing enthusiasts who find its wide expanses and deep waters a paradise, especially in the lower sections.

Era of Wooden Ships. – Pre-Loyalists and Loyalists established a great industry—the building of ships of timber cut from the region's forests, especially New Brunswick's. Beginning as mast making for British naval vessels, the industry grew, particularly at Saint John, which became one of the world's great shipbuilding centres by the mid-19C. Two brothers who opened a shipyard in Chatham were to become famous as founders of the **Cunard line**. Skilled craftsmen perfected clipper ships, schooners, brigs and barques for worldwide use as shipyards sprang up along the coasts of Nova Scotia and Prince Edward Island.

By Confederation in 1867, New Brunswick was well established and wealthy. In the latter half of the 19C, the province was the most prosperous in Canada. The prosperity did not last, however. By 1900, steam replaced sail power and steel hulls superseded wooden ones. Lack of foresight doomed the shipbuilding industry; only a few shipyards converted their operations to the newer technology. By World War I, wooden ships were no longer built, and the age of prominence was over.

Cultural Heritage. – The social fabric of New Brunswick was woven over two centuries by a diverse population of Micmac and Maliseet natives, New England Loyalists, Acadians, Scots, Irish, Germans, Danes and Dutch. Each group has left its imprint in the pioneer structures and celebrated traditions of rural communities and coastal villages throughout the province. The richness of provincial place names, such as Kouchibouguac, Memramcook, Shediac and Richibucto, stems from original Indian designations. The Brayons' custom of flying the flag of their "republic," the Acadians' yearly "Blessing of the Fleet," Canada's largest Irish festival, an annual folk music celebration and a francophone festival featuring performers from France, Belgium and Louisiana illustrate the cultural variety of the province. Traditional feasts of seafood—particularly salmon, clams, oysters and lobster—or of earth's bounty ("corn boils," strawberry fests, "spud" days and even a brussel sprout festival) are staged from May through October. Generations have enjoyed hot Hodge Podge, a mix of new potatoes and vegetables in milk. Acadian potato and clam pie, a Loyalist dish of fish chowder, and buckwheat pancakes topped with maple syrup are old-time favourites. Historic settlements such as **Kings Landing** *(p 195)*, MacDonald Farm Historic Park *(p 191)* and Acadian Historical Village preserve the pioneer skills and crafts of the province's founders.

★★ FORT BEAUSEJOUR

Map p 183

Overlooking the Cumberland Basin—an arm of Chignecto Bay—the Missiguash River Valley, and the Tantramar Marshes, this former French fort is exceptional for its impressive **panorama★★** of the surrounding country *(fog or rain may hamper visibility)*. The scant remains of the mid-18C outpost testify to its turbulent history during the Anglo-French conflict in the New World.

The fort stands on the Chignecto Isthmus, a narrow strip of land joining New Brunswick and Nova Scotia, which once marked the division between French and British lands. In 1672, the Acadians first settled in this area, which they called Beaubassin, reclaiming it from the sea by an extensive system of dikes. After the Treaty of Utrecht ceded mainland Nova Scotia to Britain in 1713, they found themselves in the middle of a border conflict. The British built Fort Lawrence on their side of the isthmus; the French built Fort Beausejour on theirs. Captured in 1755 by a British force under Col Robert Moncton, the latter was renamed Fort Cumberland. The Acadians were the first to be removed from the land under the Deportation Order *(p 184)* of that same year. Strengthened by the British, the fort withstood an attack in 1776 by New England settlers sympathetic to the American Revolution. Although manned during the War of 1812, the outpost saw no further military action. In 1926, the fort, rechristened Fort Beausejour, was designated a National Historic Park.

Access. – *At Aulac near Nova Scotia border, just off Trans-Can Hwy, Exit 550A.*

Visit. – ☞ *Open Jun–mid-Oct daily 9am–5pm.* ⬥ ☎506/536-0720. The **visitor centre** houses displays on the history of the fort, the Acadians and the region. Three restored underground casemates can be visited, and the earthworks are in good repair.

★★ FREDERICTON   Pop 46,466

Map p 182   Tourist Office ☎506/452-9500

Set on a bend in the placid Saint John River, opposite its junction with the Nashwaak River, this quiet city of elm-lined streets and elegant houses is the capital of New Brunswick. Largely because of the munificence of a locally raised benefactor, **Lord Beaverbrook**, the city is also the cultural centre of the province.

From Fort to Capital. – In 1692, the French governor of Acadie, Joseph Robineau de Villebon, constructed a fort at the mouth of the Nashwaak. Soon abandoned, the fort became an Acadian settlement called St Anne's Point, which survived until the Seven Years' War. However, Fredericton's true beginning came, like Saint John's, with the arrival of the Loyalists *(p 193)* in 1783. Upon the formation of the province in 1784, the settlement they founded, complete with a college that is now the **University of New Brunswick**, was chosen as the capital. The more obvious choice, Saint John, was considered a less central site, vulnerable to sea attack. Named Fredericton after the second son of George III, the new capital soon became the social centre for the governor and the town's military garrison. Garden parties, gala dinners and visits from royalty were commonplace. In many ways, little has changed in this century. The vast majority of the population works for the provincial government or the university.

Lord Beaverbrook. – Born William Maxwell Aitken in Ontario, and reared in Newcastle, New Brunswick, Lord Beaverbrook (1879-1964) was a successful businessman in Canada before leaving for England in 1910. After entering politics, he was elevated to the peerage in 1917, adopting his title from a small New Brunswick town. Having founded Beaverbrook Newspapers, he built a vast empire on London's Fleet Street. Influential in the government of **Winston Churchill**, he held several key cabinet posts during World War II. Although absent from the province most of his life, Beaverbrook never forgot New Brunswick. In addition to gifts to Newcastle, he financed, in whole or in part, an art gallery, a theatre and several university buildings in Fredericton.

SIGHTS *Map below. 3hrs.*

Stretching along the southern bank of the Saint John River, the strip of parkland known as **The Green★** is one of Fredericton's most attractive landscapes. This grassy, tree-lined expanse provides a lovely setting for the city's historic buildings.

★★ **Beaverbrook Art Gallery.** – *Open Jul–Labour Day Tue–Wed 10am– 8pm; Thur– Sat 10am– 5pm; Sun–Mon noon– 8pm. Off-season Tue–Sat 10am–5pm, Sun–Mon noon–5pm. Closed Christmas & New Year's. $3. ও ☎506/458-8545.* Designed

and built by Lord Beaverbrook, the original structure was his gift to the people of New Brunswick. Opened in 1959 and expanded in 1983, the gallery is a major art centre of Atlantic Canada, featuring the donor's personally selected collection of British, European and Canadian art. At the gallery's entrance is Salvador Dali's huge surrealistic canvas, **Santiago el Grande**, depicting St James on horseback being carried to heaven. Particularly strong in portraiture, the collection of British art is the most comprehensive in Canada. Paintings by Hogarth, Lawrence, Romney, Gainsborough and Reynolds are juxtaposed with striking works by Turner, Stanley Spencer, Augustus John and Graham Sutherland *(Portrait of Lord Beaverbrook).* An important collection of 18C and 19C English porcelain complements the artwork. Continental Europe is represented by paintings by Cranach, Botticelli, Delacroix, Tissot, Corneille de Lyon and Ribera. Fine European tapestries and furniture are arranged in period settings. The **Canadian Collection** features works by most of the country's best-known artists including Cornelius Krieghoff, Emily Carr, David Milne, Paul Kane and the Group of Seven.

★ **Legislative Building.** – *Open daily year-round. Closed legal holidays. ✗ ও ☎506/ 453-2527.* Opposite the art gallery stands the stately Georgian seat of provincial government, with its classical dome and double-columned portico. Constructed of

sandstone in 1880, this building replaced the old Province Hall, which was destroyed by fire. Visitors are permitted to see the assembly chamber with its tiered balcony and to view **portraits** of George III and Queen Charlotte by Joshua Reynolds. The parliamentary library is reached by a striking wooden spiral staircase.

★ **Christ Church Cathedral.**–This elegant stone church, distinguished by a copper-green spire and pointed arch windows, is surrounded by large, attractive Loyalist-built frame houses and tall shade trees. Completed in 1853, the church, modelled after the parish church of St Mary in Snettisham,

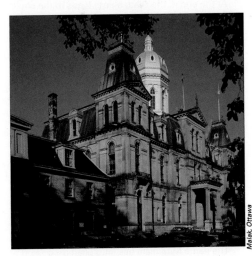

Legislative Building, Fredericton

Malak, Ottawa

Norfolk, is an example of decorated Gothic Revival architecture. The interior is dominated by a hammer-beam wooden pointed **ceiling**. At the entrance to the south transept stands a cenotaph with a **marble effigy** of the Rt Rev John Medley, the first bishop of Fredericton.

★ **Military Compound.** – *Changing of the guard daily in summer, weather permitting.* The central location of the former British military headquarters shows the importance of the infantry garrison in early Fredericton. (Today, the country's major military training area—Canadian Armed Forces Base Gagetown—lies just to the southeast.) In 1869, shortly after Confederation, the British garrison vacated the quarters. Once stretching from Queen Street to the river between York and Regent streets, the compound retains few of its original buildings.

Now a pleasant park known as **Officers' Square**, the old parade ground is the site of the former **officers' quarters**, a three-storey stone building with white arches, constructed in 1839 with additions in 1851. A few blocks to the west, the **Old Guard House [A]**, built in 1827, stands adjacent to the **soldiers' barracks [B]**, a stone building with red-painted wooden terraces. Both have been restored and furnished *(open daily late-Jun– Labour Day; ☎506/453-3747).*

York-Sunbury Historical Society Museum [M]. – *In Officers' Quarters. Open daily May– Labour Day. Off-season Mon–Sat. Mid-Oct–Apr by appointment. ☎506/455-6041.* This museum provides a portrait of the Fredericton area from its settlement by the Indian population to the present. Exhibits on the Loyalists and the garrison are included, and a World War I trench has been reconstructed. The mounted Coleman frog, which weighed 19kg/42lbs, is on display.

EXCURSION

★★ **Kings Landing Historical Settlement.** – *37km/23mi. Description p 195.*

★★ FUNDY NATIONAL PARK

Map p 182

Extending nearly 13km/8mi along the Bay of Fundy's steep seacliffs, this rolling parkland is cut by rivers and streams in deep valleys. Created by the bay's 9m/29ft tides, the vast tidal flats, explorable at low tide, contain a wealth of marine life.

Access. – *77km/48mi south of Moncton by Rte 114.*

Visit. – *☞ Open year-round. Golf, boat rental, swimming, tennis, mountain biking, hiking. Information centre (east entrance) open late-May–early-Oct daily 9am–9pm. ⚠ ☎506/887-2000. Accommodation late-May–Thanksgiving ☎506/887-2930 or 506/887-2808. Note: views described may be obscured by fog.*

Eastern Park Entrance. – From the park gate, there is a fine **view★** of the tranquil Upper Salmon River, the hills to the north, the small fishing village of Alma, Owl's Head and the bay. To appreciate the contrast, visit at both low and high tides.

Herring Cove. – *11km/7mi from entrance.* At the end of the road, there is a good **view★** of the cove from above and a display on the tides. A path leads down to a cove that has tidal pools brimming with limpets, barnacles, sea anemones and other life at low tide.

★★ **Point Wolfe.** – *10km/6mi from entrance.* The road crosses Point Wolfe River by a covered wooden bridge, below which is a small gorge forming the river's entry into Wolfe Cove. On this site a mill community once stood. To collect logs floated downstream from the north, a dam was constructed. Schooners loaded the sawn wood at wharves built in the coves. Today, only the bridge and dam remain.

At the end of the road, a path leads to the cove, providing good **views★★** on the descent. At low tide, the sand and rock pools are alive with sea creatures.

★★ HOPEWELL CAPE   Pop 757

Map p 182

35km/22mi south of Moncton by Rte 114. Directional signs en route. Morning light is best for photography. Note: Be sure to climb stairs at the posted time to avoid the 10m/32ft tides. Near this little village overlooking Shepody Bay is an interesting phenomenon known as the **Rocks★★**. Sculpted by tidal action, wind and frost, these red standstone formations, as high as 15m/50ft, stand on the beach, cut off from the cliffs. Tiny, tree-covered islands at high tide, these shapes become "giant flowerpots" at low tide, their narrow bases widening to support balsam fir and dwarf black spruce at the top. Visitors can walk around them when the tide is out and look at crevices in the cliffs that, in time, will become new flowerpots.

★ MIRAMICHI VALLEY

Map p 182

The name Miramichi has long been associated with fine salmon fishing. A major spawning ground for Atlantic salmon, the river has two branches (the Southwest Miramichi and the Little Southwest Miramichi), which together traverse the province. The area is also lumber country; Newcastle (pop 5,711) and Chatham (pop 6,544), twin towns near the river's mouth, are known for their shipbuilding past. Joseph Cunard, founder of the famous shipping line, was born in Chatham.

★ **Miramichi Salmon Museum.** – *94km/58mi from Fredericton by Rte 8 in Doaktown. Open daily Jun–Sept. $3. ⚐ ☎506/365-7787.* Overlooking a series of pools on the Miramichi River, this pleasant museum is devoted to the area's famed Atlantic salmon. Displays include boats, nets and fishing rods, migration routes, and predators. The theatre features an audio-visual show on salmon fishing, and the small aquarium contains specimens of the fish.

Central New Brunswick Woodmen's Museum. – *68km/42mi north of Frederic-ton by Rte 8 in Boiestown. Open daily May–Sept. $4.* & ☎*506/369-7214.* Set in the geographical centre of the province, this museum presents life in a lumber camp. On display is a sawmill with its original equipment and a range of tools from axes to chain saws. The re-created bunkhouse and cookhouse evoke the flavour of camp life. A small train makes a tour of the site *(runs continuously; $1).*

MacDonald Farm Historic Park. – *11km/8mi east of Chatham on Rte 11 near Bartibog Bridge. Open daily late-Jun–Labour Day; until end-Sept Wed–Sun only. $2.25.* ☎*506/773-5761.* Overlooking the Miramichi estuary, this old stone farmhouse (1820), has been restored to the period when Alexander MacDonald and his family lived in it. Beside the river, a "net" shed, complete with fishing gear, can be seen.

MONCTON

Pop 57,010

Map p 182

Tourist Office ☎ 506/853-3333

Set on a bend of the Petitcodiac River, Moncton is famous for its tidal bore, which rushes up the river from the Bay of Fundy. Named after **Robert Monckton**, the British commander in the capture of Fort Beauséjour *(p 188)*, the city is generally consid-ered the capital of Acadie.

The first settlers in the area were German and Dutch families from Pennsylvania, but they were joined by Acadians when the latter were allowed to return to British territory after Deportation. Today, one-third of the population is French-speaking, and the city boasts a French-language university, founded in 1963.

★ **The Tidal Bore.** – In the open ocean, the ebb and flow of the tide is barely notice-able, but in certain V-shaped bays or inlets, the tide enters the broad end and literally piles up as it moves up the bay. This build-up occurs in the Bay of Fundy, 77km/48mi wide at its mouth, narrowing and becoming shallower along its 233km/145mi length. Thus, the tide is squeezed as it travels the bay, a ripple increasing to a wave several feet high as it enters the rivers emptying into the bay. This wave is known as a "bore," a tidal wave of unusual height. At Moncton, the bore varies from a few inches to nearly two feet. The highest bores occur when the earth, moon and sun are aligned.

Boreview Park. – *Off Main St by the river. Bore schedules available from tourist office; arrive 15min prior to view lowest level and return 2hrs later to see high tide.* The tidal bore and the changing levels of the Petitcodiac River are best viewed from the park. A small stream at low tide, the river lies in the centre of a vast bed of red mud. At high tide, the river widens to 1.6km/1mi, and the water level increases by 7m/23ft.

EXCURSION

★ **Acadian Odyssey Historic Site.** – *20km/12.5mi southeast by Rte 106 in St-Joseph. Open daily Jun–mid-Oct.* & ☎*506/758-9783.* Located in the Lefebvre Build-ing of the **College St-Joseph**, the first Acadian institute of higher learning, the site chronicles the past struggles and present strength of this French-speaking culture. Founded by Rev Camille Lefebvre in 1864, the college trained Acadian leaders for nearly 100 years before its amalgamation with the Université de Moncton. The site of the first National Convention of Acadians in 1881, this small museum today fea-tures displays and audio-visual presentations, including those on the Memramcook Valley, one of the few regions in which Acadians maintained continuous settlement despite Deportation *(p 184).*

Harvested from the riverbanks of the Saint John in spring, edible fiddlehead ferns, boiled and topped with butter and lemon, are a New Brunswick delicacy.

★★ PASSAMAQUODDY BAY/FUNDY ISLES

Map p 192

An inlet of the Bay of Fundy between Maine and New Brunswick, this body of water is dotted with islands and indented with harbours along its irregular shoreline, which includes the estuary of the **St Croix River**. A popular resort, the area is also famous for its lobster and an edible seaweed known as **dulse**, a regional delicacy that is served in a variety of ways *(p 193).*

According to Indian legend, one day the Micmac hero-god **Glooscap** saw wolves about to attack a deer and a moose. Using his magical powers, he turned the ani-mals into islands. In 1604, Samuel de Champlain chose the bay as the site of his first settlement and spent the winter with his followers on St Croix Island (today in Maine) in the estuary of the river of the same name. However, the bleak conditions forced them to move the next year across the Bay of Fundy to Nova Scotia *(p 199).* Loyalists, arriving in 1783, settled the communities of St Stephen, St Andrews and St George, and of Deer and Campobello islands. *Fog and cold weather occur even in summer, particularly on the islands.*

★ **St Andrews.** – Pop 1,652. Situated at the end of a peninsula that juts into the bay, this charming town is lined with tree-covered residential and commercial avenues. A resort centre for summer visitors who like tranquility, and boating in pleasant sur-roundings, the town supports the **Algonquin Hotel**, one of the foremost hostelries of the province.

Founded by Loyalists, St Andrews became a prosperous mercantile and fishing town. In 1842, some of its century-old houses were floated intact across the estuary when the Webster-Ashburton Treaty declared the Canadian/US border to be the St Croix River—and some Loyalists, discovered they were on the "wrong" side of it. Among famous Canadians who have owned homes here is **Sir William Van Horne**, president of Canadian Pacific Railway from 1888 to 1899 *(p 54)*.

The town's quaint main thoroughfare, **Water Street**, mixes boutiques and cafes.

★ **HMSC Aquarium-Museum.** – *At Brandy Cove. Open daily Victoria Day–mid-Oct. $4.* ☎506/529-4285. This interesting little aquarium has fish tanks and displays on the 200-mile fishing limit, sea bird migration routes, and salmon spawning in the Atlantic provinces. The star attractions, however, are three harbour seals, which perform all kinds of antics for visitors. Films are shown regularly in the theatre.

St Andrews Blockhouse. – *On Joe's Point Road. Open daily Jun–mid-Sept.* ☎506/529-4270. Constructed during the War of 1812, the square wooden structure stands guard over the harbour. Built to protect New Brunswick's western frontier from American invasion, it is the only blockhouse remaining of the original 14 erected. Inside, there are displays on the settlement of the town and on the blockhouse itself.

★ **Deer Island.** – *Toll-free car ferry departs from Letete daily year-round 6am–6:30pm (summer until 9pm) every 30min; length of crossing 20min.* ☎506/453-2600. *From Eastport, Maine Jun–Sept daily 9am–7pm every hour; length of crossing 20min; $8/car & driver, $2/passenger* ☎506/747-2159. *Ferry from Campobello Island, see below. Note: ferries operate on first-come-first-served-basis. Lines form on weekends and peak times.* Positioned so as to nearly enclose the bay, this Fundy island is a quiet place, inhabited primarily by fishermen. The world's largest lobster pound is located on its western side.

A pleasant **trip**★ is the ferry ride to the island from Letete, among the smaller islands covered with birds. Swept by the tide in part of the narrow inlet of **Northern Harbour**, a corral where lobsters are kept year-round has been built with nets and fences. At the southern end of the island, a large whirlpool forms when the Fundy tides are running strong. Called **"Old Sow"** for the noise it makes, this vortex is visible from Deer Island Point or from the ferry to Campobello Island.

★★ **Campobello Island.** – *Pop 1,317. Car ferry departs from Deer Island Jun–Sept daily 9:15am–6:15pm every 1hr 30min. Length of crossing 45min. $11/car & driver, $2/passenger.* ☎506/747-2159. *Accessible by bridge from Lubec, Maine. Non-Americans need valid passport (p 238). See also Michelin Green Guide to New England.* Known as the "beloved island" of US President **Franklin D. Roosevelt** (1882-1945), the site is a summer resort for vacationing Americans. Sandy beaches, picturesque coves, headlands, lighthouses and an international park named in Roosevelt's honour attract numerous visitors annually.

First settled in the 1770s, Campobello was named for **William Campbell**, the governor of Nova Scotia, and for its beauty (*campo bello* means "beautiful pasture" in Italian). By the end of the 19C, it had become a retreat for wealthy Americans. In 1883, one-year-old FDR first visited the island. Thereafter, he spent summers on Campobello with his parents and later with his wife, Eleanor. He taught his five children to appreciate nature, and took them fishing, boating and swimming—activities he had done as a child. Then, in 1921, FDR contracted polio and left the island for 12 years. In 1964, the Canadian and American governments jointly established the park to commemorate him.

★★ **Roosevelt Campobello International Park.** – *Open Victoria Day–Sept 30 daily 10am–5pm.* ☎506/752-2922. Preserved as a memorial to FDR, the southern part of the island is natural parkland—forests, bogs, lakes, cliffs and beaches—crisscrossed by several lovely **drives**★★. Note the view of Passamaquoddy Bay from Friar's Head *(turn right at picnic area sign just south of visitor centre)*, and of Herring Cove from Con Robinson's Point *(follow Glensevern Rd E)*. Built in the Dutch colonial style, the red-shingled, green-roofed **cottage**★ with 34 rooms belonged to FDR. Simply furnished, the rustic interior contains personal reminders of his childhood and years as president. The west side rooms, especially the living room, have pleasant views of Friar's Bay. Films on the life of Roosevelt are shown in the **visitor centre**. North of the visitor centre, **East Quoddy Head Lighthouse**★ *(12km/7mi by Wilson's Beach and gravel road to the Point)* has a picturesque site overlooking Head Harbour Island.

★ **Grand Manan Island.** – Pop 791. *Car ferry departs Blacks Harbour six crossings daily June 26–Sept 7 (four on Sun). Off-season three crossings Mon–Sat. Length of crossing 1hr 30min. $24/car, $8/passenger.* ✗ ⅏ ☎*506/662-3724.* The largest of the Fundy islands, Grand Manan is noted for its rugged scenery that includes cliffs of 120m/400ft and picturesque harbours. A sizeable bird population inhabits the island; about 230 species have been sighted. On the island's rocky west coast, **Dark Harbour** is a processing centre for dulse, which grows on submerged rocks in the Bay of Fundy. Collected at low tide and dried in the sun, dulse has a salty, tangy flavour. Rich in iron and iodine, it can be added to soups and stews or eaten raw or toasted.

★★ SAINT JOHN
Pop 74,969

Map p 182

Tourist Office ☎ 506/658-2990

The province's largest city, this industrial centre and major port is fondly called "fog city" because of the dense sea mists that roll in off the Bay of Fundy. Its rocky, hilly site at the mouth of the Saint John River at the junction with the bay has resulted in a city with few straight roads and many cul-de-sacs.

Part of Acadie. – In 1604, Samuel de Champlain and the Sieur de Monts *(p 198)* landed briefly at the mouth of the river. Another Frenchman, **Charles de La Tour**, built a trading fort in 1630 on the site of present-day Saint John. In 1645 de Menou d'Aulnay *(p 198)*, his compatriot from Port Royal, destroyed the post. The ensuing trade rivalry among the French in Acadia was compounded by the Anglo-French struggles. Although the area was ceded by the 1763 Treaty of Paris to the English, who established their own post, Saint John records 1783 as the year of its inception.

The Loyalists Arrive. – On May 18, 1783, some 4,000 Loyalists disembarked at the mouth of the river from their square-rigged ships. Overnight, the tiny trading post became a boom town. Their wealth dissipated by the American Revolution, they possessed few pioneering skills needed to carve new lives out of the wilderness. However, they not only survived, but created a prosperous city of shipyards and social gatherings.

Thriving on trade and shipbuilding, Saint John was known as the "Liverpool of America" during the 19C. From 1860 to 1880, however, Saint John began to decline: demand for wooden ships was decreasing; an international depression had set in by early 1874; and in 1877, more than half the city was destroyed by a great fire. During the 1880s, the waterfront was modernized, a railway terminus established and by 1900, grain elevators completed. The port remained active, but not until the 1960s did the economy revive. Huge investment was made in pulp and paper, sugar and oil refining. A container shipping service was established and a deep-water terminal built for tankers.

Every July, the city recalls its founding with a celebration known as **Loyalist Days**. Inhabitants dress in 18C costumes and re-enact the landing of 1783. Street dances, sidewalk breakfasts and a large parade complete the festival.

SIGHTS *Map p 194. 1 day.*

★★ **Downtown.** – Saint John's downtown has been revitalized, making it a pleasant area for visitors to explore on foot *(contact tourist office for designated walks)*.

★★ **Market Square Area.** – Opened in 1983, the square contains an attractive shopping mall with a central atrium and several levels, a hotel, convention centre and residences. Incorporated into the complex, a row of late-19C warehouses fronts a pleasant plaza around the **market slip** where Loyalists landed in 1783. In summer, there are outdoor cafes and concerts in the plaza.

On the plaza's south side stands an 1867 clapboard structure with gingerbread decoration, **Barbour's General Store [K]**, stocked with merchandise of the period *(open daily mid-May–mid-Oct; ☎506/658-2939)*. Over St Patrick Street, a pedestrian bridge links the square with the Canada Games **Aquatic Centre** and **City Hall [H]**, which has an observation gallery on the top floor *(open year-round Mon–Fri)*. **Brunswick Square [D]** is a complex of shops, offices and hotel.

Loyalist House [E]. – *Visit by guided tour (30min) only daily June–Sept. $2.* ⅏ ☎*506/652-3590*. One of the oldest structures in the city, this house was built in 1817 by David Merritt, a Loyalist who fled New York State in 1783. One of the few buildings to escape the fire of 1877, the house has a shingled exterior on two sides, and clapboard on the other. An expensive material at the time, clapboard was installed on only the north and east sides as weather protection.

The plain exterior belies the elegant and spacious Georgian interior with its fine curved staircase and arches between rooms. Upon departure, note the solid rock foundations on the Germain Street side. All of Saint John is built on such rock.

King Square Area. – Generally considered the centre of Saint John, this square has trees, flowerbeds arranged in the form of the Union flag *(p 199)* and a two-storey bandstand. In one corner stands the old **city market [F]**, where a variety of New Brunswick produce can be bought, including dulse *(see above)*. On the other side of the square, the **Loyalist burial ground [G]** can be seen.

Fort Howe Lookout. – *From Main St, take Metcalf St, then sharp right turn onto Magazine St.* From this wooden blockhouse *(not open)* on a rocky cliff above the surrounding hills, there is a **panorama★** of the docks, harbour, river and city.

★ New Brunswick Museum. – *Open daily year-round. $2.* ♿ ☎*506/658-1842.*
Devoted to the human, natural and artistic life of the province, this museum has fine
examples of Indian birchbark, quill and beadwork. European settlement is traced
from 17C Acadia, with details of the various Anglo-French wars, through the arrival
of the Loyalists. Costume, ceramics, silver and glassware displays evoke the 19C.
The gallery of natural science features examples of the province's animal life and
geological specimens. There are exhibits of fine and decorative arts, including a
gallery devoted to Chinese costumes, porcelain, figurines and earthenware.

★★ Reversing Falls Rapids. – *To fully appreciate the rapids, visit at low tide, slack
tide (see below) and high tide. Contact tourist office for times of tides.* Where the
Saint John River empties into the Bay of Fundy the tides are 8m/28ft high. At high
tide when the bay water is more than 4m/14ft above river level, the water flows
swiftly upstream. At low tide, the bay is more than 4m/14ft below the level of the
river, so the river rushes into it. As the tide rises, the rush of river water is gradually halted and the river becomes as calm as a mill pond (slack tide) before gradually
being reversed in direction. This reversal of the river current is marked just before
the river, narrowing and curving around a bend in a deep gorge, enters the bay. The
narrow bend creates rapids and whirlpools whenever the current is great in either
direction, a phenomenon known as "reversing falls rapids."

Reversing Falls Bridge Lookout [A]. – *Parking at west end of bridge; information centre
open daily mid-May–mid-Oct.* ╳ ☎*506/658-2937. Take steps to roof.* From this lookout, fine **views★★** of the changing river current are afforded. Visitors unable to stay
for the tidal cycle will enjoy the **film** *($1.25)*, which condenses the 24-hour event.

Falls View Park Lookout [B]. – *Parking at end of Falls View Ave.* The **views★** of the rapids
from the park are not as dramatic as those from the bridge .

★ Carleton Martello Tower. – 🎦 *Open daily Jun–mid-Oct.* ☎*506/636-4011.* Built in
1813 as a defence for the city, this Martello tower *(p 209)* was used during the 19C
and in both world wars. A two-storey steel and concrete structure was added in
World War II to house anti-aircraft and fire control headquarters for Saint John.
Inside the tower, there are displays on the history of the area.
The tower stands above its surroundings, providing a **panorama★★** encompassing
the harbour, the docks, rail yards, a breakwater that leads to Partridge Island, the
bay, river and city.

*None of the Martello towers constructed in British North America
between 1796 and 1848 was ever attacked.
Of the total 16 (Halifax 5, Kingston 6, Quebec City 4
and Saint John 1), 11 remain to this day.*

Map p 182

In the south, the valley of this wide and scenic river is rolling and rural, supporting some of the richest farmland in New Brunswick. Heading north, the river traverses hilly, almost mountainous forests, the source of the province's substantial lumber industry.

Settlements sprang up throughout the valley when some 4,000 Loyalists arrived in 1783 (p 193). In the 19C, numerous steamboats moved between these communities. Traffic took to the roads in the 1940s, but the valley remains the principal transportation route since the Trans-Canada Highway parallels it for much of its length in New Brunswick.

FROM FREDERICTON TO EDMUNDSTON
285km/177mi. Allow 1 day.

Leave Fredericton (p 188) on the Trans-Can Hwy (Rte 2).

After traversing the provincial capital, the highway follows the river upstream to the Mactaquac Dam, New Brunswick's largest power project. The dam has created a reservoir, or headpond, about 105km/65mi long, affecting the valley as far as Woodstock. On the north bank of the headpond lies **Mactaquac Provincial Park**, a haven for sports enthusiasts. The Trans-Canada Highway travels the south side of the pond with fine **views★** as the country becomes increasingly rural.

Woolastook Wildlife Park. – *29km/18mi. Open daily mid-May–Sept. $4. ☎506/ 363-5410.* This is a pleasant park devoted to animals native to the Maritime provinces (p 181). From the parking lot, there is a good **view★** of the Saint John River.

★★ **Kings Landing Historical Settlement.** – *37km/23mi. Open Jun–mid-Oct daily 9:30am–5pm. $7.50. ✗ ⅙ ☎506/363-5090.* This restored village has a beautiful **site★★** on the sloping banks of the Saint John, beside a creek that joins the river via a small cove. Typical of the Loyalist riverbank settlements where lumbering, farming and some shipbuilding were principal occupations, the village provides an authentic glimpse of life in the river valley from 1783 to 1900.

After the Revolutionary War, the land on which the village stands was given to veterans of the King's American Dragoons. When the Mactaquac dam project flooded their original sites, the houses and other buildings were moved to this location.

Apart from the well-restored farms with their fields of crops, the village has a church, school, forge, store and a **theatre** with live entertainment *(ask for details at entrance).* As they carry out routine chores, about 100 costumed interpreters explain aspects of 19C rural life. Beside the mill stream is an operating water-powered **sawmill**. Activated by the large water wheel, a saw blade cuts through logs by moving along a wooden carriage. An example of a roadhouse of the period, the **Kings Head Inn** serves traditional refreshments. The commodious Morehouse residence stands near the elegant Ingraham house with its delightful garden overlooking the river.

Moored at the wharf (the "landing"), a half-sized replica of a 19C **wood boat★** typifies vessels that transported lumber from sawmills and hay from farms to market.

Between Kings Landing and Woodstock, there are excellent **views★★** from the Trans-Canada Highway of the Saint John River traversing lovely rolling country of farms and forests.

After Woodstock, leave Trans-Can Hwy and take Rte 103 to Hartland.

★ **Hartland.** – Pop 890. Settled by Loyalists, this town in the centre of the potato-growing district is known for the longest **covered bridge★** in the world. Built in 1897 and rebuilt in 1920, the 391m/1,282ft bridge crosses the Saint John River in seven spans. Until 1960, the Trans-Canada Highway was routed over it, but today it links Routes 103 and 105.

As in other provinces, the first bridges built in New Brunswick were of wood, covered to protect the large timbers from weathering. These coverings could lengthen the lifespan of a bridge by 50 or 60 years.

Upon descending the hill on Route 103, note the good **view★** of the bridge, which resembles a barnlike tunnel. The woodwork construction can be appreciated only from the interior *(cars can be driven through; no trucks).*

Take Rte 105 on the east bank to Florenceville and Trans-Can Hwy to Grand Falls.

There are fine **views★** from the highway of the river and farms of the agricultural area north of Florenceville. The Saint John gradually approaches the Maine border and enters the more mountainous country of the north.

Leave Trans-Can Hwy and enter Grand Falls.

★★ **Grand Falls.** – Pop 6,083. Built on a plateau above the river, this town is the centre of the potato belt. Here, the Saint John changes suddenly and dramatically. The previous wide and tranquil river with gently sloping banks plunges over falls and, for about 1.6km/1mi, churns through a deep and narrow gorge. A power plant has diverted much of the water of the falls, but there are two good vantage points for the gorge.

Falls Park. – *Accessible from Malabeam reception centre on Madawaska Rd. Open daily mid-May–Labour Day.* This park offers a good **view★** of the gorge and the falls below the power plant.

★ **La Rochelle Centre.** – *In Centennial Park. Accessible from Malabeam reception centre on Madawaska Rd. Open daily mid-May–Labour Day. $2.* Stairs descend into the gorge, which has walls as high as 70m/230ft in places. At the bottom, there are some deep holes in the rock called wells, but it is the **gorge★★** that is impressive.

Return to Trans-Can Hwy.

After Grand Falls, the Saint John becomes wide and placid again, marking the Canadian/US border. The towns and villages seen across it are in Maine.

Edmundston. – Pop 10,835. Situated at the junction of the Saint John and Madawaska rivers, this industrial city, dominated by the twin-spired **Cathedral of the Immaculate Conception**, contrasts sharply with the rural landscape of the surrounding valley. Once called *Petit-Sault* ("little falls") to distinguish the rapids at the mouth of the Madawaska from those of Grand Falls, Edmundston was renamed in 1856 in honour of **Sir Edmund Head**, Lieutenant-Governor of New Brunswick (1848-1854). The city's inhabitants are mainly French-speaking, although they claim Acadian, Quebecer, Indian, American, English and Irish origins.

Republic of Madawaska. – Long contested among Ontario, Quebec, New Brunswick and the US, the land south of Lake Témiscouata in Quebec and New Brunswick, and the area north of the Aroostook River in Maine were once collectively called Madawaska. When boundaries were finally fixed, New Brunswick was left with the city of Edmundston and a thumb-shaped stretch of land *(map p 182)*. The long-standing dispute forged a spirited independence among the Madawaskans, who created for themselves a legend, rather than a political entity—the Republic of Madawaska. Known as the Brayons because they crushed flax with a tool called a "brake," the Madawaskans have their own flag with an eagle and six stars (representing their different origins) and their own president, the mayor of Edmundston. The **Madawaska Museum** *(195 Herbert Blvd at Trans-Can Hwy; open daily Jun–Labour Day; $1; ☎506/737-5064)* presents the history of this region.

★ SHIPPAGAN   Pop 2,760

Map p 182

This town on the Acadian peninsula has an important commercial fishing industry, and peat-moss processing plants. A bridge leads to Lameque Island with its peat moss bogs. From there a ferry *(toll free)* crosses to Miscou Island, which has fine beaches on the Gulf of St Lawrence.

★ **Aquarium and Marine Centre.** – *Open daily May–Labour Day. Off-season Mon–Sat. $5.35.* ✗ ☐ *☎506/336-4771.* Devoted to the marine life of the gulf, this pleasant museum features exhibits on the types of ships used for fishing and their construction. An audio-visual presentation *(20min)* explains the history of the fishing industry. In a series of aquariums and an outdoor seal pool, fish native to these waters are on view. Visitors can enter the cabin of a modern-day reconstructed trawler to see the mass of electronic devices used to find and catch fish.

★ VILLAGE HISTORIQUE ACADIEN

Map p 182

This reconstructed village depicts the life of the Acadians from 1780 to 1890, a time of great hardship after Deportation *(p 184)*.
Most of the gulf shore along New Brunswick is inhabited by Acadians still living traditional lives as farmers and fishermen. Each August, nearby **Caraquet** (pop 4,556) hosts an annual Acadian festival that is opened by a **blessing of the fleet**, symbolic of Christ's benediction to the fishermen of Galilee. As many as 60 fishing boats, decked with bunting, arrive from all over the province to be blessed by the bishop of Bathurst.

Access. – *11km/7mi west of Caraquet by Rte 11.*

Visit. – *Open daily Jun–mid-Sept. $7.50.* ✗ ☐ *☎506/727-3467.* The village is entered through the **visitor centre** (centre d'accueil), where a **slide show** *(18min)* covering the entire history of the Acadians, provides a good introduction.
"Inhabited" by Acadians wearing traditional costumes, the village extends along a road nearly 1.6km/1mi long *(transport by horse and oxen-drawn carts provided)*. Houses moved from various parts of the province have been furnished to represent the period. Only the wooden church is a copy of an original building.
Over the village flies the **flag of Acadie**, the French red, white and blue tricolour with a star symbolizing the Virgin Mary at the top left corner. The flag is often seen in Acadian regions of Nova Scotia and Prince Edward Island.

Nova Scotia

Pop 899,942

Maps pp 182-183

Extending north to south, Nova Scotia consists of Cape Breton Island, and a 565km/350mi long, relatively narrow peninsula, its width never exceeding 130km/81mi. Linked to New Brunswick by the Isthmus of Chignecto, the province is surrounded by the Gulf of St Lawrence, Atlantic Ocean, Northumberland Strait and Bay of Fundy, with 7,460km/4,625mi of serrated coastline. Proximity to the sea and natural harbours have defined its historical role as largely strategic. The provincial capital, Halifax, has long served as a military stronghold.

Practical Information

How to get there. – **Air** service is provided by Air Canada and its affiliates with daily flights to Halifax and Yarmouth. **VIA Rail** connects Nova Scotia through its transcontinental train service. In Canada consult the telephone directory for the nearest office; from the US ☎800/561-3949 (toll-free). **Bus** travel is offered by Acadian Lines (☎902/454-9629).

Passenger and vehicle **ferry** service connects Bar Harbor, Maine with Yarmouth (departures mid-Jun–mid-Sept daily 8am; reduced schedule in off-season; no crossing Mar–mid-Apr; crossing time 6hrs; $75/car, $45/person) and Saint John, NB with Digby (departures daily year-round; crossing time 2hr 30min; $60/car, $20/person). For ferry schedules & reservations contact Marine Atlantic ☎207/288-3395 (Bar Harbor) or 902/742-6800 (Yarmouth). Advance reservations are recommended.

Yarmouth can also be reached by ferry from Portland, Maine (departures mid-Jun–Labour Day daily 9pm; reduced schedule in off-season; no crossing Nov-Apr; crossing time 11hrs; $98/car, $75/person, cabin extra). For reservations contact Prince of Fundy Cruises, Box 4216, Portland, ME 04101 ☎800/341-7540 (toll-free Canada/US) or 902/742-6460 (Yarmouth).

Accommodation and Tourist Information. – The official tourist office publishes a travel guide annually giving information on history, attractions, scheduled events, accommodation, farm and country vacations as well as campgrounds. For a free copy of the guide and a map contact:
Nova Scotia Department of Tourism and Culture, PO Box 130, Halifax, NS, B3J 2M7 ☎902/424-4247.
For hotel information & reservations contact toll-free ☎ 800/565-0000 (Canada) or 800/341-6096 (US).

Road Regulations. – Speed limits, unless otherwise posted, are 100km/h (60mph) on the Trans-Canada Highway, 80km/h (50mph) on highways and 50km/h (30mph) in cities and towns. **Seat belt** use is mandatory.
Canadian Automobile Association (CAA), Halifax ☎902/443-5530.

Time Zone. – Nova Scotia is on Atlantic Standard Time. Daylight Saving Time is observed from the first Sunday in April to the last Sunday in October.

Taxes. – The national GST of 7% *(rebate information p 242)* applies. A 10% health services tax is also levied. To request a rebate, non-residents should contact the Provincial Tax Commission, PO Box 755, Halifax, NS, B3J 2V4 ☎902/424-4411.

Liquor Laws. – The legal drinking age is 19. Liquor is sold in government stores.

Principal Festivals

May-Jun	**Apple Blossom Festival**	*Annapolis Valley*
Jun–Jul	**Nova Scotia International Tattoo**	*Halifax*
Jul	**Metropolitan Scottish Festival and Highland Games**	*Halifax*
	Antigonish Highland Games	*Antigonish*
	Gathering of the Clans and Fishermen's Regatta	*Pugwash*
	Moosehead Grand Prix Race	*Halifax*
Aug	**Natal Day**	*Province-wide*
	Nova Scotia Gaelic Mod	*St Ann's*
	International Buskerfest	*Halifax*
Sept	**Nova Scotia Fisheries Exhibition & Fishermen's Reunion**	*Lunenburg*

The Peninsula. – The mainland is largely flat terrain, except for a rocky, indented eastern shore, and a forested interior reaching a maximum elevation of 210m/689ft. **South Mountain** forms the northern border of this upland interior. Stretching from Cape Blomidon to the tip of Digby Neck, the **North Mountain** range parallels South Mountain for 190km/118mi along the Bay of Fundy shore. Sheltered between the ranges is the heart of the province's apple industry, the fertile Annapolis and Cornwallis river valleys. The cropped 300m/984ft **Cobequid Mountain** extends 120km/74mi over Cumberland County, which borders the isthmus.

The Island. – Northern Cape Breton Island is largely a wooded plateau rising to 532m/1,745ft above sea level, a height that permits expansive views of the wildly beautiful, often mist-enshrouded, coastline. Extending west coast-to-east coast at the northern end is **Cape Breton Highlands National Park** with its celebrated route, the Cabot Trail *(p 204)*. Culminating in the Strait of Canso, the south is predominantly lowland. A vast inland sea 930sq km/359sq mi wide, **Bras d'Or Lake** nearly bisects the island.

Sea-faring Nation. – Peopled with fishermen, sea merchants, privateers and boat-builders, Nova Scotia's colourful past is interwoven with the sea. One great industry established by Pre-Loyalists and Loyalists alike was **shipbuilding**. Blanketed by virgin forest, little of which remains today, the province used its rich timber resources to bring prosperity to its inhabitants, especially during the Napoleonic Wars (1803-1815) when Britain's need for wooden ships and ship parts was great. Along the south coast, Nova Scotia's schooners became legend, as did the sailors who manned them—universally called **Bluenoses**, an American term of derision for people who could survive the region's cold climate. More than a few fortunes were made from privateering: the east coast's plentiful coves and inlets, particularly around Liverpool *(p 203)*, once concealed many an anchored pirate ship.

Piracy diminished under threat of prosecution, and by 1900, the prominence of ship-building waned. Steam replaced sail power; steel hulls superseded wooden ones. Today, wooden vessels are still crafted on a limited basis in the Lunenburg area.

Preserving the Past. – Nova Scotia boasts more historic sites than any province in Canada except Quebec. In recent years, the Federal and provincial governments have played active roles in heritage preservation, as have countless local organizations and historical societies. Administered by the provincial museum system, more than 20 historic sites, from heritage houses to restored mills, are open to the public. **Genealogy** is popular here: local museums, schools and universities, genealogical societies, and churches have archival facilities for tracing one's roots. The migration of Nova Scotia's black population is chronicled in Dartmouth *(p 210)*, New England's planter immigrants in Kentville. Descendants of Dutch, English, French, German, Greek, Hungarian, Irish, Italian, Lebanese and Polish settlers diversify the population today.

Traditional dishes—Acadia's rappie pie, Cape Breton lamb, Scottish oat cakes and the "truly Nova Scotian" blueberry grunt—tempt visitors to partake of a **regional cookery** harking back to Samuel de Champlain's gourmandise. The gastronomy of his Order of Good Cheer *(p 199)* endures in the province's formalized food promotion entitled "Taste of Nova Scotia," offered by over 45 member dining establishments. Various cultural events and festivals preserve ancestral traditions, one of the largest being the International **Gathering of the Clans**, a tribute to the province's Scottish beginnings as *New Scotland (p 184)*. Acadian crafts and demonstrations of handiwork skills are featured in local shops and museums, particularly along the west coast of Cape Breton Island, while Gaelic wares abound along the east coast and on the mainland.

★★ ANNAPOLIS ROYAL
Pop 633

Map p 182

Tourist Office ☎902/532-5769

One of Canada's oldest settlements, Annapolis Royal has a pleasant **site★** overlooking the great basin of the Annapolis where it narrows into the river of the same name. Acadians reclaimed the marshland by building a dam across the river with flood gates to control the water level. Twice a day the Bay of Fundy tides rush in, reversing the river's flow. The quiet charm of this gracious town belies its turbulent past as site of French-English battles and Acadian struggles.

French Colonization. – The earliest settlement was a French colony at **Port Royal** *(p 199)* under nobleman, **Pierre du Gua, Sieur de Monts**, destroyed in 1613 by a force from Virginia. By 1635, the French governor, **Charles de Menou d'Aulnay**, had built a new Port Royal on the site of Annapolis Royal. Over the next century, French settlement grew, forming the region called Acadia *(p 184)*. Port Royal suffered many raids by the New England colonies to the south. The predecessor of the present Fort Anne *(see below)* was constructed by the French, but funds were insufficient to maintain it. In 1710, it fell to a New England expedition under Col Francis Nicholson. Renamed Annapolis Royal after England's **Queen Anne**, the fortified settlement became the provincial capital when the mainland was ceded to the British by the Treaty of Utrecht in 1713. Constantly threatened by surrounding Acadian settlements sympathetic to soldiers from Quebec or Louisbourg, it frequently withstood French attack. In 1749, the capital was relocated to Halifax where British military force was being strengthened. Annapolis Royal was relegated to an outpost, eventually losing detachments to Halifax. In 1854, the few troops remaining were removed to New Brunswick. Annapolis Royal had lost its importance.

Much of the area's history is evident today: de Monts' habitation has been reconstructed near Port Royal, Fort Anne has been partially re-created, and the older buildings along **Lower Saint George Street** have been renovated.

SIGHTS *1/2 day*

★ **Fort Anne National Historic Site.** – ☞ *Open daily mid-May–mid-Oct. Off-season Mon–Fri. Closed holidays during off-season.* ♿ ☎902/532-2397. A peaceful expanse of green in the centre of town, this fort was once the most fought-over place in Canada, suffering 14 sieges during the Anglo-French wars. In 1917, Fort Anne became the first National Historic Park in Canada.

Existing earthworks were built by the French from 1702 to 1708 with later alterations by the British. In one of the bastions stands a stone **powder magazine** of the French period. From the earthworks there is a **view★** of the Annapolis Basin.

★ **Officers' Quarters.** – A distinctive building with high chimneys and dormer windows stands in the centre of the fort. Built in 1797 by order of Prince Edward *(p 207)*, the quarters, now restored, house a **museum★**, which includes a display on the fort's military history.

Outside flies the flag of the Grand Union, a combination of the English cross of St George, and the Scottish cross of St Andrew. The Union Jack as we know it today did not come into existence until the union with Ireland in 1803, when the cross of St Patrick was added.

★ **Historic Gardens.** – *On Upper Saint George St (Rte 8) just south of Fort Anne. Open daily late–May–Oct. $3.50.* ♿ ☏*902/532-7018.* Situated on a 4ha/10 acre site overlooking Allain's River, a tributary of the Annapolis, this series of theme gardens exemplifies the horticultural diversity of the region's past as well as recent gardening technology.

The Acadian Garden has a traditional cottage and a replica of the dike system *(p 201)*. Formal in style, the Governor's Garden is characteristic of early 18C landscape architecture when the English governor was based in Annapolis Royal. The Victorian Garden reveals a more natural setting, a trend that became fashionable in the 19C. The Rose Garden traces the development of this ever-popular species.

★ **Annapolis Tidal Generating Station.** – *On the Causeway (Rte 1). Information centre open daily mid-May–mid-Oct.* ♿ ☏*902/532-5454.* North America's first tidal power project, this station uses a low head, straight-flow turbine generator to harness the enormous energy of the Bay of Fundy tides to produce electricity.

The exhibit area upstairs in the information centre explains the project and its construction through models, photographs and a video presentation *(10min)*. A causeway over the dam affords views of tidal activity and of the generating station.

EXCURSIONS

★ **North Hills Museum.** – *In Granville Ferry on road to Port Royal. Open daily Jun–mid-Oct.* ☏*902/532-2168.* Despite a series of modifications, this small wood-framed 18C house has retained a pioneer look. It provides a fitting setting for the predominantly 18C antique collection of a retired Toronto banker. Bequeathed to the province upon his death in 1974, the collection includes English furniture, ceramics, silver and Georgian glass.

★★ **Port Royal Habitation.** – ☝ *10km/6mi from Annapolis Royal Causeway.* The *habitation* (French word for "dwelling") is a replica of Canada's first European settlement of any permanence. This collection of dark, weathered fortified buildings joined around a central courtyard was designed in a style reminiscent of 16C French farms by **Samuel de Champlain** (c.1567-1635), captain and navigator of the expedition of de Monts.

Granted permission by Henry IV of France to set up a colony and develop the fur trade, de Monts began his expedition to the New World in 1604. The first winter in Canada was spent on an island in the St Croix River *(map p 192)* —a poor choice, as it was cut off from the fresh food of the mainland by the Bay of Fundy's storms and ice. The next year, the company moved to the Annapolis Basin where the habitation was reconstructed.

Boredom and sickness prompted Champlain to form a social club wherein members alternated as grand master and organizers of gourmet feasts. In 1606, member Marc Lescarbot wrote the first play performed in Canada, the **Theatre of Neptune.** The **Order of Good Cheer,** as the club was called, proved successful. Crops were grown, and trade with the Indians was established. Just as the settlement seemed rooted, de Monts' trading rights were revoked in 1607, and the expedition returned to France. Destroyed in 1613 by English forces, the buildings were reconstructed in 1938 by the Canadian government, using Champlain's sketch and writings as guides.

Visit. – *Open mid-May–mid-Oct daily 9am–6pm.* ♿ ☏*902/532-2898.* Over the gateway entry hangs the **coat of arms** of France and Navarre, ruled by King Henry IV (French kings held the additional title of King of Navarre from 1589 until the French Revolution). A **well** with a shingled roof stands in the middle of the courtyard. Around it are the residences of the governor, priest and artisans. The kitchen, blacksmith's shop, community room where the Order met, and the chapel can be visited as can the storerooms, wine cellar and trading room where Indians brought their furs. All furnishings are meticulous reproductions of early 17C styles.

Each building has a steeply pitched roof and, except for the storeroom, a fieldstone chimney. The walls are actually of **half-timbered** construction: upright posts placed several feet apart with spaces between them filled in horizontally with logs caulked with clay. This construction can be appreciated only from the interior, since the exterior of the buildings is covered with lapped boarding. No nails or spikes join the timbers: they are mortised and tenoned and pinned together.

★ **Kejimkujik National Park.** – ☝ *Rte 8. From Annapolis Royal 48km/30mi to park entrance, near Maitland Bridge. Open year-round. $5/day per car; $10/4 days per car. Hiking, cycling, swimming, canoeing, cross-country skiing. Canoe & bicycle rental at Jakes Landing.* △. *For information, contact the visitor centre* ☏*902/682-2772.* Recreation and beauty await visitors to this 381sq km/147sq mi forest with its accessible lakes and plentiful wildlife. For centuries, the park's waterways served the Micmac as canoe routes and still afford peaceful passage through largely untouched wilderness.

The **Mill Falls** hiking trail leads through fern-filled woods along the amber **Mersey River** to its foamy rapids. The viewing tower *(on main park road, 10km/6mi from park entrance)* permits an elevated **view★** of lovely Kejimkujik Lake.

The △ symbol indicates that campgrounds can be found on the premises of the sight described.

★★ ANNAPOLIS VALLEY

Maps pp 182-183

Flowing 112km/70mi southwest to the sea, the Annapolis River widens into the **Annapolis Basin**, a tidal lake connected to the Bay of Fundy by a narrow outlet known as Digby Gut. The area commonly referred to as the Annapolis Valley includes other rivers and extends approximately 160km/100mi from Digby to Windsor on the Minas Basin.

Some of the earliest French colonists settled in this region, only to be deported by the British in 1755 *(p 184)*. The Acadians built dikes to reclaim the marshland for agricultural production. In addition, the valley is sheltered on both sides from heavy wind and fog by the North and South mountains, a feature which has nurtured the valley's famed **apple orchards**. Today, other fruits and crops are also grown in the fertile soil, while dairy cattle graze the meadows bordering the river.

FROM DIGBY TO WINDSOR *168km/104mi. 2 days.*

Take Hwy 101 and then Rte 1.

Digby. – Pop 2,311. From this waterfront town, home of the famous scallop, ferries cross to New Brunswick. The harbour is often busy with fishing fleets. Local restaurants feature **Digby scallops** prepared in a variety of ways.

Highway 101 follows the shore of the Annapolis Basin with pleasant views until it turns inland at Deep Brook, where Route 1 continues along the shoreline.

★★ Annapolis Royal. – *Visit: 1/2 day. Description p 198.*

Remains of the old French dike system can be seen from the road. Route 1 crosses the river and continues through country that becomes more rural. Wide meadows line the riverbanks. At **Bridgetown★**, elm-shaded streets contain fine houses, many built by Loyalists. **Lawrencetown** and **Middleton** are similarly graced with trees. Apple orchards line the hills, particularly between Kingston and Waterville, where fruit-selling stands and "U-pick" farms are common. This drive is especially lovely in apple blossom time *(late May or early June)*.

Continue 14km/9mi on Rte 1 to junction with Rte 358.

★★ Excursion to Cape Split. – *28km/17mi north by Rte 358.*

★ Prescott House. – *In Starr's Point, off Rte 358, about 5km/3mi north of Rte 1. Open daily Jun–mid-Oct.* ☎902/542-3984. This attractive whitewashed-brick house, set in lovely grounds, was built in the early 19C by **Charles Prescott**, legislator, successful merchant and acclaimed horticulturalist. On this estate, Prescott experimented with new strains of wheat, planted nut trees, grapes and pears and introduced many varieties of cherries and apples. He gave away cuttings to valley farmers and is partly responsible for the development of the apple industry in this area.

The interior is attractively furnished with some original pieces. A pleasant **sun room** was added by Prescott's great granddaughter. The **garden** is also worth visiting.

Return to Rte 358 and continue north.

★★ The Lookoff. – *Approximately 14km/9mi north of Starr's Point. Follow the signs on Rte 358. Watch for paved pull-off with steel barricade.* Although there is no official marker for this site, one cannot pass by without stopping. The **view★★** of Annapolis Valley is magnificent: a 180-degree vista of patterned farmlands reaching toward the vast Minas Basin, interrupted only by the South Mountain in the distance. At least four counties are visible from this popular vantage point.

About 8km/5mi north of the Lookoff, as Route 358 descends into the tiny community of Scots Bay, there is a lovely **view★** of this bay, the Minas Channel, and the Parrsboro Shore of Nova Scotia. At Little Cove, boats can be seen resting on the channel bottom at low tide.

Cape Split. – *Rte 358 ends. Hiking trail 13km/8mi through woods to tip of cape.* This hook of forested land juts into the Bay of Fundy, edged by magnificent cliffs. Since the tides constantly ebb and flow, the bay's waters in the Minas Channel are muddied. From road's end, there are **views** of the wide bay, the shoreline of the cape, and the Parrsboro Shore.

Return via Rte 358. After about 9km/6mi, take the unpaved road on the left (Stewart Mountain Road). At junction, turn left. Road terminates at provincial park. Follow signs. Hiking trails for Cape Blomidon shown on panel in visitor parking lot.

★ Blomidon. – As the road leaves the woods and descends into flatlands, the first **view★** of the Minas Basin is grand. The patchwork farmlands of this rural coastland stretch to the cliffs of the basin. Bright red barns and two-storey farmhouses dot the landscape, dominated by the reddish cliffs of Cape Blomidon. From the end of the picnic area, the **view★★** in both directions of the wide red beach (at low tide), and the stratified pinkish-red cliffs, contrasted with the blue waters of the basin, are breathtaking.

At Blomidon junction, continue south via Pereau and Delhaven to Rte 221.

About 2km/1.2mi south of the junction, there is a **view★** from the Pereaux Small Crafts Harbour of the hole in a rock formation known locally as **Patty's Island**, fully visible at low tide.

At the junction with Rte 221, turn right to Canning for Rte 358 back to Rte 1.

★ Wolfville. – Pop 3,475. This charming town with shaded streets and heritage properties is home to Acadia University, founded 1838. Several mansions have been converted into wayside inns. Boutiques and eateries line the main thoroughfare, and during college sessions, the community is alive with scurrying students.

★ **Grand-Pré National Historic Park.** – ⚐ *Just north of Rte 1, 4km/2.5mi east of Wolfville. Park open year-round. Buildings open daily mid-May–mid-Oct.* ⚐ ☎902/542-3631. Inhabited between 1680 and 1755, the former Acadian village of Grand-Pré (French for "great meadow") has been transformed into a spacious park overlooking the flat dikelands the early settlers reclaimed. The well-maintained expanse of hedged lawns, flowerbeds and large shade trees serves as a permanent memorial to the Acadians.

Before Deportation *(p 184)*, Grand-Pré was the most important Acadian settlement in Nova Scotia, with about 200 farms along the edge of the Minas Basin. Residents who had moved here from Port Royal *(p 198)* realized the richness of the soil covered by the sea at high tide. They constructed a system of **dikes** to keep the sea out, while marsh water was allowed to escape through floodgates. The cultivated land soon supported crops, livestock and orchards. After Deportation, the farmlands were given to planters from New England, and later to Loyalists.

The American poet **Henry Wadsworth Longfellow** chose Grand-Pré as the setting for his poem, *Evangeline*. Published in 1847, the work describes a young couple's separation during Deportation and Evangeline's subsequent search throughout the eastern US for her lover Gabriel—only to find him dying. Symbolic of the tragedy of Deportation, the poem has become part of popular Acadian culture.

On the site of the first church of Grand-Pré stands a small **chapel** in a setting of horse chestnut and willow trees. Completed in 1930, the chapel is constructed of local stone in a style reminiscent of native French churches. Inside, there are **displays** illustrating Acadian settlement, the British takeover, and the final deportation. A bronze **statue** of Evangeline by **Louis-Philippe Hébert** (1850-1917) stands on the grounds.

Windsor. – Pop 3,625. Famous as the home of Thomas Haliburton, one of the foremost Nova Scotians of his day, the town is set at the confluence of the Avon and St Croix rivers. The Avon is sealed off from the Bay of Fundy by a causeway. A shipping point for lumber and gypsum mined nearby, the community was once the site of the 18C Acadian settlement of Piziquid, which was taken over by New Englanders after Deportation and renamed Windsor.

★ **Haliburton House.** – *On Clifton Ave. Follow signs from causeway. Open daily Jun–mid-Oct.* ⚐ ☎902/798-2915. At the end of a long, impressive drive stands this house, built in 1836 on the tree-covered estate of **Thomas Chandler Haliburton** (1796-1865), famous as the creator of **Sam Slick**, a fictitious Yankee peddler.

Judge, legislator, author and humorist of international renown, Haliburton started publishing stories in 1836 under the title, *The Clockmaker; or, The Sayings and Doings of Samuel Slick of Slickville*. Slick travelled all over Nova Scotia, making fun of its unenterprising inhabitants. Many of the epigrams he coined are still in use today: "six of one and half a dozen of the other," "an ounce of prevention is worth a pound of cure," "facts are stranger than fiction," "the early bird gets the worm," "as quick as a wink," and "jack of all trades and master of none" are among the most familiar. The interior of the house with its spacious entry hall, elegant dining room and sitting room reflects the man.

Shand House. – *Avon St. Street parking prohibited. Upon entrance to Windsor, watch for signs to separate parking area. Uphill walk to house. Open daily Jun–mid-Oct.* ☎902/798-8213. The most imposing of the houses atop Ferry Hill overlooking the Avon River, this Victorian dwelling was completed in 1891. The staircase is of cherry, and several rooms have oak interiors. Furnishings are those of the original and only owners. Visitors can ascend the square tower.

Fort Edward. – ⚐ *Off King St near causeway. Open daily mid-Jun–Labour Day.* ☎902/542-3631. Possessing the oldest blockhouse in Canada, this fort is situated on a hillock at the edge of town. Built in 1750 as a British stronghold in Acadian territory, it was later a point of departure for Acadians assembled for deportation.

From the grassy fortification, there are **views** of the tidal river, the causeway and Lake Pesaquid in the distance. Made of squared timbers, the dark wooden **blockhouse** is the only remaining building of the fort. The walls of its two storeys—the upper storey overhanging the lower— are pierced by square portholes for cannon and loopholes for musket fire.

Inside, there are displays on the blockhouse defence system and the fort's history.

★★ ATLANTIC SHORE

Maps pp 182-183

Nova Scotia's eastern shore is known for its rugged coastline, granite coves, sandy beaches, pretty fishing villages and attractive tree-lined towns with elegant houses built from shipbuilding or privateering fortunes. The entire coast from Canso to Yarmouth can be followed by road, but a greater concentration of quaint seaside communities is found south of Halifax.

FROM HALIFAX TO LIVERPOOL *Map p 202. 348km/216mi. 3 days.*

Leave Halifax by Rte 3. Turn left on Rte 333.

As the coast is approached, the landscape becomes wild, almost desolate. Huge boulders left by retreating glaciers and stunted vegetation give the area a lunar appearance. *Fog is least common mid-July to October, but can occur any time.*

★★ **Peggy's Cove.** – Immortalized by artists and photographers across Canada, this tiny village is unique among coastal communities, set as it is on a treeless outcropping of massive, deeply lined boulders. Its tranquil little harbour with colourful boats, and fishing shacks built on stilts over the water, is indeed picturesque.

Housing an operating post office *(mid-June–Oct)*, the **lighthouse** stands alone on a huge granite slab pounded by the Atlantic Ocean. *Sudden high waves and slippery boulders have resulted in personal tragedy. Use extreme caution when walking in this area.* Upon departing, note the **carvings** of village residents sculpted in the granite rock by William deGarthe (1907-1983).

The road follows the coast with views of the villages on **St Margaret's Bay.**

> *Rte 333 joins Rte 3 at Upper Tantallon; follow Rte 3 until Rte 329 turns off after Hubbards. Tour the peninsula and rejoin Rte 3 just before Chester.*

★ **Chester.** – Pop 10,762. Perched on cliffs rising out of Mahone Bay, this charming town has beautiful elm and oak trees and traditional New England frame houses. Founded by New Englanders in 1759, the community is a popular summer residence of Americans and a favourite retirement spot for Canadians.

> *Take Rte 12 north, 7km/4mi after Chester.*

★ **Ross Farm.** – *24km/15mi one way. Open daily Jun–mid-Oct. Admission charged.* ✆ ☎902/689-2210. Cleared from wilderness in 1816 by William Ross, this farm belonged to five generations of his family before acquisition by the Nova Scotia Museum. Maintained as a living museum of 19C agrarian life, the farm features coopering, candle making, forging, sheep shearing and other demonstrations that vary with the season. There are displays of plows and harrows, buggies and other transport, including a well-stocked peddler's wagon. Ox or horse-drawn wagon rides are available *($0.50)*.

> *Return to Rte 3.*

★ **Mahone Bay.** – Pop 1,096. Founded in 1754 by Captain Ephraim Cook, the community was once a centre of piracy and privateering. Today, this placid town is distinguished by three neighbouring churches lining the bay of the same name. Between 1756 and 1815, hundreds of small ships sailed from Nova Scotia ports to harass French, Spanish, Dutch and Americans vessels, from New England to the Caribbean. These acts of piracy were carried out with royal blessing. After obtaining a license, a privateer owner could attack only enemy ships. All prizes had to be taken to Halifax where the Court of Vice Admiralty decided their legality. Despite these restrictions, profits were enormous and coastal communities prospered.

Upon approaching the town, there is a lovely **view★** of the churches reflected in the water. Shops and restaurants, elegant frame houses, and churches are set along tree-lined streets close to the bay.

★ **Lunenburg.** – Pop 2,781. Situated on a hilly peninsula with "front" and "back" harbours, picturesque Lunenburg is named for the German hometown (Lüneburg) of the first settlers who arrived in 1753. Colourful historic houses grace the grid-patterned streets rising from the waterfront.

Once a pirates' haven, the town was sacked by American privateers in 1782. Known for its former shipbuilding industry, Lunenburg was the construction site of many schooners that fished the "banks" *(p 218)*, including the **Bluenose**, undefeated champion of the North American fishing fleet and winner of four international schooner races from 1921 to 1946. The **Bluenose II**, a replica of the original *(p 208)*, was also constructed here in 1963. Every August, the popular **Fisheries Exhibition and Fishermen's Reunion** is celebrated in Lunenburg. Dory, yacht and schooner races, fish-filleting and scallop-shucking contests, parades and displays are featured.

★★ **Fisheries Museum.** – *Lunenburg harbour. Open Jun–mid-Oct daily 9:30am– 5:30pm. $2.25.* ✆ ☎902/634-4794. Housed in a former fish-processing plant on the waterfront, this three-storey centre features a wide array of maritime displays. Exhibits range from the history of the Bluenose, and the illicit "rum-running" trade during

Prohibition to the development of the banks fishery. A sailmaker's workshop and a 1920s fish company office have been re-created, and ship models, tools and navigational equipment are on display. A theatre *(regularly scheduled films)*, working dory shop and aquarium complete the museum.

Moored at the wharf, the **Theresa E. Connor**, one of the last saltbank schooners to fish the Grand Banks, can be boarded. Built in 1938, she has been refurbished to illustrate the era of dory fishing when small, two-manned boats (dories) would haul in fish using trawl lines. The fish were salted on board a schooner, aptly called a "saltbanker," which served as a supply and delivery base. Characteristic craft that replaced dory schooners, the steel-hulled side trawler, **Cape Sable**, can also be boarded. Built in Holland in 1962, she hauled trawl nets off Lunenburg until 1982. A tiny shucking house shelters equipment and mounted scallop shells.

Follow Rte 3 and turn left on Rte 332 for 15km/9mi.

★ **Ovens Natural Park.** – *Open daily mid-May–mid-Oct. $2.50. ☎902/766-4621.* The park has a lovely site, which offers **views★** across Lunenburg Bay to Blue Rocks. A path along the cliff top leads to several sets of stairs by which visitors can descend to see the oven-like caves, cut into the cliffs by the action of the sea.

Continue on Rte 332 and then left on Rte 3.

The road follows the wide and tranquil estuary of LaHave River. Boats can be seen along this stretch of water lined with frame houses and trees. The river is crossed at **Bridgewater** (pop 7,248), a large, industrial town.

Turn left on Rte 331.

The road passes the town of **LaHave** itself, one of the earliest settlements in the province. Isaac de Razilly, Lieutenant-Governor of Acadie, built a fort here in 1632. The road continues along the coast with many pleasant views of the sea and fishing villages, especially in the vicinity of **Medway Harbour**.

Liverpool. – Pop 3,113. Founded in 1760 by New Englanders, Liverpool, like its great English namesake, is on the Mersey River. The privateering, fishing and ship repairing of the past have largely been supplanted by the modern industries of papermaking, fish processing and machine building.

★ **Perkins House.** – *On Main St. Open daily Jun–mid-Oct. ⅙ ☎902/354-4058.* This low-lying, New England frame house, with odd-shaped corners and winding hidden stairs, was built in 1767 for Col Simeon Perkins. A merchant and ship owner, Perkins moved to Nova Scotia from Cape Cod, assuming military, judicial and legislative roles beyond his business and family life. Surrounded by other elegant residences, the house is set in fine gardens among tall trees.

On display next door in the Queens County Museum is a copy of the colonel's diary, which captures life in a colonial town from 1766 to 1812.

EXCURSION TO SHELBURNE

★ **Shelburne.** – Pop 2,245. *64km/38mi south by Hwy 103. Exit 25. Tourist bureau on Dock St ☎902/875-4547.* This small waterfront town was once one of the largest 18C cities in North America. Founded by Loyalists in 1783, the community's population swelled to an estimated 10,000 when additional British sympathizers sought sanctuary in Nova Scotia from the American Revolution. The expansion was short lived, however, since many settlers moved elsewhere.

Historic homes and commercial buildings line Dock Street, former hub of the town's bustling mercantile activity. Work continues at the barrel factory and in the **Dory Shop** *(open daily Jun–mid-Oct)*, a museum spotlighting the dory's historical importance and method of construction.

★ **Ross-Thomson House.** – *Charlotte Lane. Open daily Jun–mid-Oct. ☎902/875-3141.* This two-storey structure was in use by 1785 as a combination house, store and warehouse for items of international trade. Note the two roof shapes: gambrel and gable. Visitors can tour the well-stocked interior of the old store as well as the residence. Seasonal flower and herb gardens grace the front entrance.

★ BALMORAL MILLS

Map p 183

10km/6mi southeast of Tatamagouche by Rte 311. Grounds open year-round. ☎902/657-3016. Standing beside a stream in a pleasant valley, this fully operational **gristmill** *(open daily Jun–mid-Oct)* was built in 1874. Although commercial use ceased in 1954, the mill has been completely restored.

When in operation *(a few hours daily)*, the mill is a hive of activity. Weighing over a tonne, the original millstones grind barley, oats, wheat and buckwheat into flour and meal *(for sale)*. The grain is moved from storey to storey by means of a series of buckets mounted on leather belts. Various milling processes are explained. Below the mill, the revolving water wheel can be seen.

EXCURSION

Sutherland Steam Mill. – *In Denmark, 10km/6mi northeast by Rte 311, minor road and Rte 326. Open daily Jun–mid-Oct. ☎902/657-3365.* When Alexander Sutherland built this sawmill in 1894, steam was replacing water power as the most efficient means of cutting wood. He made sleighs, carriages and sleds; his brother and partner produced doors and windows for local houses. All machinery is in working order, and the mill "steams up" once a month *(call ahead for schedule)*.

★★ CABOT TRAIL

Map p 183

Round-trip of 301km/187mi from Baddeck; allow 2 days. The trail can be driven in either direction, but visitors may prefer clockwise travel for the security of hugging the mountainside during steep, curvy stretches.

Named for explorer John Cabot, who is reputed to have landed at the northern tip of Cape Breton Island in 1497, this route is one of the most beautiful drives in eastern North America. Opened in 1936, the paved, two-lane highway makes a half-circle tour of the northern part of the island.

Initially traversing tranquil farmland, the trail then hugs the coast and winds up and down, providing scenic views of the immense Atlantic Ocean, craggy mountains, rocky inlets, magnificent headlands and dense forests. Some areas are reminiscent of the Scottish Highlands, ancestral home of many of the island's inhabitants. The east coast is especially rich in Gaelic culture. Derived from the language of the Celts in Ireland and the Scottish Highlands, Gaelic was the third most common European language spoken in Canada in the early 19C, and can still be heard here today.

★ BADDECK

Overlooking Baddeck Bay, this charming village is the starting point of the Cabot Trail. The popular resort town has a lovely **site★★** on the north shore of **Bras d'Or Lake**. This immense inland sea nearly cuts Cape Breton in two and is fed in the north by the Atlantic via two channels, the Great Bras d'Or and the Little Bras d'Or on either side of Boularderie Island.

Summer Home of Alexander Graham Bell. – Bras d'Or Lake's resemblance to a Scottish loch has attracted many settlers of Scottish origin to its shores. Among them was **Alexander Graham Bell** (1847-1922), humanitarian, researcher and prolific inventor. In 1885, Bell first visited Baddeck, where he was to conduct much of his aeronautical work. Eventually he chose the location for his summer residence, naming his home, *Beinn Bhreagh*, "beautiful mountain" in Gaelic.

His work as a teacher of the deaf led to the invention of the telephone, conceived in Brantford, Ontario *(p 105)*, in 1874, and tested in Boston the following year. The discovery brought him fame and the capital to continue other research. In Baddeck, he built kites and heavier-than-air craft, using combinations of the tetrahedron shape—an almost perfect form because it is lightweight but strong. In 1907, with other pioneer aviators, he founded the Aerial Experiment Association and sponsored the first manned flight in Canada when the **Silver Dart** flew across Baddeck Bay in 1909. Before his death, he witnessed his hydrofoil craft reach the incredible speed (for 1919) of 114km/70mph on Bras d'Or Lake.

★★ Alexander Graham Bell National Historic Site. – ☞ *On Hwy 205 in Baddeck. Open Jul–Sept daily 9am–9pm. Off-season daily 9am–5pm.* & ☎*902/295-2069.* Bell's favourite shape, the tetrahedron, is used extensively in the design of this fascinating museum. Exhibits illustrate the genius of this remarkable man.

There are models of the telephone, the vacuum jacket (a forerunner of the iron lung), the surgical probe (a device used prior to the invention of the X ray), and Bell's kites. His project to prevent stranded sailors from dying of thirst at sea is on view—a model for converting fog to drinking water, using breath and salt water. A highlight is the superb **photograph collection**, oversized black and white prints of Bell's life and work. One wing of the museum is devoted to his hydrofoil, the HD-4. Both the original hull and a reconstruction of the entire craft are cn exhibit.

From the museum's rooftop garden, there is a **view** of the wooded headland across Baddeck Bay. *Beinn Bhreagh (not open to the public)* can be seen among the trees.

★ FROM BADDECK TO CHÉTICAMP Map p 205. 88km/55mi

The Cabot Trail follows the valley of the Middle River, passes the Lakes O'Law and joins the Margaree River's lush green **valley★** of meadows and abundant salmon pools, reputed to offer some of Canada's finest salmon fishing.

North East Margaree. – Located in the heart of salmon-fishing country, the tiny rural community has two museums of note.

★ **Museum of Cape Breton Heritage.** – *Open daily Jun–mid-Oct.* ☎*902/248-2551.* This small museum displays the handicrafts of the various inhabitants of Cape Breton, primarily Micmac Indians, Acadian French and Highland Scots. Exquisite embroidery, weaving and spinning equipment, and an extensive collection of tartans are highlights. *Weaving and spinning demonstrations on request.*

★ **Margaree Salmon Museum.** – *Open daily mid-Jun–mid-Oct. $0.50.* & ☎*902/248-2623.* This pleasant little museum features a large collection of colourful fishing flies and rods—one actually 5.5m/18ft long, made in Scotland in 1880. Fishing tackle on display includes a sampling of illegal spears used by poachers. The life cycle of the Atlantic salmon is illustrated from birth to a full-grown adult's return trip upriver to reproduce. Unlike its Pacific cousin, the Atlantic salmon can make several such trips.

The Cabot Trail parallels the Margaree River northward, affording pastoral **views★** of the wide river valley and the town of East Margaree on the opposite side. The sudden vista of a wide expanse of sea, after the road ascends out of farmland, is dramatic. Upon descent, the **view★** of Margaree Harbour is breathtaking. The trail crosses the estuary of the Margaree River and heads north along the Acadian coast, with views of the Gulf of St Lawrence.

Chéticamp. – An enclave of Acadian culture, this fishing community sprawls along the coast opposite Chéticamp Island. A protected harbour and a large stone church dedicated to St Peter distinguish the town. The Acadian tri-colour flag *(p 196)* can be seen atop flagpoles scattered throughout the town. Locally made hand-hooked rugs are Chéticamp's claim to fame.

Acadian Museum. – *Open daily May–mid-Oct.* ✕ ⅄ ☎*902/224-2170.* Operated by a cooperative of Acadian women, the museum and gift shop feature a large array of hooked mats, rugs and other crafted items. There are demonstrations of hooking, spinning, carding and weaving.

FROM CHÉTICAMP TO CAPE SMOKEY *Map below. 124km/77mi.*

★★ **Cape Breton Highlands National Park.** –Spanning coast to coast across northern Cape Breton, this 950sq km/367sq mi wilderness park combines seashore and mountains. Hills ascend directly from the ocean to form a tableland more than 500m/1700ft high.

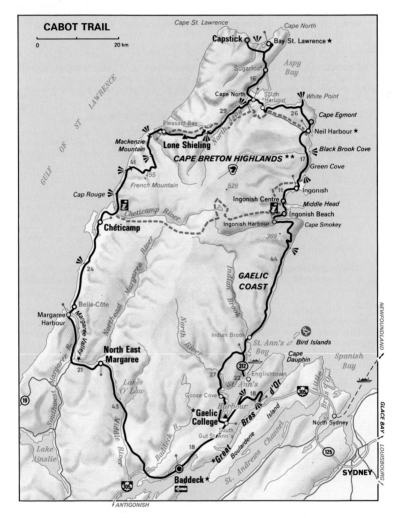

The west coast borders the relatively calm waters of the Gulf of St Lawrence. On the eastern side, the Atlantic Ocean pounds the bare rocks with great force, yet there are several fine beaches throughout this preserve. Whales, and even bald eagles, can be found on either shore.

Inland, the park is heavily forested and boggy—the realm of moose, lynx and snowshoe hare. Several trails reach the interior *(details from park office)*, but the main attraction is the beautiful coastline.

Visit. – ☞ *Open year-round. Hiking, picknicking, swimming.* △ *Information office (mid-May–mid-Oct daily 8am–9pm) at park entrances north of Chéticamp* ☎*902/224-2306 and at Ingonish Beach* ☎*902/285-2535 (summer only)* ☎*902/285-2691 (year-round). There are many designated lookouts in the park for viewing.*

From the park entrance at the Chéticamp River, Cabot Trail winds up Chéticamp Canyon to emerge on the coast and parallel the sea. Fine **views**★★ of the ocean and the road weaving up and down in the distance are afforded. From **Cap Rouge** lookout, there is an especially lovely **view**★★. The road gradually climbs French Mountain and heads inland across the plateau, the highest point on the highway.

After crossing several deep stream-lined valleys, the road descends to Mackenzie Mountain. Then, by a series of switchbacks, it reaches Pleasant Bay with outstanding **views**★★ on the descent. The **Lone Shieling**, a tiny hut of stone with rounded corners and a thatched roof *(about 6.5km/4mi from Pleasant Bay, then short walk)*, is a replica of a Scottish crofter's cottage, common in the Highlands and islands of Scotland. It was built to form a visible link between the adopted home of the Highland Scots who settled Cape Breton and their ancestral land.

205

Along its course Cabot Trail first climbs over North Mountain, descends steeply, allowing pretty **views★**, and then enters the valley of the North Aspy River, which it follows to the village of **Cape North**.

★★ Excursion to Bay St Lawrence. – *16km/10mi north.* This scenic drive rounds Aspy Bay with views of its long sandbar, and then heads inland across grassy hills spotted with pink rock to St Lawrence Bay at the north end of Cape Breton Island. Before leaving the bay, the road passes Cabot Landing Beach, supposedly the first North American landfall of John Cabot *(p 228).* Whether visited by Cabot or not, it is a refreshing scene of a long beach backed by Sugarloaf Mountain.

At the end of the road is the tiny fishing village of **Bay St Lawrence★** built around a small lake with a narrow exit to the sea. Upon the approach to the village, a large white clapboard church (St Margaret's) is prominent. From its grounds, the **view★** of the bay community is picturesque. The church's fine wooden interior has a ceiling shaped like the hull of a ship.

> *Upon leaving Bay St Lawrence, turn right and continue 3km/1.8mi to Capstick.*

Capstick. – Less populous than Bay St Lawrence, this hillside settlement consists of a few isolated houses on the grassy slopes above the seacliffs.
The dramatic **views★** of the inlets through the scraggy pines are enhanced by the beauty of the water's colour.

> *Return to Cabot Trail. After South Harbour, take coast road.*

Revealing fine **views★** of Aspy Bay, its sand bar and the long Cape North peninsula, this coastal route is a pretty drive. The road turns south after White Point through the charming fishing villages of **New Haven** and **Neil Harbour★**, the latter with an artificial harbour beside a sandy bay.

> *Rejoin Cabot Trail.*

This section of the trail is an especially splendid drive along the coast, particularly after **Black Brook Cove**. Worn, pink boulders stretch into the sea, while green forests cover the inlands. There are many little bays and coves, **Green Cove** being one of the loveliest. From Lakie's Head lookout, the narrow peninsula of **Middle Head** and towering Cape Smokey can be identified, sometimes rising from a mist reminiscent of the Scottish Highlands.

The Ingonishs. – The relative solitude of the trail is left behind in the resort area of Ingonish Centre, Ingonish Beach, Ingonish Harbour, and other Ingonish designations, popular for various forms of recreation *(fishing, boating, swimming, golf, tennis, and winter skiing).* Many cruise ships stop over at the harbour.
The bay itself is cut into two parts—north and south—by Middle Head, the dramatic setting of the **Keltic Lodge**, one of Canada's best known resort hotels. To the south, **Cape Smokey** rises 369m/1,210ft out of the sea. This headland is at times partially obscured by cloud, hence its name.

THE GAELIC COAST   *Map p 205*

From Cape Smokey to Baddeck. – *89km/55mi.* The trail climbs over Cape Smokey and then drops again, permitting several good **views★**. Descending the coast farther inland, the road passes through several fishing villages.
Offshore are the **Bird Islands**, a sanctuary where vast numbers of sea birds nest in summer. The trail rounds St Ann's Harbour, offering lovely views after Goose Cove, but especially at South Gut St Ann's.

★ **Gaelic College.** – *In St Ann's.* Founded in 1939 by Rev A. W. R. MacKenzie, this school is the only one on the continent to teach the Gaelic language and Highland arts and crafts. Attracting youth from all over North America, the college offers courses in bagpipe music, clan law, Gaelic singing, Highland dancing and hand weaving of family and clan tartans. Students can often be seen performing Highland flings, sword dances and step dancing. In August, a week-long **Gaelic Mod** is held when prizes are awarded to the best performers in each field *(for details, contact the college).*

Great Hall of the Clans. – *On campus. Open daily Jun–Oct. Off-season Mon–Sat. $2.* ♿ ☎*902/295-3411.* At the rear of the entrance is a room displaying Highlands pioneer crafts and memorabilia. Inside the large meeting hall, wall **exhibits** illustrate clan history and life. A variety of tartans and costumes are also on display. At one end of the hall stands a statue of Angus MacAskill (1825-1863), the 236cm/7ft 9in tall,193kg/425lb "Cape Breton giant" who toured the US with the midget, Tom Thumb.

★ **Alternative Route.** – *22km/14mi by Rte 312 and Trans-Can Hwy.* This road enters St Ann's Bay via a narrow spit of land that divides the bay from St Ann's harbour. At the end of the spit, there is a ferry across the 270m/300yd outlet *(24hr/day every 5min; Feb–Apr no crossing due to ice; $0.50/car;* ☎*902/929-2404).*

EXCURSIONS

★ **Great Bras d'Or.** – *Map p 205. 18km/11mi northeast along Trans-Can Hwy from South Gut St Ann's.* The road ascends Kelly's Mountain with a fine **view★** from the lookout of the harbour, spit of land and the ferry. Crossing Cape Dauphin peninsula, it descends to the Great Bras d'Or. There are good **views★** of this stretch of water, of the bridge that spans it, and, in the distance, of **Sydney** (pop 26,063), Cape Breton's principal city and the site of eastern Canada's richest coalfields, which have fostered a sizeable steel industry.

★★ The Miners' Museum. – *Map p 183. In Glace Bay, 19km/12mi northeast of Sydney. Follow museum signs from town to Quarry Point.* Overlooking the vast Atlantic Ocean from its 6ha/15-acre site, this low-lying, geometric museum stands as a monument to Cape Breton's coal-mining history.

Sprawling Glace Bay—home of the museum—has been a mining town since 1720 when French soldiers from Louisbourg found coal in the cliffs at Port Morien to the southeast. The region is underlain with bituminous coal seams that dip seaward under the Atlantic. By the late 19C, numerous coal mines were operating. When iron ore deposits were found in nearby Newfoundland *(p 185)*, a steel industry mushroomed in the vicinity of Sydney, using coal as coke in the refining process. Immigrants poured into the area in the 20C for mining jobs. By the early 1950s, use of oil and gas had reduced the demand for coal. Economic depression hit as the mines began to close. The Federal Government created the Cape Breton Development Corporation, which operated the Glace Bay colliery until 1984.

Visit. – *Open Jun–Sept daily 10am–6pm (Tue 7pm). Off-season Mon–Fri 9am–4pm. $2.75 plus $2.25 for guided mine tour. Protective clothing is provided.* ✗ & ☎902/ *849-4522.* The museum has well-presented, colourful exhibits on coal formation and mining methods. Coal samples, equipment and transport are also on display. Films *(20-30min)* about Cape Breton's mining industry and labour history are shown in the theatre.

Retired miners conduct **mine tours**, interspersing commentary with tales from personal experience. Visitors walk down a sloping tunnel under the Atlantic Ocean to see the machinery and coal face of the Oceans Deep Colliery. *Coal samples can be collected as souvenirs. Note: low mine ceilings may necessitate stooping.*

Beside the museum building, a **miners' village** has been reconstructed. The mining company supplied employee housing and owned the only store. Transactions were based on credit secured against a miner's wages. After a week of work, a miner sometimes drew no pay, finding he owed for food, clothing and other necessities. In addition to a store, a miner's house of 1850-1900 has been re-created. The restaurant serves home-cooked specialties such as "coal dust pie."

★★ HALIFAX   Pop 114,455

Map p 183   Tourist Office ☎ 902/421-8736

Situated on the east coast at about the mainland's midpoint, the capital of Nova Scotia overlooks one of the finest harbours in the world. The deep outer inlet of the Atlantic Ocean narrows into a protected inner harbour called the **Bedford Basin**. The foot-shaped peninsula upon which the city was built is dominated by a hill topped by a star-shaped citadel. These two factors—a natural harbour and a man-made fortress—were the basis of the city's founding.

Early History. – Halifax came into being because of the existence of Louisbourg *(p 210)*. New Englanders had successfully captured the French fortress in 1744, only to see it later returned to France. Their anger prodded the British government to build a fortress as a counterweight to Louisbourg. In July, 1749, the appointed governor of Nova Scotia, Col **Edward Cornwallis**, and about 2,500 English settlers constructed a fortified settlement on the site of the present-day city.

From its inception, Halifax was a military stronghold filled with soldiers from the fort and sailors from numerous naval vessels docked in the harbour. From the social gatherings of the nobility (officers in both services) to the presence of brothels along the wharves, the military shaped the town. Indeed, even law was martial; citizens were deprived of control over their affairs for nearly a hundred years, until Halifax achieved city status.

The Royal Princes. – Forbidden by their father to remain in England, two scapegrace sons of **George III** made Halifax their home. The future **William IV** spent his 21st birthday in wild revels off the port. His brother **Edward**, Duke of Kent, and later, the father of Queen Victoria, served as commander-in-chief in Halifax from 1794 to 1800. Spending a fortune on defences, he made Halifax a member of the famous quadrilateral of British defences, which included Gibraltar and Bermuda. A rigid disciplinarian, he had his men flogged or hanged for misdemeanours. He installed the first telegraph system in North America by which he could relay orders to his men from Annapolis Royal *(p 198)* or from his love nest on the Bedford Basin, where his mistress lived.

The Halifax Explosion. – The city's history has not always been so colourful, but its prosperity has coincided with times of war, whereas peace has often brought economic depression. The Napoleonic Wars, the American Civil War, World Wars I and II saw great military activity in Halifax, great wealth —and great tragedy.

During both world wars, the Bedford Basin was used as a convoy assembly point so ships could cross the Atlantic in the safety of numbers when German submarines were encountered. In December, 1917, the **Mont Blanc**, a French munitions ship, had a fatal collision in the harbour with a Belgian relief ship, the **Imo**. The *Mont Blanc* was carrying a lethal combination of picric acid, guncotton, TNT and benzol. The explosion was the world's largest, until the atom bomb was dropped on Hiroshima in 1945. The entire north end of the city was wiped out; rail yards and docks were destroyed. Windows were shattered as far as Truro 100km/60mi away; the explosion was heard over 160km/100mi. Only the *Mont Blanc's* cannon (found in Albro Lake behind Dartmouth) and an anchor shaft (which landed more than 3km/2mi away) were left. Miraculously, the crew survived, having abandoned ship in time. However, 1,400 people were killed outright, an estimated 600 died later, 199 were blinded and another 9,000 were injured. There are people in Halifax today who, injured for life as children, are still receiving compensation.

The City Today. – Halifax is the largest city in the Atlantic provinces and the region's commercial and financial capital. In addition, Halifax is the Atlantic base of the **Canadian Navy**. Nova Scotia's administrative hub and an important centre for scientific research, the capital is also a major port. The 6.5km/4mi long outer inlet of Halifax harbour is lined with docks and piers where it narrows into the 5km/3mi long, 2.5km/1.5mi wide Bedford Basin. The port has two container terminals, a grain elevator, an automobile-handling facility and oil refineries for arriving tankers.

SIGHTS   *Map p 209. 2 days.*

★★ **Halifax Citadel.** – Situated on a hill overlooking the city's commercial district, the citadel is the fourth of forts dating to 1749 to occupy this site, with its commanding views of the area. The present star-shaped masonry structure is a repository of Halifax's military history and tradition.

Begun in 1828 at the order of the Duke of Wellington, the bastioned fort was not completed until 1856. Although never attacked, the fortification served the British Army until 1906 and the Canadian military until after World War II.

Easily approached from downtown, or driven around via Citadel Road, the citadel's site offers **views★** of the city, harbour, Dartmouth, George's Island, and the Angus McDonald suspension bridge. Note the attractive **clock tower★**, the symbol of Halifax. Completed in 1803, the original was ordered by Prince Edward with four faces and bells to ring out the hours. Restored in 1962, it remains a memento to the punctilious prince.

Surrounded by a dry defensive ditch, the fortification contains a large central parade ground where soldiers attired in 19C uniforms perform military drills *(daily Jun 15– Labour Day)*.

Visit. – ☞ *Grounds open year-round. Citadel open May–Nov daily 9am–6pm. $2 (summer only).* ⚒ ও *☎902/426-5080.* This sprawling complex houses an orientation centre, barracks, ammunition magazines, a small museum and numerous other exhibits. Visitors can climb on the ramparts, look at guns that served as the citadel's main defence, and visit the outer ditches and ravelins. An audio-visual presentation *(50min), **Tides of History★**,* covers the history of Halifax and its defences.

★ **Historic Properties and the Harbour.** – Off Upper Water Street, the pedestrian area between Duke Street and the Cogswell interchange is commonly known as Historic Properties. Completely renovated, several 19C stone warehouses and wooden buildings house interesting shops, studios, restaurants and pubs, with outdoor seating overlooking the harbour.

Moored here sometimes is the **Bluenose II**, a replica of the schooner that held the International Fishermen's trophy 20 years, after capturing it in 1921. Constructed in 1963 as a goodwill ambassador for Nova Scotia, the *Bluenose II* offers summer cruises in Halifax harbour *(Jul–Aug Tue–Sun 9am, 1 & 7pm; round-trip 2hrs; $14;* ⚒ ▣ *☎902/422-2678),* when not visiting foreign ports.

From Historic Properties, visitors can walk west through a series of restored buildings to the Granville Street Mall and Scotia Square. A **boardwalk** follows the harbourfront north around the Sheraton Hotel and south past the Law Courts to reach the terminus of the passenger ferry to Dartmouth *(p 210).*

Farther south stands the **brewery market**, a former brewery now housing several restaurants, shops and a public market *(Sat & Sun 7am-2pm)* within its restored interior courtyards.

★★ **Harbour Cruise [A].** – *Departs from Privateers' Wharf Jun–Oct daily 10am–7pm. Round-trip 2hrs. $12.50.* ⚒ ও ▣ *Halifax Water Tours ☎902/420-1015.* The *Haligonian III* cruise provides interesting commentary on the Halifax shipyards where 7,000 vessels were repaired during World War II; the naval dockyards with destroyers, preservers, submarines and other ships; the National Harbours Board terminal with its huge grain elevator; the container terminal where giant gantry cranes load odd-shaped ships specially constructed to carry containers; and other points of interest seen on the tour.

The cruise rounds Point Pleasant and enters the **North West Arm★**, a lovely stretch of water extending along the peninsula's west side and bordered by expensive homes and yacht clubs.

★ **Maritime Museum of the Atlantic.** – *1675 Lower Water St. Open daily year-round. Admission charged. Closed Christmas & New Year's.* ও *☎902/424-7490.* Located on the waterfront with a view of Halifax harbour, this interesting museum presents a variety of small craft, ship models, photographs and displays on maritime history. Note the restored ship's **chandlery**, housed in an old warehouse where a range of mariner's equipment is exhibited. Sections are also devoted to the days of sail, the age of steam and naval history.

Moored at the museum's wharf, two authentic vessels can be boarded *(Jul–Aug):* the **CSS Acadia**, a steamship built in 1913 for the Canadian Hydrographic Service, and the restored **HMCS Sackville**, a World War II corvette that served in the Battle of the Atlantic.

★ **Province House.** – *Main entrance on Hollis St. Open daily Jul–Aug. Off-season Mon–Fri.* ও *☎902/424-4661.* Completed in 1819, this sandstone Georgian structure houses the Legislative Assembly of Nova Scotia, an institution that has existed since 1758.

The **Red Chamber**, where the Legislative Council used to meet, can be visited. Note the portraits of King George III and Queen Charlotte at the head of the room. In the **assembly chamber**, visitors might witness some spirited debates when the body is in session. Once housing the provincial Supreme Court, the **legislative library** was the site, in 1835, of the self-defence of journalist **Joseph Howe** against a charge of criminal libel. His acquittal marked the beginning of a free press in Nova Scotia. Later he entered politics and led a fight against Confederation but eventually joined the Dominion (now more commonly called Federal) Government in Ottawa.

★ **The Art Gallery of Nova Scotia.** – *1741 Hollis St across from Province House. Open year-round Tue–Sun. Closed legal holidays. $2.* ♿ ☎*902/424-2002.* Housed in the stately Dominion Building, this modern museum has four floors of artwork. Nova Scotia artists from the first half of the 20C and other 20C painters are featured on the first floor. Canadian art, including paintings of the well-known **Group of Seven**, occupies the second floor along with British and European works. The mezzanine features regional **folk art**—painting, sculptures, paper and textiles—and a small but excellent collection of **Inuit art.** The lower level is reserved for temporary exhibits.

Grand Parade. – Bordered by **City Hall** *(open year-round Mon–Fri; for details contact Tourist Office* ☎*902/421-8736)* at one end and **St Paul's Anglican Church** at the other, this pleasant square has been the centre of Halifax since its founding. Here the militia mustered, the town crier proclaimed the news, and city dwellers hired sedan chairs. Built in 1750, the small timber-framed church is the oldest Protestant church in Canada.

★ **Nova Scotia Museum.** – *1747 Summer St. Open daily Jun–mid-Oct. Off-season Tue–Sun. Closed legal holidays. Admission charged.* ♿ 🅿 ☎*902/424-7353.* This museum offers a comprehensive picture of Nova Scotia by covering its geology, history, society, and flora and fauna.
A beautifully restored stagecoach used in the late 19C on the Yarmouth-to-Tusket run graces the entrance. Micmac displays, furniture and glass of the early settlers, natural history dioramas, and marine life, especially whales and sharks, can be seen.

★ **Public Gardens.** – *Main entrance at corner of Spring Garden Rd and S Park St. Open daily May–Nov dawn–dusk.* Opened to the public in 1867, this 7ha/17acre park is a fine example of an immense Victorian garden, complete with weeping trees, ponds, fountains, statues, formal plantings and an ornate bandstand. Note the massive wrought-iron entrance gate.

★ **Point Pleasant Park.** – *Closed to traffic; parking on Point Pleasant Dr at Tower Rd and near container terminal. Open daily year-round.* 🍴 *(summer).* Situated at the southernmost point of the peninsula, this lovely 75ha/185 acre park has excellent **views**★★ of the harbour and the North West Arm. For many years, the park was dominated by the military, who filled it with batteries and forts, the remains of which can still be seen.

Prince of Wales Martello Tower. – 📷 *Open daily Jul–Labour Day. Grounds open year-round.* ☎*902/426-5080.* The prototype of what came to be called a **Martello tower**, this circular stone structure was the first of its kind in North America. Prince Edward ordered its construction in 1797, naming the tower for his brother—the future George IV. Its design was adapted from a tower on Mortella Point in Corsica that had proved almost impregnable. Such towers were built later in Canada and England to counter invasion by Napoleon's troops.
Exhibits portray the tower's history, architectural features and importance as a defensive structure.

EXCURSIONS

★ **McNab's Island.** – *Access by ferry from Halifax harbourfront. For schedules contact tourist office, Halifax* ☎*902/421-8736.* Located in Halifax harbour, east of Point Pleasant Park, the island has beaches, walking trails, good views and the remains of military fortifications.

Sir Sandford Fleming Park. – *5.5km/3mi by Cogswell St, Quinpool Rd and Purcell's Cove Rd (Rte 253). Open daily year-round. Walking trails, swimming, boating, picnic area.* A peaceful haven in a residential suburb of Halifax, this park is a tribute to **Sir Sandford Fleming** (1827-1915), a prominent engineer from Scotland. Instrumental in the construction of Canada's first continental railway system, he also designed the nation's first postage stamp and urged the adoption of international standard time.
The long stretch of North West Arm can be seen from **Dingle Tower** *(open daily Jun–Labour Day).*

★ **York Redoubt.** – ⍟ *11km/7mi by Cogswell St, Quinpool Rd and Purcell's Cove Rd (Rte 253). Open year-round; exhibits daily mid-Jun–Labour Day.* ♿ ☎*902/426-5080.* Located on the bluffs above Halifax harbour, this coastal fort played an integral role in the city's defensive and warning systems.
First constructed in 1793, the defences were strengthened by Prince Edward, who named the redoubt for his brother, the Duke of York. The Martello tower Edward erected in 1798 was part of his signal communication system. During World War II, the redoubt became the centre for coordinating defence of the harbour and city against German attack.
At the north end, the remains of the stone tower can be seen. Aligned along the top of the bluff, a series of gun emplacements face the harbour approach. At the south end, the **command post** contains displays on the defences, and from it *(weather permitting)* there are good **views★** of the harbour.

★ **Dartmouth.** – Pop 67,798. *Map p 183.* Site of a large naval dockyard and research centre, Halifax's twin city on the other side of the inlet has a pleasant waterfront with several shop-lined streets descending to it. Connected to Halifax by two bridges, Dartmouth is serviced by **ferry** *(daily service 6am–midnight; except Sun in winter; $0.60;* ☎*902/464-2336),* from which the views of both cities are expansive.
Quaker House. – *59 Ochterloney St. Open daily Jun–Labour Day.* ☎*902/464-2253.* This house is the sole survivor of 22 dwellings built for a group of Quaker whalers who moved to the province from New England in 1785. Its shingled exterior with paned windows is typical of the houses constructed along the coast from Massachusetts to Nova Scotia in the 18C. Note the framed walls, off-centre front door, exposed beams and narrow winding staircase.
Black Cultural Centre for Nova Scotia. – *In Westphal. Rte 7 at Cherrybrook Road. Open year-round Mon–Sat.* ♿ ☎*902/434-6223.* This sizeable museum, library and meeting hall opened in 1983 to foster the province's black history and culture. Exhibits cover early migration and settlement, military service, religion and community. There is a memorial to naval hero **William Hall** (1827-1904), the first Nova Scotian and first black to be awarded the Victoria Cross, the Commonwealth's military medal for exceptional courage.

★ **Uniacke House.** – *Map p 183. In Mount Uniacke, 40km/25mi northwest by Rtes 7 and 1. Open daily Jun–mid-Oct.* ♿ ☎*902/866-2560.* This fine example of plantation-style colonial architecture, with its wide portico rising the two storeys of the house, stands on a peaceful lakeshore estate. Completed in 1815, it was the country home of Richard Uniacke, Attorney General of Nova Scotia from 1797 to 1830.
The interior looks today as it did in 1815 with the original furnishings of the Uniacke family, including several mahogany pieces crafted by George Adams of London.

★★ **Peggy's Cove.** – *43km/27mi. Description p 201.*

★★★ LOUISBOURG FORTRESS

Map p 183

Guarding the entrance of the St Lawrence, the approach to Quebec, Louisbourg was once the great 18C fortress of New France, manned by the largest garrison in North America. The $25 million restoration project is the most expensive preservation ever undertaken by the Canadian government.

A Not-So-Impregnable Fortress. – The French had long planned a fortress in Nova Scotia, even considering Halifax as a possible site. When they lost the mainland in 1713 *(p 184),* they chose the eastern peninsula of Île Royale (now Cape Breton) and commenced construction of a fortified town in 1719.
Following fortification designs elaborated by French military engineers, the plan called for a citadel, six bastions and detached batteries. The considerable expense was still less than the cost of a French warship's six-month patrol of the Atlantic waters to guard the lucrative French fishery. Nonetheless, this massive undertaking was riddled with problems: a harsh climate, a boggy site where the mortar sometimes crumbled, scarce building materials and a few corrupt French officials who lined their pockets at royal expense. Difficult living conditions and lack of discipline among the common soldiers contributed to a mutiny in 1744.
In 1745, prior to completion, 4,000 New Englanders attacked the "impregnable" fortress. Less than two months later, the French surrendered. In 1748, the British agreed to return the fort to the island colony of King **Louis XV**. The following year, the

French reoccupied the stronghold, while the British founded Halifax as a counter-fortress *(p 207)*. Ten years later, Louisbourg was under siege again, this time by British regulars. **James Wolfe**, the second in command, managed to land, and the fortress had to be surrendered a second time. Wolfe went on to capture Quebec City in 1759 *(p 149)*. To prevent further threat to British interests, Louisbourg was destroyed in 1760.

Since 1961, one quarter of the fortress has been rebuilt according to the original plans and historical records. Furnishings are either original or reproductions.

Access. – *37km/23mi south of Sydney by Rte 22, southwest of town of Louisbourg.*

VISIT *Allow minimum 1/2 day*

🦫 *Open Jun–Sept daily 9:30am–5pm, Jul–Aug 9am–6pm. May & Oct outside walking tours only. Off-season by appointment Mon–Fri 8am–4:30pm. $6.50.* ✗ ⚙ ☎902/733-2280. *Note: Be prepared for cool temperatures, rain and fog. Comfortable walking shoes recommended.* Models of the fortress and displays on the history of Louisbourg provide orientation in the **visitor centre** *(departure point for bus to fortress; on-board commentary serves as preview of visit).*

Visitors cross a drawbridge to enter the walled town through the elaborate **Dauphine Gate**, manned by a sentry. Over 50 buildings *(most open to the public)* are constructed of wood or roughcast masonry, some furnished to their 1740s appearance, others containing themed exhibits. In the summer season, guides portray 18C

French society's leisure, propertied and working classes. Popular attractions include a **bakery**, where visitors can buy bread similar to the kind King Louis' troops lined up for in 1744. Three **period restaurants** serve 18C meals on earthenware and pewter. Along the quay stands the high wooden **Frédéric Gate**, the entrance through which important visitors to this once-bustling port were ushered from the harbour. The rich furnishings on the ground floor of the **ordonnateur's residence** include a harpsichord of the period. Archaeological artifacts recovered during reconstruction are on display at various locations.

Dauphine Gate, Louisbourg Fortress

★★ **King's Bastion.** — Once one of the largest in North America, this military stronghold has become the symbol of reconstructed Louisbourg. Quarters for the garrison provide insight into the lives of the privileged and impoverished in Old World society. The **governor's apartments** consist of ten elegant rooms, lavishly furnished. Not as comfortable but well accommodated are the **officers' quarters**. Drafty and spartan, the **soldiers' barracks** are not at all conducive to a long stay. The **prison** and a **chapel** that once served as the town's parish church can also be visited.

The beaver symbol 🦫 *indicates that the point of interest described has been designated a national park or national historic site.*

★ **MAITLAND**

Map p 183

Overlooking Cobequid Bay in the Minas Basin, Maitland was once an important shipbuilding centre. The town is best known as the site of the construction of the largest wooden ship built in Canada, the **William D. Lawrence**. Today, Maitland's fine houses attest to the wealth created by the former industry.

★ **Lawrence House.** – *On Rte 15. Open daily mid-May–Oct.* ☎902/261-2628. Surrounded by elm trees, this two-and-a-half storey house is a splendid example of the grand residences of Nova Scotia's shipbuilders and sea captains. The entrance portico with its double, curved staircase is reminiscent of a ship's bridge.

William Dawson Lawrence built this house (c.1870) to overlook his shipyard on the Shubenacadie River at the point where it joins Cobequid Bay. Believing he could double a ship's size without doubling its operating costs, Lawrence constructed an 80m/262ft ship, which weighed 2,459 tons and had three masts, the highest being over 60m/200ft. To complete the vessel, he had to mortgage his house, but the investment proved to be profitable. Launched in 1874, the ship sailed all over the world with many varied cargoes.

The house contains most of its original furnishings, including shipbuilding artifacts, pictures of 19C ships and a 2m/7ft model of the *William D. Lawrence.*

A lookout area across the road from the house affords a good **view★** of the tidal flats.

★ SHERBROOKE

Map p 183

This village occupies a pretty **site** on the St Marys River, once the location of a French fort (1655). After capture by the English in 1669, the settlement was abandoned until people were attracted by the rich timberlands in 1800. During the early 19C, sawmills sprang up and wooden ships were built. Gold was discovered in 1861, and for about 20 years, the town flourished. The gold did not last, but Sherbrooke survived as a lumber town. Today, it is a peaceful rural community and a centre for sports fishing and tourism.

★★ **Sherbrooke Village.** – *Open Jun–mid-Oct daily 9:30am–5:30pm. $2.25.* ✗ ⴠ ☎*902/522-2400.* Restored beginning in 1969, this historic village is actually an extension of the town of Sherbrooke. Streets have been closed to traffic, and only a few houses within the village are private residences.

Renovated to reflect the period, the buildings were constructed between 1860 and 1870. A church, schoolhouse, post office, blacksmith shop and several homes can be visited. Built in 1862 with separate downstairs and upstairs cells for men and women, the **jail** occupied half the jailer's house. Of particular interest is the **boat-building shop** where wooden boats are still constructed. Above Cumminger Brothers' general store, visitors can don 19C costumes and be photographed in the **ambrotype photography studio**. The process of producing a picture from a negative on dark-surfaced glass was used until c.1900. Furnished to the period, **Greenwood Cottage** is an example of a spacious house of the well-to-do, while **McMillan House** reflects the humble status of a village weaver *(spinning demonstrations)*. The hotel serves 1880s fare such as cottage pudding and gingerbread *(copies of dessert recipes upon request)*. The telephone exchange is still operable, and the court house is in use today.

Removed from the village is **McDonald Brothers' Mill★** *(.4km/1/4mi)*, an operational water-powered sawmill capable of full production. A short walk away *(3min)* through woodlands, a reconstructed **lumber camp** of the 19C shows the living conditions of loggers.

★★ SPRINGHILL   Pop 4,373

Map p 183   Tourist Office ☎902/597-8530

Located inland on the "arm" of the peninsula, east of the Isthmus of Chignecto, this town is famous as a coal mining centre that has suffered more disasters than any other place of its size in Canada.

In 1891, an enormous blast in one of the mines tore out a vast area. When a subsequent flame swept through the mine workings, 125 men died. Then, in 1916, a subterranean fire filled the galleries. No one was killed, but much damage was done. An explosion and fire in 1956 caused 39 deaths. The next year a fire wiped out most of the business district of the town. Finally, in 1958, an underground upheaval or "bump" caused the deaths of 76 men. All the mines closed after this final disaster, the death knell of an industry already doomed by conversion to oil and gas as heating fuels.

★★ **Miners' Museum.** – *On Black River Rd. Follow signs along Rte 2 (Parrsboro direction). Open Jun–mid-Oct daily 9am–5pm. $3.* ☎*902/597-3449.* This museum commemorates the tragedy of the disasters and the bravery of the rescuers through displays such as newspaper clippings and mining equipment. The highlight of the visit is the **mine tour** *(by 45min guided tour only)* conducted by retired miners. Equipped with hard hats, rubber coats and boots, visitors descend about 270m/900ft into the old Syndicate Mine via a tunnel of regular height, rather than those the miners had to crawl along.

Both old and new mining methods are demonstrated *(coal souvenirs can be removed by pick-axe).*

TRURO   Pop 11,683

Map p 183   Tourist Office ☎902/895-6328

Set on the Salmon River near its mouth, this city experiences the high tides of the Bay of Fundy and the tidal bore *(p 191)*. Site of a thriving Acadian community called Cobequid before the Deportation, Truro was later settled by people from Northern Ireland and New Hampshire. Today, this manufacturing centre is home to the Nova Scotia Agricultural College.

★ **Tidal Bore.** – *Viewpoint: leave Hwy 102 at Exit 14 and take Tidal Bore Rd (left on Robie and left again on Tidal Bore Rd, if coming from Halifax). Parking area beside Palliser restaurant; clock gives time of next bore, or contact tourist office; arrive 15min prior and if possible, stay 1hr to see high tide.* Twice a day the tide rushes up the Salmon River from the Bay of Fundy, causing a wave that may vary from a ripple to several feet in height. What is more interesting than this bore is the tremendous inrush of water and the rapid rise in water level immediately following it. In fact, high tide is reached just over an hour after the arrival of the bore.

The legend on the inside cover page explains the symbols used on the maps in this guide.

Prince Edward Island

Map p 183

The birthplace of Canadian Confederation, and Canada's smallest province, this crescent-shaped island is only 225km/140mi long; a deeply indented coastline varies its width. Separated from Newfoundland by the Gulf of St Lawrence, the Island is just 14km/9mi from neighbouring New Brunswick and 22km/14mi from Nova Scotia across the **Northumberland Strait**. Iron oxides give the soil its characteristic brick-red colour, and on fine summer days, the rolling landscape presents a stunning kaleidoscope of green fields, blue sea and sky, red soil and puffy white clouds.

Practical Information

How to get there. – **Air** service to Charlottetown from Halifax, NS is provided by Air Canada affiliates. **Ferry** service is provided by Marine Atlantic between Borden and Cape Tormentine, NB (departures mid-Jun–Oct 3 daily from 6:30–1am; reduced schedule in off-season; crossing time 45min; $17/car, $6.50/person; ☎902/855-2010). Northumberland Ferries connects the eastern part of the island at Wood Islands with Caribou, NS (departures mid-Jun–Labour Day daily from 6am–9:50pm; reduced schedule in off-season; no crossing mid-Dec–late-Apr; crossing time 1hr 15min; $25.75/car, $7.90/person; ☎902/566-3838). From Souris a ferry crosses to the Magdalen Islands, PQ *(p 159)*. **Bus** service throughout the island is provided by Island Transit ☎902/892-6167.

Accommodation and Tourist Information. – The official tourist office publishes the annual *Visitors Guide* giving information on history, attractions, festivals, sports, vacation packages and accommodation. A highway map is included. For a free copy contact:
Tourism Prince Edward Island, PO Box 940, Charlottetown, PE, C1A 7M5 ☎800/565-0267 (toll-free Canada/US).

Road Regulations. – Speed limits, unless otherwise posted, are 90km/h (55mph) or 80km/h (50mph) on highways and 50km/h (30mph) in urban districts. **Seat belt** use is mandatory.
Canadian Automobile Association (CAA), Charlottetown ☎902/892-1612.

Time Zone. – PEI is on Atlantic Standard Time. Daylight Saving Time is observed from the first Sunday in April to the last Sunday in October.

Taxes. – The national GST of 7% *(rebate information p 242)*, and a provincial sales tax of 10% are levied.

Liquor Laws. – The legal drinking age is 19. Liquor is sold in government stores.

Principal Festivals

Jun–Sept	**Charlottetown Festival**	*Charlottetown*
Jun	**Highland Gathering**	*Summerside*
	Old Home Week Provincial Exhibition	*Charlottetown*
Jul	**Summerside Lobster Carnival**	*Summerside*
Sept	**PEI Festival of the Arts**	*Province-wide*

Île-St-Jean and the Acadian Deportation. – Jacques Cartier *(p 148)* claimed the Island for France in 1534, naming it Île-St-Jean. Concerted efforts at colonization did not occur until the early 18C when French settlers founded **Port la Joye**, near the present site of Charlottetown, as a dependency of Île Royale, today Cape Breton Island in Nova Scotia *(p 204)*. France's plan to strengthen its claims in the New World brought Acadian farmers to Île-St-Jean in 1720. In 1755, the British demanded, under threat of deportation, an oath of fealty from Acadians on British territory. Several thousand Acadians chose instead to resettle on Île-St-Jean. In 1758, England captured Île-St-Jean, removing the Acadians under the Deportation Order *(p 184)*. About thirty families went into hiding—the ancestors of many of today's Island Acadians.

St John's Island and the British Regime. – Renamed St John's Island under British rule, the Island was annexed to Nova Scotia. The land was granted to wealthy Englishmen and military officers, who petitioned the British government to recognize the territory as a separate colony. In 1769, a new administration was established; and in 1799, the colony was renamed Prince Edward Island in honour of the son of King George III of England.
The Island was the site of the historic **Charlottetown Conference** in September 1864, the first of several meetings that led to Canadian Confederation in 1867.
Principal industries today are tourism and manufacturing. Annually, over 500,000 visitors are drawn to the unhurried pace of life; **farm vacations** are popular, and **lobster suppers**, held during the summer in church and community halls, provide a sampling of fresh regional seafood and abundant garden produce. Agricultural and aquacultural processing forms the backbone of manufacturing on the Island, renowned for its dairy products, lobsters and shellfish, and more than 50 varieties of **potatoes**.

Visiting the Island. – Three scenic drives established by the provincial government are a good approach to touring the Island. Organized as circuits of the three counties (Prince, Queens and Kings), the routes provide a leisurely, in-depth means of experiencing splendid scenery, charming community life, historical attractions and recreational activities.

** CHARLOTTETOWN

Map below
Tourist Office ☎902/368-4444

Located near the confluence of the West, North and Hillsborough rivers at Northumberland Strait, this gracious provincial capital is also a thriving commercial centre, its port serving as a funnel for the region's agricultural bounty. Named for the wife of King George III, the city was founded in 1768.

SIGHTS   *1/2 day*

Attractively situated along the water's edge, **Victoria Park** is home to the regal, white neoclassical **Government House**, designed by Isaac Smith as the lieutenant-governor's official residence *(not open to the public)*. From the shore, expansive **views★** extend across the harbour to the site of Fort Amherst *(see below)*.

** **Province House.** – ☞ *At the top of Great George St. Open Jul–Labour Day daily 9am–8pm; until Thanksgiving daily 9am–5pm. Off-season Mon–Fri 9am–5pm.* ☎902/566-7626. A native of Yorkshire, England, Isaac Smith designed this three-storey sandstone building (1847) in the Georgian style with neoclassical details. The **Confederation Chamber**, site of the historic Charlottetown Conference *(see 213)*, is restored to its 19C appearance with many of the original furnishings. The provincial legislature still meets in the legislative chamber.

★ **Confederation Centre of the Arts.** – *Grafton St, adjacent to Province House. Open daily year-round.* ☎902/628-1864. Commemorating the centennial of the 1864 Charlottetown Conference, this national memorial arts centre (1964) houses theatres, the provincial archives, display areas and a restaurant. Temporary exhibits in the **art gallery** feature selections from a large permanent collection of works by Canadian artists, and the main theatre hosts the annual **Charlottetown Festival** musical production, *Anne of Green Gables*.

St Dunstan's Basilica. – *Great George St.* The twin 61m/200ft spires of this Gothic-style edifice (1919) gracefully punctuate Charlottetown's skyline. Interior features include fan vaulting, streaked marble, and a stunning rose window from Munich, Germany. The contemporary stained-glass windows in the facade were designed by Island native Henry Purdy.

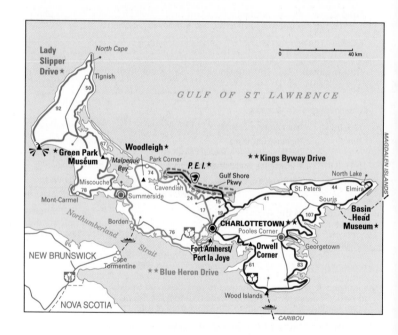

★ LADY SLIPPER DRIVE

Map above

The picturesque landscape of western Prince Edward Island is fringed with capes and beaches. Named for the province's official flower, this scenic circuit introduces the visitor to shipbuilding at Green Park; the Malpeque Bay, famed for its fine oysters; and fox farming, a major Island industry from 1890 to 1939.

288km/179mi circuit indicated by red and white signs depicting a Lady Slipper blossom. Visitor center on Rte 11 in Wilmot, 2km east of Summerside. 1 day.

★ **Green Park Shipbuilding Museum.** – *In Port Hill, 34km/21mi west of Summerside on Rte 12. Open daily Jun 15–Labour Day. $2.50.* ☎902/831-2206. Formerly the grounds of an active shipyard, Green Park is today a provincial heritage site commemorating the shipbuilding industry, the Island's principal economic activity during the 19C.

Prince Edward Island coastline

Erected by the shipyard's owner, **Yeo House** (1865) is a large, steeply gabled Victorian structure restored to reflect the lifestyle of a prominent family of the period. Maps, photographs and tools on display in the **interpretation centre** present the art and science of shipbuilding during the industry's 19C heyday. The re-created **shipyard** features pits and steam boxes for sawing, curving and shaping timbers, along with a partially completed vessel in frame.

West Point Lighthouse. – *In Cedar Dunes Provincial Park, Rte 14. Open daily mid-May–mid-Oct. $1.65. ☎902/859-3605.* This distinctive 30m/85ft striped lighthouse (1875) was automated by electricity in 1963. A narrow stairway rises past photographs and displays documenting the history of Island lighthouses. The tower itself contains numerous examples of lighthouse lenses and lanterns. From the observation platform at the summit, views stretch across the shoreline's dark red dunes.

Acadian Museum of Prince Edward Island. – *In Miscouche, 8km/5mi west of Summerside, on Rte 2. Open daily Jun 12–Sept 8. Off-season Mon–Fri. $2. ☎902/436-6237.* Erected in 1991, this modern facility for the preservation of Acadian heritage combines an historical museum with a documentation centre for genealogical research. Main gallery dioramas and texts present Acadian history after 1720, incorporating objects from an extensive collection of artifacts, photographs, textiles and journals donated by area families. Audio-visual presentations in the theatre introduce topics such as religion, education and economy, and an adjacent gallery presents temporary thematic exhibit of Acadian culture and heritage.

Our Lady of Mont-Carmel Acadian Church. – *In Mont-Carmel, on Rte 11, east of Rte 124.* Overlooking Northumberland Strait just east of Cap-Egmont, this twin-steepled brick church (1896) replaces two earlier wooden structures, the first of which was built in 1820 as a mission church for the Acadian community of Mont-Carmel. The church's symmetrical facade and rounded interior vaults are reminiscent of religious architecture in France's Poitou region, original home of most of the Island's first Acadian settlers.

★★ BLUE HERON DRIVE

Map p 214

Encircling most of Queens County and central Prince Edward Island, this scenic drive encompasses the stunning white beaches of the north coast; charming Acadian fishing villages; sights related to *Anne of Green Gables*; and the red cliffs of the southern coast, bordered by Northumberland Strait.

90km/118mi circuit indicated by blue and white signs depicting a blue heron. Visitor center at Oak Tree Place, University Ave, in Charlottetown. 1 day.

★ **Prince Edward Island National Park.** – *☞ Cavendish, 24km/15mi northwest of Charlottetown. Open year-round. Visitor center at intersection of Rtes 6 and 13; open daily mid-May–Sept. △ ☎902/963-2391.* One of Canada's smallest but most popular national parks stretches for about 40km/25mi along the north shore of the Island, fringing the Gulf of St Lawrence. Interspersed with boardwalks and paths to the water's edge, the **Gulf Shore Parkway** offers displays on shoreline ecology and views of some of eastern Canada's loveliest **beaches**, sand dunes, sandstone cliffs, salt marshes and freshwater ponds. Picnic sites are scattered throughout seaside and woodland areas, and a variety of interpretation programs are available.

Near the park's eastern entrance, a glance to the south reveals **Dalvay-by-the-Sea**, an elegant Victorian structure (1896), formerly the summer home of Standard Oil magnate, Alexander MacDonald, and now a hotel. The lobby features beautiful woodwork and an enormous fireplace with a hearth of local sandstone.

215

★ **Green Gables House.** – *In Cavendish. Rte 6 west of Rte 13, in PEI National Park. Open daily mid-May–Nov 5. Off-season by appointment.* ✕ ᕚ ☎*902/963-2391.* This small green and white farmhouse belonged to elderly cousins of **Lucy Maud Montgomery**, author of *Anne of Green Gables*. During her childhood years in Cavendish, she visited here frequently and used the house as a setting for the novel, which tells the story of an irrepressible orphan girl adopted by a strict but kindly brother and sister living at "Green Gables" farm. Once described by Mark Twain as the "sweetest creation of child life ever written," this story has become popular in 18 languages, and draws summer visitors to the Island from as far away as Japan. Today, the refurbished house re-creates scenes from the novel, including Anne's gable bedroom. In the downstairs hallway, Montgomery's typewriter and several family photographs are displayed.

Anne of Green Gables Museum at Silverbush. – *In Park Corner, Rte 20. Open daily Jun–Oct. $2.50.* ☎*902/886-2884.* Throughout her life, author L. M. Montgomery visited relatives at this spacious house; her 1911 wedding was held in the drawing room. The dwelling and its surroundings appear as settings in the *Anne of Green Gables* series. First editions of the author's books, personal correspondence, and family heirlooms are displayed throughout the house.

★ **Woodleigh.** – *In Burlington, Rte 234 northeast of Kensington. Open daily May 23–mid-Oct. $6.25.* ☎*902/836-3401.* Scattered about a pleasant, tree-shaded site are some 17 large-scale replicas of historic British structures. Highlights include an 8m/26ft replica of York Minster Cathedral, complete with 145 glass windows; St Paul's Cathedral in London; and Scotland's Dunvegan Castle. *Video presentation available on request in the theatre adjacent to the gift shop.*

Fort Amherst/Port la Joye. – ⊚ *In Rocky Point, on Blockhouse Point Rd off Rte 19. Open daily mid-Jun–Labour Day.* ☎*902/675-2220.* The first permanent European settlement on the island was established here by the French in 1720. The British, who captured the area in 1758, erected Fort Amherst, a series of defenses on the site of the original French garrison, and occupied the post until 1768. Today, only the earthworks remain—rolling, grass-covered mounds from which sweeping views★★ of Charlottetown harbour extend. In the **visitor centre**, displays offer an introduction to the site and the history of the Island during the French regime. *An audio-visual presentation (15min) is shown.*

★ KINGS BYWAY DRIVE

Map p 214

Wandering along the deeply indented bays and harbours of the Island's eastern coast, this drive offers a close look at Kings County's vibrant fishing industry. Side roads lead through lush forests past small communities with names such as Cardigan, Greenfield and Glenmartin, that harken to the province's British heritage. *375km/233mi circuit indicated by purple and white signs depicting a royal crown. Visitor center at junction of Rtes 3 and 4 in Pooles Corner. 1 day.*

Orwell Corner Historic Village. – *In Orwell, 30km/19mi east of Charlottetown on the Trans-Can Hwy. Open daily Jul–Labour Day. Off-season Mon–Fri. Closed mid-Oct–mid-May. $3.* ☎*902/651-2013.* This superbly restored crossroads village, settled in the early 19C by pioneers from Scotland and Ireland, retains the atmosphere and flavour of the Island's agricultural origins. Visitors can tour the 1864 **farmhouse**, which also served as post office, general store and dressmaker's shop, along with a church, school, community hall, blacksmith's shop, shingle mill and animal barns. Fiddle music and step dancing are features of the traditional *ceilidh* (KAY-lee) *(every Wed Jul–Sept 8pm).*

★ **Basin Head Fisheries Museum.** – *In Basin Head, 10 km/6mi east of Souris on Rte 16. Open daily mid-Jun–Labour Day; until Sept 30 Mon–Fri. $3.* ☎*902/ 357-2966.* This museum occupies a fine site overlooking the mouth of Northumberland Strait. Boats, nets, hooks, photographs and dioramas illustrate the life and work of an inshore fisherman. Outside, small wooden buildings house a salt-fish box factory, and a small craft exhibit.

Elmira Railway Museum. – *In Elmira, 16km/10mi east of Souris on Rte 16A. Open daily mid-Jun–Labour Day. $2.* ☎*902/357-2481.* Formerly the eastern terminus of a railway system linking the Island with the continent, this charming station has been transformed into a museum that recounts the railway's 19C–early 20C development. Features include a photographic display highlighting architectural differences among Island rail stations; a 1911 station log; and still-operational telegraph equipment.

Newfoundland

Map p 218

The largest of the Atlantic provinces, Newfoundland consists of a rocky island of the same name and the mountainous mainland of Labrador, with a combined landmass of 405,720sq km/156,648sq mi. The remote shores and wilderness interior of Canada's easternmost province appeal particularly to nature lovers in search of adventure.

Practical Information

How to get there. – Newfoundland and Labrador are serviced by major domestic and international **air** carriers through hubs like Toronto and Montreal. Affiliate airlines such as Air Nova, Air Atlantic and Labrador Airways provide regular connections within the province. Passenger and vehicle **ferry** service *(map p 218)* from North Sydney, NS to Channel-Port aux Basques (daily year-round; crossing time 5hrs in summer, 6hrs 30min rest of the year) connecting bus service to inland destinations (Terra Transport ☎709/737-5916). From North Sydney, NS to Argentia (mid-Jun–mid-Oct twice weekly; crossing time 14hrs). From Lewisporte, Newfoundland to Goose Bay, Labrador via Cartwright (mid-Jun–mid-Sept; one weekly crossing 32hrs). The *MV Northern Ranger* provides a weekly coastal service (passengers only) to Nain from Goose Bay. For ferry schedules & reservations contact Marine Atlantic, North Sydney, NS ☎902/794-5700 or 800/341-7981 (toll-free from US). The southern coast of Labrador is accessible from St Barbe, Newfoundland via Blanc-Sablon, PQ (twice/day Jul–Oct; off-season once/day; no service Jan 1–May 1; one-way 1hr 30min). For schedules & reservations contact Northern Cruiser Ltd, Newfoundland ☎709/722-4000.
Note: Advance reservations are recommended for all ferry services. Fuel tanks must be no more than three-quarters full.
For ferry service to **Saint-Pierre and Miquelon** *see p 226.*

Accommodation and Tourist Information. – The government tourist office publishes an annually updated travel guide giving detailed information on attractions and activities, calendar of events, and boat and adventure tours, and a listing of accommodation including hospitality homes—private homes that accept paying guests. A copy of this guide, a road map and other useful information are available free of charge from:
Department of Tourism & Culture, PO Box 8730, St John's, NF, A1B 4K2 ☎709/729-2830 or 800/563-6353 (toll-free Canada/US).

Road Regulations. – The Trans-Canada Highway Route 1 *(910km/565mi),* which traverses Newfoundland from Channel-Port aux Basques to St John's, and most secondary highways are paved. The condition of gravel roads varies according to traffic and weather. Main roads are passable during winter, but it is advisable to check with local authorities before departure (☎709/729-2381). **Seat belt** use is compulsory for all passengers. Speed limits, unless otherwise posted, are: 100km/h (60mph) on four-lane divided highways, 80km/h (50mph) on secondary and 50km/h (30mph) on gravel roads.

Time Zone. – Newfoundland Standard Time is 30min ahead of Atlantic Standard Time and 1hr 30min ahead of Eastern Standard Time. Daylight Saving Time is observed from the first Sunday in April to the last Sunday in October.

Taxes. – In addition to the national 7% GST *(rebate information p 242),* the province levies a 12% sales tax for which non-residents can request a rebate by contacting: Tax Administration Branch, Department of Finance, PO Box 8720, St John's, NF, A1B 4K1 ☎709/729-3831.

Liquor Laws. – Liquor and wine are available only from government stores except in remote areas where local stores are licensed. Beer is available in most convenience stores. The legal drinking age is 19.

Provincial Holidays *(see National Holidays p 240)*
The Queen's Birthday................ Monday nearest May 24

Principal Festivals

mid-Feb	**Corner Brook Winter Carnival**	*Corner Brook*
Jul–early-Aug	**Festival of the Arts**	*Stephenville*
Aug	**St John's Annual Regatta**	*St John's*
	Annual Newfoundland and Labrador	
	Folk Festival	*St John's*
mid-Aug	**Bakeapple Folk Festival**	*Point Amour*

The Island. – Called "The Rock" for its craggy profile, the island of the province has a 9,650km/6,000mi beautiful, deeply indented coastline, studded with bays, coves and islands. In the north and west, the coast is grandiose with towering cliffs and deep fjords *(pp 221 and 222).* From the heights of the Long Range Mountains in the west, a continuation of the Appalachians, the land slopes east and northeast. Parts of the interior are heavily forested; others are expanses of rocky barrens and boggy peatlands, a legacy of glaciers, as are the multitude of lakes and rivers.

Labrador. – A rugged land of high mountains (Cirque Mountain, in the **Torngats** of the north, reaches 1,676m/5,500ft), Labrador also possesses coastal settlements nestling under high cliffs and inland, a barren, largely treeless, terrain. Unlike the island, it forms part of the Canadian Shield *(p 14).* Labrador's 30,000 people reside primarily along the coast and around the mines in its rich iron-ore belt.

The Banks. – In Newfoundland, "banks" are not money-lending institutions but vast areas of shallow water in the Atlantic to the south and east of the province—usually less than 100m/328ft deep extensions of the continental shelf. For 500 years these waters have attracted fishermen to the fish-breeding grounds. The largest and richest of the grounds is the **Grand Banks**, an area of approximately 282,500sq km/ 109,073sq mi where the cold Labrador Current meets the warmer Gulf Stream. Sinking below the warmer one, the cold current stirs up plankton on the sea bed. The plankton rises to the surface, attracting great schools of fish. Though herring is also found, **cod** is the traditional catch. Newfoundlanders have always talked about "fishing the banks" and the boats they used were called "bankers." However, in 1992, because of depleted stocks, the Canadian government ordered a two-year moratorium on cod fishing off the northeast coast of Newfoundland. The ban will undoubtedly have far-reaching economic consequences for the province.

Inshore Fishing. – In early summer, the **caplin** "run": these small fish swim ashore to spawn, bringing with them their main predator, the cod. Using large square traps made of netting, a fisherman traditionally earned most of his livelihood during the few weeks of the run. **Cod-jigging**, slow and inefficient, is used to a limited extent at other times during the year: shiny lead "jiggers" or baited hooks on small lines attached to a trawl line attract the cod. The use of trawl lines payed out from a boat is known as **longlining**. The method of weighting nets and keeping them vertical with floats is called **gill-netting**, a more recent practice. Larger boats called **longliners**, which can stay at sea several days to pursue schools of fish, use either method. Squid, lobster, salmon and caplin (once used only as bait) are taken in as well.

Offshore Fishing. – Traditionally, large schooners left the province's ports to fish the banks for months at a time. When schools of fish were located, actual fishing was done from **dories**, small flat-bottomed open craft carried on deck. The catch was either salted on the schooner's deck and stored in the hold ("wet" fishery) or taken ashore and dried on land on wooden racks known as **flakes** ("dry" fishery). The trend since 1945 has been to use draggers, trawlers and longliners instead of schooners and dories because fish can be caught en masse. Filleting plants have replaced flakes, and refrigeration has supplanted salting.

Lifestyle and Customs. – Functional rather than fancy characterizes the lives of many Newfoundlanders. About one-quarter of the island's population of 538,349 resides in the capital city of St John's *(p 223)*; the remainder live mainly in coastal fishing villages known as **outports**. Traditionally, an outport was any community outside St John's, but today, with the rise of industrial centres such as Corner Brook, the term is applied to tiny coastal settlements with moored dories and trap skiffs, weather-beaten fishing **stages** (wooden platforms perched on poles above the water for drying fish) and colourful two-storey "box" houses. In some outports, a small "museum" preserves each community's past. Housed in historic homes or commercial buildings (often with a craft shop annexed), these collections of donated artifacts are primarily of local interest. Short on flamboyance, the articles are largely practical, reflective of the modest, hardy lives of the outport inhabitants.

Oral Traditions. – Hard times have repeated themselves over the generations of these sea-dependent people, ebbing and flowing with the size of each catch. There's rarely a depression of the human spirit, however. Reserved exuberance abounds. Visitors to Newfoundland are captivated by the wealth of unusual idioms and wonderful accents of its inhabitants. Centuries of isolation have chiselled a character that is independent, individualistic and humourous. Where else are there settlements named Stinking Cove, Useless Bay, Jerry's Nose, Cuckold Cove, Come-by-Chance and Happy Adventure, or local terms like *tickle* (a narrow waterway).

English is the first language of 98 percent of the islanders, and remarkably varied dialects enrich the provincial tongue. Some have definite Irish overtones; others are reminiscent of England's West Country (Dorset, Devon, Cornwall). Local expressions such as "to have a noggin to scrape" (a very hard task), "to be all mops and brooms" (to have untidy hair) and "long may your big jib draw" (good luck for the future) add colour and humour to every-day conversations.

Rich in tradition, Newfoundlanders possess a wealth of legend, weather lore, folk dances and songs, which attest to their wry perspective on life. Often parodies of British creations, sea shanties such as *Squid-Jiggin' Ground, Let Me Fish off Cape St Mary's, Jack Was Every Inch a Sailor* record island character and yearnings with relish, melancholy or humour.

Seafood Specialities. – Not surprisingly, cod—eaten fresh, dried or salted—has traditionally been the staple of the provincial diet. **Fish and brewis**, a mixture of boiled salt cod and hardtack (a hard, dry biscuit) soaked overnight, is a traditional dish. Of greater fame is **fried cod tongues**, a dish that should be prepared only with fish caught the same day. Arctic char, salmon, shrimp and halibut are other favourites.

After hitting an iceberg, the **Titanic** *sank 150km/93mi south of the Grand Banks on April 15, 1912.*

BURIN PENINSULA

Map p 218

The doorstep to a vast off-shore fishing industry in the **Grand Banks** *(p 218)*, this barren peninsula of isolated mountain plateaus juts down like a boot into the Atlantic Ocean from the southern coast of Newfoundland between Placentia and Fortune bays. Just off the "toe" are the island remnants of France's once-great empire in North America: Saint-Pierre and Miquelon *(p 226)*.

VISIT
203km/126mi south of Trans-Can Hwy by Hwy 210 to Fortune. Allow 3 hrs.

The drive on Highway 210 is long and deserted until **Marystown** (pop 6,660), situated on Little Bay. Its huge shipyard *(inaccessible to the public)*, where the trawlers used off Newfoundland's shores are built, is the largest in the province. South of Marystown, Route 210 crosses the peninsula and descends to Fortune Bay, providing views of the southern coast of Newfoundland. Just before entering Grand Bank, there is a view of the south coast and Brunette Island. To the west, the coast of the French island of Miquelon is just visible, weather permitting.

Grand Bank. – Pop 3,528. *199km/123mi south of Trans-Can Hwy by Hwy 210.* An important fishing centre, this community was once the home of the famous "bankers" *(p 218)*. Some of the houses from that era are examples of the Queen Anne style with their widow's walks or small open rooftop galleries from which women could watch for the return of their men from the sea.

★ **Southern Newfoundland Seamen's Museum.** – *Marine Dr. Open daily year-round.* & ☎709/ 832-1484. Housed in the former Yugoslavian Pavilion of Montreal's Expo '67, this branch of the Newfoundland Museum network features displays on the history of the Banks fishing industry. Of particular interest are the photographs of ships and fishing, and **models** of the types of ships used. A large glass-encased relief model of Newfoundland shows the Banks and the depths of the Atlantic.

Highway 210 continues to **Fortune** (pop 2,370), another fishing community with an artificial harbour, and the departure point for ferries to the French islands of Saint-Pierre and Miquelon *(p 226)*.

★★ The CAPE SHORE

Map p 218

Perhaps Newfoundland's most dramatic coastline, the southwest arm of the Avalon Peninsula from Placentia to St Bride's delights visitors with its natural wonders and historic sites. Magnificent ocean views and remnants of Europe's territorial struggles await those who travel this isolated shore.

★ **Castle Hill.** – ☻ *In Placentia, 44km/27mi south of Trans-Can Hwy by Rte 100. About 8km/5 mi from Argentia ferry. Open daily year-round.* & ☎709/227-2401. This park contains the remains of Fort Royal, built by the French at the turn of the 18C, and rebuilt and renamed Castle Hill by the British. Renowned for its commanding position overlooking the small town of **Placentia** (pop 1,954), the site affords a **panorama**★★ of the city itself, Placentia Bay and **The Gut**—a small channel that separates the bay from two long, deep inlets.

As early as 1500, Placentia's harbour, plentiful fresh water and beaches (where cod could be dried) attracted European fishermen, especially the Basques. To protect their interests in the Newfoundland fishery, the French established a small colony called Plaisance in 1662, building fortifications at sea level and in the hills. After the **Treaty of Utrecht** in 1713 confirmed Newfoundland as British territory, the British kept a small garrison at Placentia until 1811, when it was moved to St John's. Placentia settled down to a prosperous life of fishing and shipbuilding. When the era of wooden ships ended, the shipbuilding industry died, but fishing remains important today. During World War II, construction of a large American base at nearby **Argentia** brought major changes to Placentia. The centre of anti-submarine patrol during the war, Argentia was the site of the famous 1941 offshore meeting between Churchill and Roosevelt that produced the **Atlantic Charter**, a statement of peace goals adopted in 1942 by the United Nations.

Visit. – An interesting **visitor centre** with dioramas, models and panels describes the French and English presence in the area. Visitors walk uphill to the cannons and scant remains of the fort. A pleasant pathway through evergreen forests *(10min walk)* past dry stone walls leads to **Le Gaillardin**, a redoubt built by the French in 1692.

★★ **Cape Shore Drive.** – *46km/29mi from Placentia to St Bride's on Rte 100. Fuel and food available infrequently. Fog may hamper visibility.* Traversing a straggly, hilly coast, Route 100 is a spectacular ocean drive, providing numerous **views** of beautiful coves, crashing surf and windswept pines. Sparsely populated communities such as picturesque **Gooseberry Cove** *(25km/16mi south of Placentia)* dot the wide inlets of this curving coastline. Colourful flat-topped houses, wool-laden sheep by the roadside and an occasional fishing boat anchored offshore are common scenes until the road turns inland at St Bride's. The landscape then changes to isolated flatlands and pale-green hillocks, extending to the horizon.

★ **Cape St Mary's Ecological Reserve.** – *Approximately 14km/9mi east of St Bride's. Leave St Bride's via Rte 100. Turn right on unpaved road (turn-off for reserve is clearly marked) and continue 8km/5mi. Mid-June to mid-August is best season to view birds.* Located at the southwest end of the cape, this site has been an official sanctuary for sea birds since 1964 and is one of the largest nesting grounds in North America for **gannets**, relatives of the pelican family. Atop a dramatic shoreline alive with the sights and sounds of an active bird population, its pastoral **setting**★★ is unique.

What is especially thrilling about this preserve is that visitors can get within a few feet of the birds! Providing spectacular **views**★ of the rugged coast, a trail *(25min)* from the lighthouse and visitor centre over short-grass hills reminiscent of moors and often covered with grazing sheep and goats, leads to **Bird Rock**, the precarious domain of the gannets. Surrounding cliffs attract hundreds of noisy black-legged kittiwakes, common murres and razorbills.

★★ GROS MORNE NATIONAL PARK

Map p 218

Covering 1,805sq km/697sq mi along the west coast of the province's **Great Northern Peninsula**, this vast, pristine park includes some of the most spectacular scenery in eastern Canada. Designated a UNESCO World Heritage Site in 1987, the park contains geological features that have become a magnet for international scientific research. Consisting of rock 1,250 million years old, the flat-topped **Long Range Mountains** are the northernmost part of the Appalachians. Between them and the coast lies a poorly drained plain, sometimes high above the sea, with a variety of cliffs, sandy shores and little fishing communities.

Access. – *44km/27mi northwest of Deer Lake. Take Rte 430 from Deer Lake to Wiltondale, then Rte 431 to park, 13km/8mi.*

Gros Morne National Park

Western Brook Pond

VISIT *Map below. 2 days.*

🖝 *Open year-round. Hiking, cross-country skiing.* △ *Contact visitor centre (open daily year-round; closed legal holidays and Dec 20–Jan 4;* ♿ ☎709/458-2066*) near Rocky Harbour for guided boat tours, ferry crossing and trail information. Accommodation available throughout local communities.*

★★ **Bonne Bay Area.** – *Take Rte 431 from Wiltondale 50km/31mi to Trout River (food, fuel).* This is a beautiful drive along a deep fjord—a glacial trough whose several arms are surrounded by the squat peaks of the Long Range Mountains. The road travels westward along the **South Arm** from Glenburnie, offering gorgeous **views★★** of the bay. Fishing boats and small houses are set against the dark blue waters of the arm with the flat-topped mountains rising all around.

From Woody Point, as Route 431 ascends to the west, the red-brown rubble of a desert-like area known as the **Tablelands★** is abruptly visible, a jarring contrast to the lush green vegetation of the rest of the park. These mountains consist of rock that was once part of the earth's mantle—a magnesium and iron layer surrounding the planet's core—and are evidence of plate tectonics, the shifting of the plates within the earth's crust. For a closer look at the Tablelands, stop at the turnoff *(4.5km/2.8 mi from Woody Point)* where a **panel display** describes the geological history of this unique natural feature.

This vantage point offers a striking **view** of the barren expanse. A foot path leads from the parking area into the heart of the Tablelands *(for information on guided hikes, contact the visitor centre).* Beyond the little fishing village of Trout River is the long finger lake called **Trout River Pond** *(departures daily mid-Jun–mid-Sept; roundtrip 2hrs 30min; Tableland Boat Tours* ☎709/451-2101*).* Dominating the return drive to Woody Point is the vast bulk of **Gros Morne Mountain** (806m/2,644ft) to the north, the highest point in the park. From Woody Point, a ferry crossing to Norris Point *(departures daily mid-Jun–mid-Sept; 25min)* provides **views★** of the main part of the bay. For an in-depth preview of the park's

unique geology, stop at the **visitor centre** on the road to Rocky Harbour. There videos, talks, literature, photographs and rock displays are provided as well as a telescope for eyeing nearby Gros Morne Mountain, the park's namesake *(to reach the summit, take the James Callaghan trail, 3km/1.8mi south of visitor centre; 6-8hrs round-trip).* Note that Route 430 travels south, returning to Wiltondale along Deer Arm and **East Arm**, a vantage point for lovely **views★★** of Bonne Bay.

★ **From Rocky Harbour to St Paul's.** – *40km25mi by Rte 430. Fuel and food available in settlements along the way.* Overlooking a wide inlet of Bonne Bay, the small coastal community of **Rocky Harbour** (pop 1,138) functions as a service and accommodation centre for park visitors.

On a promontory just north of Rocky Harbour, **Lobster Cove Head lighthouse** *(open daily in summer)* provides expansive **views★★** of the town, Gros Morne Mountain, the mouth of the bay and the Gulf of St Lawrence.

Built on a narrow plain between the sea and the Long Range Mountains, the road affords a pretty drive up the coast past Sally's Cove, one of several little fishing communities along this coastal route. Sometimes the road is at sea level, sometimes higher above a rocky coast, but all along, the Long Range Mountains, just inland, appear like a gigantic step up from the sea because of their cropped tops. Before the turnoff to Western Brook Pond's trailhead, the rusty remains of the **SS Ethie** shipwreck can be seen on the beach. A small panel describes the fate of the ship's 1919 voyage.

★★ **Western Brook Pond.** – *29km/18mi from Rocky Harbour. 4km/2.5mi walk to boat dock – allow 40min one way. Boat trip: one departure daily Jun 1–Sept 30; Jul–Labour Day three departures daily. Round-trip 2hrs 20min; $23. Commentary on board. For schedules* ☎709/458-2730 *(jacket recommended year-round).* Western Brook runs through a spectacular gorge (which, in typical Newfoundland understatement, is called a "pond") in the Long Range Mountains before it crosses the narrow coastal plain and reaches the sea. The pond is flanked by almost vertical cliffs that rise to a desolate boulder-strewn alpine plateau where snow remains in crevices, even in August. Resembling a fjord because of these towering cliffs, this gorge is not a true fjord because it does not extend to the sea; the pond is fresh water. Bonne Bay, St Paul's Inlet, Parson's Pond (just north of the park) and the large Bay of Islands *(map p 218)* are fjords. Whether "pond" or "fjord," all of these are the result of glacial gouging in the last ice age.

A trail leads across the boggy coastal plain *(boardwalks over marshy areas)* to the edge of the pond. Gradually the deep gorge and truncated mountains become clearly visible, weather permitting. The only way to see the interior, however, is to take a boat trip. Otherwise, the sheer granite cliffs (600m/2,000ft) and the depth of the water (approaching 200m/ 600ft) cannot be appreciated. Impressive waterfalls spill over the towering peaks to the cliff bases below. Viewing the varied shapes and exposed surfaces of the cliffs from the vantage point of the pond, visitors can sense the geological uniqueness of this ancient glacial valley.

After Western Brook Pond, the road follows along the coast with views of the mountains, spotted with seasonal snow caught in crevices, and of the shore covered with rocks, boulders and driftwood. The road continues to **St Paul's**, a small fishing settlement clustered at the mouth of a deep fjord against a backdrop of mountains.

Designated "The Viking Trail," Route 430 exits the park above Shallow Bay and continues north along the coast for another 300km/200mi to L'Anse aux Meadows *(see below)*, with similar sea views but less dramatic mountain views, since the Long Range peaks are smaller and farther inland. Several native burial grounds are located at the archaeological site in **Port au Choix National Historic Site** *(135km/84mi north of St Paul's)*.

★ HEART'S CONTENT Cable Station

Map p 218

A little town founded about 1650 on Trinity Bay, Heart's Content is the site of the first successful landing, in 1866, of the **transatlantic telegraph cable**. North America's major relay site for nearly 100 years, the now obsolete station has been converted into a museum by the provincial government.

The landing was the result of years of work by the New York, Newfoundland and London Telegraph Company, led by American financier, Cyrus W. Field. The first attempt to lay a cable in 1858 failed after inaugural messages were sent between Queen Victoria and US President James Buchanan. A second attempt in 1865 also failed. Finally in the following year, Field successfully used the ocean liner *Great Eastern* to lay the cable between Valencia, Ireland and Heart's Content, where it joined a cable to New York. Messages initially cost $5 a word, and the station handled 3,000 messages a day. Improved communications technology led to the station's eventual closing in 1965.

Visit. – 58km/36mi north of Trans-Can Hwy by Rte 80, Avalon Peninsula. Open daily mid-Jun–mid-Sept. Off-season by appointment only. ☏709/583-2160 (summer) 709/729-2460 (year-round). Displays tell the story of communications with special emphasis on how long messages took to cross the ocean before telegraph was used. There is a **film** and special section on the laying of the transatlantic cables, the part played by the *Great Eastern* and the importance of Heart's Content. Costumed guides are on site for tours of the replica of the first cable office (1866) and operating room. The original equipment can be compared to the complex equipment in use at the station's closing in 1965.

★★ L'ANSE AUX MEADOWS

Map p 218

On a grassy ledge facing Epaves Bay at the northernmost tip of Newfoundland's Great Northern Peninsula, the remains of what is the oldest European settlement in North America authenticated to date are preserved for posterity. This remote site has been included on UNESCO's World Heritage List as a property of universal value.

In Search of Vinland. – In AD 900, the Vikings (also known as the Norse) from present-day Scandinavia settled in Iceland, and from there explored Greenland, Baffin Island and beyond. The account of a land sighting by a returning ship blown off course inspired **Leif Ericsson**, then residing in Greenland, to go exploring. About AD 1000, Ericsson landed at a fertile spot and built a settlement for the winter. He named the location "Vinland" for the wild grapes his crew is said to have found there. This story is preserved in two Norse tales: the *Saga of the Greenlanders* and the *Saga of Eric the Red*, which were communicated by word of mouth for hundreds of years before being recorded.

Though many scholars have tried to find Vinland, its location is unknown. Generally thought to be on the southeastern coast of the US because of the grapes, this location was, however, too far for ships to have sailed in the time suggested by the sagas. Then in 1960, **Helge Ingstad**, a Norwegian explorer and writer, and his archaeologist wife, **Anne Stine**, began a systematic search of the coast from New England northward. Led to a group of overgrown mounds near L'Anse aux Meadows by a local resident, they excavated them from 1961 to 1968. Foundations of eight sod buildings of the type the Norse built in Iceland were uncovered and several artifacts undeniably Norse in origin were found. Evidence of iron working—an art unknown to the North American Indian—was unearthed. Samples of bone, turf and charcoal were carbon dated at around AD 1000.

Though impossible to prove it is the elusive Vinland (no one can envisage grapes growing in Newfoundland), L'Anse aux Meadows is certainly a Norse settlement, and the only one ever discovered in North America. Experts believe the settlement was a base of encampment for further exploration, especially trips south in search of timber and trading goods. Occupied by about 100 men and women, the camp was probably deserted after five or ten years. Newfoundland's harsh conditions, coupled with the growing accessibility to southern European markets, most likely led to its abandonment.

Access. – *453km/281mi north of Trans-Can Hwy by Rtes 430 and 436.*

Visit. – ❂ *Open daily year-round. Visitor centre open mid-Jun–Labour Day daily 9am–8pm. Off-season by appointment only.* ⚠ & ☎*709/623-2608.* In the **visitor centre**, displays depict the Norse way of life and what a settlement might have looked like, but the collection of artifacts found on-site is the highlight. A stirring **film** on the Ingstads' search provides an enlightening introduction to the visit.

Completely excavated, the site has been preserved as grassy borders that outline the foundations of the original structures. The layout of the dwellings, work buildings and a smithy (the location of the earliest-known iron smelting in North America) can be clearly distinguished. Nearby, three **sod buildings**—a long house, a building and a workshed—have been faithfully reconstructed.

Inside, wooden platforms that served as beds line the walls. Firepits are placed at intervals in the middle of the earthen floors. A few animals skins and iron cooking utensils suggest the spartan existence of the inhabitants.

At the end of "The Viking Trail," **St Anthony** (pop 3,164), a large service centre, is the nearest city (*food, accommodation and air service*) to L'Anse aux Meadows. At the turn of the century, a British doctor, **Sir Wilfred Grenfell** (1865-1940), began his medical missionary work in the area, including Labrador. He became world renowned in his time, and today St Anthony preserves his memory through the hospital he established, a cooperative craft shop and the house local residents built for him. Now called the **Grenfell House Museum** *(open daily May–Sept; $2;* & ☎*709/454-3333),* the home contains displays about his social involvement in the province, his medical practice and his personal life.

★★ ST JOHN'S   Pop 95,770

Map p 218   Tourist Office ☎ 709/729-2830

One of the oldest cities in North America, the capital of Newfoundland sits on the northeast arm of the Avalon Peninsula, facing the expansive Atlantic Ocean. This historic sea port owes its founding to a fine natural harbour that now services an international shipping trade.

Early Years. – According to tradition, **John Cabot** entered the harbour on Saint John's day in 1497. Whether this claim is true or not, it has been established that, by the turn of the century, ships from several European countries were using the harbour as a fishing base. Under charter from Elizabeth I of England, **Sir Humphrey Gilbert** (c.1537-1583) sailed to North America, arriving at St John's harbour in 1583. Finding the crews of several countries assembled in one place, he seized the opportunity to declare Her Majesty's sovereignty, and thus is credited with giving England its first possession in the New World. Before his death at sea, Gilbert reputedly joined in the customary celebrations in St John's of fishing "admiral" elections. Determined to maintain their fishing monopolies, England's West Country merchants *(p 184)* opposed settlement of Newfoundland, aided by the captains of their ships—the fishing admirals whose often harsh and abusive rule discouraged prospective settlers. From 1675 to 1677, a formal ban on settlement was in effect. But gradually, people associated with the growing fishing industry began to take up year-round residence.

The Anglo-French Wars. – Fear of French expansion changed the attitude of the British government toward permanent settlement. The French had established fortifications at Placentia in 1662 and proceeded to mount attacks on British harbours, especially St John's. When a French force from Placentia destroyed St John's in 1696, the British realized they must have more settlers—permanent residents—to defend their territory. St John's fell twice again to the French, with the final battle in 1762 at the end of the Seven Years' War, though the city was recaptured soon afterwards. These attacks prompted the British to fortify the harbour entrance and Signal Hill *(p 225)*, a strategic promontory between the sea and the city, but St John's was never again threatened.

Devastating Fires. – In the 19C, the capital suffered five fires that virtually wiped out the entire community each time. The first in 1816 was followed by others in 1817, 1819, 1846, and the most extensive of all in 1892. A photo taken by Sir Wilfred Grenfell *(see above)* at the time shows the twin towers of the Basilica of St John the Baptist, one of the few structures still partially standing amid the devastation. Each time, the city was rebuilt, primarily in prevailing architectural styles such as Gothic Revival and, after the 1892 fire, Second Empire, styles still evident in the historic structures of the city today. The rapid expansion of St John's as a commercial centre during the 19C was reversed each time by the fires.

Confederation and the 20C. – St John's was a wealthy city in the early 20C and during World War II when it served as a base for North American convoys. After the war, the Dominion of Newfoundland's decision to enter Confederation *(p 185)* resulted in a decline in the city's economy, despite a substantial infusion of federal funds. Its industries collapsed as cheaper Canadian manufactured goods entered Newfoundland. Port activity suffered and St John's importance as a fish-exporting centre was reduced as major firms abandoned the salt-fish trade for growing whole-sale consumer markets. Today, the city's harbour serves as a supply and repair depot for international and local shipping. Over 1,000 commercial vessels of approx-imately 22 nationalities annually visit this major refueling station. Further resurgence is anticipated as a result of the discovery of offshore oil reserves in recent years.

Regatta Day. – Each year **Quidi Vidi** (KID-dy VID-dy) **Lake** is the site of the St John's Regatta, the oldest continuing sporting event in North America (since 1826). Held on the first Wednesday in August (or the first fine day thereafter), the regatta is prob-ably the only civic holiday decided that morning. The local population waits for the cry, "The races are on!" and then crowds the lakeshore to watch competitors row the 2.6km/1.6mi course, the major event of the all-day carnival.

★★ HARBOUR AND OLD CITY *Map below. 1 day.*

The city's **site★** borders a harbour almost landlocked except for a slim passage to the ocean known as **The Narrows.** Only about 207m/680ft wide, this channel is flanked by 150m/500ft cliffs rising on the north side to form Signal Hill. For about 1.6km/1mi, the harbour widens to nearly 800m/.5mi, surrounded by the steep slopes on which the city is built. Parallel to the water, **Harbour Drive** skirts the busy dock where ships from Portugal, Spain, Poland, Russia and Japan as well as Canadian ships are often berthed. Narrow streets lined with brightly painted wooden houses, topped with flat or mansard roofs, ascend the hills. Perpendicular to them, the main thorough-fares of the old city, **Water** and **Duckworth streets,** contain restaurants, shops and banks. Especially colourful, **George Street** is home to several pubs and eateries.

★ **Newfoundland Museum [M¹].** – *Duckworth St. Open daily year-round. Closed legal holidays.* ▣ ☎*709/729-2329.* Offering an insightful introduction to the province, this small museum is devoted to Newfoundland's history and prehistory. The second floor features displays on native peoples, notably Beothuk Indians and Labrador Inuit. On the third floor, re-created rooms and reconstructions such as a fishing "stage" with its flakes, ropes and nets depict the life of European settlers from the 18C onward. Replicas of a schoolroom and grocery store of the late 19C are particularly noteworthy. The ground floor is reserved for temporary exhibits.

★ **Newfoundland Museum at the Murray Premises [M²].** – *Harbour Dr. Open daily year-round.* ও ☎*709/729-5044.* Located in the **Murray Premises**, a collection of mercantile buildings (c.1847) housing shops, eateries and offices, this small branch of the Newfoundland Museum recaptures the province's maritime and military past. Highlights include a section on 16C Basques whalers who ventured to Labrador in search of whale oil, a history of fighting on provincial soil and of Newfoundland's overseas troops during both world wars.

★ **Commissariat House.** – *King's Bridge Rd. Open daily end-Jun–Labour Day.* ☎*709/729-6730.* Dating from 1821, this large clapboard house with its tall chimneys was one of the few buildings to escape the 19C fires. Used for many years by the Commissariat—the department responsible for supplying the military post of St John's with non-military provisions—the house also served as the local government pay office. After 1871, it became the rectory for adjacent **Church of St Thomas [A],** an elegantly simple edifice (1836) of painted wood.

Beautifully restored to reflect the 1830 period, the house contains the commissariat offices and kitchen *(ground floor)*, entertaining rooms and bedrooms *(second floor)*. Reconstructed on the grounds, a **coach house** lodges an exhibit on the restoration process.

Within walking distance *(Military Rd)* stand two other historic structures: the residence of the lieutenant-governor called **Government House**, a Georgian-style stone building (1830) surrounded by pleasant grounds *(only the grounds can be visited without appointment)* and the former seat of the provincial assembly, the **Colonial Building** *(open year-round Mon–Fri; & ☎709/729-3065)*, a limestone structure with a classical portico (1847-50), which now houses the provincial archives *(access weekdays only; no guided tours)*.

Basilica of St John the Baptist [B]. — *Corner Harvey Rd, Military Rd and Bonaventure Ave.* Situated on the highest point of the ridge above the city, this twin-towered Roman Catholic church has become a landmark, clearly distinguishable from the harbour, Signal Hill and other vantage points. Opened for worship in 1850, the basilica has an ornate interior with statuary and altar carving.

Cathedral of St John the Baptist [D]. – *Church Hill between Cathedral Rd and Gower St.* This imposing stone structure was originally designed in 1843 by noted British architect **Sir George Gilbert Scott** (1811–1878). Twice destroyed by fire, this Anglican church was reconstructed only in this century, a good example of Gothic Revival architecture with a finely sculpted interior, wooden vaulted ceilings and **reredos**, an ornamental stone or wooden partition behind an altar.

★★ **Signal Hill.** – Topped by Cabot Tower, Signal Hill is formed of cliffs rising steeply at the mouth of the harbour. A natural lookout commanding the sea approach, the hill permits splendid views of the city and environs by day and night.

Despite its obvious strategic value, Signal Hill was not strongly fortified until the Napoleonic Wars (1803–1815). Traditionally used as a signal station to warn of enemy ships, the hill acted in later years as a means to alert merchants to the arrival of their fleets. In 1901, **Guglielmo Marconi** chose the site for an experiment to prove that radio signals could be transmitted long distances by electromagnetic waves. When he received the letter "S" in Morse code from Poldhu in Cornwall, England—a distance of 2,700km/1,700mi—he made history.

Visit. – ☞ *Open mid-Jun–Labour Day daily 8:30am–8pm. Off-season daily 8:30am–4:30pm. & ☎709/772-5367.* The **interpretation centre** contains artifacts, dioramas, audiovisuals and panels on the history of Newfoundland, emphasizing the development of St John's.

Completed in 1898 to memorialize the quadcentenary of John Cabot's visit to Newfoundland, **Cabot Tower★** also commemorates the diamond jubilee of Queen Victoria's accession. Inside, displays on Signal Hill are complemented by information on communications, including a section about Marconi. The summit of the tower affords a **panorama★★★** of the city, the harbour and the coastline as far as Cape Spear, the most easterly point in North America *(p 226)*.

A path leads to **Ladies Lookout**, the crown of the hill (160m/525ft) and a vantage point offering views of the surroundings. From **Queen's Battery**—the fortification (1832-1833) that dominates the Narrows—there is a good **view★** of the harbour. Immediately below is Chain Rock—a white pillar in the Narrows from which a chain was stretched across the harbour entrance in the 18C to keep enemy vessels out. On the other side of the Narrows stand the remains of Fort Amherst (1763) now housing a lighthouse.

From mid-July through August, students in the 19C uniforms of the Royal Newfoundland Regiment perform a **military tattoo** *(Wed, Thur, Sat, Sun weather permitting; 45min)* consisting of fife and drum corps and military drill near the Queen's Battery. Derived from a Dutch word, *tattoo* is a bugle or drum signal to call soldiers to quarters at night.

ADDITIONAL SIGHTS *Map p 224*

★ **Quidi Vidi Battery.** – *Take King's Bridge Rd. Turn right on Forest Rd. Drive 2km/1.2mi when road becomes Quidi Vidi Village Rd. Continue to Cuckhold's Cove Rd. Turn right. Open daily Jul–Aug. ☎709/729-2977.* Built by the French during their occupation of St John's in 1762, this emplacement, with a colonial-style wooden house at its centre, stands above the community. In the early 19C, the British tried to move fishermen away from the inlet and block the channel since it provided a means of attacking St John's from the rear. The fishermen refused to budge, so the plan was abandoned and the battery strengthened. Restored to the early 19C period, the house re-creates the living quarters of soldiers stationed there.

Below is the tiny fishing community of **Quidi Vidi**, which has a narrow channel connecting to the larger Quidi Vidi Lake, site of the annual St John's Regatta *(p 224)*.

Confederation Building. – *Prince Philip Dr. Open year-round. Closed legal holidays. Information office on ground floor ☎709/729-2300.* Newfoundland's Parliament and some provincial government offices are housed in this imposing building. Constructed in 1960 and expanded in 1985, the edifice stands high above the city, providing a good **view** from its front entrance of the harbour and Signal Hill. When in session, the **legislative assembly** can be observed *(sessions Feb–May Mon–Fri, third floor Visitors' Gallery)*. Note that the government benches are to the left of the Speaker's chair. Accepted practice elsewhere is for the government to sit on the right. When the Newfoundland Assembly met in the Colonial Building *(see above)*, there was only one fireplace—to the left of the Speaker. The governing body exercised their prerogative and sat by the fire. The tradition remains.

EXCURSIONS

★ **Cape Spear.** – 🕙 *Map p 218. About 11km/7mi south; follow Water St to Leslie St. Turn left a few yards past Leslie St. Go over bridge and follow road. Park grounds open year-round. Visitor centre open daily mid-Jun–Labour Day.* ☎709/722-5367. At longitude 52°37′24″, Cape Spear is North America's most easterly point. On clear days there are marvelous **views★** of the coast and of the entrance to St John's harbour. Sometimes whales can be seen in the waters off the cape.

Walkways from the parking lot lead to the actual point, the visitor centre, an operational lighthouse *(not open to the public)* and the World War II battery where gun emplacements and bunkers remain. The visitor centre features a small display on the function and evolution of lighthouses. Restored to evoke the life of a lighthouse keeper in the 1840s, the domed, square **1835 lighthouse★** *(visit by 15min guided tour only daily mid-Jun–Labour Day)* is the province's oldest lighthouse.

The return trip to St John's *(30km/19mi)* can be made via the villages of Maddox Cove and **Petty Harbour** (pop 974), the latter a pleasant fishing village with fishing shacks and flakes—wooden racks used to dry the fish.

★ **Witless Bay Ecological Reserve.** – *Map p 218. Disembarkation on the islands is not permitted. They can be viewed only by boat. Daily departures mid–Apr–Oct. Round-trip 2hrs 30min. $25.* ⅄ Ⅹ. *Bird Island Charters* ☎709/753-4850 *or Gatherall's* ☎709/334-2887. *Embarkation from town of Bay Bulls, 30km/19mi south of St John's via Rte 10. Then watch for directional signs of your chosen boat tour company to the dock. (Shuttle service to Bay Bulls available from major hotels in St John's.)* As feeding and nesting sites, the fish-filled waters and shore islands of Witless Bay attract thousands of sea birds annually. Three barren islets house the bird population: Great, Green and Gull Islands. In summer, common murres, Greater Black-Backed Gulls, Black Guillemots and Blacked-legged Kittiwakes are plentiful. The **Atlantic puffin** colony here is reputedly the largest on the east coast of North America. Tour boats get as close as possible to two of the rocky isles where hundreds of sea birds skim the water, dive, circle overhead, or light in the crevices and crannies of the rocks.

An additional highlight of the cruise is **whale watching★★** *(late spring and summer).* The reserve is a seasonal feeding area for humpback, Minke, Pothead and Fin whales, particularly in summer. Good opportunities to view icebergs at close range may also occur *(late spring, early summer).*

★ **Marine Drive.** – *12km/8mi north on Hwys 30 and 20. Leave St John's on Logy Bay Rd. (Rte 30). After 5.5 km/3mi, turn right to Marine Dr.* A pleasant drive up the coast through residential areas north of St John's, the road ascends and descends, affording endless views of the sea, headlands, cliffs, beaches, boats and fields. The **view★** from **Outer Cove** is especially lovely. At **Middle Cove**, there is an accessible beach, good for strolling along the shore.

★ **SAINT-PIERRE AND MIQUELON** (France) Pop 6,392

Map p 218   Tourist Office ☎508/41.22.22

Few people realize that part of France lies off the coast of North America on tiny islands 48km/30mi by boat from Newfoundland. The two principal islands—Saint-Pierre, and the larger Miquelon, connected by a long sand bar to what was once a third island, Langlade—are home to a French-speaking population. A decidedly Continental flavour pervades these rocky and remote shores.

Historical Notes. – Cod fishing is the reason for settlement on these islands. From the early 16C, the archipelago was used as a base for Basque and Breton fishermen working the Grand Banks. By the Treaty of Paris in 1763, it became official French territory, but ownership changed repeatedly as France and England fought for hegemony on the continent. Although France was the loser in this battle, she retained these islands as a *pied à terre* for her fishing fleets.

During US prohibition (1920-1933), the islands experienced brief prosperity as a "rum-running" centre. Today, only tourism adds to income from the fishing industry. Until 1976, the islands were an overseas French territory. Now they are a full *departement* of France, sending a *deputé* to the French Parliament and a member to the Senate.

VISIT *2 days*

Daily passenger ferry from Fortune Jun 1–Sept 30 to Saint-Pierre island; departs Fortune 2:15pm. Next day 1pm departure from Saint-Pierre. Crossing 1hr. Round-trip $47.95. For reservations & details contact Lloyd G. Lake Ltd, Fortune ☎709/832-1955. *Warning: the sea crossing can be rough.*
Regular flights from St John's by Atlantic Airways ☎709/576-1800. *Fog can delay flights. Air service from Sydney, NS or Halifax provided by Air Saint-Pierre. For information & reservations contact Canadian Airlines International* ☎800/426-7000. *English is not commonly spoken on the islands. Telephone operators and tourist office staffs are bilingual, however. For details on hotels, pensions, etc. contact the* **Saint-Pierre Tourism Department**, *PO Box 121, 97500 St-Pierre & Miquelon, Amérique du Nord,* ☎011/508/41.22.22.

★ **Saint-Pierre.** – From the sea, Saint-Pierre appears to be a desolate island of stunted trees and low plants. Upon arrival in the harbour of the island's capital and administrative centre, also named Saint-Pierre, visitors can sense a striking cultural difference from the rest of North America. Lining the waterfront, tall stone buildings house pastry shops, fine restaurants and boutiques stocked with imported goods; the streets are narrow and full of French cars.

At the entrance to the harbour sits the picturesque islet of **Ile-aux-Marins★** *(accessible from Saint-Pierre by 10min ferry ride)*, once a community of over 800 inhabitants active in cod fishing. Villagers progressively abandoned the site for Saint-Pierre whose fishing industry continued to modernize. Today, the few remaining houses on Ile-aux-Marins are primarily vacation homes for Saint-Pierre residents. Centered in the old schoolhouse, the **museum** contains a highly poetic presentation of isle history through artifacts and memorabilia. The treeless terrain permits good **views** of Saint-Pierre and the remains of one of the more than 600 shipwrecks that have occurred in the archipelago.

Miquelon and Langlade. – *Boat departures to Miquelon and Langlade available from Saint-Pierre. In summer, daily ferry to Langlade. Transportation by shuttle van to the village of Miquelon may be arranged (contact Saint-Pierre Tourism Department).* Except for the small working town (pop 709) of the same name, the northern island of Miquelon is untouched moorland of soft hills and long beaches. Along the unpaved road from Miquelon to Langlade (25km/16mi), herds of shaggy wild horses may be spotted roaming the deserted meadows. At low tide, seals can be seen lying on the rocks of **Grand Barachois** and a variety of sea birds frequenting the shores. The road crosses the isthmus known as the Dune of Langlade, a sand bar formed in part by debris from the numerous shipwrecks that have occurred since 1800. Situated at the southern end is the "island" of Langlade, largely uninhabited except for a tiny settlement in the hills above the ferry landing. Along the east side of the dune, a wide beach stretches out in the vicinity of Anse du Gouvernement.

★ TERRA NOVA NATIONAL PARK

Map p 218

Scarred by glaciers of the past, this 396sq km/153sq mi area on the shores of Bonavista Bay is a combination of rolling country and indented coastline. Deep fjords or "sounds" reach inland, and in early summer these coastal waters are dotted with icebergs that float down with the Labrador Current. The Trans-Canada Highway bisects the park with some good views of the sounds, but visitors must leave the highway to truly appreciate its natural beauty.

Access. – *On Trans-Can Hwy 58km/36mi from Gander, or 210km/130mi from St John's.*

VISIT *1 day*
☞ *Open year-round. $5/day per car or $10/4 days per car.* △ *($10/night)* ⚅ ☎ *709/ 533-2801.*

★★ **Bluehill Pond Lookout.** – *7km/5mi from park's north entrance. Turn onto gravel road and continue approximately 2km/1mi to fire tower.* From the fire tower there is a **panorama★★** of the whole park—deep inlets, cliffs, rocks, lakes, forest, bog and hills. To the south, Newman Sound and the ocean, scattered with icebergs *(in season)*, can clearly be seen in good weather.

★ **Newman Sound.** – *12km/8mi from park's north entrance, take road to information office and Newman Sound. About 1.5km/1mi to the trail.* The beauty of this sound— a deep inlet with a sandy beach—can be appreciated by taking the walking trail along its wooded shore. Seasonal wildflowers and tiny seashells complement the setting.

Ochre Lookout. – *18km/11mi from park's north entrance; take gravel road to tower, about 3km/2mi. Observation deck.* From this lookout tower, another **panorama★** allows visitors to comprehend the vastness of the park. At this height, Clode and Newman sounds are clearly visible, weather permitting.

★★ TRINITY   Pop 326

Map p 218

Situated on a hilly peninsula jutting into Trinity Bay, this charming seaside community has a lovely **setting★** with **views** of the sea, rocks, fields and the small protected harbour. One of the oldest settlements in Newfoundland, the village evokes a feeling of a bygone era with its narrow streets, tiny gardens and colourful "box" houses.

Sufficiently established in 1615, the town became the site of the first Admiralty Court in Canada's history. Sir Richard Whitbourne was sent from Britain to settle disputes between the resident fishermen and those who crossed the Atlantic just for the season. In time, Trinity rivaled St John's in socio-economic standing, but receded in importance when the latter became the provincial capital. Today, a small fishing industry and tourism are its mainstays. It is a popular area for whale watching *(daily departures mid-Jun–Labour Day weather permitting; minimum 6 people; round-trip 3hrs-$35 or 7hrs-$80; 3-day & 7-day packages available; reservations recommended; Ocean Contact Ltd, Trinity ☎709/464-3269).*

Access. – *74km/46mi north of Trans-Can Hwy by Rte 230. Turn off Rte 230 for 5km/ 3mi.*

VISIT *1 day*

Located in a restored house overlooking the harbour, the **interpretation centre** *(open daily mid-Jun–mid-Sept; ☎709/464-2042)* has displays presenting the community's history. They chronicle Trinity's rise to prominence from the mid-18C to the early 19C as a center of commerce and society, only to be eclipsed by St John's in the 1850s. Housed in a seven-room "salt box" dating to the 1880s, the **Trinity Museum and Archives** *(open daily mid-Jun–mid-Sept; for information on walking tours ☎709/464-3720)* contains local artifacts and historical documents.

The **Hiscock House** *(open daily mid-Jun–mid-Sept; ☎709/464-2042)* has been restored to its early 1900s appearance and contains some original furnishings of the Hiscock family for whom the home was built in 1881.

In a pastoral setting with the sea in the background, **St Paul's Anglican Church** (1892) stands as a distinctive village landmark. The 31m/102ft clock spire of this large wooden house of worship towers above the town, visible from all vantage points. A small graveyard adjoins the property.

In use for over 150 years, the **Holy Trinity Roman Catholic Church** is distinguished by its detached belfry as well as the clean simplicity of its elegant tower.

EXCURSION TO CAPE BONAVISTA

From Trinity, Route 230 northbound continues inland and returns to the sea at Port Union (pop 638) and Catalina (pop 1,205), two fishing communities set along the shore. At Catalina, Route 237 crosses the peninsula, ending at Amherst Cove, where Route 235 continues northward to the cape town of Bonavista *(52km/31mi north of Trinity)*.

Bonavista. – Pop 4,597. This large seaside town is another fishing community with houses set around an outer harbour protected by a breakwater and a sheltered inner harbour for small boats.

Throughout the 16C, European fishing fleets used the harbour. By about 1600, the area had become a British settlement and remained so, despite several attempts by the French to capture it in the 18C.

Situated by the sea toward the capeside of town, the .6ha/1.5 acre **Mockbeggar Property** *(daily summer)* features a barn, a storage building and the Bradley House. Restored to the 1930s period, the house contains the personal belongings of prosperous local businessman and senator, Frederick Gordon Bradley.

> *About 5km/3mi from the town; follow Rte 235, which becomes Church St. Continue past town hall over bridge and bear right at fork.*

★ **Cape Bonavista.** – Supposedly named Bonavista ("good view") by explorer John Cabot in 1497, the cape is a superb setting with pounding waves, a clear blue sea and interesting rock formations.

Visit. – A drive through fields with **views** of the sea leads to the remote tip of the cape. A **statue** of Cabot commemorates his first North American landing, though recent research has cast doubt on the authenticity of this claim. Although he sailed under British colours, Cabot was Italian by birth. Completed in 1843, the **lighthouse★** *(open daily mid-Jun–Aug; ☎709/468-7444)* has been restored by the provincial government to portray a lightkeeper's living quarters in the 1870s. Exhibits include the construction and restoration of the lighthouse, the operation of the lamps and the lightkeeper's duties. There are sweeping **views** of the rocky coast from the lighthouse itself.

Northwest Territories

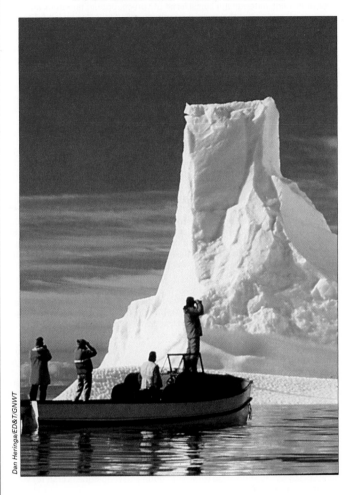

Dan Heringa/ED&T/GNWT

Contrary to the misconception that the Canadian North is a frozen wilderness, this spectacular continental rooftop abounds in varied landscape: Arctic coastline, myriad lakes, meandering rivers, massive glaciers and polar expanses, all transformed by the light of the midnight sun. A vast region encompassing over a third of Canada, the Territories sustain less than one percent of the country's population. Except for the capital city of Yellowknife, few large settlements exist in this otherwise frontier wilderness, best suited for lovers of adventure, nature and indigenous cultures. Its planned partitioning before the turn of the century will result in native administration of ancestral lands *(see Nunavut p 231)*.

GEOGRAPHICAL NOTES

Comprising lands above the 60th parallel (except parts of Quebec and Labrador), the Territories stretch from Hudson Bay to the Yukon. They include the Arctic archipelago between the mainland and the North Pole, and the Hudson and James Bay islands south of the parallel. Even larger prior to 1905, the Territories also encompassed most of Alberta, Saskatchewan, Manitoba, northern Ontario and Quebec. Mountains border this immense northland on two sides. In the east stand the glacier-strewn peaks of Baffin, Bylot, Devon and Ellesmere islands. In the west rise the Mackenzie, Selwyn and Richardson ranges—part of the rugged western backbone of North America. East of the Mackenzie Mountains is a tongue of lowlands, an extension of the plains of central Canada. Down this tongue runs the great Mackenzie River.

East of the lowlands lies the scarred face of the Canadian Shield, pitted with lakes. Glaciers that retreated from this region 10,000 years ago scoured and gouged the ancient rocks, leaving behind an intricate pattern of lakes and deep coastal fjords, which still exists today. Glacial debris—huge boulders, piles of moraine, **eskers** (narrow ridges of sand and gravel) and **drumlins** (elliptical-shaped hills inclining in the direction of the glacier's retreat)—bear witness to the region's geological history.

Permafrost. – After the last ice age, a layer of permanently frozen earth developed in all regions where the ground remains at or below 0°C/32°F for two or more years (at least 40 percent of Canada). Permafrost, as it is known, generally starts about 0.3m/1ft or more below the surface and can be very shallow or as much as 370m/1,200ft deep, as at Resolute on Cornwallis Island.

Vegetation. – The tree line crosses the Territories diagonally northwest to southeast from the Mackenzie Delta to Hudson Bay at the Manitoba border. South and west of this line extends the **boreal forest** of spruce, poplar, tamarack and jack pine. To the north and east is the **tundra**, sometimes called "the barren lands" for its bleak look in winter and lack of trees. In summer, dwarf shrubs, tiny flowers of all hues and lichens— flat, rootless growths, part fungus, part algae, which survive where no other plant could possibly grow—thrive in the surface ground above the permafrost. The latter prevents moisture from draining away. Known as **muskeg**, this surface ground is sometimes very boggy because it cannot drain.

Climate. – Annual precipitation over much of the Territories is so low (Yellowknife 254mm/10in, Inuvik 276mm/11in, Baker Lake 208mm/8in, Iqaluit 409/16in) that a great part of the region would be desert if the permafrost did not cradle what moisture there is on the surface. Generally, the winters are long, cold and dark and the summers surprisingly warm and sunny, with long hours of daylight. The southern part has 20 hours of daylight, while north, in the Arctic Circle, it never gets dark. The mean daily maximum temperatures for July are 21°C/70°F in Yellowknife, 19°C/66°F in Inuvik, 15°C/59°F in Baker Lake and 12°C/53°F in Iqaluit. The highest recorded temperature in July was 36°C/97°F in Fort Simpson; the lowest was -3°C/26°F in Holman, Victoria Island.

The Aurora Borealis. – Also known as the Northern Lights, this amazing phenomenon can usually be viewed in fall and winter. The sky "dissolves" into folded curtains of elusive, dancing lights, sometimes many coloured, other times black and white. They seem to occur when electrically charged particles, emitted by the sun, collide with atoms and molecules in the earth's outer atmosphere, causing the latter to emit radiation, sometimes in the form of visible light. Research on these displays is conducted at Churchill, Manitoba.

HISTORICAL NOTES

The first inhabitants of North America came from Asia some 15,000 years ago, across the land bridge that is now the Bering Strait. They settled south of the ice cap that covered the continent. As it retreated, some moved north. Today, these people form two distinct groups.

The Inuit. – The life of the aboriginal people of the Arctic Coast revolved largely around hunting sea mammals—especially seal and whale—as a source of food; blubber for heat and light; skins for clothing, shelter and boats; and bone or ivory for the blades of their harpoons or other tools. The smaller sea mammals were hunted from **kayaks** (one-person canoes); whales were hunted from **umiaks**, which held up to 12 men. In winter, animals were sought at openings in the ice. The occasional excursion south was made by **dogsled** to hunt caribou, the skins of which were used for clothing or bedding.

The Inuit were nomadic—several families living and moving together. In winter, they constructed **igloos**, dome-shaped snow houses made of blocks of ice, and entered by a tunnel. For insulation, the interior was lined with skins. In summer, they lived in tents made of skins. Time not spent hunting or making clothes—especially their famous parkas—was devoted to carving bone and soapstone, a craft for which they are famous today.

Since the arrival of Europeans, their lifestyle has changed drastically: a nomadic way of life is practically nonexistent, and igloos and dogsleds are no longer commonplace. Many still live by hunting, however, supplemented by income from arts and crafts. On the whole, they retain more of their traditional lifestyle than North America's other native peoples. The world's total Inuit population is estimated at 115,000. Over 6,700 of them inhabit their Quebec homeland of Nunavik *(see Michelin Green Guide to Quebec)*, a socio-cultural region established through grassroots referendum in 1986 and officially recognized by the provincial government. The creation of a homeland in the Northwest Territories *(see Nunavut, p 231)* should result in greater autonomy in the 21C for the Inuit of northern Canada.

The Dene. – The Athapaskan-speaking peoples of the sub-Arctic lived a difficult life in a meagre environment. Travelling by canoe in summer and toboggan in winter, they hunted caribou and fished, constantly on the move to find food. Home was a conical-shaped lodge similar to the teepees of the Plains Indians *(p 74)*. Today, some of these people have preserved a fairly traditional lifestyle based on hunting and fishing, but many live on the fringe of contemporary society.

The Northwest Passage. – A sea route between the Atlantic and Pacific oceans around the north of the American continent was the quest of explorers for centuries after it became obvious that America was a continent and not an adjunct of Asia. The first Europeans to visit this vast region came in search of a trade route to the Orient around the north of the continent. British sailor **Martin Frobisher** made the first attempt in 1576. His voyages were followed by those of **John Davis**, **Henry Hudson** and **William Baffin**, all of whom have left their names on the map, and Sir John Franklin in 1845. Their reports of ice-filled seas somewhat dampened enthusiasm for the passage. Except for exploration at the western end, no more attempts were made until the early 19C.

Fur Traders. – At the same time, other explorers were penetrating the interior of the Territories for skins of abundant fur-bearing animals. **Samuel Hearne** of the Hudson's Bay Company traversed much of the region, especially during his famous 1770-1772 trip from Churchill to Great Slave Lake, and later down the Coppermine River to the Beaufort Sea. Not long afterwards in 1789, **Alexander Mackenzie** of the rival North West Company travelled the river that bears his name. He named it the "river of disappointment": it led to the Arctic, not the Pacific Ocean, as he had hoped. After the two fur companies joined in 1821, several trading posts were established in the Territories, some of which remain to this day.

Naval Explorers. – Mackenzie's voyage sparked new interest in a northwest passage. The first half of the 19C saw the British Navy equipping expeditions to find a navigable route. **John Franklin** made two overland trips to explore the western end, sailing a third time, in 1845, to locate the connecting channel from the east. Years passed with no word from him. Eventually a series of expeditions, 38 in all, were sent to discover his fate. It was established that he and his entire crew had perished after years of being marooned in the frozen waters. One effect of this tragedy was the exploration by his would-be rescuers of a large part of the Territories.

Finally, a passable route of the passage was found between the Canadian mainland and the Arctic islands, but not successfully navigated until Norwegian **Roald Amundsen** did so between 1903 and 1906. Since then, many ships have followed the hazardous route, among them the schooner *St Roch (p 60).*

20C Development. – In the late 19C and early 20C, the Geological Survey of Canada mounted expeditions under such men as Joseph Burr Tyrrell, Sir William Logan (after whom Mount Logan is named), George Mercer Dawson (of Dawson City fame) and Vilhjalmar Stefansson to explore and map the Territories. By this time, both Anglican and Roman Catholic missionaries were established in the region. In the 1930s, a new breed of explorer arrived—the prospector. Several major mineral finds *(see below)* encouraged more outsiders to come to the Territories. Mineral as well as oil exploration continued to attract investment in the Territories, although the oil industry is confined largely to the Mackenzie Delta. The natural beauty and abundant wildlife are mainstays of the Territories' growing tourism, as are the arts and crafts of the native inhabitants.

Partitioning of the Territories. – In 1992, the residents of the Northwest Territories voted to divide their land by creating a new territory in the eastern portion. Stretching 2,000,156sq km/772,260sq mi nearly to Greenland from the Manitoba/Saskatchewan border, this homeland has been designated **Nunavut** meaning "our land" in the native language, Inuktitut. After a seven-year transition period, Nunavut is to be administered by its Inuit inhabitants.

Population. – Of the 57,649 inhabitants in the Northwest Territories, 59 percent claim aboriginal origin. Of these, about 21,000 are Inuit (the well-known name *eskimo,* meaning "eaters of raw meat," was given to the Inuit by the Indians of the south. *Inuit* means "the people" in Inuktitut). Another 9,800 are Dene or Athapaskan-speaking Indians. The rest are Métis and non-natives.

RESOURCES

Since the 1930s, the basis of the economy has been mining. Fur trapping, forestry, fishing, tourism and the sale of native arts and crafts also contribute, but to a much lesser extent. Deposits of pitchblende—a source of uranium—and silver were discovered on the shores of the Great Bear Lake in 1930, arousing interest in the mineral possibilities of other regions, and leading to the great gold discoveries at Yellowknife.

Today, gold is still mined at Yellowknife and at Contwoyto Lake farther north. In 1964, the vast zinc and lead deposits at Pine Point on Great Slave Lake were found. Since then, mining of these minerals has begun at Nanisivik near Arctic Bay in the north of Baffin Island and on Little Cornwallis Island. Tungsten and copper are mined near the Yukon border in the Selwyn Mountains.

Near Fort Liard, there is a natural gas extraction and processing plant, and producing oil wells and a refinery at Norman Wells on the Mackenzie. The 1968 discovery of major oil and gas fields in northern Alaska spurred the search for such resources in northern Canada. Two potentially rich areas were identified: the Mackenzie Delta–Beaufort Sea region, and the high Arctic islands. Since 1985, oil-price fluctuation and expensive drilling costs have curtailed exploration and development.

Goods are transported to and from the Territories by the Dempster Highway or by the Great Slave Lake railway. Huge strings of barges float up and down the Mackenzie River all summer. Between November and April, winter roads crisscross the frozen land, giving heavy transport access to places that can be reached only by air the rest of the year.

Handicrafts. – Largely because of their expressiveness and depiction of a disappearing lifestyle, the distinctive arts and crafts produced by the native peoples have long been popular among collectors and connoisseurs. Most famous are the **sculptures** of the Inuit. The grey or green soapstone can easily be worked with chisels and files before being polished to give it a distinctive finish.

Delicate carvings are fashioned from walrus tusks, caribou antlers or whalebone. Wall hangings and prints are also produced. Cape Dorset on Baffin Island is especially famous for the latter. Clothing suited to this climate, particularly Inuit *parkas* and Indian *mukluks* decorated with beautiful beadwork, has become popular farther south.

Principal Festivals

Mar	**Caribou Carnival**	*Yellowknife*
Apr	**Top of the World Ski Meet**	*Inuvik*
Jun	**Canadian North Yellowknife Midnight Classic**	*Yellowknife*
Jul	**Folk on the Rocks**	*Yellowknife*
	Annual Great Northern Arts Festival	*Inuvik*

Practical Information

How to get there. – **Air** service to Yellowknife is provided by Canadian Airlines International and its affiliates from major Canadian gateway cities. Scheduled and chartered service in the Northwest Territories is offered by First Air (☎613/839-3340), and NWT Air (☎403/920-2500).

Accommodation and Tourist Information. – Every year the government of the Northwest Territories publishes the *Explorers' Guide,* which lists hotels, motels, lodges, camps and outfitters. For a free copy and road map contact:

Department of Economic Development & Tourism, Yellowknife, NT, X1A 2L9 ☎403/873-7200 or ☎800/661-0788 (toll-free Canada/US).

Driving in the North. – Roads have all-weather gravel surfaces and are well maintained. Motorists are cautioned to pass other vehicles slowly to prevent flying rocks or skidding. Unless otherwise posted, the speed limit is 100km/h (60mph). Seat belt use is mandatory. Distances between gasoline stations can be great; it is advisable to fill up frequently. It is recommended that motorists carry at least one spare tire, water, first-aid kit, emergency flares and, in winter, snow shovel, parka, warm clothes, and a sleeping bag for each person in the vehicle.

Government **ferry** service (free; information ☎403/873-7799) is provided along the following highways: to reach Yellowknife, the **Mackenzie Highway** crosses the river at Fort Providence. The **Dempster Highway** crosses the Mackenzie River at Arctic Red River and the Peel River to reach Fort McPherson. Near Fort Simpson the **Liard Highway**, which connects with the Alaska Highway, crosses the Liard River. There are ice bridges across these rivers in winter. During the three to six-week freeze-up and thaw periods (November and May), the rivers cannot be crossed.

Time Zones. – The Northwest Territories span three time zones: Eastern Standard north of Quebec and Ontario, Central Standard north of Manitoba, and Mountain Standard north of Alberta, Saskatchewan and British Columbia. Daylight Saving Time is observed from the first Sunday in April to the last Sunday in October.

Taxes. – There is no provincial sales tax, but the 7% GST *(rebate information p 242)* applies.

Liquor Laws. – The legal drinking age is 19. Liquor, wine and beer are sold in government liquor stores in the larger communities. Some communities have voted for restrictions on liquor including prohibition of possession.

Provincial Holidays *(see National Holidays p 240)*
Civic Holiday ....1st Monday in August

Outdoor Activities. – The Northwest Territories are a wonderland for outdoor enthusiasts. Charter planes transport hikers, fishermen and **canoeists** (with their canoes) to remote regions. The northern summer with its 20 or more hours of daylight makes a visit to this area a unique experience. Outfitters organize and equip wilderness travel year-round. One of the world's great canoe trips is down the **South Nahanni River** *(p 235),* but other routes of varying degrees of difficulty are available. There are also opportunities for hiking, although this activity is less popular than canoeing in this land of rivers and lakes, with the exception of **Auyuittuq National Park Reserve** *(p 233).* All wilderness travellers (including boaters, canoeists and hikers,) are asked to register with the Royal Canadian Mounted Police detachment nearest their point of departure, and to notify the police when their trip is completed. Warm clothing, a sleeping bag and, beyond the tree line, a stove and fuel should be carried.

Wood Buffalo National Park *(map p 3)* has the largest free-roaming herd of bison in existence and is the last natural breeding habitat for the rare whooping crane. Owing to four North American flyways that pass through the park, the Peace-Athabasca Delta is well known for its abundance of geese, duck and other waterfowl. Park is open year-round; camping is available at Pine Lake; reservations are required. For details contact the Superintendent, Box 750, Fort Smith, NT, X0E 0P0 ☎403/872-2349.

Lodges are scattered on remote lakes and coasts from the Mackenzie Mountains to the fjords of Baffin Island, where **fishing** is superb (Arctic char, Arctic grayling, great northern pike among others). All non-resident hunters of big game (wolf, moose, caribou, Dall sheep, grizzly, black and polar bears) must be accompanied by a licensed outfitter. Details regarding seasons, package tours, accommodation, outfitters, wilderness excursions as well as hunting and fishing regulations can be obtained from the Department of Economic Development & Tourism *(see above).*

Special Excursions. – Located 48km/30mi north of the Arctic Circle, **Bathurst Inlet Lodge** offers rafting and canoeing on Arctic rivers, fishing, guided hikes and outdoor natural-history interpretations. Open mid-May–mid-Aug; 7-day packages include air transportation from Yellowknife, accommodation, meals and guided excursions. For more information, schedules and reservations contact Bathurst Inlet Lodge, P O Box 820, Yellowknife, NT, X1A 2N6 ☎403/873-2595.

In 1986, a national park reserve was created in the northern corner of **Ellesmere Island**, accessible from Resolute Bay. Covering nearly 40,000sq km/15,000sq mi of mountains, glaciers, valleys and fjords, this reserve is the world's northernmost park (latitude 82°N). For information contact the Superintendent, Eastern Arctic District National Parks, Pangnirtung, NT X0A 0R0 ☎819/473-8828.

For general information on admission, accommodation and activities in Canadian national parks, see pp 243-245.

Map of Principal Sights p 4

Named for British sailor **William Baffin** who explored coastal waters between 1615 and 1616, the island is the largest, most inhabited and scenically spectacular in the Arctic archipelago. Its mountains rise more than 2,100m/7,000ft with numerous glaciers; its coasts are deeply indented with fjords. About two-thirds of the island lies north of the Arctic Circle (66.5°N) and in the continuous daylight of summer, the tundra blooms with an infinite variety of tiny, colourful flowers.

Most inhabitants are Inuit living in small settlements along the coasts. In some respects, their lifestyle remains traditional *(p 230)*, although they have adopted certain 20C ways (dress, housing, etc). Their soapstone carvings, prints and lithographs are internationally renowned, especially those from **Cape Dorset**, a settlement on the west coast. The administrative centre and largest community is **Iqaluit** (eh-CALL-oo-it) (pop 3,552)—formerly called Frobisher Bay—where most non-natives live.

Access. – *Daily scheduled flights between Ottawa, Toronto or Montreal and Iqaluit by Air Canada, First Air ☎800/267-1247 (toll-free Canada/US) and Air Inuit ☎514/636-9445; regular service between Iqaluit and other communities. Accommodation in Cape Dorset, Iqaluit, Pangnirtung and Pond Inlet.*

SIGHTS

★★ **Pangnirtung.** – Pop 1,135. Dominated by the snow-capped mountains surrounding the Penny Ice Cap in Auyuittuq National Park Reserve, this little village occupies a spectacular **site★★** on the fjord of the same name. Situated just south of the Arctic Circle, Pangnirtung is an ideal spot for viewing the midnight "light" in summer (there is no sun at midnight, but it never gets dark). It is also a good place to study the tundra landscape and wildlife (small mammals, and some large sea mammals in Cumber-land Sound), and to purchase locally woven goods, soapstone carvings and other specialities at the Inuit cooperative.

Even if a visit to the park itself is not planned, the **trip★** down the fjord to the park entrance by boat when the ice has melted *(Jul–Sept; one-way 1hr; warm clothing essential)* or by snowmobile the rest of the year is impressive. *Outfitters' services offered year-round; for information & reservations contact Angmarlik Centre in Pangnirtung; ☎819/473-8737.*

★★ **Auyuittuq National Park Reserve.** – ☝ *Park headquarters are located in Pang-nirtung. Open mid-May–Aug 31 daily 8:30am–10pm. Off season Mon–Fri 8:30am–5pm. Closed holidays & weekends in winter. ☎819/473-8828.* A stark landscape of perpetual ice, jagged peaks of 2,000m/7,000ft and glacier-scarred valleys that be-

come deep fjords along a coast of sheer cliffs (up to 900m/3,000ft high), *Auyuittuq* (ow-you-EE-took) means "land that never melts" in Inuktitut—an appropriate name for Canada's first national park north of the Arctic Circle. Fully one quarter of its 21,470sq km/8,290sq mi is covered by the **Penny Ice Cap.** Only lichens grow on rocks bared by the ice, but in the valleys, moss heath and a few dwarf shrubs thrive during the long hours of the Arctic summer.

Inukshuk

Dan Heringa/ED&T/GNWT

Since its creation in 1972, the park has drawn climbers from all over the world to scale its rugged peaks. Backpackers and campers also come for the challenge of surviving this remote, yet breathtakingly grand landscape. The most visited region is **Pangnirtung Pass,** a huge U-shaped trench that stretches 96km/60mi across the peninsula and rises to 390m/1,280ft. By early July, the pass is usually free of ice at the south entrance of Pangnirtung Fjord, and by late July, at North Pangnirtung Fjord, although some years the ice never melts. It can be crossed by properly equipped hikers accustomed to rough mountain terrain and prepared to ford frequent streams of glacial melt water. There is constant wind, little shelter, and most of the route is on glacial moraine *(on average, 3km/2mi an hour maximum can be covered per day)*. However, this is a spectacular trip for those willing to make the effort.

Pond Inlet. – Pop 974. Situated in the northern part of the island, this community overlooks the mountains of Bylot Island—summer home of thousands of snow geese—across the inlet of the same name. Soapstone and whalebone carvings as well as Inuit parkas and footwear can be purchased in the community.

★★ MACKENZIE DELTA

Map of Principal Sights p 2

A labyrinth of channels among thousands of lakes 160km/100mi from the mouth of the Beaufort Sea, the 100km/70mi wide delta—one of the world's largest—fractures the northwest edge of the Territories' mainland. It is the estuary of the vast and fast-moving Mackenzie River, and the terminus of its 1,800km/1,100mi journey from the interior's Great Slave Lake.

One of the most prolific areas for wildlife in Canada's Arctic, the delta supports innumerable muskrats, beaver, mink, marten, fox, bear, moose, caribou and smaller mammals. Its channels and lakes abound with fish. Beluga whales calve in the warm waters, and migratory birds congregate here in the spring.

The livelihood of many of the inhabitants of the delta communities—Arctic Red River, Inuvik, Aklavik, Fort McPherson and Tuktoyaktuk—depends on trapping, hunting and fishing. However, huge reserves of oil and gas discovered under the Beaufort Sea have impacted the area's economy in more recent times.

Access. – *Dempster Highway from the Yukon (Dawson City to Inuvik 798km/496mi) open all year except during freeze-up and thaw periods (p 232). Few services on road. Motorists should be outfitted for emergencies (p 232). Also accessible by air from Edmonton via Yellowknife, and from Whitehorse, Yukon. The best way to appreciate the delta is to fly over it; charters can be arranged in Inuvik.*

VISIT

The Delta. – Viewed from the air, this delta is an amazing place. The tangle of muddy arteries belonging to the Mackenzie and the Peel rivers, which join at this point, can be distinguished from the lakes by their colour. The western edge is clearly marked by the frequently snow-capped **Richardson Mountains**, the eastern edge by the low, humped **Caribou Hills**. Heading north, the land seemingly gives way as the areas of water become greater, until the vast Beaufort Sea is reached and the land disappears completely from view.

Except for areas of tundra along the coast, the land is covered with low scrubs (dwarf willow and juniper) that turn bright yellow with the first frost (usually late August), a most attractive array. The tundra itself is full of lakes, and many colourful, multihued mosses, lichens and flowers bloom in the short but light (24 hours of daylight) Arctic summer.

Inuvik. – Pop 3,206. *On Dempster Hwy; airport; accommodation.* Meaning "place of man" in Inuktitut, this outpost lies on a large stretch of flat land beside the east channel of the Mackenzie. A thriving community, Inuvik is an administrative centre of the territorial government.

In 1954, the government moved their administrative facilities here from Aklavik, which was always being flooded. A model northern community was built and opened in 1959. Over the entire delta, the permafrost is only a few inches from the surface, causing problems for house building. The heat from a dwelling soon melts the ice, and residents find themselves living in a swamp. Therefore, the houses were constructed on pilings, steamed into the permafrost before construction. Water, sewage and heating ducts are housed together in above-ground **utilidors**, or covered corridors, to stop them from freezing.

The **Roman Catholic Church** is built in the shape of an igloo. It has a marvellously expressive **interior★** with paintings of the Stations of the Cross done in 1960 by Mona Thrasher, a young Inuit girl.

★ **Tuktoyaktuk.** – Pop 918. *Daily flights from Inuvik; ice road in winter; accommodation.* The centre for oil and gas exploration in the region, this pleasant little community on the shores of the Beaufort Sea is known simply as "Tuk" to northerners. It has a Distant Early Warning (DEW) line site forming part of a chain of radar bases guarding Canada's northern frontier. However, it is best known for one of nature's most curious phenomena: **pingos**, or huge moss- and turf-covered mounds of solid ice pushed out of the otherwise flat tundra by permafrost action. From the air, they resemble giant boils. Of the thousands in the Canadian North, the vast majority are located on the Tuktoyaktuk peninsula. At the **Fur Garment Shop**, visitors can observe Inuit women making parkas and other items of clothing.

★★★ NAHANNI NATIONAL PARK RESERVE

Map of Principal Sights p 2

A wild, remote and staggeringly beautiful place in the southwest corner of the Territories, this park, extending over 4,700sq km/1,815sq mi, covers a large section of the South Nahanni River, which flows through the Selwyn, Mackenzie and Franklin mountains before ultimately adding its waters to the Liard River, a tributary of the mighty Mackenzie. In 1978, UNESCO recognized the universal value of this reserve by designating it a World Heritage Site.

Land of Mystery and Legend. – Early in the 20C, tales of placer gold lured prospectors to the valley of the South Nahanni. In 1908, the headless bodies of two adventurers were found. Other men disappeared without trace. Stories of fierce natives and of mythical mountain men were spread abroad, and the South Nahanni became known as a place to avoid. The mystery remains and the legends are recalled by names in the park such as Deadmen Valley, Headless Range, Broken Skull River and Funeral Range.

The park's very inaccessibility is part of its beauty. Unlike other national parks, it will probably never have roads and tourist facilities. But for those willing to make the effort, one of the world's great natural glories awaits.

Access by Road and Air. – *From British Columbia: take Alaska Highway to Fort Nelson (p 28), Liard Highway to Fort Liard. From the Yukon: take Alaska Highway to Watson Lake (p 29). In the Northwest Territories: take Mackenzie Highway to Fort Simpson, or Liard Highway to Fort Liard. Air transportation available from Yellowknife, with NWT Air (☎403/920-2500) and Ptarmigan Airways (☎403/ 873-4461). Park open year-round. For details on activities & outfitters contact Park Superintendent, Postal Bag 300, Fort Simpson, NWT, X0E 0N0 ☎403/695-3151 or Economic Development and Tourism, Yellowknife, NWT (p 232).*

Access by Water. – *Various outfitters offer trips descending the river by rubber raft or outfitted canoe (equipment is flown in first). Intermediate white-water specialists can descend the river in their own canoe; permission must be obtained from the park first. For details contact the park or Economic Development and Tourism, Yellowknife, NWT.*

★★★ **South Nahanni River.** – For more than 320km/198mi, this serpentine waterway coils through the park, entering majestic canyons, cascading over a precipice twice the height of Niagara and passing a series of hot mineral springs that create surrounding vegetation unusual at this latitude (61°–62°N). Each year, this magnificent river attracts countless canoeists and raft-riders to its adventurous waters and wilderness beauty.

Visit. – ☞ *The following describes highlights of a descent of the river.* The 200km/125mi excursion downriver from Virginia Falls to Nahanni Butte is one of the world's great wilderness trips. Over this distance, the river drops more than 120m/400ft (which is why canoeists generally prefer to descend it).

The jewel of the park and one of the North's most spectacular sights is **Virginia Falls★★★**. Parted by a central pointed rock at the precipice, hectares (acres) of water plunge 90m/294ft to the gorge below. The Albert Faille Portage can be followed around the falls *(1.6km/1mi)*. From it, a trail leads to the brink of the cataract where the river can be seen in spectacular rapids, just before it cascades over the rocks. Fourth Canyon is the first of four awesome canyons with immense cliffs and depths

Virginia Falls

Nahanni National Park Reserve

as great as 1,200m/3,900ft. Then come the surging waves of Figure of Eight Rapids. The river makes a 90-degree turn known as The Gate, guarded by mighty Pulpit Rock. Third Canyon is followed by the 34km/21mi stretch of Second Canyon. **Deadman Valley**, where headless bodies were found *(p 234)*, separates Second Canyon from First Canyon, a twisting 27km/17mi channel. The river passes close to a hot spring where pools of water, at nearly 37°C/98°F, have caused ferns, chokecherries, rose bushes and flowering parsnip plants to proliferate. Before reaching Nahanni Butte, the river divides into a series of channels known as the **Splits**.

★ **YELLOWKNIFE**   Pop 15,179

Map of Principal Sights p 2   Tourist Office ☎403/873-4262

The administrative capital of the Northwest Territories lies beside Yellowknife Bay on the northern shore of the Great Slave Lake. Almost completely surrounded by water, the city has a pretty site, set on pink granite, glacier-scarred rocks topped by small trees. A pleasant "old town" (c.1934) coexists with a modern "new town," where most of the population lives, shops and works.

Foundation of Gold. – Named not for the colour of metal underlying it, but for the copper knives traded by local Indians, Yellowknife is a recent settlement. Its site was visited by Samuel Hearne in 1771, Alexander Mackenzie on his epic journey to the mouth of the river that bears his name, and John Franklin, all of whom were too preoccupied with their travels to notice the gold. Prospectors en route for the Klondike at the end of the 19C did record some sightings, but without pursuit. Not until the discovery of pitchblende in 1930 on the shores of the Great Bear Lake was there interest in the rest of the region. In 1934, exposed gold was found beside the bay and a boom town sprang up overnight.

The boom did not last, however, and the place was almost a ghost town in 1945 when new discoveries were made deep below ground. The city is still thriving from this second boom. The mining and separating process is very expensive at the two operating mines, but the price of the yellow metal makes them economically viable. When the city became the territorial capital in 1967, Yellowknife's importance was finally acknowledged.

Midnight Twilight. – The city lies just north of latitude 62° and thus in summer, experiences nearly 24 hours of daylight. Every year a golf tournament is held on the weekend closest to June 21. The tee-off commences at midnight. Among other hazards on a golf course that is largely sand are the enormous black ravens (depicted on the city's emblem) that delight in making off with the balls.

Yellowknife is also a good centre for boating, canoeing, fishing and camping. Its stores carry a fine selection of Dene and Inuit art and handicrafts.

Access. – *By Rte 3 and Mackenzie River ferry (free) in summer; "ice road" in winter. No road access during freeze-up and thaw periods (p 232). Also accessible by air from Edmonton, Winnipeg and Iqaluit/Ottawa.*

SIGHTS 1 day

** **Prince of Wales Northern Heritage Centre.** – *Entrance off Ingraham Trail. Open Jun–Aug 31 daily 10:30am–5:30pm. Off-season Tue–Fri 10:30am–5pm; weekends noon–5pm. Closed Christmas & New Year's.* & ☎403/873-7551. Overlooking Frame Lake, this attractive museum is an important archaeological and ethnological research centre. It houses displays on the history of settlement of the Territories and a fine collection of Inuit sculpture. The ways of life of Dene and Inuit peoples are described, as are the reasons European settlers came to the North.

* **Bush Pilots' Monument.** – *Steps from Ingraham Drive in Old Town.* Set on a rock that is the highest point in Yellowknife, this memorial honours the men who opened up the North. From this spot, there is a splendid **view**★ of the city, the surrounding waters and rocky site. The red-topped tower of the Cominco gold mine dominates the skyline. A hive of activity, the bay ripples with numerous small float planes arriving from the mining camps or departing with supplies for oil and gas exploration teams. Large black ravens can frequently be seen on the rocks.

From the old town, a causeway crosses to **Latham Island**, where houses perch on rocks and stilts. Here, a Dogrib Indian settlement and views of the Giant Yellowknife gold mine can be seen.

Boat Trips. – *Dinner cruise on Yellowknife Bay daily mid-Jun–mid-Sept. Roundtrip 4 hrs. $79. Cruises (7–11 days) on the Mackenzie (Jul) and the Great Slave Lake (Aug) offered. Norweta Cruises* ☎403/893-4686. *For other excursions contact Northern Frontier Visitors Association* ☎403/873-4262. These cruises enable visitors to see portions of this enormous lake (28,930sq km/11,170sq mi), which is part of the Mackenzie River system and an important fishing area.

Detah and the Ingraham Trail. – These excursions by vehicle in the vicinity of the capital allow the visitor to see the landscape in this transitional area between boreal forest and tundra. The drive to Detah provides views of Yellowknife and its bay.

Detah. – *Pop 150. 25km/16mi.* This Dogrib Indian settlement has a fine **site**★ on flat rocks overlooking the Great Slave Lake.

Ingraham Trail. – *64km/40mi to Reid Lake.* This all-weather road northwest of Yellowknife skirts five lakes—a paradise for campers and canoeists.

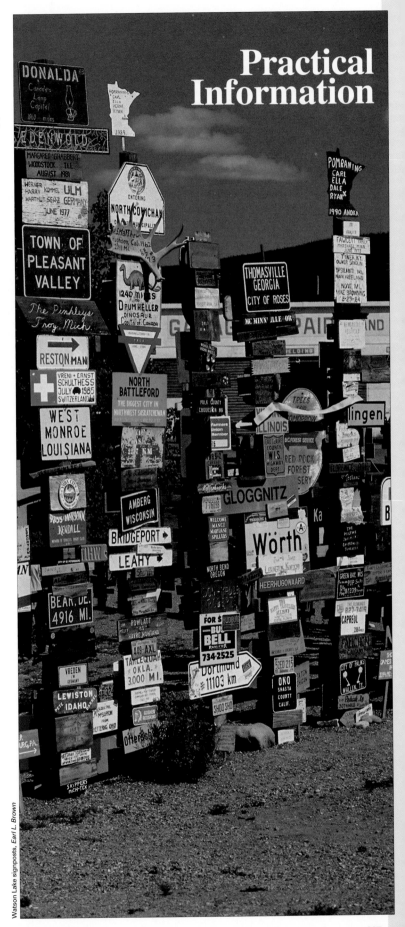

Practical Information

Watson Lake signposts, *Earl L. Brown*

PLANNING YOUR TRIP

The information provided in this section pertains to the country as a whole. Practical information specific to Canada's **provinces** may be found in the regional introductions. Detailed information is also given separately for the Queen Charlotte Islands *(p 39)*, the Rocky Mountain Parks *(p 42)* and the cities of Montreal *(p 161)*, Toronto *(p 131)* and Vancouver *(p 55)*.

Official government tourist offices operated by provincial, municipal and regional agencies distribute road maps and brochures that give information on attractions, seasonal events, accommodation, adventure travel, sports and recreational activities. All publications are available free of charge *(see regional introductions for addresses)*.

For locations in the US and Europe, contact the Tourist Department at the nearest Canadian Embassy, High Command or Consulate:

US	One CNN Center, South Tower, Atlanta, GA 30303	☎404/577-6810
	1251 Avenue of the Americas, New York, NY 10020	☎212/768-2400
	50 Fremont St, San Francisco, CA 94105	☎415/541-7708
Great Britain	Canada House, Trafalgar Square, London SW1Y 5BJ	☎071/629.9492
Germany	Europa Center, 1000 Berlin-30	☎261.1161
Australia	AMP Centre, 50 Bridge St, Sydney 2000	☎231.7022

Passports, Visas, Insurance. – Citizens of the US visiting Canada need proof of citizenship (i.e., birth certificate, voter's registration card or valid passport). Naturalized US citizens should carry their US naturalization certificate. Permanent residents of the US are advised to carry their Alien Registration Cards (US Form I-151 or Form I-551). Persons under 18 who are not accompanied by an adult should carry a letter from a parent or guardian stating name and duration of travel in Canada. Students should carry their ID.

All other visitors to Canada must have a valid passport and, in some cases, a visa. No vaccinations are necessary. For **entry into Canada via the US**, all persons other than US citizens or legal residents are required to present a valid passport. It is advisable to inquire at the Canadian Embassy, High Commission, or Consulate in your home country regarding entry regulations and proper travel documents. Visitors who wish to return to the US after staying in Canada should check with the US Immigration and Naturalization Service.

Before travelling, visitors are advised to check with their insurance company that **medical insurance** covers doctor's visits, medication and hospitalization in Canada; otherwise supplementary insurance may be necessary. Blue Cross of Canada offers insurance called *Health Plan for Visitors*, which can be purchased before departure or within five days of arrival in Canada: $3/day for individuals under 65 years ($4/day over 65 years), $8 for family; $50,000 limit. (Note: rates and benefits may not be valid if first day of coverage commences on or after March 1, 1993.) For details contact: Blue Cross of Canada, 150 Ferrand Dr, Don Mills, ON, M3C 1H6 ☎416/429-9337 or 800/668-6262 in Canada.

Embassies are located in Canada's capital, Ottawa. Most foreign countries maintain **consulates** in regional capitals.

Customs. – Personal luggage and recreational equipment, if declared upon entry, are exempt from customs regulations. Persons 16 years or older may bring into Canada duty-free 200 cigarettes, 50 cigars, or 1kg/2.2 lbs of **tobacco. Alcohol** is limited to 1.1 litres/1.2 quarts of liquor or wine, or 8.2 litres/8.7 quarts of beer. The legal drinking age varies from province to province *(see regional introductions)*. All **prescription drugs** should be clearly labelled; it is recommended that visitors carry a copy of the prescription.

Canada has stringent legislation on **firearms**. Only long guns (no permit required) may be imported by visitors 18 years or older for hunting or sporting purposes. Certain firearms are prohibited entry; restricted firearms, including handguns (a permit is required), may only be imported by a person attending an approved shooting competition. For more information contact: Revenue Canada, Customs and Excise, Ottawa, ON, K1A 0L5 ☎613/954-7129.

All animals, except domesticated dogs and cats, must be issued a Canadian import permit prior to entry into Canada. **Pets** must be accompanied by a certificate of vaccination against rabies from the country of origin. For further information contact: Agriculture Canada, Animal Health Division, Ottawa, ON, K1A 0Y9 ☎613/995-5433.

When to Visit

Climatic conditions vary greatly throughout Canada *(for climate information see regional introductions)*. From mid-March to mid-May, visitors can enjoy comfortable daytime temperatures but chilly nights in the **spring**; in some areas, spring skiing is still possible. Ontario, Quebec and New Brunswick celebrate the harvest of maple syrup with sugaring-off parties. Most visitors go to Canada during the **summer** season, extending from the last weekend in May (Victoria Day) to the first weekend in September (Labour Day). July and August are considered peak season and are ideal for outdoor activities like sailing, kayaking, canoeing or hiking. Hot and often humid days with temperatures ranging from 22°–32°C/70°–90°F can be enjoyed in most provinces. May and September are pleasant months with warm days but cool evenings. However, many tourist attractions have curtailed visiting hours, and it is advisable to phone ahead. The southern regions along the Canada/US border offer spectacular displays of **fall** colours from mid-September until early October.

For the sports enthusiast, the Canadian **winter**, generally from mid-November to mid-March, offers excellent opportunities to enjoy numerous winter activities such as downhill skiing, cross-country skiing and snowmobiling. Most provinces experience heavy snowfall. Main highways are snowploughed, but cars should be winterized and snow tires are recommended.

Note: The extreme northern regions of Canada are most accessible during July and August since the temperature rises above 0°C/32°F for only a few months each year.

Daily weather reports by Environment Canada are available through television, radio and newspapers.

... and don't forget

Athough Canada experiences severe winters, many regions are afflicted by hordes of biting insects in the summer. Late-May and June is blackfly season and in July the mosquitos arrive. For outdoor activities, **insect repellent** is a must. Sturdy footwear with non-slip soles is recommended for hiking. To protect against surprise storms or cool mountain evenings, carry raingear and warm clothing.

How to get there

From the US. – American carriers offer **air** service to Canada's major airports. Air Canada and Canadian Airlines International fly from larger US cities. Amtrak offers daily **rail** service to Montreal from Washington DC and New York City, as well as from New York City to Toronto. Aside from these direct routes, connections are offered from many major US cities. For schedules in the US ☎800/872-7245. **Bus** travel from the US is offered by Greyhound/Trailways. For information and schedules call the local US bus terminal. It is advisable to book well in advance when travelling during peak season.

From Overseas. – Major airports in Canada serviced by international airlines are: Calgary, Edmonton, Halifax, Montreal, Ottawa, St John's, Toronto, Vancouver and Winnipeg. Air Canada and Canadian Airlines International offer service to all major European cities, Latin America and the Middle East. Vancouver is the gateway city offering connections to Australia, New Zealand and the Far East.

TRANSPORTATION

Given Canada's enormous size, it is impossible to cover all of the country during one visit. *See suggested driving tours (pp 6-11) for several two-to three-week itineraries.*

By Plane. – Domestic air service is offered by Canada's two national airlines: **Air Canada** (consult local telephone directory in Canada; in US toll-free ☎800/776-3000) and **Canadian Airlines International** (toll-free ☎800/426-7000 in Canada/US) as well as affiliated regional airlines. Air service to remote areas is provided by many charter companies. Contact the provincial tourist office *(see regional introductions)*.

By Rail. – VIA Rail, Canada's extensive rail network, traverses the country with 18 major routes from coast to coast. First-class, coach and sleeping accommodation are available on transcontinental, regional and intercity trains. Fares are reasonable and trains are comfortable. Amenities offered are dome cars, dining cars and lounges, baggage handling (including bicycles), reservation of medical equipment, wheelchairs and pre-boarding aid with 24hr minimum notice. Unlimited train travel for 12 days within a 30-day period is available systemwide through **Canrailpass** (Jun 7–Sept 30 $489, off-season $329). Special rates are offered for advance purchase, youth and senior citizens. Reservations should be made well in advance, especially during summer months and on popular routes like Edmonton to Vancouver. Canada's legendary cross-country train, *The Canadian,* travels the almost 4,467km/2,700mi from Toronto to Vancouver in less than three days (one-way $404 plus sleeping accommodation surcharge). For information and schedules in Canada contact the nearest VIA Rail office. In the US call VIA Rail ☎800/561-3949 (toll-free).

VIA general sales agents abroad:

Great Britain	Long-haul Leisurerail, Peterborough	☎(0733)51780
Germany	Canada Reisedienst, Rathausplatz 2, Ahrensburg	☎04102.51167
Australia	Walshes World, 92 Pitt St, Sydney	☎(02)232.7499

By Bus. – Long-distance buses reach almost every corner of Canada. Greyhound Lines of Canada, Ltd, 877 Greyhound Way SW, Calgary, AB, T3C 3V8 operates the only trans-Canadian service and, in cooperation with Air Canada, offers **Canada Travel Passes**, sold internationally. Unlimited travel from 15 days up to 30 days is available. Peak season rates range from $197 to $329 (reduced rates during off-season and for senior citizens). For fares and schedules call toll-free in Canada ☎800/661-8747. In the US, call the local bus terminal. Voyageur services most of Quebec and Ontario and offers a 14-day TourPass for travel from May 1–October 28 ($159) ☎613/238-5900. Other regional companies supplement Canada's extensive motorcoach service *(see the yellow pages of local telephone directories)*. Most of these companies participate in the **Ameripass** program for cross-country travel, which includes a flat, discounted rate for unlimited travel, valid for specified days.

By Car. – Canada has an extensive system of well-maintained major roads. In the northern regions and off main arteries, however, many roads are gravel or even dirt. Extreme caution should be taken when travelling these roads. Foreign **driver's licenses** are valid for varying time periods depending on the province. Drivers must carry vehicle **registration** information and/or rental contract at all times. Vehicle **insurance** is compulsory in all provinces (minimum liability is $200,000, except $50,000 in Quebec). US visitors should obtain a Canadian Non-Resident Inter-Province Motor Vehicle Insurance Liability Card (**yellow card**), available from US insurance companies. For additional information contact the Insurance Bureau of Canada, 181 University Ave, Toronto, ON, M5H 3M7 ☎416/362-2031.

Gasoline is sold by the litre (1 gallon = 3.78 litres); prices vary from province to province. All distances and speed limits are posted in kilometres (1 mile = 1.6 kilometre). During winter, it is advisable to check road conditions before setting out. **Snow tires** and an **emergency kit** are imperative. Studded tires are permitted without seasonal limitations in Alberta, Saskatchewan, Yukon and the Northwest Territories, and are allowed in winter in some provinces.

Road regulations. – The **speed limit** on highways, unless otherwise posted, is 100km/h (60mph) and on trans-Canada routes 90km/h (55mph). The speed limit on most rural roads is 80km/h (50mph) to 90km/h (55mph); in urban areas 50km/h (30mph). Service stations that are open 24 hours can be found in large cities and along major highways. The use of **seat belts** is mandatory for all drivers and passengers. On Yukon highways, driving with headlights on at all times is required by law. Most provinces prohibit **radar detection devices** in vehicles. Traffic in both directions must stop (except on divided roads) for a yellow school bus. In all provinces except Quebec, **right turns on red** are allowed after coming to a complete stop. Information on highway conditions in each province can be obtained by contacting the regional Ministry of Transportation *(check the blue pages in the local telephone directories)*.

In case of accident. – If you are involved in an accident resulting in property damage and/or personal injury, you must notify the local police and remain at the scene until dismissed by investigating officers. For assistance contact the local Government Insurance Corporation. First aid stations are clearly designated along highways.

Canadian Automobile Association (CAA). – This national motor club (1775 Courtwood Crescent, Ottawa, ON, K2C 3J2 ☎613/226-7631) offers, through the offices of its member clubs, services such as travel information, maps and tourbooks, accommodation reservations, insurance, technical and legal advice, road and weather conditions. These benefits are extended to members of the American Automobile Association (AAA), clubs of the Commonwealth Motoring Conference (CMC), Alliance Internationale de Tourisme (AIT), Fédération Internationale de l'Automobile (FIA), the Federation of Interamerican Touring and Automobile Clubs (FITAC) and other affiliated clubs. Proof of membership must be presented. The CAA maintains for its members a **24hr emergency road service** ☎800/222-HELP *(see regional introductions for CAA listings)*.

Car Rental. – Vehicles can be rented at major airports, at train stations and in many cities from such international companies as Avis, Hertz and National/Tilden. Minimum age for rental is 21. To avoid a large cash deposit, payment by credit card is recommended. More favourable rates can be obtained by making a reservation before arriving in Canada, but be aware of drop-off charges.

By Ferry. – Canada maintains an extensive ferry-boat system. Contact the regional tourist offices for information and schedules *(see regional introductions for details)*.

THE BASICS

Time Zones. – Canada spans six time zones, but the coast-to-coast time difference is only 4hrs 30min because Newfoundland time is 30min in advance of the Maritime provinces. Daylight Saving Time (clocks are advanced 1 hour) is in effect from the first Sunday in April to the last Sunday in October *(see regional introductions for details)*.

National Holidays. – *For provincial holidays see regional introductions.* The following holidays are observed throughout Canada. Most banks, government offices and schools are closed:

New Year's Day	January 1
Good Friday	Friday before Easter Sunday
Easter Monday	Monday after Easter Sunday
Victoria Day	3rd Monday in May
Canada Day	July 1
Labour Day	1st Monday in September
Thanksgiving	2nd Monday in October
Remembrance Day	2nd Wednesday in November
Christmas Day	December 25
Boxing Day	December 26

Language. – Canada practices institutional bilingualism: English and French are the official languages for all federal and judicial bodies, federally mandated administrative agencies and crown corporations. The practice has spread to provincial governments and some parts of the private sector. However, in Quebec province the offical language is French.

Liquor Laws. – Each province abides by different liquor laws, which are strictly enforced *(see regional introductions)*. The legal blood alcohol limit is 0.08%.

Business Hours. – Business hours are Monday to Friday 9am–5pm. In general, retail stores are open Monday to Friday 9am–6pm (until 9pm Thursday and Friday), and Saturday 9am–5pm. However, depending on local laws, many neighborhood stores that sell groceries, small personal items and newspapers remain open in the evenings and on Sundays.

Metric System. – Canada has partially adopted the International System of weights and measures. Weather temperatures are given in Celsius (C°), milk and wine are sold by millilitres and litres, and grocery items are measured in grams. All distances and speed limits are posted in kilometres (to obtain the equivalent in miles, multiply by .6). Some examples of metric conversions are:

1 kilometre (km)	=	0.6 miles
1 metre (m)	=	3.3 feet
1 kilogram (kg)	=	2.2 pounds
1 litre (l)	=	33.8 fluid ounces = 1 quart = 0.26 gallons

Electricity. – 110 volts, 60 cycles. Most small American appliances can be used. European appliances require an electrical transformer, available at electric supply stores.

Post Offices. – Post offices across Canada are open Monday to Friday 8am–5:45pm. Sample rates for first-class mail are: letter (up to 30 grams) or postcard within Canada 43 cents, to the US (up to 30 grams) 49 cents; international mail (up to 20 grams) 86 cents. Visitors can receive mail c/o "General Delivery" addressed to Main Post Office, City, Province and Postal Code. Mail will be held for 15 days and has to be picked up by the addressee. **Intelpost** transmits documents and photographs via satellite to many Canadian, US and European destinations. **Telepost** "next day service" delivers communications anywhere in Canada or the US. Messages are telephoned to the nearest CN/CP Telecommunications Office; billing arrangements can be made when requesting service. To send a **telegram**, call the local CN/CP Telecommunications Office.

Telephones. – To call long distance within Canada and to the US, dial 1-Area Code-number. For overseas calls, dial "0" for operator assistance. All operators speak English and French. Collect calls and credit card calls can be made from public pay phones. For local directory assistance, check the white pages of the phone directory; outside the local area code dial 1-Area Code-555-1212. All 800 numbers are toll-free. A local call costs 25 cents. Visitors should be aware that many hotels place a surcharge on all calls.

Emergency Numbers. – **911** service is operative in many major cities; otherwise dial "0" for the operator and ask for the police. In most provinces a Tourist Alert Program is operated by the Royal Canadian Mounted Police from June until September. If you see your name in the newspaper or hear it on the radio, contact the nearest RCMP office immediately.

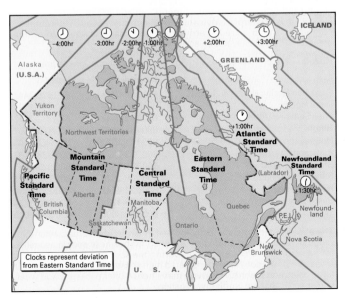

241

Handicapped Travellers. – Most public buildings, churches, restaurants and hotels provide wheelchair access. Disabled parking is provided and the law is strictly enforced. For more information contact the provincial tourist office *(see regional introductions)*.

To obtain the guide *Handy Travel* write to the Canadian Rehabilitation Council for the Disabled, 45 Sheppard Ave East, Suite 801, Toronto, ON, M2N 5W9 ☎416/250-7490. Prepayment of $12.95 plus $3 postage is required for all orders.

MONEY

Canadian currency is based on the decimal system (100 cents to the dollar). Bills are issued in $2, $5, $10, $20, $50, $100, $500 and $1,000 denominations; coins are minted in 1 cent, 5 cents (nickel), 10 cents (dime), 25 cents (quarter), 50 cents (half a dollar) and $1. It is recommended that visitors exchange money at banking institutions to receive the most favourable exchange rate.

Exchange. – The Canadian dollar fluctuates with the international money market. At press time, $1.20 Canadian equalled US $1.

Banks. – Banking institutions are generally open Monday to Friday 10am–3pm. Some banks are open on Saturday morning. Banks at large airports have foreign exchange counters and extended hours. Traveller's cheques in Canadian or American currency are accepted universally. Some institutions may charge a small fee for cashing traveller's cheques. Most principal bank cards are honored at affiliated Canadian banks.

Credit Cards. – The following major credit cards are accepted in Canada: American Express ("Lost or Stolen" ☎800/268-9820 in Canada), Carte Blanche, Diners Club, MasterCard/Eurocard and Visa.

Taxes and Tips. – Canada levies a 7% Goods and Services Tax (GST) on most goods and services. Foreign visitors can request a cash **rebate** of up to $500 per day for short-term accommodation and, for most consumer goods taken out of Canada, by submitting original receipts and identification to any participating Canadian Duty Free Shop. Rebate claims above $500 must be mailed with an application and original receipts. Provincial sales taxes vary, and are refundable in some provinces *(see regional introductions)*. For additional information and rebate forms contact: Revenue Canada, Customs & Excise, Visitor Rebate Program, Ottawa, ON, K1A 1J5 ☎613/991-3346 or 800/668-4748 (toll-free in Canada). Tips or service charges are not normally added to a bill in Canada. However, it is customary to give 10–15% of the total amount.

ACCOMMODATION

Canada offers accommodation suited to every taste and pocketbook from luxury hotels in major cities, roadside motels, quaint B&B's in the countryside, hunting and fishing lodges in remote wilderness areas, farm and country vacation houses to campsites and resorts. Many resorts operate year-round offering tennis, golf and water-sports facilities; winter activities include downhill skiing, cross-country skiing and snowmobiling.

Government tourist offices supply listings (free) that give locations, phone numbers, types of service, amenities, prices and other details *(see regional introductions for addresses)*. Canada is a vast country, and in less populated regions it may be difficult to find accommodation at the end of a long day's drive. Advance reservations are recommended especially during the tourist season (Victoria Day to Labour Day).

During the off-season, establishments outside urban centers may be closed. It is therefore advisable to telephone ahead. Guaranteeing reservations with a credit card is recommended. However, in remote areas, credit cards may not be accepted.

Hotels. – Major hotel chains with locations throughout Canada are:

	In Canada	In the US
Canadian Pacific Hotels & Resorts	800/528-0444	800/828-7447
Delta Hotels	800/268-1133	800/877-1133
Four Seasons Hotels	800/332-3442	800/332-3442
Hilton	800/445-8667	800/445-8667
Holiday Inn	800/HOLIDAY	800/HOLIDAY
Radisson International	800/333-3333	800/333-3333
Sheraton Hotels	800/325-3535	800/325-3535
Ramada International	800/228-2828	800/228-2828
Hotel Novotel	800/221-4542	800/231-5100
Best Western International	800/528-1234	800/528-1234
Westin Hotels	800/228-3000	800/228-3000

The above-listed hotels, mostly located in large urban areas, offer a full range of facilities and amenities designed for business people as well as for vacationers. Prices are higher during the summer months. In resort areas, the ski season is also considered high season. Expect to pay more in large cities and resorts. However, many hotels offer packages and weekend specials that are worth investigating.

Motels. – Along major highways or close to urban areas motels such as Comfort Inn (☎800/221-2222), Relax Inns (☎800/667-3529), Days Inn (☎800/325-2525) and Journey's End (☎800/668-4200) offer accommodation at moderate prices ($45-90). Amenities include television, restaurants and swimming pools. Family-owned establishments and small, independent guest houses that offer basic comfort can be found all across Canada.

Bed & Breakfasts and Country Inns. – B&B's and country inns can be found in cities as well as in the countryside. Most are privately owned and can be housed in an an elegant Georgian mansion, a Victorian homestead, an old mill, a restored farmhouse, a country estate or a cozy cottage by the sea. A continental breakfast is usually included in the room rate. A private bath is not always offered. Some have restaurants. Room rates vary according to the degree of comfort and amenities offered ($45–140). Some accept major credit cards, but it is advisable to check at the time the reservation is placed.

Farm Vacations and Guest Ranches. – Farm and ranch lodgings are rustic and especially suited for families with children. The visitor is a paying guest on a working farm, and participation in daily activities depends on the host's preference. Meals are included and are taken with the host family. Guest ranches may be located in rugged country but holiday packages usually include comfortable accommodation and hearty meals. A variety of activities such as hiking, trail riding and campfire gatherings can be enjoyed by the whole family.

Youth Hostels. – The Canadian Hostelling Association, affiliated with Hostelling International, offers a network of budget accommodation from coast to coast. Hostels provide basic accommodation such as separate dormitory-style rooms (blankets and pillows are provided), shared bath, social areas, laundry facilities and self-service kitchens for $4-20/night per person. In some resort areas outdoor saunas, swimming pools, interpretive programs, theatre workshops and other amenities are offered.
Advance booking is advisable during peak travel times; walk-ins are welcome. Membership is $25/year, but non-members are also admitted. To obtain an application or request the comprehensive guide-book *Hostelling North America* contact the Canadian Hostelling Association, 1600 James Naismith Dr, Suite 608, Gloucester, ON, K1B 5N4 ☎613/748-5638.

Universities and Colleges. – Most universities make their dormitory space available to travellers during summer vacation (May–August). Rates average $28-$35/day per person. Reservations are accepted. For more information contact the local tourist office or the university directly.

Campgrounds. – Canada has excellent campgrounds that are operated privately or by the federal and provincial governments. Government sites are located in the many national and provincial parks. Fees are nominal. These campgrounds are well equipped and fill up quickly *(for description of national park campgrounds see p 244)*. Commercially operated campgrounds, often located adjacent to national parks and provincial parks, are more costly but offer amenities such as electrical and water hookups, bathrooms with showers, restaurants, recreational facilities, grocery stores and gas stations. For a list of campgrounds contact the provincial tourist office *(see regional introductions for addresses)*.

Fishing Camps, Fly-in Lodges and Wilderness Camps. – Canada offers the experienced angler or the outdoor enthusiast a variety of fishing lodges and camps, some of which are so remote, they can only be reached by private boat or plane. Outfitters offer packages that include transportation, accommodation, meals, supplies, equipment and expeditions led by experienced guides.
Wilderness camps located in Canada's northern regions offer all-inclusive hunting packages. Non-residents must be accompanied by licensed guides. Permits can be obtained through the outfitter, who can also assist with game registration (required by law).
These packages are costly and the number of spaces is usually limited. It is advisable to make reservations well in advance. For information on fishing and hunting regulations and license fees, as well as listings of outfitters, contact the provincial tourist office *(see regional introductions)*.

NATIONAL PARKS AND RESERVES

Since the creation of the first national park in Banff in 1885, the amount of protected land overseen by the Canadian Parks Service has grown to 214,840sq km/82,950sq mi. Canada's 29 national parks and 7 national park reserves offer the visitor spectacular scenery, a wealth of wildlife and fauna, as well as unlimited recreational opportunities.
More than 13 million people visit the parks each year. Most points of interest are accessible by car. Well-marked hiking trails permit outdoor enthusiasts and novices alike to enjoy the backcountry. Parks are open year-round; however, some roads may be closed during the winter. **Park motor license** fees are $5/day per car, $10/4 days per car and $30 for an annual pass. Persons entering on foot, by bicycle, on horseback or by boat are admitted free. Canadian senior citizens can obtain an annual pass free of charge.

Visitor **information centres** (open daily Victoria Day–Labour Day; reduced hours during the off-season) are usually located at park entrances. Staff are available to help visitors plan activities. Trail maps and literature on park facilities, hiking trails, nature programs, camping and in-park accommodation are available on-site free of charge. Interpretation programs, guided hikes, exhibits and self-guided trails introduce the visitor to each park's history, geology and habitats. *For a listing of in-park activities see the appropriate section within each province.*

Activities and Facilities. – All **hikers** are required to register at the park office before setting out and to deregister upon completion of the trip. It is a good idea to ask park officials about trail conditions, weather forecasts and safety precautions. Trail distances are given from trailhead to destination, not round-trip, unless otherwise posted. Topographic maps and a compass are indispensable for backcountry hiking. To obtain topographic maps contact Canada Map Office, 130 Bently St, Ottawa, ON, K1A 0E9 ☎613/952-7000.

Licenses are required for **fishing** and can be obtained from the park office, sporting goods stores or other retail businesses. Some parks offer boat and canoe rentals. Hunting is not permitted within the national parks.

Most park **campgrounds** are open mid-May through Labour Day, and operate on a first-come, first-served basis. Dates are subject to change, and it is recommended that visitors check with the park superintendent. Some parks offer winter camping. Maximum stay is two weeks. Daily rates apply for all campgrounds accessible by road. Usually campsites include a level tent pad, picnic table, fireplace or fire grill with firewood, and parking space close to a water source. Most have toilet buildings and kitchen shelters. Some campgrounds are for tents only, while others allow recreational vehicles. Most campgrounds do not have trailer hook-ups but many have sewage disposal stations. Many accommodate the disabled. In some locations, certain equipment restrictions apply. Primitive campgrounds, located near hiking trails in the backcountry, can be reached only on foot. The brochure *Welcome to National Parks,* obtainable free from the Park Service *(see address below),* lists facilities of major campgrounds.

Contact the headquarters of the Canadian Parks Service, Environment Canada, Hull, PQ, K1A 0H3 ☎819/997-2800 or individual park headquarters (see listing below) to obtain additional information and descriptive brochures on services, including outfitters and activities

A word of caution. – Bears are present in many of Canada's national parks. These unpredictable animals can inflict serious injury. Few bear attacks have occurred, however. Visitors are asked to respect **wildlife** and observe park rules: don't hike alone; do not take along a dog; stay in open areas; never go near a bear cub; keep campsites clean; store food away from tent or in the trunk of your car; and always place garbage in containers provided by the park. To avoid **hypothermia**, stay dry; beware of wind, dampness and exhaustion in regions where weather changes rapidly; carry weatherproof clothing, plastic sheeting and nylon twine for emergency shelter; and eat high-calorie foods.

National Parks and Reserves

Western Regional Office
Box 2989, 220 Fourth Ave SE, Calgary, AB, T2P 3H8
☎403/292-4440

Banff *(p 43)*	Box 900, Banff, AB, T0L 0C0 ☎403/852-1500
Elk Island	Site 4, RR1, Fort Saskatchewan, AB, T8L 2N7 ☎403/992-6380
Glacier *(p 37)*	Box 350, Revelstoke, BC, V0E 2S0 ☎604/837-7500
Gwaii Haanas *(p 41)*	Box 37, Queen Charlotte City, BC, V0T 1S0 ☎604/559-8818
Jasper *(p 49)*	Box 10, Jasper, AB, T0E 1E0 ☎403/852-6161
Kootenay *(p 51)*	Box 220, Radium Hot Springs, BC, V0A 1M0 ☎604/347-9615
Mount Revelstoke *(p 37)*	Box 350, Revelstoke, BC, V0E 2S0 ☎604/837-7500
Pacific Rim *(p 62)*	Box 280, Ucluelet, BC, V0R 3A0 ☎604/726-7721
Waterton Lakes *(p 66)*	Waterton, AB, T0K 2M0 ☎403/859-2224
Yoho *(p 46)*	Box 99, Field, BC, V0A 1G0 ☎604/343-6324

Prairie and Northern Regional Office
457 Main St, Winnipeg, MB, R3B 1B5
☎204/983-3108

Aulavik (Banks Island)	PO Box 1840, Inuvik, NT, X0E 0T0 ☎403/979-3248
Auyuittuq *(p 233)*	PO Box 1720, Iqaluit, NT, X0A 0H0 ☎819/979-6277
Baffin Island *(p 233)*	PO Box 1720, Iqaluit, NT, X0A 0H0 ☎819/979-6277

Ellesmere Island *(p 232)*	PO Box 1720, Iqaluit, NT, X0A 0H0 ☎819/979-6277
Grasslands	PO Box 150, Val Marie, SK, S0N 2T0 ☎306/298-2257
Kluane *(p 71)*	Box 5495, Haines Junction, YT, Y0B 1L0 ☎403/634-2251
Nahanni *(p 234)*	Postal Bag 300, Fort Simpson, NT, X0E 0N0 ☎403/695-3151
Northern Yukon	Box 5495, Haines Junction, YT, Y0B 1L0 ☎403/634-2251
Prince Albert *(p 89)*	Box 100, Waskesiu Lake, SK, S0J 2Y0 ☎306/663-5322
Riding Mountain *(p 92)*	Wasagaming, MB, R0J 2H0 ☎204/848-2811
Wood Buffalo *(p 232)*	PO Box 750, Fort Smith, NT, X0E 0P0 ☎403/872-2349

Ontario Regional Office
111 Water St, Cornwall, ON, K6H 6S3
☎613/938-5866

Bruce Peninsula *(p 107)*	PO Box 189, Tobermory, ON, N0H 2R0 ☎519/596-2233
Georgian Bay Islands *(p 107)*	PO Box 28, Honey Harbour, ON, P0E 1E0 ☎705/756-2415
Point Pelee *(p 125)*	RR No. 1, Leamington, ON, N8H 3V4 ☎519/322-2365
Pukaskwa *(p 104)*	PO Box 39, Heron Bay, ON, P0T 1R0 ☎807/229-0801
St Lawrence Islands *(p 111)*	Box 469, Mallorytown Landing, ON, K0E 1R0 ☎613/923-5261

Quebec Regional Office
3 Buade St, Haute Ville, Quebec, PQ, G1R 4V7
☎418/648-4177

Forillon *(p 156)*	122 Blvd Gaspé, Gaspé, PQ, G0C 1R0 ☎418/368-5505
Mauricie *(p 180)*	Box 758, Shawinigan, PQ, G9N 6V9 ☎819/536-2638
Mingan Archipelago *(p 154)*	CP 1180, Havre-Saint-Pierre, PQ, G0G 1P0 ☎418/538-3331

Atlantic Regional Office
Upper Water St, Halifax, NS, B3J 1S9
☎902/426-3457

Cape Breton Highlands *(p 205)*	Ingonish Beach, NS, B0C 1L0 ☎902/285-2270
Fundy *(p 190)*	PO Box 40, Alma, NB, E0A 1B0 ☎506/887-2000
Gros Morne *(p 220)*	PO Box 130, Rocky Harbour, NF, A0K 4N0 ☎709/458-2417
Kejimkujik *(p 199)*	PO Box 236, Annapolis, NS, B0T 1B0 ☎902/242-2772
Kouchibouguac *(p 186)*	Kouchibouguac, Kent Co, NB, E0A 2A0 ☎506/876-2443
Prince Edward Island *(p 215)*	PO Box 487, Charlottetown, PE, C1A 7L1 ☎902/566-7050
Terra Nova *(p 227)*	Glovertown, NF, A0G 2L0 ☎709/533-2801

Good references for planning a visit to Canada's national parks are: **Canada's National Parks - A Visitor's Guide** by Marylee Stephenson *(Prentice-Hall Canada Inc, 1991)* and **The Outdoor Traveller's Guide Canada** by David Dunbar *(Stewart, Tabori & Chang, 1991)*.

In addition to the national parks, there are over 600 **provincial parks** to explore. More than 100 **national historic sites**, such as the French fortress of Louisbourg *(p 210)*, the site of one of the oldest European settlements in Canada *(p 199)* and homes of several Canadian prime ministers, can be found from coast to coast. Designed for day-time visit only, most sites are open from Victoria Day to Labour Day, with reduced hours in the early spring and fall. Some charge a nominal admission fee. At many of these sites interpretation centres and costumed guides provide insight into Canada's history and cultural heritage. For more information contact the appropriate regional office of the Canadian Parks Service.

INDEX

Winnipeg
Mackenzie, Alexander
98, **107**, *235*

City, town, region or other point of interest
Person, historic event or term
Page reference, **principal reference**, *illustration*

The principal sights in Montreal, Toronto and Vancouver are listed separately as are National Parks and Provincial Parks. Place names appear with the following abbreviations: AB Alberta, BC British Columbia, MB Manitoba, NB New Brunswick, NF Newfoundland, NS Nova Scotia, NT Northwest Territories, ON Ontario, PE Prince Edward Island, PQ Quebec, QCI Queen Charlotte Islands, SK Saskatchewan, YT Yukon Territory.

MANUFACTURE FRANÇAISE DES PNEUMATIQUES MICHELIN
Société en commandite par actions au capital de 2 000 000 000 de francs
Place des Carmes-Déchaux – 63 Clermont-Ferrand (France)

R.C.S. Clermont-Fd B 855 200 507

© Michelin et Cie, Propriétaires-Éditeurs 1993

Dépôt légal 4-1993 — ISBN 2-06-151705-6 — ISSN 0763-1383

Printed in the United States of America 04-93-33 by Hart Graphics, Austin, Texas